Second Edition

JUVENILE JUSTICE

Second Edition

JUVENILE JUSTICE

G. Larry Mays
New Mexico State University

L. Thomas Winfree, Jr.
New Mexico State University

WAVELAND
PRESS, INC.
Long Grove, Illinois

For information about this book, contact:
Waveland Press, Inc.
4180 IL Route 83, Suite 101
Long Grove, IL 60047-9580
(847) 634-0081
info@waveland.com
www.waveland.com

Inside front cover: Adapted from Sickmund (2003), *Juveniles in Court*. Juvenile Offenders and Victims National Report Series. Office of Juvenile Justice and Delinquency Prevention, U.S. Dept. of Justice.

Photo credits: page 1, © Robert Essel NYC/CORBIS; page 8, © Marc Asnin/CORBIS SABA; page 31, © Bob Owen/San Antonio Express/ZUMA/Corbis; page 41, © Bettmann/CORBIS; page 61, © Bob Daemmrich/The Image Works; page 97, © Laura Pedrick/CORBIS SYGMA; page 105, © Shelley Gazin/The Image Works; page 129, © Bob Daemmrich/The Image Works; page 147, © Mitch Wojnarowicz/The Image Works; page 165, © Don Murray/ZUMA/Corbis; page 185, © Jacksonville Journal Courier/Steve Warmowski/The Image Works; page 197, © Bob Daemmrich/The Image Works; page 219, © Larry Kolvoord/The Image Works; page 231, © Tom Stewart/CORBIS; page 246, © Fritz Hoffmann/The Image Works; page 265, © Hannah Gal/CORBIS; page 297, © David Turnley/CORBIS; page 331, © Jeff Greenberg/The Image Works; page 343, © Tony Savino/The Image Works; page 361, © Reuters/CORBIS; page 372, © Bob Daemmrich/The Image Works.

CONTENTS

PREFACE

TO THE STUDENTS

This book represents a long journey for us, but the path traveled by each was a bit different. For example, in the 1970s Larry Mays served as a police officer in Knoxville, Tennessee, working undercover and in plainclothes in drug enforcement, as well as in the juvenile division. These experiences sparked a lifelong interest in the juvenile justice system and the problems of youngsters processed by the system.

After completing a master's degree at East Tennessee State University, Larry received his doctorate in political science from the University of Tennessee. His major professor was Otis Stephens and his doctoral work focused on judicial politics, constitutional law, and public administration. His research focus in graduate school often turned to juvenile justice issues and, after receiving his doctoral degree, Larry researched and wrote extensively in books and academic journals on such diverse juvenile justice topics as juvenile transfer to adult courts and gangs and gang behavior. In the late 1980s, this interest culminated in *Juvenile Delinquency and Juvenile Justice*, a book he coauthored with Joseph Rogers. Over the next 10 years, Larry often thought about what that book tried to do—merge two substantive areas of academic study—and eagerly awaited the chance to put these thoughts into written words. That book afforded him just such an opportunity.

At about the same time that Larry Mays was a police officer, Tom Winfree served in the U.S. Army, stationed in Berlin, Germany. During this time he served briefly as a tower guard at Spandau Prison, a maximum security facility housing the last convicted war criminal from World War II, Rudolph Hess. Upon leaving active duty in 1970, Tom decided to pursue a graduate degree in sociology with an emphasis on drugs and society, the latter interest piqued by the relatively high levels of substance abuse he had witnessed in Europe among U.S. military personnel during the late 1960s. Academic realities and personalities intervened, changing Tom's focus to juveniles and correctional institutions. The reality was the need to develop a thesis topic in a relatively short period of time; the personality was

Charles W. Thomas, who became a driving force in Tom's early career. Tom began his research career studying juvenile responses to a secure correctional facility in Virginia.

After receiving a doctorate in sociology from the University of Montana in 1975, Tom held academic positions at the University of New Mexico, East Texas State University, and Louisiana State University before taking his current job at New Mexico State University. During this quarter century or more of teaching, research, and writing, Tom focused on the problems of contemporary youths. Returning to an earlier interest and combining it with his evolving juvenile justice research agenda, he wrote extensively on the causes and correlates of juvenile drug abuse, particularly in rural America and among Native American youth. In the early 1990s, he and Larry Mays, with the assistance of a long succession of able graduate students, began a series of gang-related research studies, culminating in Tom's participation in the National Evaluation of the Gang Resistance Education and Training program.

Throughout Tom's research and writing efforts, two themes have dominated his work. First, he grounded his studies of youthful drug use and gang activities in contemporary delinquency theory, believing that unless we attempt to provide theoretical understandings of attitudes and behavior, our explanations will fail to stand up to the test of time and changing social forces. Second, he subscribed to the belief that theory, research, and practical applications must complement each other. This latter orientation translates into an appreciation of how basic research (the study of phenomena for the sake of knowledge itself) and applied research (the search for workable answers to specific problems) can help us understand our world. In the present instance, that world is defined as the juvenile justice system. This textbook reflects both perspectives—a concern for theory and a belief that it must make sense.

We offer these brief biographical sketches to give you a sense of our orientation toward the subject matter of this text. Like many academics, we bring much personal and intellectual "baggage" to our work. We felt that it would help you understand this book a bit better if you understood us as well.

TO THE INSTRUCTOR

We would like to call your attention to several pieces of information about the authors and features of this text. First, we bring varied backgrounds and perspectives to the book. Larry Mays is a political scientist by training and worked in local law enforcement (including stints in drug enforcement and the juvenile division) in the early 1970s. Tom Winfree's academic training is in sociology, and he brings a wealth of practical and research experience to the text. We both have been engaged in gang research for most of the 1990s. The net result is different, but complementary, perspectives on the issues presented in the text.

Second, we consciously have tried to develop a new pattern for this book. As one example, rather than ignoring theory altogether or segregating discussions of theory in several introductory chapters, we lay a foundation in chapter 2 and include boxed material on theory throughout the text. Some of the essential material included in this book (e.g., police work with juveniles, the juvenile court, and juvenile probation) is present in every text on juvenile justice. However, four chapters are relatively unique.

- Chapter 8 on juvenile parole and aftercare proved one of the most difficult to write. The material is difficult to locate (what little seems to exist), so we searched high and low to find the information for this chapter. We have found that this material is absent from many of the other juvenile justice texts on the market.

- Chapter 9 on nondelinquent children in the juvenile justice process presents recent information on those youngsters who fit into the categories of dependency, neglect, and abuse. In some sense, these youngsters are victims with whom the juvenile justice system must deal.

- Chapter 10 on juvenile gangs highlights a national issue of some concern and one that students find fascinating. This material shows how theory may inform research and how research may inform policy and practice in the juvenile justice system.

- Chapter 11 addresses prevention and intervention from both philosophical and practical perspectives. We discuss what works and what does not work and some of the reasons behind program success or failure.

Third, we feel compelled to comment briefly on the references we have cited throughout the text. We have tried to incorporate those sources (some secondary in nature) that best inform us about certain issues. Therefore, we have included items from 2000 and later as well as some from the 1990s, 1980s, 1970s, 1960s, and some even earlier. We believe that each reference speaks to the issues at hand in a vital way.

Fourth, the opening vignettes we have included in each chapter may be a new feature to many of you. Before you judge too quickly, keep these two things in mind:

- It is important to get the students to read the book (we assume you will), and we have "test driven" these scenarios with students at our university and found that they pull them into the chapters.

- Each of these is loosely based on experiences we and our former students have had, and they should bring a degree of realism and relevancy to the text.

Fifth, new to this edition are the international perspective features in each chapter. Each of these items addresses a contemporary juvenile justice issue in another nation or culture, and in some instances compares this information with agencies and functions in the American juvenile justice system.

Finally, we encourage you and the students to use the critical review questions included at the end of each chapter. A quick glance will tell you that these are not really "test" questions, in that many of them do not ask for recall of substantive information. However, they should prompt interesting classroom discussions and give you some measure of whether the students are comprehending the material. Thus, these questions could be used as out-of-class assignments or for in-class small group discussions.

We both feel that it is a great disservice to our students to bore them with top-ics we feel passionately about. This book is designed to tell a story. We hope you and your students find it interesting and useful.

G. Larry Mays
L. Thomas Winfree, Jr.

ACKNOWLEDGMENTS

A book such as this, which took nearly two years to bring to closure, necessarily involves many participants beyond the authors. We would like to thank the folks at Waveland Press with whom we have worked in the course of preparing this text, including Laurie Prossnitz, who shepherded the project during the critical editing and production phases; Gayle Zawilla, who began the project with us; Jan Weissman, who provided expert assistance in obtaining the photos; Katy Murphy, who did the typesetting and created the very effective layout; and Don Rosso, who provided our cover design. We also would be remiss if we did not thank the Rowes—Carol (for whom we have great affection) and Neil (who we tolerate because he's married to Carol).

We would also like to thank the following external reviewers who read some or all of our manuscript for both editions of this book: Tom Barker, Thomas Bernard, Stephanie R. Bush-Baskette, Felecia Dix Richardson, John Holman, G. Roger Jarjoura, William Kelley, Roger J. R. Levesque, Walter B. Lewis, Jerome McKean, Roger B. McNally, Dana Peterson, Rudy Sanfilippo, Clifton Joe Scott, and Terrance J. Taylor.

We would also like to thank our students, who have helped crystalize our thinking about juvenile justice and forced us to become better teachers. In particular, the following students provided invaluable assistance to us as we prepared this manuscript—looking up references, reading and commenting on chapters, and the like: Jackie Fuhr, Amy Mercer, and Kathy Movsesian.

To all those we have named, and to the many others who have, over the years, influenced our careers and lives: Thank you. Of course, they share all the credit; we bear all the blame for any mistakes made in this text.

GLM
LTW

JUVENILE DELINQUENCY AND JUVENILE JUSTICE

* * *

The pneumatic door of the group study room hissed as it closed. The three students sitting around the table looked up as Suzie, the last study-group member to arrive, entered the room, a sheepish grin on her face. Laying her leather book bag on the table at a spot nearest the door, Suzie spoke to no one in particular, "Sorry I'm late, but, well, you know, sometimes . . ."

Arnela—Arnie to her friends—interrupted Suzie, her voice tight with displeasure, "Look Suzie. We have the room for only two hours." Arnie got up from her seat, walked around the table to where Suzie had encamped, looked down disgustedly at the latecomer, and continued, "We've still got eight essays to cover, and we're way behind schedule."

"Come on people," interrupted Jake, the only male in the study group. This was his last final for his last class; he had no patience for petty feuding. Jake continued speaking: "Each of us had 40 terms. We all did ours, made copies and everything. Where are the ones you defined, Suzie?"

Suzie opened her bag, pulled out a sheaf of papers and laid them on the table. "That's what I was trying to say. The two copiers here in the library are broken, so I had to use the one at the student center." Suzie walked around the table, dropping a packet of materials in front of each member. She took special care with the one she placed in front of Arnie.

Peace restored, Gail, the group's fourth member, took control as she had at each study session since the first test, when they had collectively blown the bottom out of the curve. Their grades had improved over the next two tests, but now they faced a comprehensive final. "OK, Arnie," Gail started, "what was it you were saying about the second question? That was one of yours, wasn't it? Remember, this question's from the first test, the one we all messed up."

Arnie, the only member of the group double-majoring in criminal justice and sociology, sorted through the stack of paper-clipped sheets in front of her, finally finding the one she sought. "Right. This question was about theories of juvenile delinquency. OK, the question as stated is: 'Which single theory of delinquency do you think provides the most comprehensive explanation for delinquent behavior? Provide support for your choice.' My answer would be predicated"—Arnie talked like that a lot—"on what I think she means by 'comprehensive.' Now, according to Webster's . . ." Arnie then launched into a 15-minute dissertation on comprehensive answers, the real meaning of "do you think," and how she felt that whatever theory each of them picked would be right if the selection was justified.

"That's great," interrupted Jake, "but what is it I'm supposed to put down for my theory? I guess I like differential association theory, but I'll be damned if I know why it is comprehensive. I need specifics. Weren't we supposed to get specific on our answers?"

Noisily shifting her papers on the table, Suzie spoke up for the first time since handing out her materials. "I personally think that power control explains a lot, especially about the differences between the delinquency of boys and girls. Look, Jake, your parents raised you to take risks. My parents raised my brothers to be risk takers, but they expected me to be, well, more conforming."

"You know what," said Gail, resting her head on the table as if she was suffering from a terrible headache—which she was, "I've got to ask this one little question: What's all this theory stuff have to do with juvenile justice? I mean, that's the name of the class, isn't it? I want to be a JPO[1] when I graduate, not a delinquency theorist. Arnie, you're a double major. You took juvenile delinquency last term. What's the difference?"

Arnie, still dumbstruck by Suzie's theoretical insights, answered Gail's question with uncharacteristic simplicity: "You know what, Gail? I thought this would be a 'twofer.' You know: same material, different classes. But they're different. As for the 'theory stuff,' that's more sociology than CJ, I think. Still, I suspect we'd better be sure before next week's test."

"Look, guys," interrupted Jake, impatience written across his face, "We have only 90 minutes left, and I still don't know what to put down for question 2. Can I get some help here?"

* * *

Some students, when they take a particular class, look for the bigger issues and broader concerns. They try to make connections between courses and academic curricula. Others get caught up in the finer points of the current course and in finding the "right" answers to specific questions, and they often lose sight of the big picture. Still others want to know what the course has to do with the real world. The study group described above evidenced a little of the conflict that can emerge when these different views converge.

Each of these concerns is important, and each has a place in any exploration of the juvenile justice system. Our goal in this chapter is to orient you to the study of juvenile justice. Two terms form the heart of this text: *juvenile* and *justice*. Both terms are defined and their relative contributions explained in detail. We also provide linkages to related courses and to the practices of the juvenile justice system. At the chapter's conclusion you should better appreciate how information from widely different sources shapes not only general society's views of the problems created by misbehaving youth, but also those held by policy makers and practitioners (and, not surprisingly we trust, you). Assessing the relative value and utility of these various information sources is an essential step toward a complete understanding of contemporary juvenile justice in the United States. By the chapter's end, you also will have received an overview of the juvenile justice system, its core elements, and the distinctive problems associated with processing youngsters who violate laws. You should not find yourself wondering, as did the students in our opening vignette, what juvenile justice is and how it is distinct from juvenile delinquency.

DEFINING DELINQUENCY: THE BASICS

The introduction to any topical area in an academic discipline should begin with the definition of the subject matter. If this were a textbook on organized crime, we would begin with definitions of what organized crime is and who the organized criminals are. Similar processes would occur for such topics as political crime, white-collar crime, youth gangs, terrorism, or any other substantive topic in criminal justice. Juvenile justice conforms to this generalization. Three questions guide our preliminary exploration of juvenile justice: What is meant by delinquency or delinquent acts? Who is a juvenile? Who is a delinquent?

WHAT IS DELINQUENCY?

The process of defining delinquency is a complex task. Consider that legally, delinquency is the failure, omission, or violation of law or duty (*Black's Law Dictionary*, 2004). A delinquent act, however, may be defined more precisely and concisely if the actor is also more carefully identified. For our purposes, an act of delinquency includes the following characteristics:

- It is an act committed by a juvenile that, if committed by an adult, would require prosecution in a criminal court. Because the act is committed by a juvenile, it falls within the jurisdiction of the juvenile court. Delinquent acts include crimes against persons, crimes against property, drug offenses, and crimes against the public order (Office of Juvenile Justice and Delinquency Prevention, 1998a:57).

- It includes juvenile actions or conduct in violation of criminal law, juvenile status, and other juvenile misbehavior; an act committed by a juvenile for which an adult could be prosecuted in a criminal court, but for which a juvenile can be adjudicated in a juvenile court, or prosecuted in a court having criminal jurisdiction if the juvenile court transfers jurisdiction; generally, a "felony or misdemeanor level offense" in states employing those terms (U.S. Department of Justice, 1981:78).

Delinquency as a legal noun describes a broad range of activities from bad debts to the failure to act in a lawful manner. One special meaning of delinquency shifts the focus to specific forms of unlawful behavior by juveniles. Perhaps the most concise way to answer the question of what is meant by delinquency is as follows: **Delinquency** is an act committed by a juvenile that, had it been committed by an adult, would have resulted in a felony or misdemeanor arrest. The added elements of where the youth would be adjudicated—another legal term for the act of sitting in judgment of someone—and the form those acts may take will be addressed later in this and other chapters.

What about the other misconduct identified in the Department of Justice definition, specifically, "actions or conduct in violation of juvenile status"? This idea has given rise to the term **status offender**, a person who by reason of his or her "tender age" is not yet legally an adult. The "offenses" of such a person, conduct in violation of his or her status as a juvenile, are technically called **status offenses,** not delinquency. To more fully appreciate this distinction, however, we must define precisely who is a juvenile in the eyes of the law and society at large.

WHO IS A JUVENILE?

Exactly when an act changes from a crime to delinquency (or vice versa) is dependent on how a given legal jurisdiction defines the accused person's legal status. Indeed, a status offense is entirely dependent upon the age of the person alleged to have engaged in it; that is, "adults" cannot commit status offenses. Four such statuses are generally important to the study of juvenile justice. First, youths are **minors** from birth until the point at which they achieve a certain age, the second status, called their **majority**. At that point, usually age 21, minors became adults in all legal respects.[2]

Adding to the confusion is a third legal status, that of the infant or immature child.[3] In most legal jurisdictions an **infant** is a human being from birth to 10 years of age. As we explain in more detail in chapter 5, infants are incapable of forming the necessary criminal intent, that is, *mens rea*, required to try a person for most crimes. Legally, they cannot be held accountable by any legal jurisdiction for their acts until they become juveniles. That does not mean, however, that no one cares if they engage in rule-breaking behavior or that no one can intervene. Typically, such children fall within the domain of social welfare or social services agencies in the local community. Staff in one of those agencies may consider whether to remove the child from his or her home or recommend some form of family or individual therapy to help remedy the situation. In order for this to happen in most jurisdictions in the United States, a family or juvenile court judge or some other member of the local judiciary with expertise in the problems of children is apprised of the situation by local law enforcement, school officials, or other concerned citizens (including parents). No matter what specific actions these officials take, every effort is made to avoid stigmatizing the child or associating his or her conduct with that of older, more legally responsible juveniles.

In most situations, infants become **juveniles**, the fourth status, on their tenth birthday. They lose that status, becoming adults, in one of three ways. First, they can grow older, naturally passing into adulthood—but not necessarily their complete legal majority—between their sixteenth and eighteenth birthdays. The exact age varies from jurisdiction to jurisdiction.[4] Keep in mind that juvenile and adult statuses are legal ones and not simply chronological factors. This concern is not unique to the United States, a topic addressed in box 1.1.

Courts of law, following two statutorily defined procedures, have the legislated power to alter a youth's legal status. The first such procedure is the **juvenile emancipation hearing**. At an emancipation hearing, a juvenile appears before a judge, again usually a family or juvenile court judge. Based on witnesses' testimony and other forms of evidence, the juvenile's lawyer makes a case that the child in question could live independent of his or her parents. One of the more common reasons for emancipation involves requests by minors to be allowed to marry. By court order, the judge can declare the youth emancipated and legally an adult.

Box 1.1 International Perspectives
Coming of (Legal) Age Around the World

There is considerable variation in the United States when it comes to defining the age of criminal responsibility, although it is generally fixed at age 10, as derived from English Common Law. Worldwide, there is much disagreement as to the age of criminal responsibility. Consider, for example, figure 1.1, which examines both the age at which youths in 125 nations assume criminal responsibility and the age at which they can get married.[5] We include the latter since it provides an interesting comparison with the age of responsibility for crime.

In terms of marriage, a plurality of nations has mixed age requirements, meaning that the age at which a youth can legally marry differs for boys and girls. In each case, girls are allowed to get married as much as two or three years younger than boys. In some cases girls can marry as young as 12 and boys at 14. However, in most cases the ages are 15–16 for girls and 18–21 for boys. No minimum age is the next most prevalent category. That is, boys and girls can get married at whatever age their parents feel is appropriate. After these two categories, the minimum age for marriage ranges between 14 and 18, with the most frequent category being 16 years of age for both boys and girls. In terms of marriage, then, most nations surveyed reported either no minimum ages or different minimums for boys and girls.

Criminal responsibility presents a different picture. The plurality is found at age 7. In fact, nearly one-half of the nations for which a determination could be made reported either no minimums or ranged between the ages of 7 and 10. For those nations indicating different marriage ages for boys and girls, none were less than age 12. It appears that for many nations in the world, children come of age for criminal responsibility before they are old enough for marriage.

Efforts by the United Nations to raise the age of criminal responsibility have been met with considerable resistance by member nations, many of whom claim that they are in the best position to know when their citizens become criminally responsible, based on the moral, religious, and cultural practices found in their own nations. As a result, in Rule 2.2(a) of the Beijing Rules, the United Nations (1986) defines a juvenile as "a child or young person who, under the respective legal systems, may be dealt with for an offence in a manner which is different from an adult." In Rule 4.1 the United Nations offers an equally vague set of guidelines to help in defining the lower limits: ". . . the beginning of that age shall not be fixed too low an age level, bearing in mind the facts of emotional, mental, and intellectual maturity." The figures cited above suggest that the world's nations exercise great variability in defining exactly what is the lower limit.

Sources: Adapted from UNICEF's Convention on the Rights of Children (1997); Melchiorre (2004).

The second means by which a child moves to adult status is the **transfer hearing**. This process also involves a legal hearing. While the legal jurisdiction determines the necessary evidentiary requirements for transfers, the basic process and possible outcomes are nearly identical in most places. The importance of the transfer hearing is addressed at several junctures in this text; however, the most detailed exploration of it occurs in chapter 5. The significance of this hearing is considerable, as it means that the former child may now be treated as an adult in all legal regards, including the administration of adult procedures and penalties.

Figure 1.1
Minimum Age of Criminal Responsibility and Eligibility for
Marriage in 125 Nations

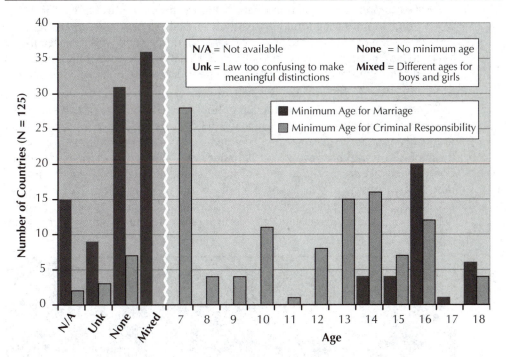

Sources: Adapted from UNICEF's Convention on the Rights of Children (1997); Melchiorre (2004).

Clearly, the legal status of juveniles provides a link between delinquency and delinquents, acts and actors. Just as clearly, defining who is a juvenile depends on such factors as chronological age, jurisdictional issues, and prior judicial actions.

WHO IS A DELINQUENT?

Determining who is a delinquent is a process with many of the same definitional mysteries and legal complexities associated with the first two terms, until we include the adjective *juvenile*. That is, anyone can be a delinquent, even an adult. Used by itself, the term simply refers to anyone who fails to do what is required of him or her by law or duty. You can be a delinquent if you do not pay your taxes or neglect to pay your rent on time. When combined with *juvenile*, the term takes on a unique meaning. Even then, we may define a **juvenile delinquent** in at least two distinct ways:

- *Social definition*: A young person who is viewed by society generally, and those responsible for the administration of justice specifically, as having a devalued or spoiled identity. Often this term is used indiscriminately by the public at large and even criminal justice practitioners, as in the statement, "They're nothing but a bunch of juvenile delinquents."

- *Legal definition*: A legal minor, over whom a specified court has legal jurisdiction, who has been found by that judicial body to have committed an act in violation of the jurisdiction's penal code; that is, a child who has been found to have been involved in delinquency. This definition also includes those acts that are considered offenses for youngsters (for example, status offenses) that are not law violations for adults.

These two definitions hint at a gap in how various segments of contemporary society view juvenile delinquents. Juvenile delinquents are (1) whomever we wish to identify as such, or (2) a narrowly defined legal category of youngsters declared by a court of law to be "involved in delinquency." Naturally, it is the latter definition that most concerns the juvenile justice system, although the former is important for reasons that will become clear in the next chapter. We must also acknowledge several groups of children who are not, strictly speaking, juvenile delinquents, but also come under the control of the juvenile justice system, some

Peers play an important role in much delinquency, especially behavior that can be viewed as social in nature, drinking alcoholic beverages for example. The question is why? Some theories, like social learning theory, focus on the physical and social benefits of the rule-breaking behavior, along with the direct influence of delinquent peers. Other theories, like self-control theory, look at the absence of effective parental controls and the personal enjoyment of risky behavior as holding clues to youthful misbehavior. What do you think is causing the youth in this picture to break the law?

only temporarily. The first group is the very young, particularly children, whose actions—*no matter what the severity of their misdeeds*—are, as a general rule, beyond the intervention of the *juvenile justice system* but are not beyond some measure of legal intervention. As mentioned, it is often the police who intervene when infants act, but the powers of the police to deal with them are limited. The fates of such children are also beyond the scope of this book.

Children who engage in acts that would not be crimes if committed by adults—**status offenders**—technically are not juvenile delinquents. However, since they are minors, they do fall under the jurisdiction of the juvenile justice system, although their treatment differs in substantial ways from that accorded to juvenile delinquents. The fate of status offenders in the juvenile justice system is a topic we explore at many points in this text. The final group, children who have not broken any rules or laws but are more correctly defined as victims of the actions or inactions of others (such as dependent or neglected children), is examined in chapter 9. These **nondelinquent children** are generally overlooked by juvenile justice textbooks. Nonetheless, they often find themselves clients of a system that is unsure what to do with them.

MEASURING DELINQUENCY: ISSUES AND INSIGHTS

How do we know the nature and extent of juvenile misconduct found in the United States? As importantly, how do we know about the nation's formal and informal responses to delinquency and related problems of youth? These questions have many answers. Beyond our own idiosyncratic and often unique experiences, the answers one finds depend on where those answers are sought. In contemporary U.S. society we have many such sources, ranging from fictional accounts portrayed by the entertainment industry to news media accounts of real events—or what are believed at the time to be real events—to government agency statistics and studies to, finally, the reports of nongovernmental organizations on the problems of delinquency.[6] We begin with a review of the mass media as a source of information about crime generally and about juvenile delinquency in particular.

CRIME, DELINQUENCY, AND THE MEDIA

The media—newspapers, radio, television, and even motion pictures and DVDs—shape both the questions asked about juvenile delinquency and the answers received. For example, "media frenzies" about real and alleged criminal events can create perceived **crime waves** (Fishman, 1976). Media-created crime waves can appear when the media highlight crimes that they previously ignored; report crimes without regard to their geographical, temporal, or social contexts; or when they fail to follow-up on their initial reports (i.e., to correct mistakes) (Kappeler and Potter, 2005:19). The media also can create the impression that isolated events are part of a larger, more pervasive pattern of crime. This attributed pattern then takes on a life of its own, becoming, in some cases, a crime wave or even a series of crime waves. Victor Kappeler and Gary Potter call these "manufactured" crime waves *myths* (2005:18).

An example of the news media creating a theme is the well-publicized school shootings in Arkansas, Kentucky, Mississippi, Pennsylvania, and Tennessee. However, the events that have come to define "school shootings" occurred at two locations: Columbine High School in Colorado in 1999, where 15 died—including the two gunmen by suicide; and Red Lake High School in Minnesota in 2005, where 7 students were shot and killed, again with the assailant taking his own life. Reporters kept the stories alive for weeks searching for answers and explanations for such events. (In chapter 12, we address the issue of juvenile violence and guns.) This topic—guns in schools—is one illustration of the impact of reporting on perceptions of youth crime.

Sometimes the news media pick up a story at its logical conclusion and perpetuate it beyond its natural life expectancy. For example, in the late 1980s local newspapers and television stations in widely separated cities began reporting the use of crack or rock cocaine by inner-city youths, often confusing smoking crack with freebasing.[7] The media entered this chapter of the "crack epidemic" when, according to scientific studies of the drug, its use had peaked, was leveling off, and was even declining in some areas (Kappeler and Potter, 2005:196–97). As Steven Belenko (1993) observed, public hysteria surrounding drug scares like that associated with crack is often whipped to near frenzy by often inaccurate media portrayals. Other cases, such as the moral panic that followed the 1989 attack of a female jogger in Central Park (the so-called "wilding" event), pander to society's worst racial, sexual, and social class stereotypes (Welch, Price, and Yankey, 2002).

Other examples of the media's influence on crime-fighting policies and practices abound, many having no real connection to "hard news." Appearing in increasing numbers over the past two decades, crime-fighting television programs that emphasize real crimes and real offenders, such as *Unsolved Mysteries* and *America's Most Wanted*, can give the impression that a particular type of crime is sweeping the nation (Kappeler and Potter, 2005:14–17). The popular "true crime" shows, such as *Rescue 911*, *Cops*, and *Real Stories of the Highway Patrol*, also have the potential to shape the public's image of crime and justice, for better or worse (Kappeler and Potter, 2005).

The government, through media leaks and official reports, also shapes public perceptions of crime. For example, a massive government-supported public relations campaign during the 1930s to criminalize marijuana succeeded largely for two reasons. First, the sheer weight of this campaign silenced the scientific community's objections to criminalizing what it viewed as a relatively harmless drug (Galliher and Walker, 1977). Second, the media blitz, which included the 1936 cult movie *Reefer Madness*, tied the drug to youthful misconduct, especially sexual promiscuity (Abadinsky, 1996:52). At the time,

> no state undertook any empirical or scientific study of the effects of the drug. Instead they [government officials and the public] relied on lurid and often unfounded accounts of marijuana's dangers as presented in what little newspaper coverage the drug received. (Bonnie and Whitebread, 1970:1021–22)

Similarly, government reports on juvenile delinquency during the 1940s and 1950s gave the public the impression that youth gangs were spiraling out of control, creating what has been referred to as "the great juvenile delinquency scare" (Mennel, 1973; Gilbert, 1986; Kappeler and Potter, 2005). These events, described in chapter 3, owe much to media accounts of congressional hearings on delinquency.

The news media have both professional standards and a professional code of ethics. However, the process of editorial oversight—a form of "informational gate-keeping"—is relatively simple, and the cloak of the First Amendment affords reporters and their sources considerable protection. Given the prominent cases of news fabrication that have appeared in the media recently, including false reports about President Bush's military record that surfaced during the 2004 elections, we should consider the information provided by such sources with some measure of skepticism, especially when the story appears to be nearly unbelievable. For example, *Washington Post* reporter Janet Cooke received a Pulitzer Prize for her story of eight-year-old Jimmy, a "third-generation heroin addict" living in one of Washington's low-income neighborhoods. As it turned out, Jimmy was, at best, a composite of children she met during her "research" for a story on heroin addiction in the District of Columbia. At worst, most if not all of her award-winning story was false. The *Post* ultimately gave back the Pulitzer Prize and fired Cooke ("Writer says drug story faked," 1981; "The Story," 1981). In recent years, the number of discredited reporters has grown to include employees at the *New York Times* and *USA Today* (Harris, 2004). To their credit, investigative reporters have played a major role in uncovering media frauds.

According to sociologist Barry Glassner (1999), the pressures to be entertaining or to be first with a raw and sensational story have created a culture of fear in America. In particular, he notes, people too often uncritically accept what they see on television as the truth. As Glassner observes:

> Fearmongers [journalists, special-interest advocacy groups, talk-show hosts] are experts at the use of poignant anecdotes in place of scientific evidence, the christening of isolated incidents as trends, depictions of entire categories of people as innately dangerous.

Although he also points out that some in the media help to debunk the fear spread by their brethren, at the end of the day we would all do well to consider the news and entertainment media highly suspect information sources about juvenile justice (and perhaps about crime generally). Even more troubling is the observation that governmental agencies may be among the fearmongers Glassner describes (see "Professor Barry Glassner," 2003; see also box 1.2).

Stanley Cohen (1980) popularized the term **moral panic** to describe a process that may be started by a complete fabrication or a story based loosely on true events. The story itself eventually takes on a life of its own apart from any ties to reality. In his case, Cohen described how British society overreacted to the problems allegedly created by the Mods and Rockers, two antagonistic youth groups of the 1960s. According to Cohen, moral panics follow a predictable pattern:

> A condition, episode, person or group of persons emerges to become defined in a stylized and stereotypical fashion by the mass media; the barricades are manned by editors, bishops, politicians, and other right thinking people; socially accredited experts pronounce their diagnoses and solutions; the ways of

coping are evolved or . . . resorted to; the condition then disappears, submerges
or deteriorates and becomes invisible. (1980:9)

Why are moral panics important? As described above, information put before
the public has a tendency to assume its own reality, without regard to the truthful-
ness or accuracy of the original information.[8] Richard McCorkle and Terance
Miethe (2002) employed this perspective in their examination of the "youth-gang
epidemic" reported in the United States during the 1980s. Some social problems
may be socially constructed, they observed, noting that "social problems are what
people think are social problems; if they don't see a problem, for all intents and
purposes it doesn't exist . . . . What is thus important is not the actual nature of the
condition, but rather what individuals say about that condition" (2002:11).

Crime waves. Moral panics. Socially constructed reality. Clearly, the generation and distribution of information about youthful misbehavior have become as
important to society's understanding of the breadth and depth of the problem as
the actual problems themselves. We turn next to social science research as an alternative method of discerning the problems of contemporary youths.

**Box 1.2   Not All Media Fakes Are Products of a Free Press:
The Role of the Office of National Drug Control Policy in Issuing
"Fake News Features"**

In early 2004, a "reporter" named Mike Morris appeared on many national media outlets,
including a spot right before Super Bowl XXXVIII, touting a new plan for a White House ad
campaign aimed at the dangers of drug use. The Office of National Drug Control Policy,
headed by a political appointee sometimes referred to as the "drug czar," issued the following lead-in statement for local media to use prior to airing the video:

> Despite the fact that marijuana is the most widely used illicit drug among
> today's youth, many parents admit they're still not taking the drug seriously.
> Now, the nation's experts in health, education, and safety have joined the Drug
> Czar to speak directly to parents about the very real risks of teen marijuana
> use. Mike Morris has more.

A person purporting to be reporter Mike Morris then narrated a brief series of interviews
with such experts.

As it turned out, except for John Walters, drug czar at that time, the rest of the people
appearing in this "news break" were essentially actors, claimed Susan A. Poling, managing
associate counsel for the Government Accounting Office (GAO), who further observed that
such packaged materials purporting to be news stories amounted to "illegal 'covert
propaganda.'" This "story" was one of seven different prepackaged "news reports" issued
by the drug czar's office. The stories or their content were not the issue. The problem was
that they were packaged to look like independent journalism when in fact they were created
by the federal government as part of an anti-drug campaign, a practice described by the
GAO as misleading at best and perhaps, as a violation of the fundamental principle of open
government, illegal.

Source: Connolly (2005).

SOCIAL SCIENCE RESEARCH

When people talk about the extent of delinquency plaguing American society, an often-quoted saying comes to mind: There are liars, damned liars, and statisticians.[9] *Statistics do not lie.* However, they can be manipulated, distorted, overlooked, and even suppressed. As used here, **statistics** is a term that refers to numerical facts or data.[10] Crime statistics, including those for juvenile offenders, encompass the type and number of complaints, arrest reports, and probation and aftercare cases; rates of violations and revocations; and rates of failure (and of successes) for a wide variety of juvenile-based programs. These levels, rates, and the like are expressed as raw numbers, percentages, means, medians, and modes. They become statistics in the reporting.

Science—like journalism—is a form of human inquiry. Science as a process and scientific findings differ in significant ways from journalistic efforts. To be scientific is to be regulated by the systematic principles that guide any discipline's fact-finding efforts (Babbie, 2004). Researchers committed to the principles of scientific inquiry refrain from prejudging what they will find or the specific answers they will seek. Instead, they frame their research questions carefully, establish the level of proof required, and report whatever answers they find.[11] Scientific inquiry also must be free and independent; an idea embodied in the **principle of autonomy** (Kaplan, 1964). That is, no individual or group should have the power to steer the eventual outcome toward one conclusion or another. Finally, unlike many nonscientific pursuits, science demands an openness that is unique and essential. Scientists encourage others to question and even challenge their research questions, methods, findings, and conclusions. The only way that a science grows, expands, and ultimately contributes to society is by the actions of those who question its findings, conclusions, explanations, and laws.[12]

Researchers also want answers that are accurate, reliable, valid, and generalizable.[13] **Accuracy** is the relative absence of mistakes: The fewer the mistakes, the more accurate the information. Researchers often take great pains to describe how their data were collected. This exemplifies both accuracy and the openness of science to criticism. Researchers usually list the steps taken to ensure that there were as few errors or mistakes in the data collection as humanly possible.

Factually accurate information is only one part of scientific inquiry. The information also should be reliable. **Reliability** refers to the research method's ability to yield the same results when used by different individuals. For example, suppose you are given a description of a specific delinquency offense and one month's worth of police reports. You sort through the reports, counting the number of times the offense occurred in that month. If, using the same instructions and stack of records, you find the same number as the person before you there is a high degree of confidence in your results: The method and findings are reliable. If the results are not the same, then we must reconsider (1) the instructions for counting or (2) the selection criteria employed by those doing the counting.

Scientific information also should be valid, and it is on this point that the statistics produced by the nation's criminal justice system often fall short of the mark. **Validity** means that the researchers' findings and the reality they seek to measure are the same. As an illustration of validity, consider a hypothetical study of American delinquency that purports to contain "all acts of delinquency committed by youths in the United States." The researcher satisfies us that the information is accurate and reliable. However, is it valid? Given 50 state governments and the federal government, how can we ever be sure that the study contains all relevant information? Indeed, determining a study's validity is one of the most difficult tasks confronting consumers of such reports. Statisticians have sophisticated techniques for determining this or that type of validity, but often consumers must decide a study's validity on the basis of whatever they can glean from the researcher's definitions and the way the information was collected.

The usefulness of a study depends largely on its **generalizability**. This trait refers to the researchers' ability to infer from recorded observations to some other set of subjects or phenomena for which they do not have similar information. For example, can a study of delinquency in a North Dakota community be generalized to the nation as a whole? How about generalizing to California or South Dakota? How about another community in North Dakota? Even the most carefully constructed and scientifically designed study may have limited generalizability, a fact that most honest researchers address as a limitation of their findings.

Lastly, before a given piece of research—a final research report or a scholarly journal report—becomes part of the scientific literature it must undergo a process of rigorous **peer review**. For their part, academic (or scholarly) research journals engage in both internal and external reviews, whereby the editor or a panel of associate editors decides whether a work submitted for publication should be sent to three or four subject area experts for careful reading and review. The recommendations of these impartial reviewers are then considered by the journal's editor and associate editors prior to a final decision to accept or reject the submitted work. Governmental agencies also subject research reports funded by federal and state money to a similar process by which area experts outside the agency read and critique the findings prior to publication and widespread dissemination. The work also must often pass an internal review process—sometimes including judging the political implications of the findings—before receiving final approval for publication. Nongovernmental organizations, sometimes referred to as NGOs, also issue research results and reports; many such groups similarly subject these works to internal and external review by involved parties, recognizing that such a process enhances their credibility.

REPORTING SYSTEMS FOR DELINQUENCY: MEASURES AND TRENDS

Systematic insights into delinquency—ones that meet the rigorous criteria of social science research—come from many sources. Some of these measures are the products of governmental agencies and others are generated by social scientists independently or under contract to a governmental agency. In order to introduce social scientific insights into the functioning of the juvenile justice system, we present three different types of information: victimization statistics, arrest statistics, and juvenile court processing statistics. The purpose of this review is twofold. First, it will provide an appreciation of the array of information available on youth crime, much of which contributes to the content of later chapters in this textbook. Second, the information reviewed in the following three sections tells us a great deal about current delinquency levels and recent trends. It gives us a base point from which to begin our study of juvenile justice. We turn first to the surveys of youthful victimization.

YOUTHFUL VICTIMS OF CRIME:
NATIONAL CRIME VICTIMIZATION SURVEYS

Surveying people about socially relevant concerns and issues is an old idea, dating back at least 250 years. The modern crime-victim survey, however, dates only to 1966. At that time, social scientists and government officials agreed that the existing formal record of crime in America, the FBI's *Uniform Crime Reports*, provided only a partial picture. Some other portion of law violations, suspected to be considerable and called the **dark figure of crime**, would require self-reporting if it were to become known. In the 1970s, researchers refined and field-tested the self-reporting survey method for studying crime victims. The **National Crime Victimization Survey (NCVS)** emerged as the primary method.

Twice a year Census Bureau employees contact nearly 60,000 physical addresses and ask about the crimes committed against all residents age 12 and older. Researchers randomly select the addresses in a scientific fashion to guarantee as representative a sample as possible. The NCVS includes two major forms of criminal behavior—personal crimes and property crimes. The four NCVS personal crimes are: (1) rape, (2) robbery, (3) assault, and (4) personal theft (purse snatching and pocket picking). The three NCVS property crimes are:[14] (1) household burglary, (2) property theft, and (3) motor vehicle theft.

Table 1.1 contains the personal victimization rates for seven age groups. The National Crime Victimization Survey includes as violent crime rape, sexual assault, robbery, and assault. Because the NCVS interviews persons about their victimizations, murder and manslaughter obviously cannot be included. Only personal victimizations make sense when comparing age groups, since the other offenses refer to property victimizations. The young are far more likely than the elderly to be violent-crime victims. Only for the crime of purse snatching/pocket picking do the rates of those 65 and older remotely resemble those of any younger age group. One could conclude from this table that American youth face a unique set of dangers. To be quite young—that is, 15 or younger—is, with a few exceptions, to be in one of the most dangerous age groups.

Our review of the NCVS is useful for at least three reasons. First, we use the results of various victimization surveys at different junctures in this book. Second, although the NCVS has its shortcomings and critics, the process of collecting self-reported victimization information over the past 30 years has helped shed light on the dark figure of crime. But victimization represents only part of the youth-crime problem. Another important element is found in the statistics created by police officers as they interact with the nation's youth, a topic to which we turn next.

Table 1.1   Victimization Rates for Persons Age 12 and Over, by Type of Crime and Age of Victims, 2004

Age of Victim	Population	Victimizations per 1,000 persons age 12 or older							Personal Theft
		Violent Crimes							
						Assault			
		All	Rape/ Sexual Assault	Robbery	Total	Aggra- vated	Simple		
12–15	17,082,980	49.7	2.2	3.8	43.6	6.2	37.5		2.1
16–19	16,256,320	45.9	2.5	4.8	38.6	11.3	27.2		3.3
20–24	20,272,750	43.0	2.5	3.1	37.4	9.4	28.0		0.7*
25–34	39,509,560	23.7	0.7*	2.4	20.6	4.8	15.8		0.6*
35–49	65,580,130	17.9	0.5	2.1	15.2	3.9	11.4		0.7
50–64	48,411,930	11.0	0.3*	1.1	9.6	1.9	7.8		0.5*
65 or older	34,590,050	2.1	0.1*	0.3*	1.8	0.5*	1.3		0.8*

Note: Detail may not add to total shown because of rounding.

* Based on 10 or fewer sample cases.

Source: Adapted from Catalano (2005:7, Table 6).

KIDS, COPS, AND CRIME: UNIFORM CRIME REPORTS

In 1870 Congress authorized the attorney general to report on crime in the nation. Throughout the late 1920s, discussions between the Department of Justice, International Association of Chiefs of Police, and the Federal Bureau of Investigation culminated in a voluntary reporting program (International Association of Chiefs of Police, 1929). Congress formally assigned to the Federal Bureau of Investigation the task of collecting crime data and reporting crime in 1930, thus creating an annual report entitled *Crime in America*, otherwise known as the *Uniform Crime Reports* (UCR). By the late 1960s, with the cooperation of the National Sheriffs Associations, the UCR achieved near-total coverage of the nation.

The UCR contains many different types of crime information, but perhaps the most important elements are the Part I and Part II offenses.[15] Part I offenses are crimes known to the police; that is, they reflect formal complaints received. Part II offenses are all other crimes that result in an arrest. The **Part I offenses** consist of four personal crimes (homicide, rape, aggravated assault, and robbery) and four property crimes (burglary, larceny-theft, auto theft, and arson). According to the FBI, Part I offenses are the ones most likely to be reported and occur with sufficient frequency for comparison (Federal Bureau of Investigation, 1998:1–2). The eight crimes included as Part I offenses also are called **index crimes** because taken together they form an index, or mathematical representation, of the nation's crime picture, generally represented as a number of offenses per 100,000 population in the United States.

Part II offenses do not meet the frequency-of-occurrence or seriousness tests, or they may be "victimless" crimes; that is, there is no clearly defined victim other than society. In addition, three Part II offenses—curfew and loitering, running away, and suspicion—are not true criminal offenses, although the first two are important for the study of juvenile justice. Remember too that Part II offenses are crimes that have resulted in an arrest.

If we accept the UCR as an indicator of the criminal justice system's ability to process known crimes, then the annual UCR is important in its own right. Consider the crime statistics summarized in table 1.2. Nearly 3 in 10 of the almost 2.2 million juveniles arrested in 2003 were females. You might want to look down the column for females and determine in which crime categories female juveniles were either overrepresented or underrepresented. For example, females accounted for 69% of the arrests for prostitution and commercialized vice and 59% of the runaways; at the other extreme, they accounted for 2% of the forcible rape arrests and gambling arrests. Indeed, any time the percent of female arrests exceeds 29% (that reported for total offenses), then they are overrepresented in that arrest category.

Similarly, consider the arrests of youths under the age of 15. About 3 in 10 of all juvenile arrests involved children less than 15 years old. Youths in this age group accounted for 61% of arson arrests, 44% of vandalism arrests, and half of the arrests for sex offenses, except forcible rape and prostitution; however, only 2% of the DUI arrests and 6% of the arrests for embezzlement involved youths under 15.

Finally, the last three columns in table 1.2 reveal the percent change in juvenile arrests for three periods: 1994–2003, 1999–2003, and 2002–2003. Like general crime trends in the United States, overall juvenile crime is going down. It is interesting to note that juvenile crime took a couple of years to "catch up" to the general crime trend, since juvenile crime had increased throughout the late 1980s and early 1990s (Snyder, 1997:2). Many of the greatest decreases are found between 1994 and 2003, as overall arrests dropped by nearly 20% over this decade. For example, consider that juvenile arrests declined for *every index crime* during the first two time frames, including murder and nonnegligent manslaughter, robbery, burglary, and motor vehicle theft. The comparison for 2002–2003 suggests that these declines have leveled off somewhat. Nonindex crime presented a slightly different story. Juvenile arrests for some offenses did indeed decline, including forgery and counterfeiting and stolen property; and some of those offense categories that experienced declines were also "traditional" juvenile offenses such as vagrancy, curfew and loitering, and runaways. Juvenile arrests for other offenses, however, increased when compared between 1994 and 2003, but by 1999 and 2003 they too were declining (e.g., liquor law violations, driving under the influence, drug abuse violations, and offenses against the family and children).[16]

CHILDREN IN COURT:
NATIONAL JUVENILE COURT STATISTICS

The National Center for Juvenile Justice, funded by the Office of Juvenile Justice and Delinquency Prevention, publishes annual reports of juvenile court statistics. These reports, initially begun over 70 years ago, give us a snapshot of the children processed by the nation's juvenile courts. The classification scheme used by the National Center maintains the general distinctions between Part I and Part II UCR offenses. Recall that a delinquent act is one that if committed by an adult would result in an arrest for a felony or misdemeanor. Consider, then, the follow-

Table 1.2   UCR Index Crime Arrests, 2003, and Trends, 1994–2003

Most Serious Offense	2003 Estimated Number of Juvenile Arrests	Percent of Total Juvenile Arrests		Percent Change		
		Female	Under age 15	1994– 2003	1999– 2003	2002– 2003
Total	2,220,300	29%	32%	−18%	−11%	0%
Violent crime index	92,300	18	33	−32	−9	0
Murder and nonnegligent manslaughter	1,130	9	11	−68	−18	−10
Forcible rape	4,240	2	37	−25	−11	−9
Robbery	25,440	9	25	−43	−8	3
Aggravated assault	61,490	24	36	−26	−9	0
Property crime index	464,300	32	37	−38	−15	−3
Burglary	85,100	12	35	−40	−15	−1
Larceny-theft	325,600	39	38	−35	−15	−3
Motor vehicle theft	44,500	17	25	−52	−15	−4
Arson	8,200	12	61	−36	−12	−3
Nonindex						
Other assaults	241,900	32	43	10	5	5
Forgery and counterfeiting	4,700	35	13	−47	−36	−8
Fraud	8,100	33	18	−29	−37	−9
Embezzlement	1,200	40	6	15	−30	−17
Stolen property (buying, receiving, possessing)	24,300	15	27	−46	−19	−5
Vandalism	107,700	14	44	−33	−11	2
Weapons (carrying, possessing, etc.)	39,200	11	36	−41	−6	11
Prostitution and commercialized vice	1,400	69	14	31	23	11
Sex offense (except forcible rape and prostitution)	18,300	9	51	2	3	−3
Drug abuse violations	197,100	16	17	19	−3	4
Gambling	1,700	2	15	−59	46	1
Offenses against the family and children	7,000	39	35	19	−24	−19
Driving under the influence (DUI)	21,000	20	2	33	−9	−4
Liquor law violations	136,900	35	10	4	−22	−6
Drunkenness	17,600	23	13	−11	−19	−6
Disorderly conduct	193,000	31	41	13	0	6
Vagrancy	2,300	25	25	−50	−20	9
All other offenses (except traffic)	379,800	27	28	−2	−12	−1
Suspicion	1,500	24	26	−77	−74	−53
Curfew and loitering	136,500	30	29	−1	−18	−8
Runaways	123,600	59	36	−42	−18	−2

Source: Snyder (2005:3).

ing four groups of offenses that are used in the annual report entitled *Juvenile Court Statistics*: (1) crimes against persons, (2) crimes against property, (3) drug law violations, and (4) offenses against the public order.[17] The National Center's annual report also includes information on status offenses. Status offenses, as we observed earlier in this chapter, are not true acts of delinquency. Rather, they are acts or types of conduct that are offenses only when committed or engaged in by a juvenile and that can be adjudicated only through a court with jurisdiction over juveniles. The report includes statistics for the following status offenses: (1) runaways, (2) truancy, (3) ungovernability, and (4) status liquor law violations.

Table 1.3 contains a summary of arguably the most serious delinquency cases processed in 1999 by the nation's courts with juvenile jurisdiction—personal offenses.[18] These figures suggest that most—but not all—personal offense categories declined throughout the 1990s. Consider, first, that for criminal homicide, forcible rape, robbery, and aggravated assault, the number of offenses declined most in the last five years of the decade and registered an overall decline as well. However, the overall personal offense figures and rates increased because the category of simple assaults, which includes unlawful intentional infliction or attempted infliction of less than serious bodily harm without a deadly or dangerous weapon, nearly doubled during the first five years of the 1990s, and continued to increase during the final five years. That is, owing to the huge volume of such offenses relative to the other personal offenses, changes in simple assaults "drove" the total numbers and rates. For example, the total number of person offenses increased over the

Table 1.3   Person Offense Cases Handled by U.S. Juvenile Courts, 1990–1999

Cases Disposed	1990	1995	1999	Percentage Change	
				1990–99	1995–99
Total Person Offenses*	249,500	387,000	387,100	55%	0%
Violent Crime Index	93,600	136,900	86,900	–7	–37
Criminal Homicide	2,300	2,800	1,800	–21	–34
Forcible Rape	5,100	6,800	4,200	–19	–38
Robbery	27,600	40,200	25,100	–9	–38
Aggravated Assault	58,600	87,100	55,800	–5	–36
Simple Assault	131,500	218,600	255,900	95	17
Case Rate**					
Total Person Offenses*	9.7	13.7	13.2	35%	–4%
Violent Crime Index	3.7	4.8	3.0	–19	–39
Criminal Homicide	0.1	0.1	0.1	–31	–37
Forcible Rape	0.2	0.2	0.1	–29	–41
Robbery	1.1	1.4	0.9	–21	–40
Aggravated Assault	2.3	3.1	1.9	–17	–38
Simple Assault	5.1	7.7	8.7	70	13

Percent change figures are based on unrounded numbers.
* Total includes other person offense categories not listed.
** Per 1,000 youth age 10 through the upper age of juvenile court jurisdiction.
Source: Puzzanchera (2003b:1).

1990s for both the number of cases disposed (55%) and the case rate (35%), while in all but one category—simple assault—the numbers and rates declined.

The figures contained in table 1.3 appear to indicate that for the most serious offenses the youth-crime problem increased in the early 1990s. In point of fact, the overall number of delinquency cases in the United States, while experiencing large increases in the 1980s and early 1990s, started a modest decline by the mid-1990s (figure 1.2). In spite of these declines, however, the nation's juvenile courts handled more than four times as many delinquency cases in 2000 as in 1960 (Puzzanchera et al., 2004:6). Stated differently, in 1960 juvenile courts processed about 1,100 cases every day; by 2000, this figure had increased to roughly 4,500. While the overall delinquency arrest figures (table 1.2) and the cases processed in juvenile court (figure 1.2) suggest a downturn in delinquency beginning in the mid-1990s, the overall level of rates and cases indicates that delinquency will remain a serious problem for the nation well into the twenty-first century.

The youth-crime statistics reviewed in this portion of chapter 1 tell only part of the story. Other issues and concerns remain to be explored, and in many instances, but not all, the sources of our insights are the same: official reports on the nature and extent of administration of juvenile justice in contemporary society. Indeed, the next section provides a preliminary understanding of the national, state, and local systems of juvenile justice.

Figure 1.2
Juvenile Cases Processed, 1960–1999

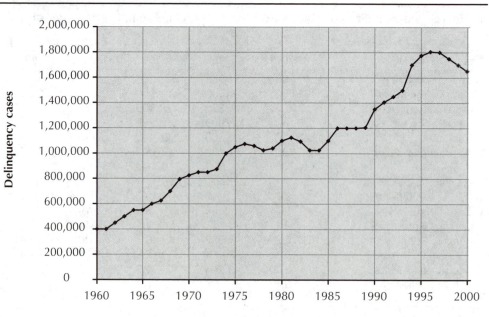

Source: Puzzanchera et al. (2004:6).

Box 1.3   Other Sources of Information about Delinquents and Delinquency

Self-report studies constitute another source of information about delinquency. Asking someone about his or her involvement in crime may seem counterintuitive: Why be honest about dishonest activities? Although this method of collecting information about crime and delinquency has been debated for more than a quarter century (Nettler, 1978), most such surveys appear to be both reliable and valid (Clark and Tifft, 1966; Elliott and Ageton, 1980; Hardt and Petersen-Hardt, 1977). They accomplish these goals by providing respondents with either **confidentiality** (the researcher knows the respondent's identity but refuses to reveal it) or **anonymity** (the respondent's identity is unknown even to the researcher).

Over the past 30 years self-report surveys have provided considerable insights into delinquency, perhaps none more so than the National Youth Survey (NYS) and the three-site Causes and Correlates study. Begun in 1976, the NYS followed members of a probability sample of nearly 2,000 youths from the time they were ages 11 to 17 to when they were 24 to 30 (Elliott, Huizinga, and Ageton, 1985). The Causes and Correlates program consisted of three coordinated, longitudinal projects in Rochester, New York; Denver, Colorado; and Pittsburgh, Pennsylvania. The Causes and Correlates researchers followed nearly 4,000 participants at regular intervals over a 10-year period beginning in 1986 (Kelley, Huizinga, Thornberry, and Loeber, 1997). Both studies have contributed to our understanding of delinquency and are cited at various points in this text.

Finally, qualitative studies, especially those involving individual delinquents or groups of delinquents or types of delinquency, provide rare insights into the social fabric of youthful misbehavior. Two of the more popular methods are the **case study** and the **observational study**. For example, in chapter 3 we recommend *The Ville*, a book with two key protagonists: a police officer and a neighborhood youth with a propensity for misbehavior. This book presents slices of both their lives in an effort to reveal the forces compelling both to act as they do. The book reads more like a novel or a journalistic account than a scholarly text on police juvenile interactions, a characterization shared by many case studies. Both case studies and observational studies, as we make clear in chapter 10, have also contributed immensely to our understanding of geographically unique forms of delinquency, such as gang behavior. However, the ability to generalize from qualitative research is questionable (Babbie, 2004).

RESPONDING TO DELINQUENCY AND DELINQUENTS

A child's parents or other family members may respond to observed, detected, or suspected delinquent acts. Often these informal first responders provide sufficient punishments—sometimes, more than enough. At other times, the acts are of such a serious nature that they cannot be handled within the circle of family and friends. Perhaps people other than forgiving relatives observe or are victims of a child's misbehavior. On such occasions, more institutionalized and formalized responders may get involved. This is the realm of the criminal justice system. The following sections provide a brief overview of the criminal justice agencies and organizations that will be addressed in a juvenile justice context later in this book.

LAW ENFORCEMENT

Most discussions of criminal justice and juvenile justice begin with the police. Police agencies supply both adult and juvenile justice systems with their raw material: accused offenders. It is important to note that police agencies exist at all three levels of government in the United States: federal, state, and local. As we will explain in chapter 3 and elsewhere, most juvenile justice activity in this country occurs at the local level (city, county, and township departments). For example, the nation's nearly 13,000 municipal agencies handle the bulk of policing and employ most of the full-time sworn personnel, including the uniformed officers who are assigned to respond to calls for service (Reaves and Hickman, 2004:v). Next in line are more than 3,000 county law enforcement agencies that are generally administered by elected sheriffs. In the early history of the United States, the sheriff was the chief law enforcement agent in the county. The authority of sheriffs in some jurisdictions has been eroded over the past 50 years and in some instances has been reduced to jail operations and tax collections. In some states in the South, West, and Midwest, and especially in rural areas, sheriffs have retained most of their powers.

Officers in the other two types of agencies, including most state police and federal law enforcement agents, are far less likely to have contact with juvenile offenders. In some regions the state police are devoted solely to highway patrol functions. In other states they have general police powers and can enforce the complete range of criminal laws, including those dealing with juveniles, throughout the state. The state police, where they have general police powers, may provide a state-level criminal investigation agency. Still, in terms of the volume of contacts, state police officers are far less likely than local officers to come in contact with juveniles. Federal law enforcement authority is spread among a variety of agencies, and no single agency has total responsibility for enforcing all federal laws. Federal agencies tend to be specialized by function (customs, drug enforcement, counterfeiting, protective services, and the like), and most agents have little or no contact with juvenile offenders, unless the miscreant child has the bad fortune to commit a criminal act on federal property.

Police officers are called on to perform at least three major functions: law enforcement, order maintenance, and public service. Law enforcement is presumed to be the major responsibility for local police personnel. In reality, most police officers spend little time enforcing the laws, including traffic laws. Some observers (see Champion, 1998:97–98) have noted that on average, police officers devote less than one-fourth of their working hours to law enforcement or crime-related activities broadly defined. If the police are not doing law enforcement, what are they doing? The vast majority of police time is consumed by order maintenance (e.g., loud parties, honking horns, traffic flow) and public service.

COURTS

Court actors include the prosecuting attorney, defense attorneys, judges, and auxiliary actors in what frequently is called the courtroom work group (Eisenstein and Jacob, 1977; M. Jones, 2004). Prosecutors, like the police, operate at all three levels of government. Again, in terms of juvenile justice processes, local prosecutors (sometimes called children's court attorneys) handle the bulk of juvenile delinquency prosecutions. The prosecutor has been characterized by many as the single most influential actor in our justice system (Katzman, 1991; Neubauer, 1999). The prosecutor has the power to decide whether or not to go forward with criminal charges. The prosecutor also influences decisions on matters such as bail, plea bargaining, and sentencing.

In some jurisdictions, as many as 80% to 90% of the minors brought to court waive their right to an attorney, often simply because they do not understand what they are waiving or what the term means (J. Jones, 2004:2). When present in court, defense representation comes about in one of two ways. If defendants (or their families) can afford their own attorneys, they can retain their own lawyers. However, for the more than 60% of defendants who are indigent, the court will appoint an attorney. Some courts maintain lists of lawyers available for appointment, but in many large jurisdictions this work is handled by appointed attorneys, contract defense attorneys, or public defenders. Unlike most local prosecuting attorneys, who are elected, public defenders typically are appointed to office (Abadinsky, 2002a; Holten and Lamar, 1991).

Judges play a vital role in processing cases for juveniles as well as adults. Prior to trial (or the adjudicatory hearing for juveniles) the judge may conduct a preliminary or probable cause hearing. This hearing requires the prosecuting attorney to present enough evidence to show sufficient probable cause to send the case forward for adjudication. The defense may choose not to present any evidence at such hearings, but to use the proceedings as an opportunity to get a preview of the prosecutor's case. At these preliminary hearings the judge will inform the accused of the charges, will address the issue of bail (typically not applicable to juveniles), and will deal with the right to counsel. After the pretrial or preadjudicatory matters are settled, the case will finally be set on the docket with a firm trial date. Beyond this point judges are less sympathetic to requests for continuances, and in all states prosecutors are battling speedy trial deadlines by which they must bring the accused to trial.

In most jurisdictions in the United States, juveniles are not granted the right to trial by jury (see the discussion of *McKeiver v. Pennsylvania* in chapter 5). However, about a dozen states do provide accused delinquents with the option of a jury trial. In many of these cases, trial procedures for juveniles and adults may be virtually indistinguishable.

After the adjudicatory hearing is completed, the judge (or jury) will decide whether the accused youngster is delinquent beyond a reasonable doubt (see the discussion of *In re Winship* in chapter 5). If the child is found to be delinquent, the court will hold a dispositional hearing to decide where along the corrections continuum the child should be placed.

CORRECTIONS

Corrections can involve a vast array of programs for youngsters. In simplest form, juveniles can be placed in community-based, noninstitutional programs or in secure, institutional placements. Community-based programs include probation, parole, shelter care, and nonsecure residential placements (halfway houses). Secure placements include detention centers (for short-term incarceration) and state training schools. Secure placements might involve farm, ranch, and camp programs as well. In addition to these two categories (or more precisely, between these two ends of the spectrum) are what are now known as intermediate sanctions. **Intermediate sanctions** include intensive probation supervision, home confinement/electronic monitoring, and correctional boot camps, among others. In the end, every adjudicated delinquent will encounter some type of correctional placement.

PROVIDING FOR JUVENILE JUSTICE:
A NATIONAL PERSPECTIVE

Four types of public and private organizations help form the nation's public policy responses to delinquency: (1) governmental committees and commissions, (2) governmental and quasi-governmental agencies, (3) professional organizations, and (4) private foundations and interest groups. Since we refer to many of these organizations by name at various points in the text, we next introduce several of the more influential ones, providing a review of their mission statements and relevant modes of information dissemination.

GOVERNMENTAL COMMITTEES AND COMMISSIONS

Special justice commissions and committees became a fact of life in the twentieth century. In the mid-1960s, these activities took on a new status when the President's Commission on Law Enforcement and Administration of Justice redefined the criminal justice landscape and provided guidelines that continue to be viable long after their publication. The president's commission issued *Task Force Report: Juvenile Delinquency and Youth Crime* (1967b), a comprehensive assessment of the juvenile court system and prevention measures. The report contained 20 appendixes written by a "who's who" of that period's leading juvenile delinquency theorists, researchers, and practitioners; many of their recommendations became policies in the 1970s. A decade later, the congressionally mandated National Advisory Committee on Juvenile Justice and Delinquency Prevention (1980) provided detailed policy recommendations, many of which we will refer to in this text.

PERMANENT GOVERNMENTAL AND
QUASI-GOVERNMENTAL AGENCIES

The Office of Juvenile Justice and Delinquency Prevention (OJJDP) provides "national leadership, coordination, and resources to develop, implement, and support effective methods to prevent juvenile victimization and respond appropriately to juvenile delinquency" (OJJDP, 1998a:1). Established in 1974 with congressional passage of the Juvenile Justice and Delinquency Prevention Act, OJJDP is organizationally under the Department of Justice's Office of Justice Programs. Missing children were added to OJJDP's mission in 1984. Four years later, Congress added the twin goals of addressing youth gang problems and preventing and treating juvenile drug abuse. In 1992, OJJDP took over responsibility for administering the Victims of Child Abuse Act. Reorganized in 1992, OJJDP added several new priorities, including developing services for juveniles in secure custody, providing gender-specific services, providing information regarding hate crimes, developing model boot camp programs, and providing effective aftercare programs. A major function of OJJDP is its Juvenile Justice Clearinghouse (JJC) (http://ojjdp.ncjrs.org/programs/ProgSummary.asp?pi=2). Established in 1979, JJC links OJJDP's publications, research findings, and program information to juvenile justice policy makers, researchers, and the public. Since the late 1990s, OJJDP has assumed a national leadership presence in coordinating efforts to define, report, and reduce the disproportionate confinement of minority group members in the nation's correctional facilities for youthful offenders, a problem known widely by the abbreviation DMC, and a topic revisited in chapter 12. The significance of OJJDP as a source of leadership and funds for the nation's juvenile delinquency intervention and prevention programs cannot be overstated.

The National Council of Juvenile and Family Court Judges was founded in 1937 as a means to address issues involving the administration of juvenile justice and family law in the United States. The national council, located on the campus of the University of Nevada at Reno, sponsors training programs and symposia for juvenile and family court judges and other justice system professionals. It also promotes policy development and continuing education programs and publishes the *Juvenile and Family Court Journal*.

PROFESSIONAL ORGANIZATIONS

For every criminal justice profession there is at least one organization. The academicians who teach in these areas—your professors—have national organizations, including the American Society of Criminology (ASC) and the Academy of Criminal Justice Sciences (ACJS). Each organization has state and regional arms, all dedicated to enhancing the professionalism of criminal justice and criminology professors. Each one publishes a newsletter, for example, *The Criminologist* and *ACJS Today*. The ASC also publishes two journals, *Criminology* and *Criminology and Public Policy*. Likewise, the ACJS publishes *Journal of Criminal Justice Education* and *Justice Quarterly*. The newsletters provide general and topical information for the membership, while the journals publish externally reviewed scholarly research and policy-related articles.

Similar professional support comes from such organizations as the American Correctional Association (ACA), the American Jail Association (AJA), the American Probation and Parole Association, the National Juvenile Detention Association, the Juvenile Justice Trainers Association, and the National Council of Juvenile Correctional Administrators, to name a few. The first two admit as members those individuals who deliver services to juveniles in various correctional settings and the community. The other four organizations have specific juvenile justice missions. Like academic organizations, these entities sponsor state, regional, and national meetings where members participate in workshops, training, and general discussions about their work. Also like the academic organizations, they provide topical newsletters and publish professional magazines, such as the ACA's *Corrections Today* and the AJA's *American Jails.*

PRIVATE FOUNDATIONS AND INTEREST GROUPS

Literally dozens of private foundations and interest groups include in their mission statements a concern for the health, safety, and welfare of the nation's youth, including the consequences of delinquency. One group stands out from the rest in the area of research and policy. Founded in 1907 and headquartered in San Francisco, the National Council on Crime and Delinquency (NCCD) "conducts research and initiates programs and policies to reduce crime and delinquency. The NCCD seeks to influence public policies that affect the nature of crime and delinquency and the future of the justice system" (NCCD, 1998:1). The council created the Children's Research Center in 1991 to work with state and local agencies on implementation of structured decision-making systems for child protection. It is also worth mentioning that many states have statewide councils on crime and delinquency that serve as watchdogs, monitoring the lives of state-level adult and juvenile offenders.

Besides maintaining a newsletter on its Web site (http://www.nccd-crc.org), NCCD also publishes two academic journals, *The Journal of Research on Crime and Delinquency (JRCD)* and *Crime and Delinquency (C&D)*. *JRCD* is described by its editorial board as including "reports of original research in crime and delinquency, and the critical analysis of theories and concepts *especially pertinent to research development in this field*" (NCCD, 1998; emphasis added); *C&D*, conversely, is a "policy oriented journal for the professional with direct involvement in the criminal justice field" (NCCD, 1998:2).

SUMMARY

Three themes have dominated this chapter: (1) defining delinquency and delinquents, (2) providing reliable and valid measures of both phenomena, and (3) describing the nation's systematic responses to the problems created by youthful offenders. The first set of definitions was both sociological and legalistic. Indeed, that is the typical approach to defining what constitutes delinquency and the identity of the delinquents. Officially, youths are not juvenile delinquents unless and until they have been adjudicated as such. Legally and socially, delinquents are whomever we choose to designate as such. These definitions and distinctions should help you (and could have helped the fictional students in the chapter's opening vignette) to make important distinctions between delinquency's definition, measurement, and explanation (often called *juvenile delinquency*) and society's formal responses to acts of delinquency and the actors themselves (often called *juvenile justice*). Even from these cursory differentiations between the goals of juvenile delinquency and juvenile justice, it should be clear that each has much to contribute to our overall picture of delinquents and delinquency in the United States. Practitioners in the juvenile justice system rely heavily on legalistic and sociological definitions, measures, and even, as we shall make clear, theories of delinquency and delinquents. The sociology of juvenile delinquency would likewise be incomplete without an appreciation for the various formal responses to juvenile misconduct. We acknowledge these symbiotic relationships, but also stress that this textbook is, in the final analysis, an exploration of the juvenile justice system.[19]

The second theme focused on the many ways to measure delinquency. Where we look for information about juvenile delinquents clearly shapes our understanding of the problem. The mass media present many images of the problem, views often influenced by economic concerns, whether we are talking about the entertainment industry or the more journalistic media outlets. Official statistics give the nation a far more complex and sometimes less sensational view of delinquency. The fact that this is a textbook on juvenile justice, however, explains our emphasis on understanding and appreciating the official picture of delinquency. Currently, it is the official statistical picture that, rightly or wrongly, determines public policy toward delinquents, with, as we observed, a little help from the mass media.

The final theme is meant to serve as a guidepost for the remainder of the text. A full understanding of the nation's response to delinquents requires an appreciation of not only the formal systemic responses to delinquency, but also those of the policy-oriented think tanks and interest groups. As the text unfolds, our goal is to make this understanding more complete.

CRITICAL REVIEW QUESTIONS

1. Why do you think there are so many different definitions of delinquency?

2. How would you respond to the person who suggests that we ought to punish 6-, 7-, and 8-year-old children as adults? Would your answer change if the crime was homicide and the victim was another child?

3. Does the social definition of the delinquent resemble any other sociological contribution found in this chapter? Explain your answer.

4. Do you think the mass media's standards are too high or too low? Have you ever read a retraction of a story that appeared in the newspaper or was broadcast on an electronic medium? What problems do you see with retractions? (*Hint*: Think about a criminal trial in which a judge instructs the jury to disregard a witness's statement after the fact.)

5. Do you take issue with the statement that scientific studies of crime and justice issues are held to a higher standard than, for example, mass media reports on these same issues? Which single element of scientific inquiry do you think is most critical in this regard? Explain your choice.

6. Compare and contrast the definitional issues raised by the following statistical sources of crime data: Uniform Crime Reports, Juvenile Court Statistics, and National Crime Victimization Surveys.

7. Each source of crime statistics in question 6 has a different audience. Identify each audience; then describe how the source meets the needs of the constituency.

8. Critique this statement, providing your opinion as to its accuracy: "Sociologists and other social scientists are more interested in self-report and case studies than official statistics."

9. Rank the four types of organizations that have helped shape the nation's policy response to the delinquency problem from (1) the organization that has the greatest potential to help shape policy to (4) the organization that has the least potential. Keep this list and check it as we progress through the semester to see if your projections were correct.

RECOMMENDED READINGS

Kotlowitz, Alex (1991). *There Are No Children Here*. New York: Anchor Books/Doubleday. This book, by a *Wall Street Journal* columnist, covers two years in the life of LaJoe Rivers and her family, especially her two youngest sons, Lafeyette and Pharoah. This true story of the Rivers family details their daily struggles in Chicago's Henry Horner Homes public housing project. While not primarily intended to be a criminological analysis, the work provides tremendous insights into the world of poverty, racism, and crime experienced by the urban underclass, or the "truly disadvantaged," in the United States.

Potter, Gary W., and Victor E. Kappeler (2006). *Constructing Crime: Perspectives on Making News and Social Problems*, 2nd ed. Long Grove, IL: Waveland Press. Consisting of 18 timely essays on a wide range of topics related to the construction of crime news and public perspectives on a wide variety of social problems, this work answers questions central to socially constructed crime reality. Of particular interest to those studying juvenile justice are several articles on drugs and crimes and the myths surrounding the initiation of gang members.

KEY TERMS

accuracy	moral panic
anonymity	National Crime Victimization Survey (NCVS)
case study	nondelinquent children
confidentiality	observational study
crime waves	Part I offenses
dark figure of crime	Part II offenses
delinquency	peer review
generalizability	principle of autonomy
index crimes	reliability
infant	self-report studies
juvenile delinquent	statistics
juvenile emancipation hearing	status offender
juveniles	status offenses
majority	transfer hearing
mens rea	validity
minors	

NOTES

[1] Juvenile probation officer (JPO) is a professional staff person who supervises conditionally released youths. This position, and its duties and obligations, is described in more detail in later chapters.

[2] Legal majority is one of those confusing terms often found in our legal system. A youth may vote and serve in the military at age 18 but, in most jurisdictions, may not take a legal drink until age 21. Some car rental agencies resist leasing vehicles to youths under 25 for "insurance reasons," meaning that they are denied full rights. The time between ages 10 and 20 is clearly a confusing one, when the former adolescent gains access to certain rights and responsibilities.

[3] While the use of the term *infant* may seem awkward, it is preferred to *child*, a term that informally covers much of a young person's early life, as in the term *childhood*. Infancy, which initially conjures up images of small babies, captures the sense of this legal status. Indeed, Webster's (2003) defines infancy as a state of early childhood before one achieves his or her majority. Thus, while calling both a 9-year-old and a 15-year-old infants would be legally correct, it would really upset the latter (and probably not make the former too happy either). When referring to children under the age of 10, we will use the term *infant*.

[4] Perhaps the best way to view the time between ages 16 or 18 and 21 is that of conditional majority. That is, persons in this gray zone are adults for some purposes and less than adults in others. The justice system is equally split on when a juvenile becomes an adult for punishment purposes. For example, in many states the juvenile correctional system maintains jurisdiction over young adults after 18 years of age and up to 21. In other states, when youthful offenders turn 18, they are released from the juvenile correctional authority to the adult one.

[5] Minimum ages are difficult to define. Typically the ages reported for the world's nations fit one of three patterns: (1) an absolute minimum age for criminal responsibility below which the child cannot form any criminal intent (*doli incapax*); (2) a minimum age for deprivation of liberty; and (3) an age of criminal or penal majority where the prosecution must show cause for proceeding with youth under that age. It is not clear from the data used in this table which of the three is reported for each of the 125 nations. These ages should not be viewed as absolutes, but rather reflect the flexibility found throughout the world on this issue.

[6] Confounding the credibility of many media sources are the heavily edited "reality" television programs that purport to show police-juvenile interactions and related juvenile justice practices and problems. Such programming, while often entertaining, should be viewed with a healthy degree of skepticism.

[7] Freebasing refers to a complicated method for chemically altering cocaine to be smoked. This technique is also quite dangerous, as the media chronicled when the drug paraphernalia of the comedian Richard Pryor exploded, setting him on fire and almost resulting in his death.

[8] Hunt (1997) explores the ways that the term *moral panic* has become part of the moral language of the media, suggesting that the media have adopted it as a way of justifying the moral and social role of the media, and even supporting the reassertion of "family values" in British culture during the 1990s. While rather philosophical in tenor, the article nonetheless extends the debate about the media's role in shaping public perceptions of a range of social problems, including crime and delinquency.

[9] Students sometimes amend this statement to: "There are lies, damned lies, and statistics" (usually after taking a statistics course). The correct quotation, "There are three kinds of lies: lies, damned lies, and statistics," is attributed by Samuel Clemens to nineteenth-century British prime minister Benjamin Disraeli (Partington, 1992:249).

[10] There is a second use of the term *statistics*. That is, those infamous statisticians (you know, worse than "damned liars") employ a science of which they are practitioners and after which they are named. As a science, statistics is "a branch of mathematics dealing with the collection, classification, analysis, and interpretation of numerical data" (*Merriam-Webster's Collegiate Dictionary*, 2003). By use of mathematical theories of probability, the science of statistics imposes order and regularity on aggregates of more or less disparate elements. In a perfect world, statisticians create order out of chaos, but they may be accused of making a silk purse out of a sow's ear. Be careful when you use both terms. It would appear from these two definitions that statisticians (the practitioners) create and interpret statistics (the products) through the use of statistics (the procedures). All this is true, except that academicians disdain definitions that use the word being defined in the definition even once, let alone twice. To avoid this confusion, we will rarely use the term *statistics* unless we are referring to the numerical products; the procedures are for other college courses.

[11] Many courses on research methods describe how some scientists prefer to use an inductive approach to scientific inquiry, allowing the real world, through data collected by the researcher, to speak for itself. This approach follows strict procedures and is not based on preconceived ideas about what will

be found. Inductionists look for patterns and groupings of findings that allow them to suggest what may be occurring in the area or topic under study. Those researchers following deductive reasoning first link their questions to theory; then they decide how they will measure the ideas and information associated with the theory. Having created something that can be measured, called variables, they then proceed to test hypotheses, or systematic and scientific guesses based on the ideas guiding the research. Once they subject these hypotheses to testing in the same real world as the inductionists, a decision about accepting or rejecting the hypotheses must be made. At that point, the deductionist must decide if the findings support or fail to support the theory.

[12] The term *law* in this context refers to a highly verified theoretical idea that resists all attempts to prove it false. Few social science theories achieve this status. The physical sciences have many such examples. However, even physical science laws are subject to revision and outright abandonment. If you want someone to amplify on this idea, talk to a physics or chemistry professor about the early laws in that person's academic discipline.

[13] Much of the discussion about accuracy, reliability, validity, and generalizability is taken from Babbie (2004).

[14] The property crimes included in the NCVS differ from UCR property crimes in three important ways. First, arson is not included in the NCVS. Second, several crimes, including burglary and theft, have definitions different from those in the UCR. Third, rather than the legalistic and broad term *larceny-theft*, the NCVS includes the more narrowly defined form of the crime.

[15] The following discussion of the UCR is taken in large part from the Federal Bureau of Investigation (1998).

[16] There are other offenses that also fit this pattern; however, the base number of offenses, often under 2,000, means that they are easily changed up or down by a relatively small number of arrests.

[17] Generally, these groupings are logical and intuitive; however, offenses against the public order may require some elaboration, as they include the following: (1) weapons offenses; (2) prostitution and commercialized vice; (3) liquor law violations; (4) disorderly conduct; (5) obstruction of justice, the intentional obstruction of court or law enforcement efforts in the administration of justice, acting in a way calculated to lessen the authority or dignity of the court, failing to obey the lawful order of the court, and violating probation or parole, other than technical violations that do not involve committing a new crime or are not prosecuted as such; and (6) other offenses against the public order, such as offenses against government administrations or regulations (for example, escape from confinement, gambling, as well as fish and game, hitchhiking, and health violations).

[18] *Juvenile Court Statistics 2000* (Puzzanchera, Stahl, Finnegan, Tierney, and Snyder, 2004:2) contains court-level or case-level information for the courts with juvenile jurisdiction operating in 48 states and the District of Columbia. These statistics represent 95% of the entire juvenile population in the United States (Puzzanchera et al., 2003:60). Collectively, this information is as close to a complete census of the nation's juvenile courts as the National Center can achieve, and even for aggregate statistics the Center must *estimate* the numbers for the missing jurisdictions. The various participating state and county agencies responsible for collecting juvenile court processing information do not use a uniform reporting system. Hence, the National Center also provides *estimates* for case-level information—that is, for each case processed by the jurisdiction—based on the counts for those jurisdictions that do provide comparable information. For example, the report contains case-level statistics for 932,550 delinquency cases handled in 1,678 jurisdictions in 28 states which represent 59% of the nation's youthful population in 2000 (Puzzanchera et al., 2004:74). For status offenders, slightly more jurisdictions (1,753) in 27 states included compatible data; courts in these jurisdictions processed more than 57% of the nation's status offenders (Puzzanchera et al., 2004:60). From both sets of court processing data, the Center creates national estimates.

[19] Symbiosis occurs when two rather dissimilar entities exist in close and mutually beneficial proximity to each other. Though the term is generally used in the biological sciences, we are using it more as an analogy—to describe a measure of interdependence—as opposed to a description of actual relationships.

chapter

2

HISTORICAL AND THEORETICAL PERSPECTIVES ON JUVENILE JUSTICE

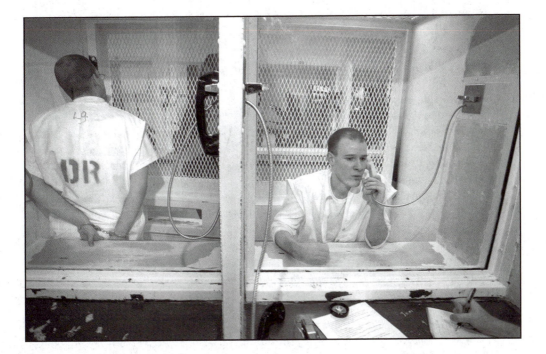

* * *

The hangman waited at the top of the stairs, his massive arms folded and resting on his ample stomach. Jess, hands bound behind his back, feet shackled, and accompanied by the sheriff, counted each step as he struggled up the steep, rough-hewn wooden staircase. One. Two. Three. *One of the men in jail had told him there would be 13.* Six. Seven. Eight. *Jess had thought the man was making a bad joke.* Eleven. Twelve. Thirteen. *This was anything but a joke.*

Sheriff Jackson had caught Jess four days ago riding Pete Amberton's prize stallion at Blue Mesa. The posse found Amberton's body the next day, half buried at the base of the mesa, where coyotes had partly dug him up. Circling vultures had given away the body's location.

The circuit judge was already overdue, so when he showed up the day before yesterday, the docket was full. There was another homicide, an "accidental" shooting after a card game gone bad; two thefts by misappropriation, one in which a teamster had misappropriated a load of freight and a case involving a local lawyer who had stolen part of the proceeds from a land sale; and two water rights violations, both involving farmers who took too much water from the all-important canal that brought water from a nearby river. The judge had saved Jess's case until last.

The trial had been mercifully short. Mr. Fedderson, the prosecutor, brought Alice Amberton to the stand first. She testified that her father and Jess, one of his ranch hands, had left a week ago to ride the wire, looking for stray cattle and breaks in the barbed wire fence. Jess's horse, a broken-down gelding, had appeared in the corral the next morning, but there was no sign of her father, his horse, or Jess. That same day she rode into town to tell the sheriff.

The sheriff had testified to the facts as he knew them. As he had done with Miss Amberton, Jess's attorney, William Howard Jones, passed on any cross-examination. Why bother, he had told Jess. They caught you with the horse, and you admitted you killed Amberton and stole his horse. Jones simply wanted to get this trial over and see what the court was going to do.

The "court" was Judge Henry Renfrew, known to all in the territory as "Hanging Hank." After Fedderson concluded the state's case and Jones rested without presenting a defense, Judge Renfrew quickly turned the matter over to the jury. The jury, after sitting through nearly an hour of testimony, stood up, looked at each other, nodded, and sat back down. The foreman boldly announced their unanimous verdict. "Jess Orville," stated the foreman, *"is guilty as sin, Judge."*

That had been two days ago. This morning, Donnegal—the man convicted of killing a bystander in a "dispute" with a crooked card dealer and the one who told Jess about the 13 steps—left for the territorial prison. Now Jess found himself peering down at the ground through cracks in the gallows's trapdoor. The hangman stood off to his left, the noose in one hand and a black hood in the other. Sheriff Jackson was finishing the public declaration of the death warrant: ". . . and, on the fourteenth day of this month, in the year of our Lord 1874, Jessup Orville shall be taken to the square opposite this courthouse, where at twelve noon, he shall be hanged by the neck until he is dead. May God have mercy on his eternal soul. Signed, the twelfth day of August, 1874, the Honorable Henry F. Renfrew, Esquire, presiding judge." Sheriff Jackson turned to Jess and asked, "Do you have any last words before the sentence is carried out?"

Jess took in the scene before him. Probably 50 townspeople filled the dusty square. He searched the crowd, looking for someone. She was not there, he noted with mixed feelings. Looking back at the sheriff, Jess began: "Well, sir, I guess I'm heartfully sorry for all the pain I caused Miss Amberton, seeing as she's an orphan and all now. I done wrong. I know it. But, hell, that lesson ain't gonna do me no good now." Turning to the sheriff, tears welling in his eyes, he continued: "You been good to me, Sheriff. I just hope I die like a man."

"Good speech, son," the hangman whispered into Jess's ear as he placed the hood over his head and adjusted the noose. Bending down at Jess's feet, he fastened two sand-filled canvas sacks to the shackles, carefully arranging them on the trapdoor. He had visited Jess in the jail the night before, sized him up for the knot and any needed weights. The sandbags added about 20 pounds, enough to snap his neck, but not enough to pop his head off his shoulders.

The hangman straightened up and walked over to the lever mounted to the side of the gallows. He looked over at the sheriff, who held a pocket watch in his hand. Sheriff Jackson raised his arm and then quickly dropped it as the minute hand touched 12.

Jess fell through the trap, the rope snapping taut with a resounding whomp. His neck did not separate from his shoulders, nor did it break. Instead, Jess hung there, kicking wildly as he slowly strangled to death. He kicked without stopping for a full three minutes, so violently that both sandbags broke loose from his shackles and thudded into the dust below. When the first bag hit the ground, the assembled crowd began to thin out, leaving only three cowboys as witnesses. Slowly the spasms became less violent, then less frequent, finally stopping after about 10 minutes.

Fifteen minutes after the trapdoor dropped, a deputy set a stepladder next to Jess's limp body. Sheriff Jackson climbed up and put his finger on Jess's neck; he could feel no pulse. He held a mirror up to Jess's mouth; it did not cloud. Pulling out a pocketknife, he cut down the body. Sheriff Jackson knew that the hangman would not want the rope returned: It was bad luck to use the same rope to hang more than one person. The deputy set the boy's body in a wheelbarrow for the short trip to the undertaker.

The undertaker's office was quiet, the solitude broken only by a woman's sobs and the sound of a rag being wrung out in a tin washbasin. The woman washed Jess's body, slowly, lovingly. Hardin, the undertaker, stood in one corner of the room; he did not want to intrude. The door opened, and a hot desert wind licked into the room. In the doorway was Miguel, the local stonemason. "Señor Hardin, I need to finish my work. I need his birth year." Hardin turned to the woman preparing the body. "Mrs. Orville, how old was Jess anyhow?"

The woman, looking far older than her 33 years, glanced up. "Why, Mr. Hardin, surely you remember. Jess was born in 1861, the summer the war back east started up."
"But señora," interjected Miguel, "that would make him only 13 years old."
Turning back to her work, Mrs. Orville spoke softly to her dead son, "You would have been 13 if you'd have lived another week."

* * *

The death of Jess Orville: fact or fiction? This case is fiction. Hundreds of youths under the age of 18 have been sentenced to die since colonial times, the youngest being convicted murderer James Arcene, a Cherokee youth sentenced at age 10, but not executed for 12 years (Regoli and Hewitt, 1997:616). The estimated number of executions involving persons who committed their crimes as juveniles is nearly 350 (Streib, 1995). Was this practice an anomaly unique to the Old West or to a young and developing nation? Hardly. For the past 100 years, with the exception of the years between 1965 and 1984, persons who committed their misdeeds as juveniles accounted for between 2% and 5% of all those executed in a given year. Nearly one-quarter of all such persons executed in this country since colonial times met their deaths in the two decades between 1930 and 1949 (Regoli and Hewitt, 1997:616). As you will learn in later chapters, several dozen current death row inmates committed their crimes as juveniles, and many state legislatures are clamoring for laws that will pave the way for the execution of subteens. However, in light of the Supreme Court's 5-4 decision in *Roper v. Simmons* (2005), it is unlikely that anyone under 18 at the time of offense will be executed for a capital crime.[1]

If you think that children have always enjoyed unique legal protections and privileges, you are wrong. If you qualify your statement by saying that throughout most of this nation's history, the fate of children has been pretty consistent, you are right but for the wrong reasons. You are closer to the truth if you qualify your original statement about children's special status by including the phrase "since the beginning of the twentieth century, . . ."

This chapter explores two topics that may not immediately seem related (or perhaps even relevant) to juvenile justice: history and theory. The history reviewed in the first half of this chapter is the evolution of social and legal ideas about youth and juveniles, terms we take for granted and defined with relative ease in the first chapter. The path to our current understanding of juvenile delinquency has been anything but straight and narrow; it has turned and twisted through the course of several thousand years and has been based on changing philosophies about how society should define and deal with children and their problems. Understanding the history of children is crucial to understanding how they are treated today— including gaining some insights into how the Supreme Court arrived at its decision about the sanctity of age 18 for full legal responsibility in capital crimes and the nineteenth century's perspective on youth like Jess Orville. The second topic—the theories of crime and delinquency—is less intuitively connected to juvenile justice, but we would submit, no less important. In Jess Orville's day a person as young as 12 could be held strictly accountable for his or her misdeeds, largely because of religious beliefs and social practices at the time. Importantly, Jess's execution would stand as a lesson to other youths in the territory who might consider stealing a horse or killing their employer. In contrast, during the 1960s children were more likely to be viewed as acted upon by an often intrusive and sometimes destructive justice system rather than as actors who perpetrated criminal deeds. The juvenile justice system provided negative labels for such children, more or less assuring their fate as adult criminals, so the theory went. In short, where we look for causal arguments about topics such as crime and delinquency is shaped by the times in which we live. Hence, like the definitions we explored in chapter 1—and their use to measure the nature and extent of delinquency—we feel it is equally important for students of juvenile justice to develop an appreciation for the history and theory that has evolved around juvenile delinquents and their acts.

At the beginning of the twenty-first century, it is difficult to think of a time when children were treated as anything but special citizens, not fully protected by the Constitution and Bill of Rights, but not fully exposed to the full force of a justice system created for adult offenders. This ambivalent view of children began at the end of the nineteenth century. It was the culmination of centuries of change in both child-rearing philosophy and practices. In order to place the current status of children into a historical context, we turn first to an overview of children's rights through the ages.

HISTORICAL STATUS OF CHILDREN: THE EVOLUTION OF CHILDHOOD

From ancient times through medieval times, the lot of children was similar to that of common property. Children were **chattel**, to be disposed of at the whim of the family patriarch. They could be bought or sold, kept living, left to die, or even killed (Watson, 1970). Typically, the child's fate was left to the family's patriarch, the oldest living blood-kin male.

Why did this situation exist? Somewhere in the darkness of prehistory, obedience became linked with the idea that the patriarch controlled the entire family, especially slaves, children, and even adult women (Newman, 1978:54). Sons, and eventually all family members, owed absolute obedience to the father first and then to the larger family unit. Only the father could decide the correct punishment for family members, and only the father could lay a hand on his chattel (Newman, 1978:56). Slaves and sons, as property with considerable value, rarely suffered harsh punishments, or at least sanctions that would decrease their economic value. Women—especially daughters—often suffered horribly for their wrongdoings (Newman, 1978:56).

CHILDREN IN ANCIENT ROME AND IN THE MIDDLE AGES

The Roman city-state embraced the child's lowly status. This status was codified in the *patria potestas*, literally "power of the father," a crucial part of the *paterfamilias* doctrine, whereby the father was the head of the family. This legal dictum placed the child under the father's absolute control as long as the father lived, but the father could emancipate the child if he so wished (see box 2.1). Children were at the bottom of the family hierarchy, below even slaves. Roman history records cases of slaves beating their master's children, a sign of the latter's status in Roman society (de Mause, 1975; Watson, 1970).

While the father was bound by practical limits as to what he could or would do to his children, the legal code remained largely unchanged for hundreds of years. In 374 CE, a law forbade the exposure of infants to the elements, a common method of disposing of unwanted children, in most cases, daughters. At about that time, the writings of early Christian philosophers, including Augustine, helped erode the *patria potestas* in favor of the more benevolent **paterna pietas**, or "fatherly love" (Mounteer, 1984:255). In spite of these fourth- and fifth-century inroads, *patria potestas* remained a central theme in Roman law through its last great revision by the Byzantine emperor Justinian I in the sixth century (Jolowicz, 1957).

The collapse of the Western Roman Empire in the fifth century—and along with it, most of the old Roman legal institutions—was the beginning of the Middle Ages. The sociopolitical power of Christianity had evolved to the point that the belief in the immortal soul of all humans meant that children suffered less brutish treatment than in earlier times. Childhood was viewed as a time for the inculcation of Christian beliefs (McLaughlin, 1975). The Roman Catholic Church even helped define the age of culpability for children. For example, medieval theologians popularized the belief that a child could not be held accountable for an act committed before the age of six or seven, given that only after this age was mortal sin possible (Ozment, 1983:144). Moreover, during this period of growing church power in the affairs of society, the father's power declined.[2] Beginning in the twelfth century, the church also recognized the validity of marriages entered into without the permission of a child's father as long as the girl was 11 1/2 years old and the boy 13 1/2 (Flandrin, 1979:131).

Medieval life generally was nasty, brutish, and short. Given the growth of cities and the poor sanitary standards of the day, deadly diseases were rampant. Plague, smallpox, whooping cough, scarlet fever, diphtheria, and measles often took more lives than they spared, and children were at particular risk for dying. The parents' love for a child, while not unknown, may not have been wise in a time when so many died so young. As Ariès has observed:

> In medieval society the idea of childhood did not exist; this is not to suggest that children were neglected, forsaken, or despised. The idea of childhood is not to be confused with affection for children: it corresponds to an awareness of the particular nature of childhood, that particular nature which distinguishes the child from the adult, even the young adult. In medieval society this awareness was lacking. (1962:128)

Even in the early 1700s, "people could not allow themselves to become too attached to something that was regarded as a probable loss" (Ariès, 1962:38).

Ariès's conclusions have been criticized as superficial and exaggerated (Pollock, 1983). Nonetheless, it is important to observe that medieval Europe lacked separate institutions for the socialization of the young (Binder, Geis, and Bruce, 1988:46). Children learned their roles and expectations by wandering through the

Box 2.1 International Perspectives
The Moral and Legal Education of Children

If a son strikes his father, one shall cut off his hands.

—Code of Hammurabi, eighteenth century BCE

A father shall have the right of life and death over his son born in lawful marriage, and shall also have the power to render him independent, after he has been sold three times.

—Law I (The *Patria Potestas*), Table IV, Concerning the Rights of a Father, and of Marriage, Roman Codes, Twelve Tables, fifth century BCE

If any heartless person, induced by extreme poverty and want, should sell either his son or daughter for the purpose of obtaining means to live, in a case of this kind the sale shall only be valid where the purchasers had a right to the service of the person sold, and he who made the sale, or the one to whom the child was alienated, shall have the right to restore it to its freeborn condition, provided he tenders its value to the owner, or furnishes him another slave in its stead.

—Book IV, Title XLIII, 2. Concerning Fathers Who Have Sold Their Children, Code of Justinian, fifth century

The first six years of life on earth
We to January would compare
For in that month strength is rare
As in a child six years from birth

—Anonymous, fourteenth century (as quoted in Ariès, 1962:22)

If any child, or children, above sixteen years of age, and of sufficient understanding, shall CURSE or SMITE their natural FATHER or MOTHER, he or they shall be put to death, unless it can be sufficiently testifyed that the Parents have been very unchristianly negligent in the education of such children: so provoked them by extreme and cruel correction, that they have been forced thereunto, to preserve themselves from death or maiming: *Exod* 21:17, *Lev* 20:9, *Exod* 21:15.

—*The Book of General Lawes and Libertyes Concerning the Inhabitants of Massachusetts*, 1641

An Alphabet of Lessons for Youth
A wise son makes a glad father, but a foolish son is the heaviness of his mother.
Foolishness is bound up in the heart of a child, but the rod of correction shall drive it far from him.

—*New England Primer*, 1762

The Cruel Boy Punished

1. An idle boy was one day sitting on the steps of a door, with a stick in one hand, and a piece of bread and butter in the other. As he was eating his bread, he saw a dog lying near him, and called out, "Come here, fellow!"

2. The dog, hearing himself kindly spoken to, arose, pricked up his ears, wagged his tail, and came up.

3. The boy held out his piece of bread and butter, and as the dog was about to take it, the naughty fellow struck him on the nose with the stick, which he had in the other hand. The poor dog howled, and ran away as fast as he could.

4. The cruel boy laughed heartily at the trick he had played. At this moment, a man on the other side of the street, who had been watching him, called out to the boy, and showing him a half-dollar, asked him if he would like to have it.

5. "Yes," said the boy, "to be sure I would." "Come and get it, then," said the man. The boy ran to him and stretched out his hand for the money, when the man gave him such a rap over the knuckles with his cane, that he roared in pain.

6. "Why did you do that?" said the boy, grinning and rubbing his knuckles. "I did not hurt you or ask you for money."

7. "Why did you strike the poor dog just now?" said the man. "Had he hurt you, or asked you for bread? I have served you just as you served him."

8. The bad boy hung his head, and seemed very much ashamed; and I have never heard of his playing any cruel tricks since.

—*McGuffey's New Third Reader*, 1857

world of adults. They played adult games, performed adult jobs, dressed like adults, and basically led adult lives from a very early age.

THE EMERGENCE OF CHILDHOOD IN THE RENAISSANCE AND THE PROTESTANT REFORMATION

The lives and fates of children began to change slowly with the end of the Middle Ages and the beginning of the Renaissance in the late fourteenth century. Historians cannot agree on precisely when, but by the late 1600s or early 1700s new concepts of the family had emerged, ones that eventually included an emotional bond between parent and child, not to mention a lessening of what some writers describe as outright adult hostility toward infants (Binder et al., 1988:47–48; see also Hunt, 1970:81). Historians also cannot agree on the forces that led to the emerging views of childhood and family. It could have been an offshoot of the intellectual explosion in arts and letters associated with the Renaissance. Then too, medical training and urban sanitary practices both improved during the late Renaissance period, increasing the survival rate for infants into childhood. Whatever forces were at work, family portraits, especially those that showed everyday life in the 1500s and 1600s, began to show distinctively childlike children as opposed to the mini-adults found in earlier works (Ariès, 1962). Treatises on child-rearing methods began to appear as early as the sixteenth century, serving as recognition of children's separate status from adults (Tucker, 1975).

The separate status of children from adults and the significance of childhood as a path toward later adulthood were only emerging ideas by the end of the 1600s. A new view of the family, one that included an emotional bond and a clear separation of childhood and adulthood, did little, however, to erode the power of *paterfamilias*. As the world moved toward European colonization of the Americas, the power of secular governments reached new heights. Not coincidentally, fathers—the kings of their households—had regained firm control of their families. Contemporary laws no longer permitted the killing of unwanted children or their sale into slavery. Yet the practice of **binding out** children—placing them in work situations for days, weeks, or even months—was common (Hanawalt, 1993). The more upwardly mobile citizens of the day used the **apprenticeship system** for their young male children. Apprenticeship often lasted a decade or more, during which the apprentice was little more than a slave (Hanawalt, 1993). In all such situations, the father's power extended to the child's new master. The legal status of children as chattel had changed little in the preceding two thousand years.

BETWEEN CHILDHOOD AND ADULTHOOD: CREATING ADOLESCENCE

The colonies of the New World were rich in natural resources. The colonial powers, however, were labor poor. Centuries of war and disease had depleted their labor pool. Moreover, the distances between the homelands and the new colonies were often too great to make the transportation of laborers an economically feasible alternative, at least in the first century or so of colonization. Consequently, colonists enslaved the indigenous peoples as a source of inexpensive labor or physically removed them from the resource-rich regions of the colonies, or both. Some colonies imported labor in the form of convicted felons and indentured servants. Later colonists, particularly those who could not afford indentured servants, rented convicts, or African slaves, turned to a time-honored source of labor, their own children.

During the seventeenth and eighteenth centuries, fertility in the North American colonies reached levels similar to those found in France and England. Two factors created a population boom in the colonies that had never been equaled in Western Europe (Flandrin, 1979:198). First, the average marriage age in the colonies was far lower than in Western Europe at the time, especially the age at which women married. This meant that even if the fertility rates were similar, the women in North America theoretically could produce more children than was the case in Western Europe. Second, infant mortality was much lower in North America than in Europe at the time. The net result was an explosion in the number of children found in the colonies, workers to aid their parents by toiling in fields and working the harvests, to be sent off as apprentices, or to be bound out as servants.

DEFINING THE "GOOD CHILD" IN EARLY AMERICAN HISTORY: 1620–1870

The definition of a "good child" during colonial times was closely tied to Puritan beliefs that originated in New England (see box 2.1). According to Puritan philosophy, children were conceived in original sin, and it was the parents' responsibility to subordinate the child to their will and Christian beliefs (Mather, 1690:117). Good meant obedient and subservient: A good child both respected and feared his or her parents. In fact, in a seventeenth-century Massachusetts legal code, a child—identified as a "son" in the code—could be put to death if he did not "obey the voice of his father or the voice of his mother," providing he was at least 16 years of age (quoted in Binder et al., 1988:50).

The apprenticeship and binding-out systems fit well with the Protestant work ethic popular among both the Puritans of New England and other Anglo-American colonies prior to the American Revolution. In exchange for food, clothing, and shelter, apprenticed and bound-out children literally became part of the new master's household. Corporal punishment, while used judiciously for nonrepentant and recalcitrant children, was the norm in both "families." As Cotton Mather, the renowned Puritan minister, observed: "Better Whipt than Damn'd." According to Binder and associates,

> Puritan teachings were encapsulated—and, indeed, spread far beyond the boundaries of New England—in the first and most widely influential early American schoolbook, the noted *New England Primer*, which was intended to teach reading and piety at one and the same time. (1988:49–50)

Some 6 million copies of this work, which was in print for over 150 years, were distributed throughout North America, England, and Scotland (Lystad, 1980).

Puritanism meant more than just increased corporal punishment for misbehaving children. It helped sweep aside centuries of indifference toward children. Colonial laws and books of that era recognized the special status of children. While such developments had occurred as early as the sixteenth century in Europe, the American emphasis on the singular importance of childhood during the late eighteenth and early nineteenth centuries was far greater than at any previous time. That the Puritans specifically and North American families generally placed so much importance on childhood signified a dramatic shift in child-rearing patterns.

European colonial powers transported more than people to the Americas. They also sent European views on young people, including the recognized rights and duties of children. For example, the previously mentioned apprenticeship system—and, to a lesser extent, the practice of binding out children—had the practical effect of extending childhood. These practices created society-wide problems: What were the social and legal statuses of these children? This dilemma—what to call children caught between childhood and adulthood and how to deal with them—extended to language. According to John Gillis,

> By the standards of today's biologically exacting vocabulary, the language of age in pre-industrial Europe was hopelessly vague. Even as late as the eighteenth century, the French and German words *garçon* and *Knabe* referred to boys as young as 6 and as old as 30 or 40. (1974:1)

Gillis further reflects that "the Latin terms *puer* (child) and *adolescens* were used interchangeably until the eighteenth century" (1974:1). One late-eighteenth-century development that changed this linguistic and social state was the Industrial Revolution.

The role of children as workers during the **Industrial Revolution** was secured early and remained unchallenged for 100 years or more until various legal jurisdictions in the U.S. created child labor laws in the late nineteenth and early twentieth centuries (Bakan, 1971). Children had been sent from their homes to be apprenticed at an early age for centuries. Thus, shifting children from apprenticeships to jobs as laborers in the emerging factories did not require a great leap in thinking. Many child laborers continued to live at home, an almost unheard of situation during the apprenticeship period. Children were also cheap and easily replaced; moreover, many of the tasks associated with the Industrial Revolution, including weaving and certain manufacturing jobs, required small, quick hands.

As the children of the emerging working class in Europe entered the job marketplace, they allied themselves with their older, more experienced peers (Gillis, 1974:92). It was in the best interests of these child-laborers to forge "a precocious identity with adult comrades," a practice that the upper class often viewed as an economic threat. At the same time, middle-class parents came to recognize that the future well-being of their children was tied to extending childhood as long as possible, in order to gain the training and skills required for success in the workplace. For middle-class children, entering the job market too early could spell economic disaster. By mid-century, then, the children of the working and middle classes "were moving in very different directions" (Gillis, 1974:93).

ADOLESCENTS AND DELINQUENTS: 1870–1900

In the final three decades of the nineteenth century, American families experienced a revolution in attitudes and practices. They discarded the *New England Primer*'s Puritanism and followed instead the more child-centered and family-centered orientations of *McGuffey's Reader* (see box 2.1). They abandoned authoritarianism and child-repressive practices and endorsed "reverence and love" between parents and between parents and children (Binder et al., 1988:55). These changes represented major shifts in the definitions of children and childhood: "Gone, then, was the fear of childish impulses, and in its place was a sense that the basis for a proper upbringing lay in the children themselves" (Binder et al., 1988:57).

In 1877, three years after the execution of our fictional juvenile criminal Jess Orville, police officers arrested the adolescent in this engraving. Apparently his mother, seen imploring the officer to release her child, had strong emotional ties to him or perhaps she was upset at the prospect of losing a wage earner from her impoverished household. The child in custody faced an uncertain future: The juvenile court was nearly a quarter-century in the future.

The time was ripe for a new term to describe an evolving legal status; the term was **adolescence**.[3] The key to understanding the emergence of adolescence lies in the drop in child mortality experienced first by the aristocracy of England and then by the middle class (Gillis, 1974:98–105). The upper class, by reason of its wealth, could absorb many children; however, the middle class recognized the need to restrict family size to pass on the improved lifestyle to the next generation. Female children were kept at home until ready for marriage. Male children were afforded greater autonomy, but their prospective "career" options and educational opportunities extended their childhood as well. While decreased child mortality increased the supply of children, adolescence seems to have emerged in response to increased educational opportunities, beginning with England's elite secondary schools. It was here that middle-class values became an integral part of adolescence, the standard against which all adolescents would come to be measured. Eventually these ideals crossed the Atlantic. By the late 1800s, children's ties to the nuclear family assumed even greater importance with the establishment of compulsory primary and secondary education and expanded postsecondary education opportunities, the latter created by the growth in colleges and universities. In this manner, late-nineteenth-century demographic, economic, and political forces defined the adolescent ideal (Gillis, 1974:118).

Bakan (1971) contends that adolescence is a uniquely American invention (see also Binder et al., 1988:63; Jensen and Rojek, 1998:37). He contends it was the creation of G. Stanley Hall, the father of adolescent psychology. Hall, whose *Adolescence: Its Psychology and Its Relation to Physiology* was first published in 1904, had influenced public thinking about the lives of "children" aged 14 to 24 since the 1880s. He believed that this age group lived in a primitive psychological state, located between savagery and civilization. Youth in this period, called adolescence by Hall (1904:I, xix), needed to be protected against "insidious dangers," many of which were described in sexual or aggressive behavioral terms. Thus, adolescence was not the sociopolitical condition described by Gillis, but rather a psychological state characterized by moral indifference, mood shifts, and willful behavior. Hall saw the adolescent's physiological changes as the "most plastic stage of both temperament and character" (1904:II, 364).

Whichever view of the evolution of adolescence is *more correct* is less important than the fact that both shared a central theme, the need for social control. By the late nineteenth century, for reasons that will become clear in the next section, American society experienced a need to define the behavior of certain groups as meriting formal intervention and control. The members of these groups—soon to be defined as delinquents—were also adolescents, many of whom were, not coincidentally, the children of working-class parents.

THE JUVENILE COURT: A NEW JUSTICE SYSTEM FOR A NEW CENTURY

By the late 1800s, three major forces helped create a means of responding to the newly defined social and legal category of adolescents—the juvenile court (Bernard, 1992; Schwartz, 1989). These forces included the Industrial Revolution and nearly unchecked immigration. In fact, it was the rapid urbanization associated with the first two forces that ultimately led to the emergence of the third element, the Progressive Movement (Platt, 1977; see also Forst, 1995). The following sections briefly review the influence of each of these social forces and reveal how the concept of a juvenile court gained widespread acceptance in the early twentieth century—not in response to an isolated incident, but rather as the result of decades of social discontent and efforts at reform.

THE INDUSTRIAL REVOLUTION

The Industrial Revolution began in earnest during the middle of the nineteenth century. This period had an indirect, but profound, effect on what was to become the juvenile justice system. During the Industrial Revolution, the nation's economy shifted from one based almost exclusively on agriculture to one relying more heavily on manufacturing. The result was large-scale relocation from rural areas and farming communities to the industrialized cities of the Northeast and Midwest. As the farming families relocated, the fathers were employed in industrial production and often so were the mothers, especially in industries like clothing and textiles. Moving from the countryside to the cities often took people away from their extended families and the child-care and support systems upon which they had come to depend.

These practices left many children unsupervised for long periods of time. Some children banded together and roamed the streets looking for excitement and entertainment. Eventually, most came into contact with the police for their "incorrigible" behavior. Reform groups in many cities campaigned to remove children from the streets and redirect them toward productive activities.

IMMIGRATION AND URBANIZATION

To compound the problems associated with increased urbanization, the period from the end of the Civil War to the turn of the century saw massive immigration from Europe and Asia. European immigrants arrived in the nation's major eastern metropolitan centers, for example on New York City's Ellis Island, and followed the emerging transportation system—first rivers, lakes, and canals and later railroads—to population centers like Buffalo, Chicago, Kansas City, and points west. Asian immigrants, largely from China and Japan, arrived in the larger West Coast cities like Seattle, San Francisco, and Los Angeles. They rarely ventured far from these cities. Wherever the immigrants ended up, they tended to congregate in high-density, older parts of the cities, where they found low-paying jobs, cheap housing, and few amenities. Rarely did they have the resources to purchase land for agriculture, the primary means of living outside the big cities. The immigrants spoke little or no English and often clung to old customs and ideas. Their children—some born in the United States and some born in the old country—learned English and adapted to a new way of life. Often the result was strain—within the family, within the neighborhood, and within society. These youngsters became **marginalized youths**: They had one foot in each of two competing cultures (Vigil, 1990).

THE PROGRESSIVE ERA

The third social movement that paved the way for the creation of a separate juvenile court has been called the Progressive Era (see for example Schwartz, 1989; Schlossman, 1977). The **Progressive Era** was a time of reform in reaction to the massive social problems besetting crowded urban centers, including crime, disease, and pollution. Part of the reform crusade manifested itself in what came to be called the child-saving movement (Platt, 1977).

The **child savers** frequently were white middle-class women who engaged in community service and other worthy causes. Many were affiliated with philanthropic and religious organizations, and they had the time and financial resources to devote to helping others. However, not everyone takes such a benevolent view of the child savers. Some critics do not view the contributions of the child savers as benign (Platt, 1977). In fact, much of the work of the child savers is seen as an attempt to impose middle-class, Protestant values on a group of Catholic immigrant children of lower socioeconomic status.

Whatever the motivations of the child savers might have been, during the last decade of the nineteenth century, groups representing the law, philanthropic societies, and the newly emerging profession of social work joined forces to establish a separate justice system for children accused of criminal—that is, delinquent—activity. This system was built around the juvenile court, a process and structure described in greater detail in chapter 5.

Moving from the belief that children were property less valuable than slaves to a rather more complex view of good adolescents and bad delinquents took centuries. Along the way, many of the individuals and institutions that contributed to defining the social and legal statuses of children also offered ideas as to why children engaged in behavior that so troubled adults. In the late nineteenth century, when social, economic, and political forces collided to create a new youthful status, new views on what to do for and with children likewise emerged. We turn next to an overview of those ideas, what we commonly call theories of crime and delinquency.

EXPLAINING DELINQUENCY, PART I: HISTORICAL VIEWS

In the opening vignette, we described the hanging of a preadolescent horse thief and murderer. Regardless of whether you felt sympathy for Jess, his mother, his victim, or the victim's daughter, did you wonder why Jess did it? What if Jess's father did not die in the Civil War, as Jess was told by his mother? What if he abandoned his family and became a road agent, a highwayman, holding up travelers in the Old West? The story of his dying in the war, then, was how Jess's mother dealt with being abandoned by her good-for-nothing husband. What if we said that Jess himself had since the age of 10 hung around a group of older and more violent young men? Lacking in formal education and having no father, Jess looked up to and emulated the misdeeds of his peers. Or, finally, what if we told you that Jess's mother had experienced a difficult pregnancy with Jess and there had been prenatal complications? Essentially, Jess was developmentally challenged and little understood the differences between right and wrong. We could continue offering diverse scenarios and insights into Jess and his family. The point is that each, in its own way, represents a slightly different criminological theory.

SPIRITUAL AND NATURAL EXPLANATIONS: PRECURSORS OF MODERN CRIME THEORIES

Social communities have long expressed the need to understand why some among them, especially their young, commit acts against the norms or rules. Religious tracts, including the Judeo-Christian Bible, the Islamic Koran, the Buddhist's "Four Noble Truths," and the Hindu's Laws of Manu, describe defining moments that speak to questions of the presence of evil in the world. For example, in the Judeo-Christian tradition, the temptation of Adam by Eve (and Eve by the serpent) brought about a chain of events that led to the expulsion of Adam and Eve from the Garden of Eden. Buddhists are perhaps the ultimate practitioners of defining reality in cause-and-effect terms. For Buddhists the *samsara* is a repeating cycle of birth and death, based on one's physical and mental actions. Those who succumb to their base desires are destined to be reborn as successively lower beings. Attainment of Buddhism's highest state, *nirvana*—a state of complete enlightenment— gives liberation from the cycle of birth and death. Cause yields effect.

From the dawn of recorded history to the beginning of the twentieth century, cultures linked crime and delinquency to a wide range of forces and factors. Historical evidence points to spiritualist and naturalist explanations. For thousands of years it was believed that evil spirits—devils and demons—possessed adults and children, causing them to act in law-violating ways. Often the evil that possessed a person was associated with sinful conduct (Johnson and Wolfe, 1996:7). Many cultures created highly specialized rituals to drive off the evil spirits, including physical (corporal) punishments, sometimes carried out in the name of a favored deity. Failing in these efforts, a surefire last-ditch option was to destroy the host (Newman, 1978).

The ancient Phoenicians, Greeks, and Romans sought causal arguments from the physical and material world. As naturalists, they sought to understand the nature of things. They placed a great premium on what could be seen and understood, using objective observation and deduction. For example, in the eighth century BCE, Homer observed in *The Iliad* that Theristes, a particularly ugly person, was also a despicable liar. The naturalist emphasis on the exterior mirroring the inner person was to have implications well beyond the time of Homer.

Ideas about crime causation changed little from the days of Homer for the next two thousand years. During the Middle Ages (c. 500 CE to c. 1500 CE), crime was tied to witchcraft and other sins against the Roman Catholic Church. Many of the more extreme punishments were restricted to offenses against the state or the church (Hinckeldey, 1993). At the other extreme was the payment of fines. More than 2,500 years ago in ancient Greece, garden-variety criminals paid fines, a practice that continued at least through the end of the Tudor period in England (1485– 1558). As Newman (1978:123) observes:

> Contrary to the popular opinion of historical penologists, the bulk of punishments up until the beginning of the seventeenth century have been economic

sanctions either in the form of fines, confiscations, or restitution. . . . The gradual escalation of capital and corporal punishments began more markedly in the early seventeenth century, coinciding with the rise of parliamentary power and the weakening of the monarchy.

It was widespread use of the gallows in eighteenth-century Europe that led at least one reformer to suggest alternatives. That person was Cesare Beccaria; his contribution was perhaps the first modern criminological theory.

CRIME AND DETERRENCE

In 1764, the 26-year-old Italian rationalist Cesare Beccaria published a modest pamphlet entitled *On Crimes and Punishments* that outlined his ideas about how punishments could serve to deter individuals from crime. Man, he contended, was a rational being who possessed **free will**, and who would always choose the path that shifted the balance from pain toward pleasure. In other words, if there was little doubt about the *certainty* that one would receive a pain, or punishment; if the punishment *swiftly* followed the illicit deed; and if the punishment was of a severity that *equaled* the harm caused by the misdeed, then a criminal sanction (1) could deter the offender (**specific deterrence**) or, failing to deter the person being punished, (2) could serve to deter the population witnessing the punishment (**general deterrence**).

Beccaria also believed that those who chose crime, in spite of possible punishments, deserved the punishment they received. However, he tempered this belief with three exceptions. First, he was opposed to the death penalty on both philosophical and moral grounds. The state, he argued, should not use its weighty resources essentially to declare war on the individual; moreover, he was not convinced of the death penalty's deterrent effect. Second, he stressed that men, women, and children should receive punishment through incarceration at different locations, a radical idea in an age when all three were sometimes housed in the same prison. Finally, he observed that not all crimes were equal. He argued that serious crimes, what we call felonies, should receive more severe penalties than other, less serious ones, offenses roughly corresponding to our misdemeanors. Beccaria's positions on deterrence, inmate classification systems, a hierarchy of crimes and punishments, and questions about the death penalty remain relevant even today.

CRIME AND BIOLOGY

Charles Darwin's mid-nineteenth-century ideas about evolution had far-reaching implications for supporters of **social determinism** and **criminal anthropology**. Determinists, as a group, believed that people became criminals due to forces beyond their control. The type of forces—social, psychological, economic, or biological—defined the form of determinism that was at work. For example, Herbert Spencer, who originated the phrase "survival of the fittest," wrote in 1864: "The quality of society is physically lowered by the artificial preservation of the feeblest members [and] the quality of society is lowered morally and intellectually by the artificial preservation of those who are least able to take care of themselves" (p. 313). In this sense, then, Spencer was a social determinist. It remained for Cesare Lombroso to link biology and evolution to the study of crime and criminals.

In 1876 Italian prison doctor Lombroso published *The Criminal Man*, in which he outlined his theory about criminals being throwbacks to earlier, more primitive beings, what he called **atavists**. This type of determinism looked at crime as a biologically predestined condition of certain individuals. On the basis of years of performing autopsies on prison inmates, Lombroso believed that a trained observer could classify criminals according to externally manifested **criminal stigmata**, or physical characteristics unique to categories of criminals. For example, property offenders had different stigmata than rapists or murderers. While later versions of Lombroso's published work acknowledged the importance of economic and social forces, the ideas that criminals were born and that certain types of offenders share certain physical characteristics with one another defines his intellectual legacy.

Lombrosian criminology and American criminal anthropology remained controversial elements of delinquency theory until after World War II (Rafter, 1992). In the 1930s, E. A. Hooton (1939) wrote that human body measurements held the key to separating criminals from the rest of society. William Sheldon, a 1940s physician, applied the science of embryonic development to delinquency studies. Delinquents, he observed, had body types that were more **mesomorphic** (that is, muscular, broad shouldered, and narrow-waisted) and less **ectomorphic** (that is, fragile and thin) than those of noncriminals (Sheldon, 1949). Sheldon received support from the delinquency studies of social scientists Eleanor and Sheldon Glueck (1949). While they affirmed the idea that mesomorphy is overrepresented in the delinquency population, the Gluecks also maintained that biological features were not causal factors, but rather set the context for delinquency. For example, muscular individuals may be overrepresented in youth gangs since this quality may be a much sought-after characteristic for delinquent youth gang "enforcers."

On the causation question, biological determinists held a position quite different from classical deterrence theorists. The former did not hold the individual responsible, since criminality resulted from uncontrollable biological forces; the latter saw crime as the offender's conscious and informed choice. One was extremely deterministic; the other gave free will top billing. Classical deterrence theory, especially as endorsed by Beccaria, placed a premium on equal legal treatment for all offenders; criminal anthropologists, conversely, advocated "that punishments be tailored to fit the offender types they had identified" (Rafter, 1992:539).

EXPLAINING DELINQUENCY, PART II: PSYCHOLOGICAL AND SOCIOLOGICAL THEORIES

At the beginning of the twentieth century, psychology and sociology offered numerous criminological explanations. At the end of that century, older arguments reemerged, joined by newer academic disciplines, and competed with psychology and sociology for the mantle of "first among equals" for the delinquency theories. We begin with the psychological explanations.

DELINQUENCY AND PSYCHOLOGY

Like classical deterrence and biogenic explanations, psychology looks within the individual for delinquency causes.[4] **Behaviorism**, a school of psychology, brought that discipline closer to the physical sciences. Proponents claim that all behavior results from learning responses to certain stimuli. A person who is disturbed has learned to respond inappropriately to incoming stimuli. **Operant conditioning**, based on the work of behaviorists John B. Watson and B. F. Skinner, stresses that **reinforcers** are stimuli that cause a behavior to continue and even increase, while **punishers** result in behavioral extinction. Some stimuli—punishers and reinforcers—are defined by their presence or absence. For example, a positive reinforcer is one that is present in the subject's environment and that serves to continue or increase the behavior. A negative reinforcer is one that by its absence is intended to accomplish the same goal. Punishers have similar positive and negative manifestations but act in the obverse fashion, eliminating the targeted behavior.

Psychopathy and personality theory are closely related. **Psychopaths** allegedly possess no conscience; they engage in norm-violating behavior without concern for morality. Many psychologists also define psychopaths as unpredictable, untrustworthy, and unstable individuals. For its part, **personality theory** is based on the assumption that our understanding of normal and abnormal behavior comes through the ways that people express habitual patterns and behavioral qualities. Using standardized tests, such as the Minnesota Multiphasic Personality Inventory (MMPI) or the Rorschach inkblot test, the tester links the subject's responses to known personality types.

In the 1950s, S. R. Hathaway and Elio Monachesi (1953) found support for the predictive value of a subscale of the MMPI. The personality type most closely associated with delinquency was the MMPI's psychopathic deviate scale, called the **Pd scale** (Tennenbaum, 1977). While official delinquency and the Pd scale are highly intercorrelated, the fact that the Pd scale includes self-reported delinquency is problematic (Waldo and Dinitz, 1967). In fact, separating the objective measurement of the psychological condition from the clinical measurement is viewed as one of the perspective's most troubling weaknesses (Hindelang, 1973). As Walter Reckless observed, "Non-Freudian oriented psychiatrists now identify formerly conceived psychopathic behavior as 'character disorders' or 'personality disturbances'" (1967:35).

Hans Eysenck (1973, 1977) proposed a personality theory that tied environmental conditions to inherited features of the nervous system. Biological aspects of the autonomic nervous system yield specific personality types, two of which are crime prone. Eysenck believed that neurotic extroverts are crime prone as a result of (1) neurological aspects of their biology, which require high levels of stimulation from their environment, and (2) a hair-trigger fight-or-flight response to threats. Psychotics also are overrepresented among criminals since, for unknown psychological reasons, they are cruel, hostile, insensitive to others, and unemotional. Placing such people in certain learning environments, where they may fail to make the necessary connection between criminal activity and aversive consequences, can lead to criminality.

DELINQUENCY, SOCIOLOGY, AND THE CONTROL OF DELINQUENCY

In the late nineteenth century, French sociologist Émile Durkheim (1897) observed that following economic upheavals and wars, the old ways of behaving no longer seemed to work, and often the result was what he called **anomie**, a general sense of normlessness. Societies lacking in effective rules tended to experience a host of troubles, from economic crises to suicides to crime. Fortunately, social groups resist any disruption in the collective order, or social equilibrium, and always seek a new balance, an outcome that may take months or years, perhaps even generations, to accomplish.

Durkheim's ideas about society and its rules inspired generations of criminologists. In the 1930s, Robert K. Merton (1938) viewed such ideas as having potency for understanding individual human actors. Merton believed that a society's culture promoted certain successes (the goals), while at the same time its institutions restricted legitimate avenues to attain those goals (the means). This strain between the goals and the means created what is called the anomic trap: There are no legal means to reconcile the strains toward success (goals) and the limited access to legitimate means. As a consequence, some people became innovators, accepting the goals but rejecting the legitimate means, a position reflected in the saying, "The end justifies the means." Many innovators embraced criminal means to legitimate ends.

Merton's **strain theory** inspired others interested in explaining how the structural elements in society caused crime.[5] Richard Cloward and Lloyd Ohlin (1960) proposed a youth gang theory that included both the **subcultural tradition** and the **cultural transmission thesis**. The former stressed that much delinquency is a natural rejection of unattainable middle-class values, while the latter explained that unlawful conduct can pass from one generation to the next through basic learning mechanisms. Cloward and Ohlin's **differential opportunity theory** redefined the anomic trap. "Delinquent subcultures," they stated, " . . . represent specialized modes of adaptation to this problem of adjustment" (1960:107).

Robert Agnew redefined strain theory by adding distinctly psychological elements and placing it in a juvenile context. Agnew's (1985, 1992) **general strain theory** can be differentiated easily from Merton's: Traditional strain theory views youths as running toward money or some other tangible goal; in general strain theory, youths often get into trouble while they are running away from undesired punishments or negative relationships with others. As children seek to avoid strains, such as the failure to achieve positively valued goals or the presence of negative stimuli, they engage in coping strategies that are themselves troubling and often delinquent. For example, exposure to chronic strains lowers a child's threshold for adversity; the next such episode could elicit a law-violating response. Children on society's margins may be prone to fits of anger and rebellion that draw the unwanted attention of law enforcers.

Durkheim's speculation that the lack of attachment to others frees people from moral constraints also influenced control theorists. Travis Hirschi (1969) defined the social bond in similar terms, as a kind of glue that holds society together. In his **bonding theory**, the social bond had four elements: (1) attachment, or affection for and sensitivity to members of social groups; (2) commitment, the investment one has in conventional norms; (3) involvement, a behavioral measure of the level of conventional activity; and (4) belief, the value attached to the correctness of social norms. Weakening one element of the social bond increases the inclination toward delinquency, no matter which bond element is involved.

Bonding theory was only one of a series of social control theories to emerge in the 1950s and 1960s. For example, Jackson Toby (1957) viewed delinquents as having a weak stake in conformity. He observed that as many youths grow up, they may be tempted to violate laws. However, because they are doing well in school and value their futures, they risk losing it all by giving into temptation. F. Ivan Nye, a contemporary of Toby's, placed social controls in a family context. Nye (1958) saw social control as existing in four forms:

- Direct controls were provided by the family and included punishments and restrictions.

- Indirect controls consisted of emotional identification with parents and non-criminals.

- Internal controls were part of the individual youth's psychological makeup and limited misbehavior through the conscience.

- Gratification of personal needs was fulfilled through legitimate versus illegitimate means.

One of the most complete social control theories of the 1960s is **containment theory**, proposed by Walter Reckless (1961, 1967). Reckless visualized delinquency as a push-pull process. Certain forces, such as the social conditions associated with living in poverty, family conflicts, or youthful delinquent subcultures, pull children away from conventional society. Other forces, including biological and psychological elements such as hostility and aggression, push them toward delinquency. Reckless theorized that two sets of countervailing forces, called inner and external containment, kept most children normative. Inner containment, reflecting as it did Freudian psychological components of ego strength and superego, along with a sense of responsibility, resembled Nye's internal control. Reckless, like Nye, also found a role for the family in his containment theory. External containment, manifested in reasonable norms and expectations, effective supervision and discipline, and the like, derived from the family.

John Hagan's **power-control theory** adds gender to control theory (1990; see also Hagan, Simpson, and Gillis, 1979). This theory acknowledges that boys and girls are socialized differently, the origins of which are in the family. The child's status mimics the parents' power relationships. For instance, in patriarchal families, where fathers are in control, both fathers and mothers control daughters more than sons. In more egalitarian families, where parents share power and have societal positions that are similarly egalitarian, the control over daughters is nearly identical to that for sons. Daughters raised in egalitarian homes should have crime rates similar to those for males. Daughters raised in patriarchal families, not encouraged to take risks and acting more in accordance with their parents' wishes, exhibit lower delinquency levels.

Theoretical Reflections
Self-Control Theory and the Family

Travis Hirschi teamed up with Michael Gottfredson to offer a general theory of crime. In what is often called **self-control theory**, they suggested that all crime is motivated by self-interest and the hedonistic desires to avoid pain and to maximize pleasure. Crime and what Gottfredson and Hirschi called analogous acts—consuming alcoholic beverages, smoking cigarettes, illegal drug use, illicit sex—offer short-term pleasures and hold certain attractions. However, those who succumb to those attractions are typically, in their words, **low self-control** individuals. These unrestrained persons have little commitment to conventionality and equally low concern for the long-term consequences of their acts, including the accidents that often flow from risky behavior.

Gottfredson and Hirschi's self-control theory has several elements that distin-guish it from other control theories. First, children's malleability ends at around 10 years of age, a contention that has important implications for any attempt to change human beings. Second, **parental management**—or mismanagement—is a causal force in delinquency. As a result of ineffective parenting, some children exhibit low self-control. These same children share certain characteristics, among which are the need for immediate gratification, an interest in material rather than spiritual matters, a propensity for risk-taking activities, a quickness to anger, and a generally impulsive nature. In the final analysis, low self-control persons engage in risky and even law-violating behaviors because these activities hold the promise of immediate pleasures for minimal effort.

Source: Gottfredson and Hirschi (1990).

DELINQUENCY, SOCIOLOGY, AND DELINQUENCY AS LEARNED BEHAVIOR

To this point, the sociological theories have defined delinquency as something that would be embraced by everyone if it were not for society and its cultural restraints. It seems as if youths, naturally inclined to misbehave, become delinquent because of the social system's failures, including ineffective parenting and defective norms. The next group of theories explains how otherwise good children become delinquent. For example, early in the twentieth century, University of Chicago researchers observed that certain parts of Chicago were and had been far more crime prone and socially disrupted than other parts. They theorized that criminal activity was the result of a breakdown in the social and physical fabric of these neighborhoods. This theoretical perspective, often referred to as **social disorganization theory**, was important in its own right, but it also helped establish another perspective on crime and delinquency that emphasized the intergenerational nature of crime in Chicago. Called the **cultural transmission thesis**, it is found in the work of Shaw and McKay (1972), who noted that groups were not delinquent but that, owing to the pervasiveness of illicit values and norms in a neighborhood, there were "deviant places."

Edwin Sutherland (1947) recast the cultural transmission thesis by extending its central thesis of the intergenerational nature of crime. He theorized that learning delinquent values, orientations, outlooks, and perspectives is essentially identical to learning nondelinquent ones. Sutherland's **differential association theory** suggests that children commit delinquent acts when the definitions favoring violations of the law outweigh those calling for conformity. The youths must have close, intimate contact with the sources of these definitions, along with a strong, emotional link. Moreover, the earlier these contacts occur in one's life, the greater the likelihood of committing delinquent acts. Not surprisingly, parents, childhood friends, teachers, and other relatives are the primary sources of such definitions.

Sutherland failed to explain why some definitions were included and others were discarded. Faced with this puzzle, Ronald Akers (1985) reframed Sutherland's theory in the vocabulary of operant conditioning and created **social learning theory**. He believed that people model some behavior on that of others around them, especially those who seem to succeed. Such modeling is vicariously rewarded and reinforced by the rewards received by others. Moreover, the behaviors that are most highly rewarded are those that are retained and repeated; those that are severely punished, again largely through the mechanisms of operant conditioning, are abandoned. Both physical and social experiences help to define certain experiences as reinforcing or punishing. Akers saw two types of definitions as essential to this process: (1) those definitions that place delinquent and other nonnormative behavior in a positive light and deserving of repetition, and (2) those that neutralize or run counter to the endorsed misbehavior.

DELINQUENCY, SOCIOLOGY, AND THE ROLE OF POWER

The final group of sociological theories acknowledges the role of power. **Power** is the relative ability of one group to carry out its collective will and attain its goals, despite opposition. Frank Tannenbaum (1938) observed that conflict ensues because what many youths define as fun or adventuresome is defined by middle-class society as evil or a nuisance. Children, lacking in power, often find their behavior being dramatized as evil. As practitioners of evil, they may receive a delinquent tag, giving such children a new status and exposing them to specialized treatment by society.

Tannenbaum's **dramatization of evil** and delinquency tagging served as one of the earliest theoretical explanations of labeling. Other explanations, however, predate even the 1930s. For example, the Judeo-Christian Bible includes the story of the first homicide victim, Abel, and the first murderer, Cain. In chapter 4 of Genesis, God's discovery of Cain's crime causes God to condemn Cain. Cain, worried about his fate among his fellow humans as much as he fears God's wrath, claims that others will kill him. God answers Cain by giving him "a token so that no one finding him should kill him." This token has been interpreted to be a physical sign upon Cain's person, the so-called mark of Cain, or the first social label.

Social groups label other groups, their members, and, generally, everyone else they encounter. As Howard Becker observed, social groups "create deviance by making the rules whose infractions constitute deviance, and by applying those rules to particular people and labeling them as outsiders" (1963:9). When these labels identify the person being labeled as one whose behavior is outside the norms of society, and when the person being labeled accepts the deviant label, then the worth of the individual is despoiled and devalued (Lemert, 1951). For our purposes, however, it is the application of **labeling theory** to the formal justice system that most interests us.

To this point, we have little explored gender's role, beyond noting that the delinquency rates for males and females are different.[6] Several theoretical perspectives acknowledge and explain these differences. Meda Chesney-Lind (1989b), in the **patriarchal society hypothesis**, defines many crimes committed by young girls as survival strategies, necessitated by a society that gives fathers nearly complete power over their children. Often trapped in abusive families or otherwise dangerous environments, female victims may attempt to flee or survive on the streets, acts that are likely to be seen as delinquency. Reliance on prostitution and drugs as survival strategies continues to influence their adult lives: Such women "possess truncated educational backgrounds and virtually no marketable occupation skills" (Chesney-Lind, 1989b:23).

At about the same time that labeling theory began to find supporters, another group of social philosophers and revolutionaries emerged. This group was the **Marxists**. Crime, they insisted, was a form of class warfare.[7] The rich and powerful, through their influence over the entire criminal justice system, sought to control the labor supply. **Capitalists**, as the owners of the means of production, "enslaved" the working class, alienating them from their work products and keeping them in virtual bondage to the capitalists' interests. Crime, even violent personal crimes, represented war against capitalism. Criminals were heroes of the revolution to come. For example, Krisberg (1975) criticized mainstream criminologists for serving the power elite's interests. Particularly damning was his criticism of liberals, who, he maintained, understood political struggle but succumbed to institutionalized cynicism. Krisberg (1975:20) placed the study of crime within "the broader quest for social justice" (i.e., the condition of equality, self-determination, and liberation that results in the elimination of all conditions of human suffering).

Throughout the 1970s, Marxist criminologists continued to question the traditional and emerging crime theories and supporting research. In the early 1980s, structural Marxists (Chambliss and Seidman, 1982; Hagan, 1989) suggested that the state provides capitalists with a means of long-term dominance to preserve their way of life. The state assumes not so much a subordinate role as an equal role to that of capitalist interests, forming a dual power structure. Through the state's "mediating influence, the worst excesses of economic exploitation, and the crises these create, are controlled in the interests of legitimating the long-term maintenance of the system of inequality" (Einstadter and Henry, 1995:231).

By the late 1980s and early 1990s, Marxism as a general social philosophy was dealt a series of deadly blows. The demise of the former Soviet Union and its allies in Eastern Europe, along with the reunification of Germany, suggested to many that Marxist philosophy was just that, a philosophy and not a practice worth imitating. If one overlooks Cuba and China, Marxism was pronounced politically "dead" by the mid-1990s.

In criminology, the radical critique of the justice system did not disappear. Rather, as we explain in "Theoretical Reflections: The Legacy of Conflict Theories," it changed shape. The new forms, like the majority of the sociological theo-

Theoretical Reflections
The Legacy of Conflict Theories

The importance of Marxists for the study of juvenile justice is their emphasis on power relations, especially the powerlessness of groups such as children. **Anarchist criminologists** view all hierarchical systems, including socialism, as evil. They argue for dismantling the justice system and replacing it with a decentralized system of negotiated justice. Juvenile delinquency, then, is a form of resistance; the enemy is the juvenile justice system. As a case in point, consider the crime of urban graffiti. Few cities lack what some call acts of wanton vandalism. Ferrell (1993) sees the phenomenon quite differently: Graffiti represents a direct attack on the existing power structure, the city's hierarchy. Threatened by this assault, the typical response of city officials is to wipe out the graffiti and target the gangs for enhanced police attention.

Left realists emerged in response to the conservative policies of Britain's Prime Minister Margaret Thatcher in the 1980s. They do not view criminals, including juvenile delinquents, as the romantic figures of the Marxists. Rather, left realists focus on the relationships between the offender, the victim, and the justice system. Criminals are neither political rebels nor champions of the underprivileged; they represent a threat to society. Left realists take crime seriously, believing that it can only be reduced by changing social policy. Holding lawmakers and law enforcers accountable for their policies is a start. Actual and potential victims of street criminals need to be mobilized in order to get their needs made a part of the emerging policies and practices. Finally, left realists assume a minimalist position with respect to implementing the state's coercive power, including the use of police and penal sanctions.

Sources: Ferrell (1993); Matthews (1987); Pepinsky (1978); Young and Matthews (1991).

ries before them, placed considerable emphasis on the social nature of adult crime, juvenile delinquency, and society's responses to both. In the next section we review theories that generally see society as of secondary importance to other factors.

EXPLAINING DELINQUENCY, PART III: THEORETICAL ECLECTICISM AND PRAGMATISM

In the 1970s, 1980s, and 1990s, criminologists began developing theories that often combined various elements of existing theories into new theoretical frameworks. Many of these emerging perspectives on crime and justice, unlike their predecessors, were not rigidly bound by the often-restrictive disciplinary boundaries of sociology, psychology, and related academic fields (Winfree and Abadinsky, 2003:301–3). The new theories were intellectually eclectic and highly pragmatic. What worked—or seemed to work—was the primary focus of these theories. They were not always, as we shall see, welcome additions to the "theoretical stew."

Many of the new explanations had ties to existing ones, but generally represented alternative ways of viewing offenses and offenders. For example, there is a direct intellectual tie between research conducted at the University of Chicago in the 1920s on the ecological causes of crime, and C. Ray Jeffery's (1971) book *Crime Prevention Through Environmental Design*. Jeffery argues that careful urban planning can make any area more defensible, that is, resistant to crime and delinquency. As an example, Paul Brantingham and Patricia Brantingham (1993) recommend locating malls and schools far from one another to avoid congregation of school-age children during lunch hours and after school, when acts of vandalism and drug use are common. However, any environmental design program's success depends upon heightened involvement of citizens in their own communities and a more efficient criminal justice system.

Besides using street-smart urban architecture, an involved citizenry, and an efficient criminal justice system, other environmental theories suggest that certain kinds of offenders seek out specific types of targets. The work of Cohen and Felson (1979) addressed offenders and their targets. They wrote that criminal motivation and the supply of potential offenders are constants, yet crime is obviously not spread evenly throughout society. Why? The probability of crime increases by placing a highly motivated offender in close proximity to a suitably attractive target without effective guardianship. Their theory—called **routine activities theory** or **opportunity theory**—gives a conceptual reason for being smart about designing against crime. As they observed: "Rather than assuming predatory crime is simply an indication of social breakdown, one might take it as a by-product of freedom and prosperity as they manifest themselves in the routine activities of everyday life" (1979:606).

A final cluster of theories exhibits ties to biology and psychology. First, biochemistry—from hormones to dietary sugars—has long been linked to delinquency (Hippchen, 1978). More recently, Ellis (1991) observed that the level of an enzyme found in the bloodstream *and* the brain, **monoamine oxidase (MAO)**, may be related to delinquent behavior. An MAO deficiency is associated with a tendency toward aggressive outbursts, often in response to anger, fear, or frustration (Brunner et al., 1994). After noting a modest association between MAO levels and inappropriate behavior, Ellis (1991) observes that:

- Males have lower MAO levels than females and higher arrest rates than females.

- MAO levels are significantly lower during the second and third decades of life, the years official statistics show are the most crime prone for these same age groups.

- African Americans, who have disproportionately high arrest, conviction, and incarceration rates, also have lower MAO activity than whites.

Second, the connection between weak minds and weak morals emerged in the first two decades of the twentieth century (Degler, 1991). Hindelang (1973) suggested that IQ determines school performance, which itself shows a high correlation with delinquency proneness. Bartol (1991) suggests that the discussion about the links between IQ and crime is, to paraphrase Shakespeare, "much ado about the wrong thing." As Bartol (1991:32) observes,

IQ scores and the concept of intelligence should *not* be confused. The term IQ merely refers to a standardized score on a test. Intelligence, on the other hand, is a broad, all-encompassing ability that defies any straightforward or simple definition. (emphasis in the original)

These warnings did not stop Herrnstein and Murray from offering one of the more controversial crime and delinquency theories of recent times. Writing with James Q. Wilson, Herrnstein posited "a clear and consistent link between criminality and low intelligence" (1985:148). In *The Bell Curve*, Herrnstein and Murray (1994) took this idea one step further. They stated that it was membership in certain racial groups that determined IQ scores; moreover, IQ scores led directly and irrevocably to underclass status, poverty, and crime.[8] The **race-IQ-crime thesis** they offer is intellectually weak; the supporting data reported are self-serving; and the authors are uncritical of the studies cited (Cullen, 1997; see also Fraser, 1995).

Herrnstein and Murray's work serves to remind us how short the distance is between the thinking of Homer's day and today. Indeed, these last two sets of causal forces—biochemistry and intelligence—are interesting, since we end this review of delinquency theory where we started it: looking for the demons within us that cause crime.

SUMMARY

We organized this chapter around two primary themes, both of which, we believe, will help sharpen your analytical and critical thinking skills for the further exploration of juvenile justice. The first half of the chapter was a historical analysis of the relationships between children and their families. Several key points are worth reviewing. First, until very recently, growing up had challenges largely unknown today, including high infant mortality and deadly childhood diseases that assumed epidemic proportions. Second, and related, parental love for one's children, particularly as we know it today, is a relatively recent development. Parents in previous times were emotionally attached to their own children; however, it appears that parents often had to harden their hearts against the prospect of losing so many offspring. This practice was particularly true in the late Middle Ages and early Renaissance, when mothers became "baby factories" simply to guarantee that parents replaced themselves in the community. Third, a little more than 100 years ago fertility and child mortality rates both declined. Compulsory education and, eventually, elective postsecondary education extended childhood, creating adolescence. It was during this historical period that American society created a unique institution, the juvenile court, to deal with the problems associated with troublesome adolescents, the delinquents.

The second theme centered on criminological theory. In chapter 1's opening vignette, Gail asks an essentially rhetorical question: "What's all this theory stuff have to do with juvenile justice?" We happen to believe that delinquency theory has a great deal to do with juvenile justice. Indeed, two primary goals guided our discussion of delinquency theory. First, we want you to feel comfortable with the idea that seeking answers to difficult and complex questions is a praiseworthy activity. You might ask, Why do some youths engage in delinquent behavior and others do not? Why do some stop? How can we help the rest desist their troubling behavior? Can we make them stop?

The second goal centers on the fact that convincing students that theory should have any role in the study of juvenile justice is a difficult task. By definition, theories are abstract and at times hard to fathom, especially at first.[9] We take the position that theoretical ideas about why juveniles become delinquent can inform us about the creative forces behind the establishment of certain laws and policies, and the use of specific practices. For similar reasons, these theories often shape future laws, policies, and practices. To reinforce this position, we provide at regular intervals in this text inserts entitled "Theoretical Reflections," the first two of which were included in this chapter. Each insert links a specific theory to some aspect of juvenile justice being addressed in that chapter. These inserts speak to the relevant theoretical arguments and the related practical aspects.

Nearly everyone has ideas, suggestions, or theories to offer as answers to questions about why juveniles violate the law. Often the answers emerge from personal experiences or observations. Perhaps one of the theories captured the essence of your own favorite explanation, the single theory that makes the most sense to you. Or you may have adopted a more pragmatic position, preferring to link specific forms of behavior to different theories. If you have not already considered these types of questions, our goal is to have you asking them by the end of the text. If you are already seeking answers, we hope that you will continue, framing your questions in even more sophisticated terms.

CRITICAL REVIEW QUESTIONS

1. Do you have an opinion about executing pre-teenagers? How about teenagers? For example, do you feel that either of these practices would be wrong under any set of circumstances? (This is the position of the death penalty opponent.) Do you think that it would be acceptable to sentence preteens or teenagers to death as long as the execution is carried out later, when they are older? Do you think that it would be acceptable to sentence and execute a preteen (assuming, of course, that the appeals process did not age the youth beyond his or her teenage years)? You might want to consider the values or ideology to which you refer when crafting your answers.

2. Prepare a time line, beginning with the establishment of the Roman Empire in 27 BCE and ending in 1900. (Scale is not important.) Identify the following historical periods on the time line: Middle Ages, Renaissance, Protestant Reformation, Colonial America, American Revolution, and Industrial Revolution. Lastly, place the key changes in definitions of children, childhood, and child-parent relations along this time line.

3. At several different points in this chapter, we mentioned fertility and child mortality rates. What appears to be the historical relationship between these terms and familial child-rearing patterns over the ages?

4. Compare and contrast the eighteenth- and nineteenth-century theories of crime with the child-rearing philosophies and practices of each century. Do you see any similarities? Any differences?

5. Obviously, prior to the 1870s and 1880s, youths passed through the biological and physiological stages associated with being adolescents without all the fuss currently associated with that stage of development. What was dif-

ferent? Did society truly create the condition about which its members were complaining?

6. The Industrial Revolution had an impact on countries other than the United States in the eighteenth and nineteenth centuries, yet it was in the United States that the juvenile court emerged. From what you have read—and the discussion of the forces that led to the creation of this unique court—why do you think it happened in the United States first?

7. What was the oddest historical fact you learned in this chapter about how children were seen prior to the nineteenth century?

8. A friend not taking this class, upon learning that you are studying a bunch of really old theories about crime, some of which were written by people who have been dead for a hundred years or more, asks you a simple question: Why? How do you respond?

9. Which general perspective on current delinquency theory do you think provides the best insights into the phenomena being studied in this text? Support your choice.

10. In the recent past, the racial and cultural-imperative implications of eugenics (literally, the systematic inclusion or exclusion of certain genetic material in the human species) were hotly debated. A more recent example might be that of genetic engineering as a method of creating the "perfect" human being. Explain how you think theoretical arguments about delinquency are treading along this path once more.

11. Have a little fun. Create a list of all the theories discussed in this chapter. Now predict which ones will have practical implications for the administration of juvenile justice. Indicate both whether you think they will have utility and where, generally, you think they will appear (for example, law enforcement, courts, corrections). As we progress through the text, check your list and evaluate your predictions.

12. At the beginning and the end of this chapter we acknowledged that some students might find the commingling of theory and history to be problematic. Now that you have completed the chapter, explain why this practice is not such a half-baked idea.

RECOMMENDED READINGS

Ariès, Philippe (1962). *Centuries of Childhood: A Social History of Family Life*. New York: Knopf. This classic sociological-historical work looks at French family life during medieval times to the early Renaissance. Through the use of letters, poems, and other documents of the day, Ariès skillfully relates what life was like for parents and children alike. This work is famous—and criticized—for Ariès's generalizations about changes in children's status during the Renaissance based on his analysis of woodcuttings and portraits.

Shoemaker, Donald J. (1997). *Theories of Delinquency: An Examination of Explanations of Delinquent Behavior*, 3rd ed. New York: Oxford. This book, while nearly a decade old, presents a sociological orientation to delinquency theories: Two chapters focus on biogenic and psychogenic theories, and multiple chapters address sociological theories. It also contains solid reviews of female delinquency and middle-class delinquency.

KEY TERMS

adolescence
anarchist criminologists
anomie
apprenticeship system
atavists
behaviorism
binding out
bonding theory
capitalists
chattel
child savers
containment theory
criminal anthropology
criminal stigmata
cultural transmission thesis
differential association theory
differential opportunity theory
dramatization of evil
ectomorphic
free will
general deterrence
general strain theory
Industrial Revolution
labeling theory
left realists
low self-control
marginalized youths
Marxists

mesomorphic
monoamine oxidase (MAO)
operant conditioning
opportunity theory
parental management
paterfamilias
paterna pietas
patria potestas
patriarchal society hypothesis
Pd scale
personality theory
power
power-control theory
Progressive Era
psychopaths
punishers
Puritanism
race-IQ-crime thesis
reinforcers
routine activities theory
self-control theory
social determinism
social disorganization theory
social learning theory
specific deterrence
strain theory
subcultural tradition

NOTES

[1] The Supreme Court had ruled nearly 16 years earlier in *Stanford v. Kentucky* that the execution of persons who had committed a capital crime at age 16 or 17 was constitutionally acceptable, but not for persons who were 15 or less at the time of the homicide. With *Roper*, some 72 persons on death rows throughout the nation had their death sentences vacated.

[2] Around 1000 CE, European nobility adopted the patrilineal ideology. Previously, they used the cognate family, in which each individual was related to everyone else in the community through both mother and father. Women were valued members of this type of family, and they enjoyed considerable power with respect to divorce and property. Friendship was stronger than kinship. The force that changed this system was feudalism (Trumbach, 1978:1).

[3] Adolescence, as an age-graded period in childhood, was recognized in the late fourteenth century: It circumscribed the ages between 14 and 21 (Binder et al., 1988:63). However, the use of this term to describe a period in human socio-legal development, created by the need to extend childhood, was unique to the late nineteenth century.

[4] Psychology is an area of scientific study chiefly concerned with the mind and mental processes—feelings, desires, and motivations. Psychiatry is a medical specialty that studies and treats mental *diseases* of varying intensity: Neuroses are mild personality disorders; psychoses are far more serious.

[5] Recall the social strains created for the children of immigrants in the late nineteenth and early twentieth centuries. Rather than view this social force in strictly Durkheimian or Mertonian terms, some

conflict theories, including Sellin (1938), saw the conflict as one between an established old-world culture and the culture of the new world.

[6] For an exception to this generalization, see Hagan's power-control theory and its implications for the treatment of females in contemporary society.

[7] Much of the following is based on Quinney (1973) and Taylor, Walton, and Young (1973).

[8] Gordon (1987:92) states: "It is time to consider the black-white IQ difference seriously when confronting the problem of crime in American society."

[9] Some criminologists might view these explanations as cursory and simplistic. They would be correct. We see our task as introducing the student to the theoretical constructs and ideas. If students—or their professors—wish to build on these basics, more power to them.

JUVENILE OFFENDERS AND POLICE PROCESSES

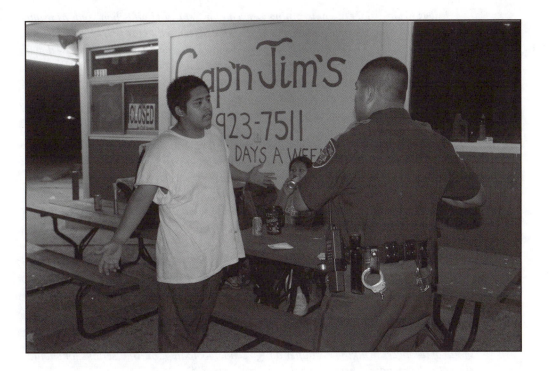

* * *

It was Friday night of homecoming weekend for Central High School and, as usual for this time of year, the police radio crackled with calls related to the festivities occurring all over town. At 12:15 AM one patrol car was dispatched to check out a keg party "down by the river," and very quickly the officers in this car called for backup. Eventually three cars, with a total of six officers, arrived at the party and observed 40 to 50 juveniles and young adults celebrating Central's victory over Madison.

As it turned out, the police cars approached from different directions and with their lights out. Therefore, the officers were on top of the party before any of the celebrants realized they had company. When the realization set in some in the crowd ran furiously into the dark and got away, a few unfortunately leaving their cars behind. Others froze in their tracks. Some cried, and one young man vomited.

By the time it was all over the six officers had arrested 22 youngsters under the age of 18 and had charged some with marijuana possession and all of them with a variety of alcohol-related offenses. Also taken into custody were four people who were between the ages of 18 and 20, and two more who were over 21.

Since Elmwood did not have its own juvenile detention facility, all of those arrested were transported to the county jail for booking. The parents of the juveniles were called to pick them up, and the adults all posted small cash bonds.

After the process was completed, three groups—the arresting officers, the jail personnel, and some of the parents—all were wondering the same thing: Was it worth it? Should the police have made the arrests? Should they have ignored the behavior? Is a group of teenagers drinking beer after a high school football game that serious, or should the police be spending their time fighting "real crime?"[1]

* * *

When we consider the nation's crime problem, we need to note that a substantial portion of the crime reported is youth crime. In 2003 police departments in the United States arrested roughly 2,220,300 people under the age of 18. Figures from the *Uniform Crime Reports* indicate that about 16% of all arrests for that year were of juveniles. The number of juvenile arrests for violent crimes declined 9% from 1999 to 2003, but remained unchanged from 2002 to 2003. Overall, from 1994 to 2003 there was a decrease of 32% in the number of arrests of juveniles for index crimes of violence. Table 3.1 provides a snapshot of the recent crime trends for youngsters in the United States.

Judges and the juvenile courts receive much of the attention in the juvenile justice system. Police officers also are key actors: Juveniles are more likely to encounter the police than any other actors in the criminal justice system. That fact has profound implications for the ways in which youngsters are or are not processed by the juvenile justice system. For the time being, we need to explore a brief history of police–juvenile interactions, the general role played by the police, and the specific procedures employed in processing juvenile offenders and non-offenders.

A BRIEF HISTORY OF POLICE WORK WITH JUVENILES

Most police agencies in the United States developed during the early to mid-1800s. Initially, most major-city policing was done on foot or with horse patrols. This approach to law enforcement put the cop on the beat in close contact with community residents. Police officers were more often problem solvers than crime fighters (see Trojanowicz, 1983).

Following World War II, police departments nationwide began to expand and specialize, and one of the first specializations for most large departments was a juvenile unit. A variety of factors occurring during the 1940s and 1950s caused police departments to focus more attention on the activities of delinquent youngsters. One of these factors was the prominence of gang activities in cities such as New York, Boston, Philadelphia, Detroit, and Chicago. New ethnic gangs—made up of the children of immigrants from the Caribbean Islands, of Eastern European and Asian asylum seekers, and of African-Americans from the Deep South—joined the traditional Italian and Jewish gangs of the inner cities.[2]

Gangs were only part of what was perceived to be a larger delinquency problem. Indeed, the 1940s and 1950s witnessed what has been called "the great juvenile delinquency scare" (Binder, Geis, and Bruce, 1988:240–44; see also Mennel, 1973). As Binder and associates (1988) observe:

> With the coming of the 1940s, and particularly of World War II, Americans began to develop a heightened consciousness of juvenile delinquency as a problem in their midst and as a problem that threatened the very fabric of American life.

In the 1950s, this concern reached crisis proportions. After nearly a decade of congressional hearings, commissions, and reports, the cascading delinquency problem began to be linked to sympathetic and even glamorous portrayals of antisocial and delinquent lifestyles by the mass media (Gilbert, 1986). By the 1960s, scholars began to question whether media accounts of heightened levels of teen violence, racism, rampant illegal drug use, and an ineffective juvenile justice system had exaggerated the delinquency problems of the 1940s and 1950s. There was reason to believe that levels of delinquency in past decades may not have been as bad as was portrayed by the media (Binder et al., 1988:241).

Table 3.1   Juvenile Arrests, 1994–2003

Most Serious Offense	2003 Estimated Number of Juvenile Arrests	Percent of Total Juvenile Arrests		Percent change		
		Female	Under Age 15	1994–2003	1999–2003	2002–2003
Total	2,220,300	29%	32%	−18%	−11%	0%
Violent Crime Index	92,300	18	33	−32	−9	0
Murder and nonnegligent manslaughter	1,130	9	11	−68	−18	−10
Forcible rape	4,240	2	37	−25	−11	−9
Robbery	25,440	9	25	−43	−8	3
Aggravated assault	61,490	24	36	−26	−9	0
Property Crime Index	463,300	32	37	−38	−15	−3
Burglary	85,100	12	35	−40	−15	−1
Larceny-Theft	325,600	39	38	−35	−15	−3
Motor vehicle theft	44,500	17	25	−52	−15	−4
Arson	8,200	12	61	−36	−12	−3
Nonindex						
Other assaults	241,900	32	43	10	5	5
Forgery and counterfeiting	4,700	35	13	−47	−36	−8
Fraud	8,100	33	18	−29	−37	−9
Embezzlement	1,200	40	6	15	−30	−17
Stolen property (buying, receiving, possessing)	24,300	15	27	−46	−19	−5
Vandalism	107,700	14	44	−33	−11	2
Weapons (carrying, possessing, etc.)	39,200	11	36	−41	−6	11
Prostitution and commercialized vice	1,400	69	14	31	23	11
Sex offense (except forcible rape and prostitution)	18,300	9	51	2	3	−3
Drug abuse violations	197,100	16	17	19	−3	4
Gambling	1,700	2	15	−59	46	1
Offenses against the family and children	7,000	39	35	19	−24	−19
Driving under the influence	21,000	20	2	33	−9	−4
Liquor law violations	136,900	35	10	4	−22	−6
Drunkenness	17,600	23	13	−11	−19	−6
Disorderly conduct	193,000	31	41	13	0	6
Vagrancy	2,300	25	25	−50	−20	9
All other offenses (except traffic)	379,800	27	28	−2	−12	−1
Suspicion (not included in totals)	1,500	24	26	−77	−74	−53
Curfew and loitering	136,500	30	29	−1	−18	−8
Runaways	123,600	59	36	−42	−18	−2

Source: Snyder (2005).

A third factor was the introduction of women into policing. For most of its history—and here the United States is fairly typical—policing has been a male-dominated field. Nevertheless, beginning in the early 1900s women were employed in police departments in the United States, often to work with female arrestees and juveniles.

There is some debate about who the first female police officer in the United States actually was. However, the two women frequently mentioned as the "firsts" were Lola Baldwin and Alice Stebbin Wells. Baldwin was hired in 1905 by the Portland (Oregon) Police Department and was put in charge of a group of social workers hired to protect the "moral safety" of the city's young women during the Lewis and Clark Exposition (National Center for Women & Policing, 2004:1).

In 1910 the Los Angeles Police Department hired Alice Stebbin Wells, who was given the designation of "policewoman." Wells, like many of the other women working in early law enforcement, was part social worker and part police officer. Many of these first policewomen were responsible for "cases relating to women and children, such as young runaways, shoplifting, and prostitution" (National Center for Women & Policing, 2004:2).

During the decades of the 1930s, 1940s, and 1950s, police departments hired larger numbers of female employees, particularly following World War II. Women's involvement in the civilian and military workforces during the war opened doors never before fully opened to them. However, many of the women hired were assigned support positions such as dispatchers, file clerks, and the "women's bureau." Thus, "the role that women police officers originally filled as social workers still strongly defined how women were used in the police force" (National Center for Women & Policing, 2004:2).

Historically, female officers dealt with juvenile offenders. These assignments allowed police administrators to introduce women to the police workforce in positions for which they were "suited" but kept them out of traditionally male-dominated areas that might be considered too dangerous. It also allowed police departments to minimize criticisms of gender discrimination, sometimes by placing female officers in limited enforcement positions. Most of the jobs for female officers were fairly visible, and this was good public relations for police departments. They could say, "Not only do we hire women, we place them in meaningful positions." Women's employment in law enforcement got a big boost in 1972, when Congress amended Title VII of the Civil Rights Act of 1964 to prohibit discrimination against women in recruiting, hiring, promoting, and working conditions by public agencies. A quick review of female involvement in police work shows that since the mid-1970s women have been assigned to the full range of police duties (National Center for Women & Policing, 2004:2–3).

Virtually every police department of any size in the United States now has one or more juvenile units. In a report entitled *Police*, the National Advisory Committee on Criminal Justice Standards and Goals recommended that "a police agency with 75 or fewer personnel should establish a juvenile unit if warranted by local conditions; however, for agencies with more than 75 personnel, full-time juvenile investigators are essential *unless the community clearly has no problem with juvenile delinquents*" (1973:223; emphasis added). In departments with 200 or more officers, juvenile units or sections are usually part of the Criminal Investigation Division or Special Operations Division; these departments may also have specialized antigang units (Sanders, 1994). No matter how many units exist to deal with juveniles, the number of officers assigned to them is typically quite small, perhaps fewer than 5% of the sworn officers in even a large department (Bittner, 1990).

POLICE ROLES AND JUVENILE OFFENDERS

Many students reading this book already have had an introductory course in policing. For them this section will provide a brief review. For others it will introduce some of the functions performed by the police and then tie these functions to the various ways the police interact with juveniles.

POLICE FUNCTIONS

While police officers perform a variety of tasks, most of their responsibilities can be summarized in terms of three major categories: law enforcement (or crime fighting), order maintenance, and public service (see Peak and Glensor, 2004; Walker and Katz, 2005).

Law enforcement is the function most members of the public (and even many police officers) think of when they consider policing in the United States. Television shows, movies, and novels about policing tend to perpetuate the myth that police work is all about crime fighting. However, Walker and Katz note that "only about one-third of a patrol officer's activities are devoted to criminal law enforcement" (2005:5–6). What does this mean in terms of police contacts with juveniles? First, it means that police officers will encounter some juveniles breaking the law, but the vast majority of their arrests will involve adults. In fact, Snyder (2005) says that in 2003 only about one arrest out of every six involved a juvenile. Second, most of the police–juvenile encounters will involve relatively minor violations of the law, including status offenses. Third, even when serious offenses are committed, juveniles tend to be overrepresented in arrests for some crimes (arson, vandalism, motor vehicle theft, burglary, larceny/theft, disorderly conduct, robbery, and weapons violations) and underrepresented in arrests for other crimes (murder, aggravated assault, forcible rape, and drug crimes) (Snyder, 2005:4). In other words, juveniles tend to be the least serious among even the serious offenders.

Order maintenance is a necessary part of police work, but one not necessarily highly valued by police officers. These calls can range from traffic control at the scene of an accident or sporting event, to neighborhood (or family) disputes, and loud parties. In the end, the complainant wants the police to "do something" (see Walker and Katz, 2005:233). Order maintenance responsibilities may bring the police into contact with juveniles when youths congregate in parks or on street corners. Officers may order them to "move along," though the youngsters may feel that they are not doing anything wrong and should not be hassled by the police.

Finally, public service or calls for service is the catchall category in policing. These calls may involve everything from animal control issues to dented garbage cans. This has been an area that has been shunned by some departments and ignored by others. Nevertheless, the emergence of the community policing movement in the early 1980s brought a renewed emphasis on the police as community resources and problem solvers (see H. Goldstein, 1993; Peak and Glensor, 2004; and Trojanowicz and Bucqueroux, 1990). In the juvenile arena, the police may be called on for dependency, neglect, and abuse cases (see chapter 9) and they may find themselves acting as social workers and community organizers. This is consistent with the community-oriented (or problem-oriented) model of policing but often is viewed as inconsistent with the crime-fighting model.

POLICE STYLES AND THEIR IMPLICATIONS FOR POLICE–JUVENILE CONTACTS

Our opening scenario and the brief history of police work with juveniles begs another question: How should police officers act when they come in contact with minors, whether or not they are suspected juvenile offenders? Should we fault the officers for making arrests for what might be perceived as youthful good-natured fun?

Several aspects of police work can confound the police–youth relationship. During the 1960s and 1970s, police researchers focused on police roles, or styles of policing (Wilson, 1973). The different styles reflect divergent orientations by individual police officers as well as particular departments. A number of these styles have been applied to police–juvenile interactions. Second, law enforcers serve as gatekeepers for the juvenile justice system. If the police fail to act, many children escape the juvenile justice system's attention. Third, given the sheer volume of "juvenile business" that involves the police, the individual officer's discretion plays a crucial role in police–juvenile interactions. As we continue our discussion by examining police processes, we will more fully explore these concepts since they will contribute to our understanding of both *how* the police operate and *why*. We start with police styles.

Law, departmental policies, and local customs shape police dispositional choices. They also are influenced by officers' personalities, predispositions, and policing styles. This section addresses the traditional policing styles and contrasts them with the recent emphasis on community policing.

The **Law Enforcement Assistance Administration (LEAA)** defined traditional policing in terms of the preventive patrol concept. Its definition of preventive patrol is "the routine movement of uniformed officers by vehicle or on foot through delineated geographic areas" (LEAA, 1976:6). Preventive patrol has five goals: "(1) deterrence of crime; (2) apprehension of criminal offenders; (3) satisfaction of public demands for non-crime-related services; (4) maintenance of a sense of community security and confidence in the police; and (5) recovery of stolen goods" (LEAA, 1976:6).

To accomplish these goals, uniformed patrol services have two apparent responsibilities. First, crime suppression, also called **proactive policing**, has long been an important objective. By their physical presence on the streets and through crime prevention programs, today's police practice proactive policing. Second, most law enforcement involves **reactive policing**, including, for example, apprehending an armed robbery suspect, recovering stolen goods, or, more commonly and less glamorously, dealing with the aftermath of drunk driving or other motor vehicle code violations. Even on patrol, police officers have to change to a reactive mode in the event they observe a crime or its consequences. Police work's reactive nature means that in most instances police resources are not mobilized until after law violations have occurred.

We can make several assumptions about policing styles. First, police officers will use different styles when dealing with offenders, victims, and witnesses. Second, the officers' levels of education, socioeconomic backgrounds, personalities, and job assignments may influence these styles. Third, agency structure and management orientation can influence an individual officer's orientation and perspective. Finally, some officers may utilize inflexible policing styles, while others see their orientation as largely defined by the situation.

What can we derive from an examination of the different policing styles in relation to police–juvenile encounters? First, some police officers will make few distinctions between law violators who are juveniles and those who are adults; they are **rule-applier cops**. These officers do not differentiate in their responses to rule enforcement on the basis of the offender's age, or, for that matter, any other observable or readily discerned external characteristic, including gender, race, religion, or sexual orientation (see Gaines and Kappeler, 2003:332).

Second, some officers will see themselves as the kindly parents of erring youngsters. These officers, functioning as **problem-solving cops**, may feel like more can be accomplished by not making an arrest. Their approach is more than simply a turn-your-back-and-do-nothing technique; it may emphasize counseling and personal interaction more than a strict law enforcement orientation. In curfew violation cases and minor thefts or acts of vandalism, these officers may decide the most time-saving and outcome-effective solution is to deliver children to their parents. This option can have a dramatic impact, especially when the child is brought home after midnight and sleeping parents must be awakened.

Lastly, officers can be characterized as **ambivalent enforcers**. Like problem-solving cops, these officers will counsel or threaten and subsequently release most of the youngsters with whom they have contact, since many of the violations are relatively minor. When presented with serious delinquent offenses, ambivalent enforcers do not hesitate to make a juvenile arrest. In other words, arrest is the response of last resort for this type of police officer.

THE POLICE AS JUVENILE JUSTICE SYSTEM GATEKEEPERS

The term *gatekeeper* often appears in social science literature. In simplest terms, a **gatekeeper** is one who decides who comes in and who stays out. The gatekeeper has control over how many people are admitted and at what rate. In the juvenile justice system, the police exert the greatest influence over the number of juveniles formally or informally processed by the system. As gatekeepers, they determine which youths will (or will not) be arrested and the procedures for handling the different types of children with whom they have contact. How the police operate has an impact on the rest of the juvenile justice system.

For the most part, we can say that the police process virtually all the juvenile justice system's clients. Families and schools can make direct referrals to the juvenile court, but in most cases, referrals come from the police. Therefore, it is important to stress the vital role the police play in determining the juvenile justice system's workload. A key to this role of police as gatekeepers is discretion.

POLICE DISCRETION

Discretion is a commonly misunderstood notion in the criminal justice system. In fact, many people confuse discretion with discrimination, and people outside the justice agencies in the United States may feel that discretion should be tightly controlled through departmental policies. While discretion and discrimination share some common properties, discrimination is almost always considered negative, while discretion can be treated as a neutral idea.

Some definitions and a brief discussion will illustrate what we mean. **Discrimination** is the

> unfavorable treatment of groups of people on arbitrary grounds such as race or religion, a form of control that keeps the groups socially distant from one another. This separation is accomplished through institutionalized practices that attribute inferiority on the basis of notions that frequently have little or nothing to do with the real behavior of those who are discriminated against. (Rush, 2003:115)

Discrimination implies that police officers apply the law to the disadvantage of one person or group compared to the way others are treated. By contrast, **discretion** is

> an authority conferred by law on an official or an agency to act in certain conditions or situations in accordance with the named official's or agency's considered judgment or conscience. (Rush, 2003:114)

Thus, discretion means that criminal justice officials have choices to make, and in the course of their duties they make those choices. In fairness, we must note that sometimes the choices involve discrimination, but often they do not.

Many factors influence the choices made by police officers when handling accused juvenile offenders. For instance, laws can influence the ways in which juvenile offenders are treated and determine which youths are classified as offenders. State laws and local ordinances play critical roles in defining the parameters of juvenile justice. Additionally, police department policies will define the outer limits of the acceptable exercise of discretion. Police agencies are always in the process of developing and refining policies, and some of these policies will be directed at processing youngsters suspected of having violated the law.

Furthermore, local practices may influence the exercise of discretion. As one example, a city may have a curfew law for teenagers below a certain age. The law would dictate citations or actions such as taking youngsters into custody and notifying their parents. Departmental policy typically would support this type of response. However, the practice as understood by the officers and their supervisors might suggest that curfew violations are not very serious and unless there are other violations or justifications for action, curfew violations should be ignored.

We also need to acknowledge that personal attitudes and characteristics can influence the exercise of discretion. If officers believe that little will happen to juvenile arrestees, they may be less inclined to take formal action. Police officer attitudes concerning appropriate or inappropriate behavior by youngsters, the numbers and ages of their own children, and perhaps whether they are having a bad day might also affect discretionary decision making.

How important is police discretion? The research reveals a rather consistent pattern. In all police–juvenile encounters when a crime is suspected, arrests occurred in 15% to 16% of the cases. If a felony was suspected, arrests ranged from 75% to 100% of cases (Black and Reiss, 1970; Lundman, Sykes, and Clark, 1978). For similar situations involving adults, the arrest rates were slightly higher than those reported for juveniles (Black, 1968).

As we conclude this section, we need to emphasize a few points that will be critical to our understanding of police roles and processes in the juvenile justice system:

- Police work involves a lot of unsupervised, low-visibility decision making.
- Uniformed patrol officers will always exercise much discretion.
- Discretion is particularly broad in cases involving relatively minor offenses.
- Police discretion with juvenile offenders is even broader than that pertaining to adults.

Therefore, discretion is central to the police gatekeeping role, and uniformed patrol officers best exemplify the exercise of discretion.

POLICE DISCRETION, AGE, GENDER, AND RACE: A CAUTIONARY NOTE

A youthful suspect's age may limit the officer's options. Researchers indicate that older juvenile suspects are more likely to be arrested than younger ones (Piliavin and Briar, 1964; Terry, 1967). Other researchers, however, suggest that age is a poor predictor of police decisions to act (Hohenstein, 1969). All other things being equal, however, if the suspect is 12 years of age or younger, formal police intervention is far less likely (Binder et al., 1988:383). Perhaps the inconsistency is due to the fact that older youths are typically involved in more serious law-violating behavior or have more extensive prior delinquent histories.

Race and gender are strong and poorly understood predictors of police decision making. Minority youths and males experience formal processing far more often than whites and females. If a given police officer has a black male and a white female in similar situations, typically the black male will receive formal processing and the white female will receive an informal action.

Differences by race are troubling. Wilson (1973) suggests that in the 1960s, traditional police departments (those with relatively low levels of professionalism) selected juveniles for arrest according to race, since they viewed African Americans as alien and homeless. Black and Reiss (1970:68), in their study of arrest decisions, reported that the arrest rate in police–black encounters was 2.5 times higher than for police–white encounters. Wolfgang and associates (1972), in an early analysis of a birth cohort of Philadelphia males, found that nonwhites were arrested more

> **Box 3.1   International Perspectives**
> **Kids and Cops in the Netherlands**
>
> Police confrontations and interactions with groups of young people present problems in nations other than the United States. For example, in the Netherlands there is a conspicuous population of families who have moved there from the North African nation of Morocco. The police often confront the boys from these families and accuse them (rightly or wrongly) of breaking into cars, assaults, and robberies. Additionally, much like George Kelling and James Q. Wilson's (1982) discussion of community disorderliness, or "broken windows," the police believe that Moroccan boys cause disturbances and harass people.
>
> A research project by Stol and Bervoets (2002) examined "what works" in responding to the problems of interactions among the police and Moroccan youths living in the Netherlands, and they observed that most of the police responses were not effective at best, or counterproductive at worst. In the end they made several recommendations: (1) the police culture has to change in order to respond effectively to situations involving Moroccan youngsters, (2) the police have to get to know these juveniles personally, (3) officers must respond to youths with respect if they anticipate being treated with respect themselves, and (4) "a zero-tolerance policy does not work: it is more important to be clear than to be strict."
>
> Source: Stol and Bervoets (2002).

frequently than whites and received more severe dispositions. Thornberry (1979) reanalyzed the cohort data and noticed that the most lenient dispositions were associated with white minor offenders, and the most severe with black serious offenders. Finally, Black and Smith (1981) observed that by the late 1970s the national trend seemed to be toward equal treatment, and bias in court referrals favoring whites over blacks was disappearing.

Considerable evidence suggests that differences in arrest and detention rates for minorities versus whites are due to more than the suspect's race. Theodore Ferdinand and Elmer Luchterhand (1970) report that if the charges are serious, the legal factors dominate. If the case is minor, then race emerges as a prime factor. What accounts for the high number of cases in which police take formal action against black juvenile suspects? The answer may lie within the black community's cultural values. Researchers suggest that the high arrest rate of African-American youths is at least in part related to the large number of black complainants who demand formal police action (Black and Reiss, 1970; Lundman et al., 1978). The prevailing opinion is that "factors other than race weigh most heavily in the police decision-making process" (Griswald, 1978:65–66; see also Wilbanks, 1987).

Gender's role in police decision making remains a little-understood phenomenon. Most comprehensive studies of police decision making fail to find a gender bias, although the ratio of male to female arrestees would seem to contradict that finding (Black and Smith, 1981). One argument stresses the influence of the notion of chivalry. This argument, called the **chivalry hypothesis** by some (Visher, 1983), is as follows: Women (and girls), being the weaker sex, need protection; fathers and other males in authority positions, being in the business of protecting the weaker sex, treat women (and girls) paternalistically. However, if a woman, by her demeanor and deeds, demonstrates that she does not deserve a chivalrous police response, she receives the full force of the criminal justice system. That is, if the female suspect violates police gender expectations, her actions are likely to result in an arrest.

What evidence exists to support this hypothesis? By itself, probably very little. However, when gender is included with age and race, several patterns emerge. First, white female offenders receive preferential treatment from the police, especially when compared with their black counterparts (Smith, Visher, and Davidson, 1984). Second, both age and race appear to interact with gender to influence arrest decisions (Visher, 1983). A hostile, antagonistic female is far more likely to be arrested than a compliant one. This finding fits the general demeanor test as well: Overall, the police are less likely to arrest an adult or juvenile, male or female, if that person is respectful, compliant, and deferential to the officer's authority.

POLICE AND JUVENILE CONTACTS

Citizen contacts with patrol officers generally include calls for service as well as preventive patrol and officer-initiated activities (Gaines and Kappeler, 2003; Walker and Katz, 2005). Juveniles with whom the police have contacts, regardless of how those contacts occur, are likely to include both those creating problems and those needing assistance. For our purposes, we can define these two groups even more narrowly into troublesome youths and crime victims.

TROUBLESOME YOUTHS AND THE POLICE

During routine patrol, police officers are more likely to encounter juveniles than adults for several reasons. First, youngsters are likely to commit offenses in public. Juveniles tend to be much less secretive about many of their deviant acts, either discounting the likelihood that they *will be* apprehended or discounting the seriousness of the consequences if they *are* apprehended.

Second, compared with their adult counterparts, juvenile offenders tend to commit unsophisticated crimes. Most law-violating youngsters commit property crimes that generally require few, if any, specialized skills. Their most common offenses are larcenies, residential burglaries, and auto thefts as opposed to commercial burglaries or safecracking.

Third, most of the offenses juveniles attempt involve several youngsters and, at times, even large groups of individuals. Large groups are easier to detect, and individuals may be more likely to be apprehended as the group's size increases.

Fourth, like many naive or immature offenders, youthful or otherwise, many of their offenses are crimes of opportunity. That is, an opportunity presents itself to a highly motivated offender, and it may be too good to pass up. For example, a group of high school students are coming home after their team has lost a big basketball game. They pass a car loaded with students from their archenemy's school, and one of them tosses a glass soda bottle at the vehicle, smashing the windshield: The car was in the wrong place at the wrong time.

Green (1985:46) examined the ages of persons arrested as included in the *Uniform Crime Reports* "to ascertain whether UCR arrestee figures reflect accurately the relative criminal involvement of juveniles (those under 18 years of age) and adults (all others) in the crimes of forcible rape, aggravated assault, and robbery." His conclusions for these three offenses are as follows:

1. Juveniles are not disproportionately likely to be reported for forcible rapes, but when they are reported, juveniles and adults appear equally likely to be arrested.
2. Juveniles are underrepresented in cases involving aggravated assaults.
3. Juveniles appear to be reported less often than adults for robbery, but once reported they seem to be arrested more often.

While he urged caution with regard to these preliminary results, Green suggests that UCR figures for persons arrested by age may be fairly representative.

The police do not *detect* most offenses. Violations are most likely to come to police attention through citizen complaints, and the behaviors most likely to be reported are delinquent offenses. Citizens consider these unlawful activities serious, and so do the police: The more serious the offense, even when it involves juveniles, the more likely the police are to investigate, make an arrest, and press for prosecution. This scenario is most likely to unfold with residential burglaries or auto thefts, school vandalism, and drug dealing.

JUVENILE CRIME VICTIMS

Another situation in which the police encounter juveniles involves youngsters as crime victims. Juveniles are victims of property crimes—especially when they have bicycles, backpacks, and electronics equipment stolen—but they are the victims of personal crimes as well. Adolescents are particularly susceptible to assaults, strong-arm robbery or extortion by threat, and rape.

How susceptible are juveniles to victimizations? Take another look at the data in table 1.1, which came from the 2004 National Crime Victimization Survey. The point that is readily apparent from this table is that youngsters (including 18- and 19-year-olds who technically are adults) are more than twice as likely to be victimized for most crimes compared with adults over the age of 25. In fact, the differences really become dramatic when comparing those aged 12 to 15 with groups more than 35 years of age.

It is vital to note that most crime is both intraracial and intragenerational (Jerin and Moriarity, 1998:116–17). That is, people of one race are most likely to be victimized by members of the same race, and youngsters are most likely to be victimized by other youngsters (Catalano, 2005; OJJDP, 2000). The conventional wisdom about crime victimization has been that the urban elderly are disproportionately likely to be crime victims. However, Wilson points out that "the victimization of the elderly has been reduced by the anticipatory actions of the elderly themselves who have decided to live behind locked doors" (1983:35).

In view of the findings about crime and the elderly, juvenile criminal victimization best can be explained by the concept of exposure. Youths are apt to become crime victims because they frequent places and associate with people likely to increase their vic-

Theoretical Reflections
Juveniles and Risk-Taking Behavior

In the 1930s, Chicago researchers observed that gang members and other delinquents showed an affinity for dangerous behavior. Thirty years later, Walter Miller reported that trouble (as in getting into trouble) and excitement (as in doing things that are risky and dangerous) are **focal concerns** for lower-class youths. This class-based argument, however, failed to explain risk taking among middle- and upper-class youths. More recently, Thomas Bernard (1992:168) has emphasized the risk-taking nature of youngsters in general, saying that it is appropriate to think of "the vast majority of juvenile offenders ... as *naive risk taker[s]*" (emphasis in the original).

Other researchers have explored the link between risk-taking behavior and self-control. **Parental management** is a central feature of Gottfredson and Hirschi's self-control theory. They define effective parental monitoring to include such things as the monitoring and recognition of deviant behavior in one's child, the use of appropriate punishments in response to inappropriate behavior, and a strong emotional bond between child and parent. Poor parental management, they claim, leads to **low self-control**, elements of which are risk taking (see Miller, 1958; Bernard, 1992) and the need for physical stimulation, behaviors that can lead to law-violating behavior.

Sources: Bernard (1992); Miller (1958); Gottfredson and Hirschi (1990).

timization. Additionally, youngsters often have feelings of invincibility that cause them to minimize their fear of crime and underestimate their likelihood of being victims.

A variety of factors complicate police interactions with juvenile crime victims. For example, much crime is never reported to the police (see Kappeler and Potter, 2005), and juveniles may be reluctant to report victimization or fear embarrassment, retaliation, and further victimization. Additionally, many times they know, and are known by, their victimizers, and they all may be involved in ongoing relationships (for instance, schools and neighborhood living arrangements) from which they find it very difficult if not impossible to extricate themselves. There also may be a feeling of intimidation or distrust of the police as adult authority figures, particularly when the confrontation involves minority youths and nonminority police officers.

POLICE RESPONSES TO DELINQUENCY

Some departments have specialized police–juvenile officers, while in others there is very little specialization. At one level, it does not matter whether a department is specialized. Many officers come into contact with youthful law violators, and by default these officers become "juvenile" officers. More than likely, however, the first police officers to encounter most young law violators are members of the police department's uniformed patrol division. Police–juvenile encounters can occur in various contexts, but for our purposes we classify them into four categories: citizen-initiated, family-initiated, school-initiated, and police-initiated encounters.

CITIZEN-INITIATED ENCOUNTERS

Most police work is reactive; it is safe to assume that most police–juvenile encounters are reactive as well. Therefore, most police contacts with juvenile offenders or suspected juvenile offenders will be the result of citizen complaints. Black and Reiss (1970:66) report that, excluding traffic offenses, citizens initiated more than 75% of all police encounters in their study. The term *citizen* includes any complainant other than police officers, school officials, or family members.

Citizen complaints may involve activities that fit within the jurisdiction's definition of delinquent behavior, or they may be disorderly behaviors that really are not of a criminal nature (see Gaines and Kappeler, 2003). Some complaints may involve disruptive, but not illegal, behavior, such as youths playing in the street or hanging out on street corners. These behaviors are especially disturbing to older citizens, who see such youngsters as being on the verge of committing delinquent acts if they have not done so already. Citizens also complain about behavior that is marginally illegal—conduct that is technically against the law but otherwise harmless (for example, playing loud music, engaging in boisterous parties, driving cars with loud stereo systems). Certain types of activities, neighborhoods, and complainants tend to generate regular complaints involving youths engaged in bothersome activities.

Police interest in criminal acts committed by minors or adults is easy to justify. Some critics question whether the police should be concerned at all with public disturbances and other local ordinance violations when there are so many "real criminals" that need catching. Kelling and Wilson, among others, would take exception with this characterization of the appropriate emphases for police work—in particular, police interfaces with the community. They observe two crucial points about crime and incivility: (1) **community disorder**—such as public drunkenness, vagrancy, suspicious persons, youth gangs, graffiti—contributes to a climate of fear in inner-city neighborhoods; and (2) crime and disorder "are inextricably linked, in a kind of developmental sequence" (1982:38; see also Wilson, 1983). The key to losing control over any neighborhood, note Kelling and Wilson, is the presence of broken windows in local buildings and homes: "If a window in a single building is broken *and left unrepaired*, all the rest of the windows will soon be broken" (1982:38). When a neighborhood is left untended, when no one seems to care or be concerned about disorder, then disorder grows, and crime grows with it. Police response to noncriminal and quasi-criminal behavior, from this perspective, is critical in creating and maintaining a sense of community.

Early research found that citizen-initiated complaints were likely to draw severe reactions (such as arrests) from the police (Black and Reiss, 1970). Richard Lundman and his colleagues (1978), in a replication of the research by Black and Reiss, found that what the citizen complainant asked the police to do largely determined the type and severity of the response.

FAMILY-INITIATED ENCOUNTERS

According to most state codes, families can make referrals directly to the juvenile justice system. In particular, they can ask for the juvenile court's assistance when they have an ungovernable or incorrigible child. In some states the petition filed with the court alleges that the child is beyond the control of the parents or guardian.

The reality, however, is that parents often involve the police to serve as intermediaries for a child they want referred to the juvenile justice system. One reason for this parental response is that they believe the police will know whom to consult concerning a child's problems; for example, officers may be able to make a referral either within the juvenile justice system or to an agency outside the system. Additionally, parents may feel that calling the police to deal with a wayward child will add some shock value to their threats to do something about the child's behavior.

SCHOOL-INITIATED ENCOUNTERS

Later in this chapter we will explore some of the functions police officers may serve in local schools. In chapters 6 and 11 we also will discuss the role of schools as intervention forces in the juvenile justice system's responses to nondelinquent youths who come under its jurisdiction. For the time being, however, it is important to note that the police are occasionally called to respond to school-based delinquency.

School authorities, like the family and the general public, can directly petition the juvenile court for action on behalf of a child. Like families and other private citizens, schools often turn to the police to handle matters that will be referred to the juvenile court. Some police agencies assign school liaison officers, also called school resource officers, to handle school-based delinquency. In other jurisdictions schools may have their own system-wide security staffs to handle disciplinary problems that otherwise would be referred to the local police. Whatever the policing arrangement, it is important to note that schools will be a regular source of contacts for many law enforcement agencies. We suspect that in the wake of shooting and bombing incidents such as those that transpired in the late 1990s, armed police officers on campus will be a common sight.

POLICE-INITIATED ENCOUNTERS

Some police–juvenile contacts will be initiated by police officers themselves. These confrontations can take many forms and occur in various locations. In this section we will examine some of these situations.

Uniformed patrol officers frequently come into contact with juveniles during **routine preventive patrol**. When not answering calls, police officers may check **hot spots**[3] on their patrol beats (Sherman, Gartin, and Bueger, 1989). For example, juveniles may "hang" at video arcades, skating rinks, amusement parks, and very often at shopping malls. In order to anticipate problems and to prevent complaints from citizens and business owners, uniformed patrol officers may check these spots periodically to see if juveniles are loitering in the area.

Routine preventive patrol can result in police officers seeing youngsters in the act of committing a crime. These situations are usually minor and, as we have indicated, the use of discretion provides the officer with a variety of responses from which to choose. However, before we dismiss such acts as "minor," recall Kelling and Wilson's observation about broken windows and community disorder. Is such behavior, from that perspective, really all that minor? Conversely, is it all that serious?

Box 3.2   The Impact of Police–Juvenile Contacts on Youthful Perceptions of Law Enforcers

In the past, did you ever find yourself in a situation remotely similar to the one in the opening scenario of the chapter? Were you ever pulled over for a speeding ticket or other traffic violation? Did you ever feel that you were being hassled by the police? If you answered yes to any of these questions, those negative contacts probably influenced you. By contrast, what if you wandered off on a camping trip as a child and a park ranger found you and reunited you with your parents? Perhaps you were stranded on the side of a busy interstate highway and a police officer came to your assistance. Would those events have shaped how you feel about law enforcement officials?

Besides employing simple yes/no protocols for determining youthful contacts with police, nearly all the research into the effects of juvenile–police contacts has lacked a theoretical base and has employed simplistic statistical analyses. Michael Lieber, Mahesh Nalla, and Margaret Farnworth offer an exception to this generalization. Employing a sophisticated multivariate analytic model, grounded in theoretical ideas from social environmental and delinquent culture perspectives, Lieber and associates report that for predictions of both respect for police and police fairness, police-juvenile interactions did play a significant role. However, the youth's race or ethnicity was the most consistent predictor: The ability of social environment theory, delinquent culture theory, and juvenile–police interactions to predict the attitudes of minority youths was markedly lower than that reported for white youths. This finding "reinforces past findings that minority status in itself differentiates public responses to law enforcement" (Lieber et al., 1998:171).

Source: Lieber, Nalla, and Farnworth (1998).

In cases where the police–juvenile encounter is officer initiated and where the offense is minor, a warning or something less than an arrest is likely to occur. Nevertheless, certain situations dictate that officers arrest juvenile suspects, and when they do, careful consideration must be given to the procedures employed in processing these youngsters. In the next two sections we will examine police procedures in regard to arrest and restraint as well as those involving criminal investigation processes. Our goal is not only to explain the procedures used with youngsters, but also to contrast them with the ways adults are handled.

ARREST AND RESTRAINT: ISSUES AND PRACTICES

How do the police process juvenile offenders? How are these procedures different from those for adults? In this section we will answer such questions. Three particular issues will guide the discussion:

1. the use of force and restraints by police officers making an arrest
2. the use of routine identification procedures such as fingerprinting and photographing suspects
3. the development and maintenance of records on juvenile offenders

POLICE USE OF FORCE

In the process of making arrests, police officers may be required to use physical force, up to and including deadly force. The basic rule is that officers may use a reasonable amount of force whenever they encounter resistance from a person they are trying to arrest, whether the suspect is a juvenile or an adult. Many police departments and sheriff's offices require that anyone—male or female, adult or juvenile—taken into custody must be handcuffed. In the remaining departments, officers may use their discretion not to handcuff if the flight risk is low and if they reasonably believe the unrestrained suspect poses no threat to the officers or others.

The decision to use force is almost entirely left up to the officer, although many departments have specific policies about the use of carotid choke holds, pepper spray, stun guns, and similar techniques or devices. Other uses of force, including wrestling, arm twisting, and even the use of painful thumb and finger holds, may be authorized and even preferred, based on the level of resistance offered by the suspect, juvenile or otherwise.

Deadly force may present moral and legal dilemmas. For these reasons, most law enforcement agencies have developed policies concerning the use of deadly force (Gaines and Kappeler, 2003; Walker and Katz, 2005). Police officers *may use lethal force* in attempting to make juvenile arrests. However, the Supreme Court has spoken very forcefully on this issue, and its ruling in the *Tennessee v. Garner*, 471 U.S. 1 (1985) case that deadly force is not to be used against fleeing, nondangerous felons is now the law for juveniles and adults.

POLICE IDENTIFICATION PROCEDURES

When booking adults into county jails or police lockups, law enforcement officers typically fingerprint and photograph suspects. These documents become part of a permanent arrest record, and most police departments retain fingerprints and photographs even if the criminal charges are dropped or the suspect is found not guilty. Furthermore, it is a common police procedure to send sets of fingerprints to the Federal Bureau of Investigation's Criminal Justice Information Services Division, where they join the more than 250 million fingerprint cards on file (Federal Bureau of Investigation, 2004).[4]

Fingerprinting and photographing are such routine procedures that most law enforcement officials do not give them a second thought. However, for juvenile suspects, different laws or guidelines often come into play. As we will learn in chapter 5, the original juvenile court was created to be confidential, informal, and non-adversarial. These characteristics influenced other parts of the emerging juvenile justice system as well, and in many states the police traditionally were prohibited from fingerprinting and photographing juvenile suspects. Still, as the Bureau of Justice Statistics notes, many agencies now photograph and fingerprint juveniles, and the "laws in 40 states expressly authorize police to take fingerprints when arresting a juvenile" (1997:23).

The guidelines proposed by the National Advisory Committee on Criminal Justice Standards and Goals, which tightly proscribed police authority in the area of suspect identification, are an illustration of the traditional approach. The National Advisory Committee (1976:221) recommended that

> fingerprints and photographs of juveniles should be taken for investigative purposes only. Juveniles should not be subjected to these procedures unless they are taken into custody for a violation of the law, or the [juvenile] court has determined there is probable cause to believe that the fingerprints or photographs must be taken to establish the court's jurisdiction.

These guidelines, and similar ones developed by the Institute for Judicial Administration/American Bar Association (1996), emphasized that the police practice of fingerprinting and photographing juvenile suspects

- was not to be a routine arrest and booking procedure
- was to be done with strict statutory or judicial guidance
- was to be a short-term investigative or identification procedure (that is, once the fingerprints and photographs had served their purpose, they were to be destroyed)

The assumption was that treating juveniles the same as adults would stigmatize these youngsters—something the juvenile justice system was created to avoid. Therefore, a basic premise of the IJA/ABA (1996) guidelines is that juveniles should be provided at least the same protections as adults processed by the criminal justice system, if not more.

These recommendations and many state juvenile codes have produced intended and unintended consequences. First, law enforcement agencies have had to develop different processing procedures for juveniles. Second, these restrictions make it difficult to conduct photographic lineups, as is often done with adults. Third, despite such restrictions, photographs and fingerprints can be taken by court order to establish an individual's identity or to assist in the solution of a crime, but for only a limited time period. In other words, these identification tools cannot be retained in criminal history files the way they can for adult suspects.

POLICE RECORD KEEPING[5]

Police record-keeping issues with juveniles go beyond fingerprinting and photographing and include the compilation and dissemination of an individual's total criminal history. For adult arrestees, law enforcement agencies typically maintain sets of fingerprints, booking photographs, and what frequently are called rap sheets. The total package constitutes the offender's criminal history.

Police records for juvenile suspects are usually available only under court order or for purposes of national defense. The **national defense exception** allows armed forces recruiters to check the criminal records of older teenagers who want to enlist in the military. Otherwise, the policy is to maintain police juvenile records solely for law enforcement purposes.

Laws and regulations governing juvenile record keeping are changing, much like policies governing identification procedures. Most police departments seldom destroy juvenile records unless under court order. According to a Bureau of Justice Statistics report specifically on this topic, "Sealing and expungement laws, like other laws governing juvenile justice records, are more likely to apply to juvenile court records than to law enforcement records" (1997:16). Therefore, when a juvenile's records are expunged from court or probation files, this does not mean the police record has been erased also. Indeed, it may take the actions of an attorney, which suggests that the complete expungement of a juvenile's police record could be class biased, because few lower-class or even middle-class families can afford an attorney to ensure that all copies of the juvenile record are destroyed or sealed.

When it comes to juvenile offenders, the creation, maintenance, and distribution of criminal history records may require procedures different from those for adults. A few particular policy issues must be addressed in this area. The following three questions and answers highlight some concerns facing police departments:

1. If fingerprints and photographs cannot be included, what information can be contained in a criminal history file for juvenile offenders? The usual information includes the following: (1) general physical characteristics, such as height, weight, color of hair and eyes, and distinguishing marks or tattoos; (2) date and place of birth; (3) parents' names and addresses; (4) school- or education-related information, such as highest grade achieved, school attended or attending; and (5) general criminal history, such as prior charges, and court dispositions.

Theoretical Reflections
Labeling Theory—Police as Drug-Law Deviance Amplifiers

Describing the police as "deviance amplifiers" is almost to belabor the obvious. The role played by police is very powerful, capable of redefining the public's image of a given youth and the youth's own self-image. Aaron Cicourel notes that many juvenile activities

> that might go unnoticed or [be] regarded as "minor" pranks will not be so viewed by juvenile officers . . . because [the juvenile may fit] their conception of the potential delinquent, and they will seek him out whenever there is reported "trouble" in his neighborhood. Routine juvenile activities, therefore, can be turned into serious "delinquent acts." (1976:190)

Jock Young's (1971) description of police actions in drug-law cases as examples of **deviance amplification** has direct applications to juvenile–police interactions. He notes that police occupy a relatively isolated position in the community; therefore, they may form stereotypes about a variety of human social behaviors, including drug use and delinquency. They also occupy a relatively high position of power and may be called upon to "negotiate" the physical and testimonial evidence of someone's conduct—the reality of the delinquent behavior—to fit a preconceived stereotype, much in the manner described by Cicourel. As a result, there is an intensification of the youths' views of themselves as norm violators. Such youths may even try to live up to these stereotypes as self-fulfilling prophecies—"If enough people call me delinquent often enough, maybe I am delinquent and should act accordingly." Through police amplification of delinquency, Young believes, myth becomes reality.

Sources: Cicourel (1976); Young (1971).

2. If departments do maintain criminal histories for juveniles, where will these files be stored? The basic choices are (1) in a separate filing system within the agency's juvenile division; this practice allows limited general access and virtually complete control by juvenile division officers; and (2) in the agency's general filing system. In the information and computer age, a central data bank within the department's records division maintains these records.

3. Wherever the files are maintained, what is the procedure for gaining access to juvenile information? In most agencies, general files are maintained with a limited-access code, and officers who want to review these files must demonstrate not only a *desire* to know, but also a *need* to know in order to gain access.

INVESTIGATION OF JUVENILE OFFENSES

The identification and record-keeping issues discussed previously are very important when it becomes necessary to investigate offenses involving juvenile suspects. As most police investigators realize, crimes are solved more by information than by inspiration. Therefore, one of the key information sources—the police record-keeping system—is not very helpful in the investigation of many of the offenses involving juvenile suspects. Given a juvenile suspect, the police may have to look elsewhere for information, and when that involves eyewitnesses, the information can be spotty and often unreliable. Because of these limitations, the police have to rely even more heavily on interrogations and confessions. As a result, a number of other potential problems are raised.

EVIDENTIARY PROCEDURES AND THE RIGHTS OF JUVENILE SUSPECTS: THE BASICS

For most crimes, investigators seek physical and testimonial evidence. Physical evidence includes footprints, fingerprints, tire impressions, fabric remnants, tool marks, and bloodstains. Simply obtaining comparison points from juvenile suspects may be problematic. Given the expanding use of **DNA profiling**, new technologies may supersede the old restrictions on juvenile identification procedures (Bureau of Justice Statistics, 1991; see also Purcell, Winfree, and Mays, 1994).

Again, as long as the purpose of such techniques is to affirm or deny positively a person's identity and include or exclude a person as a suspect, the collection of such information from juveniles may not pose a problem. Since the mid-1990s, many states have started to create DNA data banks, usually taking samples from convicted and released sex offenders. Such data banks, it is proposed, will serve not only a reactive function (that is, identifying offenders from physical evidence collected at the crime scene), but a proactive, deterrent function as well (that is, criminal justice officials propose that offenders may think twice about committing a new crime knowing that their DNA is already in a database, making positive identification a certainty). Whether, or to what extent, these databases will include juvenile suspects' DNA is an issue that the juvenile justice system will have to resolve as their use expands.

Testimonial evidence comes from witness interviews and suspect interrogations, an area of great importance with juveniles and one requiring that the police exercise particular caution. When the police conduct an interrogation with an adult suspect, a whole range of procedural guarantees and protections comes into play. An obvious consideration is the warnings provided in *Miranda v. Arizona*. However, as Smithburn notes,

> A juvenile's rights during interrogation predate both *Miranda v. Arizona*, 387 U.S. 436 (1966) and *In re Gault*, 387 U.S. 1 (1967). In an early case, the U.S. Supreme Court acknowledged that juveniles were entitled to certain protections under the Fourteenth Amendment. The Court in *Haley v. Ohio*, 332 U.S. 596 (1948), overturned the conviction of a fifteen-year-old boy whose confession the police obtained after an all-night interrogation session. (2002:91)

In its decision in the *Miranda* case the Supreme Court tried to minimize police misconduct in the process of conducting **custodial interrogations**. *Miranda* and other cases tried to ensure that suspects could not be held incommunicado and that an attorney's presence during questioning was one way to protect suspects' rights. The bottom line for adults in the interrogation process is that any admission or confession must be freely, knowingly, and voluntarily given in order to be legal. In fact, the last question typically asked of a suspect is, "Do you understand these rights, and are you willing to make a statement at this time?" The difficulty comes in applying this standard to juvenile offenders.

Gardner (2003:227) says that the Supreme Court never expressly has applied *Miranda* to juvenile interrogations, but that "the lower courts have interpreted *Gault* as requiring the *Miranda* safeguards in delinquency cases, and a number of states have statutorily implemented the safeguards." While some people consider juveniles to be fairly sophisticated, youngsters often do not fully understand their *Miranda* rights and the consequences of waiving those rights. In fact, Feld (2003:116) says that most juveniles who receive the warnings do not understand the language, much less the legal concepts, well enough to waive their rights in a "'knowing and intelligent' manner." Consequently, interrogations of juvenile suspects raise the following questions:

- Can the police ever interrogate juveniles?
- Can juveniles waive their rights under *Miranda*, especially the right to remain silent?
- Must juveniles have an attorney present if they request one, or can some other adult (such as a parent) protect their rights?
- Should parents or guardians be present during all interrogations? What role should the parents play in encouraging or discouraging juveniles to make incriminating statements?
- Whose rights are being protected, the parents' or the juveniles'?
- How do we know (or can we know) if juveniles understand their rights during the process of custodial interrogation?

These questions illustrate the complexity of the interrogation process with accused juvenile offenders. While we cannot give definitive answers to all these questions, we can shed some light on this somewhat murky situation. For example, the U.S. Supreme Court examined the validity of juvenile confessions in the case of *Fare v. Michael C.*, 442 U.S. 707 (1979). In that case instead of asking to speak to an attorney, the juvenile being interrogated asked to speak to his probation officer. Eventually, before he spoke with the probation officer, Michael C. confessed to a murder. The Supreme Court was asked to decide if the confession given under these circumstances (the absence of an attorney during the interrogation) was admissible. The response was that this was a valid confession, but when courts examine juvenile confessions, they should employ what is known as the **totality of circumstances test**. Two other California cases decided 10 years or more before *Fare v. Michael C.* illustrate this concept. In *People v. Lara*, 432 P. 2d 202 (1967) and *In re M.*, 450 P. 2d 296 (1969) the California Supreme Court held that "from the totality of circumstances in this case we conclude that there is substantial evidence that appellant had the capacity to understand the meaning of the *Miranda* warnings given him, and that he knowingly and intelligently waived [his] rights." These cases did not sanction the use of juvenile confessions; they simply provided the standard by which courts, particularly appellate courts, should look at all the circumstances surrounding a confession to see whether it was given in a constitutionally acceptable manner.

In simplest terms, the totality of circumstances test means that the trial court judge will examine all the factors surrounding the interrogation, including characteristics of the juvenile being interrogated, to determine whether the confession was freely, knowingly, and voluntarily given. The circumstances fit into two categories: the surroundings where the questioning took place and the youngster's personal characteristics.

THE INTERROGATION ENVIRONMENT

Police custodial interrogations can take place in many locations, including at the crime scene, in a police car, or at a suspect's school, home, or workplace. The most threatening environment for both adult and juvenile suspects is a police station. In examining the totality of circumstances, a judge should inquire into the physical surroundings of the locality where the interrogation took place. Was the suspect made comfortable? Were threats made, or was there any hint of intimidation? Were witnesses present, and if so, who were they? Did the youngster request an attorney? Once again, the key question is whether any circumstances contributed to an involuntarily given confession.

One element of the interrogation environment that must be considered is the presence of adults, other than police officers, during the questioning. Obviously, having an attorney present would protect juveniles' rights, but what about a parent or guardian? The National Advisory Committee on Criminal Justice Standards and Goals, the standards proposed by the American Bar Association, and some state juvenile codes require a responsible adult's presence during the juvenile suspect's questioning. This requirement raises additional questions: Instead of an attorney, would parents or guardians be sufficient? Can only an attorney look after the child's best interests? Should both parents or guardians and an attorney be present?

A few considerations are apparent. First, most police officers believe that having an attorney present during questioning has a chilling effect on an interrogation. After all, an attorney's main task during a custodial interrogation is to guarantee that the police respect a suspect's Fifth Amendment rights. If an adult must be present, most police officers would prefer dealing with a parent rather than an attorney, since the parents may be sympathetic to the police. Additionally, in this sort of situation it is difficult to determine whether the parents are concerned with the child's rights and whether they can qualify as neutral, disinterested parties (Gardner, 2003:225–32).

The essential question concerning the attorney's presence during the juvenile suspect's custodial interrogation is: Whose interests are being protected, the child's or the parents'? While the answer might seem obvious at first, remember that the parents may be responsible for retaining an attorney for the child, and they may be concerned about their own liability from the child's actions. Therefore, the parents may be concerned about the child's rights, or they may be interested in protecting their own interests, since some states now hold parents or guardians civilly liable for damages their children cause (see Feld, 2003:124).

PERSONAL CHARACTERISTICS OF THE SUSPECT

In determining a confession's voluntariness, the judge must also consider the attributes of the juvenile being interrogated (see *Fare v. Michael C.*, 1979). That is, what was the youngster's age? How criminally sophisticated was the suspect? In other words, has this juvenile been processed by the police before, perhaps on more than one occasion? Furthermore, was the suspect intoxicated or under the influence of drugs at the time of the arrest? What is the juvenile's level of intelligence or understanding? While the personal characteristics are not directly legally relevant, they do speak to the totality of the circumstances issue.

Not all these qualities can be measured with certainty, either by the police or by court personnel. However, as McCarthy, Patton, and Carr assert,

> There appears to be general agreement . . . that a juvenile is entitled to the *Miranda* warnings concerning the right to remain silent, the use of any statements against him or her and the right to presence of counsel, to be appointed in case of indigency. (2003:452)

This means that it is essential that the juvenile court judge be assured that a confession resulting from a police interrogation is legally admissible. In effect, we are asking the judge to make a determination on factors that might not lend themselves to easy determination.

SEARCHES INVOLVING JUVENILE SUSPECTS

Searches involving juvenile suspects are subject to varying standards, depending on the setting and who is conducting the search. We will discuss police-school interactions in the following section, but it is important to examine the rights of juveniles in search situations and the degree to which schools and law enforcement agencies may differ. Nothing illustrates the differences more than the U.S. Supreme Court decision in *New Jersey v. T.L.O.*, 469 U.S. 325 (1985).

In this case a school administrator searched the purse of a female student suspected of smoking in the restroom and found cigarettes, rolling papers, a small amount of marijuana, a paper with lists of names and dollar amounts, and several other items that indicated that T.L.O. was both using and selling drugs. The question that came before the Supreme Court was whether a warrantless search such as this was a violation of the Fourth Amendment to the Constitution. Justice White, writing for the Court's majority, said: "Against the child's interest in privacy must be set the substantial interest of teachers and administrators in maintaining discipline in the classroom and on school grounds." He added that "it is evident that the school setting requires some easing of the restrictions to which searches by public authorities are ordinarily subject." He concluded that school searches did not have to be conducted with warrants and that the traditional probable cause requirement need not be the standard by which reasonableness must be judged.

However, before we conclude that the Constitution stops at the schoolhouse door, it is important to remember that the search of T.L.O. was conducted by a school official, not a law enforcement officer. If the police are called to campus to investigate a crime, or if they are present as school resource officers (see the discussion in the following section), they are bound to conduct searches in strict adherence to the U.S. Constitution. In simplest terms this means that police officers must have probable cause, and perhaps warrants, when conducting searches of students.

Are there other circumstances in which the search warrant requirements might differ in school and nonschool settings? Clearly there are. Another area where the U.S. Supreme Court has spoken fairly clearly is in the random drug testing of students involved in extracurricular activities such as athletics. For example, in *Vernonia School District 47J v. Acton*, 515 U.S. 646 (1995), the Supreme Court upheld the random, suspicionless drug testing of student athletes in grade schools and high schools. The Court believed that this policy was a reasonable response to a perceived drug problem in a community and that it promoted the safety of students participating in team sports. Justice Scalia, writing for the six-member majority, concluded that "the decreased expectation of privacy, the relative unobtrusiveness of the search, and the severity of the need met by the search" promoted a policy that was "reasonable and hence constitutional."

The basic conclusion from cases like *New Jersey v. T.L.O.* and *Vernonia School District 47J v. Acton* is that the courts will give deference to school officials when it comes to the investigation of criminal activity, but that these public officials do not possess a blank check when it comes to infringement on constitutional protections. Furthermore, law enforcement agencies do not enjoy the same relatively broad discretion when it comes to dealing with schoolchildren. Having made these observations we now turn to some of the circumstances and situations under which the police work with schools in their jurisdictions.

POLICE–SCHOOL INTERACTIONS

Schools play a critical role in addressing delinquent behavior and often are the first place in which delinquency appears. Quite often the police and the schools engage in a love-hate relationship. School administrators have been reluctant to call on the police for fear of creating hostility and damaging the trust relationship between the students and school officials. The police have been reluctant to get involved in incidents on school campuses because they believe that many occurrences are of a relatively minor nature (which most are), and that school personnel may not support them in whatever actions they take. The result of this uneasy relationship has been the development of at least two models of police–school interactions.

While much recent national attention has focused on drugs, gangs, and violence, most police contact with school officials is of a more routine, much less serious nature. Ongoing and persistent crime problems plaguing schools include vandalism (much of which occurs after school hours) and school property thefts. A police presence and a beefed-up security apparatus—especially during school hours—may have little impact on these offenses.

Perhaps the most common police–school interaction involves truancies (Flores, 2004). Since states have compulsory school attendance laws, students who habitually fail to attend may be petitioned to the juvenile court for truancy. Schools typically are diligent in carrying out attendance requirements because funding is dependent on average daily attendance figures.

Truancy enforcement mechanisms vary widely across the nation. Some school districts have their own attendance enforcement officers, and some even go so far as to have their own truancy police. Others rely primarily on local police departments to carry out truancy enforcement. These rules and other types of infractions bring the police into regular contact with the schools. Aside from the police themselves, schools may be the juvenile justice system's most frequent source of delinquency referrals. The police–school interface must be effective if both institutions are to discharge their duties and responsibilities.

SCHOOL POLICE DEPARTMENTS

As noted previously, some very large school districts operate their own police departments. These police personnel may be school district employees, or they may be contract security personnel. Early on, many school police officers essentially were security guards. They typically were in uniform but quite often were not equipped with automobiles, radios, or firearms. These officers were assigned to patrol hallways before and after school and during class and lunch breaks. They primarily were charged with preventing or breaking up fights and patrolling parking lots to prevent vehicle break-ins.

This model has been modified as both the perception and reality of violence have increased dramatically in some of the nation's larger school districts. The result has been a move to a true school system police force. The new model includes both officers who are in uniform and plainclothes investigators. Typically, all are armed. In effect, they become a small town police agency and are responsible for handling all crimes occurring on school property, including fights, thefts of personal property, thefts or destruction of school property, and possession of weapons or drugs in violation of school policies or state laws. The only exception to having the school police handle cases would be if the agency or school administrators asked for assistance from another local agency, such as a municipal police department or sheriff's office.

POLICE OFFICERS IN THE SCHOOLS

Since the 1960s some public school district administrators have requested the regular assignment of police officers, called **school resource officers (SROs)**, especially in middle schools, junior high schools, and high schools (Walker and Katz, 2005; see also National School Safety and Security Services, 2004). Some school districts have gone so far as to pay the salaries for police officers assigned to campuses in an effort to offset the costs to financially strapped police departments. SROs now represent one of the nation's fastest growing segments of law enforcement, and the National Association of School Resource Officers (2004) represents nearly 15,000 members who work in this area.

The model of assigning local law enforcement officers to schools offers some distinct payoffs. For example, SROs may provide a proactive, first line of defense in many volatile school situations. These situations can include guns, gangs, drugs, or fights involving fairly large groups of students. First and foremost, the SROs are to provide prevention, but when situations escalate they should provide swift and effective intervention. The National Association of School Resource Officers (2004) promotes interactions among law enforcement officers, teachers, and counselors in order to "educate, counsel, and protect" the nation's schools.

As previously mentioned, SROs can intervene in situations involving gangs, drugs, or firearms on campus or can alert local law enforcement agencies to the emergence of such problems. In the event of a violent school-based incident, such as occurred at Colorado's Columbine High School in 1999, a school resource officer can be a first responder and coordinate other emergency response efforts.[6] Furthermore, individual officers may establish rapport with students in the school setting. This rapport can enhance police–community relations and give police officers access to reliable, confidential information sources normally not available to them. In this chapter's final section we will discuss a number of innovative programs involving police–juvenile interactions; several of these efforts are school-based.

BEST PRACTICES

Quite often, juvenile justice textbooks focus on the policies and practices that do not work, to the detriment of those that do. In this section we especially want to focus on some innovative police programs that have been implemented to decrease the amount of delinquency and to improve police–juvenile contacts. Most of these programs can be characterized as occurring within the course of normal police operations; others clearly fall outside the police domain. This difference will soon be made clear.

POLICE–JUVENILE PROGRAMS

Some police–juvenile contacts result from normal police duties. For example, the **Law Enforcement Explorers** program allows teenagers to gain exposure to potential career fields. Several local law enforcement agencies sponsor Explorer posts. This program gives teenagers the opportunity to do ride-alongs and perform other non-enforcement jobs in order to experience actual police duties firsthand. Involved police officers develop rapport with community youngsters, and some of these youths go on to pursue law enforcement careers.

While the Explorers program is certainly a worthwhile one, it has some limitations. One limitation is that, because of the nature of police work, youngsters will not be able to participate in the full range of police duties. Perhaps the greatest limitation is that this project is most likely to appeal to youngsters who hold fairly strong law-abiding values. Law Enforcement Explorer groups are not likely to attract the most at-risk youngsters. This might be good or bad depending on your personal perspective, but if programs like the Explorers are meant to strengthen bonds between the police and youths who might eventually become clients of the juvenile justice system, such a weakness is very serious.

Police Athletic Leagues (PALs) come in many forms and operate in different ways depending on the locality. PAL programs may consist of traditional team sports like baseball, football, and basketball, or they may include such athletic activities as soccer, boxing, skateboarding, or BMX motocross bicycle racing. Some programs have police sponsorship in terms of team names, uniforms, and so forth. In some locales police officers actually coach the various sports. When officers are personally involved, activities normally take place in their off-duty time, but some departments encourage participation to the degree that they allow a few officers at a time to be involved in these activities while on duty.

With both Explorers and PALs, police officers interact with community youths in their official or unofficial capacities as officers. Thus, the police role is always a prominent one. However, the police have increasingly expanded their community interactions and now deal with some youngsters in other settings.

EMERGING POLICE ROLES

It is commonly said that police officers are always police officers whether they are on duty or off duty, whether they are in uniform or plainclothes, and whether or not they are operating in a traditional police setting. However, two programs developed since the mid-1980s not only have taken police officers out of their traditional environment and placed them in the school classroom but also have added the role of teacher-trainer. These two programs are **Drug Abuse Resistance Education (DARE)** and **Gang Resistance Education and Awareness Training (G.R.E.A.T.)**. In this section we will discuss the various elements incorporated into these projects and what we know about their effectiveness. Box 3.3 provides overviews of the DARE and G.R.E.A.T. programs.

Both DARE and G.R.E.A.T. share a common pedagogy. First, both efforts center on the belief that elementary or middle school/junior high school students should be exposed to real-world information concerning drugs and gangs. The implicit message is not only that there are essential lessons that youngsters need, but also that there are legal and social consequences for getting involved in drugs or gangs. Second, beyond building children's resistance to drugs and gangs, the lessons emphasize decision making and problem solving. Rather than simply telling children to say no to drugs or gangs, the course materials present students with alternatives and also help them reason through why individuals might or might not want to get involved in these activities.

A second element common to both programs is that specially trained uniformed law enforcement officers deliver the lessons.[7] Only certified peace officers may instruct in both programs. Using uniformed officers is believed to enhance their credibility with students.

Both of these police-taught, school-based programs have been in existence long enough to evaluate them and to draw some conclusions. There is reason to be both optimistic and pessimistic about these emerging police initiatives. For example, early analyses of DARE were not positive (Aniskievicz and Wysong, 1990; Ennett,

---

Box 3.3   Cops in the Classroom: DARE and G.R.E.A.T.

Project DARE was created in 1983 through the combined efforts of the Los Angeles Police Department and the Los Angeles Unified School District. The curriculum, taught by specially trained uniformed police officers, is offered to fifth- or sixth-grade students. There are 17 lessons, taught once per week for about 50 minutes: (1) personal safety, (2) drug use and misuse, (3) consequences, (4) resisting pressure, (5) resistance techniques, (6) building self-esteem, (7) assertiveness, (8) managing stress, (9) media influences, (10) decision making and risk taking, (11) alternatives to drug abuse, (12) role modeling, (13) forming a support system, (14) ways to deal with pressures from gangs, (15) Project DARE summary, (16) taking a stand, and (17) graduation.

In 1991 the Phoenix (Arizona) Police Department, in conjunction with the federal Bureau of Alcohol, Tobacco, and Firearms, developed the Gang Resistance Education and Awareness Training program (G.R.E.A.T.). The National Institute of Justice conducted a longitudinal study of G.R.E.A.T. based on several selected sites nationwide and, as a result, in 2000 the program underwent a curriculum review and expansion.

The program is structured to help youngsters set goals for themselves, learn how to resist peer pressure, learn how to resolve conflicts, and understand how gangs may affect their lives. There is a third- and fourth-grade curriculum that consists of four 40-minute lessons: (1) What is a gang? (2) Families and why they are special, (3) My future, and (4) Do you know me? The primary delivery system is the seventh-grade curriculum, which originally consisted of nine sessions but now has been expanded to the following 13 sessions taught in roughly 1-hour blocks: (1) Welcome to G.R.E.A.T. (gangs, violence, drugs, and crime); (2) What's the real deal? (message analysis); (3) It's about us (community roles and responsibility); (4) Where do we go from here? (setting realistic and achievable goals); (5) Decisions, decisions, decisions (impact of decisions on goals); (6) Do you hear what I am saying? (effective verbal and nonverbal communication; (7) Walk in someone else's shoes (active listening, emotions, and empathy); (8) Say it like you mean it (body language, tone, refusal skills); (9) Getting along without going along (influences and peer pressure); (10) Keeping your cool (anger management and cooling off); (11) Keeping it together (recognizing and calming anger in others); (12) Working it out (consequences of fighting and conflict resolution); and (13) Looking back (program review).

Sources: Ennett et al. (1994); Moorhead-Nord (1994); Phoenix Police Department (2004); Winfree and Lynskey (1999).

Tobler, Ringwalt, and Flewelling, 1994; National Institute of Justice, 1994). The only supportive finding provided by the federally funded study of DARE was that program participants reported a slightly more positive view of the police (National Institute of Justice, 1994).

Herman Goldstein (1993) also raises questions that apply to DARE's program *intensity* and program *integrity.* Program intensity deals with the amount of treatment provided students. The DARE program is designed to be administered in one 45- to 60-minute session per week for 17 weeks (see box 3.3). Researchers have asked whether this exposure is sufficient to dissuade students from drug involvement. Program integrity addresses the issue of whether the course content is delivered exactly the way it was envisioned. Given the number of agencies and officers presenting the DARE material, great care must be taken that officers do not ad lib and that they present the curriculum as it was intended. Obviously, this is not an easy task.

While not specifically addressed by G.R.E.A.T. researchers, the same questions of integrity and intensity could be raised about this program. Indeed, initial assessments on G.R.E.A.T. also questioned its effectiveness (Palumbo and Ferguson, 1995). The National Institute of Justice, working with the Bureau of Alcohol, Tobacco and Firearms, has funded a multiyear, multisite evaluation of G.R.E.A.T. (Esbensen, 1995). Finn-Aage Esbensen and D. Wayne Osgood (1999), in a first-

---

Theoretical Reflections
Social Bonding, Social Learning, and Police–Juvenile Contacts

Social bonding theory is often linked to programs intended to strengthen youthful bonds—or a general sense of social connectedness—to legitimate social institutions, including the police. The four elements of the bond include their attachment, commitment, and involvement in the institutions, as well as the legitimacy the youths accord their associated moral beliefs. Programs like Law Enforcement Explorers and the Police Athletic Leagues stress all four elements.

Recent studies have demonstrated linkages between social learning theory and adolescent involvement in youth gangs, owing to that theory's emphasis on the learning environment, the reinforcers and punishers associated with the learning processes, and the significant role played by one's associations in that learning. Perhaps the same learning mechanisms can be employed to intervene between youths and gangs. For this reason it can be argued that police officer-instructed programs like G.R.E.A.T. owe a conceptual debt to social learning theory, a linkage we will explore in more detail in chapter 10. For now it is sufficient to say that police officers, in close association and personal contact with youths, provide lessons intended to reinforce certain behaviors and exclude others. They provide alternative definitions that support law-abiding behavior, not only questioning law-violating behavior but also giving youths weapons to resist its temptations. The learning mechanisms through which youths might learn to violate the law are instead being used by the police to strengthen social prohibitions against law breaking. At least, one could argue, that is the theory.

Sources: Winfree and Abadinsky (2003); Winfree, Esbensen, and Osgood (1996).

look assessment of a single group of program participants and a matched group of nonparticipants, maintain that program participants report more pro-social attitudes and lower rates of some types of delinquent behavior, including self-reported gang membership, than those in the comparison group. On the basis of these preliminary results, we are likely to see law enforcement agencies utilizing programs like DARE and G.R.E.A.T. and developing other projects based on these models.

Suppose, however, that further evaluations demonstrate that innovative police programs like DARE and G.R.E.A.T. are ineffective. Should we abandon such efforts? Probably not. Most departments already have discovered that there are benefits to the agencies and to the officers who conduct these programs, even if the students exposed to them do not receive a long-term inoculation from drug and gang involvement. These efforts place officers in the schools, and students as well as teachers benefit from the interaction. Therefore, while most law enforcement agencies will not commit major resources to these types of projects, many will continue to exert some effort in this regard. Especially in agencies dedicated to the community policing concept, innovative police–juvenile programs will be part of the ongoing departmental mission.

Community policing repackages old ideas about police and the public they serve and protect (Walker and Katz, 2005). While community policing definitions abound, they do not always contain the same content and describe the same programs (Gaines and Kappeler, 2003). One definition is quite useful: **community-oriented policing (COP)**

> is a collaborative effort between the police and the community that identifies problems of crime and disorder and involves all elements of the community in the search for solutions to these problems. It is founded on close, mutually beneficial ties between police and community members. (Community Policing Consortium, 2004:1)

Given this orientation, it is easy to envision youth-focused community policing. Indeed, such programs exist. The Department of Justice's Youth-Focused Community Policing (YFCP) initiative is one example. A collaborative effort of the Office of Juvenile Justice and Delinquency Prevention, the Office of Community Relations Service, and the Office of Community Oriented Policing Services, YFCP has the following goals:

- Promote information-sharing strategies that support comprehensive, proactive partnerships among police, youth, and the community.
- Establish locally based interagency working groups to identify and address juvenile crime issues.
- Develop strategies consistent with the principles of community policing.

Still in the developmental and testing stages, YFCP is being implemented in eight communities: Boston, Massachusetts; Los Angeles, California; Kansas City, Kansas; Oakland, California; Mount Bayou, Mississippi; Houston, Texas; Rio Grande, Texas; and Chicago, Illinois. Each location offers a slightly different community-based and community-generated version. For example, the Los Angeles initiative "established a county-wide multidisciplinary structure to address youth

Many cities have implemented community-policing projects, like bike patrols, to increase officer visibility and interaction with citizens of all ages. Policing open spaces like parks and playgrounds allows officers to interact with juveniles in ways other than through law enforcement.

crime, delinquency and victimization" (Community Policing Exchange, 1999:1). The Los Angeles Commission on Children, Youth and Their Families, the sponsoring organization, divided the school district into 27 clusters, each of which formed its own planning team to address that cluster's unique problems and challenges. In Kansas City, YFCP targets high-risk youths through an intensive police/probation field-supervision and monitoring program. The key to all YFCP programs is the development of "comprehensive, collaborative efforts to problem solving. Communities participating in YFCP have systematically assessed and identified local juvenile issues and concerns, and they have designed effective and appropriate community responses" (Community Policing Exchange, 1999:8).

Preliminary evaluations of community policing–youth interaction programs are instructive and speak to the concerns created by such collaborative, cooperative efforts. For example, as described in box 3.4, the relationship between officers and children is little understood. Other research on community-based police–youth programs suggests that the children and officers who participate are themselves better off as a result. A second-year assessment of a Spokane, Washington, program entitled Community Opportunities for Youth (COPY Kids) by Giacomazzi and Thurman (1994:17) suggests that while a "sincere attempt was made to reach out to children from economically disadvantaged areas of Spokane," the program's

---

Box 3.4   Cops and Kids: An Assessment

In an assessment of one community policing model, researchers interviewed 59 patrol officers regarding the officers' roles "in resolving complaints about a rowdy group of juveniles" (Belknap, Morash, and Trojanowicz, 1987:213). This research discovered five role orientations assumed by the officers: "peacekeeper and problem solver, competent law enforcer, authority figure, friend or peer, and knight in shining armor" (Belknap et al., 1987:219). Belknap and her research associates discovered distinctive orientations for foot patrol officers (community policing program) and for motor patrol officers (traditional preventive patrol). They found the community policing officers were more likely to employ a problem-solver or peacekeeper style and the motor patrol officers to be predominantly law enforcer-oriented. They concluded that the foot patrol officers they interviewed were different in their orientations from the motor patrol officers "and that these differences are apparent in work with teenagers" (1987:239).

While Belknap and her associates note differences among officers in their orientations toward handling rowdy teenagers, they issue two qualifications in regard to their research. First, the main difference in outcome, as opposed to orientation, was that foot patrol officers counseled the teenagers more often than did motorized patrol officers. Therefore, the difference in handling these cases may be more one of degree rather than of kind. Second, it is difficult to know whether the officers' orientations are shaped by their assignments or whether there is a self-selection process through which officers with certain orientations are attracted to the community policing program.

Source: Belknap, Morash, and Trojanowicz (1987).

---

positive effects appeared to have been short-term. This demonstration project, intended to intervene with youth at risk for abusing alcohol or illegal drugs or joining a criminal gang, assigned **neighborhood resource officers** to specific problem areas. The officers worked with neighborhood youths referred by school administrators and community center directors. The children worked with the police for one week on neighborhood cleanup projects, received a meal, engaged in recreational activities, were provided a savings account with $40, and had a graduation ceremony. The children, their parents, and the officers involved felt good about the program, but there is no evidence of long-term behavioral changes, results that mirror those for DARE evaluations.

SUMMARY

The police are the juvenile justice system's front line of defense in the battle against delinquent behavior. Police officers are the juvenile justice system's most common referral source, and they frequently serve as intermediaries between families, neighborhoods, schools, and law-violating juveniles. The police emphasis on law enforcement has caused them to exercise a great deal of discretion in relation to accused juvenile offenders. In cases where the behaviors are minor, even if annoying, the police may simply threaten and release, turn youngsters over to their parents, or do something else short of making an arrest. When more serious offenses are suspected or alleged, officers are more likely to arrest juveniles much as they would adults.

Police discretion and officers' responses to juvenile offenders will depend on various factors. State laws and departmental policies will influence officers' actions in many situations. However, individual biases and predispositions also will play a part, as will different styles of policing displayed by officers. Whatever factors enter into the picture, one conclusion is inescapable: Police officers exercise a great deal of discretion, and nowhere is this fact more evident than in police–juvenile contacts.

Police procedures in processing juvenile offenders continue to be a point of concern. Should the police photograph, fingerprint, and interrogate juveniles the same as they do with adults? Or should the noncriminal ideals of the earliest juvenile codes be applied? The policies regarding the processing of juvenile offenders continue to evolve, and while the door has not been opened completely, many states now allow the police greater latitude in identification and record-keeping procedures for juvenile suspects than in the recent past.

One of the areas where we see police–juvenile contacts changing is in school-based programs with nondelinquent children. For most of our nation's history, police departments have concentrated their efforts on law enforcement. However, with the advent of community policing, or problem-solving policing, the emphasis has shifted in some departments to community service, such as the Youth-Focused Community Policing initiative. If this movement becomes an institutionalized part of American police efforts, officers may devote more of their time to delinquency prevention and intervention efforts than in the past. The result may be that cases involving juveniles may no longer be viewed as merely nuisance calls but rather as integral parts of the fundamental police mission.

CRITICAL REVIEW QUESTIONS

1. Now that you have finished the chapter, what do you think about the officers' response in the opening scenario? Was the course of action taken justified or unjustified? Would you have handled the situation differently? If so, what would you have done?

2. Can community policing help reduce delinquency? Explain how this is possible or impossible.

3. How do the practices of gatekeeping and discretion intermix to create the clients of the juvenile justice system?

4. How troubling is the relationship between police discretion and each of the following: (a) age, (b) gender, and (c) race?

5. What single fact about juveniles as victims most surprised you? (*Hint*: Your answer can be a single statistic or a general pattern.)

6. With respect to the four situations likely to generate police–juvenile encounters:

   (a) Are police responses to incivility and community disorder real police work?

    (b) How would you respond to someone who maintained that some families rely on the police to handle conflicts and issues that are best resolved within the family?

    (c) What troubles you most about the idea of school-initiated juvenile–police encounters?

    (d) What are some hot spots in your community for youthful incivility and disorder?

7. Explain briefly how each of the three issues related to police arrest and restraint help us understand the police role as deviance amplifiers.

8. What do you think of the idea of police officers as antidrug/antigang teachers for middle school/junior high school students? (*Hint*: Not all teaching takes place in the classroom.)

9. Which criminological theory do you believe provides unique insights into police–juvenile interactions?

RECOMMENDED READINGS

Gardner, Martin R. (2003). *Understanding Juvenile Law*, 2nd ed. New York: Matthew Bender and Co. Gardner's book principally is a law school text on juvenile law. He covers a wide range of legal topics, but his treatment of police procedures such as interrogations, searches, and seizures, is thorough and insightful. This is a very useful reference work for anyone who chooses a career in the juvenile justice field.

Kenney, John P., Donald E. Fuller, and Robert J. Barry (1995). *Police Work with Juveniles and the Administration of Juvenile Justice*, 8th ed. Springfield, IL: Thomas. Although this edition is a decade old, this book is still the "Bible" for juvenile officers. It provides the reader with an insider's view of police work with juveniles. The chapter on interviewing, for example, is quite detailed and includes checklists and other practical guides.

Lawrence, Richard (1998). *School Crime and Juvenile Justice*. New York: Oxford University Press. This book primarily is about crimes committed in and around schools. Nevertheless, it contains two chapters on the juvenile justice system within which is a brief but enlightening discussion of the role the police can play in preventing and responding to school crime. The final chapter deals with school-based delinquency prevention programs (like DARE and G.R.E.A.T.).

KEY TERMS

ambivalent enforcers	DNA profiling
chivalry hypothesis	Drug Abuse Resistance
community disorder	Education (DARE)
community policing	focal concerns
community-oriented policing (COP)	Gang Resistance Education and
custodial interrogations	Awareness Training (G.R.E.A.T.)
deadly force	gatekeepers
deviance amplification	hot spots
discretion	Integrated Automated Fingerprint
discrimination	Identification System (IAFIS)
disorderly human behavior	Law Enforcement Assistance Administration

Law Enforcement Explorers
low self-control
national defense exception
neighborhood resource officers
parental management
physical decay
Police Athletic Leagues (PALS)
proactive policing

problem-oriented policing
problem-solving cops
reactive policing
routine preventive patrol
rule-applier cops
school resource officers (SROs)
totality of circumstances test

NOTES

[1] For an expanded discussion of this particular problem as it is being addressed by law enforcement, see Johnson (2004).

[2] We will explore the development of gangs in the United States and juvenile justice responses to them in chapter 10.

[3] The concept of hot spots is closely related to the routine activities theory of crime (Roncek and Maier, 1991).

[4] The Criminal Justice Information Services Division is also responsible for the development and implementation of the **Integrated Automated Fingerprint Identification System**, known as IAFIS. This system will completely replace the current paper-based system for identifying and searching criminal history records. IAFIS will also support any law enforcement agency's ability to digitally record fingerprints and electronically exchange information with the FBI. Considering how difficult, if not impossible, it is to remove a physical fingerprint record, consider what will happen when it is digitized, stored, and transmitted electronically.

[5] This section is based in large part on a 1997 report entitled *Privacy and Juvenile Justice Records: A Mid-Decade Status Report*, prepared by the U.S. Bureau of Justice Statistics.

[6] Having an officer at school may not deter an act of violence. For example, at Columbine High School, an SRO was in place and exchanged shots with one or more of the teenage shooters within minutes of the first shots being fired. Whether this officer's presence saved additional lives is a point of much speculation; however, just having an officer present in the schools is obviously not enough to stop a determined offender, adult or juvenile.

[7] Most jurisdictions use municipal police officers or sheriff's deputies. However, in some localities, federal agencies such as the Border Patrol provide a uniformed officer to teach these courses; in overseas and military post operations, military police and security police personnel deliver the program to the juvenile dependents of military service members.

chapter

4

PREADJUDICATION DETENTION AND DIVERSION PROGRAMS

* * *

Jerome cocked his head slightly toward the steel door. He heard the sound of high-heeled shoes, ricocheting off concrete, coming from the hallway. Like the other nine residents of Detention Pod 10, he knew what that meant. Too early for mail, outside "play time" in the yard, or dinner. Evening showers never came before dinner. Too late for visitations from the family or, for the chosen few, attorneys. The detention officers wore sensible crepe-soled or soft rubber-soled shoes. Their shoes squished or made a distinctive sucking noise when one of the officers walked the line. Only one person who regularly came down that hall wore high-heeled shoes—Ms. Johnson, the preadjudication caseworker. She was coming for someone on "The Block," what all the detainees called this section in the city's modern Youth Detention Center complex.

Concentrating, Jerome could barely make out a second set of footsteps. Squish. Squish. Squish. *A correctional officer was coming with Ms. Johnson to unlock the cell door. Both sounds stopped in front of Pod 10. Jerome looked around the room. No one else seemed too interested in what was happening; they continued to watch the television bolted to the wall four feet above the floor in one corner of the bay-like communal cell, to read, or to listen to music on headsets. Then it hit him. He was the cell's only preadjudication resident; he had yet to have his day in court. Everyone else had been "convicted"—that is, "found to be involved in delinquency." They were all awaiting transfer to Spotsford, the always-overcrowded state school for boys.*

Jerome heard a hand slam against the cell door, followed by a gravelly voice, slightly muffled by the steel door. It was Fudpucker—actually, Detention Center Officer Hunsicker, but Fudpucker was the nicest name the boys on The Block called him behind his back: "All boys back from the door and on their bunks," he ordered. Ms. Johnson was coming for him.

The key rattled in the lock, then caught on the tumblers' teeth with a loud metallic click. In a single smooth movement the door opened and slammed loudly against the doorstop on the wall. Fudpucker strode quickly into the cell and stood just inside the steel doorjamb, his back to the open door. Over his shoulder, Jerome could see Ms. Johnson in the hallway, a tiny figure silhouetted by the door frame. She seemed to be held back by an invisible barrier, but more likely by the stale smell of urine and human sweat. "Jerome Esteban," she intoned, her voice taking on a somewhat officious tone. "Follow me," she ordered.

Jerome slowly pulled himself from his bunk. He had not been looking forward to this session. He had met with Ms. Johnson on two other occasions. They had discussed his "options" at their first meeting, shortly after he arrived on The Block. Ms. Johnson had reminded Jerome—like he needed reminding—that he was charged with a very serious crime, although it was unlikely that he would be tried as an adult. Unlikely, she repeated, but still possible. On her second visit she had explained that if Jerome would do an allocution, or admit to the crime in open court, the actual sentencing would be deferred for six months. At that time the formal finding of involvement in delinquency—the conviction—would be held in abeyance, contingent, of course, on Jerome's successful completion of the program.

The program had been the sticking point. Ms. Johnson wanted Jerome to do mediation with the victims of his house burglary, the Arnauds. Jerome, however, wasn't too interested in the program. He just wanted to do his six months at Spotsford and get on with life. Ms. Johnson had persisted. If he would have a series of meetings with the Arnauds, make restitution for the property he had damaged in the burglary—Jerome had smashed up the house because he was angry at the Arnauds for having so little worth stealing—and help clean up a downtown park damaged in a recent flood, he would have to do only six months of unofficial but supervised probation. Finally, Jerome would have to successfully complete an anger-management class run by the Department of Juvenile Probation. Ms. Johnson had failed to see the humor in his response: "Do I look like a trash-picking, weak-minded, psycho nut? Do I look like someone's slave?"

Today it was do or die. Jerome's hearing was scheduled for early next week. He would have to opt for the program she was offering or, in all likelihood, join his cell mates at Spotsford. As he followed Ms. Johnson down the hall, Fudpucker's feet squishing behind him, Jerome started having second thoughts. Maybe, he said to himself, just maybe I'll give the program a try. As long as they don't make me say I'm sorry.

* * *

Jerome's story revolves around preadjudicatory choices. Much of the juvenile justice system's attention is focused on juvenile court procedures and what happens *after* youngsters have been adjudicated delinquent. However, most of what happens in the juvenile justice system occurs before adjudication, and much of this activity is of relatively low visibility to the general public or agencies outside the juvenile justice system. This chapter's central focus is on the procedures that occur after an arrest but before formal adjudication (a trial, for a juvenile) happens. As with most activities in the juvenile justice system, there will be variations from jurisdiction to jurisdiction. Therefore, we will describe this stage of offender processing in general terms.

WHY PREADJUDICATION DETENTION?

How serious an issue is pretrial detention? In 1995 the average daily population in jails in the United States was nearly 510,000 individuals. Of this number 56% were unconvicted and in some type of pretrial detention status. By 2003, the average daily population of U.S. jails had grown to just over 680,000 people, and of that number 60.6% were held in pretrial detention status. This means that 412,000 adult men and women, along with juveniles, are in jail but unconvicted on any given day (Harrison and Karberg, 2004:8–9).

The main release mechanism for these pretrial detainees is bail. Bail is not an absolute right for either adults or children. For adults, the reasons given for pretrial detention generally fall into one of three categories (Meyer, 2002): (1) the judge has set bail, but the accused is unable to make the bail amount; (2) the judge has refused to set bail for a specified reason, usually suggested by the prosecutor, the practice of so-called **preventive detention**; or (3) the charge is so heinous that the punishment upon conviction is death and the evidence so overwhelming that by statute or custom the judge will not set bail.

For many jail-bound adults, bail is an economic impossibility. First, judges may set very high bail amounts based on the serious nature of the alleged offense, the public outrage at the crime victim's fate, the perceived danger to the community, or the likelihood that the accused will fail to show up for the next court date. Second, the definition of "incredibly high bail amounts" varies from person to person, situation to situation. What is incredibly high for the average person may not be incredibly high for Bill Gates, Donald Trump, or other affluent individuals. Consequently, many pretrial detainees are unable to make what are viewed as modest bail amounts.

Federal and state laws often provide mechanisms whereby the judge may simply refuse to set bail if public safety or flight risk is a significant issue. In *U.S. v. Salerno* (481 U.S. 739, 1987), the Supreme Court ruled provisions of the Federal Bail Reform Act of 1984 constitutional, permitting federal judges to deny pretrial release. The basis for this denial was the finding that there was no way to guarantee community safety from the threat posed by some detainees. Concern over the question of preventive detention for adults has become quite apparent. Such detention for juveniles, however, continues almost without challenge.

Finally, not only is there no absolute right to bail, but many states automatically exclude certain crimes from bail eligibility or limit its use for those previously convicted or those who have committed a crime while on bail. By local custom or statute, persons accused of such crimes may be denied access to bail. Feld notes that, statutorily, states have taken "three different positions on juveniles' right to post bail to secure pretrial release: some allow bail as a discretionary matter similar to adults; some deny youths any right to bail; and most are silent on the issue" (2003:160). Gardner adds that those courts which have ruled on the issue of bail for juveniles have held that youngsters "do not have a right to bail under either federal or state constitutional provisions extending the right to persons accused of crimes" (2003:238).

Both delinquent and nondelinquent juveniles are subject to the same reasoning that guides adult pretrial-detention decisions. For example, the Institute for Judicial Administration/American Bar Association (1996) in its standards on juvenile justice administration says that there are three justifications for detention of a youngster: (1) to preserve the jurisdiction and processes of the court (that is, to prevent flight and to assure a youngster's appearance in court); (2) to reduce the likelihood that the juvenile will harm others; and (3) to prevent the youngster from being harmed by others (in other words, protective custody).

However, for youngsters there are considerations that may not apply to detained adults. For example, in a study of juveniles detained in Jefferson County (Birmingham), Alabama, McCarthy (1985:49) found the second most frequently cited reason for detention was the lack of alternative placements. Schwartz, Harris, and Levi (1988:144) also found this to be a problem in Minnesota: Many youngsters who probably should not be detained prior to adjudication are held simply because there are no other programs or facilities into which they can be placed. Schwartz and his associates also found that in Minnesota the youngsters held the longest were probation and parole violators (1988:141). In such cases, extended detention may result from delays occurring in other parts of the juvenile justice system. Locating bed space in the state system so that a violator's sentence may be continued (as in the case of parole violators) or started (as in the case of probation violators) may take time. Finally, as Feld notes, a monetary bail system for juveniles simply may be irrelevant since many accused delinquents come from poor families, and the inability to make bail will cause these youngsters to be detained anyway (2003:161).

Whatever the possible justifications for juveniles' preadjudication detention, one thing is certain: The courts and other juvenile justice agencies treat juveniles and adults differently. This especially became apparent in the U.S. Supreme Court case of *Schall v. Martin* (467 U.S. 253, 1984). In this case a challenge was brought against Section 320.5(3)(b) of the New York Family Court Act that authorized pre-adjudication detention of juvenile suspects "based on the finding that there is a 'serious risk' that the child 'may before the return date commit an act which if committed by an adult would constitute a crime.'" Justice Rehnquist, writing for the Court's six-member majority, observed that "Preventive detention under the FCA [Family Court Act] is purportedly designed to protect the child and society from the potential consequences of his criminal acts." The Court concluded that the detention was nonpunitive, that the state had in place procedures to "provide sufficient protection against erroneous and unnecessary deprivations of liberty" and, thus, "preventive detention under the FCA serves the legitimate state objective, held in common with every state in the country, of protecting both the juvenile and society from the hazards of pretrial crime."

PLACES OF DETENTION

The practice of detaining youngsters prior to adjudication has not been without controversy, and Roush maintains that juvenile detention is "ignored, maligned, and misunderstood" (2004:218). Furthermore, "It is embattled, abused, neglected, underfunded, understaffed, and overcrowded." There are debates over detention as a process (as was the case in *Schall v. Martin*) as well as the places of detention.[1]

Adults facing pretrial incarceration normally are held in one of two types of facilities: Some may be detained for short periods in police lockups, while others will be incarcerated in city, county, or regional jail facilities (Mays and Winfree,

2005). Youngsters are detained in *at least* three types of facilities: (1) detention centers designed specifically for accused offenders or other juveniles needing secure care, (2) designated juvenile units within adult jails and police lockups, or (3) secure or nonsecure shelter care facilities.

JUVENILE DETENTION CENTERS

The Office of Juvenile Justice and Delinquency Prevention defines **detention** as "the placement of a youth in a restrictive facility between the time of referral to court intake and case disposition." Roush says that a detention center is "a secure facility with (1) controlled ingress and egress, (2) security hardware and locks on windows and doors, (3) cement, steel, and cinder block construction, and (4) communications and technology systems representative of secure correctional facilities" (2004:219).

Some people (see for example Krisberg, 2005:74–76) feel that very few juveniles warrant secure detention. Many youngsters now detained could be released with no threat to public safety. Furthermore, none of the children detained should be status offenders or nondelinquents, and perhaps only the delinquents accused of the most serious offenses (some estimate between 5% and 10%) should be detained. When secure placements are warranted, the preferred facility seems to be a detention center built specifically for juveniles and operated by specially trained staff members. Nevertheless, the problems with such facilities are extensive.

First, most separate **juvenile detention centers** exist in large, populous counties. Often these counties have a vast network of agencies and organizations that can supplement or supplant secure incarceration. Smaller, rural counties quite often have neither the facilities nor the alternative agencies and organizations to adequately address the needs of the accused.

Second, some juvenile detention centers are little more than warehouses for youths awaiting court dates. They have one security level—essentially, maximum security—and very little in terms of health care, recreation, or treatment programs and resources. Consider our fictional detainee, Jerome. While accused of a serious crime, it was a property crime rather than a violent crime. Nevertheless, Jerome found himself in a congregate cell with postadjudicated juveniles awaiting transfer to the state's highest-security juvenile facility. In this case, fiction closely parallels reality.

Third, well-trained, highly motivated, and adequately compensated personnel may be scarce. Some juvenile detention centers share personnel on a rotating basis with adult facilities. Many centers find that qualified staff members are difficult to recruit and retain. Those who suffer most are the detainees, a fact not lost on many judges, who sometimes refuse to detain special-needs children unless the resources exist to meet those needs. This scenario presumes that judges know about the presence or absence of such staff and programs.

ADULT JAILS

In some jurisdictions, the juvenile detention center is simply a separate part of the adult jail. This is especially true in smaller and more rural jurisdictions that do not have the budget or the demand to operate separate juvenile and adult facilities.

Without a doubt, the greatest controversy surrounding preadjudication detention involves housing juveniles in adult jails (Howell, 1998). At this point several issues concerning juveniles in adult jails should be mentioned.

In 1998, the average daily population of juveniles in the nation's adult jails was just over 8,000 (Austin, Johnson, and Gregoriou, 2000). However, over the span of a year there may be several hundred thousand individual juveniles booked into adult jails. As impressive—or, given existing federal and state laws, disturbing—as these numbers may be, the truth is that they are only estimates, and we do not have accurate counts for jails in many states.

Juveniles detained in adult jails fit into one of two categories: those youngsters held in jail as adults, and those held as juveniles. As table 4.1 shows, the group of youngsters held in adult jails is substantial.

Juveniles held as adults typically have committed very serious, often violent, offenses. Most are 16 or 17 years of age, and they have committed homicides, armed robberies, rapes, or other serious crimes. As such, they are viewed as too great an escape risk to be held in juvenile detention centers or too great a threat to the health and well-being of the other juvenile inmates. In order for a juvenile who has committed a serious crime to be held in an adult facility, a hearing first must be conducted, depending upon law and local custom, by a juvenile court judge or a juvenile referee. Once this person decides that the accused is not a suitable candidate for the juvenile detention facility, the youngster is remanded to the adult authority. It is worth noting that this process alone does not automatically place the youth in the care and control of the adult court system. In order for a change in judicial authority to occur, nearly all jurisdictions require that a separate transfer hearing be conducted.

The youngsters held as juveniles in adult jails frequently are victims of geography (Feld, 1999c; see also Krisberg, 2005:79–80). They live in rural counties that cannot afford a full array of juvenile services. In these counties the dilemma facing

Table 4.1 Average Daily Population of Juveniles in Local Jails, 1983–1998, 2000, 2002, 2003

Year	Juveniles	Year	Juveniles	Year	Juveniles
1983	1,736	1990	2,301	1996	8,100
1984	1,482	1991	2,350	1997	9,105
1985	1,629	1992	2,804	1998	8,090
1986	1,708	1993*	4,300	2000	7,615
1987	1,781	1994	6,700	2002	7,248
1988	1,676	1995	7,800	2003	6,869
1989	2,250				

Note: Prior to 1993 only juveniles held for juvenile court adjudication were included in the count. Beginning in 1993 the jail census included the number of juveniles held for transfer to adult courts. For instance, of the 7,800 youngsters detained in 1995, 5,900 were awaiting transfer to adult courts or were under adult court jurisdiction for sentencing. In 2000 this number was 6,126; in 2002 it was 6,112; and in 2003 it was 5,484.

Sources: Austin, Johnson, and Gregoriou (2000:5); Harrison and Karberg (2004:8).

judges and other criminal justice decision makers is the choice between jail and doing nothing. Most of the time the "safe" choice is made, and the child is detained in jail. Schwartz and his colleagues found in Minnesota that jail frequently was chosen because of a "lack of readily available alternatives . . . [including] on-call crisis intervention and screening services, home detention, family oriented shelter care, and staff operated shelter care" (1988:144–45).

The American Correctional Association (2004), in the fourth edition of its *Performance-Based Standards for Adult Local Detention Facilities*, endorses a policy that would prohibit housing accused offenders under the age of 18 in adult detention facilities. Nevertheless, in the absence of such a policy some jurisdictions continue the practice of detaining juveniles in jails that also hold adult prisoners. When they do, there must be sight and sound separation from adults, a difficult standard to meet in most jails.

The "sight and sound separation" standard has been advanced for some time by groups such as the National Advisory Committee on Criminal Justice Standards and Goals (1976) and the National Advisory Committee on Juvenile Justice and Delinquency Prevention (1980). Sight and sound separation can only be achieved in many jails by placing juvenile detainees in virtual isolation. In the end, however bad juvenile detention centers may be, things generally are worse for those youngsters housed in adult jails. Krisberg summarizes the problem by saying that

> minors placed in adult jails have experienced much higher rates of violence and sexual exploitation than youths placed in specialized youth facilities. The suicide rate for juveniles in jails is much higher than [that for] youths in juvenile detention centers. (2005:77)

POLICE LOCKUPS

The police lockup is a frequently overlooked place of juvenile detention. Nationwide there are probably between 15,000 and 16,000 police lockups (Mays and Winfree, 2005). These facilities often hold people for less than 48 hours and do not hold people after they have been formally charged (Champion, 2005). Schwartz (1989:80) notes that "virtually no attention has been focused on the number of juveniles housed in local police and sheriff's lockups" despite the pervasiveness of lockups. He adds, "With the exception of a few states, there are no reliable data regarding the number of juveniles admitted to these facilities and, as yet, there has been no national and systematic attempt to gather such information" (1989:80).

While thorough and current information on police lockups may be difficult to obtain, we do know certain things about these institutions and can speculate on their impact on juveniles detained in them. First, police lockups typically are much smaller in cell size and overall space than county jails. Second, they often have no classification systems and little in the way of meaningful segregation. Therefore, juveniles detained in lockups must be kept in virtual isolation. Third, very few lockups offer food, bedding, or treatment services of any kind. More often than not, lockups are little more than steel cages in the corner of a precinct building or small, inadequately ventilated cells. They were never intended to be used for more than very brief periods of time, and many do not even have rudimentary plumbing.

Like many of their adult counterparts, juveniles held in detention often must meet with their attorneys in less-than-ideal circumstances.

Finally, lockups are dangerous, even though the average stay is brief. Juveniles and adults who are depressed, intoxicated, or under the influence of controlled substances are checked only periodically. Suicide is a particular concern. In 1999, of the 934 inmate deaths reported by all jails in the United States, 326 were the result of suicide, and estimates are that a dozen or so of these involved juveniles, although the exact juvenile numbers are unknown (Stephan, 2001). Another 1,000 or so individuals die in lockups, although again this figure is an estimate, and the number of juveniles is unknown (Charle, 1981; Davis and Muscat, 1993). It does appear that the risk of suicide is greatest within the first 24 hours of arrest, when inmate stress, embarrassment, isolation, and shock are greatest. Given these observations and the relative absence of antisuicide measures (see box 4.1), the probability of a *successful* suicide is much greater in lockups than in jails. While neither institution is particularly suited for the average juvenile detainee, lockups are especially dangerous.

No matter what type of facility is utilized, juvenile detention serves many of the same functions for accused delinquents as jails do for accused adult offenders. Detention is used to provide protection to the community from predatory juvenile offenders, make certain the juvenile appears in court for the next scheduled hearing, and provide for some type of preliminary evaluation of the juvenile's needs. Like adult jails, juvenile detention centers provide temporary, secure custody for youths awaiting dispositional decisions in their cases (Krisberg, 2005; Roush, 2004; Sickmund, 2003).

Box 4.1 Suicide by Youthful Detainees: Can We Predict Its Occurrence?

Some experts on jail suicides believe that suicide-risk profiles allow jail administrators to identify and isolate special-risk detainees and inmates. However, these instruments miss as many cases as they catch, employ questionable assumptions about suicide, and lead to a false sense of security among jail staff and administrators. Suicide-proof detention facilities could be constructed, but they would be dehumanizing, leading to other behavioral problems.

Other steps may reduce suicide's likelihood. A survey by Dale Parent and his colleagues of public and private detention facilities, reception and diagnostic centers, and training schools found the following:

• Suicide behavior was lower at institutions that practiced suicide screening at admission and employed staff trained in suicide prevention.

• Suicide behavior was higher among youngsters housed in isolation.

• Written policies mandating close supervision of suicidal residents did not reduce suicide behavior, but may have reduced completed suicides, since the policies are often formalized after a risk comes to the attention of facility administrators.

Lindsay Hayes suggests that besides building a suicide-resistant physical structure, planners must provide (1) training for all staff who come in contact with residents; (2) mental health assessments for new residents; (3) ongoing observation for changes in behavior and for presuicidal behavior; (4) special-alert status for at-risk youths; (5) referrals for suicide-risk assessment, intervention, and treatment; (6) contingency plans to deal with the contagion syndrome after suicide attempts and completed suicides; and (7) regular prevention plan reviews.

Sources: Hayes (1994); Parent, Leiter, Kennedy, Livens, Wentworth, and Wilcox (1994).

DETENTION DECISIONS: DELINQUENTS VERSUS STATUS OFFENDERS

During recent years the number of juveniles detained prior to adjudication has been increasing. In 2000 the number of youngsters detained in alleged delinquency cases was 329,800, up from 234,600 in 1985. On average, children committed to publicly operated detention facilities remain for 15 days (Sickmund, Snyder, and Poe-Yamagata, 1997). Table 4.2 shows the breakdown by percentage of accused delinquents detained in 1985, 1989, 1994, 1998, and 2000 and the most serious offense with which they were charged.

As is obvious from this table, property offenders are the most likely group to be detained. Personal offenders and youngsters charged with public order offenses have nearly identical percentages of detention. Furthermore, it is important to touch on the use of secure detention with status offenders. Although table 4.2 does not show the numbers of youths detained for status offenses, the numbers for 2000 (the most recent year for which data are available) provide something of a mixed picture. During this year 17% of the youngsters charged with being runaways were detained, along with another 3% charged with truancy, 10% charged with ungovernability, and 7% charged with liquor violations (Puzzanchera et al., 2004:68). Males were slightly more likely than females to be detained for running away and

Table 4.2   Percentage of Delinquency Cases Detained, 1985, 1989, 1994, 1998, 2000

Most serious offense	1985	1989	1994	1998	2000
Person	19%	21%	27%	27%	28%
Property	52	48	42	36	33
Drugs	7	11	10	13	11
Public order	22	21	21	24	28
Number of cases	234,600	261,500	308,000	327,700	329,800

Source: Puzzanchera et al. (2003:22; 2004:26).

liquor violations, and blacks were more likely than whites to be detained for running away and liquor violations (Puzzanchera et al., 2004:68–69). The plus side is that the number of detained status offenders is fairly small and has declined in recent years. The minus side is that many jurisdictions still hold status offenders in secure detention facilities.

ALTERNATIVES TO SECURE DETENTION

At least three factors justify the use of detention alternatives: (1) secure detention is an expensive proposition, with a typical cost of $50 to $100 per day depending on the facility's size and the services delivered; (2) secure detention is a scarce commodity, and most jurisdictions simply do not have an unlimited amount of bed space available for juvenile detainees; and (3) detention can be physically and emotionally detrimental to many youngsters who are not prepared for the rigors of secure confinement. Detention alternatives seem preferable in all but the most extreme cases.

A major alternative to detention prior to adjudication is **third-party custody**, in which the minor is released into the custody and control of someone other than a state-sponsored legal entity. The third party will be parents or legal guardians, including other relatives, in virtually all cases. This alternative is comparable to release on recognizance (ROR) for adult offenders. With an ROR release, the accused offers his or her word to appear in court for the next scheduled hearing. For juvenile offenders, this promise is backed by an adult signatory's word. The vast majority of juvenile offenders can be released into the custody of a third party with little danger to the community and little possibility of flight from prosecution. Most accused delinquents simply do not have the resources to go far or hide long from adjudication, and most parents are responsible enough to ensure the appearance of the accused offender.

Juvenile court workers, especially intake staff members, readily recognize that some youngsters should not be returned to their homes prior to a hearing on their charges. The parents may be unwilling or unable to provide the child with the necessary supervision. Some accused delinquents live in homes where one parent is absent; where one or both parents have drug, alcohol, or mental health problems; or where one or both parents may be engaged in some type of criminal activity themselves. In these situations, the intake staff may recommend an alternative residential placement for the youngster awaiting adjudication. Some of these residential placements may have limited-security arrangements (usually the presence of staff members and locked doors is enough), but many such placements are nonsecure. These **group homes** give youths a place to stay and provide academic and other types of support while they are awaiting their court dates.

A final alternative might be shelter care in a private home, sometimes called a **foster home**, for a limited number of youngsters. The primary problem with this arrangement is that foster homes are in extremely short supply, and very few potential foster families are interested in housing an accused delinquent.

DETENTION DECISION MAKING

Preadjudication decision making typically has several phases, with several people providing input into the process. In most jurisdictions, when a police officer brings a juvenile to the detention center, a staff member may have the court's permission to order detention instead of releasing the child immediately. This authority may be very tightly defined, however. In other jurisdictions, court staff members such as the intake caseworkers may be responsible for the initial preadjudication detention authorization. These staff members are a logical choice for this function, since they often will make decisions concerning the filing of petitions and scheduling of meetings with the judges for various hearings. Intake workers may be probation officers who specialize in this area, and as we will see in later chapters, these personnel not only work *with* the juvenile court judges, but in some instances work *for* them.

DETENTION SCREENING

Screening for placement in juvenile detention is a critical decision for all parties. In most jurisdictions, the decision to detain in custody or to provide an alternative placement is made at the intake screening. Intake screening determines (1) if the court has jurisdiction; (2) if the evidence warrants a court hearing; (3) if the charges are serious enough for a court hearing; (4) if the accused is a suitable candidate for an informal disposition, given the current charges and evidence; and (5) if the accused is a candidate for detention, given positive answers to the first three questions and a negative answer to the fourth. Normally, the case manager or juvenile probation officer assigned to the case answers all five questions. This individual makes a recommendation to the court on detention status. Remember, the youth is already in custody. The question remaining is: What do we do with the juvenile now?

A common practice is to screen all juveniles for detention. The screening process determines each youth's suitability for detention. The juvenile's mental state and physical condition must pose no health threat. Having determined that there are no overriding reasons why detention is inappropriate, the case manager reviews the case to determine whether the youth (and the charges) meet the detention criteria. These criteria vary from jurisdiction to jurisdiction, but most involve the risks created by leaving the accused at large in the community. Such criteria include the following: (1) the youth is wanted by another jurisdiction for a delinquent act, (2) the youth requests in writing to be taken into protective custody, or (3) the youth is charged with a very serious violation of law, such as murder, rape, or some other equally violent offense, perhaps involving the use of a firearm.

Some states prohibit the use of detention under certain conditions. Consider the guidelines used in King County (Seattle), Washington Superior Court (2004).[2] Use of detention is authorized if the youth:

- commits an offense that would result in automatic adult court jurisdiction
- commits an offense involving possession of a firearm
- is charged with a sexual offense other than indecent exposure
- is charged with domestic violence
- has an active warrant for out-of-jurisdiction hold, parole hold, escape charge, or violation of conditions of release; is a material witness; or has failed to appear for another court hearing

Juveniles also can be detained if they have two or more warrants on their present charge, if they have had a warrant within the past six months on a class C or above felony, or if they previously have been adjudicated on a felony offense.

Use of detention is prohibited when:

- the present offense is a misdemeanor
- the present offense is a class C or lower felony, especially if there is an issue of proper notice to the parents or guardians
- there are no outstanding warrants or administrative holds
- there have been no felony adjudications in the past three months and there currently are no pending charges

A detention recommendation also may be influenced by mitigating or aggravating factors associated with either the accused or the alleged offense. Among possible mitigating factors, or those that would suggest that detention is inappropriate, are those occurring when:

- the juvenile did not cause or threaten serious bodily harm and the victim expresses no fear of harm
- the parents are able to supervise the youngster until the next court hearing
- the police are not fearful that the youngster will cause harm
- there has been at least one year since prior court-imposed sanctions

The overall detention assessment, along with any mitigating or aggravating factors, becomes part of the documentation presented to the court at the detention hearing.

PREDETENTION HEARINGS

No matter who orders the initial detention, the decision to continue detention beyond 24 to 48 hours rests with the juvenile court judge. When either the police or the prosecutor request preadjudication detention, the juvenile court judge typically schedules a detention hearing as quickly as possible, but usually no more than 24 to 72 hours after the initial arrest. A longer stay may be required if an evaluation process is ongoing and if the judge believes that additional information is necessary to make the detention decision (see Feld, 2003; Gardner, 2003).

Detention hearings are frequently somewhat mechanical and routine. The intake officer or other court official presents the results of the screening process, and the judge decides whether the child is a threat to himself or herself or to others, is a runaway possibility, or is in danger of being victimized by someone else. Like the intake officer, the judge may decide to release or detain the child, and not to file, dismiss, or forward the petition for processing. Given the potential for the child to lose his or her liberty, many state authorities have mandated that the right to counsel at this stage is essential (see, for example, McCarthy, Patton, and Carr, 2003:517ff.).

ASSESSING PREADJUDICATION DETENTION

After a review of both the screening process by which many youths are recommended for detention and the legal proceeding that determines whether detention will be imposed, several important questions remain. First, to what extent are the legal factors, including the offense seriousness and prior record, associated with who receives detention? Second, to what extent are extralegal factors, including the juvenile suspect's age, race, and gender, associated with this decision? Third, to what extent are status offenders likely to find themselves in preadjudicatory detention? We begin with the role of legal factors.

THE ROLE OF LEGAL FACTORS

Offense seriousness appears to play a variable role in detention decisions. During the 1960s and 1970s, many researchers found that the detention rates for status offenders were consistently higher than for those accused of more serious offenses (Ferseter, Snethen, and Courtless, 1969; see also Sarri, 1974; Pawlak, 1977). The higher detention rates for youths accused of less serious offenses compared with those accused of serious offenses do not appear to have been a function of the higher occurrence rate of the former over the latter (Cohen, 1975a; 1975b). A decade later researchers also found that offense seriousness, prior record, demeanor in court, and even prior adjudications were largely unrelated to detention decisions (see for example Bailey, 1981; Fenwick, 1982; McCarthy, 1985). Only the most serious forms of delinquency, for example, burglary, larceny, robbery, and sex offenses, by themselves showed a consistent link to higher detention rates (Bailey, 1981). These findings lend credence to the suggestion that detention was being used as an unofficial punishment, especially for status offenders who faced few real sanctions (Sarri, 1983).

Other researchers found that one legal variable, prior record of offenses, and one extralegal variable, current living arrangement, gave the best insights into detention decisions (Black and Smith, 1980). A study of metropolitan courts in Denver and Memphis found that in both jurisdictions the juveniles most likely to be detained had prior offense records and were not attending school (Cohen and Kluegel, 1979). These same jurisdictions, however, used very different criteria when considering status offenders. A study of Florida detention decisions also tapped prior offense record as related to the detention likelihood, as were the offense seriousness and the number of offenses charged (Frazier and Cochran, 1986).

How can these different findings about the role played by legal factors be reconciled? Frazier (1989:153) suggests that

> it appears likely that detention could be determined in part by the particular structure of the juvenile justice system in a jurisdiction (such as whether the structure involves police in the decision process or not) and the general philosophies of juvenile justice held by various types of justice officials (police versus probation officers). This implies, of course, that there should be wide variations in rates across jurisdictions, in the characteristics of juveniles selected for detention across jurisdictions, and in both rates and detainees' characteristics over time.

The findings reported for legal factors suggest considerable support for this hypothesis. We turn next to a consideration of the extralegal factors to see if they, too, support Frazier's ideas.

THE ROLE OF EXTRALEGAL FACTORS

Detention decisions may also take into consideration such extralegal variables as living arrangement, school attendance and truancy rates, and extracurricular work record. Some personal characteristics of accused delinquents are less legitimate and, in fact, are troubling if considered at all in pretrial release decisions. For instance, basic equity questions surround the degree to which age, gender, and race or ethnicity enter into the decision-making process, although the court may have to consider the child's age in the preadjudication release decision. Given the complexities of the issues, it may be easiest to illustrate the concern over offender characteristics by asking a series of questions:

1. Are younger juveniles (10 to 13 years old) more likely to be detained because they are perceived to be in need of protection, or are older juveniles (14 to 17 years old) more likely to be detained because their acts of misconduct are viewed as more threatening since these youths are older and should know better?
2. Are females more likely to be detained than males?
3. Are racial or ethnic minorities more or less likely to be detained than nonminorities?

A persistent concern is whether younger juveniles are held for longer periods of time "for their own protection." Puzzanchera and colleagues (2004) found that in 2000, 19% of the youngsters detained in the United States were 15 years of age or younger, compared with 22% of those 16 and older. In just one decade these numbers had decreased from 22% for the younger group and 25% for the older group.

The type of offense with which the youngster is charged may influence the detention decision. As we saw in table 4.2 the number of youngsters detained increased 41% from 234,600 in 1985 to 329,800 in 2000. However, overall percentage of delinquency cases detained remained virtually unchanged (20% in 1985 and 21% in 2000). One factor of great interest is that those detained for personal offenses increased from 19% in 1985 to 28% in 2000. By contrast, youngsters detained for property offenses (the largest number of "serious" offenses coming before juvenile courts) decreased from 52% in 1985 to 33% in 2000 (Puzzanchera et al., 2004:26).

A report by the National Center for Juvenile Justice (Puzzanchera et al., 2004) also found that males are slightly more likely to be detained than females. In 2000, 21% of the delinquency cases involved males who were detained versus 17% of the delinquency cases in which females were detained. This compares with 24% of the males detained and 18% of the females detained in 1990 (see table 4.3).

The situation involving females and preadjudication detention often is confounded by a host of other factors, including age and the nature of the offense. Based on their numbers throughout the juvenile justice system, females are substantially underrepresented in offender populations. Frequently, females are detained longer and for less serious offenses than their male counterparts. Chesney-Lind (1988), in looking at figures from around the United States, found two very important factors relating to the detention of juvenile females. First,

---

**Box 4.2   International Perspectives
Detaining Youths in Australia**

Are the problems associated with juvenile detention unique to the United States? Hardly. All we have to do is look to Australia. In fact, Australia's situation is instructive because it is dealing with some of the same dilemmas facing the United States, but the overall situation is different.

A 2002 report by the Australian Institute of Criminology noted that the maximum jurisdictional age varies among Australia's states and territories: for some the maximum age is 16 and for others it is 17. Nevertheless, some of the nation's juvenile detention centers hold people beyond their eighteenth birthdays, in Victoria up to age 20.

One of the issues plaguing juvenile detention in the United States and Australia is the overrepresentation of minority youngsters. In the United States this is particularly a problem for African-American youths. In Australia the problem appears in "indigenous populations." Indigenous youths represent about 2% of the juvenile population in Australia, but they have a detention rate of 284 per 100,000 youths in the target population. This compares with a non-indigenous youth detention rate of 16.3 per 100,000. In other words, indigenous youngsters are over 17 times more likely to be detained than non-indigenous youths.

In both the United States and Australia, about 25% of the total population is under age 18. Unlike the United States, however, Australia generally has a very low number of juvenile detainees. In fact, on June 30, 2001, there were 604 juveniles in detention centers throughout Australia. Nevertheless, like the United States, 90% of the detainees were male. So what can we conclude? The detention population size difference clearly is notable between the United States and Australia, but some of the problems facing the juvenile justice systems are common to both nations.

Source: Cahill and Marshall (2002).

Table 4.3   Percentage of Delinquency Cases Involving Detention by Gender, 1990, 1995, 2000

Most Serious Offense	Male			Female		
	1990	1995	2000	1990	1995	2000
Delinquency	24%	18%	21%	18%	12%	17%
Person	29	23	26	20	17	20
Property	20	15	18	14	8	12
Drugs	39	22	20	28	16	15
Public Order	28	20	24	26	15	22

Source: Adapted from Puzzanchera et al. (2003:23; 2004:28).

although boys are arrested for more serious offenses than are girls, still almost 17% of the youngsters detained are female. Second, larceny-theft and running away from home have accounted for almost half of the arrests of girls since 1975 (Chesney-Lind, 1988:150). Concluding her analysis of nationwide data, Chesney-Lind writes:

> In general, these state-by-state accounts suggest large numbers of girls continue to be held in adult jails. It also seems fairly clear that these girls are charged with far less serious offenses than their male counterparts, and, in many states, they are being held in adult facilities for status offenses. Girls are on the average younger than their male counterparts. They may stay as long as boys despite their less serious offense backgrounds. Finally, it appears that as restrictions are placed on the jailing of youth, the number of girls held in these adult facilities may drop sharply. (1988:161)

In 2000 females were most likely to be detained in cases involving personal offenses and public order charges, but overall they still were less likely to be detained than males (80% of the youngsters detained were male). Nevertheless, between 1990 and 1999 the percentage of females detained increased at a greater rate than the rate for males. Why? Some researchers (see for example Chesney-Lind, 1988) have suggested various reasons, but the most persistent cause is the juvenile justice system's paternalistic nature. Females are assumed to need more care and protection, from themselves and others, than males.

The biggest discrepancies for youngsters detained appear when race is taken into account. As table 4.4 also shows, the percentages for black youngsters and those of other races are much higher than those for white youngsters. Puzzanchera and associates (2004) found that in 2000 25% of black youngsters arrested were detained for cases of accused delinquency compared with 24% for other races and 18% for whites. However, the greatest disparity in detention use in 2000 was in cases involving drug charges. Detention was used in 15% of the drug cases involving white juveniles, 32% of the cases involving blacks, and 22% of the cases involving youngsters of other races (Puzzanchera et al., 2004:29).

As table 4.4 indicates, the general trend for all races is decreased detention between 1990 and 1999. Nevertheless, blacks and other races consistently lead whites in the percentages of youngsters detained. In some cases the differences are

Table 4.4   Detention Rates by Race and Offense, 1990, 1995, 2000

Most serious offense	White			Black			Other races		
	1990	1995	2000	1990	1995	2000	1990	1995	2000
Delinquency	20%	14%	18%	29%	22%	25%	29%	21%	24%
Person	24	19	23	31	25	25	38	29	32
Property	17	12	15	24	17	21	25	16	18
Drugs	27	14	15	52	34	32	35	17	22
Public order	26	17	21	31	20	29	33	29	28

Source: Puzzanchera et al. (2003:24; 2004:19).

small, and at other times the differences are substantial. There is no easy explanation for why this is the situation. For example, the discrepancies could be the result of discriminatory detention decision making or discrimination during earlier processing decisions (arrest and intake, for example). Higher detention rates also could be the consequence of higher offense rates, lack of alternative placements, lack of family stability or support services, or some other undiscovered or unexplained causes (Lieber and Jamieson, 1995).

McCarthy (1985:50) found that race and social class were not significant factors in the cases of 109 juveniles detained in Jefferson County, Alabama. Schwartz and his colleagues (1988:142–43) discovered that during 1986 almost 90% of the youngsters admitted to adult jails and police lockups in Minnesota were white (out of a total of 3,941). In terms of minority populations, 6.3% of the youths were Native Americans, less than 5% were black, and "others" accounted for less than one-half of 1% (0.2%). Many of the Native American youngsters were detained in county jails and most of the blacks were detained in police lockups, perhaps indicating the state's racial or ethnic dispersion patterns.

While the studies in Minnesota (Schwartz and Merriam, 1984; Schwartz et al., 1988) stop short of accusing the juvenile justice system of discrimination, the researchers do note that (1) Native American youths were detained longer, on average, than white youths; (2) the counties near American Indian reservations have high juvenile incarceration rates; and (3) black juveniles were incarcerated longer, on average, than whites. Aside from geographical considerations, the explanations for racial or ethnic disparity seem somewhat elusive. Schwartz and his colleagues suggest that "state lawmakers and the public interest groups should conduct inquiries into the nature and scope of these disparities and determine what action steps need to be taken in order to correct the problem" (1988:147).

REFLECTIONS ON THE USE OF PRETRIAL DETENTION

A few observations about pretrial detention seem warranted. First, substantial numbers of youngsters are detained every year prior to adjudicatory hearings on delinquency charges. Second, most detained youngsters are charged with delinquent offenses (violations that would be crimes for adults), but a substantial number of them are status offenders. Third, detention may be based on the perceived seriousness of the offenses with which these juveniles are charged; however, three out of every four youngsters detained were charged with something other than a personal offense. In other words, only 25% of the youths detained were held for crimes against persons. Fourth, the odds of being detained seem to have remained relatively stable over time, decreasing slightly during the 1990s. Fifth, males are more likely to be detained than females, and nonwhites are more likely to be detained than whites. This might lead us to conclude that juvenile court judges consider minority males more dangerous than other groups, or it may mean that judges and court personnel perceive the families of these youngsters as being less stable. Therefore, detention might be more a function of family status and stability than of seriousness of the offense with which the youngster is charged. In any event, evidence suggests that preadjudication detention is predicated on more than just community risk factors.

WHY PREADJUDICATORY DIVERSION?

Now that we have examined preadjudication detention, it is time to turn our attention to alternatives to the adjudication process itself. The area of **preadjudication diversion** has witnessed explosive growth within juvenile justice, particularly since the mid-1970s. Diversion is not confined exclusively to the juvenile court but extends across many aspects of the juvenile justice system. For our purposes, however, it seems most appropriate to address diversion prior to commencement of adjudication, since once adjudication begins, attempts at true diversion end.

DIVERSIONARY PHILOSOPHY

Diversion, as an alternative to formal processing, is a policy whose roots are easy to trace. The first clear articulation of the diversionary philosophy came in the report of the President's Commission on Law Enforcement and the Administration of Justice (1967a:80–82). This report, entitled *The Challenge of Crime in a Free Society*, viewed justice system processing of accused delinquents, especially relatively minor (status) offenders, as stigmatizing and held that this stigmatization had continuing and future consequences for delinquency (see also Anderson and Schoen, 1985). This philosophy was emphasized in the report of the Task Force on Juvenile Delinquency (1967), and became the basis of federal policy with passage of the Juvenile Justice and Delinquency Prevention Act of 1974 and its subsequent amendments.

Most of the impetus for developing diversionary alternatives came from the work of Edwin Lemert and his exploration of labeling theory. Labeling theory's suppositions are that many adolescents at some point commit deviant acts. Some of these youngsters are apprehended by the justice system and given some type of official label. As a result of the label being applied and subsequently reinforced, the child comes to behave as the label suggests he or she is to behave.

If, indeed, this is the case and stigmatization is entirely negative, then it makes sense to remove as many children as possible from the formal adjudication system. Such an approach may help them improve their behavior by providing the services they need, and it may prevent them from getting worse by preventing recidivism resulting from the labeling process.

Theoretical Reflections
Labeling Theory and Diversion

To understand fully the diversion efforts that have marked the past 30 years, one must understand **labeling theory** and the influence it has had on juvenile justice policy. In simplest terms, people who adhere to labeling theory's tenets believe that the first tentative explorations of an individual into deviance or crime—or delinquency—represent acts of **primary deviance**. Generally, the actor has no great commitment to a criminal career, nor does he or she pose a long-term threat to society. However, the more frequent the contact a youngster has with the juvenile justice system and the deeper the penetration into that system, the more likely the youth is to acquire a delinquent label and to act in accordance with that label. This condition is what Edwin Lemert (1951) calls **secondary deviance**.

Lemert popularized these terms in his influential work *Instead of Court: Diversion in Juvenile Justice* (1971), which became a blueprint for diversion programs in the 1970s. Labeling theorists assume—since many of labeling theory's elements are untested—that once youngsters have obtained a delinquent label, juvenile justice system actors will treat them as delinquents and eventually the youngsters will come to see themselves as delinquents as well. Therefore, diversion programs aim to minimize labeling and reduce the stigma associated with a delinquent label in order to avoid exposing low-risk offenders to formal adjudication and disposition.

Source: Lemert (1951; 1971).

DIVERSIONARY PURPOSES

Before we examine existing diversion programs, it is important to first deal with a very simple question: What do we want diversionary programs to achieve? First, diversion provides an alternative to incarceration (see Roberts, 2004). Locking children in secure juvenile correctional facilities is presumed to have many negative consequences. Secure confinement may be detrimental to the child emotionally and psychologically as well as physically. Incarceration with hardened delinquents may increase the child's law-violating inclinations, to say nothing of increasing his or her delinquency skill levels. Correctional confinement additionally may create a stigma that no amount of time or treatment can erase (DeAngelo, 1988:24). Thus, incarceration is often viewed as a last resort, and then only for the most serious juvenile offenders.

Second, diversion should provide the kinds of services needed by certain adolescents, services that might be unavailable in an institution or inaccessible without the intervention of the juvenile justice system (Roberts, 2004). This purpose carries on the juvenile justice system's tradition of acting in the child's best interests.

Third, informal (diversionary) handling of many youngsters should reduce juvenile justice system costs (DeAngelo, 1988:24). Cost savings should result from less intensive probation supervision of diverted youths, fewer prosecutorial and court resources needed for adjudicatory hearings, and substantially lower costs than those associated with secure correctional confinement (upwards of $25,000 per year per child in most states). If diversion works—as measured by recidivism, one of the traditional yardsticks of success—the community should feel safer, be safer, and suffer fewer property losses as well. Binder and his associates examined one juvenile diversion program in Orange County, California, and found that "the desired goal of cost savings with the new program was not attained at the expense of increased criminal behavior" (1985:10).

Fourth, scarce juvenile justice resources can be focused on some of the system's most pressing problems. This practice may allow for greater attention to be given to juveniles who have committed serious acts of delinquency, particularly violent personal crimes.

Recall that diversion is based on the assumption that (1) in every case formal processing will result in a label being applied to youngsters passing through the system, (2) this label will stick, and (3) this stigmatization process is, by its very nature, bad. The intent, then, is to reduce the stigmatizing of children entering the juvenile justice system by removing them from formal processing. However, there are other considerations that would indicate diversion from the juvenile justice system may not be all that positive, particularly for minor (status) offenders. For example, consider the following brief points about the labeling and stigmatization process:

- We cannot assume that all stigmatization is bad. It may be that some youngsters turn from law-violating behavior as a result of being held up to public scorn.

- We cannot assume that the labels applied by the justice system are well known and recognized by either the juveniles who are processed or by the general public.

- We cannot assume that even if youngsters know the labels they will accept them as legitimate. Young people have a remarkable capacity to define and redefine things to suit themselves.

- The diversion movement might result in removing one label or set of labels only to apply another label. Juveniles might no longer be considered delinquent, but they now might be viewed as having a conduct disorder.

Given these competing sets of assumptions, what do we know about the nature and extent of diversion programs and their effectiveness? The following sections will explore these questions.

FORMAL DIVERSIONARY PROGRAMS: A CREATED NEED?

Prior to 1974 very few diversionary projects for juvenile delinquents existed. Pre-1974 programs were small, widely scattered geographically, and not especially well known. When the Juvenile Justice and Delinquency Prevention Act (JJDPA) of 1974 was passed, the federal government provided a new source of operational funding (Roberts, 2004). The result was that quite a number of entrepreneurs got into the juvenile justice diversion business (Curran, 1988:367).

The 1974 act provided three main thrusts in relation to the diversion of juvenile offenders. First, a major consideration was the **jail removal initiative** (Schwartz, 1991). At the time of the JJDPA's passage, roughly 3,000 youngsters were housed in adult jails on any given day in the United States. Most of these detainees were housed in jails not because they were the "worst of the worst," but because there were no other places to detain them prior to adjudicatory hearings. Many jurisdictions did not operate juvenile detention facilities, so the adult jail became the default detention option. Therefore, the jail removal initiative was designed to divert youngsters from confinement in facilities where they might be exposed to adult offenders.

A few points need to be made about the jail removal initiative. It did have an impact on juvenile justice processes in many states. The numbers of youngsters housed in adult jails on a daily basis dropped from about 3,000 to between 1,500 to 1,700 (Austin et al., 2000; Harrison and Karberg, 2004). However, the numbers stalled at that point because the remaining jurisdictions did not have the financial resources or the population numbers to justify separate juvenile detention centers. Furthermore, the federal jail removal deadlines were altered on a number of occasions (see for example Schwartz, 1989; 1991). The original legislation said that federal funding for state juvenile justice initiatives would end if states did not comply with the jail removal initiative by 1980. In 1980 the JJDPA was amended to extend the deadline for removing juveniles from jails to 1985. When the deadline arrived, some progress had been made, but not all state and local governments had been able to move swiftly enough to meet the JJDPA's demands. In a typical response, Congress again extended the deadline.

Writing in 1991, Schwartz noted that the goal of full compliance had yet to be achieved, and that statement holds true today. In the 1990s the numbers of juveniles being housed in adult jails rose steadily, and have only recently begun to decline (see table 4.1). However, in fairness to localities, a new counting method by the Bureau of Justice Statistics includes those youngsters who, although they technically still are juveniles, are to be tried as adults. By the current counting method, the one-day count of juveniles in adult jails is just under 7,000, and only 1,385 of these youngsters were held as juvenile offenders (Harrison and Karberg, 2004:8).

The **deinstitutionalization of status offenders (DSO)** is the second most frequently discussed diversion component of the JJDPA of 1974. In the mid-1970s it was not uncommon for many states to have juvenile correctional populations of which at least half were status offenders. Some of these youngsters were habitual truants, but the bulk of the status offenders were females and runaways. A number of the runaways were actually "throwaways" who came from chaotic and dysfunctional homes. These children needed treatment and frequently an out-of-home placement. What they did not need was to be locked in secure institutions with youngsters who had committed serious criminal acts. Therefore, the JJDPA both encouraged and prodded states to develop alternatives to secure incarceration for status offenders, and the DSO component sought to divert youngsters from incarceration with adjudicated delinquent offenders.

The DSO effort achieved several ends, not all of them intended. First, the DSO movement has been successful in that the number of youngsters, particularly females, housed in state juvenile correctional facilities has declined dramatically. However, before we celebrate the victory we should note that the number of these youngsters in private correctional placements has increased proportionately. Therefore, it seems that the DSO effort has moved status offenders into the private facili-

Theoretical Reflections
Explaining Decarceration and Deinstitutionalization

In the 1970s, deinstitutionalization and decarceration proponents viewed labeling theory as the conceptual base for their beliefs about the evils of correctional institutions. From both perspectives, institutionalizing both status offenders and juvenile delinquents has three clear consequences. First, society tends to view them as dangerous cast-offs regardless of the youths' actual legal status as delinquents or minicriminals. In short, these youths have spoiled identities that incarceration only worsens. Second, the police, juvenile courts, and allied professionals serve as deviance amplifiers, making others aware of the youths' deviant status. Finally, incarceration facilitates the youths' movement to secondary deviant status, at which time they come to see themselves as others see them.

Besides labeling theory, other theories support both deinstitutionalization and decarceration. First, differential association and general cultural deviance theories suggest that immersion of impressionable and essentially noncriminal children in an environment filled with negative role models and criminal learning mechanisms will only help confirm criminal values. Second, some deinstitutionalization proponents support incarceration's deterrent effect but argue that it should be used only as a last resort, rather than indiscriminately and widely; moreover, other options may help cement a child's stake in legitimate versus illegitimate opportunities, a difficult goal in a youth prison. In this second set of observations, we see deterrence theory, opportunity theory, and social bond theory.

Sources: Coates (1981); Finckenauer (1984); Winfree and Abadinsky (2003).

ties that are now much more available, and at the same time has freed additional bed space in public facilities for more delinquent offenders. In classic fashion, this policy change has increased our capacity to punish or, as we frequently say, it has "widened the net."

The DSO movement also is somewhat flawed because, though judges cannot incarcerate youngsters for committing status offenses, they have a backdoor through which they can still accomplish the same objective. In most states, when a judge adjudicates a status offender, a condition of the disposition is that he or she not violate the conditions of probation by committing any other offense, including status offenses. If the youngster does so, the judge can treat this as contempt of court and order the youth incarcerated (Feld, 2003:46). Therefore, some juvenile correctional populations will contain these relabeled status offenders.

The final component of the diversion initiatives spelled out by the JJDPA is what might be called **decarceration**. Decarceration is somewhat like status offender deinstitutionalization in that it aims to remove youngsters from secure institutional confinement.[3] However, unlike DSO, decarceration is much more broadly based, and its goal is to minimize incarceration for a wide spectrum of adjudicated delinquents. In simplest terms, decarceration directs judges and other juvenile justice personnel to seek the least restrictive placement for youngsters coming before the juvenile court. This means that the preferred placement option for most youngsters will be their own homes, and that institutionalization will be ordered as a last resort. Therefore, decarceration seeks to divert youngsters from the secure confinement system.

The result is that federal initiatives, followed by state practices, formalized what had been informal: the process of removing some youngsters from the juvenile justice system at various stages in the process, from prearrest to postadjudication. Whether called diversion, deinstitutionalization, or decarceration, such practices often failed to achieve the standards set by the rhetoric of change.

DIVERSIONARY PROGRAMS

Once federal dollars became available after passage of the JJDPA, diversionary projects started to spring up. Most of these programs serve as (1) service brokers, helping juveniles in need of services and their families make connections with service-providing organizations; or (2) direct service providers, helping children who need particular kinds of assistance. The diversity of program structures and services makes it difficult to generalize about their nature; for example, some are residential and others are nonresidential. The types of services provided include victim-offender restitution efforts; community service requirements; educational programs, especially tutoring and remedial education; and a variety of counseling programs, such as individual, group, substance abuse, family, and employment counseling (see Cummings and Clark, 1993; Roberts, 2004).

Although referrals to diversion programs can come from families, schools, or community agencies, the most frequent referral sources are the police and juvenile probation departments. This linkage makes some diversionary endeavors extensions of the juvenile justice system. Acknowledging that diversion's presumed benefits have not always been realized, nevertheless many observers maintain hope for the concept. Yet, diversionary efforts are not without critics. We will address these shortcomings after first exploring diversion's operational forms.

OPERATIONAL PERSPECTIVES

Diversion programs can take many different forms. The following list provides five of the typical goals for diversion (see Sullivan, 2002):

1. to avoid negative labeling
2. to reduce unnecessary social control
3. to reduce recidivism
4. to provide needed services
5. to reduce juvenile justice system costs

The Juvenile Justice and Delinquency Prevention Act of 1974 put the federal government in the business of promoting innovation and providing funding for state and local juvenile diversion programs (Binder, 1998; Roberts, 2004). Nevertheless, it is important to point out that there are formal diversion programs as well as informal "nonprograms." We will provide examples of each of these categories.

Box 4.3   Community-Based Diversion Efforts

Before the JJDPA was law, Sherwood Norman provided the blueprint for the first widely accepted diversion mechanism in *The Youth Services Bureau: A Key to Delinquency Prevention*. Norman defined **Youth Services Bureau** (**YSB**) as "a noncoercive, independent public agency established to divert children and youth from the justice system by (1) mobilizing community resources to solve youth problems, (2) strengthening existing resources and developing new ones, and (3) promoting positive programs to remedy delinquency-breeding conditions" (1972:8). Hundreds of YSBs appeared throughout the 1970s. Dunford, Osgood, and Weichselbaum observed that children were diverted into less coercive, less controlling, and more client-oriented agencies, but diversion was no more successful than previous programs in "avoiding stigma, improving social adjustments, or reducing delinquent behavior" (1982:16).

As Law Enforcement Assistance Administration funding dried up in the early 1980s, all but a few YSBs closed their doors. According to Binder and his associates, **new diversion** has largely disappeared. **Traditional diversion** continues to funnel children out of formal processing through the discretionary acts of police and probation officers. Juvenile court judges practice diversion through **informal adjustments**. Other contemporary diversion options include formal mediation between the juvenile, the complainant, and a trained mediator. The goal is to resolve the conflict to the satisfaction of all parties, a difficult goal in any situation, let alone one involving law violations.[4]

Sources: Binder, Geis, and Bruce (1988); Dunford, Osgood, and Weichselbaum (1982); Norman (1972).

At the most informal or nonprogram level are efforts exerted by the police. As we have mentioned, the police are the principal agents of diversion from the juvenile justice system. As expected, given their involvement very early in the processing of most juvenile offenders, they are also the juvenile justice system's primary referral agents. We discussed the concept of police discretion in chapter 3, but it is worth mentioning again that police officers often informally adjust or divert many of the cases they encounter. This may be the ultimate exercise of diversion.

Most police diversion responses to juvenile cases can be characterized as nonprogrammatic approaches. This means that the police handle many encounters—especially with minor juvenile offenders—in some manner other than arrest. For these confrontations there is no record, no formal action is taken, and presumably there is no stigmatization. The informal, street-corner adjustment of encounters with juveniles is utilized daily by uniformed patrol officers with virtually no oversight or review.

In contrast with the nonprogrammatic diversion approach, juvenile courts and community service agencies frequently have established much more formalized juvenile diversion programs. Some of these programs utilize small paid staffs, supplemented with volunteers. The types of services commonly provided by these programs are individual, group or family counseling, and academic assistance (Patenaud, 2003).

ASSESSING PREADJUDICATION DIVERSION

Diversion programs are designed primarily to keep certain categories of youthful offenders out of the juvenile justice system's formal adjudicatory mechanism. However, as we would expect, these efforts have had both intended and unintended outcomes.

One criticism often leveled at diversion is its self-perpetuating nature. Once the project starts, it is in the staff's best interests to generate a sufficient caseload to stay in business, or even to expand (see Binder and Geis, 1984:640). The drive for self-perpetuation can cause some personnel to lose sight of their initial objectives, such as minimizing the stigma attached to minor juvenile offenders, and to develop different agendas, such as getting additional governmental grants.

A second consequence of some diversion programs has been to bring more children under some form of social control, in other words, to widen the net. **Net widening** is said to occur any time youngsters who otherwise would not fall within the system's control are brought into the juvenile justice system (Sullivan, 2002). This consequence clearly is unintended and is one that concerns many juvenile justice reformers. Lundman (1976:436) observed that "diversion may magnify rather than correct existing problems." Polk remarks that diversion in practice is different from diversion in principle; therefore, many diversionary efforts are not "meeting [the] original goal of deflecting cases away from juvenile justice processing" (1984:655). The result is an increase rather than a decrease of stigmatization (Vito, Tewksbury, and Wilson, 1998).

Some of the research done over nearly three decades indicates that net widening does occur in many diversion programs (Sullivan, 2002). However, the findings are not always definitive. Two problems that have appeared in some of the evaluations are inadequately defined concepts and poorly developed evaluation methodologies (Frazier, Richards, and Potter, 1983). The bottom line seems to be that net widening is a very real, but not necessarily automatic, result of diversion programs. However, this is an issue worthy of ongoing research and continuous monitoring.

A third outcome of diversion programs is the development of a **second system** (Rogers and Mays, 1987). By a "second system" we mean an agency network that operates in conjunction with, but outside of, the formal juvenile justice system's processes and protections. Many second-system agencies manifest the original juvenile justice system's ideals of privacy, confidentiality, and informality. The second system provides a nonstigmatizing way to deal with many nonserious juvenile offenders. The net result of the second-system approach is greater discretion and less legal and administrative oversight to agencies dealing with diverted youngsters (Vito et al., 1998:16–18).

Notwithstanding the advantages that attend the second system for processing youngsters, the greatest danger seems to be the lack of due process guarantees. It almost seems as though the youngsters diverted from the formal juvenile justice system leave behind all the constitutional protections extended to them in cases like *Kent*, *Gault*, and *Winship*, cases discussed at length in chapter 5. Therefore, the net effect may be that minor offenders are dealt with less harshly and more informally but with few, if any, procedural protections.

A fourth outcome attributed to diversion is expanded coercion. Implicit in most diversion programs is voluntary participation and low levels of compulsion. In exchange for increased leniency, youngsters may have to submit to greater levels of constraint than normally would be expected. For instance, in order for juveniles to participate in many diversion programs, they first must admit to the allegations against them, even though there may not be enough evidence to prove delinquency should the case go to court. Consequently, juveniles may admit to delinquent behavior that is hard to prove in order to avoid going to court and taking a chance on being found delinquent. Often the parents and juvenile probation officers are part of the coercion when they perceive an easy way out for the child accused of relatively minor delinquent behavior.

Lack of program evaluation is the fifth problem. Polk (1984:657) best summarizes diversion evaluations when he says, "The contradictory record of juvenile diversion is not easy to read or interpret." Even two of diversion's most ardent supporters observe that "the empirical evidence concerning the consequences of diversion tends to be less than satisfactory" (Binder and Geis, 1984:626). We can infer from this statement that either one or both of the following are possibilities (see especially the debate between Binder and Geis, 1984; Polk, 1984):

- The research methods employed in studying and evaluating diversion have been deficient; thus, there is a lack of clarity or there are contradictory results.

- Research has been thorough and adequate, and some projects have been helpful to the children involved. By the same token, some efforts have had no effect, and some have been shown to be detrimental.

In the end, as policy makers and the public demand greater accountability, diversion programs will have to undergo thorough and ongoing evaluations.

A final contention is that diversion programs simply do not work, or—even worse—they cannot work: that is, they can demonstrate no positive outcomes for the children participating in them. Curran believes that diversion has not worked because it has not really been tried: "The system did not fail because of the concept; the concept failed because of the system" (1988:374). Others (for example, Polk, 1984) view diversion as a fatally flawed ideal. It was a noble experiment, they note, but it has unanticipated, negative consequences. These juvenile justice system observers suggest that we have enough research concerning the negative nature of most diversionary programs to abandon most such endeavors immediately.

Part of the difficulty in the area of diversion is that there may be lingering definitional disagreements or lack of consensus among the justice agencies involved in the diversion process. It is important to remember that after three decades of experience, there are still definitional differences over what constitutes diversion. Two conclusions we might be able to draw from our experiences nationwide are that (1) diversion programs are highly desirable and that they should be part of the juvenile justice system, but (2) we do not always agree on what these programs should do and with whom.

SUMMARY

Sometimes we view the steps early in the juvenile justice process as not being very important. Therefore, our focus is deflected to the more "serious" decisions occurring during and after adjudication. It is important to remember that only a fairly small number of youngsters ever make it to the point of a juvenile court delinquency hearing, and before a delinquency case ever makes it to court, a lot of decisions are made and actions taken by individuals in the juvenile justice system. These decisions and actions can have major consequences for accused delinquents, who can be turned away from formal processing or can be pulled further into the system at this point. For them, and indeed for all children processed by the police and the juvenile court's intake mechanism, the preliminary processing stages are significant.

Two preadjudicatory alternatives—detention and diversion—are especially momentous for suspected youthful offenders. After arrest, virtually all youths will be released into their parents' or guardians' custody awaiting the next court hearing. The immediate assumption in most cases is that only the most dangerous juveniles, or those with the highest risk of flight, are to be detained, but this turns out not to be the case.

Some of the most dangerous youngsters will be held in secure detention prior to adjudication, but so will many nondangerous youths. Many of the adolescents facing detention will spend from a few hours to a few weeks in a juvenile detention center with other youngsters awaiting adjudication. Some will spend time in police lockups or county jails. Generally speaking, those youths undergoing preadjudication detention will be processed further into the juvenile justice system, but why do nonserious offenders get detained as well? There are no simple answers to this question, but there are some obvious explanations.

First, preadjudication detention is used to teach some youngsters a lesson. Parents, the police, and juvenile justice workers may believe that a little taste of incarceration will deter most youths from future misbehavior. This assumption may be correct, but what if it is not? Some of the juveniles held in detention will suffer serious physical or emotional harm as a result of even a short confinement period.

Second, many jurisdictions in the United States do not have adequate alternatives to secure detention, so the choice is to detain or do nothing. To be safe, detention will be authorized if there seems to be any possibility of future misbehavior or flight by the accused delinquent. In many jurisdictions that do not have secure confinement alternatives, there is no separate juvenile detention facility. Therefore, to make a bad situation even worse, juveniles who are detained will be housed in the adult jail.

Once a detention decision has been made, court intake workers, often in conjunction with the prosecuting attorney's office, will decide whether to file a petition, and what charges to allege. The prosecutor's office plays an increasingly important role in this process, and now legal sufficiency often overrides the social concerns that may be raised by court workers.

The next chapter deals with the youngsters against whom delinquency petitions are filed, but what about youths who need some type of service but do not need formal adjudication and incarceration? A whole network of agencies and programs has developed nationwide since the mid-1970s to divert the least serious offenders from the formal juvenile justice process. These diversionary projects have removed large numbers of first offenders, minor offenders, and particularly, property offenders from the juvenile court's purview. The youngsters who have ended up in these programs have been required to make restitution to crime victims, to perform community service, and to be involved in various kinds of counseling. While diversion efforts have deflected many adolescents from the formal criminal justice system, those adolescents often have reappeared in the second system of private or quasi-private agencies that materialized when state and federal diversion dollars became available.

Many diversion programs began with an almost religious zeal. As with many other innovations in juvenile justice, diversion programs began with a great deal of promise but eventually raised many questions about their intentions and effectiveness. Diversion advocates cannot afford to ignore the criticisms, even though they may result in some programs being discontinued and others being modified.

Today diversion programs are a conspicuous part of the juvenile justice system, but questions regarding net widening and effectiveness continue to haunt many of these programs. In the end, we must ask ourselves what we intend diversion to accomplish. A follow-up to this is to determine how we can make sure diversion performs up to our expectations. To do less is to allow projects to exist that are ineffective or, worse, counterproductive.

In all likelihood diversion is with us to stay, but in cases where tax dollars are being expended there may be additional calls for accountability. Are these programs simply accepting the best cases and then proclaiming success? Can they be effective (and less costly) when dealing with tougher delinquency cases? Should diversion programs also handle the tougher cases, or are they dealing with the appropriate populations now? These and similar questions will continue to confront us for decades to come.

CRITICAL REVIEW QUESTIONS

1. After reading the chapter, review Jerome's situation. How likely is such a scenario?

2. What do you see as the major difference(s) between adult pretrial detention decisions and those for juveniles?

3. What juvenile detention facilities are best equipped to handle the problems of youngsters? Which are the worst equipped? What are these unique problems?

4. Would you add or remove characteristics or qualifications for those who should not be detained and those who may be detained? What would you add to or subtract from the lists of mitigating and aggravating circumstances?

5. Compare and contrast the legal and extralegal factors that have an impact on the use of pretrial detention. Did any factors on either list surprise you?

6. Labeling theory appeared several times in this chapter. Also, the 1967 presidential commission report acknowledged the role of criminal associations,

suggesting that diversion may remove youths from corrupting influences. How do you respond to critics who suggest that these arguments constitute a smoke screen for the real reasons behind diversion, deinstitutionalization, and decarceration? (*Hint*: Check out one of the endnotes in this chapter.)

7. Compare and contrast diversionary philosophy, purposes, and practices, including in your answer what you consider any inconsistencies.

8. In what ways were each of the following policies ill conceived: jail removal initiative, deinstitutionalization of status offenders, and decarceration.

9. Is there a simple answer to the question, Does preadjudicatory diversion work? (If yes is your answer, give it. If you answer in the negative, tell why a simple answer is difficult.)

RECOMMENDED READINGS

Feld, Barry C., ed. (1999). *Readings in Juvenile Justice Administration*. New York: Oxford. This edited book is useful for two reasons. First, Feld provides a compilation of many seminal works on the juvenile court and juvenile justice. Second, the work contains a number of very useful recent articles with legal perspectives on juvenile justice. Of particular interest to this chapter are the entries entitled "Detention" (by Snyder and Sickmund) and "Preventive Detention and the Judicial Prediction of Dangerousness for Juveniles" (by Fagan and Guggenheim).

Feld, Barry C. (2003). *Juvenile Justice Administration*. St. Paul, MN: West Group. Feld's book primarily is a text designed to give law school students a quick summary of the juvenile justice system and juvenile justice processes in the United States. However, this little paperback book is easily readable and understandable by undergraduate students as well. Chapter 4, "Preliminary Procedures: Intake and Diversion" and chapter 5, "Pretrial Detention" are especially pertinent to the material covered in the present chapter.

Roberts, Albert R., ed. (2004). *Juvenile Justice Sourcebook*. New York: Oxford University Press. In essence, this is a one-volume encyclopedia on juvenile justice. Of particular interest to students concerned about detention and diversion are chapter 8 by Roberts entitled "The Emergence and Proliferation of Juvenile Diversion Programs," and chapter 10 by David Roush, entitled "Juvenile Detention."

KEY TERMS

decarceration
deinstitutionalization of
    status offenders (DSO)
detention
detention hearings
foster home
group homes
informal adjustments
jail removal initiative
juvenile detention centers
labeling theory

net widening
new diversion
preadjudication diversion
preventive detention
primary deviance
second system
secondary deviance
third-party custody
traditional diversion
Youth Services Bureau (YSB)

NOTES

[1] See Roush (2004) for an extended discussion of this distinction.

[2] The King County conditions under which detention may be used have been edited for simplicity and to provide more generalizable statements.

[3] Scull (1977) provides a brilliant and disturbing critique of decarceration. He argues that decarceration of both the mentally ill and criminals—whom he calls "the mad and the bad"—was motivated not by liberal ideology and the need for change, but by money. That is, Scull believes the state saw decarceration as a way to save money and pass along the costs of treating the mad and the bad to existing community-based welfare mechanisms.

[4] A reconciliation meeting, like the one proposed in our opening vignette by Ms. Johnson for Jerome and his "victims," is similar to a mediation session, although there is less question of conflict and more concern for reestablishing community harmony and balance in reconciliation than in mediation. The concept of balance is discussed at length in the final chapter of the text.

JUVENILE COURT PROCESSES

* * *

Sixteen-year-old Denise Watson had been charged with shoplifting more than $200 worth of compact discs. Although she had been in legal trouble twice before in the past year, this was her first trip to juvenile court. The first time she had been arrested, also for shoplifting, the store management dropped the charges after her mother told the store owner that Denise had never before been in trouble with the police (true) and a shoplifting "conviction" would ruin her chances for getting into college (probably false). After a second arrest two months later, this time for curfew violation and solicitation for prostitution, Denise had been screened into a pretrial diversionary program for suspected gang members after a 20-minute meeting with a probation officer. She attended all the sessions but found it hard to give up her friends. Indeed, at the time of her third arrest, Denise had been with four friends who were engaged in a blitz shoplifting spree—in the same store as her first arrest. Only Denise had been caught, and she had refused to give up her friends—hence today's trip to court.

Denise sat quietly next to her mother and older brother (who also had been to juvenile court), looking around the crowded courtroom. Some youngsters were represented by attorneys, usually public defenders; some were not. Some had both parents with them, but many did not. It was a bewildering array of activity, not much of which made sense.

Denise had been assured by her mother, brother, and the public defender that the court had much more serious cases than hers, and that in all likelihood she would receive probation. Nevertheless, in the back of the teenager's mind were questions: Which judge would be there that day? Would the judge be a man or a woman? Would the judge be in a good mood or a bad one? What if the judge was in a bad mood? Might he or she decide to send Denise to the state training school for girls? The cool, confident demeanor that had been so evident when she was arrested had now given way to genuine fear.

A wave of movement interrupted her thoughts as people sitting around Denise physically shifted their attention to the front of the courtroom. The din of conversation stopped as if a switch had been thrown. A woman in a uniform like that worn by sheriff's deputies had casually shifted her body from leaning against a doorjamb at the front of the courtroom to a more upright position. She spoke in a loud voice: "All persons having business before this court please rise. The Honorable Jason McCord, presiding."

At that moment, as if on cue, a tall, slender man in a partially fastened black robe entered the courtroom from the door next to the bailiff. Denise could see that he wore blue jeans and a casual shirt under the trappings of public office. On his feet were expensive name-brand sneakers. He stumbled slightly as he stepped up to the elevated desk in front of the courtroom. "This guy doesn't look much like a judge," Denise observed, speaking softly to herself as she, along with the rest of the "audience," sat down.

"He's a real cherry. He was just sworn in as a juvenile judge 'bout two months ago," said a woman sitting to Denise's right. Denise sat upright, shocked and embarrassed, not realizing that she had spoken her thoughts aloud. The older woman shifted her body toward Denise and continued, her voice a conspiratorial whisper: "I always come to watch the new ones. They're a real treat. I read in the paper that he just returned from some kind of judge's school out in Nevada. Guess this one needed to learn 'bout being a judge. Looks of him, he flunked most of the courses," she said, chuckling.

Denise watched intently as Judge McCord shuffled through a stack of papers on his desk. He paused, looking out at the assembled court watchers, defendants, family members, and attorneys. His lips moved but Denise could hear nothing. The bailiff leaned over to the judge, holding her hand in front of her mouth. Nodding, Judge McCord flicked a switch at the base of the microphone stand on his desk, causing a loud, crackling electronic noise to fill the courtroom. "As I was saying," Judge McCord said, his unwavering voice taking on an authoritative air, "this session of juvenile court will come to order. We have a busy docket, and I would like to expedite matters a bit by asking all of you accused of first-time possession of alcohol by a minor to stand."

About one-third of those in attendance stood, accompanied by the sounds of shuffling feet and nervous whispers. The judge spoke again: "Great. OK. Do you waive the reading of the formal petitions? All those who wish to respond in the affirmative, raise your right hand."

After a few seconds of discussion among the accused persons and their family members or lawyers, a flurry of right hands appeared in the crowded courtroom. "Great," continued Judge McCord, "I now find in favor of the charges and specifications contained in your respective petitions. You are hereby ordered to participate in the county's 'Smart Choices' alcohol education program and return within one month with a certificate of completion. Anyone failing to complete this program will be fined the maximum allowable under the law and, for those with driver's licenses, lose all driving privileges for six months. Those of you returning with your certificates will have this petition expunged from your records. Is this clear?"

The youths standing responded with a mixture of "yeahs," "yes, sirs" and silent head shakes. "I said, 'Is this clear?'" Judge McCord inquired, his voice taking on an insistent tone that left no question as to the answer he wanted. "YES, SIR!" came the reply in unison.

"Fine. Now please clear the courtroom because we have a number of serious cases remaining on the docket. We'll go in reverse alphabetical order. First, there is the matter of the State versus Denise Watson. Are Ms. Watson and her counsel present today?"

"Looks like I was off the mark," the old woman said to Denise. "Guess he didn't flunk all them classes."

Denise looked down at her feet. It was going to be a long day.

* * *

America's juvenile courts are filled daily with youngsters like Denise. Her case is so common that any name could be substituted and the facts would look virtually the same. In this chapter we will examine the creation, structure, and operations of juvenile courts in the United States from the beginning until the present.

In some ways, the juvenile court is the cornerstone upon which the juvenile justice system has been built. As it was originally established, the juvenile court was a unique entity in purpose and design. In the following sections we will deal with the notion of age as a distinguishing factor in the law and provide a brief overview of the creation of the first juvenile courts.

AGE AND THE LAW

As we have noted elsewhere, for much of recorded history children held no legal status apart from their parents. Furthermore, in terms of criminal law children were treated the same as adults. These two factors had clear implications in terms of Anglo-American law and the development of the first juvenile courts.

First, since children did not hold independent legal status, they were not able to transact business. There were also legal difficulties regarding their inheritance rights. As a result, the king would appoint one of his chancellors to safeguard the children's legal rights. These functions eventually evolved into **chancery law**, or equity law. The doctrine of *parens patriae*, which loosely translated means "father of the country," developed out of chancery law. Under this notion, the king was the father of the country, and his chancellors discharged his responsibilities in regard to children. With the juvenile court's development, the judge becomes the "father" (or "mother") of those children coming before the court.

Second, the notion of *mens rea*, a component of English law, was incorporated into the development of law in the United States. Dressler (2001) says that *mens rea* is viewed as having two meanings. The broad meaning of *mens rea* involves "a general notion of moral blameworthiness," while the narrow meaning is directed at the state of mind required by a criminal offender (Dressler, 2001:116–17).

Roman law originally provided an age-specific delineation for criminal intent. Later, under English common law, this distinction was refined. Briefly, common law held that:

1. Children under the age of 7 were *deemed incapable* of forming criminal intent. Thus, any act that normally would have constituted a crime—if committed by a person younger than 7—would not be a crime.

2. Children between the ages of 7 and 14 were *presumed incapable* of forming criminal intent. However, the state could produce enough evidence to convince the judge (or jury) that the child was capable of forming intent. As with most elements in criminal trials, the prosecutor had the burden of proof in the infancy defense.

3. Over the age of 14, children were *presumed capable* of forming criminal intent. In these cases, children were treated the same as adults before the law (see, for example, Feld, 2003:32–33).

Because the law did not treat older children any differently from their adult counterparts, concern began to emerge in the mid-nineteenth century over the criminal law's harshness. During this period, the concept of *parens patriae* was extended

---

Theoretical Reflections
Courts and Justice Gendering

Feminists—people who advocate social and political rights for women equal to those of men—have long viewed the judiciary as a source of **justice gendering**; that is, it imposes justice for women differently than it does for men. Liberal feminists contend that in criminal justice matters, women receive more lenient treatment prior to trial, such as less frequent use of pretrial jail detention. At sentencing, however, the results are less clear. Generally, given similar charges and criminal circumstances, women's sentences are less harsh than men's. There are two general exceptions to this observation: Women often receive harsher sanctions than men (1) if they engage in nontraditional female crimes (that is, those not normally engaged in by women, such as violent crimes or others largely in the domain of men), or (2) if they violate female sexual norms (that is, rules intended to control female sexuality). According to liberal feminists, the differences can be traced to a paternalistic court system that treats women and young girls as if they were the judges' wayward daughters.

Critical feminists look at the ways courts consolidate power in the hands of men, including male judges. Often the locus of control is the family, supported by the decisions of judges. For example, women who are dependent upon their fathers or husbands are more likely to receive probation than nondependent women. Other decisions that address the hardships caused by loss of the female family member also "genderize" the justice process by linking it to the family. Women are responsible for the care and comfort of others, while men provide for the family's financial well-being. Conse-

quently, men and women without family responsibilities receive harsher sentences.

Outright gender-based discrimination may not cause differential treatment. What may be occurring instead is a concerted but uncoordinated effort to preserve and protect the nuclear family and its associated values system. This orientation has become pervasive in both the adult and juvenile justice systems. Perhaps nowhere is this perspective more evident than in the family preservation movement. This movement, long advanced by juvenile court judges, includes among its most important ideologies the notion of keeping the family unit together *at virtually any cost*. Failing in this, children are assigned to the female parent, largely on the basis of the bias noted by feminists for viewing women as caregivers and men as providers.

Two criminological perspectives, one in the feminist tradition and one in the social control tradition, suggest that this is a flawed policy. First, liberal feminists such as Chesney-Lind warn us that many of the behaviors engaged in by young girls that eventually come to be viewed as deviant and delinquent behaviors are survival strategies, ways to live away from the homes and parents that pose real threats to their lives. Second, Agnew's general strain theory suggests that children, by running away from troubling family arrangements, may place themselves in delinquency's path. In both cases, forcing the child back into the family in the name of family preservation may create even worse criminogenic situations, sometimes deadly ones.

Sources: Agnew (1992); Bernstein et al. (1977); Chesney-Lind (1989a); Daly (1987, 1989); Nagel (1983); and Simpson (1989).

to a newly emerging social welfare movement in the United States. The result was the creation of the first juvenile court. In the following section we will examine the forces that combined to give rise to the first court exclusively for children.

A NEW COURT IS ESTABLISHED

In chapter 2 we identified the social, economic, and political forces behind the creation of Chicago's juvenile court in 1899. This innovation took as its primary legal philosophy the English common-law doctrine of *parens patriae*. As a result of this orientation the court was not concerned with the determination of guilt and punishment, as were adult criminal courts. Instead, the juvenile court was to be nonpunitive, nonstigmatizing, and therapeutic. Children coming before the court were not held fully liable for their actions, and the primary presumption was that children who violate the law are in need of treatment more than punishment.

Three procedural features defined the juvenile court's helping philosophy:

1. Court hearings were *confidential*—the feeling was that children accused of offenses should not be held up to public scorn. Therefore, the names of accused delinquents were not reported to the news media, and court hearings were closed to all but the parties involved in the case.

2. Court hearings were *informal*—informality was expressed in the absence of formal courtroom trappings (such as the judge's robe and bench) and also a lack of adherence to formal legal procedures such as jury trials and rules of evidence.

3. Court hearings were *nonadversarial*—in simplest terms, an attorney represented neither side.

In order to demonstrate more fully how the court was designed to work and why some of its initial ideals were not fulfilled, in the next sections we review the original juvenile court.

JURISDICTION OF THE JUVENILE COURT

With any court discussion, the concept of **jurisdiction** is critical. Champion (2005:139) says that jurisdiction is "the power of a court to hear and determine a particular type of case" and that it also "refers to [a] territory within which [a] court may exercise authority." Thus, jurisdiction deals with the legal authority to hear certain kinds of cases (see Sanborn and Salerno, 2005:50–65). Jurisdiction is not a singular concept, however. When considering juvenile courts, we can treat the jurisdictional issue as having three dimensions: geography, age, and subject matter.

GEOGRAPHICAL JURISDICTION

Geographical jurisdiction is a concern in every criminal case, and while it is technically not synonymous with venue, it must be considered in conjunction with venue. According to Champion, **venue** is "the area over which a judge exercises authority to act in an official capacity" or "the place where a trial is held" (2005:260).

AGE JURISDICTION

We have previously discussed the importance of age as a factor in processing juvenile cases. Age is a fairly straightforward issue in some ways, and in other ways it is very complicated. Historically, for juvenile courts, three particular ages have been important:

- minimum age jurisdiction
- maximum age jurisdiction
- age at which juveniles can be tried as adults

We will consider each of these in turn, beginning with the minimum age.

Minimum Age Jurisdiction

With juvenile courts, minimum age jurisdiction is the least definitive of the age factors that must be addressed. By this, we mean that there is great variation in the minimum age jurisdiction specified from state to state. For example, at the end of 1999 only 16 states specified a minimum age for juvenile court jurisdiction:

- age 6—North Carolina
- age 7—Maryland, Massachusetts, and New York
- age 8—Arizona
- age 10—Arkansas, Colorado, Kansas, Louisiana, Minnesota, Mississippi, Pennsylvania, South Dakota, Texas, Vermont, and Wisconsin (Sickmund, 2003:3).

All other states do not specify a minimum age at which the juvenile court's jurisdiction begins. They rely on case law or the common law classifications. This approach may require judges to decide on a case-by-case basis whether the child is appropriate for juvenile court disposition.

Walker discusses the concept of *innocentia consilii*, or "innocence of purpose." He says that 7 years old "was the age at which both Roman law and the Church assumed that a child began to know good from evil" (Walker, 1983:23). Therefore, as various states began to develop their juvenile codes, many adopted 7 as the minimum age of juvenile court jurisdiction (see Gardner, 2003).

The reporting system of the Office of Juvenile Justice and Delinquency Prevention (OJJDP) handles the variation in minimum age by creating a category entitled "youth at risk population." Because there are so few youngsters under the age of 10 processed for delinquent or status offenses, OJJDP considers the **youth at risk population** to be the number of youngsters between the ages of 10 and the upper age limit for the juvenile court (OJJDP, 2004).

Maximum Age Jurisdiction

Unlike juvenile courts' minimum age stipulation, the maximum age limit is very clearly defined by each state. Table 5.1 shows the upper age limits utilized by the various states. As is readily apparent, the most common age at which juvenile court jurisdiction ends is 17. Thus, in 37 states and the District of Columbia, individuals 18 years old will be processed as adults.

Table 5.1   Maximum Jurisdictional Age for Juvenile Courts

Age 15	Age 16	Age 17	
Connecticut	Georgia	Alabama	Montana
New York	Illinois	Alaska	Nebraska
North Carolina	Louisiana	Arizona	Nevada
	Massachusetts	Arkansas	New Jersey
	Michigan	California	New Mexico
	Missouri	Colorado	North Dakota
	New Hampshire	Delaware	Ohio
	South Carolina	District of Columbia	Oklahoma
	Texas	Florida	Oregon
	Wisconsin	Hawaii	Pennsylvania
		Idaho	Rhode Island
		Indiana	South Dakota
		Iowa	Tennessee
		Kansas	Utah
		Kentucky	Vermont
		Maine	Virginia
		Maryland	Washington
		Minnesota	West Virginia
		Mississippi	Wyoming

Source: Sickmund (2003:3).

Although the maximum jurisdictional age is defined by state juvenile codes, there may be deviations from this standard in three situations. First, some states exclude certain offenses from juvenile court. At the least serious end of the scale, traffic offenses are commonly excluded from juvenile court. In most jurisdictions, juvenile traffic cases appear in the same courts designated to hear adult traffic cases or in specialized juvenile traffic courts. At the other end of the scale, some states exclude very serious offenses, such as murder, particularly when committed by older juveniles (see Feld, 2003:179–80).

Second, the juvenile court often has jurisdiction over nondelinquent acts. In cases involving dependency and neglect, juvenile courts may exercise jurisdiction over adults who contribute to a child's status. Additionally, the juvenile court may exercise jurisdiction in those cases where an offense was committed by a 17-year-old who became 18 before adjudication could occur. Although these cases are not uncommon, juvenile courts do not necessarily deal with them in large numbers.

Third, the juvenile court has another option for dealing with adult-like behavior: It can transfer youngsters who have not yet turned 18 to adult criminal courts. **Transfer** is also known as waiver of jurisdiction, certification, remand, or binding over for criminal prosecution (Sickmund, 2003:4).

Age at which Juveniles Can Be Tried as Adults

Generally speaking, states can employ one of four methods (or some combination of methods) for deciding which juveniles should be transferred to adult court. The most common method of deciding transfers is through **judicial waiver.** This system is utilized by 46 states and the decisions can be discretionary, presumptive, or mandatory. At the end of 1999 every state except Massachusetts, Nebraska, New Mexico, and New York (along with the District of Columbia) had provisions for judicially waiving juvenile offenders to adult courts (Sickmund, 2003:4).

In judicial transfers, state statutes give juvenile court judges the authority to conduct hearings to determine the suitability of transferring jurisdiction to criminal court. In most instances, only two grounds will support these transfers: public safety and lack of amenability to treatment. The public safety justification is utilized in cases where a youngster has committed an especially serious personal crime, such as homicide, armed robbery, or rape. In these instances, the juvenile need not have an extensive history of delinquency. One serious offense is sufficient to justify trying some juveniles, particularly 16- and 17-year-old youths, as adults. It is important to note that these cases constitute a very small portion of all the cases transferred yearly to criminal courts.

The lack of amenability to treatment justification typically is applied to youngsters who have persistent offense histories. Often these are property offenders who have passed through the juvenile justice system multiple times and for whom the juvenile court has imposed a variety of different sanctions. Transfers give the juvenile justice system an option for dealing with youngsters who are bothersome, although not particularly dangerous, offenders. At some point, as these youths get older, the juvenile judge and the court staff tire of dealing with persistent offenders and order them to stand trial as adults based on a lack of amenability to treatment in the juvenile justice system.

Fifteen states also utilize concurrent jurisdiction whereby cases can be filed in juvenile court or directly in the adult criminal courts. This second transfer system is called **prosecutorial waiver** or **direct file.** This mechanism allows the prosecuting attorney to decide in which court the case will be filed. In states such as Florida the juvenile courts and the adult criminal courts have concurrent jurisdiction over many delinquent offenses. Therefore, the prosecutor has the option of taking a case to the juvenile court or filing charges directly with the criminal court. This system is used in only 15 states and the District of Columbia, but it illustrates the "get-tough" orientation many jurisdictions have taken toward juvenile offenders (Bishop et al., 1999; Butts and Mears, 2001).

In the states that provide for concurrent jurisdiction, juveniles as young as 12 and as old as 16 may be eligible for adult court processing. Interestingly, in the OJJDP's report *Juveniles in Court*, Sickmund notes that "no national data exist on the number of juvenile cases tried in criminal court under concurrent jurisdiction provisions" (2003:9). However, Florida—the state that probably employs this approach most frequently—had more than 4,000 cases filed in adult courts by prosecutors in the 1998–99 fiscal year.

Increasingly, in many states the largest number of transfers to adult court comes under legislative provisions excluding certain offenses from juvenile court jurisdiction, known as the **legislative waiver** or **statutory exclusion.** These automatic waivers occur in 29 states, and they typically include the most serious offenses (such as murder and other crimes against persons) and the least serious offenses (such as traffic and game and fish violations). Whether it is to demonstrate toughness toward serious juvenile crime or to preserve the juvenile justice system's resources, legislatures often define certain offenses as outside the juvenile court's jurisdiction.

The final transfer mechanism is **demand waiver.** A small number of states allow juveniles and their parents or guardians to request a transfer to adult court. While this seems like an inconceivable option, it is likely to be requested for at least two reasons. First, in states that do not provide juveniles with jury trials, a demand waiver will give a youthful offender the chance to present his or her case to a jury. Second, it is possible that in some cases there are treatment resources available in the adult system (for example, for sex offenders) that might not be available in the juvenile system. Table 5.2 summarizes the provisions under which juveniles may be transferred. Table 5.3 lists the ages and offense criteria for transferring juveniles in each state. Note that many states employ the concept of "once an adult, always an adult." This means that juveniles who have already been tried as adults must be tried as adults for subsequent offenses. In nearly all cases, the juvenile must have been convicted on the initial offense in order for this provision to apply.

SUBJECT-MATTER JURISDICTION

It is in the area of subject-matter jurisdiction that we see the greatest distinction between adult criminal courts and juvenile courts. For the most part, adult courts deal with criminal matters. Some cases may be felonies and some misdemeanors, but in every instance there are clearly defined norms and clearly described penalties. This is not the situation for cases over which the juvenile court has jurisdiction. Historically, juvenile courts had jurisdiction over cases that fit into categories such as delinquency, dependency, neglect, or abuse. In this section we will define each category to illustrate the breadth of the court's jurisdiction and the difficulty the juvenile court has had in being all things to all people (see, for example, Butts and Mears, 2001; Fox, 1996).

Delinquency

This is the easiest term to define. As we noted in chapter 1, a delinquent act is any act committed by a child (a person under a specified age who is subject to the juvenile court's jurisdiction) that would be a crime if committed by an adult. Puzzanchera and associates say that a delinquent act is

> An act committed by a juvenile which, if committed by an adult, would be a criminal act. The juvenile court has jurisdiction over delinquent acts. Delinquent acts include crimes against persons, crimes against property, drug offenses, and crimes against public order. (2004:79)

As originally conceived, the juvenile court's delinquency jurisdiction extended to offenses that *would not* be crimes if committed by adults. These acts were known as **status offenses** and they included behaviors like running away from home, truancy, tobacco and alcohol violations, and other ambiguous categories such as ungovernability, unruliness, or incorrigibility. The treatment of status offenses and status offenders in the United States has undergone many changes over the past three decades. For this reason we will spend additional time later in the chapter addressing the juvenile court's jurisdiction over status offenses.

Table 5.2 Summary of Transfer Provisions, 1999

State	Judicial waiver			Direct File	Statutory exclusion	Reverse waiver	Once an adult/ always an adult
	Discre- tionary	Man- datory	Pre- sumptive				
Total states	46	15	16	15	29	24	34
Alabama	n				n		n
Alaska	n		n		n		
Arizona	n		n	n	n	n	n
Arkansas	n				n	n	
California	n		n		n		n
Colorado	n		n	n		n	
Connecticut		n				n	
Delaware	n	n			n	n	n
District of Columbia	n		n	n			n
Florida	n			n	n		n
Georgia	n			n	n	n	
Hawaii	n						n
Idaho	n				n		n
Illinois	n	n	n		n		n
Indiana	n	n			n		n
Iowa	n				n	n	n
Kansas	n		n				n
Kentucky	n	n				n	
Louisiana	n	n		n	n		
Maine	n		n				n
Maryland	n				n	n	n
Massachusetts				n	n		
Michigan	n			n			n
Minnesota	n		n		n		n
Mississippi	n				n		n
Missouri	n						n
Montana	n			n	n	n	
Nebraska				n		n	
Nevada	n		n		n	n	n
New Hampshire	n		n				n
New Jersey	n	n	n				
New Mexico					n		
New York					n	n	
North Carolina	n	n					n
North Dakota	n	n	n				n
Ohio	n	n					n
Oklahoma	n			n	n	n	
Oregon	n				n	n	n
Pennsylvania	n		n		n	n	n
Rhode Island	n	n	n				n
South Carolina	n	n			n	n	
South Dakota	n				n	n	n
Tennessee	n					n	n
Texas	n						n
Utah	n		n		n		n
Vermont	n			n	n	n	
Virginia	n	n		n		n	n
Washington	n				n		n
West Virginia	n	n					
Wisconsin	n				n	n	n
Wyoming	n			n		n	

Legend: "n" indicates the provision(s) allowed by each state as of the end of the 1999 legislative session.
Source: Sickmund (2003).

Table 5.3   Judicial Waiver: Minimum Age and Offense Criteria, 1999

State	Any criminal offense	Certain felonies	Capital crimes	Murder	Certain offenses Person offenses	Property offenses	Drug offenses	Weapon offenses
Alabama	14							
Alaska	NS				NS			
Arizona		NS						
Arkansas		14	14	14	14			14
California	16	16		14	14	14	14	
Colorado		12		12	12			
Connecticut		14	14	14				
Delaware	NS	15		NS	NS	16	16	
District of Columbia	16	15		15	15	15		NS
Florida	14							
Georgia	15		13	14	14	15		
Hawaii		14		NS				
Idaho	14	NS		NS	NS	NS	NS	
Illinois	13	15						
Indiana	14	NS		10			16	
Iowa	14	15						
Kansas	10	14			14		14	
Kentucky		14	14					
Louisiana				14	14			
Maine		NS		NS	NS			
Maryland	15		NS					
Michigan		14						
Minnesota		14						
Mississippi	13							
Missouri		12						
Montana	NS							
Nevada	14	14			14			
New Hampshire		15		13	13		15	
New Jersey	14	14		14	14	14	14	14
North Carolina		13	13					
North Dakota	16	14		14	14		14	
Ohio		14		14	16	16		
Oklahoma		NS						
Oregon		15		NS	NS	15		
Pennsylvania		14			15	15		
Rhode Island		16	NS		17	17		
South Carolina	16	14		NS	NS		14	14
South Dakota		NS						
Tennessee	16			NS	NS			
Texas		14	14				14	
Utah	14			16	16	16		16
Vermont				10	10	10		
Virginia		14		14	14			
Washington	NS							
West Virginia		NS		NS	NS	NS	NS	
Wisconsin	15	14		14	14	14	14	
Wyoming	13							

Note: "NS" indicates "none specified."
Source: Adapted from Sickmund (2003); Griffin (2000).

Dependency

The second category of traditional juvenile court jurisdiction involves **dependency** cases. Dependency is not something a child does; it is a condition in which the child is found. Some legal scholars have defined dependency as a state of want or need in which a child is found, but which exists through no fault of the parents or guardians (McCarthy, Patton, and Carr, 2003:347). Dependency might exist where the parents fail to provide adequate clothing and shelter for the child but, given their financial limitations, are unable to do so. With this kind of jurisdiction, the juvenile court can intervene to help the child and the family as well. Dependent children can also include youngsters who have been abandoned or who are orphaned (Smithburn, 2002:385ff.).

Neglect and Abuse

The third category of subject-matter jurisdiction for the juvenile court includes **neglect** and, in its most extreme form, **abuse**. Like dependency, neglected children are in a state of want or need. Unlike dependency, neglected children are in this condition as a result of a deliberate act, or failure to act, on the part of the parents or guardians (McCarthy et al., 2003; Smithburn, 2002).

In most dependency and neglect cases, the juvenile court intercedes with the family through some social services agency. In child abuse or endangerment cases, the court may remove children from the home temporarily or may permanently suspend the parents' rights. In extreme abuse cases, particularly when a child has been killed, the prosecuting attorney will move the case to the criminal courts and prosecute under the state's child abuse or endangerment statutes.

For the most part, the contemporary juvenile court's jurisdiction focuses almost exclusively on delinquency cases. As a result, there is an ongoing debate over the court's role in nondelinquency matters. Although delinquency may be related to abuse and neglect, there is disagreement over whether the juvenile court can or should deal with such cases (chapter 9 will address this issue at length). Most people agree that social services agencies are much better equipped than courts to deal with such cases.

THE ACTORS IN THE JUVENILE COURTS

Many professionals play critical roles in the processing of juvenile court cases. Some of these individuals would be present in practically any juvenile court you might attend. Others might appear on occasion or only in certain courts. Given local variations, it is nearly impossible to describe all the people who potentially could be involved in juvenile cases. Therefore, we will deal with the major participants in the juvenile court process.

JUDGES

Perhaps the one person who has defined the juvenile court throughout its history is the juvenile court judge. Such judges have faced several issues in the first

100-plus years of the juvenile court's existence, but one of the most crucial has been their qualifications.

The first juvenile courts were confidential, informal, and nonadversarial. Judges presiding over these original courts were expected to act as kindly, protective parents who were concerned with the child's best interests. Therefore, the primary qualification sought was an orientation to children. Julian W. Mack (1909), one of the nation's first juvenile court judges, emphasized the juvenile judge's significant role in carrying out the court's benevolent *parens patriae* philosophy.

**Box 5.1   International Perspectives
Juvenile Courts in Singapore**

We have a tendency to think of the juvenile court as unique to the United States. However, the model of a separate court for youthful offenders has been embraced by many nations around the world. A good example is the juvenile court of the Republic of Singapore.

Singapore originally was a British colony, eventually a crown colony, and finally a part of the Commonwealth of Nations. In 1965 Singapore separated from Malaysia and became a sovereign nation; however, the British influence is still apparent in its governmental structure, particularly its courts. The juvenile court of Singapore was created in 1949 by the Children and Young Persons Ordinance. Unlike juvenile courts in the United States, the juvenile court of Singapore is presided over by a magistrate and two lay advisors appointed by the President of the Republic.

The juvenile court of Singapore has jurisdiction over children, defined as persons under 14 years of age, and young persons, defined as persons above 14 but below 16 years of age. Much like juvenile courts in the United States, the juvenile court of Singapore deals with youngsters who have violated the law as well as those who are beyond parental control and those in need of care and protective orders. The latter category includes juveniles who have been neglected or abused.

In making decisions about the court's disposition of juvenile cases, the court takes into consideration the following seven factors:

• rehabilitating and reforming offenders

• removing youngsters from undesirable circumstances

• promoting the child's education and welfare

• providing victim compensation

• protecting the public

• decreasing the risk of future offending

• punishing law violators

The juvenile court of Singapore has a number of dispositional options when it comes to discharging juvenile cases: (1) the case may be dismissed, (2) the youngster can be placed in the care of a relative "or other fit person," (3) community service can be ordered, (4) the juvenile can be placed on probation, (5) detention (including weekend detention) can be imposed by the court, (6) the offender can be committed to a "Reformative Training Centre," or (7) the juvenile can be ordered to pay a fine, damages, or associated costs.

Source: "Subordinate Courts of Singapore—Juvenile Justice" (2004)
(http://www.juvenilecourtofsingapore.gov.sg/).

Fox (1996), in commenting on another of the country's first juvenile court judges, Ben Lindsey—the first such judge in Denver, Colorado—said that Lindsey viewed these children as "fundamentally good human beings whose going astray was largely attributable to their social and psychological environment." Lindsey "had no specific statutory authority to adopt his social worker-friend approach to the children who came before the court," but his view was that "formal adjudication of the charges was of minimal importance, and rehabilitation was everything" (Fox, 1996:35).

Many of the first juvenile courts were created as limited jurisdiction courts. That is, they had a narrowly defined subject-matter jurisdiction, procedures were informal, they did not conduct jury trials, they were not courts of record (they did not produce verbatim transcripts), and in most instances there were no attorneys present. In many ways, these early juvenile court judges resembled modern-day justices of the peace or magistrates. As a result of a long historical tradition in the United States, judges in juvenile courts were not required to be licensed attorneys or even to have attended law school.

Lack of legal training on the part of these lay judges was not viewed as a problem for much of the juvenile court's history, since the child was presumed not to be in legal jeopardy and the doctrine of *parens patriae* was assumed to govern all proceedings. However, as the U.S. Supreme Court imposed a constitutional due process orientation on the juvenile court during the 1960s and 1970s, the deficiencies of nonlawyer judges became increasingly apparent.

Most states now require juvenile judges to be licensed attorneys, even where the juvenile court is a court of limited jurisdiction. Anticipating the coming trend, as early as 1976 the National Advisory Committee on Criminal Justice Standards and Goals recommended that judges in juvenile or family courts "should be lawyers who possess a keen and demonstrated interest in the needs and problems of children and families" (1976:284). Therefore, the emphasis today is to a much greater extent on legal formality and the adversarial nature of the adjudication process, and juvenile court judges must possess some legal training in order to perform their duties adequately.

For decades, judges' attitudes, behaviors, and qualifications have been debated. Should the judge be a kindly, protective parent figure as originally envisioned, or should the judge be an individual trained in the law and committed to the constitutional principles of due process and equal protection? Are the two roles incompatible? While these questions have been settled in some jurisdictions, the debate over roles and qualifications continues in a few areas. Table 5.4 gives an overview of the qualifications of juvenile court judges in several states.

PROSECUTORS

Since the original juvenile court was to be nonadversarial, attorneys typically were not present for either side. In most instances the police served as "prosecutors" for the cases they brought before the court; some police departments had designated liaisons or court officers who, in effect, became the prosecutors.

Owing to cases like *Kent v. United States* (383 U.S. 541, 1966) and *In re Gault* (387 U.S. 1, 1967), the Supreme Court affirmed that a juvenile has the right to be

Table 5.4   Qualifications of Juvenile Court Judges in Selected States

State	Court name	Law degree required and other legal requirements
Colorado	Denver Juvenile	Yes; 5 years as state bar member
Delaware	Family Court	Yes; 5 years as state bar member
Georgia	Juvenile Court	Yes; 5 years as state bar member
Hawaii	Circuit Court and Family Court	Yes; 10 years as state bar member
Louisiana	Family Court	Yes; 5 years as state bar member
	Juvenile Court	Yes; 5 years as state bar member
Maryland	Orphan's Court	No; state bar member
Massachusetts	Juvenile Court	No; none
Mississippi	Family Court	Yes; 5 years in practice
Nebraska	Separate Juvenile Court	Yes; 5 years in practice
New York	Family Court	Yes; 10 years as state bar member
	Surrogate's Court	Yes; 10 years as state bar member
Rhode Island	Family Court	Yes; member of state bar
South Carolina	Family Court	Yes; 8 years as state bar member
Tennessee	Juvenile Court	Yes; qualified to practice law
Utah	Juvenile Court	Yes; member of state bar

Source: Rottman, Flango, Cantrell, Hansen, and LaFountain (2000).

represented by an attorney in delinquency proceedings. Therefore, because an accused delinquent is entitled to a defense attorney, most jurisdictions routinely provide a prosecuting attorney as well.

Historically, court intake or probation workers dominated the decision whether to file a petition on behalf of the child and what the appropriate charges should be. In the years following *In re Gault* and *In re Winship* (397 U.S. 358, 1970), prosecuting attorneys appeared with increasing frequency and eventually came to dominate the juvenile prosecution process (Butts and Mears, 2001).

Two factors about the prosecution of juvenile offenders must be mentioned. First, having a prosecutor present certainly defines the case as being adversarial. However, even though a prosecuting attorney represents the state, this does not mean that there will be a vigorous prosecution. Juvenile court judges are well known for constraining overzealous prosecutors and defense attorneys. Second, prosecuting attorneys' offices around the nation follow similar patterns in assigning assistant prosecutors to the juvenile court. In most instances the youngest, least-experienced assistant district attorney (or whatever the precise title) becomes the juvenile court prosecutor. This happens because of a long-standing tradition and a general feeling that less experienced attorneys can do the least damage in juvenile court.

DEFENSE ATTORNEYS

When juvenile courts maintained the myth that accused delinquent youngsters were not in legal jeopardy, it made very little sense to have defense attorneys represent these children. However, as the juvenile court's legal abuses of youngsters became more widely known and much criticized as a result of cases like *In re Gault* (discussed below), the need for defense attorneys became apparent. Two major Supreme Court decisions established and affirmed the right of juveniles to be represented by attorneys.

Kent v. United States

The U.S. Supreme Court heard its first juvenile justice case in 1966. In *Kent v. United States* the Court was asked to decide procedural due process rights for juveniles in a very narrow context. Kent was 16 at the time he was accused of committing a number of very serious crimes, including burglary and rape. When Kent came before the juvenile court in the District of Columbia, the judge ordered the case to be transferred to the U.S. District Court. Three fundamental issues were raised by this case:

1. Should there have been a transfer hearing, as set out in the District of Columbia juvenile code?

2. Should Kent have been provided an attorney during juvenile court proceedings?

3. Should defense attorneys for juvenile clients be provided access to the social records compiled for, and used by, the courts?

Justice Abe Fortas wrote the Court's majority opinion and addressed each of these issues. First, he noted that the juvenile court judge did not hold a transfer hearing and that no justification was given for the waiver. This action was in violation of the District of Columbia's juvenile code.

Second, Kent was interrogated without an attorney present, as was commonly done at that time, and also appeared before the juvenile court judge without legal representation. Justice Fortas emphasized that the right to counsel "is not a formality. It is not a grudging gesture to a ritualistic requirement. It is the essence of justice." As a result, the Court for the first time applied the right to counsel to all accused law violators irrespective of age.

Third, the Supreme Court felt that for an attorney to be effective in representing accused juveniles there must be access to the child's social history records. Probation officers and the court's staff typically compile these records, and they may contain unsubstantiated assertions and opinions. While these reports are not counted as evidence, they may serve as the basis for the court's disposition of the juvenile's case.

Kent v. United States is an important case for two reasons. First, it firmly established the right to counsel for juvenile offenders. Second, it called into question the juvenile court's nonadversarial nature and its supposed reliance on the underlying legal doctrine of *parens patriae*. What the Supreme Court did not do was challenge the juvenile court's essential nature. Instead, the Court emphasized ways in which procedural deficiencies could be corrected. However, *Kent* provided the mechanism for a broad-based assault on the traditional procedures of the juvenile court. That assault came the next year in the *Gault* case (see especially Manfredi, 1998).

In re Gault

Gerald Gault was 15 years old when he was arrested for making obscene phone calls to a neighbor. The arrest occurred while his parents were both at work, and at no time were they notified of the arrest. A probation officer filed a petition alleging Gault's delinquent behavior but never fully specified the nature of the delinquency. At the first hearing the complainant did not appear to testify against Gault, and at a second hearing six days later the juvenile judge committed Gault to the Arizona Industrial School until his twenty-first birthday "unless sooner discharged by due process of law." This disposition far exceeded that applicable in the case of an adult. An adult charged with the same offense could have received a fine of between $5 and $50 and a maximum jail sentence of two months.

Among the due process rights alleged to have been denied Gault were:

- notice of charges
- right to counsel
- right to confront and cross-examine accusing witnesses
- protection against self-incrimination
- right to a transcript
- right to appellate review

Justice Fortas, who had written the majority opinion in *Kent*, wrote again for the majority in *Gault*. Fortas emphasized that constitutional due process protections, as provided for in the Bill of Rights and applied to the states by way of the Fourteenth Amendment, were not just for adults. Therefore, the right to notification of charges and the right to counsel were both affirmed. In regard to the right to counsel, the Court said:

> In respect of proceedings to determine delinquency which may result in commitment to an institution in which the juvenile's freedom is curtailed, the child and his parents must be notified of the child's right to be represented by counsel retained by them, or if they are unable to afford counsel, that counsel will be appointed to represent the child. (387 U.S. 41, 1967)

In addressing the issue of confrontation and cross-examination, the Court said that "no reason is suggested or appears for a different rule in respect of sworn testimony in juvenile courts than in adult tribunals" (387 U.S. 56, 1967). The Court clearly stated that "it would be surprising if the privilege against self-incrimination were available to hardened criminals but not to children" (387 U.S. 47, 1967). Thus, it affirmed that the protection against self-incrimination applied to juveniles as well as to adults.

The *Gault* decision opened the juvenile court to a whole range of due process procedures and protections. Perhaps the most significant conclusion the Court drew was that "juvenile proceedings to determine 'delinquency,' which may lead to commitment to a state institution, must be regarded as 'criminal'" (387 U.S. 49, 1967) in regard to due process protections. Although the Court declined to fully declare the juvenile court a criminal court on a par with adult courts, Justice Fortas noted, "Under our Constitution, the condition of being a boy does not justify a kangaroo court."

In concluding this section on defense attorneys in the juvenile court, we need to make several observations. First, like their adult counterparts, juveniles now have the right to counsel when they are accused of delinquent behavior (Rubin, 1996). This puts them on equal footing with adult criminal defendants. However,

Police officers encounter juvenile suspects in a variety of situations. The most serious of the youngsters processed end up in court accused of delinquent offenses.

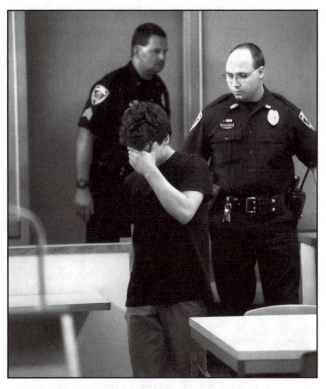

research by Barry Feld (1999b, 1999c) indicates that the right to counsel and actual representation by counsel are two different things (Manfredi, 1998). Feld (1999b) conducted a study in the 1980s that examined six states and the way in which the mandates of *Gault* had been carried out by juvenile courts. He concluded, "In the two decades since *Gault*, the promise of counsel remains unrealized." In fact, "In many states less than 50% of juveniles adjudicated delinquent receive the assistance of counsel to which they are constitutionally entitled" (1999b:117–18). One reason is that some judges who hold traditional values may harbor hostility toward the presence of attorneys in juvenile proceedings. Furthermore, there may be some role ambiguity created in trying to reconcile the competing goals of rehabilitation and punishment. Thus, attorneys may feel that they cannot be effective advocates in a system where *parens patriae* values still are very much present.

Additionally, actors such as juvenile probation officers and court intake workers may undermine the role of counsel by advising youngsters and their parents that cases can be disposed of more quickly and smoothly if attorneys are not involved. Finally, it appears that the attorneys' presence may make dispositions more severe for youngsters who are adjudicated delinquent (Rubin, 1996). On this point, however, Feld warns that this may be a spurious relationship. In fact, juveniles who appear with attorneys may be charged with the most serious offenses, so severe dispositions—once they are found to be delinquent—would be logical (see especially Feld, 1999c:138).

Another point that should be emphasized about attorneys and delinquency proceedings has already been inferred but now needs to be made explicit. A great deal of research has touched on the types of attorneys who take criminal cases (see, for example, Cole, 2004). Generally speaking, these are lawyers in small firms or solo practices that may depend on low fees and high case volume to make a living. For the most part, the practice of criminal law is a low-status part of the legal profession, a fact doubly true for juvenile cases. Most youngsters charged with delinquent offenses do not have the means to hire their own attorneys, nor are their families able to help. Even when families can privately retain an attorney, the available pool willing to accept such cases may be incredibly small. The result, unfortunately, is that youngsters accused of delinquent offenses may get the least experienced attorneys and those least willing or able to mount a vigorous defense on their behalf (Rubin, 1996).

The lack of financial resources results in heavy reliance on public defenders or other appointed attorneys to handle the bulk of delinquency cases. Research on public defenders who represent indigent adult defendants indicates that they "get the job done and done well" (Hanson and Ostrom, 2004). These attorneys have regular and ongoing contacts with the prosecutor's office and they obtain a lot of courtroom experience in a short time. Nevertheless, public defenders frequently labor under incredibly heavy caseloads. As a result, Feld concludes, "Even in jurisdictions where counsel are routinely appointed, there are grounds for concern about their effectiveness" in representing accused delinquents (1999b:126).

Intake Worker and Probation Officers

As you learned in chapter 4, intake typically is the first contact offenders have with the juvenile court. Intake serves as a basic screening mechanism, and it may be performed by a specially designated probation officer or someone classified as an intake worker. Intake is designed to assess the child's status and to help determine whether a petition should be filed and whether detention should be utilized. An intake worker necessarily will have to make a hasty preliminary appraisal in order to expedite the processing of the child's case.

Detention status must be decided fairly quickly. Some states require that these decisions be made within the first 24 to 48 hours; others require them in as little as six hours. Intake workers will make recommendations based on public safety or flight risk, and the judge will decide the appropriateness of the detention. Often staff opinions and judicial decisions will err on the cautious side and suggest detention for youngsters who might not need it.

The juvenile court's intake function is especially important when we consider that in 2000 only about 58% of the delinquency cases referred to juvenile courts resulted in formal processing—that is, the filing of a petition (Puzzanchera et al., 2004). The intake staff will make the initial recommendations on who gets detained and for how long. They also will decide (1) which cases merit diversion, (2) which charges may be held in abeyance while treatment or diagnostic work is started, and (3) which cases warrant filing a petition for formal adjudication. The recommendations are influenced by legal factors such as the youngster's offense history and the type of offense with which the youngster is charged, as well as extra-legal factors such as race, age, and gender (Puzzanchera et al., 2004). In the following paragraphs we will consider the consequences of each of these recommendations.

Intake workers may decide a particular case deserves diversion, what the Office of Juvenile Justice and Delinquency Prevention (2004) calls **immediate sanctions**, based on the minor nature of the offense, the lack of a delinquent history, and the child's family situation and broader support systems. Immediate sanction programs currently available in the United States include family group conferences, peer mediation/conflict resolution, restitution/community services, teen/youth court, victim impact panels, and victim offender mediation (OJJDP, 2004). Such programs may be operated by the juvenile probation office, or probation officers may serve as facilitators.

Intake workers' diversion recommendations can have an impact on youngsters in other ways. For example, diversion workers may reduce the time juveniles spend in detention (Bazemore and Dicker, 1996). Diversion also can reduce the physical and emotional trauma that some youngsters experience in the juvenile court adjudication process. In the chapter's opening scenario Denise Watson started to experience some of the anxiety that may be associated with appearing before a juvenile court judge.

Motions to hold charges in abeyance may be formally or informally presented to the juvenile court judge. Intake staff members may feel that they lack sufficient information to make a rapid decision about the child's future in the juvenile justice system. Intake workers may ask the judge not to detain the child, assuming this is appropriate, but to allow them time to have diagnostic work done concerning the child's needs. This recommendation has the effect of interrupting the flow of adjudication for the case. The result may be that no formal charges will be filed. Other possible results may be diversion into a community-based program for delinquent offenders or referral to a community mental health or other social services agency. Holding charges in abeyance gives the court continuing jurisdiction over youngsters, but it also has the effect of keeping children in a state of limbo.

Finally, the case may move forward if it seems appropriate to file a petition. This decision customarily has hinged on two considerations: social factors and legal sufficiency. Historically, court intake workers were called upon to decide the relative weights of both of these concerns. Now, with the presence of prosecuting attorneys, there is a division of labor: Intake workers assess the child's social situation and the prosecutor weighs the legal sufficiency of the case. Once the decision to move forward is made, a date for an adjudicatory hearing will be set.

Intake workers' recommendations can have a tremendous impact on the youngsters referred to the juvenile court. These decisions are of low visibility and involve a great deal of discretion. Perhaps no one other than the juvenile court judge will have this much influence on delinquency case processing.

DETENTION CENTER STAFF

Historically, many of nation's juvenile courts have operated their own detention centers, an arrangement that the National Advisory Committee on Criminal Justice Goals and Standards (1976) recommended against. Nevertheless, some juvenile courts still operate detention centers, and detention center staff members work for the court and ultimately answer to the judge or an administrative officer such as a court manager. Again, as a reminder, we discussed the role and scope of detention and detention staff in chapter 4.

TYPES OF HEARINGS

Most juvenile courts conduct four types of hearings on a regular basis. These include detention, transfer, adjudicatory, and dispositional hearings.

DETENTION HEARINGS

Detention hearings typically are held within a few hours or, at most, a day after a juvenile is taken into custody. Normally the police will take to the detention center any youngster who has been arrested and who is not to be immediately released to the parents.

The detention staff personnel will alert the court to the child's presence, and an intake officer will hastily try to assemble enough information to make a decision. The juvenile court judge usually conducts the detention hearing, but in some very large jurisdictions a hearing officer, sometimes called a **referee**, handles such routine court matters. Essentially, the hearing officer is trying to determine whether there appears to be sufficient legal justification to detain the child and whether there are social factors, such as community safety and family stability, that must be considered as well.

One of the important things to remember is that most of the youngsters arrested by the police do not need to be detained prior to the delinquency adjudication. Some, however, will have to be detained because they pose a public safety risk to the community or they are likely to flee the jurisdiction if they are released.

TRANSFER HEARINGS

One of the most controversial aspects of juvenile court proceedings is the use of the **transfer hearing**. These hearings decide which youngsters should be tried as adults. *Kent v. United States* sent the juvenile justice system a mandate to hold a hearing before a youngster could be transferred to a criminal court's jurisdiction. In the *Kent* decision the Supreme Court provided a list of "determinative factors" that judges should consider in making transfer decisions. These factors include:

- The seriousness of the alleged offense to the community and whether the protection of the community requires waiver.
- Whether the alleged offense was committed in an aggressive, violent, premeditated, or willful manner.
- Whether the alleged offense was against persons or against property, greater weight being given to offenses against persons especially if personal injury resulted.
- The prosecutive merit of the complaint, i.e., whether there is evidence upon which a grand jury may be expected to return an indictment . . .

- The desirability of trial and disposition of the entire offense in one court when the juvenile's associates in the alleged offense are adults . . .
- The sophistication and maturity of the juvenile by consideration of his home, environmental situation, emotional attitude, and pattern of living.
- The record and previous history of the juvenile, including previous contacts with . . . law enforcement agencies, juvenile courts and other jurisdictions, prior periods of probation . . . or prior commitments to juvenile institutions.
- The prospects for adequate protection of the public and the likelihood of reasonable rehabilitation of the juvenile (if he is found to have committed the alleged offense) by the use of procedures, services and facilities currently available to the juvenile courts (*Kent v. United States*, 383 U.S. 541, 566–67, 1966).

There are two justifications for transferring juveniles to adult courts: (1) public safety, and (2) lack of amenability to treatment. The public safety provision is fairly self-explanatory. This is raised as a concern with youngsters who have committed very serious personal crimes such as armed robbery, rape, or homicide. The lack of amenability justification is somewhat ambiguous. In simplest terms, it means that within the juvenile justice system there are no services or agencies to provide appropriate treatment for the youngster. For some judges, lack of amenability to treatment signals a desperation disposition: They have tried everything else; now they are willing to give the adult system a chance.

As we conclude this section, it is important to note three points about transfers. First, they have declined from a high of 12,000 in 1994 to around 6,000 in 2000. Second, while transfers are still numerous nationwide, they represent only about 1% of all delinquency cases processed by the juvenile courts (Puzzanchera et al., 2004). Finally, the use of transfers represents a major philosophical break with the traditional role of the juvenile justice system as rehabilitative rather than punitive.

ADJUDICATORY HEARINGS

Like many other elements of the juvenile justice system, juvenile procedures have names different from those of adult procedures. Therefore, what would be called a trial for adults is considered an **adjudicatory hearing** for juveniles. It is at this hearing that the child is called into account for the alleged delinquent behavior.

Several features have distinguished juvenile proceedings from criminal trials; we touch briefly on two of them. First, as we have mentioned previously, the original juvenile court was nonadversarial in nature. Theoretically, all parties were on the juvenile's side. This stands in contrast to adult criminal trials where lawyers are present for both sides, and the give-and-take of the trial is designed to arrive at the truth. Second, in criminal law all crimes are prosecuted by the state and with the public's best interests in mind. In juvenile proceedings everyone is supposed to act in the child's best interests.

DISPOSITIONAL HEARINGS

Another instance where terminology distinguishes the juvenile justice system from the adult criminal justice system is in case dispositions. When an adult defendant has been found guilty, the judge will sentence the offender to the appropriate sanction. Juvenile courts do not impose sentences; rather, a youngster who has been found "delinquent" will receive a **disposition**. The disposition is the sentence the juvenile will serve, whether probation or some period of incarceration in a state training school or other juvenile correctional facility.

Once the juvenile probation office has completed the child's case history, the judge will schedule a dispositional hearing. The judge will review this report in making the disposition decision. It is important to note again that juvenile courts have a much narrower range of **dispositional options** than do the adult criminal courts.

Probation is a frequent disposition for both adults and juveniles. Juvenile probation will be covered more fully in chapter 7, but it is important to emphasize that this is the most common juvenile court disposition. In fact, national juvenile court statistics from 2000 indicate that 393,300 cases (63% of the cases formally petitioned to juvenile courts) received probation as a disposition, as well as over 227,000 informally processed (nonpetitioned) cases (Puzzanchera et al., 2004).

In addition to probation, judges may impose fines, order restitution, place the child in a nonsecure residential setting, and require the child and perhaps the family to undergo some type of counseling or, in extreme circumstances, order institutionalization.

Economic sanctions might be employed in a variety of cases. For instance, fines might be used for adults and juveniles in traffic cases. Another economic sanction is **restitution**. Restitution typically is a probation condition, and it is designed to pay back the victim for losses suffered, to increase the juvenile's sense of accountability for commission of the offense, and where possible, to reduce recidivism (see, for example, Butts and Mears, 2001; OJJDP, 2004).

Restitution is appropriate and most effective for vandalism, burglary, and larceny. But there are difficulties in restitution programs when youngsters come from low-income families, since restitution is based on the assumption that the offender can pay the restitution order. As an alternative, adjudicated delinquents may be required to assist the victim in doing yard work or household chores to provide a payback. Either approach can be effective if the victim feels that justice has been served and the offender feels a sense of accountability for the crime.

Community service programs also have been used with delinquent youths. These programs often are tied to probation, and they may suffer from some of the deficiencies that plague restitution efforts. For example, while community service has been praised as an effective, nonstigmatizing way to deal with minor property offenders, we do not have solid evidence of the impact of these programs on future law-violating behavior. One common problem with community service efforts is that their results are compared with those of institutional programs. Yet most children placed on probation, whether or not they are ordered to do community service, are good candidates for future law-abiding behavior, while those youngsters whose dispositions include institutionalization are more likely to engage in future law-breaking behavior. The major payoff may be that community service programs get businesses and community groups involved in the process of addressing delinquency problems.

Juvenile court judges may also order the out-of-home placement of some youngsters. While these types of placements seem most appropriate for dependent

Theoretical Reflections
Labeling Theory and Court Hearings

A troubled youth stands in front of a juvenile court judge to receive the disposition. The child has traveled a long road to this point. Much of what happened can be understood in the language of labeling theory, especially that theory's emphasis on negotiated outcomes.

Before exploring these linkages, we must review the reasons for court appearances. Children appear in court because of (1) delinquency charges, (2) status offenses, or (3) conditions of dependency, neglect, and abuse. In the first two cases, the court's job is to determine (1) the extent of a child's culpability and legal responsibility and (2) the appropriate disposition. In the third instance, parents, legal guardians, and others receive the court's attention.

What about youths whose alleged behavior involves combinations of these legal statuses? Charles Thomas studied more than 2,000 youths appearing in one of two juvenile courts at least once over a five-year period. He based his analysis on a longitudinal comparison of three groups: (1) those whose first appearance involved a felony charge, (2) those whose first appearance involved a misdemeanor charge, and (3) those whose first appearance involved a status offense. Thomas found little to no support for the notion that different kinds of children populate these three groups:

> To the contrary, with relatively minor exceptions, the findings indicate that many of those who appear before the courts because of alleged involvement in behavior proscribed by status offense statutes have previously appeared for quite different types of offenses and

that those whose initial appearance involved a status offense frequently return for other types of alleged misconduct. (1971:454)

Are status offenders different? Thomas's conclusion appears to be no; they are essentially the same as other offenders. As he observes, those whose first recorded court appearance is related to a status offense "are more likely to recidivate than those *first charged with a misdemeanor or felony*" (Thomas, 1971:438; emphasis added).

So how do some youths come to be categorized as delinquents or status offenders, especially if the legal questions involve both types of charges? Labeling theorists suggest that a child's ultimate status is negotiated in court. For example, Robert Emerson notes that the court must decide if the juvenile defendant was (1) a normal child accidentally involved in delinquency, (2) a criminal-like child likely to continue along this evil pathway, or (3) a disturbed child in need of professional help. Emerson observes that the court's final decision need not be proved in the legal sense. Rather, the respective statuses are negotiated among the concerned parties, including the court, the public schools, the reform school, the social services system, and other community services. Emerson's negotiation process is similar to what other labeling theorists have observed about the court's role in moving people from being among the discreditable to the discredited, often as a result of public or semipublic shaming ceremonies.

Sources: Emerson (1969); Garfinkel (1956); Goffman (1963); Thomas (1971).

and neglected children, they are used with delinquent children as well. Children may be removed from the home when the parents are found to be contributing to their delinquent or dependent status, or when there is a need, such as substance abuse or psychiatric treatment, that necessitates residential care. These placements typically are operated as part of foster home placements, in residential treatment centers (RTCs), or in group homes and halfway houses.

The ultimate juvenile court sanction is commitment of a child to the state juvenile correctional authority. Juveniles, like adults, can be sentenced to either indeterminate or determinate incarceration periods. An **indeterminate sentence** is "a sentence of imprisonment to a specified minimum and maximum period of time, specifically authorized by statute, subject to termination by a parole board or other authorized agency after the prisoner has served the minimum term" (MyLawTerms.com, 2004). In most cases, a paroling authority decides, within the sentencing range, when the prisoner actually will be eligible for release from custody.

Indeterminate sentencing was the most common adult and juvenile correctional disposition throughout the twentieth century. However, beginning in the late 1970s dissatisfaction with rehabilitative efforts led several states to abandon indeterminate sentences and the traditional concept of parole in favor of sentences of definite or fixed lengths.

Determinate sentences, and the related concept of **presumptive sentences**, have been implemented in a small number of states for juvenile offenders (see Mears, 2002). These sentences specify a set amount of time to be served by the incarcerated individual. There still may be a paroling authority, but release generally is achieved through completion of the entire sentence or through the accumulation of good-time credits, resulting in a mandatory release date (Champion, 2005).

Regardless of the sentencing system used in a jurisdiction, adults can be sentenced to terms from a few days for misdemeanors up to life in prison for serious felonies. In most states juveniles can be sentenced to no more than two or three years, no matter how serious the offense. Furthermore, in adult criminal courts the death penalty is available for certain very serious crimes. The death penalty is not available in juvenile court.

Institutional confinement can occur in various facilities, from those with low security to those with fortress-like security. Low-security programs may be operated as farms, ranches, or camps. The high-security facilities—frequently called state industrial or training schools—resemble adult prisons. The youngsters sent to these facilities are supervised by correctional officers, and the buildings are surrounded by fences and other security measures.

ORGANIZATION AND STRUCTURE OF JUVENILE COURTS

Now that we have discussed what juvenile courts are and what they do, we need to turn our attention to how juvenile courts are organized. In some ways, the most difficult issue is the juvenile court's status within state court structures. No one pattern prevails. Instead, we have clusters of juvenile court organizational patterns. Table 5.5 shows something of the organizational diversity of the nation's juvenile courts.

Table 5.5   Diversity of Juvenile Court Organization

State	Court name	Court type
Colorado	Denver Juvenile Court	General jurisdiction
Delaware	Family Court	Limited jurisdiction
Georgia	Juvenile Court	Limited jurisdiction
Hawaii	14 district family judges	General jurisdiction
Louisiana	District Court	
	Juvenile Court (4 courts)	General jurisdiction
	Family Court (1 in Baton Rouge)	General jurisdiction
Maryland	Orphan's Court	Limited jurisdiction
Massachusetts	Juvenile Court	Limited jurisdiction
Mississippi	Family Court	Limited jurisdiction
Nebraska	Separate Juvenile Court	Limited jurisdiction
New York	Family Court	Limited jurisdiction
	Surrogate's Court	Limited jurisdiction
Rhode Island	Family Court	Limited jurisdiction
South Carolina	Family Court	Limited jurisdiction
Tennessee	Juvenile Court	Limited jurisdiction
Utah	Juvenile Court	Limited jurisdiction
Vermont	Family Court	General jurisdiction

Source: Rottman et al. (2000).

Juvenile courts may be classified into one of two categories depending upon whether they are courts of limited jurisdiction—that is, hearing delinquency, dependency, and neglect cases only—or courts of broader jurisdictional boundaries, such as **family courts**. Family courts often handle the traditional juvenile court caseload and, in addition, are responsible for divorces, paternity suits, custody cases, child support, and adoptions.

Another way of classifying juvenile courts is to determine whether they are independent courts, along the lines of the traditional juvenile court model, or whether they are located within general trial jurisdiction courts. General jurisdiction courts (sometimes called district or superior courts) are empowered to hear a broad range of both civil and criminal cases (Champion, 2005). These are the courts that process felonies in most states, they are structured to conduct jury trials, and they are courts of record (that is, they produce verbatim transcripts of proceedings).

In some jurisdictions, juvenile courts operate as totally separate entities within the state or local court organization. Some of these separate courts are confined to hearing juvenile matters only, and their structure is equivalent to that of an adult court of limited jurisdiction, such as a justice of the peace, magistrate, or municipal court. Rubin says that this sort of placement "may well represent the lowest-status end of the lowest-status court" (1985:350).

Some states, like New Mexico, have eliminated specialized courts; they merged these court functions into the general trial courts. Such states typically follow one of two models. First, there may be only one judge or, in some multi-judge arrangements, a particular judge or division may be specifically designated as the juvenile or family division. Second, in some multi-judge courts each judge takes turns hearing juvenile cases, or the juvenile caseload is evenly distributed among all the judges. This arrangement allows judges neither to develop specializations nor to become juvenile law experts.

A final issue dealing with juvenile court organizational structure or status involves the degree to which the courts have sole jurisdiction over juvenile matters. That is, does the juvenile court have the exclusive right to hear all cases involving youngsters—aside from those to be transferred to adult court—or does it share that jurisdiction with other courts? In states such as Florida, where juvenile courts have concurrent jurisdiction with adult courts in many cases, prosecutors do not have to file a transfer motion (Bishop et al., 1999; Butts and Mears, 2001). They simply can bypass the juvenile court and file charges in the adult criminal courts. Such an arrangement clearly undercuts the juvenile court's status and authority.

ISSUES FACING THE JUVENILE COURT

At this point we want to turn from concerns over structures and functions to address some of the major issues facing juvenile courts today. In most instances, these issues will continue with us for some time to come, and those of you who choose to work in the juvenile justice system may well find yourselves grappling with them.

REDEFINITION OF JUVENILE COURT JURISDICTION

Obviously, one of the most fundamental issues with which we are confronted is what the juvenile court will look like now that it has passed its one hundredth anniversary. As is readily apparent to most people interested in juvenile justice, the juvenile court—and indeed, the entire juvenile justice system—is in search of a guiding philosophy. The court's future status will depend to some degree on the philosophy adopted by the court, or imposed on the court by legislative bodies. The two major philosophies can be classified as treatment and punishment.

If the juvenile court retains the original rehabilitative ideal proposed for it, then a treatment philosophy is likely to prevail. Several consequences seem likely if this happens. A treatment philosophy would dictate that juvenile courts retain status offense jurisdiction. The difference might be more in the final disposition of status offenses, rather than in how they are adjudicated. A number of dispositional alternatives are already available for status offenses, and more might be created if the juvenile court retains jurisdiction over these behaviors.

Additionally, a treatment orientation might lead states to move from a narrow juvenile court model toward a more broadly based family court. This court would have jurisdiction over delinquency, dependency, and neglect/abuse cases; divorces, custody, child support, and paternity suits; and wills and inheritances. Such an approach would treat children in the context of the family as opposed to treating them in isolation.

Finally, a juvenile court focusing on treatment could still provide due process protections. However, in such a court the emphasis would be more on the juvenile justice system's treatment aspects than on the child's legal rights. Attorneys could be present and a formal procedural structure could be applied to cases, but treatment would be the primary concern.

Since the early 1980s, punishment increasingly has been the guiding principle of juvenile justice. If this punitive philosophy persists, the juvenile court could be facing changes of a different kind. For instance, the juvenile court might operate with a very narrow focus, dealing almost exclusively with the most serious delinquency cases. These are offenses that would be misdemeanors or felonies for adults, and a punitive juvenile court would provide serious penalties for juveniles committing these offenses (Gardner, 2003). In this type of court, youngsters would be provided the full range of legal protections that adults receive. By the same token, they could receive punishments very similar to those of adults. The result would be fewer children coming before the juvenile court, but those found to be delinquent would be punished more severely.

ELIMINATION OF THE JUVENILE COURT

Some would suggest that a more punitive juvenile court, one that resembles an adult criminal court, eliminates most of the justification for a separate court (see, for example, Feld, 1999a). In other words, if the juvenile court is going to resemble the adult court, why have both? The U.S. Supreme Court, in a series of cases discussed earlier in this chapter, has applied a broad range of due process guarantees to youngsters accused of delinquent behavior. However, it has not granted juveniles all constitutional rights extended to adults, and the Court has refused to suggest the juvenile court has outlived its usefulness. Therefore, the juvenile court's future seems somewhat murky. It could be greatly modified, or it could be eliminated.

STATURE OF THE JUVENILE COURT

Unfortunately, for most of its history the juvenile court has suffered from a status problem. Many criminal justice system actors refer disparagingly to the juvenile court as "kiddie court." Juvenile court judges may not be held in the same esteem as their criminal court counterparts. In fact, juvenile court judgeships are not highly sought-after positions in most jurisdictions. The fact that we place the most junior of the prosecuting attorneys in juvenile court also says something about the court's stature.

Therefore, if the juvenile court is to survive and flourish well into the twenty-first century, one issue that must be addressed is the court's status relative to other courts in the judicial hierarchy. In order for the juvenile court to enjoy greater respect, prestige, and status, it must be fully a court of law, and one with general trial jurisdiction. Furthermore, as we will address in the following section, juvenile and family court judges must possess qualifications equivalent to those of criminal court judges.

QUALIFICATIONS OF JUDGES

As we noted earlier in this chapter, there has been a long tradition of nonlawyer judges in certain courts throughout our nation's history. When juvenile courts first came into being, and until the due process revolution of the 1960s and 1970s, judges frequently were not required to be law school graduates. The result was that some juvenile courts truly were inferior courts, both in their stature and in the quality of the justice they dispensed. Given the increasingly adversarial nature of juvenile court processes, juvenile judges today overwhelmingly are licensed attorneys. Where this is not the case, controversy will continue to surround the juvenile courts and the nonlawyer judges that serve them. Most groups today advocate the highest level of qualifications for juvenile court judges. These qualifications include not only a law degree but also a requirement that the person selected has been a practicing attorney. Furthermore, there is additional pressure from the legal profession and the judges themselves to require specialized training for juvenile court judges. The National Council of Juvenile and Family Court Judges is one group that has led the way in advocating appropriate qualifications and compensation for the nation's juvenile court judges.

ATTORNEYS IN THE JUVENILE COURT

We have already discussed the U.S. Supreme Court's rulings in *Kent v. United States* and *In re Gault* requiring a more conspicuous role for attorneys in the juvenile court. However, there still are a few remaining issues involving lawyers' presence and activism in juvenile court. First, the presence of lawyers for both sides obviously has made juvenile court proceedings more adversarial in nature. For some observers, lawyers' involvement undermines the juvenile court's fundamental nature and is further justification for its elimination. However, it seems safe to say that attorneys will be part of juvenile court processes as long as there is a juvenile court. Second, although defense attorneys frequently appear in juvenile courts, not every youngster accused of delinquency will be represented by counsel.

Furthermore, it is important to note that even juveniles with privately retained attorneys or public defenders do not always receive the most vigorous defense in their cases. Therefore, the precise role attorneys will play in future delinquency proceedings seems uncertain. Are they to serve as officers of the court and provide for smooth case processing, or are they to provide their clients a spirited defense?

TRANSFERRING JUVENILES TO ADULT COURT

The final issue we will address is transferring juveniles to criminal courts. From the juvenile court's earliest days, there have been provisions in state juvenile codes for transferring juveniles to the criminal courts. National statistics on juvenile court cases processed show that in 1985 32% of all transferred cases involved crimes against persons, and property crimes constituted the most common offenses for which waivers were sought (45%). Overall, the general trend of cases waived for property crimes has been downward, declining from 45% in 1985 to 36% in 2000. By contrast, transfers for crimes against persons increased from just over 30% in 1985 to 40% in 2000 (Puzzanchera et al., 2004).

The transfers that involve serious or repeat juvenile offenders let the juvenile justice system off the hook in situations where nothing seems to work, or no juvenile treatment seems to be appropriate (see Bortner, 1986).

Given the number and types of cases transferred from juvenile court to adult court, we must raise this question: What really happens to those youngsters tried as adults? It is important to remember that one of the primary justifications for transferring juvenile cases to adult courts is so that more severe sanctions can be applied. Is this what actually happens? Let us look at the evidence.

Box 5.2   Juveniles and the Death Penalty

A number of justifications are given for transferring juveniles to adult courts. Among the most common is that transfers allow youngsters to receive harsher penalties than they typically would receive in juvenile court—where one to two years of secure confinement in a state training school is often the maximum. By contrast, in the adult court system youthful offenders can receive long prison terms, including life in prison, or even the death penalty. Courts have wrestled with the question of death for youngsters for over two decades and, as is often the case, thorny social issues such as this eventually make their way to the U.S. Supreme Court.

The Supreme Court was asked in 1982 to decide the first in a series of death penalty cases for juvenile offenders. In *Eddings v. Oklahoma*, 455 U.S. 104 (1982), a 16-year-old youngster was charged with and convicted of killing an Oklahoma State Highway Patrol officer. The U.S. Supreme Court in its review of this case did not decide precisely on the issue of the constitutionality of the death penalty for juveniles, nor did it determine the precise age that should serve as a cutoff. Instead, the Court ruled that age must be considered a mitigating factor by jurors in such cases.

The next juvenile death penalty case to come before the Supreme Court was *Thompson v. Oklahoma*, 487 U.S. 815 (1988). Wayne Thompson was convicted along with his brother of killing his brother-in-law, whom the Thompsons suspected of abusing their sister. Wayne Thompson was 15 at the time of the killing, and under Oklahoma law he was tried as an adult and given the death penalty. On appeal to the Supreme Court, Thompson's attorneys asked the Court to issue a ruling declaring unconstitutional the execution of any person whose crime was committed before the age of 18. The Court declined to issue such a broad ruling, instead dealing with the issue at hand and holding that the death penalty was constitutionally inappropriate for persons under 16 years of age.

The cutoff age of 16 was reaffirmed in *Stanford v. Kentucky*, 492 U.S. 361 (1989) and its companion case, *Wilkins v. Missouri*. In these two cases the Supreme Court again refused to set 18 as the minimum age for crimes warranting executions, and allowed states to impose capital punishment for crimes committed by 16- and 17-year-olds. At this point the issue seemed to be settled, and indeed it was until March 1, 2005.

In *Roper v. Simmons*, 543 U.S. ___ (2005) the Supreme Court again was asked to deal with the question of capital punishment for youthful offenders, and by a 5–4 vote the Court ruled that 18 years of age should be the minimum at which executions should be imposed. Referring to the practices of other nations, the laws of most states that impose capital punishment, and the notion of "evolving standards of decency," the Court held that imposition of the death penalty on youngsters age 16 or 17 at time of the offense was disproportionately harsh and constituted cruel and unusual punishment. Thus, for the time being it seems that while youngsters still can receive long prison terms when they are tried as adults, they no longer can be executed for their crimes.

Sources: Champion and Mays (1991); *Eddings v. Oklahoma* (1982); *Roper v. Simmons* (2005); *Stanford v. Kentucky* (1989); *Thompson v. Oklahoma* (1988); and *Wilkins v. Missouri* (1989).

As we have already seen, older juveniles who are persistent property offenders likely will be transferred to adult court. When these youngsters get to adult court, they are often "reborn," either because their juvenile record does not follow them in some states, or because they do not look like serious offenders compared with the adults being tried in criminal courts. Therefore, the overwhelming evidence indicates that the juvenile property offenders tried as adults get lenient sentences. In fact, many receive probation (see Champion and Mays, 1991).

By contrast, a study by the National Center for Juvenile Justice (Snyder, Sickmund, and Poe-Yamagata, 2000) found that in the four states they examined, transfers were reserved for juveniles who had been accused of committing serious personal crimes, and typically these youngsters received some period of incarceration. However, these youths would have received some period of secure confinement—although perhaps not as long—in the juvenile justice system as well.

Therefore, what can we conclude about transfers? First, a small group of offenders will receive severe sanctions in the adult system. These will be 16- and 17-year-old youths who have committed notorious or very serious crimes, such as killing their parents or a schoolteacher, or that very small group of children who have histories of violent delinquent behavior. Second, many juveniles transferred to the adult system are persistent property offenders, and often they will receive probation. Thus, given the actual outcomes of transfers, this policy is more symbolic than practical. It is designed to give the appearance of a tough, no-nonsense approach to juvenile crime—an approach that may satisfy those who believe the juvenile court's orientation should be punitive rather than rehabilitative but which likely has little impact on the juvenile crime rate.

SUMMARY

When the juvenile court was created more than 100 years ago, it was hailed as one of the greatest innovations in the history of American jurisprudence. Finally, society had found a way to deal with children who violated the law without treating them as harshly as adults. Do most people feel that this is appropriate today? Apparently not.

The juvenile court was created as a mechanism to protect children. The child-saving movement of the late 1800s and early 1900s envisioned a court that would focus on *who* the child was rather than on *what* the child had done. This view was assumed to be the underlying principle of the court's operation until the late 1960s, when several legal challenges were raised regarding the juvenile court's procedures.

The current juvenile court model combines elements of both rehabilitation and due process. In simplest terms, the juvenile court is trying to be all things to all people. The result is that there seems to be a growing disenchantment with the juvenile court. On the one hand, conservative critics charge the court with coddling and sheltering young criminals. On the other hand, liberal critics maintain that the juvenile court punishes in the name of treatment, and that very little treatment is actually delivered.

This chapter ends with a short review of the trends that currently affect the juvenile court and are likely to be with us for some time:

- The juvenile court's jurisdiction has been narrowed in many locations, which includes removing the least serious offenses (status offenses). Some states have attempted to end all status offense jurisdiction for the juvenile courts. At the same time, the most serious offenses have been removed through transfers (see Butts and Mears, 2001; Gardner, 2003).

- As a result of redefinitions or reclassifications, most juvenile courts are employing less coercive interventions with nondelinquency cases. This is particularly true for dependent, neglected, and abused children. Alternatives include the use of social welfare, mental health, and substance abuse programs rather than the formal juvenile court adjudication process.

- Nationwide the trend has been toward decreasing the age at which juveniles can be transferred to adult court, or decreasing the maximum age of juvenile court jurisdiction. New Mexico, for example, has created the categories of "youthful offender" and "serious youthful offender (SYO)," and these groups of youngsters can (and in the case of SYOs will) receive adult sanctions including prison time (see Mays and Gregware, 1996). This trend illustrates the more punitive attitudes prevalent in many states in cases involving serious juvenile offenders.

- In some states, changes in dispositional procedures for convicted delinquents have mirrored the trend for adult offenders regarding a move toward determinate sentencing (see Mears, 2002). As a result, parole or aftercare may be substantially restricted for juveniles. Furthermore, for crimes like armed robbery, states are imposing mandatory sentences on juvenile offenders just as they do on adults.

These four trends present a picture of the contemporary juvenile court that is substantially different from that of the first court in Cook County. One consequence of these trends is that some youngsters will serve significantly longer sentences than they would have two decades ago. As a result, the juvenile corrections apparatus—probation, institutionalization, and parole—has been and will continue to feel the impact. We will see the consequences of changes in juvenile court dispositions in the following chapters.

CRITICAL REVIEW QUESTIONS

1. Define the following two legal concepts and explain their implications for the creation of a juvenile justice system: *parens patriae* and *mens rea*.

2. Remember Jess Orville, the 12-year-old boy executed at the start of chapter 2? Given what you learned about *mens rea* in this chapter, how do you think that the judge and jury justified their decision and his fate? (We asked a similar but more general opinion question at the conclusion of chapter 2. Here we are asking for your informed legal opinion.)

3. Review the three defining characteristics of the juvenile court. Then reread the opening vignette. It contains three intentional errors; that is, descriptions of events, people, or processes that were inaccurate when considering the normal practices of juvenile courts. (There may be others, but we

intentionally included three in the vignette.) Find them and link each to the appropriate defining characteristic. (*Hint*: Two of the errors involve the judge and one involves someone else in the courtroom, not the accused or a member of her family.)

4. *Kent v. United States* is obviously an important Supreme Court decision about the rights of juvenile suspects. The case raised three crucial questions. Provide brief summary answers to each question. Why is this case so important to juvenile justice?

5. Would you want to be a defense attorney primarily handling juvenile cases? Explain why you feel as you do, grounding your answer in the material discussed in this chapter.

6. We identify transfer hearings as one of the most controversial aspects of the juvenile justice system. What is it about this proceeding that leads us to this characterization? Do you find it controversial? How so?

7. Create a three-column table with the various dispositional options available for juveniles. In the left-hand column, place the name of the disposition. In the center column, give an example of the disposition. In the right-hand column, state briefly the theoretical or philosophical origins of that disposition.

8. What kind of organizational structure for juvenile courts can provide justice that is in the best interests of juveniles? In providing your answer, first define *best interests of juveniles*; then explain your response to the question.

9. We explored six issues that need to be addressed by the juvenile court, issues certain to continue for decades to come. Rank them in order from the issue *most likely to be resolved* (number 1) to the one *least likely to be resolved* (number 6). Explain the basis of your ranking.

10. Having answered question 9, now rank these same issues in order from the one that merits the most attention to the one that is least critical. Again, provide the basis of your ranking, but this time compare the list prepared for question 9 with the one prepared for this question.

RECOMMENDED READINGS

Gardner, Martin R. (2003). *Understanding Juvenile Law*, 2nd ed. New York: Matthew Bender and Co. This book primarily is intended for law school courses on juvenile law. Nevertheless, undergraduate students will find it readable and very useful. A number of chapters are especially relevant to the topics we have covered in this chapter. Particular attention should be paid to chapter 6 (Constitutional Rights), chapter 7 (The Juvenile Court Movement), and chapter 8 (Jurisdiction).

Hemmens, Craig, Benjamin Steiner, and David Mueller (2004). *Significant Cases in Juvenile Justice*. Los Angeles: Roxbury. Hemmens and his colleagues provide abbreviated versions of 121 federal and state appellate cases dealing with juvenile justice. As you would expect, major cases such as *Kent v. United States*, *In re Gault*, *In re Winship*, and *McKeiver v. Pennsylvania* are included, but the book also provides case coverage of issues such as juvenile curfews, detention, conditions of confinement, and the death penalty.

KEY TERMS

abuse
adjudicatory hearing
chancery law
delinquency
demand waiver
dependency
detention hearings
determinate sentence
disposition
dispositional options
family courts
immediate sanctions
indeterminate sentence
judicial waiver
jurisdiction

justice gendering
legislative waiver
mens rea
neglect
parens patriae
presumptive sentences
prosecutorial waiver
referee
restitution
status offenses
statutory exclusion
transfer
transfer hearing
venue
youth at risk population

Juvenile Probation

* * *

Beverly Carman is a junior, majoring in criminal justice at State University. As one of her assignments for juvenile justice, Beverly must attend five sessions of the local juvenile court and write a summary paper that is due before the end of the term. "Piece of cake," she thought to herself when Professor Johnson covered the syllabus and class requirements. "Twenty percent of my grade for doing something cool like going to court. I can live with that assignment."

Now, however, it is Friday of the week after the midterm exam, and Beverly has been to only three court sessions. Her observations have caused her to question what Professor Johnson wanted and whether she was clear on basic requirements he had described in the syllabus. With only three more weeks before the assignment is due, Beverly is understandably anxious as she waits for Margaret Anderson at Caffeine Corner, the student union building's coffee bistro.

Margaret, also a junior and fellow traveler across the landscape of the criminal justice curriculum for the past two years, took juvenile justice the year before. Beverly frequently consults with her friend about this and other courses. Given their conflicting Monday-Wednesday-Friday schedules and the fact that both have campus jobs on Tuesdays and Thursdays, they are able to get together for coffee only on Friday afternoons. Beverly was deep into her third high-test espresso when she spotted her friend approaching.

"Hey, Bev," called out Margaret as she crossed the nearly deserted commons, an insulated paper cup of foamy cappuccino in her right hand, "been waiting long?"

"Hi, Margaret. Yeah." Her voice taking on an impatient tone, Beverly pulled back a chair so Margaret could sit. "Look, I've got a bit of a crisis, and I could use your help."

Margaret took a seat next to Beverly, noticing the furrowed brow and worried look on her friend's face. This must be serious. "OK, what's up?"

"Remember how I told you that I've been meaning to go to juvy court," Beverly continued. "I thought, well, now that it's a requirement for juvenile justice, I'll do it."

"Yeah right. It took me all semester to find the time to do that assignment. I warned you weeks ago it wasn't a 'piece of cake' like you said." Margaret stopped, assessed the effect of what she had said on her friend, and decided that this was no time for recriminations. She would take another approach. "What can I do to help?" she asked.

Beverly then recounted her experiences in juvenile court. After her first visit, which lasted about two hours, Beverly started to believe that all the cases coming before the judge were following some kind of script. In fact, the case processing was so routine that Beverly discussed with her professor why she needed to do more than one juvenile court visit. The answer, of course, was, "It's a requirement for everyone in this class."

"Yeah, I remember Johnson telling me the same thing when I complained. That dude needs to work on his comebacks 'cause . . ." Margaret looked at Beverly, noticed her ever-deepening frown and stopped. "So, uh, he told you it was a requirement for everyone in class and . . . ?"

Beverly continued her tale of woe. By the third court visit, Beverly had become adept at predicting the outcomes of most of the cases on the court's docket. In fact, she would say to her classmates and others sitting in the courtroom, "Here's what the judge will do now." While she was not 100% accurate, her predictions missed the mark in only one or two cases.

Of particular interest to Beverly was the number of cases that received probation as the sole disposition. It seemed like a lot, and after she started keeping track, she found that 5 or 6 of every 10 cases resulted in a disposition of probation. "What's going on?" she thought. "Are all these kids getting a slap on the wrist? What happened to punishment? Surely some of them get punished!" Beverly came away with the feeling that not much of consequence really happens to most of the youngsters who go through the juvenile court.

"So Margaret, the point is this: Do I really write up what I saw? I'm wondering if I've missed something. That somehow I saw only some really unusual court sessions. I mean, I went to two different judges, one a guy and the other a woman. Did I miss something someplace?"

"Look, Bev," Margaret began, "I love juvenile justice, and I want to be a juvy court judge someday, but, well, at times I think the judges I observed just didn't have time to, you know, dispense real justice. Seems like it's 'Johnny, you get probation; Sarah, you get probation; and, oh yeah, Billy, you get probation too.' When I'm a judge, it'll be different, I promise you that." Margaret, noticing that her little speech did little to reverse her friend's blue mood, changed her approach once again. "Oh, all right, let's see what we can do to make good old Professor Johnson happy. Now about those final two court visits. Go do them. Maybe you just don't stay for the whole session. My bet is you probably won't see anything different. Then write it up. Johnson's probably seen so many papers describing what you and I saw, he won't read it anyhow."

Margaret saw an immediate change in her friend's mood; Bev's face relaxed as she realized she was on the right track and would, in fact, complete the assignment. "So how's the espresso today?" Margaret asked, changing subjects.

* * *

Experts often describe the juvenile court as the hub of the juvenile justice system. If that characterization is accurate, then juvenile probation is the wheel rim surrounding that hub. The spokes joining the hub and the wheel rim are the multiple formal and informal ways that youngsters find themselves on probation. In fact, juvenile probation developed in such close collaboration with the juvenile court that the two are virtually inseparable in their philosophies and operations. A report by the Office of Juvenile Justice and Delinquency Prevention (OJJDP) characterized juvenile probation as the workhorse of the juvenile justice system, underscoring this significance (Torbet, 1996). What does this characterization mean? Consider the fact that of the more than 1.7 million delinquency cases processed annually by juvenile courts in recent years, virtually every one of them involved some contact with a juvenile probation officer (Puzzanchera, 2003a:1). This involvement, which can come at many different decision points in the process, illustrates the crucial role played by juvenile probation officers and agencies throughout the juvenile justice enterprise.

Probation plays a vital role in the administration of juvenile justice, a fact not necessarily understood or appreciated by many key players within the U.S. criminal justice system. Therefore, in this chapter we consider the following points: (1) the historical development of juvenile probation; (2) the types of services performed by juvenile probation officers; (3) the nature and extent of the use of probation; (4) juvenile probation organizational patterns; and (5) the future of juvenile probation.

DEFINING PROBATION: THE BASICS

In many jurisdictions the same personnel deliver juvenile probation and parole services, employing very similar rules and conditions. In spite of these similarities, probation and parole (or aftercare as it is often called for juveniles) are different. The Bureau of Justice Statistics (BJS) defines **probation** as "the conditional freedom granted by a judicial officer to an alleged or adjudged adult or juvenile offender, as long as the person meets certain conditions of behavior." BJS adds that "juvenile probation is often designated as 'informal' or 'formal,' depending upon the authority granting it and the nature of the conditions" (BJS, 1981:170).

We will distinguish between formal and informal probation later in this chapter. Now, however, we present three basic features that are crucial for a complete understanding of probation:

1. Probation is *conditional*. Juveniles granted probation have certain restrictions placed on their freedom. They have conditions imposed on them by juvenile probation officers and backed by the court's authority, and their freedom is dependent on the degree to which they live up to those conditions.

2. Probation is a *sentence*. In fact, it was the most severe disposition ordered by juvenile and family court judges in over 60% of the cases handled in 1999 (Puzzanchera, 2003a:1). Juveniles on probation remain under the court's supervision enforced through juvenile probation officers' surveillance.

3. Probation is *ordered and monitored by the courts*. This fact makes probation a judicial function, in contrast with parole (or juvenile aftercare), which is essentially an executive function.

These features shape the nature of juvenile probation. While accused or adjudged juvenile offenders are free from incarceration, that freedom has limits. If they fail to abide by the probation conditions, they may be incarcerated.

A BRIEF HISTORY OF PROBATION

Probation's exact historical creation is a little hard to pinpoint. Probably one of the primary historical antecedents is **judicial reprieve**, used by the early English courts. Under that system, judges would suspend imposition of a sentence until the convicted person had the opportunity to appeal the conviction to the Crown. Ultimately, the practice evolved into one of suspending the sentences that judges might consider unfair. Use of suspended sentences, while not based on statutory authority, also became common in the United States (Abadinsky, 2002b).

Many people contributed to the development of probation in the United States. Most criminal justice historians trace the notion of probation to the volunteer work of John Augustus, a Boston boot maker. Augustus is often called the "father of probation." His work began when he started asking the judge of the Boston police court to release convicted individuals into his custody. Beginning in 1841 Augustus took into his care and supervision literally thousands of reformation candidates (Allen, Eskridge, Latessa, and Vito, 1985; M. Jones, 2004:63–67).

As far as we know, most of Augustus's "clients" were adults. He did influence juvenile probation, however, because he spoke for and assisted juvenile girls in legal trouble by supervising, guiding, and counseling them. Thus, Augustus's principles and practices have been applied to both juvenile and adult cases in modern times.

Augustus's approach had four fundamental features. First, he was cautious in selecting those individuals to be released into his custody. Second, he assembled a social history on those he was considering in the selection process, a kind of predispositional investigation report. Third, Augustus himself supervised the offenders he selected, and he helped them find jobs and other needed services. Fourth, he regularly reported his clients' progress to the courts, which maintained records for them (Abadinsky, 2002b; Allen et al., 1985).

Based on the work of people like Augustus, Massachusetts established a paid probation officer position for Boston in 1878; in 1880 probation officers were established throughout the entire state. In 1899 Illinois and Minnesota followed the lead of Massachusetts and established probation procedures, but exclusively for juvenile offenders. Michigan's contributions to the development of probation are noted in box 6.1.

Although Augustus's methods seemed successful, the probationary alternative to incarceration did not catch on in most states until the twentieth century. In fact, the juvenile court movement helped speed up the development and expansion of probation, and "by 1927, all but two states had passed enabling legislation to establish both juvenile courts and juvenile probation" (Allen et al., 1985:44). The result was that as the juvenile court movement spread nationwide, the use of probation increased for adults and juveniles.

JUVENILE PROBATION SERVICES

Juvenile probation operates on both the "*front end* of the juvenile justice system for first-time, low-risk offenders [and] the *back end* as an alternative to institutional confinement for more serious offenders" (Torbet, 1996:1). The responsibilities of juvenile probation officers (JPOs) include (1) intake and case screening, (2) social histories and other investigations, (3) client supervision, and (4) service delivery (Allen et al., 1985:45). In this section we examine each responsibility.

Box 6.1   Michigan County Agent

Most juvenile justice textbooks go back to the 1840s and Bostonian John Augustus to describe the evolution of probation services. The next significant step occurred in 1869, when the Massachusetts Board of State Charities created the position of "state-supervising agent." The following year the Massachusetts state legislature gave juveniles separate trials from adult offenders. In 1878, the probation movement took off with the appointment of the first paid full-time probation officer in Boston. From this point to the creation of the juvenile court, we know little about probation services. Historians such as David Rothman and Steven Schlossman have observed that as important as juvenile probation is for a full understanding of juvenile justice, we have few insights as to its use during the period from 1869 to 1899.

The state of Michigan made substantial contributions to expanding and formalizing the duties of those who provided probation-like services. In 1873 it created the position of "county agent," a role that, according to Hurl and Tucker (1997), had many of the same powers and duties as a twenty-first century probation officer. Operating at the county level under the State Board of Charities and Corrections (SBCC), the county agents took charge of boys younger than 16 and girls younger than 17 who had been paroled by the court. According to Hurl and Tucker, by creating the SBCC the Michigan legislature intended

> to find a means to prevent children from entering [correctional institutions], or, failing that, to get them out quickly once they were admitted. Such a mechanism would serve the anti-institutional sentiment of leaders in Michigan's child-saving movement, and save the state the costs of building or expanding children's institutions. (1997:908)

While agents initially served without compensation, except legitimate expenses, by 1875 the state began paying a per-case fee with a fixed maximum amount. Also, the occupational ranks of the county agents shifted from physicians, lawyers, and clergy to teachers, clerks, and insurance agents. While people from professional and white-collar occupations had dominated the county agent ranks for the first quarter century, by 1900 the gradual broadening of the occupational spectrum became apparent as more lower-middle-class agents appeared on the state rolls. Hurl and Tucker also observed that by 1900, when the concept of juvenile courts was beginning to gain popularity throughout the nation, the Michigan county agents clearly viewed themselves as a new occupational group.

Hurl and Tucker make three important points regarding juvenile probation. First, while Massachusetts may have had the first probation officer, Michigan had developed a comprehensive statewide system only four years later. Second, Illinois adopted much of what defined the Michigan system, and these ideals became part of the child-saving movement that was the impetus for the first juvenile court. Third, much of the Michigan system, including paid agents, did not become common practice elsewhere until well into the first decade of the twentieth century. Clearly, we need to reconsider the commonly accepted origins of both juvenile probation services and probation in general.

Sources: Folks (1902); Hawes (1971); Hurl and Tucker (1997); Rothman (1980); Schlossman (1977).

INTAKE AND CASE SCREENING

Juvenile probation officers frequently serve as the juvenile court's intake decision makers. Historically, juvenile probation officers exclusively were responsible for **case screening**. Since probation officers were not trained in the law, the traditional emphasis in screening cases was on **social factors**. Social factors relate to the youngster's personal history and family situation. Although a presumption that cases would be screened for legal sufficiency is inherent in the system, in practice this element is often missing.

Owing to the increased emphasis on due process and procedural regularity concerns, in recent years the **legal factors** associated with the case have received greater attention. The current trend is for the prosecuting attorney's office to play a much more significant case-screening role. Some jurisdictions use a two-stage screening process, with the juvenile probation officer focusing on the case's social factors and the prosecutor focusing on its legal factors. The increased presence of defense attorneys in the juvenile court has also created a more adversarial approach. Prosecutors have become far more attentive to due process rights than the creators of the juvenile court intended. In some jurisdictions the prosecutor's office has taken over case-screening activities (Rubin, 1980; Torbet, 1996:2).

During the case screening and intake process, the juvenile probation officer starts to collect personal information on the child and the family situation. This is the point at which some decision also must be made about the child's detention status, making case screening crucial to the juvenile justice process. In 2000, for example, 42% of the delinquency cases (or roughly 693,000 cases) did not have a petition filed as a result of case screening (Puzzanchera et al., 2004:30).[1] This practice means that the juvenile probation office, sometimes in consultation with the local prosecutor's office, is responsible for screening out those cases that do not seem appropriate for formal juvenile court disposition.

Placing sufficient resources in the juvenile intake unit should maximize the court's effective control over the numbers and kinds of cases that go to adjudication. To decide who gets what, case-screening officers must consider the interests of the child, the family, the victim, and the community. If this is done carefully, the result should be less stigmatization for first and minor offenders and the elimination of unnecessary detention time.

Once the case-screening process is complete, the judge or the juvenile court staff can decide whether (1) the case should be dismissed, (2) informal handling seems to be the best option, or (3) a petition should be filed and a formal hearing held. Another crucial decision made during intake and case screening involves detention. Although not all children are detained at intake, for those who are, the probation intake staff arranges for an interview with the child at the earliest possible time, typically within 24 hours. The intake worker decides alone, or in consultation with the judge or a screening committee, whether to release the child into the parents' or guardians' custody and whether a petition should be filed. In some jurisdictions a petition must be filed if the child is going to be detained.

SOCIAL HISTORY AND OTHER INVESTIGATIONS

Once intake and case screening are completed—and sometimes during the process—the probation staff begins the investigation function. During **case investigation**, the intake staff compiles a preliminary **social history** to help the court in making decisions. This report must be expanded for those youngsters who are adjudicated delinquent. For delinquent youngsters, the court typically requests that the probation officer complete a predisposition report. **Predisposition reports** are similar to **presentence investigation reports (PSIs)** compiled on adult offenders.[2] The process of compiling the child's case history begins early in the process, but the judge rarely sees it until after adjudication.

The National Advisory Committee on Criminal Justice Standards and Goals (1976:651–52) recognized the critical position of the intake and investigation functions and recommended that the juvenile court intake unit be responsible for preparing the predisposition reports. Preparation of a dispositional report by the intake unit is a good idea for several reasons. First, most of the facts surrounding the child's situation can be gathered early and pursued comprehensively. Second, a thorough report, completed early in the process, should provide a basis for making an informed detention decision. Finally, beginning the report at an early stage should cut down on hurried, incomplete, and inaccurate reports.

In making a decision to grant probation, the judge often relies on the juvenile probation officer's predisposition report. These reports should include:

- the child's history of delinquency
- the family situation, including stability and any other factors that might be contributing to the child's delinquent behavior
- school status and academic problems
- treatment and services needed for the child and the family
- an opinion about how the child may act under probation supervision, including the appropriate levels of surveillance necessary (Allen et al., 1985:46)

If the judge decides that the youngster should be given probation, the juvenile probation officer provides supervision or surveillance. Probation supervision by JPOs is more than simply a mechanism for keeping probationers on a short leash or a means to catch youngsters engaged in prohibited behaviors. When done properly, supervision should help JPOs monitor their clients' progress and identify the areas in which they are having adjustment problems (Allen et al., 1985:46).

CLIENT SUPERVISION

Probational client supervision can take a variety of forms. At times probation officers schedule their probationers to appear at the juvenile probation office. This type of meeting may be for the JPO's convenience, or it may be mandated by the need to administer drug tests. Given their highly structured and formal nature, these visits usually provide little information about the client's behavior or adjustment problems. To see youngsters in their natural environment, probation officers occasionally make home visits. In the home setting, the youngster's progress can be addressed not only with the probationer but also with the parents and siblings. Surveillance also takes the form of field visits to the probationer's school and, where appropriate, to the job site or job-training program. Again, the goal is to give the probation officer a sense of how the youngster is doing on probation.

In some jurisdictions JPOs conduct **intensive supervision** with 20 to 25 clients. As the name suggests, officers provide far closer supervision than is common in regular probation. Curfews, multiple weekly contacts, strict enforcement of probation conditions, unscheduled drug testing, and other restorative justice elements are common parts of intensive supervision (Petersilia and Turner, 1990). Such programs may be effective alternatives to incarceration, although cost-effective ISP programs may require a large-scale diversion of youths who otherwise would be incarcerated (Wiebush, 1993). Intensive supervision for juveniles has become so popular that the National Council on Crime and Delinquency has prepared a planning guide that outlines the philosophy and practices associated with an intensive supervision model (Krisberg, Neuenfeldt, Wiebush, and Rodriguez, 1994).

SERVICE DELIVERY

The final probation function—**service delivery**—typically is the one that students think of when they consider a juvenile probation career. Many prospective JPOs believe that much of their time will be spent helping wayward youngsters. Often, this goal is more illusion than reality, more easily discussed than attained.

Most client assistance in juvenile probation is based on social work's **casework service model**. Using this approach, juvenile probation officers attempt to "diagnose, treat, and handle the juvenile and related case matters through home visits, conducting interviews, working with the school, discussions with parents, and making referrals to treatment-delivery agencies" (Allen et al., 1985:46–47). The casework service model facilitates the performance of three tasks:

- *Diagnosis.* Through client and family interviews and the use of psychological tests, some determination will be made about the source of the probationer's problems.

- *Treatment.* Once the diagnosis has been made, the JPO will develop and carry out a treatment or client service plan with the client and appropriate family members.

- *Referral.* In those cases where the JPO does not possess the specialized skills needed, the probationer will be referred to the appropriate treatment agencies.

The reality is that probation officers have too little time and too many cases to deliver anything that resembles therapeutic treatment for the youngsters on their caseloads. Often a cursory attempt is made to diagnose the youngster's problems. This task may be performed through referral to an organization such as a community mental health agency. Attempts at treatment are limited by the time JPOs have to spend with each client and the other demands on their time, such as court appearances and the predisposition report preparation. Occasionally, probation officers may have the time but lack the expertise or the willingness to provide client services. Whatever the constraints under which they operate, most JPOs currently

Theoretical Reflections
The Medical Model Rears Its Head

How is the casework service model related to the medical model? The probation officer's role is to diagnose the illness. Local custom or state law usually will dictate whether they use psychometric testing, systematic observations, experience, or some combination of these tools. The officer, alone or with other professionals, devises a treatment or client service program. In theory, the program is tailor-made for the client's needs; practically speaking, a similar and common "prescription" is generally provided for all youths presenting similar symptoms.

Few probation officers have the time, inclination, or training to deliver more than a rudimentary form of individualized or group therapy. Much of their time outside the office is spent in making home visits and otherwise keeping tabs on clients. Consequently, they find themselves, like physicians who make referrals to specialists,

sending their seriously troubled clients to other more skilled professionals. They must review the reports of these specialists, reports that describe the services they rendered and progress made by the patient.

Is this model necessarily bad? It depends on the ideology of the person to whom you address this question. Liberals tend to view it as a form of mind control and the misapplication of science to social ills. Conservatives view the casework service model as counterproductive pampering of offenders, even youthful ones. The conservative position won the day during the 1970s for adult corrections, as the federal government and states scaled back their medical model-based treatment programs. In juvenile probation the medical model is alive and well.

Sources: Abadinsky (2002b); McShane and Krause (1993); Mays and Winfree (2005).

serve as **service brokers**. Instead of providing diagnosis and treatment themselves, they make referrals to other agencies and organizations that may better serve juvenile probationers' needs.

DELIVERING PROBATION SERVICES

In this chapter's introduction, we referred to a description of juvenile probation as the workhorse of the juvenile justice system, and we alluded to both formal and informal probation. In fairness, then, we must distinguish between these two workhorses. Of course, anyone who has spent time on a farm or knows anything about horses understands that if we team up two horses, they should be a matched set, working together. Otherwise, the quality and quantity of their work are negatively affected. Unless both are pulling the load, the wagon quickly gets off track. This analogy works well for the juvenile justice system.

FORMAL VERSUS INFORMAL PROBATION

Formal probation is nearly identical for both juveniles and adults. **Formal probation** occurs after the judge adjudicates and sentences the accused to probation.

The judge, in consultation with the probation officer, imposes the conditions of probation. The fact that this is *formal* probation does not tell us anything about the restrictiveness of the specific conditions or how much surveillance will be employed. For instance, youths on formal probation may have minimal conditions imposed and sporadic supervision, or they may suffer what the probationers view as harsh conditions, such as the loss of their driving privileges, imposition of a strict after-school curfew, and regular check-in times with the juvenile probation authority.

Children on informal probation often have the same range of conditions as those on formal probation. Thus, it is not the conditions of their probation that separate the two. Rather, the key factor that distinguishes informal from formal probation is the point during the process at which it is imposed. **Informal probation** (sometimes called a **consent decree** or **voluntary probation**) is carried out in one of two ways (see Binder, Geis, and Bruce, 1988:298; Simonsen and Gordon, 1982:297–98). First, the juvenile court intake staff may initiate it before a petition has been filed with the court. Second, a youth can be placed on probation while the petition is suspended and, therefore, before an adjudicatory hearing has been held. In this latter case, the case status may be listed as "not petitioned" and the supervisory status listed as "voluntary probation" (Puzzanchera et al., 2003:38).

The consent decree—or any other informal probation mechanism, including voluntary probation—allows the intake officer to divert appropriate cases before the youngsters further penetrate the formal juvenile justice system. The court may use this method to dispose of first-time (nonserious) offenders, status offenders, and children whose problems stem from family circumstances. This method also expands the juvenile court's options for dealing with the less serious delinquency cases. As an added incentive, those youths who successfully complete informal probation find that they face no further threats of legal action from the juvenile court.

Informal probation generally is not used if the youth denies the allegations. Furthermore, if the alleged offense is serious or is a violent crime, an informal probationary diversion typically is not appropriate. Informal probation may not be suitable for a youngster previously on informal probation and for whom such an approach does not seem to work. In such situations, a formal adjudication petition—and whatever sanction the court deems necessary—may be the only recourse (Abadinsky, 2002b). Informal probation's effectiveness depends on program structure and the availability of probation resources. Quite often, informal probation consists of merely warning a juvenile not to commit future violations. Supervision is practically nonexistent, and enforcement is reactive. If resources allow, informal probation provides a means to develop counseling and referral plans for youths and, sometimes, their families. The result is that informal probation often resembles other diversion programs for nondelinquent and marginally delinquent children.

While informal probation appeals to many youngsters and their parents, its use has been criticized. In many jurisdictions, before juveniles can be placed on informal probation or a consent decree, they must admit to the allegations set forth in the police report or the petition. Consequently, juveniles may be faced with the same dilemma that faces adults in plea-bargaining situations (Abadinsky, 2002b; Mays and Winfree, 2005): Should one admit delinquency involvement to forego adjudication and a potentially more severe sanction? Concern about the potential for coercion and abuse led the Institute of Judicial Administration/American Bar Association (1980) to recommend the elimination of nonjudicial probation entirely.

In spite of calls for its elimination, informal/voluntary probation remains a central feature of many states' youth or children's codes (Sickmund et al., 1998:15). To silence critics, some states provide children due process protections, especially concerning self-incrimination. A key method for achieving this is the removal of the original hearing judge. For example, in New Mexico a judge who elicits or examines materials that would be inadmissible in a hearing on the allegations is not allowed to participate in the adjudication phase. Removal of a judge can happen when the child objects to that particular judge's continuation in the case and one of the following conditions exists: (1) a consent decree has been denied, the child claims innocence, and the outcome has yet to be decided, or (2) a consent decree is granted but the delinquency petition is subsequently reinstated (*New Mexico Criminal and Traffic Law Manual*, 2004:1168–69).

As the examples contained in "International Perspectives" make clear, probation can be implemented in many ways. The divisions and concerns expressed by critics of the U.S. system of juvenile probation—formal versus informal, supervised versus unsupervised release, professional versus volunteer staff—are found in other nations as well.

TRENDS IN PROBATION

Figure 6.1 summarizes the manner in which the nation's juvenile courts handled delinquency cases between 1990 and 2000 (Puzzanchera, 2003a:1; Puzzanchera et al., 2004:52).[3] This figure includes (1) probation as the most severe sanction; (2) other sanctions (e.g., payment of restitution or a fine, participation in a treatment or counseling program); (3) out-of-home residential placement; and (4) waiver to criminal court. The probation statistics are summary measures that include three types of probation: (1) formal probation that results from an adjudication finding (i.e., the child is a delinquent); (2) formal probation as a result of a not-delinquent finding (i.e., the child is not determined to be a delinquent but some sanction, including probation, is ordered by the court); and 3) informal probation where the child's case is not petitioned but some sanction, including probation, is "offered" to the child through voluntary probation or a consent decree.

The trends depicted in figure 6.1 suggest that probation became increasingly important throughout the 1990s and into the 21st century. This movement toward more formal processing was first observed in the mid-to-late 1990s. In 1986, for example, over one-half (53%) of the cases were processed informally (Sickmund et al., 1998:15). By 1995, this percentage had dropped to 45%, and it dropped further to 43% by 1999. Residential placements were less common by the end of the 1990s, accounting for about one in four dispositions for adjudicated delinquents compared to nearly one-third in 1990. Other sanctions, while used frequently by 2000, still proportionately counted for about the same percentage of all delinquency adjudications at the end of the decade as at the beginning. Clearly, the difference was not attributable to waivers, as these numbers changed little throughout the 1990s, and the actual percentage being waived dropped. Most of the increase, both numerically and proportionately, came from adjudicated delinquents placed on probation. The number of court-order probation cases increased by 80% from 1990 to 2000. The number of cases where informal probation was ordered increased about 12% during this same period (Puzzanchera, 2003a:1; Puzzanchera et al., 2004:52). If, as Torbet (1996) claimed, probation was the workhorse of juvenile justice in the mid-1990s, it was pulling an even greater share of the load by the end of the decade.

Box 6.2   International Perspectives
Probation: Comparing Three Nations

Probation may be the workhorse of the U.S. juvenile justice system, but it is far from that for the rest of the world. For example, England, a common-law nation, began phasing out probation for young offenders in the early 1970s, replacing the practice with a supervision order. Such an order may be used for up to three years or until the person reaches his or her eighteenth birthday. The person enforcing the supervision order may be a probation officer but it is not required, as caseworkers from the local social-work authority may function as supervisors. In either case, supervisors must advise and assist their clients and, if such clients fail to abide by the conditions of their supervision, return with them to court, where supervisees may be fined or placed under an "attendance center order" by the local magistrate. Local police or another social service agency operate the attendance centers on the weekends only and offer physical education and craft programs. Another option is the "care order," which terminates parental rights; places the child in the care of local authorities; and provides for housing at a community home, voluntary home, or foster home. Is this probation by another name? Apparently the British do not think so, as they reserve "formal" probation for adult offenders. Juveniles receive the less rigid conditions associated with supervision orders and the use of nonprobation authority personnel, and they have alternative plans for youth such as the attendance center order or care order.

Japan, a nation whose legal system includes elements of both civil law and common law, uses probation but puts its own cultural stamp on the practice: They use volunteers to assist the professional workers. Juvenile justice experts in Japan, however, worry that the use of increasingly older volunteers creates a generation gap between the probationers and their supervisors. It is important to note, however, that formal probation is used in less than 10% of all cases handled by Japanese family courts. A second option does exist in Japan. This is "conditional probation," where a child is placed in the custody of a family court probation officer, so that he or she may observe the conduct of the child and make a recommendation to the court as to the next course of action.

China, a communist nation, essentially does not use probation for adults or juveniles. Legal authorities in China do resort to informal and formal methods of "supervising" youthful offenders in the community. An informal support group—called the *bang jiao*—may be created to assist a youth returning from incarceration or one who has been identified as "at risk." The group consists of the youth's parents; a member of the local neighborhood committee, a sociopolitical entity; a local police officer; the child's work supervisor, if employed; and the head of the local school, even if the child is not in school at the time. Youthful offenders' warranting something more formal find themselves under "public surveillance," China's version of probation. Imposed for a period of time ranging from three months to two years, an order of public surveillance requires that the youth report to the local police on a regular basis; moreover, coworkers would be expected to participate in the surveillance.

Source: Terrill (2003).

Figure 6.1
Judicial Outcomes, 1990–2000

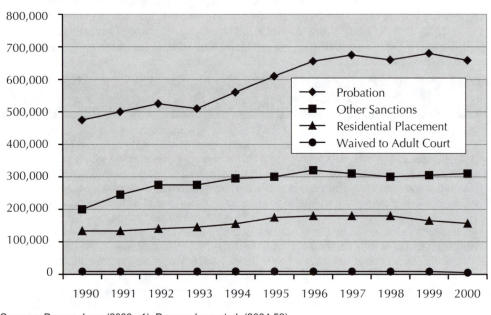

Sources: Puzzanchera (2003a:1); Puzzanchera et al. (2004:52).

PROBATION CONDITIONS

Probation conditions are at the heart of any formal probation system. They are the rules probationers must follow to avoid incarceration, and they define the relationship between the probationer and the probation officer. In a sense, the conditions establish a binding contract among the probationer, the judge, and the probation officer. The specific conditions imposed on juvenile probationers are related to the ever-present concept of discretion. This fact is evident in the development, imposition, and enforcement of probation conditions. Although juvenile probation is defined both by laws and administrative regulations, JPOs exercise a great deal of authority in carrying out their duties. Therefore, what the JPO says often becomes "the law." Yet JPOs are more than rule enforcers. They may serve as adult role models for their clients. They set limits and expect results, working with the family to reinforce these "lessons" at home. They monitor the child's academic progress or level of participation in treatment. The multiple roles that JPOs perform can make the job one of the most challenging in the criminal justice system.

THE PROBATION PLAN

In most juvenile probation offices a probation plan is developed to guide each offender's treatment. These probation plans are based on several factors. For instance, the diagnostic and dispositional reports prepared by the intake and detention staffs may be reviewed. Additionally, the probation officer should determine the availability of community treatment services for the probationer. Finally, each probationer should take part in developing the probation plan by which he or she must abide.

Once the probation plan is formulated, consideration must be given to the probation conditions imposed by the juvenile court judge and the JPO. In a perfect world the probation conditions would reflect individualized justice and meet the unique needs of each youngster. Unfortunately, in our imperfect juvenile justice system we are often forced to make do. Nevertheless, probation conditions should be reasonable and related to the current offense. Consider the typical probation conditions listed in box 6.3.

The length of a formal probation disposition varies by both statute and practice among jurisdictions. Statutory limits also exist for most types of informal probation, although it is fairly easy to extend these. Most youngsters are on probation for one year or less. Commonly, the upper age limit of juvenile court jurisdiction determines the maximum term of probation.

ASSESSING THE CONDITIONS OF PROBATION: HOW GOOD MUST THEY BE?

Throughout the history of the juvenile justice system, the presumption that youngsters were dealt with as individuals and consequently received individualized dispositions has stood at its core. When it comes to probation, however, the reality is that many agencies have photocopies of probation condition forms. Often these forms are handed to the new probationers on their first visit to the juvenile probation office. The list of typical conditions we have provided in box 6.3 shows the constraints under which juvenile probationers may be placed.

We traditionally assess probation conditions as being either general or specific. Moreover, most rules address either new acts of delinquency or probation condition violations. With respect to the first concern, general conditions are those imposed on all probationers. Most of the conditions provided in box 6.3 are general conditions. Virtually any juvenile placed on probation would be expected to abide by them.

Specific conditions apply to particular youngsters. Consider the case of a juvenile who has been placed on probation for shoplifting CDs from a music store at the local mall. As a specific probation condition, this youngster might be prohibited from entering that or any other music store, or possibly even enjoined from visiting shopping malls. Driving restrictions constitute typical probation conditions. For such restrictions to be viewed as fair—and, therefore, have some ameliorative effect—they should be related to the offense. For example, a youth who was found to have been driving drunk would be forbidden from driving at all. Or, suppose a youth provided transportation for peers to engage in an act of vandalism some distance from their community. The youth may need the car to get to work and school. If that's the case, driving is allowed for work and school but at no other time. Finally, in some specific cases and depending upon community resources, the

---

Box 6.3   Typical Conditions of Supervision for Probation Services

The following list has been assembled from various probation documents, and the individual items illustrate the diverse approach taken toward dealing with juvenile probationers.

1. Probationers may be ordered to pay fines or make restitution or reparations.
2. Probationers may be ordered to submit to physical and/or mental examinations and treatment.
3. Probationers must obey the orders of the probation officer.
4. Probationers may not leave the court's jurisdiction without prior permission.
5. The privilege of operating a motor vehicle may be suspended for probationers.
6. If the probationer is arrested, he or she must immediately report it to the probation officer.
7. Older juveniles may be required to work in addition to, or instead of, attending school. Juveniles falling under compulsory school attendance laws must regularly attend school.
8. Probationers must refrain from using alcoholic beverages or controlled substances.
9. Possession by a probationer of any firearm or other weapon is forbidden.
10. Probationers may not associate with known criminals or, possibly, other probationers.
11. Probationers must meet regularly with the probation officer and allow probation officers to visit their homes, schools, or places of employment.
12. Probationers must follow orders issued by the court.
13. Probationers must obey their parents and observe all curfew restrictions.
14. Probationers must submit to searches on demand by governmental agents.
15. Probationers must refrain from violating federal, state, or city laws or ordinances.

---

child may be ordered to participate in a specialized treatment program, such as an antidrug or antigang program, or even sex offender therapy.

Not only can probation conditions be classified as general or specific, but failure to abide by them can be categorized as either delinquent (criminal) violations or technical violations. The final condition in box 6.3 illustrates a "criminal" probation violation. In other words, youths on probation violate a primary probation condition when they break any other law, including curfews and failure to attend school for those youngsters governed by compulsory school attendance laws. Traffic tickets may or may not count here, depending on the nature of the original offense for which the youngster received probation.

Technical conditions exist because the judge and the juvenile probation officer want them; the court's authority, not a legislative enactment, supports their imposition and enforcement. Violations of technical conditions include leaving the jurisdiction without permission, failure to report at specified times, failure to keep counseling appointments, or changing jobs without prior notification. While a single technical violation might not warrant formal action by the JPO, an accumulation of technical violations may result in a sanction.

Theoretical Reflections
The Conditions of Probation and Criminological Theorizing

We believe that many probation conditions have clear, if unstated, links to criminological theory. Before making these links, we need to issue a series of warnings. First, we do not contend that probation officers and judges have systematically consulted criminology textbooks or read the general criminological theory literature. Trial and error, common sense, good observational skills, and a general appreciation for human social behavior have led to these conditions (and, we suspect, to much criminological theorizing). Second, we offer these linkages to stimulate discussion about the probation rules. Third, because of space limitations, we have collapsed some rules into groups. Finally, we recognize that many theories could be offered in support of more than one condition; we are just making the linkages that occur to us.

The links include the following:

1. Fines and reparations are part of the accountability thesis and are central elements in both restorative and balanced justice. They also are an outgrowth of the classical position that all acts have consequences, and of the just-deserts notion of retribution or payment for one's sins.

2. Physical examinations are part of the biological theories' search for organic bases of delinquency, while mental functioning or competency exams reflect the psychologists' tendencies to look for defective or deficient thinking processes and mental abilities.

3. Requiring probationers to obey authority, to follow society's rules, to limit their free-ranging movement throughout society, and to meet regularly with social-control agents are all time-honored ideas with roots in the Judeo-Christian tradition, among others. They also are central themes in social-control theories. The existence and enforcement of rules by social-control mechanisms, contend control theorists, hold society together.

Offenders also must respect and obey these same sets of rules if they are to succeed. Some rules, such as controlling probationers' movements in society, have ties to routine activities theory (limit offenders' proximity to likely victims). Restrictions may also be counterproductive. For example, restricting driving privileges may be viewed as punishment for its own sake. Such restrictions become what Agnew's general strain theory calls the removal of a positively valued stimuli, which can cause delinquency.

4. As Akers and other behaviorists have observed, drugs are nonsocial reinforcers. Bad behavior usually follows excessive drinking and illicit drug use. Refraining from the use of illicit drugs and alcohol may also reflect the idea that some individuals have addictive personalities. Keeping them away from drugs reduces the likelihood that they will become intoxicated and, in that state, commit an offense.

5. The "known associates" rule exhibits ties to several theories, perhaps the most obvious ones being differential association and social learning. To break the delinquency cycle, one must cut off the youth from illicit definitions and other criminal reinforcers, most of which come from known criminal associates. The rule could also help reverse the movement toward a criminal career, given that known criminal associates are a recognized pathway to crime. Lastly, peer controls, the presence of unconventional peers and the absence of conventional ones, are important to understanding the social bond. Upsetting negative peer controls and allowing for the substitution of prosocial ones reads like both a probation condition and a principle of Hirschi's social bonding theory.

Source: Winfree and Abadinsky (2003).

PROBATION REVOCATION

Most legal authorities define a **probation violation** as "an act or failure to act by a probationer which does not conform to the conditions of his probation" (Bureau of Justice Statistics, 1981:175). A violation of *any* probation condition could result in a revocation of probationary status. Probation officers frequently distinguish between technical violations and criminal violations, with additional criminal violations being considered the more serious of the two types. Nevertheless, the most important point to emphasize is that most violations do not result in revocation for at least four reasons.

First, the probation officer may feel that the youngster deserves another chance. In such a case the JPO will likely mandate more stringent conditions, closer supervision, or additional forms of treatment. Second, the JPO may feel that the violation was a result of factors beyond the juvenile's control. Third, the juvenile may need treatment services that are that are available in the community but unavailable in an institution. Finally, juvenile probation officers may harbor doubts about secure incarceration's effectiveness for most juvenile offenders. JPOs may believe that institutionalization should be the last resort, reserved only for the most serious delinquents.

If any of the probation conditions are violated, particularly in those situations where there is a persistent violation pattern, the JPO can request that the juvenile court judge review the youth's probationary status. Because of the legal protections extended to both juvenile and adult probationers, revocation proceedings have become much more formal than they traditionally were (del Carmen, Parker, and Reddington, 1998).

PROBATION REVOCATION: THE LEGAL ISSUES

When juveniles commit further criminal violations, JPOs may temporarily detain them while the court decides their fate. In the end, they may be institutionalized with or without adjudication on the new charges. Simply committing another delinquent act is sufficient for the judge to order the probationer's incarceration. Before a formal probation revocation occurs, however, a whole set of legal procedures comes into play.

The **probation revocation** process within the juvenile justice system operates under the same legal guidelines as in the adult criminal justice system. The U.S. Supreme Court, beginning with *Mempa v. Rhay* (389 U.S. 128, 1967), set forth due process standards that apply to both probation and parole revocation proceedings.[4] The majority opinion in *Mempa v. Rhay* held that the sentencing procedures followed by the State of Washington should have allowed Mempa to have an attorney present during his probation revocation hearing. In reality, *Mempa v. Rhay* applied only to a very narrow range of circumstances; specifically, the right to counsel during probation revocation hearings. Nevertheless, it provided the basis for extending other constitutional due process protections to the probation revocation process.

Mempa v. Rhay was followed by *Morrissey v. Brewer* (408 U.S. 471, 1972). Since *Morrissey* applied to parole revocations, it is discussed in detail in chapter 8. However, for the time being it is important to note that the Supreme Court articulated due process protections in *Morrissey* that later were applied to probation revocations. Chief Justice Warren Burger wrote for the 8 to 1 majority in *Morrissey* and noted that to ensure constitutional due process, the individual facing revocation proceedings must:

- be given written notice of the alleged violations
- be told about all the evidence relating to the alleged violations
- have the opportunity to present his or her case and to call witnesses and provide documentary evidence on his or her behalf
- be allowed to confront and cross-examine accusing witnesses
- have a neutral hearing body review the case (presumably, for parole violations this would be the parole board, and for probation violations it would be the court having jurisdiction over the case)
- have a written record of the case findings and the grounds or justifications for those findings (see Davis, 1980; del Carmen, Ritter, and Witt, 1993)

Two points are especially noteworthy about *Morrissey*. First, as the Supreme Court noted, parole—and probably probation—revocations are "not part of a criminal prosecution and that the full panoply of rights due a defendant in such a proceeding" (408 U.S. 481) do not apply. While revocation proceedings are governed by constitutional protections, they are not subject to the full range of due process rights. Therefore, a revocation hearing is different from a trial, and the attendant procedural protections are provided to a lesser extent. Second, although *Mempa v. Rhay* provided the right to counsel in probation revocation hearings, it did not say whether this right applied to hearings involving indigent individuals. In fact, as Chief Justice Burger wrote in the *Morrissey* majority opinion: "We do not reach or decide whether the parolee is entitled to the assistance of retained counsel or to an appointed counsel if he is indigent" (408 U.S. 490).

Another significant case concerning probation revocation rights is *Gagnon v. Scarpelli* (411 U.S. 778, 1973). This case was decided the year after *Morrissey* and it raised two important issues with regard to due process rights for probationers facing revocation proceedings. Perhaps the most significant point was that the Supreme Court explicitly noted that due process guarantees applied to both probation and parole revocations. The second point was significant for what the Court did not say. Regarding the issue of the right to counsel, the Supreme Court refused to accept a blanket requirement of the right to counsel, and instead said that trial and appellate courts would have to resolve this question case by case.

THE SCOPE OF PROBATION

Probation—as practiced by John Augustus and envisioned by the juvenile court founders—was intended for a small numbers of offenders in close contact with and under close supervision by a probation officer. Modern probation scarcely resembles the original ideals. In fact, in many juvenile probation offices the work experience resembles an assembly line in a busy factory. What is the impact of offense type on the decision to impose probation? As table 6.1 shows, adjudicated delinquents were placed on formal probation in more than half of all cases. Throughout the 1990s, the likelihood of formal probation increased for all offense types. For example, in 1990 the range between the offense type most likely to receive probation (property offenses) and the offense least likely to receive probation (public order offenses) was 6%. In 2000, property offenses and public order offenses were still the most and least likely, respectively, to receive probation, but the difference between them shrunk to 5%. At the start of the new decade, probation was more likely than any other sanction, regardless of the offense type.

Table 6.1   Percent of Adjudicated Delinquency Cases Placed on Formal Probation, 1990, 1995, 2000

Most serious offense	1990	1995	2000
Delinquency	56%	54%	63%
Person	55	54	64
Property	58	56	65
Drugs	54	54	62
Public order	52	50	60

Source: Puzzanchera et al. (2004:49, 52, 54).

Table 6.2 shows the breakdown by referral age and offense for the years 1990, 1995, and 2000. The smallest percentage of youngsters on probation—and the only groups in this table to drop below one-half—involved juveniles 16 or older who were adjudicated for public order or person offenses in 1995 (47% and 49%, respectively). As a general observation, children who are 15 or younger are more likely to be placed on probation than adjudicated delinquents older than 15. In fact, the differences between these two groups grew more marked by 2000, when 2 of every 3 adjudicated delinquents 15 and younger received probation, contrasted with 59% of those 16 or older. The differences by offense type were small compared to the differences by age.

Table 6.2   Percent of Adjudicated Delinquency Cases Resulting in Formal Probation, by Referral Age and Offense, 1990, 1995, 2000

Most serious offense	1990		1995		2000	
	15 or younger	16 or older	15 or younger	16 or older	15 or younger	16 or older
Delinquency	57%	54%	57%	51%	66%	59%
Person	56	52	56	49	66	59
Property	60	56	58	53	67	61
Drugs	54	55	57	52	66	60
Public order	52	52	52	47	65	55

Source: Puzzanchera et al. (2004:50).

Noting the gender differences that arise in the juvenile probation process is important, as the juvenile justice system has a long history of treating male and female offenders differently. Once petitioned, females are *slightly less likely* to be formally adjudicated than males (68% to 62%), and once they are adjudicated, they are *more likely* to be placed on formal probation (Puzzanchera et al., 2004:50). Between 1989 and 1993, the number of female probationers increased 26%, while their male counterparts increased 16% (Poe-Yamagata and Butts, 1996:13). Table 6.3 contains the percentage differences for adjudicated male and female delinquents for 1990, 1995, and 2000.

Another important analysis of juvenile probation involves the race of the probationers. Table 6.4 presents the percentages of youngsters placed on probation by race and type of offense for 1990, 1995, and 2000 (Puzzanchera et al., 2004:51). As is apparent from this table, by 2000 white youngsters and those of other races were

A juvenile and her probation officer talk about whether to extend or terminate the girl's house arrest. House arrest—restricting a person to his or her home except for specific or limited purposes—is sometimes used by the juvenile court as a means of controlling a child whose misbehavior warrants a legal intervention short of incarceration. In this case the girl, aged 15, allegedly assaulted a school counselor at an alternative school for students with truancy and behavior issues. The Morgan County (Illinois) Juvenile Court placed the girl on house arrest until she and her mother met with the court's probation officer, at which point the girl was allowed to leave her home again.

Table 6.3   Percentage of Adjudicated Delinquency Cases Resulting in Formal Probation, by Gender and Offense, 1990, 1995, 2000

Most serious offense	Female			Male		
	1990	1995	2000	1990	1995	2000
All Offenses	60%	59%	68%	55%	53%	62%
Person	63	60	69	53	52	62
Property	62	60	70	58	55	64
Drugs	59	59	66	54	53	62
Public order	53	54	63	51	49	59

Source: Puzzanchera et al. (2004:50).

slightly more likely than juveniles who were black to receive probation. Additionally, from 1985 to 1995 the percentage of white juveniles placed on probation stayed virtually the same, declining from 56% to 55% (Butts et al., 1996:32; Sickmund et al., 1998:32). During this period, black youths on probation declined from 58% to 52%, and youngsters of other races decreased from 55% to 53%.

By the late 1990s, any substantial variation by race had all but disappeared, a pattern also found in 2000. This statement, however, does not hold up for all of the offense-specific comparisons. Take, for example, black youths adjudicated for drug offenses as their most serious law violation in 2000. Only 56% of them received probation, compared to 64% of the white youths and 68% of the youths of other races. Clearly, the courts were not treating these children equally. The question that is not answerable from these statistics, however, is whether the actual offenses charged were identical. Nonetheless, these differences are troubling and fit with the pattern of disproportionate minority confinement—especially for black males—that will be addressed in greater detail in chapter 12. In no other offense-specific comparisons by race are the differences greater than two or three percent.

This apparently unequal treatment for black youths adjudicated for drug offenses seems dramatic, but neither OJJDP nor the National Center for Juvenile Justice explores the legal factors (for example, present offense or offense history) or extralegal factors (such as age, income, and family status) that might account for

Table 6.4   Percentage of Adjudicated Delinquency Cases Resulting in Formal Probation, by Race and Offense, 1990, 1995, 2000

Most serious offense	White			Black			Other		
	1990	1995	2000	1990	1995	2000	1990	1995	2000
Delinquency	57%	55%	63%	55%	52%	62%	55%	53%	64%
Person	56	55	64	53	51	66	54	53	65
Property	58	57	65	58	55	64	55	53	62
Drugs	59	58	64	51	48	56	57	56	68
Public order	51	50	60	53	50	60	57	52	63

Source: Puzzanchera et al. (2004:51).

this variation. Should this trend continue, and the disparities become greater, future researchers should address these factors for probation as they have for incarceration.

The Organization of Juvenile Probation Agencies

The nation's legal jurisdictions organize juvenile probation agencies and deliver juvenile probation services in several ways. Table 6.5 shows some structural arrangements and types of agencies responsible for juvenile probation. Generalizing about the delivery of juvenile probation services is difficult, since there are state-to-state and even county-to-county variations. Making generalizations about the organization of these programs is nearly impossible.

First, as table 6.5 shows, there are probation programs at the local and state levels. As this table illustrates, local juvenile courts are responsible for administering juvenile probation services in 15 states and the District of Columbia. In New York and Oregon juvenile probation is managed locally as an executive function. Seven states (Connecticut, Hawaii, Iowa, Nebraska, North Carolina, South Dakota, and Utah) house juvenile probation within a state-level judicial agency, typically the administrative office of courts. Ten states provide juvenile probation services through a statewide executive agency, such as a corrections department, youth authority, or similar agency. The rest employ various arrangements, and some states (for example, Arkansas, California, Kentucky, and Washington) appear in multiple places on this table and are in bold type.

Second, probation and parole agencies differ in the types of clients they serve and the functions they perform. A basic distinction for most of these agencies is whether they handle only juveniles, only adults, or both juveniles and adults. Of those agencies handling a single function (for our purposes, juvenile probation), 50% have juvenile responsibilities only. Slightly more agencies handle two or more functions, although fewer manage adult and juvenile probation than administer juvenile probation alone.

Although listing all the possible variations for delivering juvenile probation services is impossible, we can offer three categories within which most of these agencies fall. These categories include (American Correctional Association, 2003):

- *A single state agency.* The most comprehensive method for administering probation and parole services is through a single statewide agency (normally the department of corrections). This agency manages both adult and juvenile offenders and is responsible for supervising probationers and parolees.

- *A juvenile justice services agency.* The chief distinction between this type of organization and a single state agency is that a juvenile justice services agency (sometimes called the youth authority, as in California) has jurisdiction only over juvenile offenders. Also, this type of agency may be concerned with youth problems other than delinquency (dependency, status offenses, and neglect, for example).

- *Local provision of services.* The most decentralized approach is through the local court apparatus. This arrangement gives the judge and juvenile proba-

Table 6.5   State-By-State Organization of Juvenile Probation

State Administration		Local Administration	
Judicial Branch	**Executive Branch**	**Judicial Branch**	**Executive Branch**
Connecticut	Alaska	Alabama	**California**
Hawaii	**Arkansas**	Arizona	**Idaho**
Iowa	Delaware	**Arkansas**	**Minnesota**
Kentucky	Florida	**California**	**Mississippi**
Nebraska	**Georgia**	Colorado	New York
North Carolina	**Idaho**	District of Columbia	Oregon
North Dakota	**Kentucky**	**Georgia**	**Washington**
South Dakota	**Louisiana**	Illinois	**Wisconsin**
Utah	Maine	Indiana	
West Virginia	Maryland	Kansas	
	Minnesota	**Kentucky**	
	Mississippi	**Louisiana**	
	New Hampshire	Massachusetts	
	New Mexico	Michigan	
	North Dakota	**Minnesota**	
	Oklahoma	Missouri	
	Rhode Island	Montana	
	South Carolina	Nevada	
	Tennessee	New Jersey	
	Vermont	Ohio	
	Virginia	**Oklahoma**	
	West Virginia	Pennsylvania	
	Wyoming	**Tennessee**	
		Texas	
		Virginia	
		Washington	
		Wisconsin	
		Wyoming	

Note: States listed in bold print provide probation services in a variety of ways. Some large counties operate local probation departments, and smaller counties have probation services provided by a state agency.
Source: Torbet (1996:2).

tion staff more flexibility, but at the expense of a narrow funding base. Local control may mean that salaries and hiring are handled locally, and this can lead to relatively low pay, political favoritism, and the lack of qualified staff.

THE FUTURE OF JUVENILE PROBATION

In the final section of this chapter we engage in a little crystal ball gazing to see what the future may hold for juvenile probation in the United States. Although predicting the future is a risky proposition, in some fields—and juvenile probation may be one of those—there are many unmistakable trends that seem likely to persist. In particular we are going to look at (1) greater specialization and job differentiation in juvenile probation, (2) the increasing uses of technology in probation, (3) service delivery coordination, (4) consolidation of youth-serving functions, (5) the parents' role in the juvenile probation process, and (6) the serious investment in or reinventing of juvenile probation (DiIulio, 1997; Schaffner, 1997).

SPECIALIZATION AND JOB DIFFERENTIATION

Several changes are taking place in the juvenile justice system that may have a profound impact on probation service administration and delivery. In many jurisdictions the most serious and least serious offenders are being removed from the juvenile court's jurisdiction. Many states automatically try as adults those youngsters accused of homicide, rape, and other serious crimes. The least serious offenders are being diverted into community-based programming. Together, these practices leave the juvenile court and juvenile probation officers to deal with youngsters who have committed "normal" acts of delinquency. Given the relatively large number of these youths in comparison to the number of JPOs available, juvenile probation agencies are going to have to make some tough choices about how to process and supervise these cases. Two options seem worth exploring.

First, juvenile probation departments must pay more attention to **case classification**. Institutional personnel have long recognized that not all inmates can be housed together and treated similarly. By contrast, many probation agencies treat new probationers as just additional clients on the caseload, without consideration for the clients' treatment needs and the level of supervision necessary. Therefore, to maximize the use of scarce personnel resources, juvenile probation agencies must begin a client classification process.

Second, after establishing a classification process, juvenile probation officers will need to differentiate job responsibilities, meaning that some JPOs will be assigned relatively small caseloads of high-risk offenders who need close supervision. Other JPOs may have many low-risk clients who need only minimal contact, surveillance, and service delivery, similar to those on informal probation. The idea of caseload equalization will be based on overall workload, not simply on equal distribution by numbers of cases. This approach, when combined with case classification, should allow probation agencies to put personnel resources into those areas of greatest need or where the maximum impact can be achieved.

INCREASING USE OF TECHNOLOGY

Along with the use of caseload classification and job specialization, juvenile probation agencies are facing a future that will be much more technology driven than is currently the case. While the ideal of probation work has always been face-to-face contact with clients, resource limits and increasing caseloads may require the adoption of new technologies to replace or supplement the human touch.

One example where technology already has been applied to both adult and, to a lesser extent, juvenile offenders concerns electronically monitored home confinement, or house arrest (Lilly and Ball, 1987; Lilly, Ball, and Wright, 1987). Home confinement has allowed the criminal justice system to punish more severely some

offenders—such as drunk drivers—who otherwise might receive traditional probation. Moreover, home confinement—combined with electronic detection devices—
provides a highly desirable alternative to incarceration for many juvenile offenders.
Is this method less expensive than incarceration? Not necessarily, especially when
we factor in the threat to the community. Does it provide an expansion or extension of probation supervision? In all likelihood, electronic monitoring of home
confinement is merely the first wave of technology for juvenile probation services.

COORDINATION OF SERVICE DELIVERY

One juvenile justice reality is that the system barely resembles a system. A major
future challenge is to create a much more consistent and coherent service delivery
system for youthful probationers. One example of coordinated services brought
together by a common philosophy is the American Probation and Parole Association's so-called balanced approach to juvenile probation, highlighted in box 6.4.

The greatest difficulty in coordinating services is that so many different groups,
all of them with their own agendas, are responsible for providing assistance to juvenile probationers. Most of these organizations lie outside juvenile probation's
domain, so coordination has to come through informal contacts. Coordination

---

**Box 6.4   A Balanced Approach to Juvenile Probation:
Punishment Philosophy Meets Practice**

The American Probation and Parole Association's **balanced approach probation
model** incorporates both liberal and conservative philosophies toward juvenile offenders.
Marilyn McShane and Wesley Krause identified four principles at the heart of this approach:

• *Accountability*. This brand of **juvenile accountability** draws from the restorative justice
perspective and emphasizes restitution and community service; however, the youth must
manifestly and overtly take responsibility for his or her own actions.

• *Community protection*. Part of the 1970s and 1980s conservative agenda, **community
protection** allows probation officers to select from among different options, including house
arrest, electronic monitoring, substance abuse testing, curfews, mandatory school attendance, and intensive supervision, as part of a total package for the youthful probationer.

• *Competency development*. In the balanced approach, competency development largely
replaces rehabilitation. **Competency development** emphasizes learning academic,
vocational, social, and other daily living skills.

• *Individualization*. To better tailor probation to individual offenders, **individualization**
includes (1) *legal classification*, or the specific type of offender involved; (2) *treatment prescription*, or any specific treatment required for the offender, including drug treatment,
individual or family counseling, and interpersonal skills training; and (3) *risk assessment*,
or the risk posed to community and offender.

Many states include balanced elements in their codes or are considering their adoption.
A few states, Florida for example, have incorporated the philosophy throughout the juvenile
justice system.

Sources: Freivalds (1996); McShane and Krause (1993:267–68); Mays and Winfree (2005:220).

really becomes problematic when dealing with private agencies. Juvenile probation agencies have no legal authority over private service providers, so JPOs must constantly engage in networking with their counterparts in these organizations.

CONSOLIDATION OF YOUTH-SERVING FUNCTIONS

Related to the issue of service coordination is the trend toward the consolidation of many diverse agencies and organizations responsible for delivering services to youngsters. Some states have made a move toward establishing a state agency similar to the California Youth Authority. This organization would provide juvenile probation and parole services, juvenile correctional facilities, and social services designed to meet the needs of children and families involved in dependency, neglect, and abuse cases. The "one-stop shopping" approach helps bring together various services and organizations that might be dealing with the same clients at different times or under different circumstances.

A serious problem facing probation is the lack of resources. Juvenile probation officers often spend the bulk of their time with the most serious offenders on their caseloads, especially those on formal probation. The result is that less serious cases, particularly youngsters on informal probation, get relatively little attention. Therefore, if less serious offenders' needs are to be met, then one of two likely approaches must be employed. One option is to make informal probation a program unto itself. In this way a budget could be developed and a staff employed to address these youngsters' service needs. A second choice is to use community volunteers to assist youngsters on informal probation.

THE ROLE OF PARENTS IN JUVENILE PROBATION

At least 10 states and several municipalities have adopted laws mandating parental responsibility for delinquency (Dundes, 1994; Geis and Binder, 1991; Sanborn, 1996).[5] States are increasingly willing to hold parents civilly liable for damages caused by their children in cases such as vandalism. Some states, such as Alabama, Hawaii, Louisiana, Oregon, and Wyoming, have adopted laws threatening fines or prison terms for being a negligent parent, although some of these laws have been struck down by appellate courts ("Some states target parents," 1999). Additionally, California requires parents to attend court-ordered parenting classes operated by juvenile probation offices. Often the parents may feel that the state is their adversary rather than their ally in dealing with children who have been adjudicated delinquent (see, for example, Schaffner, 1997). Frequently, a single parent may be struggling financially to keep a family afloat and struggling to maintain disciplinary control over the children as well. The juvenile probation office can probably lend assistance in such situations. However, as Schaffner (1997) found in one California program, most of the parenting classes are spent telling the parents what a poor job they have done in raising their children. The result is an overwhelmingly negative message with little positive support or guidance.

Whatever else may happen in the juvenile justice system, parents increasingly will be held accountable for their children's law violations. If this outcome occurs with regularity, the juvenile probation officer's role may expand from simply guiding and counseling delinquent youngsters to dealing in a much larger context with "delinquent families." The present staffing and structure of most juvenile probation offices make this virtually impossible.

REINVENTING JUVENILE PROBATION

John DiIulio (1997:40), a conservative critic of many criminal justice policies, has said that "the U.S. spends next to nothing on the adult and juvenile probation systems, and gets about what they pay for." However, rather than endorsing further get-tough approaches and scrapping the juvenile system, DiIulio calls for three initiatives:

- closer surveillance and more "face-to-face oversight" for probationers, especially those charged with serious offenses
- smaller caseloads to allow for closer surveillance and more meaningful contacts between probationers and probation officers
- better pay for juvenile probation officers (DiIulio, 1997:40–42)

Following these recommendations would require a major capital infusion and a reversal of two or three decades of practices. These actions would, in essence, reinvent probation.

SUMMARY

Envisioning the juvenile justice system without the juvenile court's pivotal role is difficult. Similarly, thinking of the juvenile court's development in the United States without considering juvenile probation's vital role is nearly impossible. In effect, the juvenile court and probation services have developed hand in hand for 100 years to give us the juvenile justice system we have today. What can we now say about the role juvenile probation has played in the past and the role it will play in the future? Several possible answers to this question are worth mentioning.

First, juvenile probation historically has allowed the juvenile court to express its *parens patriae* philosophy of acting in the child's best interests. Often, juvenile probation has been the means through which the best and most noble intentions envisioned by the juvenile court were manifested. However, at times, in the name of benevolent and regenerative care, juvenile probation officers have undercut whatever legal protections have existed for youngsters accused of delinquency.

Second, from the very beginning, juvenile probation officers have played a major role in the juvenile court's intake process. This function has involved decisions about holding youths in detention and, ultimately, about whether a petition should be filed for the child. The real focus, as far as juvenile probation officers are concerned, has been on the social factors surrounding the child and the child's family. Over the past two decades intake decisions increasingly have become dominated by legal considerations, and the prosecuting attorney now plays a substantial role in the process (see Rubin, 1980). Nevertheless, probation officers still are active and involved in the juvenile court's intake process, and their influence should not be underestimated.

Third, the heart of juvenile probation has been investigation (compiling social histories and predisposition reports) and supervision. These two responsibilities continue to dominate resource allocation and discussions about juvenile probation today. Investigation and supervision are the responsibilities most people envision when they think of juvenile probation.

Fourth, as we begin the new century, juvenile probation's investigation and supervision functions must change. It is possible that information-gathering tasks will be automated, and much of the information may be collected by phone or computer by paraprofessionals, such as college students doing internships in juvenile probation offices. By contrast, supervision occupies much of the JPOs' workdays, and this function will become increasingly sophisticated and stringent. Technology will allow JPOs to provide very close surveillance for those youngsters who need to be kept on short leashes. The result will be that much of what will pass for juvenile probation will begin to resemble its adult counterpart, and many duties will be more oriented toward law enforcement than toward treatment or service delivery. For some potential JPOs this approach will be more attractive; for others it will be less attractive.

Finally, as we have suggested in some places and explicitly said in others, the juvenile court's second century will see major changes for juvenile probation. Caseload size and the continuing limits on personnel resources inevitably will mandate changes. JPOs must adapt to a changing environment, or their role will be redefined for them by others. Will these changes take us "back to the future," with small caseloads and intensive supervision as envisioned by John Augustus? Or will probation services increasingly be provided in an environment dominated by technology, with very little of the human touch?

CRITICAL REVIEW QUESTIONS

1. To what extent were the services rendered by Augustus different from modern probation work?

2. We describe probation as both a front-end and back-end operation for the juvenile justice system. First, what do these characterizations mean? Second, how do the various categories of probation officer responsibilities inform both operations?

3. Compare and contrast traditional probation services and the program described as a balanced approach to juvenile probation.

4. The conditions of release stand at the core of any probation plan. Provide a response to the following contention: To improve the success of juvenile probation, we need only to eliminate the technical violations and concentrate on new acts of delinquency.

5. The juvenile probation system's revocation process is nearly identical to that found in the adult system. Is that good or bad, and why? (That is, why should juveniles be exempt from or protected by the Supreme Court decisions governing adult probation?)

6. What do you make of the recent trends in formal probation?

7. What specific information about the trends for different offenses by age, gender, and race do you find most informative? Why did you pick those trends?

8. Various states have adopted three main models for providing juvenile probation services. Which one makes the most sense to you? Support your choice with your own observations or material from the text that buttresses your position.

9. Which single aspect of crystal ball gazing in which we engaged do you think holds the most potential to improve the quality of probation services rendered juveniles? ("None" is not an appropriate answer. Make a judgment and support it with your own analysis of the problem and the solutions.)

10. In retrospect, how do you respond to the questions posed about the opening vignette? Why do you think Beverly and Margaret have similar feelings about juvenile probation?

RECOMMENDED READINGS

Abadinsky, Howard (2002). *Probation and Parole: Theory and Practice*, 8th ed. Upper Saddle River, NJ: Prentice-Hall. We are unaware of a textbook on probation or parole dedicated exclusively to juveniles. Abadinsky wrote the first edition of this book while he was a senior parole officer with the New York State Division of Parole. The current edition retains the gritty realism and no-nonsense approach to the tasks performed by adult and juvenile probation (and parole) officers. Chapter 4 ("The Juvenile Courts and Juvenile Justice") and chapter 5 ("Juvenile Probation, Institutions and Aftercares") are the only chapters related exclusively to juvenile justice issues. However, Abadinsky integrates juvenile justice practices and programs throughout the book.

Torbet, Patricia McFall (1996). *Juvenile Probation: The Workhorse of the Juvenile Justice System*. Washington, DC: Office of Juvenile Justice and Delinquency Prevention, U.S. Department of Justice. While a decade old, this document does an excellent job of summarizing the issues related to probation's role in juvenile justice, and not a great deal has changed in the intervening years. Torbet, a staff member at the National Center for Juvenile Justice, produced this official OJJDP publication. She does an excellent job of summarizing the definition of juvenile probation, service delivery models, questions of caseload sizes, and the influences of county size. Torbet also provides an overview of the probation officer's job (including salary ranges) and the characteristics of youngsters on probation.

KEY TERMS

balanced approach probation model
case classification
case histories
case investigation
case screening
casework service model
community protection
competency development
consent decree
formal probation

individualization
informal probation
intensive supervision
judicial reprieve
juvenile accountability
legal factors
predisposition reports
presentence investigation
   reports (PSIs)
probation

probation revocation
probation violation
service brokers

service delivery
social factors
social history

NOTES

[1] The percentage of non-petitioned cases changed little throughout the 1990s, although the case numbers did fluctuate somewhat: 700,000 in 1994 to 750,000 in 1996 and to slightly more than 700,000 by 1999 (Puzzanchera, 2003a; Sickmund et al., 1998).

[2] In some jurisdictions the reports are called **case histories**; in others the *presentence investigation report* nomenclature may be used with both juveniles and adults. We have chosen to use *predisposition reports* to emphasize the distinction between juvenile and adult processes.

[3] Given considerable variability in data collection and storage across the nation, the data obtained by the National Center for Juvenile Justice cannot support national estimates of trends and volume figures for status offenders. As a general observation, probation is far more likely in the case of a status offense than any other disposition, whether formal or informal. Incarceration occurs in very few cases of petitioned status offenders. For all four types of status offenses examined by the National Center (i.e., runaway, truancy, ungovernability, and liquor-law violations), formal probation was the most likely outcome. In 2000, for example, nearly 8 in 10 adjudicated status offenders whose most serious offense was truancy were placed on probation; roughly 6 in 10 adjudicated status offenders whose most serious offense was a liquor-law violation received probation. For more on status offenders see Puzzanchera et al. (2004:65–72).

[4] This case dealt with an appeal from an adult offender, but like *In re Gault* (1967), it extended these kinds of guarantees to juvenile court proceedings.

[5] For example, the New Mexico Statutes Annotated (NMSA) 1978, Section 322.27 provides, in part:

Any person may recover damages not to exceed four thousand dollars ($4,000) in a civil action in a court or tribunal of competent jurisdiction from the parent, guardian or custodian having custody and control of a child when the child has maliciously or willfully injured a person or damaged, destroyed or deprived use of property, real or personal, belonging to the person bringing the action.

Furthermore, NMSA, Section 322.28 provides that:

In any complaint alleging delinquency, a parent of the child alleged to be delinquent may be made a party to the petition . . . if the child is committed for institutionalization, [the parent may be ordered to] participate in any institutional treatment or counseling program including attendance at the site of the institution. The court shall order the parent to support the child committed for institutionalization by paying the reasonable costs of support, maintenance and treatment of the child that the parent is financially able to pay.

These statutory provisions mirror those enacted by many other states.

JUVENILE INSTITUTIONAL CORRECTIONS

* * *

Margaret Jamieson exited the dilapidated taxi and walked up to the gate of the Rockridge State Training School for Boys. She looked at her watch. It was almost the start of visiting hours. Margaret had taken two buses and three hours to get to the school, located just outside the tiny farming community of Rockridge. In two hours, the southbound bus—the only bus she could take today to return home—would arrive in town. The taxi driver had promised that he would come back by to pick her up in 90 minutes.

Margaret identified herself to the gatehouse officer, who directed her to the visiting room. Following a brick-lined concrete walk, Margaret was struck once again by how much the training school looked and felt like the prisons she had seen on television. She passed a building that looked like a school complex and detected greasy-food smells coming from what John, her oldest son, had called the dining hall. Margaret had never seen the upholstery shop where John spent half his day, after going to high school classes in the morning.

Fifteen-year-old John was at Rockridge—what the inmates called "the Rock"—for armed robbery of a convenience store. This was Margaret's fourth trip to Rockridge in the past five months. Given bus fares and the $20 she had to pay her cousin to watch her four other children while she was away all day, monthly visitations were becoming too costly. This trip would be the last one for a couple of months, and Margaret had yet to figure out how to tell John.

Entering the visitor's room lobby, Margaret observed that four people, a man and three women, sat in white plastic chairs along the room's pale green walls. Margaret checked in with the female civilian employee at the reception desk. John, she learned from the receptionist, would soon arrive. She directed Margaret to cubicle 12.

The visitation room consisted of a dozen small cubicles, each with a metal stool bolted to the room's concrete floor and a telephone handset affixed below the thick glass window separating the inmate from his visitor. On the other side of the glass partition was an identical set of cubicles, each with its corresponding handset. No one was sitting on the metal stool in the prisoner's cubicle number 12, so Margaret sat down on the cold, uncomfortable stool and waited.

About five minutes later, John and three other inmates suddenly appeared on their side of the partition. John looked down the line, saw his mother, and smiled. Margaret could not believe that this smiling child had done the terrible thing for which he had been imprisoned. Sure, he had a couple of past scrapes with the law, but nothing very serious, she reasoned. The juvenile court judge had not been so forgiving. Given his previous record, his unwillingness to take responsibility for his acts, and the offense's serious nature, she had given John a six-year sentence. It just doesn't seem fair, Margaret thought to herself.

John sat awkwardly on the small stool, causing Margaret to reflect that her son looked older than 15. Many questions echoed in her head each time she visited. What is happening to my son in this horrible place? When will John get out? What will he be like when he finally does get out? For a moment, mother and son sat looking at each other and then, at the same instant, reached for their respective handsets. As she heard her son's thready voice amplified in the phone, tears welled up in Margaret's eyes and spilled down her cheeks. A more immediate worry flashed through her mind: How can I tell him I won't be coming to visit next month?

* * *

The history of juvenile custodial corrections is not particularly attractive or appealing. Nevertheless, correctional facilities are very much a part of the nation's contemporary juvenile justice system. Therefore, rather than praising or condemning juvenile corrections, we are going to examine the reasons for this sanction's use and the development of current correctional programming.

Our goal in this chapter is to provide a thorough and thoughtful examination of various custodial approaches to correcting delinquent behavior. Somewhere between "nothing works" and "everything works" is the vast juvenile correctional landscape we explore in this chapter. Either of these extreme positions is difficult to defend. Furthermore, these extremes convey unrealistic pictures of the nation's institutional response for juveniles.

HISTORICAL DEVELOPMENTS IN JUVENILE CORRECTIONS

The evolution of juvenile corrections in the United States reflects the changes that have occurred in attitudes toward misbehaving children. We presented an overview of these changes in the first two chapters. Here we deal in more detail with the development of juvenile correctional institutions and with some of the people and groups that have shaped these facilities. Four general eras have come to define the history of juvenile correctional institutions, each corresponding to societal views of children at that time.[1]

THE PRE-INDUSTRIAL ERA AND FAMILY-CENTERED PUNISHMENTS (1600s TO 1820s)

For more than 200 years, especially during the colonial period, the family was the seat of power for dealing with children (see chapter 2). Colonial courts upheld the absolute parental authority over children, even extending this power, through the doctrine of *in loco parentis*, to the masters of apprenticed children. In theory, a court could order the death penalty for a disobedient or disrespectful child, although there is little evidence that such executions occurred (Krisberg and Austin, 1993:13). The formal justice system of this period treated children 10 years and older as adults, confining them in prisons and jails.

THE JACKSONIAN ERA AND THE HOUSES OF REFUGE (1820s TO 1850s)

John Griscom and Thomas Eddy, nineteenth-century Quaker prison reformers, led the Society for the Prevention of Pauperism, a group whose focus was on those people who received aid from funds designated for the poor, or **paupers** (Bernard, 1992:60). From the standpoint of Griscom, Eddy, and other reformers of that time, paupers did not engage in criminality because they were poor; instead, they were poor because of vices in their lives (Bernard, 1992:60). The cure for pauperism and other social ills was to remove children from the corrupting influences of their wicked and ineffective parents.

The society changed its name to the Society for the Reformation of Juvenile Delinquents in 1824, and a year later, the new society established the first **house of refuge** in New York City (Pickett, 1969). This institution, the prototype for subsequent ones in Philadelphia and Boston, emphasized discipline and hard work, elements common to other social programs of the **Jacksonian era** (Bernard, 1992; Schlossman, 1977). Most of the organizations primarily responsible for the creation of the houses of refuge espoused specific lessons for youngsters who were paupers or who were in danger of becoming paupers, especially children of immigrants. Bernard (1992:63) says this orientation toward youthful reformation shared three features:

1. Youngsters were confined for an indeterminate time, as opposed to the fixed sentences more often given in adult criminal courts.

2. Nondelinquents were often confined with few legal formalities.

3. There was a heavy emphasis on work.

The lessons and values of the house of refuge mirrored the **Protestant work ethic**, or redemption through hard work, thrift, industry, and self-criticism (Platt, 1977).

THE VICTORIAN-ERA CHILD SAVERS AND REFORM SCHOOLS (1850s TO 1890s)

As often happens with policy innovations, enthusiasm gives way to reality, and reality gives way to disillusionment. The house of refuge supporters had traveled this path by the 1850s. Despite being rooted in common-sense ideology, the houses of refuge had virtually no impact on the juvenile crime problem in the cities where they existed. Young criminals, "at that time . . . men up to the age of thirty" (Walker, 1998a:96), did not seem to be deterred from their law-violating ways, and dependent and neglected youngsters suffered from exposure to the law violators (Bernard, 1992).

In addition, by the 1850s the **cult of domesticity** defined the Victorian view of children. Obedience and morality remained the chief goals, as they had been in the Jacksonian era. Persuasion, kindness, and empathy—what Schlossman (1977:52) calls **affectional discipline**—replaced physical punishments as the means to domesticate a willful child. Shame, guilt, and love were added weapons in the arsenal of affectional discipline. The most appropriate locus for these practices was the family; the most logical practitioners were parents.

After the American Civil War, many policy makers and practitioners favored a more punitive, separate system of formal institutions. This response collided with the beliefs of the Victorian-era **child savers**, so named because they wished to save children from "depraved and criminal lives" (Krisberg and Austin, 1993:21; see also chapter 2). This clash of philosophies reshaped the emerging reformatory system. Even the name accorded these institutions held out the hope that they could change law-violating youngsters.

Reformatories, sometimes called **reform schools**, differed from houses of refuge. As Platt (1977:54–55) observed, the underlying principles of reformatories also derived from the Protestant work ethic. Hence, reformatory supporters segregated young offenders from the corrupting influences of adult criminals, removed them from their homes, imprisoned them for their own good and protection, assigned them to reformatories without trial and with minimal legal requirements, and gave them open-ended sentences to encourage cooperation in their own reform. However, the mandate for reformatories also included the following tenets:

- Do not confuse reformation with sentimentality.
- Protect inmates from idleness, indulgence, and luxuries through military drill, physical exercise, and constant supervision.
- Build the cottage-style reformatories in the countryside.
- Change inmates through labor, education, and religion.
- Teach the values of sobriety, thrift, industry, prudence, and realistic ambition.

The location of reformatories in rural America sometimes created reintegration problems. As contemporary critics noted, after living in a rural setting and learning skills appropriate to farming, the ex-reformatory inmates invariably returned to city life.

The criminal or noncriminal status of the inmates in early reform schools, like those found in houses of refuge, was not always clear (Krisberg, 1995). These facilities housed children sentenced for a wide range of offenses. Also confined with these young offenders were children guilty of nothing more than being truant, vagrant, abandoned, or abused.

Private charitable or religious groups owned and operated many of the first reformatories. This arrangement fit with the movement's religious focus, whose members saw the **family reform school** as a viable, if less than ideal, alternative to the house of refuge (Platt, 1977; Schlossman, 1977). However, conflicts arose with local Catholic leaders, who believed that many of these private facilities served as proselytizing agents for their Protestant sponsors (Schlossman, 1977:42–53). Only the creation of state reform schools dampened this criticism.

Reliance on financial support by community groups or private philanthropies often meant meager funding and little accountability. These two shortcomings— poor financing and the dearth of adequate program evaluations—persisted into the twentieth century and continue to plague public and private correctional programs. In the mid-1970s, struggling correctional agencies "rediscovered" private juvenile corrections, but these contemporary facilities operated more along the for-profit business model than along charitable lines.

THE PROGRESSIVE-ERA CHILD SAVERS AND TRAINING SCHOOLS (1880S TO 1920S)

In the 1880s, new waves of immigrants flooded the urban centers of the Northeast and north central parts of the nation. These new urban residents came from southern and eastern Europe. Against this backdrop of urban development and the influx of non-English-speaking immigrants, the pluralistic **Progressive movement** delivered the second generation of child savers. Educational progressives like John Dewey emphasized that industrial training, agricultural education, and social education provide children with a reconstruction of an ideal life. Child-saving progressives applied similar principles and practices to youthful misbehavior. Historians and social critics of this era (see, for example, Platt, 1977; Schlossman, 1977) have described these second-wave child savers in both flattering and unflattering terms:

- well-intentioned humanitarians who sought to help mainstream the newly arrived immigrants' disadvantaged children
- frightened members of the upper-class establishment who, like the supporters of the houses of refuge, viewed immigrant children as racially and socially inferior beings who needed to learn middle-class values and lower-class skills and aspirations
- middle-class women who desperately needed to find socially acceptable roles in a new and changing society

All three perspectives contain some truth, as many participants had more than one motive for their involvement (see Smith, 1989).

The product of the second-wave child-saving movement, with its progressive agenda, is undeniable: the juvenile court.[2] This newly created judicial body had a rehabilitative orientation; a very broad clientele of troubled, victimized, and criminal youth; and a singular lack of concern for the legal rights of its constituents. As Finckenauer observed:

> The juvenile court quickly became bureaucratized and professionalized in the same manner as had the earlier houses of refuge and reform schools. It did not get rid of the existing and largely failed childcare establishment that preceded it, but instead sustained and nourished that bureaucracy. This resulted in "treatment" continuing to be a mere euphemism for "punishment." (1984:119)

A logical outgrowth of the newly bureaucratized juvenile court, and the next major historical milestone in juvenile corrections, was the creation of government-operated **training schools**, or **industrial schools**. These facilities represented a shift toward a more punitive, formalized, and structured response to juvenile misbehavior. Training schools, following the progressive agenda, provided inmates with "realistic" education and "class-appropriate" vocational training; they resembled non-cottage-plan reform schools. Training schools were a return to an institutionalized, state-sponsored delinquency response. Moreover, they started two trends. First, governments entered the business of juvenile corrections, largely ending private philanthropic operations. Second, although the emphasis was on rehabilitation, state training schools firmly established a form of regimented, punitive corrections, anchored in the twin Progressive Era pillars of general education and vocational training.

THE "MODERN ERA" OF JUVENILE INSTITUTIONS (1920 TO 1970S AND BEYOND)

The intent of training schools was to house a state's most dangerous juvenile offenders. By the mid-1970s that intent was clearly at odds with common practice. Seventy years after their creation, up to half of the training schools' residents were status offenders (Schwartz, 1989). The long and difficult process of **decarceration** began in the 1970s, following federal guidelines contained in the **Juvenile Justice and Delinquency Prevention Act of 1974.**[3] No longer could local, state, or federal authorities imprison youths simply because they were incorrigible, beyond the control of their parents, or otherwise juvenile status offenders. Some states, like Massachusetts, experimented with **deinstitutionalization**, a policy that essentially closed all that state's juvenile institutions in favor of community-based alternatives (Feld, 1977; Miller, 1991).

Training schools are central to juvenile corrections in most states today and for the most part house a state's most serious (and allegedly more dangerous) juvenile offenders. Many states also operate juvenile facilities based on the 150-year-old family reform school/cottage plan. Some experts would argue that while the states call them training schools and provide some measure of vocational training, such facilities have not kept to the spirit of the original model. See, for example, the different evolution of training schools in Germany as discussed in box 7.1.

THE PURPOSES OF SECURE CORRECTIONAL PLACEMENTS

If any issue ought to be firmly established, it would seem to be the reason for having secure juvenile correctional facilities. However, this issue is far from settled. A long-standing debate continues over the existence of the entire juvenile justice system, let alone its institutional component (Bernard, 1992; Krisberg and Austin, 1993). Box 7.2 lists the five main rationales for corrections. This list prompts the following question: To what degree does the system of juvenile corrections, particularly institutional corrections, achieve these purposes?

RETRIBUTION

It is apparent that incarceration is one way of expressing society's disapproval of criminal behavior. The public seems to support the incarceration of youthful offenders, sometimes for lengthy sentences. The oft-repeated phrase, "If you're old enough to do the crime, you're old enough to do the time" reflects this sentiment. The clear implication is that the state should punish youngsters who commit adult-like (serious felony) offenses in a manner similar to that of adults. This viewpoint accepts that juvenile corrections should rely heavily on secure institutional settings and be punishment oriented.

INCAPACITATION

The goal of incapacitation often manifests itself in different policies. For example, a movement toward determinate instead of indeterminate sentencing clearly signals the incapacitation philosophy. Emphasis on early identification of career criminals is another way of trying to achieve this goal. Researchers tell us that the most crime-prone years are between ages 15 and 25 (see, for example, Winfree and

---

Box 7.1   International Perspectives
Vocational Training in the United States and Germany

In the 1850s, as reform schools replaced houses of refuge, the apprenticeship model dominated the American work world. It should not be surprising, therefore, that reform schools—and later industrial schools—included vocational training programs. The German principalities and city-states had a long tradition of apprenticeship programs, and their inclusion in juvenile corrections was only a logical extension of that tradition. In the 1840s, Germany saw the development of a family reform school at the Rauhe Haus outside Hamburg.

After World War I, but particularly after the Great Depression, the apprenticeship model began to lose popularity in the United States. Only certain vocations kept the tradition alive, and their hold was tenuous and largely enforced by trade unions. As the number of union-controlled vocations decreased, the few remaining apprenticeship programs disappeared. However, juvenile corrections continued to emphasize vocational training tied to the now largely defunct apprenticeship method for entering certain vocations, including barbers, bricklayers, carpenters, plumbers, and electricians. Moreover, the equipment found in most juvenile institutions represented old technologies, decreasing the likelihood that participants would find employment. Other aspects of these programs were problematic. For example, during the 1970s the Virginia School for Boys at Beaumont had a barber apprenticeship program, even though most successful graduates would not be eligible for state licensing for at least three years due to their age.

Contrary to the American experience, in post–World War II western Germany apprenticeship programs remained strong. The German education system emphasized early tracking into pre-vocational/technical training and pre-college curricula. Even today, young persons interested in technical vocations enter the highly competitive vocational training schools only after passing difficult written examinations, and apprenticeship program graduates must pass stringent state-monitored tests. German youth prisons, such as Justizvollzuganstalt-Adelsheim in the German state of Baden-Württemberg, allow inmates access to these same apprenticeship programs, often learning and practicing side by side in the facility with non-inmate students. Given the competitive and difficult nature of many of the state licensing examinations, the equipment found in these institutional-based apprenticeship programs is often state-of-the-art.

Thus, while reform schools in Germany and the United States both began in the era of apprenticeship programs, only those in Germany have remained faithful to that model, and only in Germany does the emphasis within the institutional context resemble that found outside the institution. In the United States, the rhetoric of the youth correctional facility vocational programs and the reality of the free-world job market do not appear to resemble one another as well as they do in Germany.

Sources: Bernard (1992); Justizvollzuganstalt-Adelsheim (1998).

Box 7.2   Five Main Purposes of Corrections

Correctional experts agree that correction practices fulfill *at least* five purposes:

1. **Retribution** (also called **just deserts**), its meaning found in such words as *revenge* and *vengeance*, is punishment for punishment's sake. The Babylonian King Hammurabi's Code and Mosaic Law included eye-for-eye, tooth-for-tooth, and life-for-life repayments.

2. **Incapacitation** (also called **selective incapacitation**) works on the theory that incarcerating youngsters during their most offense-prone years will mean that they cannot engage in the same level of delinquency as they would if they were in free society.

3. **Deterrence** involves "demonstrating the certainty and severity of punishment to discourage future crime by the offender (**specific deterrence**) and by others (**general deterrence**)."

4. **Rehabilitation** makes future criminality less likely by providing offenders with psychological or educational assistance or job training. Rehabilitation, like deterrence, is future oriented; unlike deterrence, the emphasis is on helping, not on punishment or the threat of punishment.

5. **Restitution** refers to the offender's repayment in money or services to the victim or community. While most restitution orders are part of a conditional disposition, they may be included in a custodial disposition. For example, the state may set aside some of an inmate's earnings to pay court-ordered restitution.

Source: Bureau of Justice Statistics (1988:90).

Abadinsky, 2003:85–87, 144–45). If that is the case, then incarcerating 16- and 17-year-old youngsters should minimize their ability to commit offenses during their high-offense-rate period of life.

Incapacitation is a testable notion. For instance, if an apprehended youngster had been committing an average of one crime per month, then incarcerating that youngster for two years would prevent 24 crimes. While this notion is appealing, we must acknowledge certain limitations about the assumptions concerning incapacitation (or selective incapacitation):

- Selective incapacitation assumes that if we can identify the most persistent offenders, we can target them for special attention, including lengthy incarceration terms.

- If we can incarcerate the high-rate offenders who have long-term criminal careers (the so-called career criminals), then we can prevent a substantial amount of crime committed by a relatively small group of offenders.

- Incapacitation implicitly assumes that if we incarcerate the high-rate offenders, then there are no other high-rate offenders ready to take their place.

However, some researchers (see Greenwood and Zimring, 1985) see these assumptions as ill conceived and only tenuously reflecting reality. Although incapacitation does affect some youngsters' offense patterns, especially late in their juvenile offense careers, the major problem is that incarceration's impact on the overall crime rate is largely unknown.

DETERRENCE

Deterrence is very much in vogue in today's juvenile justice system. The clearest examples of policies and programs that involve a deterrent approach are longer sentences for juvenile offenders and more regimented confinement programs, such as boot camps. The certainty, swiftness, and severity of the correctional punishments provided in state juvenile codes may deter some juvenile offenders. However, to speculate that this is true for all juvenile offenders is to assume that (1) practically all youngsters *know* the punishments provided in the juvenile codes, and (2) they are rational in assessing the true risk of being apprehended and in weighing the consequences of their actions. Knowing teenagers' abilities to overestimate the benefits and underestimate the costs would lead us to believe that most youngsters do not behave in completely rational ways, even when they know the potential penalties involved (and few may actually know the penalties). Therefore, deterrence as a correctional philosophy may hold out much symbolic hope but deliver very little actual delinquency prevention.

REHABILITATION

The concept of rehabilitation had fallen out of favor with many in the criminal justice system but is enjoying a resurgence of sorts (however, see, Cullen 2005; Cullen, Golden, and Cullen, 1983). Nevertheless, both secure and nonsecure custodial correctional placements have rehabilitative elements. Nearly every state's juvenile justice authority includes rehabilitation as a goal for juvenile custodial corrections. Indeed, rehabilitation may be more realistic for juveniles than for adults, as the former may be more open and amenable to change than the latter. However, rehabilitation services represent an option that the state can only *offer* offenders, not something achievable by force, rule, or legal ruling. That is, we can help people in the rehabilitation process, but we cannot force a successful result. With this in mind, institutional corrections hold out at least some measure of hope for youngsters *who want to change their lives.* Counseling, substance abuse treatment, and educational programs may help juveniles leave the delinquent lifestyle.

RESTITUTION

Many conditional juvenile dispositions include a restitution order. Judges may order juveniles to pay restitution when property was stolen or damaged. Having already addressed this idea in chapter 6, we will skip restitution's impact as a conditional disposition in this chapter. We revisit its place in the future of juvenile justice in chapter 12.

ORGANIZATIONAL GOALS: CUSTODY VERSUS TREATMENT

Correctional institutions for juvenile offenders have two primary organizational goals. First, they must maintain legal and physical control over the inmates, the **custody** domain. The type and number of custodial arrangements—for example, the absolute number of custody staff and the ratio of custody staff to inmates;

the presence of a perimeter wall or fence; guard towers; perimeter patrols; secure (that is, locked) working, living, and sleeping areas; the extent to which inmates move freely about the institution—determine a correctional facility's security level. Thus, we can place custodial goals on a continuum, from low to high: The greater the reliance on custodial arrangements to contain inmates, the higher the facility's security level. For example, most cottage reform schools were relatively low-security facilities, although they normally contained secure cell blocks for punishment. The custodial arrangements found in houses of refuge, non-cottage-style reform schools, and most training schools were far more severe and restrictive of individual liberties.

Treatment is the second generally acknowledged organizational goal for juvenile corrections, including correctional institutions. Treatment is a term borrowed from medicine by early penal reformers and refers to customized therapy based on a diagnosis. Juvenile correctional institutions typically offer inmates a wide range of treatment programs, including the two constants—education and vocational training—and, on an individual level or group level (or, on occasion, both levels), drug and alcohol abuse treatment, sex offender treatment, gang intervention counseling, and medical and psychiatric treatment. Equally important is the absolute number of treatment staff present at the facility as well as the ratio of treatment staff to inmates.

Theoretical Reflections
Linking Correctional Treatment and Delinquency Theory

James O. Finckenauer links delinquency theory and correctional practices as follows:

- Biological theories might prompt such treatment methods as (1) chemotherapy as a means to accelerate the autonomic nervous system's arousal rate, and (2) megavitamin and diet therapies.

- Psychological theories might undergird such approaches as (1) the use of token economies and the systematic reinforcement of desired behavior in behavior modification programs and (2) intensive individual and group therapies to correct erroneous thinking processes.

- Sociological theories can be linked with (1) use of peer groups as the locus for intensive group therapies; (2) encouragement of the bonds of attachments and commitment to family, conventional peers, school, and work; and (3) emphasis on defusing the culturally deviant peer group found in most juvenile correctional institutions.

Finckenauer's overall assessment of correctional programming is mixed. He finds much promise in Maine's Elan program, an individual-centered therapeutic community orientation in which inmates actively participate in treatment. However, Finckenauer criticizes Scared Straight, an individual-centered program in which inmates of New Jersey's Rahway Prison, through their words and living conditions, provide a type of special deterrence for visiting at-risk youths. He also questions the utility of New York State Division for Youth's Higher Horizons, a wilderness-training program, and New Jersey's Highfields, a modified form of group psychotherapy called Guided Group Interaction.[4] Their importance, he notes, is not so much in what they have accomplished as that "they are good illustrations of corrections programs using social factor theories to guide their treatment processes."

Source: Finckenauer (1984:209).

While treatment is an organizational goal, it relates to other correctional goals. For example, many facilities use the phrase "rehabilitative treatment" to describe inmate programs. Applying this term, boot camps provide treatment, yet, as we will see later in this chapter, they have deterrent and rehabilitative goals as well. Since many juvenile authorities also stress that corrections should teach personal responsibility and individual accountability, restitution may qualify as treatment, especially if the youth participates in restitution from within an institution.

Treatment—like custody—is also variable, depending upon the facility's resources and orientation. Consequently, we can also place treatment on a continuum, meaning one correctional institution or a unit within such an institution may place greater or lesser emphasis on treatment than another. Depending on the number of incarcerated youths and the resources available, a state may operate one or more facilities for each gender. However, some states farm out female offenders (a generally small proportion of all juvenile offenders) to other states or the private sector. Still others maintain multiple facilities spread throughout the state, each one catering to a geographic location, housing a different type of juvenile offender, or providing a specific type of treatment. In such cases, a centralized reception and diagnostic center determines the inmate's appropriate institutional or unit placement.

TRENDS IN JUVENILE CORRECTIONS: POLICIES AND PRACTICES

The general trend nationwide since the mid-1970s has been for the juvenile justice and adult criminal justice systems to become more alike. The current get-tough movement has caused a blurring in the distinctions between juvenile and adult justice institutions and policies (Schwartz, 1989; see also Bernard, 1992:147–51). However, it is in the area of correctional facilities and programs where we still see the greatest differences between the two systems. For example, a **determinate sentence** specifies a single time quantity, which becomes the maximum one would have to serve, for example a five-year sentence or a twenty-year sentence. By contrast, an **indeterminate sentence** is an order for incarceration where the time of commitment ranges between a minimum point and a maximum point, for example, two to five years or fifteen years to life. The clear trend in the adult criminal justice system has been toward using determinate sentences and either curtailing or eliminating indeterminate sentences (Mays and Winfree, 2005). The juvenile justice system overwhelmingly relies on indeterminate sentences.

Two other dimensions are important when examining the nature of juvenile correctional facilities. First, institutions can be categorized by the length of the inmates' stay; that is, short-term and long-term facilities. **Short-term facilities** are most often either detention centers or reception and diagnostic centers. They hold youngsters who are awaiting adjudication or who are awaiting transfer to a long-term custody institution. **Long-term facilities** are primarily state training schools but also include many outdoor programs, such as farms, ranches, and forestry camps. These correctional facilities and programs are designed to hold juveniles who have been adjudicated delinquent (or whatever their appropriate status) and who are serving **custodial dispositions**.

Second, juvenile facilities differ in terms of the type of correctional environment they employ. The two primary classifications here are institutional and open environments. **Institutional (secure) environments** incorporate security restrictions that may constrain the movements of the youngsters confined in the facility, as well as limiting the public's access to the facility and its residents. Normally, institutional environments are far more central to the operation of detention centers, reception and diagnostic centers, and state training schools than to other types of facilities. **Open (nonsecure) environments** permit the youthful inmates a high degree of physical freedom. Furthermore, these facilities may be more accessible to community members—including the youngsters' families and volunteers—than would be typical of institutional settings. Open environment facilities usually include shelters, halfway houses, and group homes, as well as farms, ranches, and forestry camps (Bureau of Justice Statistics, 1988:110). According to the American Correctional Association (2003:68), among 62,000-plus juveniles under supervision in 2002, nearly 39,000 were in secure facilities and most (80%) of those were in training schools.[5]

In summary, there are four principal types of juvenile correctional facilities currently found throughout the nation. **Detention centers** are facilities that hold juveniles for short periods; generally, the security arrangement is high, similar to that found in a local jail for adults. They serve various types of inmates, including those awaiting judicial action or those already adjudicated but who remain incarcerated pending a final disposition, placement, or transfer. **Reception and diagnostic centers** generally serve as places of short-term confinement, while children who have been committed await their initial screening and assessment. As noted previously, reception and diagnostic centers may be physically separate from other forms or a unit within a larger facility. **Training schools** are places of long-term confinement. The emphasis tends to be on custody and security, but such institutions typically also provide a broad range of treatment programming and vocational training. The final category is the **residential training center**. These long-term residential facilities generally operate at a lower level of security than training schools and include such programs as ranches, camps, farms, and boot camps. Children placed in residential training centers often enjoy more contact with the community.

INCARCERATED JUVENILES: TRENDS AND INMATE CHARACTERISTICS

Much like their adult counterparts, juvenile correctional facility populations grew throughout the 1980s and early 1990s, although the rates of population increase were nowhere near that experienced in the adult system (Mays and Winfree, 2005:3, 141–42). One of the interesting things about this increase is that it was occurring at a time when the nation's pool of possible juvenile offenders was decreasing (Krisberg, DeComo, and Herrera, 1992:2). The rate of increase slowed in the 1990s. Nationally in 1997, 368 juveniles were in custody for every 100,000 in the population (Snyder and Sickmund, 1999). Between 1997 and 1999, 20 states had decreased or stabilized incarceration rates, and the overall rate increased a modest 1% (Sickmund, 2004:7). By 1999, the per capita rate for the nation was 371, ranging from a high of 704 (District of Columbia) to a low of 96 (Vermont and Hawaii). This 1999 per capita figure represents an increase of about 4% over the course of the 1990s.

The per capita rates tell part of the story. The sheer numbers of young people—persons under 21 for purposes of OJJDP reporting—residing in the nation's juvenile facilities had been, until the early 1990s, growing at a steady rate. Paralleling the demand for bed spaces was a growth in their supply from the private sector. Since the passage of the Juvenile Justice and Delinquency Prevention Act of 1974, the private sector has taken on an increasing proportion of the juvenile custodial population. For example, between 1991 and 1999, the number of delinquent offenders in both the nation's public and private youth facilities increased by 50%.[6] Private-facility populations grew the most, increasing the number of residents in this time by 98%, while public-sector institutions experienced a 38% increase in residents. Most of this growth in both the public and the private sectors occurred in the mid-1990s. At the same time, status offenders became even less of a part of the correctional scene, dropping off 40% between 1997 and 1999, with the decline actually beginning in 1995. These two trends had another interesting impact on the populations of public and private facilities. That is, by the late 1990s and early 2000s, they were far more alike than at any previous time for which there are records. That is, in 1995, delinquents accounted for 76% of the private sector and 97% of the public-sector juvenile offender populations. By 2001, 90% of the private-sector inmates were delinquent, compared to 98% of those in the public sector.

TRENDS FOR DELINQUENT OFFENDERS

Offense-specific analyses tell an equally interesting story. Table 7.1 summarizes the nation's public and private juvenile facilities at four points in time: 1995, 1997, 1999, and 2001. The following trends warrant special attention:

- Between 1995 and 1999, the absolute number of delinquent offenders increased from 84,019 to 104,073. However, in 2001 OJJDP reported a decrease of some 5%. Some minor decreases occurred as early as 1999 in many offense categories for inmates residing in public facilities and some offense categories for private facility inmates, particularly for criminal homicide, robbery, aggravated assault, and all property offenses. This trend is worth watching.

- In the mid-1990s, the private sector had far fewer offenders who had committed a person offense. By 2001 these differences had all but disappeared. Moreover, in the mid-1990s property offenders generally accounted for a large portion of the private sector's inmate population; however, by the beginning of the new decade, these differences had largely disappeared. In most offense categories, the public- and private-sector institutional populations either kept pace with each other or moved toward each other, so that at the beginning of

Table 7.1   Juveniles in Correctional Custody by Type of Most Serious Delinquency Offense (Committed and Detained): One-Day Counts for Public and Private Facilities, 1995, 1997, 1999, and 2001

	1995		1997		1999		2001	
	Public	Private	Public	Private	Public	Private	Public	Private
Delinquency	66,235	17,784	74,522	24,361	75,537	28,536	71,331	27,807
Person	42%	33%	37%	33%	37%	35%	36%	33%
Index	26	5	29	20	27	19	26	19
Property	32	43	31	37	30	32	29	31
Index	22	23	26	31	25	27	24	26
Drug	9	9	9	11	9	11	8	12
Public order*	9	7	10	11	10	11	10	11
Technical	9	3	14	9	14	12	16	13

*Alcohol and other delinquency offenses for 1995 were included as public order offenses.

Key:
Delinquency—only those juveniles who violate a juvenile code where, had they been adults, the offense would have been a crime
Person—murder, nonnegligent manslaughter, negligent manslaughter, forcible rape, robbery, aggravated assault, assault, and sexual assault
Person index—criminal homicide, violent sexual assault, robbery, aggravated assault
Property—burglary, arson, larceny-theft, motor vehicle theft, vandalism, forgery, counterfeiting, fraud, stolen property, and unauthorized vehicle use
Property index—burglary, arson, larceny-theft, and motor vehicle theft
Public order—alcohol or drugs, driving under the influence, weapons, other public order offenses
Technical—violations of probation, parole, or valid court orders

Sources: Adapted from Austin et al. (1995); Sickmund, Snyder, and Poe-Yamagata (1997); Sickmund (2004); Sickmund, Sladky, and Kang (2004).

the twenty-first century the public- and private-sector populations were much more similar than at any time for which comparable information exists.

- In the mid-1990s, technical violators accounted for 9% of delinquents in the public sector and 3% of the delinquents found in the private sector. By 2001 these proportions had increased to 16% and 13%, respectively.

While it is true that, taken as a whole, the delinquent populations in both public and private sectors have become very similar, two exceptions are worth noting. First, the private sector had a larger percentage of drug offenders than the public sector by 2001, whereas in 1995 there was no difference between the two. The drug-offender proportion of the total population did not change over the six years reported in table 7.1; only the percentage in private facilities increased. This is not a trivial point, since drug offenders generally require more sophisticated treatment than do other offenders, which often translates into increased resources for the facility. Second, person index-crime offenders, while more common in private institutions in 2001 than in 1995, accounted for a smaller proportion of the private-sector population (19%) than of the public sector (26%). This difference is worth noting because such offenders often are more difficult to control and may require higher security arrangements. Indeed, whether a child is detained in a locked or staff-secured arrangement owes more to offense than any other factor (Sickmund, 2004:17). As general observations, then, the differences between the two juvenile correctional systems has become less evident over the years; however, the public sector tends to house the more violent and potentially dangerous youthful inmates, while both are housing proportionately more inmates whose only offense is violating a technical condition of their release.

TRENDS FOR STATUS OFFENDERS

Table 7.2 summarizes several recent trends for status offenders. As previously observed, the nation's courts are increasingly reluctant to order incarceration for status offenders, as the number has dropped from 7,485 in 1995 to 5,082 in 2001. The courts are most likely to incarcerate for incorrigibility. The table also highlights the following interesting trends:

- Underage drinking became far more popular as the most serious charge for which to incarcerate minors during the 1990s.

- Contrary to stated concerns about using curfews to curb gangs, courts were no more likely to use them in 2001 than in 1995.

- Private-sector facilities proportionately hold more youths whose most serious status offense was incorrigibility than do public-sector facilities, a trend that has not changed since the mid-1990s.

Table 7.2   Juveniles in Correctional Custody by Type of Most Serious Status Offense (Committed and Detained): One-Day Counts for Public and Private Facilities, 1995, 1997, 1999, and 2001

	1995		1997		1999		2001	
	Public	Private	Public	Private	Public	Private	Public	Private
Status Offenses	1,785	5,700	1,782	5,094	1,623	3,063	1,998	3,084
Running away	23%	25%	27%	20%	29%	20%	29%	17%
Truancy	15	18	23	18	18	20	9	20
Incorrigibility	27	36	26	47	26	47	24	49
Curfew	2	4	4	2	4	2	3	2
Drinking	2	4	6	4	12	6	11	9
Others	31	13	14	9	11	6	24	4

Key:
Running away—leaving the custody and home of parents, guardians, or custodians
Truancy—violation of compulsory school attendance law
Incorrigibility—being beyond the control of parents, guardians, or custodians
Curfew—violation of local ordinances concerning where minors may be at certain times
Drinking—possession, use, or consumption of alcohol by a minor
Others—any offenses not listed above, including underage smoking, unruliness in school

Note: Columns may not sum to 100% owing to rounding errors.

Sources: Adapted from Austin et al. (1995); Sickmund, Snyder, and Poe-Yamagata (1997); Sickmund (2004); Sickmund, Sladky, and Kang (2004).

- By 2001, public-sector facilities were much less likely to hold someone accused of truancy than in previous years, while this offense category accounted for roughly the same proportion of private-sector inmates in all four years.

Generally, the nation's public and private institutions for youthful offenders and children held far fewer status offenders by 2001 than at the beginning of the previous decade (Sickmund, 2004:5). Incorrigibility and running away—two similar behaviors—account for over one-half of all status offenders and over two-thirds of those sent to private-sector facilities.

GENDER: TRENDS AND INMATE CHARACTERISTICS

Gender presents an interesting paradox when we compare the adult and juvenile systems. In adult prisons and jails, the proportion of women inmates has increased steadily over the past 20 years. In 1983, they accounted for about 6% of the jail population; by 2002, nearly 12% of adult jail inmates were females (Mays and Winfree, 2005:331). In state prisons, similar patterns occurred over these same two decades, as the proportion of women increased from 4% in 1983 to 7% in 2002 (Mays and Winfree, 2005:142). By contrast, the proportion of girls residing in the nation's juvenile institutions decreased from nearly 20% in 1985 to 14.5% in 2001 (Krisberg et al., 1992; Sickmund et al., 2004). However, by 2001 girls accounted for a larger proportion of the youth institutional population than did women within adult facilities. This holds for girls who are detained (18.6%) and committed (12.9%), the equivalents of jail and prison populations respectively (Sickmund et al., 2004).

What do we know about the girls and boys sent to the nation's youth facilities? First, female inmates in residential placement tend to be younger than their male counterparts, a pattern observed throughout the 1990s.[7] For example, in 1999, 30% of the females were younger than 14. This contrasts with 21% of the males. The peak placement ages for females were 15 and 16, whereas boys peaked at 16 and 17. Second, the ratio of male-to-female inmates in private institutions is slightly higher than in public ones. That is, about 16% of private-facility inmates are female, whereas 12% are female in public facilities. Third, females account for 40% of admissions under a diversion agreement. Fourth, while minorities dominate the institutional populations, minority females make up a smaller share of the institutionalized female population than minority males. In 1999, 64% of those children in residential placement were minority males, contrasted with 53% of the females. Race and ethnicity are significant features of residential placement for youths, a fact we explore again later in this chapter.

Offense trends reveal additional gender-based differences. Figure 7.1 summarizes the most serious offenses for detained and committed youths in 1997 and 2001.[8] Boys changed little over these five years. The alleged or actual offenses of over 60% of the boys were either personal or property crimes in 1997 and 2001. There were small fluctuations in the percentage of public order, drug, status offending, and technical violation offenses. Status offending played a small but relatively stable role in the detention and commitment decisions for boys.

Figure 7.1
Offense Types by Gender: One-Day Counts for Public and Private
Facilities, 1997 and 2001

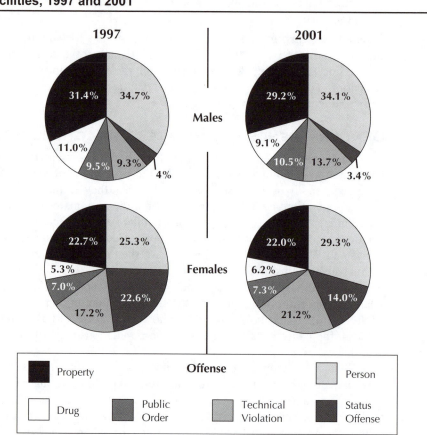

Sources: Department of Justice (1997); Sickmund et al. (2004).

The statistics for girls present a slightly different array of offense patterns and several interesting changes between 1997 and 2001. First, personal and property offenses account for about one-half of all charges against females, about 10% less than for males. Generally, then, delinquent acts are slightly less important in the detention and commitment decisions involving females than males. Status offenses and technical violations attach themselves far more often to females than males. Drug and public order violations account for rather small portions of the charges against girls, and certainly smaller percentages than reported for males. The changes, however, portend something quite different. First, between 1997 and 2001, status offenses, which have long been a significant part of the landscape of charges against girls, assumed a less important role in their detention and commitment, down from about 23% in 1997 to 14% in 2001. Second, technical violations increased from 17% to 21%. In sum, delinquency was accounting for more of the charges against girls in 2001 than in 1997. Even with this trend (and time will tell if it is a trend or an aberration), the offense records of female juvenile residential inmates differ in substantive ways from those of their male counterparts.

RACE AND ETHNICITY:
TRENDS AND INMATE CHARACTERISTICS

The role race and ethnicity play in the administration of justice is part of the ongoing debate about race relations in the United States, and this is true for both adult and juvenile offenders (Mays and Winfree, 2005:352–81). In 2002, blacks accounted for about 40% of jail and federal prisoners, and nearly half of all state prisoners. The trend toward **disproportionate minority confinement (DMC)** began in the 1970s, and the gap between black and white inmates in the nation's adult prison system has grown larger ever since (Mays and Winfree, 2005:360–61). A similar pattern exists in the juvenile correctional system. In 1985, African Americans accounted for 31% of all juvenile residents; by 1991 that number had increased to 40%, where it has remained for over a decade (Krisberg et al. 1992; Sickmund, 2004; Sickmund et al., 2004).[9] Black youth ages 13–17 account for only 14% of the juvenile population nationwide (Sickmund, 2000).

Where does this disproportionality begin? Part of the problem appears to lie with offending levels. Between 1980 and 1998, black juveniles offended at a rate 4.1 times higher than did whites (Lynch, 2002). The disproportionality was even greater for arrests, as the arrest rate for black juveniles was 5.7 times greater than for whites for these same years. In the early 1990s, the high degree of disproportionately in arrests and offending began to narrow, although only slightly. Before we blame the police we must consider other sources of information, specifically the NIBRS. The National Incident-Based Reporting System is a far more comprehensive method of collecting crime data from the police. Specifically, it is an event-driven method that looks at many more elements of each crime than does the *Uniform Crime Reports* (UCR), as discussed in chapter 1. For example, NIBRS includes information about all offenses alleged to have been committed in a single criminal event, as well as information about all of the participants, victims, and offenders.[10] An analysis of NIBRS data reveals no direct evidence of racial bias in arrests of juveniles for violent offenses (Pope and Snyder, 2003). We return to the topic of DMC in chapter 12.

Figure 7.2 compares the racial or ethnic composition of the juvenile custodial populations for 1997 and 2001 by offense type. In both years, minorities accounted for the greatest proportion of inmates. However, changes did occur. In 1997, we observe the following percentages by race and ethnicity among the nation's 105,790 juveniles in residential placement: white (38%), black (40%), Hispanic (18%), and other (4%). By 2002, these percentages were as follows: white (40%), black (39%), Hispanic (17%), and other (4%). Between 1997 and 2001, the number of white youths increased, as did their share of the total. The number of blacks and Hispanics decreased, as did their percentages of the total. The overall number of children in residence was down slightly from 105,790 in 1997 to 104,413 in 2001.

What were the offenses? Consider the following observations from figure 7.2:

- The percentage of personal and property crimes reported for white juveniles did not change much between 1997 and 2001: about 6 in 10 white juveniles

**Figure 7.2
Race and Ethnicity of Juvenile Inmates by Offense:
One-Day Counts for Public and Private Facilities, 1997 and 2001**

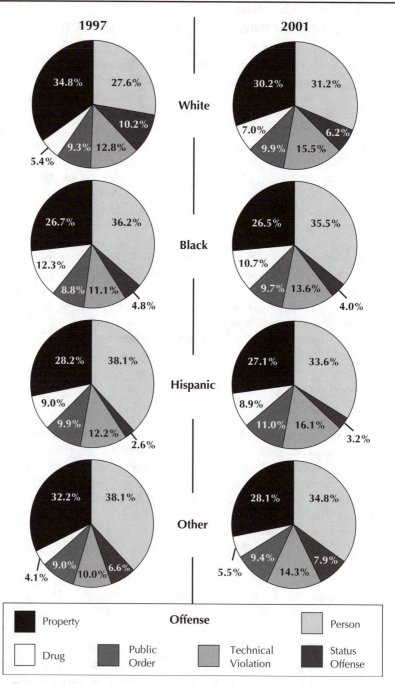

Sources: Department of Justice (1997); Sickmund et al. (2004).

had been committed or detained for a personal or property crime. These same offenses showed up for about 7 in 10 black, Hispanic, and other juveniles in residence in 1997. By 2001, their proportions were far more similar to whites than in 1997.

- Drug offenses are more common for blacks than for other groups, followed in order by Hispanics, whites, and others.
- Public order offending is relatively static over time and among the various racial and ethnic groupings.
- Technical violations became an increasingly important offense for all groups over time, but especially for "other" and Hispanic juveniles.
- Status offenses for white juveniles became less important in 2001. Minorities experienced much smaller shifts in their status-offense proportions. Indeed, very few incarcerated black or Hispanic juveniles are accused or committed status offenders. Juveniles in the "other" category exhibited proportions of status offending charges far more similar to whites than other minorities.

Generally, delinquency defined the law-violating activities of all racial and ethnic groups, although there were variations by race. The increasingly important role technical violations play as a reason for detention and commitment bears watching, particularly if other gender-specific and general trends previously reported continue into the decade.

INSIDE JUVENILE INSTITUTIONAL CORRECTIONS

For most workers and residents inside the walls or fences of a youth prison, the term *institution* has a particular meaning. Adding the adjective *total* creates a unique term, the **total institution**. Erving Goffman (1961) popularized this term, using it to describe a distinct form of social institution that includes religious orders, the military, and prisons. A total institution is "a place of confinement or partial confinement where persons of a specific type live, following a formalized life routine under the control and direction of a bureaucratic staff, and having limited contact with the rest of society" (Theodorson and Theodorson, 1969:207).

Goffman (1961) warned that total institutions often have a profound influence on their inmates. That is, the institution's rituals, customs, rules, and laws—its culture—are so ingrained in some inmates that they are largely incapable of functioning outside its protective womb. Donald Clemmer described the inmates he studied as belonging to a unique prison community; he described **prisonization** as the process by which the inmates "take on in greater or lesser degree the folkways, customs and general culture of the penitentiary" (1958:299). The resulting prison community was mainly negativistic, with both the prison staff and the free society as the most common targets. The prison community was capable of turning on its own if members strayed from the **prison code**. For its part, the inmate code provided those who would live by its precepts with a fairly narrow range of acceptable behavior (for example, be tough, be a man, be loyal to fellow cons) and unacceptable behavior (for example, don't rat on a fellow con, don't break your word, don't try to look good for the guards and other staff). Violations of these precepts resulted in quick and often violent punishments (Sykes, 1958).

In the 1970s and 1980s, researchers observed an inmate social system, replete with prison code, in juvenile correctional facilities (see, for example, Feld, 1981; Thomas, Hyman, and Winfree, 1981). However, the contemporary prison social system is many generations removed from that studied by Clemmer (McCorkle, Miethe, and Drass, 1995). The current prison climate is prone to violence, as **state-raised inmates**—offenders who have come to view violence as a means of satisfying their social, economic, and sexual urges—increasingly populate the nation's prisons and jails, including its youth facilities (McCorkle, 1993; Faulkner and Faulkner, 1997). While the qualities admired by inmates—physical and mental toughness, self-sufficiency, an exploitative nature, and loyalty to a few, close friends—are similar to those reported by Clemmer, the origins may be different (Clear and Cole, 2002). Rather than loyalty based on social status in the inmate subculture, prison gangs based on race, ethnicity, politics, and geography form the core of overlapping violent subcultures found in many adult and juvenile facilities today (Esbensen, Tibbets, and Gaines, 2004; Fong and Vogel, 1995; Pelz, 1996).

WHO IS AT RISK? CLASSIFYING AND ASSESSING INMATES

Much like adult prisons, juvenile correctional facilities face a number of ongoing problems that affect confinement conditions. There is almost no limit to the issues we could address, but in this section we focus on three major ones: (1) crowding; (2) institutional violence, including gangs; and (3) the impact of inmate programming. Before examining these problems, we take a brief look at two critical practices that have the potential to impact confinement conditions: inmate classification and suicide-threat assessment.

Inmate classification is a major institutional concern for the adult prison and jail system. Early in the twentieth century prison authorities began employing **psychometrics**, the measurement of psychological characteristics using standardized intelligence and personality tests, to help determine where to place an inmate. Classification systems expanded in the post–World War II era, when the notion of treatment gained popularity. However, prisoner litigation during the 1970s highlighted problems with the existing systems, particularly their failure to meet inmate needs and the tendency to classify inmates to far more restrictive security levels than necessary (Mays and Winfree, 2005:120–23).

By the 1980s, classification systems in adult prisons had less to do with distinctions between treatment and custody than with levels of custody, as the nation's prisons largely abandoned rehabilitation in favor of retribution and just deserts. The irony is that the juvenile system, which maintained at least a semblance of concern for the treatment of incarcerated juveniles throughout these years, primarily relied on a simplistic classification system called **case classification** that generally assesses offender risks and needs at intake. Reassessment was and is rare (Flores, Travis, and Latessa, 2004). Moreover, as Binder, Geis, and Bruce pointed out, classification staff members tend to use only legal variables when assigning a

Juvenile offenders wait their turn to begin psychological testing and evaluation at the Marlin Orientation and Assessment Unit in Marlin, Texas. The Texas Youth Commission (TYC) operates the Marlin Unit for chronically delinquent or serious juvenile offenders. The youths, ages 10-17 when committed, undergo a 50- to 60-day average stay. At Marlin they receive a physical evaluation and survey of medical history; educational testing and assessment; psychological evaluation and social summary; introduction to TYC programming; and assessment for specialized treatment, such as sex offender behavior, chemical dependency, mental retardation, or violent crime. About 80% of offenders are assigned to a TYC secure correctional facility, and 20% go into facilities and programs run by contract providers.

youth to an institutional program rather than relying on the more program-relevant personal characteristics of an offender (2001:320). In short, the adult prisons and jails, including those that house females, have fairly well-developed and thoroughly tested classification systems, while this important activity for juveniles remains relatively rudimentary and fragmented in its application.

Suicide and self-injury risk-assessment should be a concern for all detention facilities. Suicide is a leading cause of death for children in and out of detention: it is the fourth leading cause of death for juveniles over age 6. The number of children ages 7 to 17 who committed suicide between 1981 and 1998 was 20,775, meaning that nearly as many children killed themselves as died from homicide or cancer (Snyder and Swahn, 2004). Most of the victims—over 75%—were males. About 60% died from a self-inflicted gunshot wound, while a quarter suffocated, usually from hanging, and most of the rest died from poisoning. The suicide rate for white juveniles was nearly twice that reported for black and Asian youth; however, American Indian youths killed themselves at a rate that was nearly twice that of whites. Most juveniles who kill themselves are between the ages of 15 and 17.

In spite of the fact that suicide is a well-researched topic, until recently we knew little about suicide by confined children. Hayes (2004) reports on 79 juvenile suicides occurring throughout the nation between 1995 and 1999.[11] All but one child died by hanging. Nearly 80% were in a detention center or training school at the time of the suicide, about half in each type of facility. As with the national statistics, most suicides involved white youth, with a disproportionate share being American Indians. Nearly two-thirds were male, a figure similar to that reported for young people generally. Confinement suicides also resembled their free-world counterparts in terms of age, as 70% were between 15 and 17 years old.

Do institutions take the appropriate steps to prevent detention suicides? A 1998 national survey of health care in juvenile correctional facilities found that initial mental health screening was available in 64% of the facilities; mental health staff provided clinical evaluation in 74%, while over 80% had provisions for psychotropic medication. Nearly 7 in 10 facilities surveyed had on-site access to psychiatrists, psychologists, or social workers (Goldstrom, Jaiquan, Henderson, Male, and Manderscheid, 2001). While gaps in mental health services for juveniles existed, the 1998 figures represented significant improvements over 1983 (Anno, 1984). Detention centers, in particular, have unique problems with juvenile suicides, yet as Hayes (2004) observed, few that had suicides also had a comprehensive suicide prevention program—one that included, among other components, intake screening for suicide risk and staff who are well-trained to recognize predisposing factors, high-risk periods, and warning signs and symptoms.

A juvenile suicide serves as a **sentinel event** for the facility. That is, the death of one of their inmates is a "wake-up call" for the institution's administrators and staff, who often radically change the climate of the facility in the wake of the child's death. Preventing a determined person from committing suicide is a difficult task. Relying on a single method—a suicide risk-assessment upon entry, for example—is probably a bad strategy. As Hayes observed, "The challenge for those who work in the area of juvenile detention and corrections will be to conceptualize the issue requiring a continuum of comprehensive suicide prevention services aimed at the collaborative identification, continued assessment, and safe management of youth at risk for self-harm" (2004:51).

Central factors in both proper inmate classification and suicide prevention are adequate screening, follow-through, and follow-up. Improper classification, or the failure to reclassify inmates when their needs and behavior have changed, threatens the institutional climate. Suicides, perhaps more than any single event at a juvenile facility except for a mass disturbance (riot), can send a palpable shiver throughout the entire inmate population.

CONDITIONS OF CONFINEMENT IN JUVENILE CORRECTIONS

As the figures suggest, secure correctional facilities for juveniles represented a growth industry throughout the 1990s and into the twenty-first century. Virtually every state experienced growth in juvenile correctional populations, though many were able to stabilize their growth *rate* in the late 1990s. Authorities opened new facilities, and renovated and expanded old facilities; moreover, the public sector increasingly turned to the private sector for additional bed spaces. However, if we have learned anything about corrections during the 1990s, it is that we cannot build our way out of a crowding crisis (Mays and Gray, 1996; Shichor, 1995). In fact, most juvenile correctional facilities today face the prospect of having to let one resident go for each new person committed. This means that, at least for the near future, crowding will remain a problem for juvenile corrections in the United States.

Violence is often associated with institutional crowding. However, before we jump to the conclusion that violence is a recent feature of juvenile corrections, it is important to note that violence always has been a reality of institutional life, and the levels of violence encountered in the 1970s were at the heart of some states' efforts to close or downsize training schools. Yet the exact extent and nature of violence found in the nation's youth facilities remain an understudied phenomenon. Researchers report that acts of violence relate in predictable ways to offenders' records of prior violence, even controlling for the institutional security level: The greater the history of violence, the higher the levels of aggressive conduct (MacDonald, 1999; Poole and Regoli, 1983). Moreover, it appears that while acts of violence and serious injury do occur in juvenile institutions, most reported incidents involve verbal harassment and property theft; and those most likely to be victimized have the highest levels of fear and experience the "pains of imprisonment" most severely (Maitland and Sluder, 1998).

So why is violence of such concern to us today? First, with the removal of nearly all status offenders from secure custodial confinement, most juvenile facilities have seen a "distilling effect." Distilling low-alcoholic-content beverages increases the concentration of alcohol; as heat drives out water and other impurities, the vapors condense into a liquid. In other words, the distillation process increases the resulting liquid's potency. In the case of juvenile corrections, the removal of status offenders means that the nation's juvenile correctional facilities hold substantially fewer "minor" offenders and far more serious offenders. The "potency" of the juvenile correctional population has increased dramatically. Changes in laws and incarceration patterns have left the nation's juvenile corrections officials with more hardened, increasingly violent offenders (MacDonald, 1999; Maitland and Sluder, 1998).

Second, we have seen in adult prisons that gangs—called "security threat groups" in the adult sector—are a prominent part of the corrections environment today (Mays and Winfree, 2005:180–83; see also Fong and Vogel, 1995). This is true in juvenile facilities as well. With the incarceration of gang members, we have both the importation of the violent subculture of the streets and the deprivations associated with incarceration (MacDonald, 1999). In this case, the youthful gang members' penetration into the culture of the prison should occur even more rapidly than for other young offenders, except perhaps for state-raised youths. Furthermore, the presence of members from competing gangs inevitably will lead to intergang rivalries and conflicts. As a result, the levels of violence will be even higher than we normally would expect in a secure correctional environment.

Finally, **inmate programming** will remain a point of contention for decades. Inmate programming includes treatment programs ranging from traditional education and vocational training to individual-level sex offender therapy. Some inmates might argue that basic living arrangements, food, clothing, and shelter are part of inmate programming. Also included in this category are the following types of more specialized programs and services: medical and dental care, speech and physical therapy, specialized dermatological and gynecological services, recreational programs, independent-living skills training, college course work, remedial education, and English proficiency programs, including English as a Second Language. In simplest terms, the issues facing us are (1) the presence and quality of the programming presented or program availability, and (2) the consequences of inmate programming efforts.

In theory, some aspects of programming for children are more expensive than for adults. While only some adults must participate in or qualify for custody educational programming, nearly all juveniles by state law must have access to it. What does this mean in practice? Consider that in 2002, the states spent $10.5 billion on all juvenile correctional programs and $35.8 billion for adult services (American Correctional Association, 2003:22, 26). For adults, 23% of the total budget went for custody and security expenditures, compared to 15% for juveniles. Health care consumed more of the adult budget than that for juveniles (7.5% versus 3%). The states spent 6% of their entire budget for juveniles on institutional treatment programming, but only about 3% of the adult budget. Juvenile community programming receives 11% of the juvenile budget, but this amount is only 5% of the total money spent on adults. The states clearly see the needs of juveniles and adults in different terms.

In the final analysis, juvenile offenders often do not have access to the range of treatment programs offered to adults, and frequently the treatment programs for juveniles are of questionable quality. Most youngsters in custody understand the facts of institutional life, learning early in their delinquency careers that when it comes to correctional programming outside of basic education, juvenile offenders constitute a nearly forgotten population. In terms of vocational training, we need only repeat what we observed earlier: Little of what passes for vocational training in contemporary, long-term juvenile institutions bears any resemblance to the needs of workers in the early twenty-first century. In the end, however, the primary way of assessing correctional treatment programs is the degree to which they have an impact on future law-violating behaviors.

Two conclusions seem warranted about correctional treatment program assessment. First, few programs in juvenile facilities are subjected to systematic evaluation. When researchers conduct **outcomes-based evaluations** on custodial corrections programs, they tend to be performed by in-house personnel whose independence and objectivity are questionable. Our knowledge of treatment success may be limited to recidivism, or the failure rate of those youngsters who reoffend and reenter a correctional facility. More often than not, when an institution has a spectacular failure such as a staff homicide at the facility, a mass escape, or a series of inmate suicides (what we have referred to as a sentinel event), legislators and others want to know why. The fact that it takes such tragedies to attract public and political interest in juvenile corrections is not lost on the youths incarcerated in these facilities. For example, although researchers questioned the utility and claims of boot camp programs for a decade, it took serious injuries and even deaths for some states to reconsider their use (see box 7.3 for more on boot camps).

Second, correctional treatment does not seem to be especially effective. In response to this concern, we return to the point made by Lipton, Martinson, and Wilkes (1975) over three decades ago: The available evaluation research suggests that not much seems to work in terms of correctional programming.[12] Does this mean that nothing works? Hardly. But it indicates that one of the major challenges facing juvenile corrections in the future will be to design and implement effective

---

Box 7.3   Boot Camps: On Their Way Out?

One response to the perceived need for a get-tough policy toward youthful offenders has been the creation of **boot camp programs** for juvenile offenders. In the period from 1983 to 1995, boot camps grew from a single 50-bed program in Georgia to 75 programs operated by 32 states and the federal government serving over 7,500 participants. Boot camps initially confined and treated first-time nonviolent, young adult and juvenile offenders. The program elements generally associated with boot camps are:

- military-style training environments
- separation of boot camp participants from general prison population inmates if the two facilities are located together
- representation of the boot camp to participants as an alternative to a longer period of traditional institutional confinement
- participation in hard labor

What have we learned about boot camps in over 20 years of operation? An OJJDP boot camp evaluation conducted by Bourque and associates found that juvenile boot camps—what some jurisdictions call **shock incarceration programs**—offer several positive features when compared with secure institutional confinement. First, boot camps serve both juveniles and adults. Second, they had lower daily costs than state and local institutions. These features would seem to indicate that juvenile boot camps could drive down correctional costs and reduce institutional crowding. However, juvenile boot camps also have proven to be deficient in several regards. For instance, many programs cannot balance the emphasis on military discipline with rehabilitation, favoring discipline and physical fitness over rehabilitation. High staff turnover rates have compounded this problem. That is, there is a reliance on staff members with military experience, and many of them do not stay with the program long enough to support fully the rehabilitative efforts. Not all juveniles respond favorably to confrontational, military tactics. Finally, recent evaluations have been unable to demonstrate convincingly that boot camps have a positive impact on long-term behavioral change among program participants.

By 2000, Georgia had abandoned the juvenile boot camp model, as have California, Colorado, Florida, North Dakota, and Arizona. Only 15 programs existed in 11 states by 2002. In early 2005, the Federal Bureau of Prisons announced it was abandoning the strategy altogether. In the final analysis, after 20-plus years of operation, boot camps may soon enter the graveyard of tried but failed correctional programs. It is interesting to note that juvenile institutions in the nineteenth century used military-style training, even to the point of marching with wooden rifles. One wonders if some correctional specialists 50 or 75 years from now will rediscover boot camps.

Sources: American Correctional Association (2003); Bourque, Han, and Hill (1996); Mays and Winfree (2005); Parent (2003); Peters, Thomas, and Zamberlan (1997); Willing (2005).

correctional programs and to evaluate those programs thoroughly and independently on an ongoing basis.

UNRESOLVED ISSUES AND LEGAL DILEMMAS

In this section we explore two issues juvenile corrections will confront well into the twenty-first century: the influence of the Civil Rights of Institutionalized Persons Act (CRIPA) on juvenile corrections and the issue of juveniles in custody who have disabilities under the Americans with Disabilities Act (ADA).[13] We selected these two for a very straightforward reason: though the effects of CRIPA and ADA are well understood in the adult system, we can only speculate about how the juvenile justice system will respond to what are likely to be two of the major legal challenges to correctional facilities in the coming years.

THE CIVIL RIGHTS OF INSTITUTIONALIZED PERSONS ACT

Correctional facilities have experienced a great deal of inmate litigation since the mid-1970s. In both adult and juvenile institutions there have been improvements because of court actions, but the adult facilities seem to have benefited the most. Therefore, this litigation will give juveniles an additional basis to challenge correctional practice. There are a number of legal mechanisms available to inmate litigants, and we explore two of them briefly—habeas corpus and the so-called Section 1983 lawsuits—before turning to the Civil Rights of Institutionalized Persons Act.

Beginning in 1871 and continuing for nearly 100 years, judges infrequently and reluctantly heard cases involving state prison inmates.[14] In the 1960s, an activist Supreme Court became receptive to inmate lawsuits, and more inmates turned to the writ of habeas corpus as a mechanism for prison litigation (Mays and Olszta, 1989). **Habeas corpus writs** have long provided a powerful mechanism for inmates to bring their cases into court (Mays, 1984). However, two factors limit successful use of habeas corpus writs. First, the writ challenges the very fact of the inmate's incarceration. Therefore, if the inmate is successful, he or she would gain freedom from custody. Because of this rather drastic remedy (at least in the minds of some people), judges often were unwilling to find on behalf of the inmate litigants. Second, most of these cases were highly particularized. In other words, the person suing was challenging the fact of confinement in his or her own individual situation. Thus, it was difficult to bring broad-based challenges to correctional institutions and procedures.

By the mid-1970s, inmates discovered that a more direct approach to institutional reform litigation lay in 42 U.S.C. 1983, the codification of the Civil Rights Act of 1871 (Mays and Olszta, 1989). Rather than challenging the fact of incarceration, these civil rights actions allowed inmates to confront the confinement conditions that troubled them. The growth of these actions has been nothing short of explosive, and beginning in 1977 civil rights suits surpassed habeas corpus suits in terms of sheer numbers (see Mays and Winfree, 2005:304–7). State-prisoner habeas corpus petitions increased 204% between 1980 and 2000. Today, nearly 1 in every 10 lawsuits filed in federal district courts is an inmate suit, and most are **Section 1983 lawsuits**.

In 1980, Congress passed the **Civil Rights of Institutionalized Persons Act** to provide statutory protection for institutionalized persons, including juveniles and those in private facilities (Puritz and Scali, 1998:1). CRIPA authorizes the U.S. Department of Justice to sue state and local governments for violations of the civil rights of institutionalized persons. The institutions covered by CRIPA include:

- facilities holding the mentally ill, disabled, retarded, or chronically ill or handicapped
- a jail, prison, or other correctional facility
- a pretrial detention facility
- for juveniles, facilities where they are held or awaiting trial; whether residing in such facility or institution for purposes of receiving care or treatment, or residing for any state purpose (other than for educational purposes)
- facilities providing skilled nursing care, intermediate or long-term care, or custodial or residential care [42 U.S.C. Section 1997 (1)(A)]

Given these specifications, CRIPA explicitly covers juvenile detention and correctional facilities. While the Justice Department may not represent individual juvenile litigants, it may bring suits designed "to remedy systemic problems" (Puritz and Scali, 1998:1).

If the Justice Department conducts an investigation and finds systemic civil rights violations, is has one of two ways to resolve the alleged infractions: negotiation or litigation. In order to prevent showdowns with state and local governments, Congress provided for a mediation process to remedy the conditions causing the civil rights violations. There is no time limit placed on this process by the federal law, as investigations and negotiations may continue for years (Puritz and Scali, 1998:3).

Most CRIPA investigations end with negotiated settlements. At the next level of formality, the parties may enter into court-endorsed agreements or consent decrees (Puritz and Scali, 1998:3). If both these measures fail, litigation begins. If the Justice Department successfully takes a governmental entity to court, only equitable relief is available.[15] This means that CRIPA allows for "injunctions against certain practices, affirmative orders to upgrade facilities, and orders to increase staff size" (Puritz and Scali, 1998:4).

What can we conclude about the rights of incarcerated juveniles? First, many juvenile facilities suffer from structural and programmatic deficiencies. As a result, many of the facilities holding adjudicated delinquents probably would not pass constitutional muster. Second, litigation has become a regular part of the correctional landscape in the United States. State prison inmates routinely have turned to the courts to redress their grievances concerning confinement conditions. Juvenile institutions also have come under the courts' scrutiny and, in all likelihood, there will be more litigation by juvenile correctional clients, their families, and public-law interest groups. Third, the preferred method for bringing lawsuits against correctional agencies probably will remain the Section 1983 civil rights actions. Nevertheless, the Civil Rights of Institutionalized Persons Act of 1980 also serves to protect juveniles' rights.

DISABLED JUVENILES IN CUSTODY

In the mid-1990s, correctional agencies in the United States made a startling discovery: The **Americans with Disabilities Act (ADA)** applies to them. Therefore, with increasing frequency, secure institutions have had to make structural modifications and programmatic changes to comply with ADA requirements. The guiding standard for the Act is the phrase "reasonable accommodations," and what constitutes a reasonable accommodation may be subject to debate by corrections professionals, advocacy groups for disabled persons, and the courts. In this section, we examine some of the potential ramifications for detention centers and juvenile correctional facilities (such as state training schools) as they respond to compliance with the ADA.

Congress passed the Americans with Disabilities Act in 1990, an act called "perhaps the most sweeping civil rights legislation passed since the enactment of the Civil Rights Act of 1964 nearly 30 years before" (Rubin, 1993:1). Employment discrimination and access to public accommodations are the primary targets of this legislation, but it also applies to correctional facilities and inmate programming (Rubin and McCampbell, 1995). Those covered under the ADA must have "a physical or mental impairment that substantially limits one or more major life activities" (Rubin, 1993:2). Based on these specifications, juvenile correctional agencies must be concerned about facility accessibility by staff members, the public (including attorneys, family members, and other visitors), and any youngsters ordered confined in a facility (Rubin and McCampbell, 1995).

In most instances, program participation cannot be limited because of disabilities possessed by institutional residents. For instance, facilities that offer educational classes, substance abuse counseling, recreation and art therapy classes, work projects, work release programs, boot camps, and religious observances must make these activities accessible to inmates with disabilities (Rubin and McCampbell, 1995:6). However, providing program access "is not required if it would fundamentally alter the nature of the program, service, or activity, or if it would cause undue financial and administrative burdens on the governmental entity" (Rubin and McCampbell, 1995:3). Consequently, a reasonable accommodation to ensure the ability to participate cannot entail undue burdens or excessive financial costs.

ADA legislation equally applies to mentally disabled persons. The ADA defines a mental disability as "any developmental or psychological disorder, such as retardation, organic brain syndrome, emotional illness, or specific learning disability" (Rubin and McCampbell, 1995:1). Some people estimate that nationwide between 6% and 13% of detainees have a severe mental disability, although no separate estimates for juvenile justice facilities are currently available. Given the ADA's language, even juvenile "correctional facilities must do more than just identify mentally disabled inmates . . . they must also provide mental health screening, evaluation, and treatment" (Rubin and McCampbell, 1995:1).

SUMMARY

The nation's juvenile corrections system seems to be in a state of considerable flux in the early twenty-first century, provoking more questions than answers. Therefore, it may be productive to frame these questions in the most useful manner rather than attempt to answer questions that seem to be without straightforward answers.

At the most basic level, we are dealing with the historical roots of our juvenile corrections system. Private corrections—so much at the heart of the origins of the juvenile correctional system—has reemerged as a major player; moreover, rather than being underwritten by charitable and religious groups, current privatization efforts are linked to for-profit businesses. It may be appropriate to say at this point that despite centuries of experience with juvenile corrections, the system has not come very far. Juvenile corrections today still relies very heavily on secure confinement facilities, such as state training schools, that often resemble juvenile prisons. Whatever the official philosophy behind this view of penology, the message conveyed to young offenders is one of punishment.

These generalizations should not paint a picture that is all punishment and no treatment, however. The rehabilitative ideal is still very much alive in juvenile corrections, and this fact is particularly evident in the less secure facilities. Nevertheless, security is still the paramount concern for most correctional personnel, even if it means sacrificing the treatment goals. Two strong—and opposing—trends seem to be at work in juvenile corrections. On the one hand, substantial efforts have been expended to deinstitutionalize and decarcerate many youngsters who are appropriate candidates for community-based programming or other nontraditional justice alternatives. Along with these developments, some states have placed youngsters in less secure institutional settings whenever possible. On the other hand, we have continued to build, expand, and modify secure custodial settings as a way of proving that we are tough on juvenile crime. Thus, if someone asks, "Which way does the juvenile correctional system in the United States seem to be heading?" an appropriate answer would be, "Both ways at the same time!"

The "both ways" characterization is crucial because of what we call the **rubber-band effect**. If you pull a rubber band with both hands, it will stretch a relatively fixed distance in both directions from a fixed midpoint before it breaks. You can move either hand a greater distance either left or right before the band reaches its breaking point by only moving in one direction at a time, essentially giving one side more flexibility of movement than the other one. The nation's various juvenile correctional jurisdictions are employing the former approach rather than the latter. That is, rather than moving left or right from a fixed midpoint, say in the direction of *either* a building binge of secure facilities *or* deinstitutionalization, we are currently moving in both directions simultaneously. This trend begs another question: How long before the rubber band breaks—in this case, the public's willingness or ability to provide financial, political, and social support for this two-way policy?

Finally, the real questions facing juvenile corrections in the coming years are not how many bed spaces we will have or at what level of security they will be provided. Rather, we need to ask: whom do we want to lock up and why? The general public, public policy makers, and corrections professionals all must come to grips with fundamental policy choices on the extent to which we want to rely on secure custody. Is the get-tough approach reducing the juvenile crime rate? If so, then getting tough seems to be completely logical. However, if longer terms in secure facilities do not translate into reduced juvenile crime rates, correctional policy makers may need to consider less expensive (if not more effective) options very seriously and very soon.

CRITICAL REVIEW QUESTIONS

1. Go beyond the information provided in the opening narrative: What is the likelihood that John Jamieson will leave behind his criminal tendencies once he walks out the gate at Rockridge? Ground your answer in the material provided in this chapter. (Bonus question: The visiting room described in this narrative is normally found only in high-security youth prisons and lockups [jail-like facilities] for youthful detainees. What is the visiting area like in the institutional correctional facility for youths nearest your campus?)

2. Which disposition recommended by the National Advisory Committee on Criminal Justice Standards and Goals do you believe would most benefit the majority of adjudicated juvenile delinquents today? What criminological theory supports your choice?

3. Compare and contrast the nineteenth-century cult of domesticity with the concept of family values so popular in the 1980s and 1990s.

4. Decarceration and deinstitutionalization sound like similar ideas. How similar are they?

5. Provide a continuum of purposes for institutional juvenile corrections. On the left side put those most likely to be achieved, and on the right side those least likely to be achieved. Justify, in writing, your placement of the five purposes on this continuum.

6. Which single piece of information most surprised you about current trends in juvenile correctional populations? Explain your choice.

7. Respond to the following observation about the privatization of juvenile corrections: "It just doesn't seem right that the private facilities take the kids with minor problems, leaving the state with the hard-core delinquents!"

8. Besides racism, what other reason or reasons might explain the disproportionate minority confinement problem?

9. What would be the worst thing about serving time in a juvenile correctional facility?

10. After reading about what works in juvenile correctional facilities programming, are you optimistic or pessimistic that such institutions can serve as positive social change agents?

11. Which of the two legal dilemmas do you think will have the most profound impact on the future of juvenile correctional institutions? Which one *should* have the most impact?

RECOMMENDED READING

Schwartz, Ira M. (1989). *(In)Justice for Juveniles*. Lexington, MA: Lexington Books. This book does not specifically address the field of juvenile corrections. However, Schwartz deals with many of the contemporary policy initiatives concerning juvenile justice in the United States. The author was administrator of the Office of Juvenile Justice and Delinquency Prevention during the Carter administration, and Schwartz provides important insights on the federal jail-removal initiative under the Juvenile Justice and Delinquency Prevention Act of 1974.

KEY TERMS

affectional discipline

Americans with Disabilities
    Act (ADA)

boot camp programs

case classification

child savers

Civil Rights of Institutionalized
    Persons Act (CRIPA)

cult of domesticity

custodial dispositions

custody

decarceration

deinstitutionalization

detention center

determinate sentences

deterrence

disproportionate minority
    confinement (DMC)

equity

family reform school

general deterrence

habeas corpus writs

house of refuge

incapacitation

indeterminate sentence

industrial schools

inmate classification

inmate programming

institutional environments

Jacksonian era

just deserts

Juvenile Justice and Delinquency
    Prevention Act of 1974

long-term facilities

open environments

outcomes-based evaluations

paupers

prison code

prisonization

Progressive movement

Protestant work ethic

psychometrics

reception and diagnostic center

reform schools

reformatories

rehabilitation

residential training center

restitution

retribution

rubber-band effect

Section 1983 lawsuits

selective incapacitation

sentinel event

shock incarceration programs

short-term facilities

specific deterrence

state-raised inmates

total institution

training schools

treatment

NOTES

[1] Clear and Cole (1990:530–35) identified four eras: refuge period (1824–1899), juvenile court period (1900–1959), juvenile rights period (1960–1979), and crime control period (1980–present). Krisberg and Austin (1993:8–34) divided the years between the colonial period and the early 1920s into four

periods: pre-refuge period (1600s to 1820s), refuge period (1825–1860), child-savers period (1860–1890), and progressive era (1880–1920).

[2] For more on the juvenile court see chapters 1 and 5.

[3] For Regoli and Hewitt (1997:598), *decarceration* refers to removing all status offenders from correctional institutions, shifting them to community-based programs. Others employ the term *deinstitutionalizing status offenders* (or DSO) to describe this same policy (Holden and Kapler, 1995; Krause and McShane, 1994). We use *decarceration* to refer to the removal of status offenders from correctional institutions, saving *deinstitutionalization* to describe policies ranging from system-wide attempts to close juvenile correctional facilities to severely restricting the use of incarceration for even violent juvenile offenders (see Binder, Geis, and Bruce, 2001:330–32).

[4] Highfields' emphasis on group influences became the model for many treatment programs. For example, Empey used many aspects of Highfields in both the Silverlake Experiment in California and the Provo Experiment in Utah. In both cases, youths in the experimental groups failed or recidivated at rates consistent with or worse than those in the control groups. However, in the case of the Silverlake Experiment, part of the problem appears to have been that program administrators were only partly successful in providing positive rewards for desired behavior (Finckenauer, 1984:99).

[5] Alaska, Connecticut, and New Mexico failed to report the number of children in confinement.

[6] This material derives in part from Sickmund (2004).

[7] This material derives in part from Sickmund (2004) and Sickmund et al. (2004).

[8] Beginning in 1997, the Bureau of the Census and OJJDP initiated the Census of Juveniles in Residential Placement (CJRP). The methods employed in the CJRP were slightly different from those previously used to explore the nation's juvenile correctional facilities, the latter method known as the Children in Custody (CIC) census. Rather than collect aggregate data, as had been the case in the CIC, the CJRP collected individual information. The definitions of inmates were slightly different in both instruments. While Sickmund (2004) argues for the general comparability of the two methods, we chose to restrict our offense-related information to that provided by the CJRP, the most recently available one published for the 2001 CJRP.

[9] There is virtually no difference whether the children in question are detained or committed residents (Sickmund et al., 2004).

[10] Unfortunately, the breath of coverage for the NIBRS is not as great as for the UCR. That is, only 17% of the nation is included in the annual NIBRS report, while the *Uniform Crime Reports* coverage is slightly over 94% (http://www.fbi.gov/ucr/cius_02/html/web/summary/summary.html; http://www.as.wvu.edu/~jnolan/nibrsparticipation.htm). As a result, the Pope and Snyder (2003) study of race and NIBRS may be flawed for breadth of coverage.

[11] Hayes discovered records of 110 total suicides between 1995 and 1999 but was only able to get complete information on 79.

[12] Bear in mind that while Martinson's summary of the report suggests that not much appears to work, the larger report is on the lack of good evaluations, not the shortage of good programs.

[13] This section relies heavily on a report entitled *Beyond the Walls: Improving Conditions of Confinement for Youth in Custody* (Puritz and Scali, 1998) prepared for the Office of Juvenile Justice and Delinquency Prevention and the American Bar Association.

[14] The Supreme Court held in 1871 that prisoners are slaves of the state and have no more rights than slaves. At the time of their incarceration, they suffer civil death, forfeiting many of their rights as citizens (see Mays and Winfree, 2005:202).

[15] **Equity** is a legal doctrine that focuses on fairness. Historically, it has been "available in cases in which the law did not act or was ineffective" (Altschuler and Sgroi, 1996:24).

chapter

8

JUVENILE PAROLE AND AFTERCARE

* * *

The newspaper headline proclaimed, "Parolee, 15, Commits Brutal Rape, Murder." Frank Parsons, a math teacher at Central High School, slopped his cup of coffee on the kitchen table as he held up the morning paper, showing it to his wife. "Look at this story. I can't believe it! This 15-year-old kid had been up at the state training school for boys only six months. Six months! And they released him. Put him on parole. 'Aftercare,' they called it. Some care. Nobody cares is my bet. They just put him back into the community. Our community!"

Frank continued talking: "Seems he did some house burglaries last summer. Now, just two weeks after getting out, he raped and bludgeoned to death an old lady a block from his parent's house over on Maple Street. Geez, that's only four blocks from here. Lemme see. Uh, yeah, here it is: 'The authorities theorize that she came home early from a canceled therapist's appointment.' Seems the old lady went twice a week. The cops think he knew she'd be out. Listen to this." Frank's voice became louder, more strident, as he read from the newspaper:

> *Detective Arthur Nelson, senior investigator on the case, reported that the alleged rape-homicide occurred at approximately 3:30 PM yesterday. The crime did not appear to be well planned. "What we have here," Detective Nelson told this reporter, "is your typical daytime house burglary gone bad. Very bad."*
>
> *Police arrested the accused, Terrence Alexander Baker, age 15, less than 30 minutes after Alice Anderson, the victim's sister, discovered the body and dialed 911. Baker, released just two weeks ago from the State School for Boys, had known the victim for at least 10 years. For the past four summers, he had performed light yard work for her. According to previously sealed court records turned over to this reporter late yesterday afternoon, all of Baker's burglary victims last summer were also clients in his booming yard-care business. It was this fact that led police to question and arrest young Baker.*

Frank balled up the newspaper and tossed it in the trash, a disgusted look on his face. He turned to his wife and asked: "But why did he rape and kill her? What were the authorities—the police, the courts, those guys up at the state school, whoever it was made that decision—thinking? Where were their heads when they released a dangerous kid like that after so little time? Six months for four burglaries and now this: rape and murder!"

Helen, Frank's wife, saw the consternation on her husband's face. Then it struck her, like an electric shock: "What was the kid's name?"

Frank retrieved the newspaper from the trash can and smoothed it out on the table. "Oh my God." His voice was almost a whisper. "It was Terrence Alexander Baker. That's Alex Baker! You know, Jim and Anne Baker's son. He took algebra from me last year."

Frank got up from the table and started pacing back and forth in the small kitchen, almost like a caged animal. "Should we call the Bakers?" he asked his wife. "What would we say? We've known them for 20 years; we've known Alex since he was born. This is a kid from a 'good family.' Does that mean it could happen to anyone? Could it happen to us?" Frank spit the words out nonstop.

Helen could not answer Frank's questions. Moreover, she was not sure he wanted her to respond. Instead, he simply seemed to be grasping for answers where there were none. She walked purposefully over to the phone, dialed a number from memory, and when someone answered, said: "Hi, Anne. Yes, it's me, Helen Parsons." A pause. "Yes," she continued, "we saw the paper. Frank and I would like to come over and help if we can." Another brief pause. "OK, see you in 10 minutes."

Turning to her husband, who had returned to the kitchen table and the morning newspaper, Helen said, "Come on Frank. You want answers. Let's start with the Bakers."

Frank crumpled the newspaper again, tossed it once more in the trash, and joined Helen as she headed for the garage. Neither he nor Helen would ever read the story buried on page 9 of the Local News section: "Reintegrative Living Center for Juvenile Parolees Called Success: '1,000 Clients Served and No Problems,' says Unit Manager."

* * *

In this chapter we will deal with many Alex Bakers as we examine the release of committed youthful offenders. The ultimate release of all committed juveniles eventually is a given, whether it comes from death, executive clemency, completion of sentence, or parole. Of these methods, the most likely is **parole**, or as it is known in roughly one-half of the states, **juvenile aftercare** (National Center for Juvenile Justice, 2005).

Parole is "the status of an offender conditionally released from a prison by discretion of a paroling authority prior to expiration of sentence, required to observe conditions of parole, and placed under the supervision of a parole agency" (Bureau of Justice Statistics, 1981:144). Parole is the main form of conditional release from incarceration. It is also "the status or program membership of a juvenile who has been committed to a treatment or confinement facility, conditionally released from the facility, and placed in a supervisory and/or treatment program" (Bureau of Justice Statistics, 1981:144).

The quality and quantity of supervised aftercare for juvenile offenders is virtually the same as parole for adult offenders (Abadinsky, 2002b). However, aftercare is "generally linked to a rehabilitative goal and implies much more than traditional parole surveillance and supervision" (Castellano, 1995:S2). Juvenile aftercare and adult parole differ in that "juvenile aftercare [has] placed greater emphasis on achieving rehabilitative and treatment ends than was necessarily true of adult parole" (Ashford and Le Croy, 1993:181; see also Ashford, 1996). For example, the Florida Department of Juvenile Justice's (1998) aftercare services come from private service providers or state agencies, and they begin after juveniles have completed their prescribed confinement. The department's program manual asserts that "the objectives of the aftercare program are to plan, guide, and assist juveniles with successful readjustment to community living, including appropriate educational and vocational programs" (Florida DJJ, 1998:4–5). While the terms and practices vary from state to state, we will use the terms *juvenile parole* and *aftercare* as virtually synonymous throughout this chapter. The following paragraphs will give you a better overall understanding of parole.

In practically all states, parole is a privilege, not a right. Therefore, rather than automatically being granted parole after a certain number of months or years in detention, individuals being considered for parole must demonstrate that they have changed and are ready for release. For these reasons, it is common for juveniles to receive institutional sentences of indeterminate length, limited only by state laws defining the upper age limit for releasing a young adult.

Unlike probation, which is a judicial function, parole is *generally* viewed as an **executive privilege** granted after some period of confinement.[1] State executive administration is the most common structure, found in over two-thirds of all states. A few states allow the judiciary to supervise parole. A small number of states use some combination of local and state executive control. While judges *impose* probation, paroling authorities (typically called parole boards) *grant* parole, although there are exceptions to even this distinction.

While probation is a community-based sentence *in lieu* of confinement, parole is a community-based *extension* of confinement. Parole is not, technically speaking, a form of community corrections. In theory and in practice, parole—including aftercare—provides a released offender with the opportunity to readjust to life in the free community. As a practical matter, parolees may live at their homes or at an alternative location in a semi-secure facility similar to a community-based correctional facility.

The same officers or agents often supervise both juvenile probationers and parolees. In part this practice is due to state laws that refer to conditional release from a secure institution as probation or aftercare probation. In some jurisdictions, the number of parolees is so low that it is sound fiscal practice to have the same agents supervise both probationers and parolees. In still other jurisdictions, upon release from secure institutional facilities, juveniles return to the court's control; thus, their conditional release is legally a form of probation.

Both probation and parole involve the supervision of offenders under conditions imposed by the appropriate judicial or executive authority. The general conditions fundamentally are the same, and as we will see later in the chapter, there may be similar additional specific conditions as well as legal and technical conditions.

In spite of these similarities, parole officers and their charges differ from probation officers and probationers in at least two respects. First, parole officers work at a greater physical distance from the paroling authority—the corrections department or state parole board—than do probation officers, who normally have frequent and ongoing contact with the judges who impose probation. Second, the two types of clients are somewhat different. Parolees have been incarcerated, making them high-risk clients with unique adjustment and reintegration problems that probationers often do not face (see, for example, Latessa and Allen, 2003).

All forms of conditional release, no matter who the releasing or supervising authority, share a common element: If you mess up, there will be consequences. The loss-of-freedom threat is a constant. In order to better understand this threat, we turn to parole's origins.

THE DEVELOPMENT OF PAROLE

The practices that we now call probation and parole developed around the same period in history. However, parole grew out of correctional practices in Europe, while probation largely originated in the United States. Most authorities credit Bostonian John Augustus as the "father of probation," while several individuals contributed to the development of parole. First was Alexander Maconochie, a former English naval officer. In 1840, Maconochie arrived in Australia to serve as the superintendent of the Van Diemen's Land penal colony. During the eighteenth and nineteenth centuries, **transportation** or **banishment** to a penal colony was a frequent practice (Mays and Winfree, 2005). For the British, that meant sending their criminals to colonial America. However, when the United States declared independence, the English had to find other places to send prisoners, and Australia was the preferred location.

Maconochie approached his new job with correctional notions that were very progressive for his time, including less physically harsh treatment of prisoners and the ability of inmates to earn early release. Unfortunately, his progressive attitudes toward preparing offenders for release back into society soon got him into trouble with Sir John Franklin, the lieutenant governor of Van Diemen's Land (Barry, 1958). Maconochie subsequently was appointed superintendent of the English penal colony on Norfolk Island, where he established a system of marks of commendation that inmates received for good behavior or forfeited for bad behavior. Accumulation of a sufficient number of marks could help an inmate earn a **ticket of leave** for additional freedom or early release. His less punitive orientation toward prisoners resulted in criticisms of Maconochie's methods and eventually led to his recall to England in 1844. After he was relieved of his administrative duties, the Norfolk Island penal colony returned to its earlier punitive system of inmate control (Taylor, 1978a, 1978b; see also Mays and Winfree, 2005).

In the mid-1800s, two occurrences furthered parole's development. The first was the implementation of the **indeterminate sentence**, which stipulated a minimum and maximum range of imprisonment rather than a fixed number of years. Second, in 1853 the English Parliament passed the **Penal Servitude Act**, whereby prisoners could receive early release under the supervision of local law enforcement officials. The British Home Office then commissioned Walter Crofton to study living conditions in Irish prisons. Later Crofton was made director of the Irish prison system and expanded on the idea of early release (Dooley, 1978). Crofton's ticket-of-leave system had three stages, each one using decreasingly restrictive incarcera-

> **Box 8.1   International Perspectives**
> **Juvenile Parole: A Missing Practice or an Absent Need?**
>
> Juvenile parole—like probation—is relatively rare outside of the United States. In many of the world's nations, children simply reenter the community without supervision once they serve their sentences. This is due partly to the fact that few nations incarcerate children for more than a few weeks or months, preferring instead to use community-based alternatives to incarceration. This is not to say, however, that parole does not exist. As in the United States, other nations use parole in more than one form, and the "social tether" extended to parolees leads back to several different legal authorities. For example, in France the juvenile judge continues to maintain oversight of committed youth. The judge's authority extends into the correctional facility, called a *foyer*. Judges occasionally retrieve a committed youth and order probation or community service. Russian youth prisons, where commitments average less than a year, use parole as a release mechanism for their woefully crowded facilities. However, formal aftercare supervision is limited. Few nations in the world can afford or have the need for the kind of juvenile parole services found in the United States.
>
> Source: Terrill (2003).

tion. As a prisoner's behavior and willingness to comply improved, he moved up a stage. Crofton's final stage was the issuance of a ticket of leave, or conditional release into the community, much like that used by Alexander Maconochie (Carpenter, 1872; see also Barry, 1958).

One of the first places in the United States to utilize indeterminate sentencing along with early release was New York State's Elmira Reformatory, which opened in 1876. The superintendent of the Elmira Reformatory was Zebulon Brockway, a man long associated with penal innovations. Brockway, too, developed a system of good-time credits for early release.

Two generalizations about the history of parole frustrate those who study it. First, in terms of the historical record, we have more information about probation than parole. Second, what we do know about parole is largely restricted to adult offenders. We suspect that one reason for this historical gap is that during parole's formative years, prison authorities made few age-based distinctions between law violators. Consequently, juvenile parole's history is largely indistinguishable from that for the adult system, until the juvenile court's creation in 1899.

PURPOSES OF PAROLE

Defining the purposes of parole is a difficult task. In some sense, juvenile parole serves a range of functions. First, parole is one way to extend punishment beyond incarceration. Parolees who violate the conditions of their release face the possibility of administrative hearings and recommitment. Therefore, parole provides the means to remove youngsters from juvenile correctional facilities but also keep them in a legal status of restricted freedom.

Second, by determining the potential risks and making release decisions based on those risks, juvenile parole provides for public safety. The surveillance provided by parole officers is the front line of public safety. The imposition of restrictive conditions, combined with regular supervisory contacts, allow parole officers to determine when or if a parolee poses a public safety threat while in the community.

Third, effective parole systems should prevent future law-violating activity. However, as the opening scenario to this chapter suggests, parole is often a hard sell to politicians and the public, both of whom tend to view offenders recently released from secure correctional facilities as a major source of subsequent criminality. Nonetheless, the prevention of additional delinquent behavior should be a logical outgrowth of restrictive conditions and regular surveillance.

Fourth, by providing treatment and supervision, parole officers are in a position to assist their clients with **reintegration** into the home and community. Such treatment services as counseling, education, job training, and life skills exemplify the types of rehabilitative programs that can be associated with parole. Of course, cynics and critics question how you can reintegrate someone never fully integrated or only marginally integrated in the first place. If ex-inmates were outsiders when they left for the youth correctional facility, what will it take to make them part of the community when they return?

While each of these goals would seem to be worthy in and of itself, a few unresolved dilemmas foil juvenile parole's smooth operation and administration, and some of these problems are fundamental to the concept of parole. Many conservative critics argue that parole undermines the sentencing authority of the courts and the notion of truth in sentencing. Thus, when a youngster receives a two-year commitment to a state training school, in most instances this translates into a six- to nine-month period of incarceration followed by parole. For conservatives, parole is another example of a juvenile justice system "slap on the wrist" for youngsters who may have committed serious offenses (see Walker, 1998a:220–23).

Liberals level their criticism of parole along another dimension. To them, the most unacceptable element of parole is the discretionary—and some would say discriminatory—nature of the process. Parole boards may base their decisions on what they believe to be crucial factors for success (such as family stability) without having evidence that these factors actually are important. Therefore, at best, the decision-making processes of parole boards are guesswork substantiated by documentation provided by the correctional facility staff.

Other problems associated with parole concern the nature of its goals. The available methods for evaluating parole performance make it nearly impossible to document most cases of success or failure. As we have seen throughout this text, problems of definition and measurement continue to plague all parts of the juvenile justice system, and these issues will remain a challenge for juvenile justice system professionals for decades to come. Simply defining a released offender as a parole success or failure, short of some catastrophic event such as that described in the opening vignette, is often a difficult task for researchers and practitioners alike.

We next turn our attention to the trends in parole caseloads. Nationwide, both juvenile and adult parole have faced something of a roller-coaster ride for over two decades. As parole fell out of favor and states increasingly turned to determinate sentencing, the numbers of parolees fell in many jurisdictions. However, with growing correctional populations and additional pressures to house or release inmates, both adult and juvenile systems frequently have turned to parole as a backdoor or safety valve for controlling inmate crowding.

THE USE OF PAROLE AS A PRERELEASE MECHANISM

Parole has been associated with indeterminate sentencing nearly from its inception. Therefore, it is significant to note the changes in sentencing that occurred throughout the criminal justice system during the 1970s and 1980s. Beginning in the mid-1970s states began to move from indeterminate sentences, with reliance on parole for early release and community supervision, to determinate sentences. The result was a decrease in release decisions made by adult parole boards (Bureau of Justice Statistics, 1988:105).

Changes in juvenile sentencing practices typically parallel those for adults. It is important to note, however, that not as many states moved to determinate sanctions for juveniles and the pace was much slower than it was for the changes in adult sentences. Nevertheless, the movement toward determinate sentences implied a profound philosophical shift within the juvenile justice system. Yet, even with the adoption of determinate sentencing systems, juvenile parole supervision is present in one form or another in virtually every state (Ashford and Le Croy, 1993:194).

When examining juvenile parole statistics, it is important to note that we have very few reliable numbers. In 1992, the nation's juvenile justice system reported about 37,000 parolees, although this figure is misleading since many states classify children released from custody as probationers or aftercare probationers (Maguire, Pastore, and Flanagan, 1993). In 2002, figures for 25 states indicated that they collectively supervised around 69,000 juvenile parolees (American Correctional Association, 2003:74). Consider for a moment that in the adult system, the ratio of parolees to probationers is about 1 to 6 (Glaze, 2003; see also Mays and Winfree, 2005:210–13). If this ratio holds for juveniles, and given nearly 700,000 juvenile probationers, the figure of 69,000 juvenile parolees may be low by upwards of 30,000 children.[2] One final clue lies within the Census of Juveniles in Residential Placement, which estimates that secure and residential facilities release nearly 100,000 youth a year (Sickmund, 2000). Given the shorter average sentence lengths served by juveniles in comparison to those of adults and the relatively greater proportion of juveniles released each year, this final estimate seems reasonable. In terms of who these parolees are, we suggest you return to chapter 7 and its description of the gender, race, and ethnicity breakdowns for one-day counts of the nation's public and private facilities.

THE ADMINISTRATION OF JUVENILE PAROLE

The National Advisory Committee on Criminal Justice Standards and Goals (1976:675) recommended that a single state agency administer juvenile community-based correctional supervision, with local delivery of services. Implicit in this recommendation was a merger of juvenile probation and parole, in spite of the fact that juvenile parole, more so than juvenile probation, tends to be a state-level executive function. Nevertheless, many states continue to offer separate juvenile probation and parole services.

COMMITMENT LENGTH AND PAROLE DURATION

To illustrate these different administrative arrangements, we examine the ways different states determine parole eligibility. There are three basic models: indeterminate sentences, determinate sentences, and a combination of indeterminate and determinate sentences. However, even within these models there are some variations. For example, straight indeterminate-length states include Alabama, Hawaii, Idaho, Illinois, Kentucky, Maine, Michigan, Minnesota, Mississippi, Montana, Nebraska, Nevada, New Hampshire, New York, Oklahoma, Utah, Vermont, and Wyoming. The District of Columbia also employs this method. As a rule, the only restriction in these states is the upper age limit for confining a person as a juvenile. In most of these states, a statewide agency determines the actual commitment time. A second group of states with indeterminate sentencing uses a maximum commitment time, including Alaska, Arkansas, California, Connecticut, Oregon, Virginia, Washington (which sets maximums and minimums), West Virginia, and Wisconsin. The maximum sentence is typically that accorded an adult for the same offense. A third group employs indeterminate sentences that fix the minimum commitment time, including Arizona, Delaware, Georgia, Maryland, Massachusetts, Missouri, North Carolina, Ohio, and Pennsylvania. The releasing authority generally may not consider parole or aftercare until the children serve the minimum sentence.

Six states use only determinate sentencing, and even here, there is some variability. For example, Iowa uses "pure" determinate sentencing. Kansas has a set minimum. Colorado, New Jersey, and New Mexico have determinate sentences with set maximums. New Mexico is unique in that children receive maximum sentences of either one year or two years in state custody, depending on the seriousness of the offense and offender characteristics.

A final group uses both indeterminate and determinate sentencing, with the distinction generally being that the former is for less dangerous, first-time offenders and the latter is reserved for repeat offenders or dangerous ones. States using this method include Florida, Indiana, Louisiana, Rhode Island, South Carolina, South Dakota, Tennessee, and Texas.

Indeterminate sentencing dominates the nation's juvenile sentencing and release mechanisms, as 44 states and the District of Columbia use it in one form or another. Ashford and Le Croy (1993) observed that the various sentencing methods contain several themes. First, while there has been some movement away from indeterminate to determinate sentencing systems, most states rely on indeterminate lengths of parole supervision. Second, relatively few states have implemented determinate periods of parole supervision, as the general rule is to supervise youth until the threat for recidivism has been minimized. Third, the periods of juvenile parole have changed very little, even in the face of sentencing changes. Finally, some states have adopted determinate or presumptive sentences and have eliminated or severely curtailed parole for adult offenders. Nonetheless, all states have retained some form of juvenile parole or aftercare supervision, regardless of their sentencing methods.

GRANTING JUVENILE PAROLE

Across the nation, the processes associated with granting parole exhibit considerable diversity. Five models dominate juvenile aftercare at the state level, the primary focus in this chapter.[3] The first and most popular model is to invest the releasing power within a state-level or districtwide agency. In most cases, personnel within the agency alone make the release decision. This model is used in Alabama, Connecticut, the District of Columbia, Florida, Hawaii, Massachusetts, North Dakota, Oklahoma, Washington, and Wisconsin. In another cluster of states, the state agency must notify the committing court, get its approval, or otherwise work with the court in deciding on the release date. These combination decisions occur in Arkansas, Delaware, Georgia, Iowa, Kansas, Kentucky, Mississippi, Missouri, North Carolina, Ohio, Oregon, Rhode Island, Vermont, West Virginia, and Wyoming. In South Dakota, either a state agency or the committing court may authorize release. Finally, in New Jersey, the agency must obtain the court's permission if the youth served less than one-third of the sentence. Release by the state agency responsible for oversight of the correctional facility is the most common model, whether or not the court has a role.

The second model places the decision-making within the youth confinement facility. That is, upon the advice of a caseworker or other treatment staff member, a senior administrator at the correctional facility—usually the superintendent— makes a recommendation for the child's release. This model operates in Maine, Maryland, Minnesota, Montana, Nebraska, Nevada, Texas, and Virginia. Tennessee uses a variant on this theme to release committed youth: when the releasing authority—the superintendent—makes a recommendation for release, the committing judge and the commissioner of corrections must be consulted.

Parole boards are a third release mechanism. As a rule, parole boards are independent bodies, affiliated with neither the correctional institution nor the supervision agency. The governor appoints and a legislative authority confirms or approves all parole board members for staggered terms. Two types of parole boards make decisions about juvenile releases from confinement. The first works only with juveniles, as is the case in Colorado, New Hampshire, New Mexico, South Carolina, and Utah. The second type, like the parole board itself, reflects the linkage between juvenile and adult inmates; it is a combined adult and juvenile parole board. Largely a relic of the past, this combined board currently is found only in Illinois.

A fourth release mechanism has several different names, including the juvenile review board, supervisory review board, youth authority board, custody review board, and prisoner review board. One of these independent boards makes parole decisions in Alaska, Arizona, and California. In Idaho, a custody review board makes aftercare decisions for 19- and 20-year-olds who are high-risk offenders.

In several models reviewed so far, the commitment courts either exercise advisory roles or are final decision makers once another entity makes a recommendation. The fifth model gives control over the conditional release process to the commitment court only. For example, even though juvenile parolees in Iowa are under the supervision of the division of adult, children, and family services, the county court retains jurisdiction and must order any changes in placement. Similarly, in Louisiana the juvenile and family court sets the date for release, even though a separate executive authority provides supervision.

SERVICE PROVIDERS

A common way of providing juvenile parole is through the same agency responsible for adult probation and parole, often the state department of corrections. Under such an arrangement, juvenile parole typically becomes the lowest priority in the competition for funding dollars and staff positions. For this reason, some critics characterize juvenile parole as the "poor stepchild of the juvenile justice system" (Simonsen and Gordon, 1982:266; see also Armstrong and Altschuler, 1998). As a rule, juvenile parole is the least developed segment of the largely underdeveloped juvenile corrections system (Altschuler and Armstrong, 1994; Armstrong and Altschuler, 1998).

Juvenile parole services are delivered through various administrative arrangements. According to Altschuler and Armstrong (1994:5), such arrangements include:

- housing correctional institutions and aftercare supervision in the same agency
- housing correctional institutions and aftercare supervision in different agencies
- managing aftercare as a responsibility of either the executive or the judicial branches of state government
- delivering aftercare services on a county-by-county basis
- administering parole regionally, but operating aftercare as a distinct function on a statewide basis

Table 8.1 summarizes the various supervision providers for juvenile aftercare in the 50 states and the District of Columbia.[4] This information allows for several important generalizations.[5] In 10 states and the District of Columbia the same state-level, executive branch of government that is responsible for secure institutions, probation, and other services for delinquent youth also provides juvenile parole or aftercare. These are the so-called centralized jurisdictions; however, decentralization of services is the far more common pattern. Thus, more than a quarter century after the National Advisory Committee on Criminal Justice Standards and Goals (1976:675) made its recommendation, only 10 states follow its model. The District of Columbia and 12 states view juvenile aftercare as a social services issue, placing the service provider under the administrative control of agencies that have broad missions to provide for the state's general health, human, and social services needs. In eight states a unique department provides protective services for children and youth, plus the administration of juvenile corrections. Another nine states delegate parole functions to the state department of corrections, an agency that also oversees adult and juvenile institutions. The largest single category included in table 8.1 is the juvenile justice or youth services department with 18 states. However, only four states—Florida, Maryland, Oregon, and South

Carolina—operate independent, full-service departments of juvenile justice. Finally, the sentencing courts in six states provide aftercare services through either standard probation services or aftercare probation, the latter being a more intensive form of community release. These courts, as is the case for traditional probation, maintain legal control over the released youths until termination of supervision.

Table 8.1   Parole and Aftercare by Type of Provider

	Health & Social/ Human Services Department	Family & Children Department	Corrections Department	Juvenile Justice Department	Judicial Agency
Centralized states/District	**Alaska** District of Columbia **New Hampshire** Vermont	Delaware Rhode Island	Maine	Florida Maryland Oregon **South Carolina**	
Decentralized states	Arkansas **Colorado** Hawaii Mississippi Missouri Nebraska Nevada **Utah** Washington	Connecticut Michigan **New Mexico** New York Tennessee Wyoming	**Illinois** Indiana Louisiana Minnesota[1] Montana North Dakota South Dakota Wisconsin	**Arizona** **California** Georgia[2] **Idaho**[3] Kansas[4] Kentucky Massachusetts New Jersey North Carolina Ohio Oklahoma Texas Virginia West Virginia[5]	Alabama Georgia[2] Iowa Kansas[4] Minnesota[1] Pennsylvania

Note: States using either parole boards or review boards are in boldface.

[1] Minnesota operates three different systems, depending on county option: (1) Court Services Department, (2) Community Corrections Department, and (3) contracts with Department of Corrections.

[2] Depending on the location in Georgia, either the court or the Department of Juvenile Justice administers aftercare.

[3] Idaho uses a custody review board for 19- and 20-year-old high-risk youths; all others are assigned an anticipated release date by the Department of Juvenile Corrections.

[4] Kansas uses conditional release, which is administered at the local level through the Court Services Division or by the Juvenile Justice Authority, depending on the specific program.

[5] West Virginia uses a combination system for parole. Usually a probation officer from the Division of Juvenile Services provides aftercare supervision; however, some counties choose not to provide aftercare upon release from DJS.

Source: National Center for Juvenile Justice (2005).

PAROLE OFFICERS AND SUPERVISION

The National Advisory Committee on Criminal Justice Standards and Goals (1976) included juvenile probation and parole officers under the title of "community supervision staff." The committee also recommended that all community supervision staff have a minimum of a bachelor's degree in "psychology, social work, counseling, or criminal justice" (National Advisory Committee, 1976:692). Others have recommended that juvenile probation and parole officers have a master's degree in social work or a related field (see, for example, Trester, 1981:61–76). Most state agencies require a bachelor's degree for virtually all entry-level community supervision positions.

The clear trend in the juvenile justice system has been to require higher levels of education for those who work with delinquent youngsters (see, for example, DeLucia and Doyle, 1998; Robertson, 1994). This trend may unintentionally produce two problems. First, the requirement of a college degree may disproportionately exclude minority candidates. Given the conspicuous number of minority youngsters in juvenile institutions and on juvenile parole, it would seem highly desirable to have minority parole officers supervising some of these youngsters. Second, higher levels of education may create greater social distance between parole officers and the youngsters on their caseloads. Many juvenile parole officers

---

Box 8.2   Conflicting Roles of Parole Officers

Howard Abadinsky views parole officers as fulfilling three sometimes-conflicting roles. First, officers are treatment agents, although they rarely have treatment-specific training or education. Therapy is possible, says Abadinsky, if we define therapy as "the purposeful use of self to improve the social and psychological functioning of a client" (2002b:332).[6] Second, the parole system often expects officers to be brokers, whereby they help parolees secure, participate in, and complete various educational, treatment, community or social services, or mental health programs. Intensive aftercare programs heavily emphasize the broker role, a topic to which we return later in this chapter. Finally, Abadinsky observes that parole agents often must play the law enforcement role. After all, parole agents must enforce rules and, at a minimum, initiate the sanctioning process in the event the parolee violates the rules.

Do these roles create a conflict for parole officers? Abadinsky believes that those who refer to this conflict are typically nonpractitioners, and, he intimates, they do not understand the real work of parole practice. As Todd Clear and Edward Latessa observe, all professions have some form of role conflict. It is in the balancing of various roles that one learns to be a professional and practice that profession with some level of competence. Finally, as Altschuler and Armstrong found, sometimes when separate aftercare workers and surveillance officers were assigned the roles of broker and rule enforcer, the surveillance officers established better rapport with, for example, family members. They viewed this blurring of roles as an illustration of "how some forms of surveillance and service programming can benefit each other" (Altschuler and Armstrong, 1994:17).

Sources: Abadinsky (2002b); Altschuler and Armstrong (1994); Clear and Latessa (1989).

will come from middle-class backgrounds or will have acquired middle-class values because of their college experience. Since many delinquent youngsters come from society's lowest economic strata, additional education for parole officers may increase their level of professionalism but also may have the unintended result of increasing the social distance between juvenile parolees and their parole officers (Abadinsky, 2002b)

The lack of resources is a persistent problem for juvenile parole, as it is in almost all parts of the juvenile justice system. Juvenile parole may be the most neglected facet of the whole network of justice agencies in the United States (Armstrong and Altschuler, 1998). However, in order to understand this inadequacy, we need to examine the areas in which personnel and program resources are lacking.

JUVENILE PAROLE SYSTEMS AND RESOURCE ALLOCATION

The median caseload for parole officers handling juvenile cases is an elusive figure. The American Correctional Association (2003:76) notes that for 15 reporting states the median is 31 parole cases, ranging from a high of 99 in Idaho to a low of 9 in Maryland. Intensive parole caseloads are lower for the 15 reporting states: the median is 15, with a range from 4 in Wisconsin to 31 in Indiana. The National Advisory Committee (1976:684) recommended active caseloads from 25 to no more than 50. The American Probation and Parole Association (APPA, 1999) argues that the crucial factor is *workload*, not *caseload*. The APPA provides the following example to illustrate how three different caseload sizes could translate to the same 120-hour monthly workload, depending on the classification of the cases:

	Supervision caseload	
Case Priority	**Hours per month**	**Total caseload**
High	4 hours	30 cases
Medium	2 hours	60 cases
Low	1 hour	120 cases

While there will be ongoing debate over appropriate caseload sizes, it is apparent at this point that even among community supervision professionals there is disagreement over the size and composition of the ideal parole caseload.

Another piece of this caseload/workload puzzle comes from research on the intensive aftercare program (IAP), a form of supervision utilized for released juvenile inmates that resembles intensive probation. Henry Sontheimer and Lynne Goodstein (1993), in a study of Pennsylvania's juvenile intensive aftercare probation, noted that IAP officers are restricted to a caseload of no more than 12 offenders, when the regular aftercare workload is between 70 and 100 cases. However, even in the case of intensive aftercare, one caseload size may not fit all. As Altschuler and Armstrong (1994:9) observe about intensive aftercare for high-risk juveniles, there are four levels of parole supervision: intensive, maximum, medium, and minimum.[7] Obviously, depending on where the parolees are in the process, the level of supervision and the workload may vary greatly from agent to agent, let alone agency to agency.

Aftercare often includes halfway houses and group or foster home placements. Such arrangements are crucial when family problems—on the part of the parents, the child, or both—seem to be the root of the delinquency. Parole officers may be called upon to help find suitable alternative living situations for youngsters making the transition from institutional life.

The use of halfway-out or **reintegration living placements** is an important transition phase for youngsters released from secure confinement (Selph, Winfree, and Mays, 1996). Such placements provide structured living arrangements that allow juveniles to remain in residence for up to one year. These living conditions allow the youths to reestablish community contacts by attending school, working full-time or part-time, and receiving counseling services. Such placements are an extension of parole, not a substitute for it.

PAROLE CONDITIONS AND REVOCATIONS

As with probation, release on juvenile aftercare is conditional. Parole conditions place legal limits on the behavior of parolees and can include both standard requirements applied to all persons under a given agency's jurisdiction and special requirements pertaining to certain individual parolees (Bureau of Justice Statistics, 1981:146). Ideally, the paroling authorities craft the conditions to meet the needs of each individual child. Realistically, as with probation, most parole agencies maintain standard forms, occasionally called **parole contracts**, that spell out both the general requirements and special conditions that apply to particular parolees.

PAROLE CONDITIONS

Juvenile parole conditions are very similar to those for probation. That is, there are technical conditions and prohibitions against committing further delinquent acts. The following list contains frequently utilized parole conditions for juvenile offenders (Bureau of Justice Statistics, 1981:144):

- Parolees must abstain from the use of drugs and alcohol.
- Parolees must attend school and/or work.
- Parolees must get along with their parents and siblings.
- Parolees must refrain from undesirable associations, meaning abstain from associating with known offenders or others specified under the terms and conditions of parole.
- Parolees must regularly report to their parole officers.
- Parolees must remain in the jurisdiction and not change location or other conditions without prior notification and approval of their parole officers.
- Parolees must not commit any violations of local, state, or federal laws.

If a parolee violates any of these conditions, the parole officer may request a hearing. At this hearing, a decision is made to revoke parole and reincarcerate the youth or to continue parole.

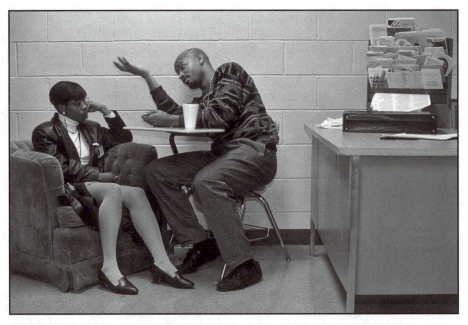

A counselor from the "I Have a Future" (IHAF) program counsels a teenage girl about issues involving her boyfriend. Begun in the late 1980s at Nashville's Meharry Medical College, IHAF evolved into a 12-month, community-based, comprehensive health initiative. IHAF targets youths ages 6 to 17 living in public housing or in economically depressed areas where most of the young people are considered at-risk for early pregnancy, HIV, and other sexually transmitted diseases; alcohol or other substance abuse; crime and violence; school dropout; and unemployment. Programs like IHAF also serve parolees as they reenter the community.

Lawrence Travis and Edward Latessa (1984) conducted a national survey of parole restrictions. While this survey dealt with adult authorities, many of the same conditions are imposed on juvenile parolees. Travis and Latessa found that most conditions are either **standard conditions** (applied to all parolees) or **special conditions** (applied to only certain parolees), and serve the following purposes (1984:592, 599):

1. They serve to notify parolees concerning their conditional release status.

2. They provide a basis for supervision of parolees by parole officers (that is, they establish the rules of the game).

3. They promote good citizenship among paroled offenders.

4. They prevent crimes and this, in turn, should minimize risk to the public.

5. They provide the basis for action in instances where parole revocation becomes necessary.

Over the years, states have tended to increase the number of conditions imposed on parolees. However, the most important consideration is not the number of conditions, but the relevance of the conditions to producing law-abiding behavior (Travis and Latessa, 1984:598–600).

The enforcement of parole conditions requires parole officers to recognize that the educational and job-training needs of parolees must be met. Facilitating parolees' educational needs can be problematic for juvenile parole officers because in many cases school authorities are unenthusiastic about having formerly incarcerated offenders back in the classroom (see Trester, 1981:121–31). In order to help the juvenile successfully complete the conditions of parole, the parole officer may have to arrange to place the youngster in a school other than the one he or she previously attended. Furthermore, if the juvenile did not make educational progress while in the institution, it may be necessary to place him or her in a grade level lower than the youngster's chronological age. This approach causes two problems: (1) it causes embarrassment for the juvenile returning from the correctional facility, and (2) it causes concern on the part of the educational authorities about this person corrupting the younger students (Trester, 1981:131).

For older juveniles who may not be in school, parole officers may be able to locate appropriate job-training programs. Such placements often are essential for most youngsters to gain parole.

PAROLE REVOCATIONS

Failure to comply with the conditions of parole may lead to curtailment of the parolee's freedom through the revocation process. Most parole officers consider revocation as the last resort, when other, less severe options have not worked. However, it is crucial to note that in most states "aftercare workers still are granted broad discretion in making decisions affecting the liberty and life chances of delinquent youth on parole" (Ashford, 1996:650). Confronted with obvious violations of parole conditions, parole officers may face a direct conflict between their law enforcement and treatment roles (Colangelo, 1998). No matter which role parole officers normally may emphasize, when revocations become necessary they must begin an investigation on behalf of the paroling authority to determine the legal sufficiency of the case. This requirement places even the most treatment-oriented parole officers in what parolees must see as an adversarial position (Trester, 1981:124, 129).

During the 1960s and early 1970s, activist courts increasingly legalized and formalized probation and parole revocations. Due to cases like *Morrissey v. Brewer* (408 U.S. 471, 1972), a variety of due process rights have been extended to adult parole revocation hearings. The Supreme Court held in *Morrissey* that revocation proceedings do not deprive individuals of absolute liberty, as would be the case in a criminal trial, but deal only with the conditional liberty that exists because of the conditions of early release. Nonetheless, the majority opinion did suggest the following as minimum due process requirements:

1. Provide the parolee with written notice of the alleged violations of conditions.

2. Disclose all evidence against the parolee.

3. Afford the parolee the opportunity to make a personal statement and to present witnesses and documentary evidence to support his or her claims.

4. Allow the parolee under normal circumstance to confront and cross-examine witnesses.

5. Hold the hearing before a neutral and detached body, typically the parole board.

6. Provide written findings when revoking parole.

In order to protect juveniles' constitutional rights, spelled out in cases like *In re Gault* (1967), the *Morrissey* guidelines should apply to juveniles as well as to adults. If a state's juvenile codes do not specify the due process rights for youngsters in aftercare status, it seems reasonable that they should be granted the same rights as adults on parole (see Ashford, 1996:643), although this is not always the case.

A primary objective of juvenile parole is to help transition youthful offenders back into family and community. Parole violations may signal persistent personal or family problems. Often we view parole as the end of the corrections continuum, but it is more accurate to view corrections as a circular process, since failure to correct the child's delinquent behavior will result in additional intervention (Armstrong and Altschuler, 1998). Parole revocations mean that not only have individual parolees failed, but so have the parole officers and aftercare programs. Therefore, juvenile parole officers may choose not to begin revocation proceedings since they recognize the possibility that incarceration alone has failed to address the child's problems.

There are several possible reasons why youngsters do not successfully complete parole. The following list provides some explanations for such failure:

1. *Unsatisfactory placement.* The correctional facility in which the youngster was confined did not meet the offender's particular needs. Placing a low-risk youngster incorrectly in a secure facility rather than in a community-based program or open residential setting is an example of this problem.

2. *Lack of institutional rehabilitation.* Insufficient rehabilitation often results from a lack of specialized programming and from trying to fit offenders into established programming efforts, rather than developing programs to meet offenders' needs. Rehabilitative failures also may result from improper diagnoses and the inability of correctional facilities to offer a full complement of treatment programs.

3. *Inadequate community supervision.* This situation occurs when caseloads are larger than community-supervision personnel or parole officers can manage. Many people believe that supervision automatically leads to success, and therefore, increased supervision should promote greater success. The real key to success seems to be the energy and commitment of parole officers and the levels of training and support they receive. In other words, caseload size may be important, but it does not necessarily equate with success or failure.

4. *Lack of justification for parole.* What are the grounds for parole decisions? Because of institutional crowding, many states release juvenile offenders in order to make room for new or anticipated arrivals. Some states employ truly indeterminate periods of confinement, and when they admit one youngster, they release another. This means that the timeliness of release may be an important factor in treatment efforts and parole success.

5. *Incorrigibility of the child.* This condition occurs when the youth fails to cooperate in treatment efforts. It does not necessarily mean that the youngster is

beyond hope. However, it is realistic to assume that some adjudicated delinquents are not interested in cooperating with staff efforts at "curing" them.

6. *Family and community conditions.* These influences may have contributed to the child's delinquency in the first place. An example of such influences would be a youngster who was gang-involved prior to incarceration and who establishes the same relationships with the gang upon release on parole.

This list strongly suggests that revocations may be due to individual, family, community, institutional, and peer influences. Peer influences, in particular, are often critical to initial delinquent acts and continued misconduct. These circumstances highlight the need for a multipronged approach to reintegrate released offenders, or intensive aftercare supervision.

INTENSIVE AFTERCARE SUPERVISION

Juvenile parole, like juvenile probation and adult probation and parole, has suffered from much criticism, at least since the mid-1970s. The criticisms center on two issues: (1) the way authorities make parole decisions and (2) lingering doubts about community safety. In this section, we will focus on community safety after a brief look at parole decision making.

DISCRETION AND PAROLE DECISION MAKING

Parole involves much discretion, and this is particularly true of decisions to grant early release. Critics of the parole system—both liberals and conservatives—have problems with the decision-making process for granting parole and the elements that factor into these decisions. For liberals, parole is invariably discriminatory. Liberals contend that minorities and youngsters from the lowest economic strata have a much more difficult time making parole because they do not have the financial resources and family support that would make them good candidates. When such resources are lacking, parole boards err on the side of caution, and they do not grant parole to those individuals who do not seem to be ideal cases (see Ringel, Cowles, and Castellano, 1994; Walker, 1998). Conservatives, by contrast, say that parole undermines truth in sentencing (see, for example, Fox, 1989; Mays, 1989). The sentence imposed by the court is not the sentence that youngsters will serve due to early-release provisions like parole. To this group, parole represents the juvenile justice system's soft-on-crime philosophy. As a result, parole has many enemies and few friends.

PAROLE AND PUBLIC SAFETY

Related to conservative criticisms of parole is the issue of community safety (Colangelo, 1998). Some of us are aware of cases, like that described in the opening scenario in this chapter, where someone released on parole commits a very serious crime. Concern over community safety invariably is linked to the ability to predict who should be released and when. At one end of the spectrum we could have parole board decisions that are completely subjective, based on the instincts or hunches of institutional correctional personnel and members of the parole board.

A completely objective system would be at the other end of the spectrum, and while this system would be highly desirable, it is not attainable. Nonetheless, some jurisdictions have developed instruments for predicting parole readiness and success (Hoffman and Adelberg, 1980). Instruments like the **salient factor score** scale, presented in figure 8.1, are similar to the actuarial tables used by insurance companies. The federal government developed the salient factor score scale to assist in granting adults parole. Washington state's juvenile rehabilitation administration created a similar tool, called the **community risk assessment**, to determine when youngsters are ready for community placement (Schmidt, Boesky, Brunson, and Trupin, 1998).

These types of instruments are useful for predicting group behavior, with an accuracy of 80%, and they attempt to make parole decisions more objective than they traditionally have been. Nevertheless, it is important to remember two things about prediction instruments. First, while the instruments may successfully predict group behavior, they may not be able to predict successfully the behavior of any individual member of the group. Second, all evaluations of human nature and predictions of human behavior are ultimately subjective.

Attempts to predict parole success can lead to two types of errors. The first type of error occurs when the paroling authority reports a high likelihood for success when in reality the youngster is not ready for release. The second type of error occurs when the paroling authority decides that a youngster is not ready for release when in fact he or she could adapt to early release and supervision. Both types of errors are possible, but the second type is more likely. How do we respond to the criticisms that parole is too soft on young offenders, and that it does not provide sufficiently for public safety? Some have suggested that we need to reinvent parole (see, for example, DiIulio, 1997). Such sentiments have no doubt contributed to the development of the intensive aftercare program.

OJJDP's Intensive Aftercare Program

Intensive supervision is appropriate for both probationers and parolees (Goodstein and Sontheimer, 1997). Public safety questions make intensive supervision particularly appealing for monitoring parolees' behavior (Altschuler and Armstrong, 1994). Almost by definition, parolees are more dangerous than probationers, thus agents frequently exercise higher surveillance levels. The most obvious way to achieve closer monitoring is to place parolees in small caseloads, supervised by one or two officers. This allows parole officers to have regular (perhaps even daily) contact with parolees and to visit them at varying times, on different days of the week, and in a variety of locations. Such an approach not only should achieve closer monitoring of parolees' behavior but also should reduce the levels of undesirable or illegal activity. While intensive supervision is an **intermediate sanction** between incarceration and traditional community supervision, little evidence exists to date that such programs reduce parolees' recidivism rates. Ironically, intensive supervision may even result in more revocations, particularly in cases where parolees give evidence of drug use through urinalysis (Castellano, 1995).

Figure 8.1
Salient Factor Score

Register Number _____ Name_____

Item A
No prior convictions (adult or juvenile) = 3
One prior conviction = 2
Two or three convictions = 1
Four or more prior convictions = 0

Item B
No prior commitments (adult or juvenile) = 2
One or two prior commitments = 1
Three or more prior commitments = 0

Item C
Age at behavior leading to first commitment (adult or juvenile):
26 or older = 2
18–25 = 1
17 or younger = 0

*Item D
Commitment offense did not involve auto theft or check(s)
(forgery/larceny) =1
Commitment offense involved auto theft [X],
or check(s) [Y], or both [Z] = 0

*Item E
Never had parole revoked or been committed for a new offense
while on parole, and not a probation violator this time = 1
Has had parole revoked or been committed for a new offense while
on parole [X], or is a probation violator this time [Y], or both [Z] = 0

Item F
No history of heroin or opiate dependence = 1
Otherwise = 0

Item G
Verified employment (or full-time school attendance) for a total of
at least 6 months during the last 2 years in the community = 1
Otherwise = 0

Total Score

Note: For purposes of the Salient Factor Score, an instance of criminal behavior resulting in a judicial determination of guilt or an admission of guilt before a judicial body shall be treated as a conviction, even if a conviction is not formally entered.

*Note to Examiners:
If Item D and/or E is scored 0, place the appropriate letter (X, Y, Z) on the line to the right of the box.

Source: Hoffman and Adelberg (1980:49).

Theoretical Reflections
Criminological Theory and Intensive Aftercare for High-Risk Juvenile Offenders

Over 50 years ago, Donald Cressey, a former student of Edwin Sutherland's and a practitioner of Sutherland's differential association, proposed that his mentor's theory could help us understand adult parole success and failure. Cressey maintained that prison inmates should be exposed to prosocial definitions in a group context while still in prison. If antisocial definitions and associations are the cause of criminality, then those same learning mechanisms should work to reverse the process, assuming new prosocial definitions and associations. The changes begun in the prison would then carry over to the world outside prison.

Serious, chronic juvenile offenders pose similar challenges with regard to parole success and failure. As David Altschuler and Troy Armstrong note, "One of the major problems besetting the juvenile correctional system has been the inability to transition offenders from closely monitored and highly regimented life in a secure institutional environment to unstructured and often confusing life in the community" (1994:7). Altschuler and Armstrong observe that many explanations of delinquency and change include elements of social control, strain, and social learning theories. Their own theory-based intensive aftercare program (IAP) links chronic delinquency to (1) weak controls produced by inadequate socialization, social disorganization, and strain; (2) strain, which can have a direct effect on delinquency independent of weak controls and which is also produced by social disorganization; and (3) peer influences that intervene as a social force between youth with weak bonds and/or strain on the one hand and delinquent behavior on the other.

These relationships form Altschuler and Armstrong's integrated theoretical framework: "The integrated IAP framework highlights the fact that the joint occurrence of strain, weak controls by conventional others, and strong bonds to delinquent groups produces a greater probability of delinquency or recidivism than any of the three alone" (1994:3).

Like Cressey before them, Altschuler and Armstrong believe that theory not only provides unique insights into why people commit crimes but also can help change offenders for the better. IAP, which includes an institutional component, relies heavily on a series of underlying principles that "embody the theoretical assumptions regarding both the multiple causes of, and behavioral changes associated with, reoffending" (1994:4). These principles include:

- preparing youth for progressively increased responsibility and freedom in the community
- facilitating youth–community interaction and involvement
- working with both the offender and targeted community support systems (e.g., families, peers, schools, employers) to establish constructive interaction and helping youth adjust successfully to the community
- developing new resources and supports where needed
- monitoring and testing youth and the community on their ability to deal with each other productively

What is also interesting about IAP is that it targets the highest-risk youths, those chronic offenders who are most at risk for failure upon release. Thus, it is hard to criticize IAP as a program designed to take only those likely to succeed.

Sources: Cressey (1955); Altschuler and Armstrong (1994).

What makes intensive supervision intensive? Altschuler and Armstrong (1994) provide some answers to this question. First, their intensive aftercare program (IAP) serves high-risk, chronic offenders who have committed serious delinquent acts. Such children, they note, often face many problems, persistent and severe delinquent activity being only one.

Second, the program begins at sentencing, well before the youths arrive at the juvenile institution's gates or at home on parole. Staff members assess each youth's reoffending risk. Practitioners of this art form acknowledge that risk-assessment instruments, such as the salient factor score scale (figure 8.1), may not be successful when addressing the unique problems of hostile and impulsive youthful offenders. Nonetheless, these instruments contain the crucial predictive elements: age at first adjudication (i.e., early age of onset), the number of prior adjudications, and the number of prior commitments (Altschuler and Armstrong, 1994:8). Since this program's goal is to facilitate the reintegration of at-risk youths into society, having a high-risk score does not disqualify a youth from the program. Similarly, placing a youth in a risk-based aftercare program after only one serious offense "may be regarded as a misuse of risk-based aftercare" (Altschuler and Armstrong, 1998:1).[8]

Third, staff members assess the youths' needs. Needs assessment devices are not predictive scales; rather, they allow staff members to identify, define, and prioritize the most frequently encountered problems juvenile parolees face. Altschuler and Armstrong (1994:11) report the following list as a cumulative rank ordering of the most heavily weighted items:

1. substance abuse
2. emotional instability
3. family problems
4. school problems
5. intellectual impairments[9]

The product of these assessments and evaluations is an **individual case plan**. That is, in IAP, one size does not fit all customers. The planning must begin early in the process and continue, along with the assessments, throughout the period of institutionalization. This is the approach followed, for example, by the Eckerd Youth Development Center in Florida. Staff members assess children after 15, 30, and 90 days of confinement, and every 90 days thereafter until release (Altschuler and Armstrong, 1994:13). Indeed, this risk and needs assessment process can play a role in the decision to release a youth on parole, given the regular and exhaustive nature of the reviews and reassessments.

The service delivery part of IAP consists of three paired elements. First, parole agents must integrate surveillance and services with risk factors. As Altschuler and Armstrong observe:

> The real question to ask about IAP is not simply whether there are more restrictions, surveillance, and consequences, but to what extent and how IAP programming addresses need-related risk factors, such as those linked to family and home situation, school and learning difficulties, negative peer influences, work opportunities, substance abuse, etc. (1994:17)

This supervision method requires more than a highly committed and proactive surveillance monitor. The agent must know both the youths' needs and the public safety risks.

Second, following the operant conditioning principles established in Akers's social learning theory, Altschuler and Armstrong's IAP includes positive reinforcements and incentives. Their approach avoids unrealistic and unenforceable conditions and rejects technical violations as meriting reconfinement. Incentives might include earning privileges valued by young people, including tickets to sporting events and discounts or subsidies toward purchasing CDs, clothing, and jewelry (Altschuler and Armstrong, 1994:19). The plan must balance incentives against graduated sanctions, which move up and down a meaningful scale of punishments. Staff members use these same sanctions for only a fixed and limited time; otherwise, they lose their deterrent effect. For example, control agents should use electronic monitoring and drug or alcohol testing "only on a selective, short-term basis" (Altschuler and Armstrong, 1994:20; see also box 8.3). At the end of this continuum of graduated sanctions stands temporary placement in a secure environ-

---

Box 8.3   An Assessment of Intensive Aftercare Parole: Success, Failure, or Mixed Results?

In 1995 an assessment of the Intensive Aftercare Program began. Ten years later, after a five-year data collection effort, Wiebush and his associates reported rather meager findings. The evaluation initially included four pilot states funded by the Office of Juvenile Justice and Delinquency Prevention; one of those states, New Jersey, was dropped from the study; hence, the evaluation examined the IAP programs in Colorado, Nevada, and Virginia. Youths were randomly assigned to either IAP or a control group. However, the total number of youths included in the study, at 435, was disappointing to the researchers and certainly had an impact on the power of the statistics generated by the study.[10] Program administration in Colorado proved problematic as there was "seepage" of the treatment from the IAP group into the control group, providing a threat to the experiment's internal validity. In short, the evaluation was solid in design and flawed in implementation.

In terms of findings, the researchers failed to find statistically significant differences between the treatment groups and the control groups. IAP youths were no more successful on parole than were their untreated cohorts. This generalization was true regarding (1) nature of the most serious subsequent offense; (2) the mean number of felony arrests, criminal arrests, or total arrests; and (3) the number of days to first felony or criminal arrests. The researchers did report some significant differences in institutional misbehavior and positive test results for a controlled substance while on parole.

Despite these rather negative findings, the researchers do not recommend abandoning IAP. Rather, Wiebush and his associates—after reviewing the problems with the study and the absence of significant findings—observe that their research was a first and perhaps not the best effort at evaluating a complex intervention model. In short, they call for additional studies that build on their findings and miscues. The fact that IAP has been implemented in at least six other states—including Idaho, Kentucky, Maryland, Minnesota, New York, and West Virginia—supports their conclusion.

Source: Wiebush, Wagner, McNulty, Wang, and Le (2005).

ment for the serious IAP violator. Called the "reflections unit" in Colorado, this sanction is the IAP equivalent of time-out. Not quite a youth prison, but also not like living at home, this sanction is for a fixed period, usually a 60- to 90-day maximum stay.

Finally, the twin concepts of brokerage and linkage are essential to IAP. Aftercare caseworkers must do more than simply provide a list of possible services or link the child and the service provider. Often, they must assume a more active role, such as the one addressed earlier in box 8.2. That is, the caseworker may need to serve as a broker among the various agencies, the client, and his or her family to ensure that the child receives the needed services at the appropriate time. In accomplishing these two goals, the caseworker must also work to ensure the integration of the youth into the community. "Reinforcement and support from family, peers, teachers, and employers may be key to seeing that the youth's readjustment to the postinstitutional community is successful and that gains achieved both in the institution and in aftercare persist" (Altschuler and Armstrong, 1994:22). In light of the high-risk youths served by IAP, we cannot complain that this program only "creams" the low-risk children from the youthful offender population. Success is not a given, and indeed it may be elusive (see box 8.3).

SPECIAL-NEEDS POPULATIONS

By definition, almost all parolees have greater difficulty adjusting to community supervision than do probationers. There are a number of reasons why this is the case. First, many of these youngsters have prior experience with various parts of the juvenile justice system, including multiple sentences to probation. Therefore, they already have demonstrated something of a commitment to a delinquent lifestyle. Second, periods of incarceration make reintegration into the family and community a key consideration in ensuring successful completion of parole. Furthermore, the longer society incarcerates a youngster, the more difficult reintegration typically will be. Third, some youngsters come into the corrections system with more substantial problems than others. Therefore, in this section we will consider the particular problems facing special-needs parolees. Specifically, we will consider the situation facing sex offenders, chemically dependent offenders, mentally ill or mentally retarded offenders, and those youngsters who are or have been involved in gangs.

SEX OFFENDERS

Youthful sex offenders pose unique problems for both institutional corrections and community supervision personnel. First, these youngsters may suffer from a number of social and psychological deficiencies (Stops and Mays, 1991). Some of them are sexual abuse victims themselves, and quite a few suffer from having inappropriate sex roles and relationships modeled for them by parents or guardians (Barbaree and Marshall, 2005). When we incarcerate youthful sex offenders, we find that most juvenile correctional facilities do not have treatment programs geared to their specific needs (Heinz, Ryan, and Bengis, 1991). In fact, nationwide there is a tremendous shortage of correctional bed spaces for sex offenders, both adult and juvenile (Mays and Winfree, 2005:388).

Second, once released from secure custody, these youngsters face the same problem that all sex offenders face: rejection by a community that fears further offenses. The challenge for parole officers is to find living arrangements where youthful sex offenders can continue their treatment regimens, where they can reestablish family and community contacts, but where the public will be safe from future predations (Greer, 1991).

The state of Florida has acknowledged the difficulty of providing a smooth transition for juvenile sex offenders. For these youngsters, transitional planning must begin 90 days prior to release from secure confinement, in contrast to 60 days for other youthful offenders (Florida DJJ, 1998). The reality is that many youthful sex offenders will be faced with the prospect of being placed in an open residential setting, such as a group home, but not being able to return to the home in which their parents live. Communities have become very sensitive to the release and return of sex offenders, and demonstrations outside the homes in which convicted sex offenders live are increasingly common. Therefore, providing public safety and finding alternative living arrangements is a major responsibility for parole officers.

CHEMICALLY DEPENDENT OFFENDERS

Juvenile correctional facilities are more likely to have drug and alcohol treatment programs than they are to have programs for youthful sex offenders. Nevertheless, drug and alcohol treatment may be in high demand, and some facilities may not have enough space in such programs to meet the demand. For the chemically dependent juvenile offender, the most important period may not be the time spent in an institution. These youngsters especially should benefit from carefully supervised and well-planned aftercare programs. This means that in the case of youths with drug and alcohol problems, the challenge is not only to get illegal substances out of their bodies, but also to get them off their minds.

MENTALLY ILL AND MENTALLY RETARDED OFFENDERS

Does it strike you as unusual that society treats mentally ill and mentally retarded youthful offenders as a special-needs group? In fact, these juveniles have special needs both during their incarceration and during aftercare (Greene, 1991). Joan Petersilia (1997a:358; 1997b) estimates that California has 22,000 adult and juvenile offenders who are mentally retarded.[11] This number represents about 2% of the probationers and 4% of those in custody. Petersilia also estimates that between 1–2% of the population at large could be classified as mentally retarded (1997a:359). By contrast, she reports national prevalence rates for the mentally retarded in correctional institutions at between 4% and 10%, and some report rates as high as 30% (Petersilia, 1997a:359).

The mentally ill and mentally retarded constitute two distinct groups of offenders, and we should not confuse the two. Nevertheless, their treatment needs may be similar during periods of confinement and during aftercare as well. Mentally ill offenders are mentally ill both because of who they are organically (genetically) and psychologically, as well as what some of them have done (for instance, engaged in intense periods of drug or alcohol abuse). Given these diverse populations, correctional treatment programs must be targeted at those factors that are correctable (substance abuse, for example), and a plan must be developed to manage those factors that are not correctable (that is, genetic makeup).

One fact that is apparent to those who study the juvenile justice system is that there has been a shift away from treating all problems of delinquency as simply criminal behavior, toward treating some delinquents as products of mental disorders. Schwartz, for one, says that this shift represents a process of delabeling and relabeling. The result is that some youngsters go from being "bad" to being "mad" (1989:143–46). The danger, of course, lies in misdiagnosing (overclassifying or underclassifying) youngsters who need mental health treatment.

Aftercare programs may include outpatient treatment segments for youngsters who need continuing mental health treatment once they leave the institution. As with many other juvenile justice programs, problems persist: (1) small communities may not have outpatient mental health programs for youthful offenders, and (2) even when community mental health agencies exist, the demand for services may far exceed the ability to provide those services. At times, youngsters get lost in the shuffle when the needs of adults seem more immediate and severe.[12]

Mentally retarded youngsters seem to be poor candidates for correctional intervention, but on the basis of the limited knowledge we do have, they seem to appear regularly in secure juvenile correctional environments. For mentally retarded offenders, secure institutional confinement is not likely to bring about much improvement in their behavior. In fact, mentally retarded offenders are likely to exhibit poor institutional adaptations and behavior. Without proper care, their mental state actually may deteriorate during periods of incarceration.

Petersilia (1997a, 1997b), in her study of mentally retarded offenders in California, paints a very gloomy picture. These inmates have disciplinary problems, participate in very few institutional programs, and are likely to make poor presentations in parole board hearings. Her conclusion is that "offenders with MR [mental retardation] do more time, do harder time, get less out of their time, and are more likely to return to prison after release than persons who are not mentally handicapped" (Petersilia, 1997a:362). On the basis of these insights, drawn largely from adult populations, we must conclude that many mentally retarded youngsters who start out in the juvenile justice system are likely to graduate to the adult criminal justice system.

Placing mentally retarded youngsters into appropriate aftercare routines as soon as possible is essential. This means that juvenile parole officers have to spend a disproportionate amount of time (given the size of their caseloads) with mentally retarded offenders—getting them settled into a routine or finding appropriate alternative living arrangements for them.

GANG-INVOLVED YOUTHS

Chapter 10 examines the broader issue of gangs as a special juvenile justice problem today. Here we address the issue of how juveniles who have been gang members prior to incarceration can successfully make the transition back into the free world without reestablishing gang ties and violating conditions of parole. Specifically, gang-involved youths often take their gang values and identities into secure correctional facilities. There they may find members of rival gangs or a unique brand of prison gang (Fong and Vogel, 1995; Hunt, Riegel, Morales, and Waldorf, 1993). Most juvenile correctional facilities are aware of these problems and have a variety of mechanisms for addressing them. However, the real problems of adjustment may come once juveniles reenter their home communities where the members of the old gang still live, and where the temptations of the gang lifestyle still exist.

Some juveniles who were gang-involved before incarceration want to get rid of their tattoos upon release and get out of the lifestyle. Others feel that they have made a lifetime commitment to the gang. The "blood in, blood out" gang philosophy is pervasive in principle if not in practice (Curry and Decker, 2003; Decker and Lauritsen, 1996). Therefore, the rule that calls for keeping youngsters in the jurisdiction from which they were sentenced may have to be reexamined, and the parol-

---

Box 8.4   Technology: An Alternative or a Parole Add-on?

One of the major movements in parole supervision nationwide is the increasing use of technology to supplement (if not supplant) client monitoring by parole officers. Technological applications, such as electronic monitoring bracelets, can enforce house arrest. The same systems are applicable for parolees, either to maintain in-home confinement or to provide around-the-clock location tracking through some type of global positioning system (GPS). While most such programs have focused on adult offenders, we are applying these concepts to juvenile offenders as well, especially when coupled with electronic monitoring. Supporters see such efforts as an alternative to extended periods of incarceration for youngsters. Critics see these so-called intermediate sanctions as another example of widening the net for offenders who might otherwise escape confinement, or who face release from confinement under some traditional form of aftercare.

What can we say about technology's application to juvenile parole? First, technology clearly expands our capacity to punish. The application of technology to juvenile corrections allows us to maintain "walls" outside the traditional walls of juvenile correctional facilities. Second, concerns over public safety—perhaps more than any other issue—seem to drive the application of technology to both adult and juvenile corrections. Third, technological devices such as electronic monitors do allow us to release some youngsters from correctional facilities who would otherwise face traditional parole practices. However, the impact of technology on issues such as treatment or rehabilitation seems unclear. While juvenile offenders may have access to programs and services in the community that might not be available in institutions, we have relatively little evidence that the use of electronic monitoring really makes a difference in terms of taking advantage of these programs, or that participating in such programming efforts substantially contributes to rehabilitation.

Further technology applications to juvenile parole may keep youngsters under closer surveillance, but these practices may contribute little to treatment outcomes or delinquency reductions. Unless we learn more about how to prevent failures on juvenile aftercare, we will probably come to view electronic surveillance technology as just another gimmick promoted by clever hardware manufacturers.

Sources: Apgar (1998); Clear (1988); Colangelo (1998); Montes (1996).

ing authority may have to enter into an **interstate compact** in order for the youngster to be placed with relatives away from the home-turf gang. Considerations such as these make gang-involved delinquents a special-needs population.

MANAGING SPECIAL-NEEDS OFFENDERS

How do parole agencies handle special-needs offenders? We see two main approaches. First, juvenile parole agencies may treat the special-needs cases as not so special and simply incorporate them into the regular caseload for parole officers. This approach deals with the issue of delinquent behavior but, for the most part, ignores other considerations in the youngster's life. Second, some agencies differentiate the caseloads of parole and probation officers, and they further specialize their respective responsibilities. For example, Florida provides four classifications for youngsters placed in aftercare: (1) maximum supervision, (2) intensive day treatment, (3) intensive community supervision, and (4) community supervision (Florida DJJ, 1998:3). Similarly, Arizona has developed a decision tree model to determine into which of four levels of parole supervision—intensive, maximum, medium, and minimum—youngsters should be placed (Ashford and Le Croy, 1988:48).

In arrangements such as these, some parole officers will have small caseloads of similar offenders (such as youthful sex offenders) with whom they can interact regularly. This allows parole officers to develop a certain level of expertise in dealing with particular problem areas (Clear, 1997). Given the trends in adult parole, we are likely to see the use of some of the same techniques of case classification and supervision specialization with juvenile offenders as well.

SUMMARY

In some ways, this chapter represents one of the most difficult juvenile justice topics to study. Juvenile parole is the end of the line as far as juvenile corrections is concerned. It supervises the smallest number of offenders (substantially less than the number of juvenile probationers), and it often receives the smallest budget allocation of any part of the juvenile justice system (see, for example, Ashford and Le Croy, 1988). Moreover, juvenile parole is a poorly studied phenomenon. In fact, with a few notable exceptions (for example, Altschuler and Armstrong, 1994; Armstrong and Altschuler, 1998; Ashford, 1996; Ashford and Le Croy, 1988, 1993; Hurst and Torbet, 1993; Wiebush et al., 2005), it is difficult to find recent research articles or other publications addressing the issues of juvenile parole, juvenile parolees, and the agencies and personnel handling this function. Therefore, in this summary we will highlight what we know about juvenile parole and issue a challenge to those of you taking this course to investigate further this crucial area of offender treatment.

While adult parole went through a long period of disfavor beginning in the mid-1970s, parole for juveniles has remained a viable component of the juvenile corrections apparatus. Juvenile courts and correctional agencies have continued to rely on indeterminate sentences, even in states where the adult sentencing system largely is determinate in nature. The continued use of indeterminate periods of confinement for juvenile offenders has kept juvenile parole alive, but at times just barely. Juvenile parole continues to be the least-funded element of the entire criminal justice system in the United States.

In looking back, we find it difficult at times to distinguish a clear historical path for juvenile parole. In all likelihood, parole for juvenile offenders developed as an outgrowth of parole for adults who were released early from prison under community supervision. Thus, as an extension of society's punishment response, juvenile parole has a somewhat indistinct past.

What about the future? Juvenile parole is certainly facing organizational and philosophical changes. In terms of philosophy, parole agencies need to define their purposes very clearly. They must ask themselves: What are we trying to accomplish with juvenile parole? Is it to provide treatment that will eventually lead to rehabilitation? Or is it designed primarily to promote public safety by closely supervising offenders released from secure custody? Are these two objectives compatible? Can they both be achieved? The next decade will bring us face-to-face with dilemmas raised by such questions.

Three factors may shape the future of juvenile parole. First, states should professionalize the parole decision process by making service on the paroling authority, where practical, a full-time job. States should require that parole board members possess backgrounds that relate in some way to juvenile justice. The use of staggered and overlapping terms also promotes consistency and minimizes overt attempts at political influence.

Second, the continued viability of parole is dependent on the development and implementation of valid and reliable predictive instruments for use in parole decision making. The salient factor score scale and similar instruments must be refined to aid in making appropriate and timely parole decisions. Juveniles should be released from correctional facilities when they are ready to be released, not before, and certainly not after.

Third, juvenile aftercare programs should contain evaluation components. In general, these programs need adequate documentation to support their successes and to identify and correct their failures. Without evaluation research data, parole agencies are subject to the funding whims of legislative committees and their research components.

All these considerations include the assumption that juvenile sentencing will continue to be largely indeterminate in nature. Although there is every indication that it will, some states have moved in the direction of establishing determinate sentencing patterns for both adults and juveniles. The danger seems to be that public and political sentiment, which often is fickle, runs against parole because it appears to provide overly lenient treatment for many juvenile offenders.

Allen Breed (1984), former chair of the California Youth Authority, warned us that in our haste to get tough on juvenile crime we should not do away with juvenile parole. He suggests that states should adopt the explicit parole guidelines model (Ashford and Le Croy, 1993). The Breed model (1984:13) incorporates due process protections with fewer parole conditions and calls for fewer revocations for violations of technical conditions. Breed further maintains that we should retain parole because it offers the best hope for managing offenders both in institutional settings and in the community. Under the Breed model, parole boards actually would have more, not fewer, responsibilities. For example, paroling authorities would be given guidelines to help them monitor and reduce sentence disparities. The use of parole would continue to provide a back door, or safety valve mechanism, to prevent institutional crowding (Breed, 1984:14–15).

As we conclude this chapter, a few issues are unresolved. Whose interests are being served in the parole decision-making process—the interests of the individual or those of the community? In the adult system, there must be a balance between the benefit to the individual and the concern for public safety. Given the historical emphasis on the best interests of the child, is public safety a legitimate issue in the juvenile justice system? More and more frequently, the public and elected lawmakers emphasize public safety when dealing with juvenile offenders.

Juvenile parole seems to be one of the most besieged parts of the embattled juvenile justice system in the United States today. However, we must remember that juvenile parole frequently receives the most serious offenders but has the fewest resources of any part of the juvenile justice system. The result is a great deal of concern over the failure of parole and the consequences of that failure, as depicted in the opening scenario of this chapter. However, do the criticisms and the level of concern translate into action? As should be obvious by now, the answer frequently is no. Therefore, if juvenile parole is to continue as the method for providing community supervision for offenders released from juvenile correctional facilities, it must address both the changes that have taken place within parole agencies and those that have occurred in the broader social and criminal justice environments.

CRITICAL REVIEW QUESTIONS

1. Now that you have completed the chapter, go back and read about Alex Baker in the opening vignette. What do you think went wrong? What could the authorities have done to prevent or forestall Alex's return to crime? What do you think about the last paragraph? Why do you think we often overlook the many successes for the few failures?

2. "Parole and aftercare are similar but not quite the same." How would you respond to this statement?

3. "Probation and parole are really quite similar. In fact, in some jurisdictions, there are no qualitative differences at all." How would you respond to this statement?

4. One could argue that the history of parole is brief because the practice is related to society's willingness to allow criminals who were once believed to be bad enough to deserve imprisonment to live once more among us. Simply put, we are not, as a civilized nation, all that forgiving. How would you relate this position with current views on the abolishment of parole and, indeed, the movement by some states toward this very end?

5. Of the stated purposes of parole, which one do you find the most defensible? Which one do you find the least defensible? Provide the basis of your decision in both cases.

6. "It would appear that taken in its entirety, the nation's system of juvenile aftercare falls far short of the recommendations made by the National Advisory Committee on Criminal Justice Standards and Goals." Support this statement with facts taken from the following processes: decisions to grant parole, hierarchical arrangement of service providers, and policies concerning parole duration.

7. What's your view on the conflict between the various roles played by a parole agent (or probation officer, for that matter)? Before answering this question, you might want to talk to a juvenile parole or probation officer.

8. Which would you rather supervise, a probationer or a parolee? The conditions for each are usually very similar. What is it about the one correctional client versus the other that shaped your answer? (*Hint*: Before you answer this question, you might want to review the six reasons behind failure provided in this chapter.)

9. Community safety is a critical part of parole or aftercare. Intensive supervision programs were created to meet the treatment needs of specialized offender populations and help maintain public safety. Do you think that they are up to the task? If yes, how do they contribute to public safety? If no, how do they fail?

10. Many special-needs children present multiple problems. Suppose you were given the choice of selecting a client from among the four special-needs groups: sex offender, chemically dependent offender, mentally ill or mentally retarded offender, or gang-involved offender. Which one do you think would create the greatest challenge for you and why? Which one do you think would be the easiest client to manage and why?

RECOMMENDED READINGS

Ryan, Gail D., and Sandy L. Lane, eds. (1991). *Juvenile Sexual Offending: Causes, Consequences, and Correction*. Lexington, MA: Lexington. This edited work looks at the complexity of the contemporary sex offender. The various authors provide wide-ranging contributions to our understanding of this disturbing social problem. Of particular interest with regard to parole or aftercare are the sections on the etiology (causes) of sexual offending and its treatment, both in secure facilities and in the community.

Wiebush, Richard G., Dennis Wagner, Betsie McNulty, Yanqing Wang, and Thao Le (2005). *Implementation and Outcome of the Intensive Aftercare Program: Final Report*. Washington, DC: Office of Juvenile Justice and Delinquency Prevention. Normally research reports are dry and boring, and in some ways, this one is no exception. However, it does include a very good description of the rationale behind IAP and similar programs. Moreover, it gives unique insights into the problems of doing this kind of research, especially projects using an experimental design. Without such research, evidence-based juvenile justice is impossible (see chapter 11 for more on this concept).

KEY TERMS

banishment

community risk assessment

determinate sentences

executive privilege

indeterminate sentences

individual case plan

intensive supervision

intermediate sanction

interstate compact

juvenile aftercare

parole

parole contracts

Penal Servitude Act (1853)

reintegration

reintegration living placements

salient factor score

special conditions

standard conditions

ticket of leave

transportation

NOTES

[1] This information comes from the National Center for Juvenile Justice (2005).

[2] In the first edition of this book, we reported that while the nation's juvenile correctional system held a fraction of the inmates found in the adult system, the volume of children through that smaller system was higher than for adults (Mays and Winfree, 2000:259). Hence, it makes sense that the ratio of probationers to parolees must at least approximate those found in the adult system if not exceed it. Of course, many aftercare probationers are more accurately parolees. Owing to this fact alone, the exact extent of juvenile aftercare may be unknowable.

[3] In some jurisdictions, juveniles are even "paroled" from county and city jails. A thorough discussion of the various legal authorities would extend this chapter to unreasonable lengths and add little to the discussion.

[4] The information reported in this section includes many changes from the previous edition, as over one-half of the states have made some change in their juvenile parole or, more generally, juvenile justice systems since the mid- to late-1990s.

[5] The typology used in table 8.1 owes much to Hurst and Torbet's (1993:7–8) analysis of the administration of juvenile services.

[6] Behind most therapeutic models is the establishment of trust relationships and the extension of confidentiality. Critics of the parole officer as treatment agent argue that such relationships and levels of trust are nearly impossible in parole work (see Dietrich, 1979).

[7] Postrelease intensive aftercare receives special attention later in this chapter.

[8] Alex Baker, the youthful repeat offender in the chapter's opening vignette, committed several burglaries. Had IAP been available for him, he would have been eligible. Where youthful offenders clearly do not qualify, "inclusion of such offenders may also mean that intensive aftercare is used punitively for social control to satisfy the public outcry about getting tough on youth crime" (Altschuler and Armstrong, 1998:1).

[9] Special-needs populations, who may present multiple symptoms, include the (1) drug and alcohol dependent, (2) developmentally disabled, (3) learning disabled, (4) emotionally disturbed or cognitively challenged, (5) neurophysiologically impaired, and (6) convicted sex offenders. These six categories of youthful offenders present unique sets of problems, and they are treated later in this chapter. Intensive supervision programs must also recognize the special services and concerns created by such parolees.

[10] Used in this way, power refers to the ability of various statistical techniques to tell if observed differences are real or perhaps random. Small samples, such as those found in the IAP evaluation, make such determinations difficult.

[11] As is the case with much of what happens in juvenile corrections and aftercare, a true and accurate picture of the mentally challenged is lacking. What we have—and what we are forced to present—are fragments, often drawn from the adult system. In the present case, we must rely on one complete and comprehensive picture of a single correctional system found in California. The absence of a national picture for the mentally ill is tragic and telling.

[12] See, for example, the discussion of such children in the juvenile justice and welfare systems in Golden (1997).

NONDELINQUENT CHILDREN IN THE JUVENILE JUSTICE SYSTEM

CHAPTER OUTLINE

- Dependent Children
- Neglected and Abused Children
- The Responsibilities of Investigating Agencies
- Juvenile Court Jurisdiction Issues

* * *

Marilyn Jones, one of five on-duty 911 operator-dispatchers at the unified police-fire-emergency communications center, received the call at 6:02 PM. The distraught caller told Marilyn that a police officer was needed "as quickly as possible" at 412 Maple Street. Marilyn spent only three minutes calming down the caller and gathering information she knew would be important to the responding officer, such as whether 412 Maple Street was a single residence or an apartment building, who would meet the officer, and the like.

Officer Thomas Ryan heard Marilyn's radio broadcast at 6:06 PM. He was about five blocks from the 400 block of Maple and took the call. After they had switched to an alternate channel, the operator-dispatcher told Ryan that the caller was a woman named Rita Ramirez; she was afraid that the children of her next-door neighbor were in danger. One of them had been screaming nonstop for the past 30 minutes. Repeated knocks on the apartment door brought no response. Then suddenly, about 10 minutes ago, the apartment became very quiet.

Officer Ryan arrived at 412 Maple Street and was met at the curb by an elderly His-panic woman, her face awash in tears. The woman—Mrs. Ramirez—explained that she had lived in the building for over 25 years and had seen a lot in her days, but "that Wright woman was a very bad mother," she observed. "Come on. We have to walk up three floors and there's no elevator."

As they walked into the building, Mrs. Ramirez told Officer Ryan that the woman who lived across the hall from her, Dolores Wright, often left her two children alone in the house when she went shopping. Her husband worked construction and was often out of the state. "They are such sweet kids," Mrs. Ramirez told Ryan. She continued her story, in between gasps for air and stops on the stairs: "Bobby, the four-year-old, is so grown up. He is the man of the house and tries to help everyone, even me. Little Stevie is only two. That witch treats them both like they was dirt."

Leaving Mrs. Ramirez on the landing between the second and third floors, Ryan quickly proceeded to apartment 3-B by himself. He knocked on the door but received no response. Trying the doorknob, he found it locked; moreover, a dead bolt also secured the door. Putting his head to the door, he could just make out a scratching noise on the other side. He called out, "Bobby, is that you?"

"Yep," came a reply.

"Open the door, Bobby. I'm a police officer and I need to see that you are OK. Is your mommy home?"

"Can't open the door. Mommy said not to open the door to anyone but her."

"But I'm a police officer, and I'm here to help."

"I know you're a pleez offsir," Bobby replied, proudly. "I saw you through the little round window in the door. Mommy showed me how. And I can see the flashin' lights on your car from my window. They're real pretty."

"Bobby, I've got to see that you and your brother are OK. So if you don't let me in, I'll have to break down the door, and your mommy won't be happy if that happens."

There was silence for what seemed like five minutes. By now Mrs. Ramirez had rejoined Officer Ryan. Suddenly they both heard a clicking noise, followed by the sound of a dead bolt being turned. The door opened slowly to reveal a frightened Bobby, standing alone in the doorway. He looked fine.

"Where's Stevie? Where's the little one?" asked Mrs. Ramirez.

"Oh, he was a bad boy, an' I hadta put him in jail. He was cryin' and wouldn't stop. You know, Mr. Pleezman, if you're bad, ya go to jail. Right? That's what Mommy says."

"Where's the jail, Bobby?" This time, the question came from Officer Ryan.

"Back down the hall. It's really a closet, but Mommy calls it the jail. There's a little lockie thing on the outside."

Rushing down the hallway, Ryan found the closet without difficulty in the small apartment. The door was secured with a hasp. He unlocked it, opened the door, and directed his flashlight into the closet. The stench that poured out of the room overcame him. An old mattress covered the floor and went partway up the two opposite walls. It was urine-soaked and had other stains of various origins. Stevie lay in the far corner of the closet, his body curled in the fetal position. He remained oddly quiet as Ryan gently picked him up. If this is a two-year-old, something is wrong, thought Ryan, feeling the baby's weight and noting his silence.

Returning to the apartment entrance, Ryan used his portable radio to contact Marilyn, the operator-dispatcher: "They're both OK," he said. "Call the shelter care facility, and tell them I will be bringing in two children, ages two and four. Then leave a message on the child protection service's voice mail so that someone can contact one of the on-call foster-care families. These kids need to be taken out of here."

As Officer Ryan and Mrs. Ramirez exited the apartment building carrying the children and walked to his police unit, they passed a small crowd. After he had secured the children in the back seat, the crowd parted as a woman, about 30 years old, pushed her way through the onlookers.

"What the hell are you doin' with my kids?" yelled the woman. Glancing at Mrs. Ramirez, Ryan knew from the look on her face that this was Dolores Wright.

"Mrs. Wright," he said, "I must inform you that I have found your children in what I determined to be an abandoned state. Moreover, judging from what I observed in your apartment, this apparently is an ongoing condition. Therefore, pursuant to the laws of this state and in the best interest of these children, I am taking them into protective custody. Here is my card." He extended his hand to Mrs. Wright. "If you have any questions," he continued, "or wish to see your children tomorrow, call this number after 8:00 AM and you will be told what to do. Good evening." Mrs. Wright took hold of his card, but it almost fell out of her unclosed hand. She collapsed and sat on the curb, tears welling in her eyes.

Moving quickly and deliberately to the driver's side of his unit, Officer Ryan prepared to leave the scene before the situation deteriorated. Starting the vehicle, Ryan observed that Dolores Wright stood by the side of the street about 10 feet behind his vehicle, tears now streaming down her face, looking as though she could not believe what was happening.

As he drove off, he looked in his rearview mirror and saw Dolores Wright entering the street, shaking her fist in the air. He could not hear what she was saying, but he could imagine its content. Well, he thought, as he drove to the shelter care facility, the good guys won this battle, but I'm not sure about the war.

* * *

Is the opening scenario an example of appropriate police intervention? Would an officer typically have the authority to act as Officer Ryan did? Would the juvenile court have jurisdiction over nondelinquent children? Should it? In this chapter we will consider these questions as they pertain to **nondelinquent children** in the juvenile justice system. As a category of youthful clients, this term represents one of the many aspects of the juvenile justice system that distinguish it from the criminal justice system. At one level, nondelinquent youngsters could include all children who come to the juvenile court's attention and have not committed an act that, had they been adults, could have resulted in a criminal charge. However, we are not concerned here with true status offenders or with those youths who have been found to have violated a juvenile code specifically created to protect them as minors. Rather, this chapter focuses on dependent, neglected, and abused children, all of whom, like their delinquent and status-offending peers, find their fates being decided by the juvenile court.

Figure 9.1 graphically captures the immensity of the nation's child maltreatment problem. According to the Coordinating Council on Juvenile Justice and Delinquency Prevention (1997), official agencies receive almost 3 million neglect and abuse reports a year, involving nearly 2 million children. Investigators' evidence supports roughly one in three reported incidents. Their findings include over

Figure 9.1
Child Abuse and Neglect Pyramid

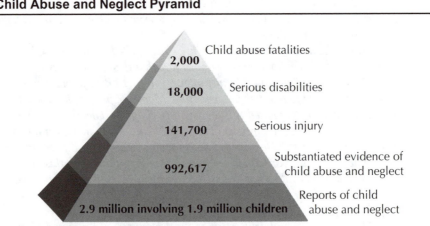

Source: Coordinating Council on Juvenile Justice and Delinquency Prevention (1997).

140,000 serious injuries to children, over 10% of which result in serious disabilities. Finally, some 2,000 children a year die from maltreatment. These figures are not only sad and troubling, but as we shall learn in this chapter, such numbers represent only part of the total dependency, neglect, and abuse problem facing the nation today.[1]

Before considering these categories of cases, it is valuable to note two very crucial points:

1. Nondelinquent cases normally do not involve children's actions, but rather a status or condition in which the children are found.

2. If the cases are serious enough and involve adult offenders, the charges may be heard in a criminal court rather than in the juvenile or family court.

With these preliminary considerations behind us, let us now turn our attention to the juvenile justice system's response to nondelinquent children.

DEPENDENT CHILDREN

Juvenile courts always have had dependency jurisdiction (Krisberg, 2005; Mack, 1909). The National Advisory Committee on Criminal Justice Standards and Goals (1976:335–36) considered dependent and neglected children together in defining these statuses as existing in the following situations:

1. A child has no substantial ties to a parent, a **guardian**, or other adult who is available and willing to care for him or her.

2. A child has suffered or is likely imminently to suffer physical injury, inflicted intentionally by his or her parent, that causes or creates a substantial risk of disfigurement, impairment of bodily functioning, or severe bodily harm.

3. A child has suffered or there is a substantial risk that the child will imminently suffer disfigurement, impairment of bodily functioning, or severe bodily harm as a result of conditions uncorrected by the parents or of the failure of the parents to supervise or protect the child adequately.

4. A child is suffering serious emotional damage, evidenced by severe anxiety, depression or withdrawal, untoward aggressive behavior toward self or others, and the parents are unwilling to permit and cooperate with necessary treatment for the child.

5. A child has been sexually abused by a member of the household.

6. A child is in need of medical treatment to cure, alleviate, or prevent serious physical harm that may result in death, disfigurement, substantial impairment of bodily functions, or severe bodily harm, and the parents will not permit medical treatment.

We provided a brief definition of dependency in chapter 5, but for our purposes here we need to consider a more thorough definition. The Office of Juvenile Justice and Delinquency Prevention (Puzzanchera et al., 2004:79) views **dependency** as:

Those cases covering neglect or inadequate care on the part of parents or guardians, such as abandonment or desertion; abuse or cruel treatment; improper or inadequate conditions in the home; and insufficient care or support resulting from death, absence, or physical or mental incapacity of the parents.

Champion says that dependency is the "legal status of juveniles over whom the juvenile court has assumed jurisdiction because the court has found their care by parents or guardians to be short of the standard of reasonable and proper care" (2005:76). He adds that a dependent child may be one "who needs special care and treatment because the parent, guardian, or custodian is unable to provide for his or her physical or mental conditions." Dependency also may result from parents or guardians who "desire to be relieved of legal custody for good cause." In the end, dependent children are found in a status of need that results from "no fault of the parents, guardian, or custodian" (2005:76); that is, they are incapable of providing a higher level of care.

Although some experts include "abuse and cruel treatment" under a broad dependency umbrella, we will distinguish between dependent children and those who are neglected or abused in separate sections in this chapter. Furthermore, as we will discuss later, dependency has changed somewhat over the years, but is still very much a part of the juvenile justice system.

THE POLICE RESPONSE

As the scenario at the beginning of the chapter demonstrates, the police may be called upon to deal with dependent or neglected children. Police responsibility occurs early in the process, and at times it does not extend beyond the initial investigation. In fact, not all cases of dependency, neglect, or abuse are reported to the police. As Snyder and Sickmund (1999:42) note, schools identified the largest number of child maltreatment cases in 1993 and child protective services agencies investigated one-third of the total number of cases reported. Maltreatment cases may be handled by social services agencies, and there may or may not be statutory requirements that the police are notified. However, when a child is reported to the police as being dependent, neglected, or abused, an investigation will be started, and in 1993 52% of the child maltreatment cases reported in the United States were investigated by police and sheriff departments (Snyder and Sickmund, 1999:42). In some jurisdictions, the police may be responsible for handling the case all the way through adjudication. In other jurisdictions, once the police investigation is completed, the case will be turned over to child protective services or some other social services agency. If this latter arrangement is followed, the investigating police officer becomes a witness, and the child welfare specialist assumes primary responsibility for managing the case.

As far as police responsibilities go, there are three critical issues. First, police officers often have the authority to remove children from the home immediately, a power that others may not have. Second, this added responsibility means they must receive adequate training in order to be able to identify dependency and neglect cases. Third, police agencies need to have carefully developed policies and procedures for handling these cases (Krisberg, 2005).

THE JUVENILE COURT RESPONSE

While delinquency cases account for much of its time, the juvenile court also is responsible for protecting dependent, neglected, and abused children. Throughout much of the juvenile court's history, little distinction was made among these statuses, and often youngsters were housed in the same institutions regardless of their situation or need (Feld, 2003). Today dispositional alternatives for different kinds of cases include both in-home and out-of-home options.

In-home placement generally is most appropriate for the dependent child, especially where there is no immediate danger to the child's health or well-being. The philosophy expressed in most states' juvenile codes, like that of the National Advisory Committee on Criminal Justice Standards and Goals (1976), favors leaving youngsters in their own homes if possible. In these cases, improving the home situation is the court's main objective, one which can be accomplished through counseling or other types of treatment rather than further disrupting the child's life by removing him or her from the family.

For abuse cases there are different concerns. When abuse is alleged or confirmed, the primary consideration is for the child's health and safety, which may require a temporary out-of-home placement. **Out-of-home placement** for abused children—and sometimes for dependent and neglected children as well—usually is in foster homes or group shelter care facilities.

Juvenile court dispositions for dependent, neglected, and abused children may present unique sets of difficulties. On the one hand, the original *parens patriae* doctrine mandates the court's concern for the best interest of the child. On the other hand, courts often are ill equipped to provide the services needed by these children, and exercising jurisdiction in these cases gives the court a wide reach. The following sections will describe the changes that have occurred in defining and processing dependency cases, and the future challenges the juvenile court faces when dealing with these cases.

CHANGES IN DEPENDENCY STATUS

Dependency status clearly has undergone changes, especially over the past 30 years. Given the media's emphasis on chronic delinquent behavior, there may not be much public attention paid to the problem of dependency. As a consequence, two primary changes have occurred. First, as we discussed in chapter 5, the original juvenile court treated status offenses as a part of delinquency jurisdiction. However, as a result of court rulings and legislative changes in the 1970s, status offenses now often are treated as a form of dependency. Thus, the dependent children category has grown in the past three decades through inclusion of cases that previously would have been considered at least marginally delinquent (Gardner, 2003:201–6).

Second, because of the changing views and attitudes toward status offenders, few states house dependent children in secure custodial placements. In fact, relatively few of these cases result in out-of-home placements of any kind. From 1989 to 1998, between 7% (for liquor violations) and 26% (for running away or "ungovernability") of the status offenders coming before the juvenile courts in the United States received out-of-home placements. By contrast, from 56% (for running away) to 78% (for truancy) of these youngsters were placed on probation (Puzzanchera et al., 2003:57).

Theoretical Reflections
Defining the Role of Parents

That parents shape their children's lives is often an unspoken and unchallenged fact in juvenile justice. In public policy terms, this "fact" has led some state legislatures to punish parents for their children's misconduct. Juvenile court judges have long chastised parents—present or absent—for failing to exercise good judgment or control over their children. With recent legislative trends, parents could face real sanctions, including fines and jail sentences, for the acts of their legal dependents.

Criminologists offer unique insights about parents as informal social control agents. Some social control proponents argue that direct parental controls, including parent-based rules and sanctions, can regulate behavior (Nye, 1958; see also Patterson, 1982; Rankin and Wells, 1990). Children who are strongly attached to their parents also may imitate parental conduct, including harmful behavior such as smoking (Forshee and Bauman, 1992). From this perspective, punishing parents for their children's misdeeds seems defensible.

So how much control should we give parents? In the eighteenth and nineteenth centuries, a husband's absolute power over his wife was partly based on the legal reality that he was responsible for the misconduct of his chattel (that is, possessions), including slaves, children, and wife. Do we want to return the child to the status of chattel? If not, how do parents protect themselves from criminal liability for their child's acts? If parents can lose their liberty as a result of their children's misconduct, should the parents not be allowed to use punitive restraints, such as chains? How about locking children in the basement or the attic? What, then, becomes of children's rights?

Self-control theory brings a different twist to this problem. In other words, the cause of a child's misconduct may be inadequate parenting and poor parental management skills during critical periods in the child's development. That is, between the ages of 8 to 10, a child's self-control—the inclination to avoid or engage in a range of roughly analogous behavior, from cigarette smoking to chronic truancy to delinquency—is fixed and unchangeable (Gottfredson and Hirschi, 1990). Evidence of this causal argument's validity is building. Therefore, sanctioning a parent for the acts of a 15- or 16-year-old means that society is punishing a person for being a poor parent during the child's formative years; they may not have been much more than children themselves when they were learning to be parents. In effect, the punishment functions as retributive justice only, since no matter what the parent does now, the child will be unresponsive, his or her self-control level having been established years before.

Whose causal argument is right? We suspect that both have merit. That is, children with low self-control may be beyond the reach of their parents' control or, for that matter, the juvenile justice system. Children with higher self-control levels are not delinquency free but may respond to parental and other sanctions. Depending on the relative number of low-self-control children in the population, this speculation may explain why parental controls by themselves are low-to-moderate delinquency predictors.

Sources: Forshee and Bauman (1992); Gibbs, Giever, and Martin (1998); Giever (1995); Gottfredson and Hirschi (1990); Patterson (1982); Rankin and Wells (1990).

These changes are consistent with both the **least restrictive placement**[2] approach and the **family preservation movement** in juvenile justice and social services. The aim has become to keep children in the home whenever possible and to deal with the distresses and dysfunctions faced by both the child and the family. Should family preservation be one of the primary goals in responding to dependency cases? What are the advantages or disadvantages of this approach? What other strategies might be explored along with or in place of family preservation?

Answers to these questions lie in the future. The family preservation movement has had a relatively brief history. With more experience the impact of the family preservation approach will become more apparent and answers to these questions should become clearer.

NEGLECTED AND ABUSED CHILDREN

While some uncertainty exists regarding the juvenile court's role with dependent children, the necessity to intervene in neglect and abuse situations is unquestioned. In fact, some people believe that if the court does not intercede when dependency occurs, neglect and abuse are likely to follow. We will next address four critical issues regarding the justice system's response to neglected and abused children: (1) the definitions of neglect and abuse, (2) the problem's current scope, (3) the responsibilities of various agencies in responding to neglect and abuse, and (4) the appropriate legal forum for dealing with these cases.

DEFINITIONS OF NEGLECT

Neglect and abuse are different degrees of the same phenomenon, what many have come to call **child maltreatment** or **child endangerment**. The Office of Juvenile Justice and Delinquency Prevention (OJJDP) says, "Child maltreatment occurs when a caretaker (a parent or parent substitute, such as a day-care worker) is responsible for or permits the abuse or neglect of a child" (Snyder and Sickmund, 1999:40). In effect, abuse is the most extreme form of neglect, and both imply intentional acts on the part of the parents or guardians (see, for example, McCarthy, Patton, and Carr, 2003:237–39, 266–84; Smithburn, 2002:377–447).

One of the problems with child neglect and abuse appears to be too many definitions. Not only are there different meanings for these terms, but also different purposes for the words. In some instances the definitions for abuse are very broad and encompassing; in other cases the terms are very narrowly defined. At times the definitions are modified to help child protective services agencies intervene to shield a child from harm. At other times the definitions provide a basis for criminal prosecution against the abusive caretaker (see, for example, Lazar, 2004). The problems associated with definitions make it more difficult to establish effective policies, which in turn makes it more difficult for law enforcement and social service agencies to respond to maltreatment (see Lazar, 2004).

For our purposes, neglect is defined as "failure to provide for a child's physical needs. This includes lack of supervision, inappropriate housing or shelter, inadequate provision of food, inappropriate clothing for season or weather, abandonment, denial of medical care, and inadequate hygiene" (Childhelp USA, 2004). By contrast, abuse "consists of any act of commission or omission that endangers or impairs a child's physical or emotional health and development. Child abuse includes any damage done to a child which cannot be reasonably explained and which is often represented by an injury or series of injuries appearing to be non-accidental in nature" (Childhelp USA, 2004).

Children experience three common types of neglect. First, there is **physical neglect**. This may involve "abandonment; expulsion from the home; delay or failure to seek remedial health care; inadequate supervision; disregard for hazards in the home; or inadequate food, clothing, or shelter" (Snyder and Sickmund, 1999:40). Snyder and Sickmund report that in 1993, 70% of the child maltreatment cases in the United States involved neglect (1999:40). The numbers are astonishing. In 1986 there were 917,200 reported cases of neglect. By 1993 this number had increased 114% to 1,961,300. Of this number, 1,335,100 cases involved children who were physically neglected. This was up from 507,700 cases in 1986, or an increase of 163% (see table 9.1). The group Parents Anonymous (2004) says that physical neglect fundamentally is "failure to provide the necessities of life."

Physical neglect also includes failure to provide for nutritional or medical needs. Robert ten Bensel's comments on these topics are especially instructive. He

Not all children who come before the juvenile court are delinquent. Some are dependent, neglected, or abused. Even status offenders such as runaways in reality may be "throwaway" children.

says that if parents do not provide food, or if they withhold food as punishment, this constitutes "nutritional neglect." Additionally, "medical neglect" exists if the parents fail "to provide consent to medical treatment which would cure, alleviate, or prevent their children from suffering physical harm" (ten Bensel, 1984:25).

Some of the physical and behavioral indicators of physical neglect are (Parents Anonymous, 2004):

- poor personal hygiene
- inappropriate dress
- lack of supervision
- physical or medical problems that have not been addressed
- falling asleep in class
- drug and/or alcohol abuse
- delinquency

Before concluding that physical neglect is simply the result of inadequate or improper parenting, we must consider the resources and life situations in which most neglectful parents find themselves. As Golden (1997:19, 47) reminds us, child neglect is very closely associated with poverty. This view is echoed in a report from the Office of Juvenile Justice and Delinquency Prevention. The authors of this report found that children in families with annual incomes of $15,000 or less were much more susceptible to all types of maltreatment than were children from families with higher incomes. In fact, the rate of neglect was more than three times higher for children in the lowest family income category compared with other groups (Snyder and Sickmund, 1999:41).

Not everyone believes that poverty alone is the issue. One observer says that while neglect is associated with poverty and unemployment, "there are other more subtle erosions to family life that affect the phenomena of child abuse and neglect" (Antler, 1981:51). Even considering family pressures, we recognize that neglect is not always a matter of what parents *will not* do for their children; it is what they *cannot* do. Thus, while parental actions may contribute to neglect, legally there is less intentionality implied in neglect cases than there would be for abuse.

The second type of neglect is **emotional neglect**. Emotional neglect exists where there is "inadequate nurturance or affection," where the parents or guardians permit "maladaptive behavior, and other inattention to emotional/developmental needs" (Snyder and Sickmund, 1999:40). This is an area where there may be very little consensus among child welfare specialists over definitions, but where we might encounter terms such as *inadequate nurturance* or *allowance of maladaptive behavior* (*delinquency*) as evidence of emotional neglect (Weisz, 1994:67). In 1986 there were 203,000 reported cases of emotional neglect (21% of the child maltreatment cases that year). By 1993 this number had increased 188% to 584,100 cases (Snyder and Sickmund, 1999:41; see table 9.1).

Although written over 20 years ago, ten Bensel (1984:26) provides a summary of factors related to emotional neglect that have retained their relevancy:

- Emotional neglect very frequently is associated with the presence of mental illness and alcohol and drug abuse in the home.

- In families that experience chronic alcoholism and drug addiction, children inevitably demonstrate behavioral problems.

- Emotional neglect may not be easy to detect, nor is it easy to link to children's behaviors or misbehaviors.

The third type of neglect that must be considered is **educational neglect**. This situation often involves "permitting chronic truancy or other inattention to educational needs" (Snyder and Sickmund, 1999:40). As table 9.1 shows, in 1993 there were nearly 400,000 reported cases of educational neglect in the United States.

Educational neglect may occur in households where one of the oldest children is kept out of school to be the parent's caregiver or the babysitter for younger siblings. Children who are found in these situations may even experience role reversals with their parents. In these circumstances—with the parent's immaturity or incapacitation resulting from mental illness or substance abuse—the child takes over parenting responsibilities and becomes the adult's caretaker.

Whatever the causes of truancy, chronic school absences may result in juvenile justice system problems. For example, a report from the OJJDP characterizes truancy as "the beginning of a lifetime of troubles" and as a "stepping stone to delinquent and criminal activity." Furthermore, youngsters who are truant "are at higher risk of being drawn into behavior involving drugs, alcohol, or violence" (Garry, 1996:1). Thus, dealing with educational neglect not only has immediate consequences but may have an impact over the individual's entire life cycle as well.

DEFINITIONS OF ABUSE

Now that we have examined three types of neglect, we will turn our attention to the most common types of abuse encountered by the justice system. As we will see, juvenile courts, adult criminal courts, and a variety of social services agencies may be involved in dealing with more serious forms of child maltreatment. We do not mean

Table 9.1   Reports of Child Maltreatment, 1986 and 1993

Maltreatment type	Number of victims of maltreatment		Percent change
	1986	1993	
Total	1,424,400	2,815,600	98%
Abuse	590,800	1,221,800	107
Physical	311,500	614,100	97
Sexual	133,600	300,200	125
Emotional	188,100	532,200	183
Neglect	917,200	1,961,300	114
Physical	507,700	1,335,100	163
Emotional	203,000	584,100	188
Educational	284,800	397,300	40*

* Indicates that increase did not reach statistical significance.

Note: Victims were counted more than once when more than one type of abuse or neglect had occurred.

Source: Snyder and Sickmund (1999:41).

to minimize the significance of neglect cases, but allegations of abuse are usually much more likely to attract the attention of private citizens and public institutions.

An OJJDP report entitled *Juvenile Offenders and Victims* identified three types of abuse: physical abuse, sexual abuse, and emotional abuse. **Physical abuse** results from "physical acts that caused or could have caused physical injury to the child" (Snyder and Sickmund, 1999:40). Childhelp USA (2004) adds that physical abuse is "any nonaccidental injury to a child. This includes hitting, kicking, slapping, shaking, burning, pinching, hair pulling, biting, choking, throwing, shoving, whipping, and paddling."

As table 9.1 reveals, in 1993 there were over 1.2 million abuse cases reported in the United States, and more than 614,000 of these youngsters were physically abused. In investigating physical abuse cases, the police and other child welfare specialists must not only examine the current injury reported, but also whether the child has experienced a pattern of injuries. This determination, along with the story provided by the caretaker, will give some evidence as to whether the injuries that occurred were unintentional or intentional (see Lazar, 2004).

Ten Bensel (1984:28) provides definitions for several degrees of physical abuse:

- Mild abuse is generally a once-in-a-lifetime episode, even if the instance is moderate or severe.

- Moderate abuse usually refers to open-hand spankings, slaps, hair pulling, and ear jerking; these usually stop by age 8 or 9.

- Severe beating usually includes beating with an instrument, such as a belt, a paddle, a hairbrush, kitchen implements, or a closed fist, and usually continues from childhood through or past puberty.

- Extreme abuse typically results in substantial injuries, such as broken bones, extensive burns, lacerations, mutilation of sex organs, head injuries, or internal injuries.

Although Snyder and Sickmund (1999:40) found that children in the 0 to 2 age category (and those from 15 to 17) had the lowest incidence of maltreatment in 1993, the Administration for Children and Families (ACF, 2005) identified children in the 0 to 3 age bracket as having the highest rate of victimization. The police and child protective services should be particularly concerned with abuse reports involving young children, since the group from 0 to 11 years of age is much more vulnerable and susceptible to endangerment than the group from 15 to 17 years of age.

Sexual abuse involves children in "sexual activity to provide sexual gratification or financial benefit to the perpetrator, including contacts for sexual purposes, prostitution, pornography, or other sexually exploitative activities" (Snyder and Sickmund, 1999:40). The OJJDP reports that 11% of the child maltreatment victims in 1993 were sexually abused. Females were reported as victims more than three times as often as males (19% versus 6%). Of those children victimized by their biological parents, 5% were sexually abused. By contrast, one-fourth of the child victims maltreated by caretakers other than biological parents were sexual abuse victims (Snyder and Sickmund, 1999).

In 1979 Congress made child sexual abuse an explicit part of the federal government's neglect and abuse definitions. Beginning in 1990 the Children's Bureau in the U.S. Department of Health and Human Services started to collect case-level data through its National Child Abuse and Neglect Data System. Using information from this system, Finkelhor and Jones (2004) found that the number of *substantiated* sexual abuse cases in the United States peaked at 149,800 in 1992 and then declined by 2–11% annually through 2000 (this was the last year for which data were available). They assert that the decrease in the number of sexual abuse cases accounts for a substantial portion of the overall 15% decline in child maltreatment cases.

What accounts for the decline in substantiated sexual abuse cases? Finkelhor and Jones (2004:7) offer six possible explanations:

- There has been an increasing conservatism in state child protective services agencies, and these agencies are taking fewer cases where there are divorces or custody fights, or where the initial evidence is weak.

- If the perpetrator was not a caregiver, some states assign a law enforcement agency to the investigation instead of child protective services. This means that different reporting systems have data on sexual abuse cases, and there may not be a final compilation or correlation of the data.

- Child protective services agencies have moved from a three-category classification system—substantiated, indicated, unsubstantiated—to a two-category system (substantiated or unsubstantiated). This redefinition may have caused some cases to be dropped from the reporting system.

- The backlash against people (especially professionals) who report sexual abuse may have resulted in fewer cases being reported.

- The number of older, unreported cases has been reduced.

- As a result of prevention and intervention programs, there has been a true decline in the number of sexual abuse cases.

From among these possible explanations, which one seems to be the most plausible or accurate? Finkelhor and Jones believe that each explanation is possible, but that no single one is totally convincing. However, they note that "based on the strength of current evidence, one of those factors was probably a true decline in the occurrence of sexual abuse." They also add that "the decline has been so widespread geographically and has occurred across so many categories of children, offenders, types of abuse, and types of evidence that a true decline can be considered as at least one part of the overall picture" (Finkelhor and Jones, 2004: 20).

Chesney-Lind and Shelden (2003), in their research on females and delinquent behavior, identify some of the significant consequences of child sexual abuse. They assert that sexual abuse is much more likely to occur with girls than with boys and is "more likely to be perpetrated by family members." The result is that the abuse is likely to last longer. Additionally, sexual abuse of juvenile females is associated with running away from home and other status offenses. They maintain that "sexual abuse . . . appears to be the most common element in the lives of girls who run away."

Although running away is one way to deal with sexual abuse, it is not the most dramatic consequence for girls who are sexual abuse victims. Some of them turn to prostitution to support themselves while they are runaways, and this may become a prolonged way of life. Sexual abuse is also related to adult offenses other than prostitution. Chesney-Lind and Shelden (2003) note that over 60% of the women in prison report being physically or sexually abused as youths. This means that the

---

Box 9.1   Consequences of Abuse:
Links to Delinquency and Other Problem Behaviors

Novelists, essayists, psychologists, sociologists, and other social scientists have long maintained that there is a strong link between being abused as a child and future misconduct. Researchers suggest that there is fire in all that smoke. Cathy Spatz Widom (1995) studied 908 individuals who, when they were 11 years old or younger, experienced abuse or neglect; their cases had been officially adjudicated between 1967 and 1971. The adult criminal records of these individuals were subsequently compared with those of a control group of individuals who were closely matched in age, sex, and approximate family socioeconomic status but did not have an official record of abuse or neglect.

Widom found that people who had been maltreated as children were more likely to be arrested as adults (26% of the abused or neglected versus 16.8% of the controls). Those who had been sexually abused as children were no more likely to have arrest records as adults than other maltreatment victims; consequently, the defining status was victim of maltreatment alone. Widom also reported that experiencing any form of abuse or neglect increased the likelihood for sex crimes. Youthful sex-crime victims, as a group, were more likely than any others to have adult prostitution arrests. For rape or sodomy, physical abuse was the key defining experience. Finally, Widom found that abused or neglected children were more likely to run away than were controls, and the prostitution arrests of sexually abused children were higher than for controls. However, none of the runaways were arrested for prostitution as adults. Widom concludes that while childhood sexual abuse puts these children at greater risk of arrest as juveniles and adults, criminal behavior is not inevitable: The majority of sexually abused children in her study did not have official criminal histories as adults (Widom, 1995:7).

A longitudinal study of adolescents undertaken by a team of researchers involved in the Rochester Youth Development Study (Kelley, Thornberry, and Smith, 1997) explored the links between child maltreatment prevalence and a series of negative outcomes. The study's subjects were 1,000 seventh- and eighth-grade youths (75% boys and 25% girls) attending Rochester's (New York) public schools; they were studied every six months between 1988 and 1992. Besides the survey data collected in face-to-face interviews, the researchers obtained official records data from the public school system, the police department, social services, and other agencies that had contact with the subjects.

Without exception, more maltreated than nonmaltreated youths self-reported official delinquency (45% versus 32%), serious delinquency (45% versus 33%), and violent delinquency (70% versus 56%). With regard to outcomes other than delinquency, more maltreated youths than nonmaltreated youths reported, for girls, pregnancies (52% versus 32%), and for all students, lower academic achievement (33% versus 23%), self-reported drug use (43% versus 32%), and mental health problems (26% versus 15%). Overall, the researchers estimate that "childhood maltreatment is associated with an increased risk of at least 25% for each of these investigated outcomes" (Kelley et al., 1997:11).

Sources: Kelley, Thornberry, and Smith (1997); Widom (1995).

sexual abuse of male and female youngsters has repercussions for the juvenile justice and criminal justice systems.

It is crucial to note two final points about child sexual abuse. First, many cases occur within the family, the vast majority never being reported or investigated. Snyder and Sickmund (1999:41) report that in 1993 birth parents accounted for 78% of the reported child maltreatment cases. Of the cases reported, 5% involved sexual abuse situations. In all likelihood this represents the tip of the iceberg. Second, the entire criminal justice system should be concerned with these cases. This concern derives from the observation that some sexual abuse victims go on to become sexual offenders (Stops and Mays, 1991).

The final type of abuse is **emotional abuse**; it may be very pervasive, but as ten Bensel notes, "We have little data about emotional assault of children" (1984:26). Snyder and Sickmund define emotional abuse as "acts (including verbal or emotional assault) or omissions that caused or could have caused conduct, cognitive, affective, or other mental disorders" (1999:40). Even with this definition it is important to recognize that emotional abuse, since it leaves no physical marks, may be extremely difficult to identify precisely and measure accurately.

In 1993 there were 532,200 reported case of emotional abuse in the United States (see table 9.1). This number accounted for 19% of all of the maltreatment cases reported in 1993, an increase of 183% over the numbers reported in 1986. The increase in emotional abuse cases was second only to emotional neglect in the largest percentage increase among child maltreatment cases.

Ten Bensel (1984:26) says that emotional abuse is the active rejection of children by their parents or guardians and is manifested in "constant verbalization of criticism, disapproval, disrespect, and denial of the worth and sensitivity of children." As with emotional neglect, this type of maltreatment often is related to mental illness or to alcohol or other drug abuse by the child's caretaker.

Prenatal substance abuse represents a fourth form of abuse (Weisz, 1994), a type of maltreatment that has gained attention as a result of news reports concerning infants born already addicted to drugs, such as the so-called crack babies of the 1980s and 1990s (Walker, 2001:252). Weisz estimates that one out of every 10 babies born in the United States has been exposed to drugs as a fetus; the mother's multiple drug use, including alcohol, can adversely affect fetal development, and the resulting impairments can be long lasting (1994:67). As a result, some states now include prenatal substance exposure in their child abuse definitions, and this may be grounds for removing a newborn child from the mother.

While we already have made some references to the extent of abuse and neglect cases in the United States, in the following section we will examine more closely what we know about the extent of child maltreatment. As the figures summarized in table 9.1 already demonstrate, we are dealing with a substantial and apparently growing problem.

THE SCOPE OF THE CHILD MALTREATMENT PROBLEM

In 1996 there were about 3 million reported child maltreatment cases in the United States, up from just over 1.2 million cases reported in 1980. Does this mean

Theoretical Reflections
New Directions in the Study of Child Maltreatment

Criminologists come from a variety of philosophical perspectives. Among those criminologists who refuse to accept status-quo answers to America's juvenile justice questions is a group broadly (and perhaps arbitrarily) called *critical criminologists*. Critical criminologists counsel us to consider carefully the impact of common wisdom and accepted practices on the juvenile justice system's clients. They also suggest that much juvenile misbehavior may constitute reasonable—or at least understandable—responses to child maltreatment.

Critical criminologists challenge us to reexamine and, perhaps, reinterpret what we think we know about abuse, neglect, dependency, and delinquency. For example, Meda Chesney-Lind's (1989a) **patriarchal society thesis** centers on how our patriarchal society's laws serve to oppress females. Add economic inequalities and racism to the equation, and delinquency becomes a survival strategy for many young girls. Running away and getting involved in petty delinquency, such as shoplifting, drug use, and prostitution, may be perfectly reasonable alternatives to staying at home and being subjected to physical, mental, and sexual abuse. Chesney-Lind warns that these adolescent survival strategies, especially prostitution and drug use, can continue into adulthood. We should not be surprised to find that many adult women are arrested for these crimes since, as Chesney-Lind (1989a:23) observes, these women "possess truncated educational backgrounds and virtually no marketable occupation skills."

Robert Regoli and John Hewitt (1994), in their **theory of differential oppression**, provide another way of viewing children's undesirable and even illegal acts. Their view is that society endorses stereotypes of children as inferior; these stereotypes inform parents that they must impose adult concepts of order on their children, even if extreme and often oppressive measures must be taken. If children would simply "get with the program," there would be no trouble. However, many children, overwhelmed by feelings of powerlessness, show their disregard for the "adult way" by engaging in sexual misconduct, drug use, and delinquent acts. They may also strike a blow for adolescent freedom by retaliating against their parents or virtually any symbol of adult authority, or gain potency by getting other children into trouble. From this perspective, some children come to the juvenile justice system's attention because they do not passively accept their inferior status as the objects of adult oppression.

Even more moderate criminologists suggest that we may need to redefine some of our ideas about delinquency. For example, Robert Agnew's (1992) **general strain theory** is a recasting of strain theory, which tells us that those faced with anomic strains may seek legitimate goals by illegitimate means. Agnew turns this idea around: in his view, delinquents are often running from undesired punishments and negative relationships with others, not toward legitimate goals. They may have failed to achieve a positively valued goal, for example, the difference between an actual outcome and what is perceived to be the fair and just outcome. Whatever the type of strain, attempts to avoid it may move the child closer to delinquency. When some youths are placed in a highly agitated and often negative emotional state, they see delinquency as an opportunity to (1) regain something lost or forbidden, (2) retaliate against the source of the strain, or (3) escape from an undesired state or condition (Paternoster and Mazerolle, 1994).

Sources: Agnew (1992); Chesney-Lind (1989a); Paternoster and Mazerolle (1994); Regoli and Hewitt (1994).

that the number of neglect and abuse cases more than doubled in the United States during this period? Possibly, but not necessarily. We may be dealing with both *increased incidence* and *increased reporting* when we consider this problem's magnitude.

The development of better and more reliable reporting mechanisms may also account for some of the increases. Figure 9.2 depicts another set of ever-increasing child maltreatment statistics; it also offers support for the speculations regarding at least some of the 161% increase. Specifically, between 1980 and 1987, the National Study on Child Neglect and Abuse Reporting was the major source of child maltreatment reports, supplemented (beginning in 1985) by the Annual 50-State Survey. The Annual 50-State Survey alone provided this information between 1988 and 1991, when it was joined by the National Child Abuse and Neglect Data System (NCANDS) report, an annual publication of the National Center on Child Abuse and Neglect. The NCANDS report has served as our primary window on the nation's child maltreatment problem since 1992. The first NCANDS report was

Figure 9.2

Maltreatment Reports and New Reporting Mechanisms: 1980 to 1996

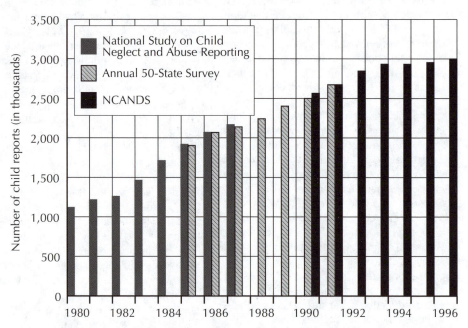

• Reports of alleged maltreatment increased 161% between 1980 and 1996. The increasing trend in child maltreatment reports is believed to be the result, at least in part, of a greater willingness to report suspected incidents. Greater public awareness both of child maltreatment as a social problem and of the resources available to respond to it are factors that contribute to increased reporting.

Note: Child reports are counts of children who are the subject of reports. Counts are duplicated when an individual child is the subject of more than one report during a year.

Source: Snyder and Sickmund (1999:45).

based on 1990 data. Since then, the maltreatment reports have fluctuated by only a few hundred thousand per year, suggesting that this method has provided a stable view of child maltreatment. Also, the NCANDS gives both summary and case-level information, which is essential if we are to understand who is being victimized, by whom, and under what circumstances.

According to both 1996 summary data and case-level reports from NCANDS, in 1996 there were about 3 million reports for neglect and abuse. Of the total number of reported child maltreatment cases, 50% involved neglect (including physical and medical neglect). The remainder involved physical abuse (26%), sexual abuse (29%), and psychological abuse (37%).

Another way to look at the child maltreatment problem is to examine the number of children who were subjects of maltreatment investigations and the total number of victims. Table 9.2 presents data from the Administration for Children and Families (ACF) of the U.S. Department of Health and Human Services. Between 1990 and 2003 (the last year for which data are available), the number of children who were subjects of maltreatment investigations increased steadily each year from 2,316,000 to 3,353,000. Interestingly, the total number of victims increased annually from 1990 to 1994, then began a gradual downward trend (ACF, 2005).

Race and ethnicity do not yield differences much greater than we would expect if the problem were randomly distributed in the population: The majority (54%) of the victims were white, followed by blacks (26.5%), Hispanics (11.5%), and other racial or ethnic groups (2.5%). However, several other factors seem related to substantiated or indicated child maltreatment. The victim's gender is one of those variables. While sexual abuse was more common among females than among males (19% versus 6%), emotional neglect was more common among males than among females (61% versus 53%). Overall, 53% of the maltreatment victims were females.

Age is also a factor in the likelihood of child maltreatment. Children under the age of 11 are more frequently at risk of endangerment than those over 15 years of age. Most maltreatment victims (53%) were under the age of 7, and one in five was 2 years of age or younger. Nearly one-half (43%) of the maltreated children who died were under the age of 1 year; nearly all (81%) were under 4 years of age. However, older children were more likely than younger ones to report having been physically (28% versus 17%) or sexually abused (18% versus 9%). That is, children who are victims of general neglect or are killed are more than likely quite young; victims of physical abuse or sexual abuse are likely to be older (Snyder and Sickmund, 1999).

Family income is also related to reported child maltreatment cases. Snyder and Sickmund (1999) maintain that all kinds of child maltreatment reported in 1993 were significantly more likely to occur in families with annual incomes less than $15,000. In fact, "The abuse rate in these lowest-income families was two times the rate in other families, and the neglect rate was more than three times higher." Furthermore, "Children in the lowest-income families had higher injury rates in every injury category except fatalities" (Snyder and Sickmund, 1999:41).

A factor strongly associated with both the number of parents present in the household and family income is family size. Children living in the largest families were more likely to be neglected or abused. In fact, in families with four or more children, youngsters were three times more likely to be physically neglected than

Table 9.2   Rates of Children Subjects of an Investigation or Assessment and Rates of Victimization, 1990–2003

Reporting Year	Child Population	Investigation Rate	States Reporting	Total Children Subjects of an Investigation or Assessment	Victim Rate	States Reporting	Total Victims
1990	64,163,192	36.1	36	2,316,000	13.4	45	860,000
1991	65,069,507	38.2	39	2,486,000	14.0	46	911,000
1992	66,073,841	41.2	41	2,722,000	15.1	48	998,000
1993	66,961,573	42.1	42	2,819,000	15.3	47	1,025,000
1994	67,803,294	42.1	42	2,855,000	15.2	46	1,031,000
1995	68,437,378	42.2	43	2,888,000	14.7	47	1,006,000
1996	69,022,127	42.0	42	2,899,000	14.7	46	1,015,000
1997	69,527,944	41.9	44	2,913,000	13.7	45	953,000
1998	69,872,059	42.1	51	2,939,000	12.9	51	904,000
1999	70,199,435	41.0	50	2,878,000	11.8	50	828,000
2000	72,346,696	42.0	49	3,039,000	12.2	50	883,000
2001	72,616,308	43.2	48	3,137,000	12.5	51	905,000
2002	72,894,483	43.9	50	3,200,000	12.3	51	897,000
2003	73,043,506	45.9	49	3,353,000	12.4	50	906,000

Victimization and investigation rates were computed by dividing the respective counts of children by the population and multiplying by 1,000.

Source: Administration for Children & Families (2005).

children in one-child families. The sad reality is that children in the largest families have the highest potential for endangerment (Snyder and Sickmund, 1999:41).

Child maltreatment perpetrators share several interesting characteristics. More than 6 in 10 perpetrators are women. However, age appears to play a role in relation to the perpetrator's gender: If perpetrators are under 40, more than likely they are a woman; perpetrators over 40 are most often men.

Birth parents account for most (78%) maltreatment victimizations. Other parents (14%) and other perpetrators (9%) make up the remainder. However, if the maltreatment is suffered at the hands of one's birth parents, more than likely it was neglect rather than abuse. If other parents are involved in the maltreatment, the reverse is true: The most common form of maltreatment suffered by children at the hands of parents other than birth parents is physical abuse. In spite of these differences, when birth parents injure their children, they are twice as likely to kill or seriously injure them than are either other parents or other perpetrators (Snyder and Sickmund, 1999:42).

Finally, the type of maltreatment varies by the perpetrator's relationship to the victim. Among relatives, general neglect cases accounted for most (57%) of the reports, followed by other maltreatment (24%), physical abuse (22%), sexual abuse (13%), medical neglect (5%), and emotional maltreatment (4%). Nonrelated perpetrators presented a slightly different set of proportions. General neglect was the most common form, but at 30%, the percentage was far less than that reported for relatives. The remaining maltreatment types, in declining order, are sexual abuse (27%), physical abuse (26%), other maltreatment (22%), medical neglect (15%), and emotional maltreatment (3%). The greatest disparities were noted in sexual abuse cases (more common for nonrelated perpetrators) and other neglect (more common for relatives) (Snyder and Sickmund, 1999).

THE RESPONSIBILITIES OF INVESTIGATING AGENCIES

Meriwether (1988:9) indicates that the creation of reporting statutes was the most significant nationwide development in the child protection movement. Currently, both the federal **Child Abuse Prevention and Treatment Act of 1974** (and subsequent amendments) and state laws mandate the reporting of child neglect and abuse (see, for example, McCarthy et al., 2003:272–84; Smithburn, 2002:379–85). In simplest terms, this means that anyone who becomes aware of or even suspects child maltreatment is legally obligated to report it. The reporting mandate is problematic for several reasons. First, as we have indicated previously, not all the definitions are sufficiently clear to indicate what should be reported and by whom. Tzeng and his colleagues (1991) note that while federal and state laws provide definitions, "child abuse terminology remains complex and ambiguous." Second, because of ambiguous wording, there may be problems with reporting inappropriate cases—those not involving abuse—and not reporting appropriate cases—those involving abuse (Meriwether, 1988:9). Finally, we must recognize that reported cases do not disclose the full extent of the problem.

With these factors in mind, the questions before us in this section are: (1) to whom should suspected child maltreatment be reported? and (2) who should have the primary responsibility for investigating such incidents? As we will see, the answers to these and similar questions can be quite complicated. In order to more fully explain the complexities involved, we will examine the responsibilities of family members, friends, and neighbors; school authorities; the police; medical personnel; and finally, child protective services.

FAMILIES, FRIENDS, AND NEIGHBORS

This group includes the people closest to suspected child endangerment and maltreatment cases, and we can assume two things about these individuals. First, they are the most likely to know about neglect and abuse cases and, therefore, they should be under the greatest obligation to report their knowledge or suspicions. Second, since they are in close—and sometimes intimate—relationships with the offender, they may be the least likely to report their observations or suspicions, perhaps until it is too late. This fact means that no amount of legislation or regulation is going to overcome kinship ties or bonds of friendship, and that the existence of laws does not guarantee reporting. Nevertheless, in 2003 family members (parents and other relatives) did report 15.4% of the child abuse and neglect cases, and friends and neighbors reported another 5.6% of these cases (ACF, 2005).

At times, family members, friends, and neighbors are reluctant to report suspected child maltreatment for fear that they might be mistaken. They also may feel that the activity simply involves family discipline and that it is none of their business (see, for example, Portwood and Reppucci, 1994:7). Besharov asserts that "child protective decisions often must be based on incomplete and misleading information, and that there are many borderline cases." He concludes: "The chance of human error is always present" (1988:89). Fear of retaliation also may keep spouses and other children from reporting child maltreatment. Finally, the maltreatment—especially if it involves sexual abuse—may be unknown to family members, friends, and neighbors. Therefore, how can we learn about the less visible forms of child maltreatment? The next section provides some answers.

SCHOOL OFFICIALS

Schools play a vital role in recognizing and reporting child maltreatment cases. In 2003, 16.3% of the maltreatment cases were identified by educational personnel, the largest single category of individuals reporting these cases (ACF, 2005). The next largest group identifying neglect and abuse cases was law enforcement agencies with 16% of the cases.

Obviously, schools are crucial in dealing with abuse and neglect problems. What places schools in this advantageous position? The primary factor is that the schools have extended periods of exposure to youngsters for most of the day and throughout much of the year. Consequently, teachers, coaches, and school nurses have the opportunity to observe unusual behaviors or injuries that might indicate maltreatment. Additionally, as abused and neglected children develop trusting relationships with teachers and other students, they may begin to disclose maltreatment incidents occurring at home.

In the final analysis, school officials have two major obligations. First, every school employee, from teachers and coaches to secretaries and cafeteria workers, should be given periodic training on how to identify neglect and abuse. This training would sensitize school personnel to various types of maltreatment and the signs of neglect or abuse. Second, school systems must have fully developed and carefully articulated policies on what to do in suspected or identified child maltreatment cases. These policies should cover who should interview suspected maltreatment victims, where the interviews should take place, who should be present, and to whom reports should be submitted. At least once per year these policies ought to be reviewed and presented to teachers, principals, and school health personnel.

LAW ENFORCEMENT AGENCIES

Local law enforcement personnel become aware of suspected child maltreatment cases through several different means. First, some concerned citizen may alert them. As we have discussed previously, this could include family members, friends, or neighbors. The fictionalized scenario that opened this chapter illustrates the kind of report the police may receive. Second, the police may be notified of an injured child by a frightened parent, from emergency medical services (EMS) employees, or from hospital emergency room personnel. We will consider health care officials in the next section. Suffice it to say that the police regularly receive "injured child" reports from hospital and clinic emergency rooms.

The police role is vital to resolving child maltreatment cases, since they frequently will be responsible for determining whether a crime has been committed, what the appropriate charges are, who will be arrested, and when and where an arrest will take place. Snyder and Sickmund (1999:42) note that law enforcement agencies have the highest investigation rates once neglect and abuse are reported. In 1993 police departments and sheriffs departments investigated 52% of the cases known to them. By contrast, child protective services agencies investigated 33% of cases reported to them. The lowest actual investigation rates were by public health agencies (4%) and day care centers (3%). In all likelihood, given the lack of trained investigators within these organizations, either nothing was done or, more likely, these cases were turned over to law enforcement agencies or child protective services.

HEALTH CARE AGENCIES

Three types of health care organizations typically come into contact with child maltreatment incidents: hospitals, mental health agencies, and public health facilities. These three groups reported 11.2% of the child maltreatment cases identified in 2003 (ACF, 2005). Although this percentage is somewhat low, we must note that hospitals investigated 46% of the neglect and abuse cases they identified, and mental health agencies investigated 42% of the cases they discovered. Obviously, trained medical personnel play a key role in both the identification and treatment of injuries suffered in maltreatment cases. Because these professionals are both first responders and medical practitioners, their testimony can have a profound impact on the court's decision as to the appropriate short-term action.

CHILD PROTECTIVE SERVICES

One might assume that **child protective services** agencies play the primary role in dealing with neglect and abuse cases. However, as we already have noted, schools identify maltreatment cases more frequently than any other community agency or organization, and the police are responsible for a large number of the criminal investigations when there are child maltreatment allegations.

Nevertheless, the role played by child protection agencies is still a vital one. In 2003, child protective agencies reported 11.6% of the child maltreatment cases (ACF, 2005). Such agencies typically investigate a very high percentage of the cases they identify. There were five possible outcomes for these cases (ACF, 2005):

- *Alternative response nonvictim.* This disposition results when a child is not identified as a victim after there is a response other than an investigation.

- *Alternative response victim.* In this type of case the child is identified as a victim after a response other than an investigation.

- *Indicated.* In these cases maltreatment cannot be substantiated under state law, but there is reason to believe the child has suffered maltreatment or was at risk for maltreatment.

- *Substantiated*. The investigation has been able to establish, according to state law, that a case of maltreatment has occurred.
- *Unsubstantiated*. The investigation establishes that there is not sufficient evidence, under state law, to conclude that maltreatment has occurred.

In 2003, 6.2% of reported maltreatment cases nationally were determined to be alternative response nonvictim, 0.1% were alternative response victim, 4.1% were indicated, 26.4% were substantiated, 57.7% were unsubstantiated, and the remainder were intentionally false, closed with no finding, unknown or missing, or other.

AGENCY COOPERATION

It should be apparent from the previous sections that many groups and individuals have either informal or formal responsibilities for identifying, reporting, and investigating child maltreatment cases. Two problems continue to confront those interested in deciphering this part of the juvenile justice puzzle. First, some cases fall through the cracks of the juvenile justice and child protection systems. Newspaper stories periodically report on cases where the mechanisms for detecting maltreatment fail and a child dies.

The second problem is in some ways the opposite of the first. In some cases many different agencies get involved in the identification of, and intervention with, neglect and abuse cases. In these situations the problem becomes one of interagency cooperation. Since the police, school officials, medical personnel, and child protective services workers are not organizationally linked, each is free to pursue an investigation and prosecution independently of the others.

Cooperation among these entities is vital, but turf disputes may make cooperation problematic. National interest groups dedicated to the issues of children have attempted to fill the gaps left by such disputes (see box 9.2); however, since many problems are local, the solutions must be local. Lack of cooperation will result in less-than-efficient handling of maltreatment cases, and endangered children will suffer the most.

JUVENILE COURT JURISDICTION ISSUES

The fact that the juvenile court has jurisdiction over delinquent and status-offending juveniles is beyond dispute. Several issues emerge, however, once we consider whether that court has jurisdiction over nondelinquent children and their parents or guardians.

JURISDICTION OVER NONDELINQUENT CHILDREN

The main tasks confronting juvenile and family courts throughout much of their history were (1) to determine if children had been abused or neglected and (2) in abuse and neglect cases, to decide whether it was in the best interests of the children to remove them from the home, place them under the court's supervision, and find alternative placements. The status quo was changed in 1980 with the passage

---

Box 9.2   Professional Organizations and Private Foundations as Interest Groups

In chapter 1 we observed that numerous interest groups provide aid and assistance, sometimes unsolicited, to the juvenile justice system. Two such organizations are the American Bar Association and the Children's Defense Fund.

The **American Bar Association** (**ABA**) represents an interesting blend of the ad hoc committee and the professional organization. In 1977, the Institute of Judicial Administration (IJA) and the American Bar Association, as part of the Juvenile Justice Standards Project, issued 23 volumes of standards dealing with a variety of juvenile justice issues. These standards addressed not only alleged delinquency cases but also situations involving neglected, abused, and dependent children and their families. The IJA/ABA standards were designed to guide the actions of the justice system, as well as parents, foster parents, and guardians *ad litem*. There is no way to measure how many jurisdictions have adopted the standards, in whole or in part, nor their impact. However, such a comprehensive set of recommendations is likely to become a benchmark for many other groups, especially those concerned with juvenile justice system reforms.

On a continuing basis, the ABA operates the **Center on Children and the Law**. Established in 1978, the center has as its mission "to improve children's lives through advances in law, justice, knowledge, practice and public policy" (ABA, 2004:3). The center researches and disseminates information on laws, policies, and practices that affect children. Some of the topics addressed by the center in recent years are legal representation of children, parents, and child welfare agencies; improvement of attorney-caseworker teamwork; legal training for child welfare caseworkers; and domestic abuse and child custody mediation. The center "integrates law, public policy, and social science research" (ABA, 2004:3) as it works to improve the legal system's response to the problems of the nation's youth. For example, in 1996 the center finished a three-year study on how the criminal justice system handles parental abduction cases and evaluated the use of videotaping and closed circuit television in child sexual abuse trials.

The **Children's Defense Fund** (**CDF**) was created in 1973 by Marian Wright Edelman. A private, nonprofit organization, CDF considers itself a "strong and effective voice for all children of America, who cannot vote, lobby, or speak for themselves" (Children's Defense Fund, 2004:1). This group disseminates information on a broad range of child-related matters, including the health care conditions of the nation's children and the nature and extent of poverty. Among their online services is an extensive database containing youthful crime and victimization data for each state.

Sources: American Bar Association (2004a); Children's Defense Fund (2004).

---

of the **Adoption Assistance and Child Welfare Act**, after which juvenile and family court judges had to ensure that every abused or neglected child found placement in a safe, permanent, and stable home. In theory, juvenile and family court judges can stay involved in cases for years; in practice, they spend an average of 10 minutes on the 35 to 40 cases on their daily dockets (Coordinating Council on Juvenile Justice and Delinquency Prevention, 1997).

In view of the time spent on such cases, we must ask whether the juvenile court should continue to serve as the ultimate legal guardian for dependent, neglected, and abused youngsters. Would some other court or social services agency be better suited? Although it is impossible to provide definitive answers, in this section we will give you some options to think about as the juvenile court begins its second century.

There has been much discontent during the past three decades over the juvenile court's performance with delinquency cases (see, for example, Ainsworth, 1999; Feld, 1999d). However, there seems to have been an equal amount of disaffection with its treatment of nondelinquency cases. Why is this the case, and what can be done about the criticisms that have been leveled at the juvenile court?

One of the lingering issues facing the juvenile court is whether the best interests of the child are being represented, or whether other institutional imperatives are being served. Quite often the juvenile court's jurisdiction over nondelinquent children allows the court to maintain a full docket, which keeps the court's staff busy and employed. Furthermore, some courts oversee shelter care placements and programming efforts for dependent, neglected, and abused children, and this provides funding and increased community support for juvenile court efforts. Thus, once these programs are created, they may take on lives of their own.

A second issue is that of effectiveness. Is the juvenile court having a positive impact on the lives of dependent, neglected, or abused children? If not, how can we change that? Perhaps a different way of looking at the problem would help. Maybe we should treat dependency, neglect, and abuse not as the child's problem but rather as a family problem. Such an approach would lend support to expanding the juvenile court's jurisdiction into that of a family court (see Feld, 2003; Smithburn, 2002). In the family court context, children's problems would not be considered in isolation from those of their parents or guardians. This arrangement would expand the court's jurisdiction over adults in such cases.

Another option in the handling of dependency and child maltreatment cases would be to remove these cases from the courts' coercive legal jurisdiction altogether. Instead of resolving these cases through litigation, social services agencies would be responsible for attending to the needs of these nondelinquent youngsters and their families.

The nonlitigation, social services approach is not without problems as well. For instance, Golden emphasizes that "what constitutes the child's best interests depends on your point of view" (1997:21). In her assessment of the U.S. child welfare system, she says that the bureaucratic mandates of state and local social services agencies quite often override what is best for either the child or the family. As a consequence, when children are removed from abusive homes, they may end up in "foster care drift" where the "caseworkers often lose track of a child." The result is that "babies grow to school age and float through four or five foster placements" (1997:22).

What can we conclude? Is there no hope for a more responsive system to deal with these special-needs children? The past two decades have left us with several general observations about the current system's approach. First, there is broad-based agreement that nondelinquent children should not be confined in secure correctional settings (see especially Schwartz, 1989; Schwartz, Harris, and Levi, 1988). Second, while social service agencies can provide valuable assistance to the courts, nondelinquency cases should not all be dumped onto a child welfare system that itself is having difficulties (Golden, 1997). Third, in all likelihood, some coercive legal authority will have to be maintained in order to provide assistance to these children and support for their families. Fourth, a more broadly defined family court—one dealing with a range of family-based issues—seems preferable to a juvenile court largely focused on, and overburdened with, delinquency cases. Therefore, removing nondelinquency cases from the juvenile court, or changing the court's mandate relative to the way in which these cases are processed, seems to be a preferable course to pursue.

The Coordinating Council on Juvenile Justice and Delinquency Prevention (1997) notes that among the many strategies and programs for dealing with child maltreatment, the following seem to be the most effective and promising:

- *State court improvement.* Given the increased role assumed by juvenile and family courts since 1980, improvement of the services provided by those courts seems the prudent course of action. The Omnibus Budget Reconciliation Act of 1993 (Public Law 103-66) created a grant program to improve the services rendered by state-level courts handling adoptions and foster care.

- *Unified family courts.* This promising strategy involves the creation of a one-stop, full-service court for family-related legal matters. Such courts can address the needs of the child within the family context. However, to be effective, unified courts must have judicial authority and trained staff equal to that of the highest general jurisdiction trial courts.

- *Children's advocacy centers.* These centers provide community-based consolidation of all necessary services to better meet the needs of abuse and neglect cases. The goals are varied: investigations and prosecutions should be

---

Box 9.3   International Perspectives
Child Victimization

In this chapter we examine the statuses of dependency, neglect, and abuse. The ultimate victimization occurs when a child is killed. In the United States most of the homicides of young children (ages 5 and under) are committed by family members. In fact, 71% of these victims die at the hands of family members. Finkelhor and Ormrod (2001) found that the most common method of death is by "personal weapons," such as hands or feet that often are used to "batter, strangle, or suffocate victims." Boys and girls die in almost equal numbers, but female offenders are disproportionately represented for this offense.

To provide a point of comparison, the Centers for Disease Control and Prevention examined the homicide and suicide rates for children in 26 industrialized nations. For children 0 to 4 years of age, the rate of homicides in the United States was 4.10 per 100,000 children. This compared with the rate of 0.95 per 100,000 in the other 25 industrialized nations. The rates for homicides by firearms were very low for both groups (0.43 versus 0.05), but still nearly 10 times greater in the United States. The homicide rates in cases not involving firearms were even more dramatically different: 3.67 per 100,000 children in the United States compared with 0.05 per 100,000 in the other nations, or more than 70 times greater. Clearly, children in the United States are more likely to be victims of violence than children in other industrialized countries.

Sources: Finkelhor and Ormrod (2001); Snyder and Sickmund (1999).

increased; the immediate and long-term needs of victims and their families should be addressed; community awareness of abuse and neglect problems should be raised; and collaboration among local governmental agencies should be increased.

- *Court-appointed special advocate (CASA) programs.* **CASA programs** use court-appointed trained volunteers, sometimes called **guardians** *ad litem*, to reduce the trauma in the victims' lives. Handling only one or two cases at a time, the guardians *ad litem* provide a thorough and independent investigation and recommend a plan based on the best interests of the child. Once the court makes known its wishes, the volunteers monitor compliance and report regularly to the court.

- *Family preservation, family support, and independent living.* The key to family preservation is, first and foremost, children's safety. After ensuring their safety, the focus is on changing the family's behavior. Family members may be required to participate in structured programs that provide them with conflict-resolution skills, communications skills, and parenting practices necessary for healthy cognitive, emotional, and behavioral development.

- *Early family strengthening and support.* Sounding like a manual for the development of high levels of self-control within the family context, programs like Prenatal/Perinatal Healthy Family and Healthy Babies basically tell mothers what their own mothers forgot to tell them or did not know themselves about raising babies. Prenatal and perinatal health care is emphasized, along with intensive health care education for the mothers, the rest of the family, and all others who will have contact with the child or children. The goal is to enhance parenting skills, something emphasized by self-control theory (OJJDP, 1995).

- *Victimization prevention programs.* One thing should be obvious from the preceding discussion of child maltreatment: Any program intended to reduce general victimization will address the children's needs. Most victimization programs are not specifically related to the courts; however, Teen Court and similar peer-based adjudicatory programs include lessons about crime and victimization problems.

As the juvenile court moves through its second century of existence, it will continue to grapple with the most effective ways to meet the needs of nondelinquents under the court's jurisdiction. Related to this, and equally vexing, is whether or to what extent the juvenile court should have jurisdiction over adults.

JURISDICTION OVER PARENTS AND GUARDIANS

Since its creation, the juvenile court has had authority over adults within a fairly narrow range of cases. For example, juvenile courts have had jurisdiction not only over children in delinquency, dependency, and neglect cases, but also over adults who have contributed to the delinquency, dependency, or neglect of minor children (Gardner, 2003). How often do juvenile courts exercise such jurisdiction? Probably not very often. Is this an appropriate exercise of jurisdiction? It depends. If the juvenile court is a court of limited or inferior jurisdiction, in contrast to being a general jurisdiction trial court, then it may not have much to offer in the way of sanctions for adults. In all likelihood, the cases of adults who contribute to the delinquency, dependency, or neglect of a minor—especially child abuse or endangerment cases—should be heard in adult criminal courts. This mandate seems to be a more appropriate exercise of age jurisdiction, since all other cases with adult offenders and child victims are tried in criminal courts. It also provides a broader range of sanctions and more severe sanctions for those adults found guilty of offenses related to dependency and maltreatment.

If the court's jurisdiction is that of a broadly defined family court, as we have suggested, then jurisdiction over both children and adults is perfectly justifiable. Otherwise, juvenile courts should not retain jurisdiction over adult offenders.

SUMMARY

In this chapter we have provided definitions for the various types of nondelinquency cases handled by the juvenile courts. It might be useful for you to review these definitions now. Clearly, dependency cases are the least serious but in some ways the most difficult of the nondelinquency cases. Even though dependency exists largely through no fault of the child's caretaker, these cases do not seem to lend themselves to easy solutions. In fact, there is some concern that dependency situations will grow worse if timely and suitable interventions are not provided.

By contrast, neglect and abuse cases are much more serious than dependency cases and may even be life threatening. Debate continues over the most appropriate solutions to such child maltreatment cases. Should the child (or children) be removed from the home immediately, and should the parents' rights be terminated in situations involving mental illness or drug and alcohol abuse? Or is it preferable to leave the child in the home and provide the types of "housing, day care, jobs, decent schools, . . . and health care" (Golden, 1997:22) that these parents often need to do an adequate job of raising their children?

We also have examined the different groups—including family members, friends, neighbors, school authorities, law enforcement, and health care providers—who may be in a position to detect dependency, neglect, or abuse situations. Most states now legally mandate that anyone with knowledge of these conditions must report them to the appropriate agencies, which typically are defined within the statutes.

Furthermore, the chapter included a discussion of those agencies with authority to investigate allegations of neglect and abuse. One of the greatest dangers in the investigative area is that no agency will take responsibility for neglect and abuse investigations, with the result that children are injured or killed. The other danger is that several agencies will rush in to handle these cases and interagency turf battles will erupt.

We ended the chapter by considering whether juvenile courts should deal with dependency, neglect, and abuse cases or whether other organizations are more suited to this task. A related concern is whether juvenile courts should have jurisdiction over adults involved in these cases.

Most of the juvenile court's attention is on youngsters accused of delinquency, and perhaps that is appropriate. However, as we have pointed out here and in chapter 5, juvenile courts must often disentangle moral, legal, and social problems involving nondelinquent youngsters, their parents or guardians, and other community institutions, such as the schools, social services, policing agencies, or mental health providers. The basis for this aspect of the court's jurisdiction is the *parens patriae* doctrine and the child-saving movement of the late nineteenth and early twentieth centuries. Today there seems to be other courts or agencies better equipped to handle these cases than juvenile courts. Nevertheless, juvenile courts continue to deal with dependency, neglect, and abuse cases literally on a daily basis.

We have no easy answers to the problems these cases create for the juvenile justice system nor for the personal grief these youths must suffer as that system tries to resolve their problems. And the debate goes on. All too frequently we must face the kinds of ethical, legal, and social dilemmas that confronted Officer Tom Ryan at the beginning of this chapter. What should he have done? What should we do?

CRITICAL REVIEW QUESTIONS

1. Looking back, what do you think about Officer Ryan's solution to the parental neglect—and possible abuse—case he encountered? Is there another resolution he could or should have taken?

2. The National Advisory Committee on Criminal Justice Standards and Goals listed six conditions that defined dependent and neglected children. Which one of these conditions is an officer in the field best equipped to determine exists? Which one, in all likelihood, would challenge the skills of the best-prepared police officer? Explain your choices.

3. How can we reconcile the family preservation movement and the concept of least restrictive placement with (a) the differing views of the parents' roles in creating the problem child and (b) the research on family structure (that is, single- versus two-parent families), family stress, and children's mental health?

4. Can you think of any reasons why there are so many different definitions of child neglect and abuse? Why is it troubling to have so many definitions? Do the definitions presented in the chapter clarify matters or muddy the waters?

5. Is poverty an excuse for physical neglect? No matter how you answer this question, provide support for your position.

6. If neglect is an omission or failure to do something, and this includes physical neglect, emotional neglect, and educational neglect, isn't it possible that at some time or another, nearly everyone has been the victim of neglect? What, then, distinguishes the family encountered by Officer Ryan from the rest of us?

7. Here's a hard one: Rank from the most unacceptable to the most acceptable the four forms of physical abuse, recognizing that society condones none of them. How did you come up with your ranking? Does your ranking system accommodate the varying degrees of abuse within each major category?

8. What statistic about child maltreatment in the United States did you find most shocking? What correlate of maltreatment did you find most amenable to correction? That is, where can we spend our child protective services dollars to get the best return?

9. We discuss seven groups or individuals with the duty or responsibility to report child maltreatment. Review them and provide the themes or elements common to the reporting responsibilities of each.

10. A number of possible solutions are proposed for the issue of juvenile court jurisdiction over nondelinquent children. Are any of these alternatives available in your community? Which one do you think has the greatest potential to reduce the burden on the already overtaxed juvenile court system?

RECOMMENDED READINGS

Chesney-Lind, Meda, and Randall G. Shelden (2003). *Girls, Delinquency, and Juvenile Justice*, 3rd ed. Belmont, CA: Wadsworth. This volume primarily focuses on why girls commit delinquent acts and why the juvenile justice system responds the way it does. Nevertheless, Chesney-Lind and Shelden provide a very thorough discussion of physical and sexual abuse and the role they play in the lives of adolescent girls.

Golden, Renny (1997). *Disposable Children: America's Welfare System*. Belmont, CA: Wadsworth. Golden's book provides a look into the history and contemporary operations of America's welfare system and its impact on the lives of children and their families. Of particular importance is the interface between two systems—juvenile justice and social welfare—that often are portrayed as being very distinct. This book also discusses the family preservation movement.

Levinson, David, ed. (2002). *Encyclopedia of Crime and Punishment*. Thousand Oaks, CA: Sage Publications. This four-volume encyclopedia provides brief articles on a number of criminal justice and juvenile justice topics. Particularly of interest to the topic of this chapter are the entries in Volume 1 on "Child Maltreatment," "Child Neglect," "Child Physical Abuse," and "Child Sexual Abuse." These short but scholarly entries provide students and others with summary information that serves as a useful starting place for the study of these topics.

KEY TERMS

Adoption Assistance and
  Child Welfare Act of 1980
American Bar Association (ABA)
CASA programs
Center on Children and the Law
Child Abuse Prevention and
  Treatment Act of 1974
child endangerment
child maltreatment
child protective services
Children's Defense Fund (CDF)
dependency
educational neglect

emotional abuse
emotional neglect
family preservation movement
general strain theory
guardian
guardians *ad litem*
indicated charges
in-home placement
least restrictive placement
neglect
nondelinquent youngsters
out-of-home placement
patriarchal society thesis

physical abuse	sexual abuse
physical neglect	substantiated charges
prenatal substance abuse	theory of differential oppression

NOTES

[1] One of the unfortunate realities of this topic is that more recent, complete national statistics are not available. Students might go online and search the Web for statistics that may be available for their states.

[2] See Gardner (2003:283–84) for a discussion of the "least drastic alternative" to incarceration notion.

chapter 10

GANGS

A SPECIAL JUVENILE JUSTICE PROBLEM

* * *

The two officers sat quietly in their patrol unit, its conspicuous profile hidden by the dark alley in which it was parked, the vehicle's hood just out of the light cast from a nearby streetlight. The older of the two officers sat behind the wheel. He didn't like to drive, but he didn't completely trust the driving skills of the rookie to his right. He had backed the unit into the alley about dusk on this quiet spring evening. They had just driven over from a nearby take-out Chinese restaurant and were taking a quick food break before resuming a crisscrossing patrol pattern of their assigned sector.

Across the street and slightly to their right, 10 teenage boys sat on the curb or played basketball in a nearby playground. Those youths not playing basketball were engaged in animated conversations. They did not appear to have noticed the police unit, or if they had, they didn't seem to care.

"Jeez, Bill," snarled Alvin Jones to his field training officer, "looks like we'll have to bust the lot of them gang-bangers. It's a weeknight, almost curfew, and I'll guarantee you none of them is more than 17."

Bill Straight, a veteran of 10 years on the force, finished his order of dim sum, crushed its paper container, and lofted it flawlessly out his open window into a nearby trash container. Two points, he thought to himself as the trash fell silently into the barrel. He wanted to straighten out this rookie but thought better of it, and he started to work on his fortune cookie. Maybe the numbers printed on the back would come in handy when he placed his bet on the lotto this weekend.

"Come on," continued A. J., "they're beggin' for us to do somethin'. What d'ya say we . . ."

"Chill, A. J.," interrupted Bill, his voice almost a whisper. "Look," he continued, "those kids aren't gang members. And I really don't want to process a dozen juvie complaints tonight."

"Not gang-bangers? Look at their clothes. And they've been flashing gang signs at each other all night. I think I know a bunch of gang-bangers when I see them." Officer

Straight took a deep breath, sucked the remaining bits of his meal from between his widely spaced teeth, and turned his considerable girth toward the rookie sitting next to him. "First of all, those kids don't belong to any local gang. The clothes are all wrong, more like something you'd see on television than on gang kids from this neighborhood. Second, the age is all wrong: They're way too young. All core members of the K-Street Warriors—the KSW's the big gang for six square blocks—are three years older than those kids. Could be wannabe gangsta kids, but I think they just want to look tough. You know, posturing for their friends, lookin' cool." Officer Straight paused for a moment to let the probationary officer absorb what he'd just told him; then he continued, never changing the inflection of his voice, never sounding preachy or condescending. "And you know what's most important?" he asked rhetorically. "Those kids ain't broken the law. And I can't see how they plan to do anything that would make me get my big butt outta this unit. If we leave right now, we'll never even see 'em breaking curfew."

As if to punctuate his last statement, Bill started up the police unit, eased it into gear and out of the alley, turning right. As he slowly passed the group of youngsters across the empty street, Bill turned on the unit's rooftop lights and dropped his left hand down below the window, flashing the KSW sign. One of the youngsters returned the gesture, while several others dropped to the ground, convulsing with laughter. A. J., oblivious to what was transpiring, stared out the front window of the unit. "I wonder where he learned all that stuff about gangs," he said, more to himself than to his partner. "They sure didn't teach us that in the academy."

* * *

Was Officer Straight right or wrong? What is the truth about youth gangs? Are all gangs law enforcement problems? How long has society had to deal with gangs? What are we doing about them? Annual reports released by the National Youth Gang Center provide an ongoing assessment of the extent of the nation's gang problem. The 2002 report concludes that roughly 731,500 individuals are in the nation's 21,500 gangs (Egley and Major, 2004). No state is gang-free; few large cities are gang-free. Gangs are not just a big-city problem and may be found in rural areas (Mays, Winfree, and Jackson, 1993; Weisheit and Wells, 2004). However, for the most part, gangs form in major urban areas and the small cities and suburbs surrounding urban areas (Egley, 2002; Egley and Major, 2004). Nevertheless, 27% of the jurisdictions with populations of 2,500 to 49,999 reported youth gang problems in 2002, as did 12% of rural county police and sheriff's departments (Egley and Major, 2004).

According to the National Youth Gang Center, the 10 states with the most gangs are (in order) California, Texas, Illinois, Colorado, Arizona, Florida, Missouri, Washington, Oregon, and Utah. The 10 states with the most gang members are (in order) California, Illinois, Texas, Ohio, Indiana, New Mexico, Arizona, Florida, Nevada, and Minnesota.[1] Few of you were probably surprised by California's appearance as first on both lists, and that Arizona, Illinois, and Texas also made both lists. But what about Colorado, Oregon, and Utah as states with the most gangs? Or how about New Mexico, Indiana, and Minnesota as states with the most gang members?

Anyone who follows news accounts about youth gangs might assume that they are a relatively modern-day phenomenon. A quick glance at the juvenile delinquency literature, however, reveals that gangs in one form or another have existed for most of our nation's history, and the early part of the twentieth century was a golden era of gang research.

THE GOLDEN ERA OF GANG STUDIES

One interesting feature of gang research in the 1920s and 1930s is that virtually all of it occurred in cities like Chicago, New York, and Boston. This has left the lasting public impression that gangs are largely, if not exclusively, a big-city problem. Furthermore, many of the early delinquency researchers employed personal interviews and direct observations, a technique called **field research** (Thrasher, 1927; Ashbury, 1928; Whyte, 1943). These early works focused on description of the gang phenomenon as much as on its explanation. For example, Herbert Ashbury (1928) described life in the Five Points, the Irish and Italian neighborhood of New York City that was home to many of the most notorious mobsters of the 1920s, including Paul Kelly, Lucky Luciano, and Al Capone. Ashbury provided rich and detailed descriptions of the area's gangs and youthful misconduct. In so doing, he made an important distinction between youths who found a home and social support in the street gangs and criminals who organized into gangs as a means of escaping the crushing poverty of the Five Points.

William Foote Whyte's (1943) classic field study of a Boston street corner captures more than the youth gang members' illegal activities. Whyte vividly portrays the daily lives of a group of Italian-American young men, whose quest for a better life was put to the test by the Great Depression's grinding poverty. Some of these young adults, called college boys, squarely addressed life's adversities through legitimate means, such as education and hard work. Corner boys, by contrast, facing the same challenges, engaged in the slum neighborhood's illegal activities, largely by participating in widespread gambling enterprises.

Field research was a hallmark of the University of Chicago's Sociology Department, and many of the gang and delinquency studies conducted before World War II—before the growth of the social survey—relied upon this journalistic-like fact-finding method. For example, Clifford R. Shaw wrote *The Jack-Roller: A Delinquent Boy's Own Story* (1931) and *Brothers in Crime* (1938), two highly individualistic accounts. Frederick Thrasher's (1927) *The Gang: A Study of 1,313 Gangs in Chicago*, a massive study of Chicago-area juvenile groups, stands as the wellspring for later generations of gang researchers.[2] Thrasher, a former newspaper reporter, employed an anti-psychological approach to youth gangs, a view that stressed Shaw and McKay's (1942) ideas about delinquency as social phenomena with origins in group conflict. While Thrasher emphasized that most Chicago gangs originated as amorphous, ill-defined groups largely of boys, conflicts with other groups often helped unify the groups—essentially creating the gangs themselves—and defined the gangs' territories. As Thrasher observed: "To become a true gang the group as a whole must . . . meet some hostile element which precipitates conflict . . . . Con-

Theoretical Reflections
The State of Gang Theory in the 1950s and 1960s

Albert Cohen, literally a student of both Robert Merton (anomie theory) and Edwin Sutherland (differential association theory), believed that the same culture that created prosocial youngsters created delinquent ones. Some lower-class youths, held up to the middle-class measuring rod of success, face failure. They subsequently turn the middle-class value system on its head and, in rejecting it, find others who express similar levels of frustration and ambivalence. Like ideas about gang formation in the 1930s and 1940s, Cohen's **reaction formation theory** stresses that gangs provide the status and self-respect missing in their members' lives. "The delinquent subculture," Cohen wrote, "with its characteristics of non-utilitarianism, malice, and negativism, provides an alternative status system and justifies, for those who participate in it, hostility and aggression against the sources of their frustration" (1955:26).

Richard A. Cloward and Lloyd Ohlin updated and expanded on themes first used by Chicago gang researchers. Ohlin had been one of Sutherland's students and was a University of Chicago graduate; Cloward studied under Merton at Columbia. They combined Merton's anomie theory with the differential structures element of the Chicago school's belief in the significance of social transmission to limit one's choices. The result was **differential opportunity theory**. Like Merton and Cohen, they emphasized the intense frustration felt by lower-class youths; however, its source was to be found in the disparities between what lower-class youngsters are led to believe is important and what they can reasonably achieve. Like Sutherland, Cloward and Ohlin acknowledged that "criminal behavior is partially a function of opportunities to commit (that is, perform) specific classes of crime, such as embez-zlement, bank burglary, or illicit heterosexual intercourse" (1960:147). In other words, illegitimate opportunities were differentially available, because not everyone had access to the same illegal means to goals for tangible success. That is, upper-class criminals use illegitimate means that are unavailable to those in the lower classes, and vice versa.

Walter B. Miller, a University of Chicago-trained anthropologist, differs from Cohen and other strain theorists in that he does not subscribe to the idea that lower-class youths engage in delinquent acts simply to flout middle-class values. On the basis of fieldwork studies in Roxbury, Massachusetts, Miller wrote that lower-class delinquents adhere to behaviors that are *supported within their subculture* (for example, getting into trouble, being tough, taking risks, and expressing autonomy from external controls). Often, but not always, these behaviors—and accompanying values—place them in conflict with formal control agents, including police and school administrators. The focal concerns of the lower class—actual behaviors as opposed to abstract values—represent a patterning of concerns unique to lower-class culture. These focal concerns can exist, claims Miller (1958:19), only because the lower class values and rewards them. "No cultural patterning as well-established as the practice of illegal acts by members of the lower class corner groups could persist if buttressed by negative, hostile, or rejecting motives; its principal motivational support, as in the case of any persisting cultural tradition, derives from a positive effort to achieve what is valued within that tradition, and to conform to its explicit and implicit norms."

Sources: Cohen (1955); Cloward and Ohlin (1960); Lilly et al. (1995); Miller (1958).

flict, as already indicated, comes in clashes with other gangs or with common enemies such as the police, park officials, and so on" (1927:50).

By the early 1940s, pop culture, criminal justice practitioners, and academics alike shared an enduring picture of youth gangs in the United States. Gangs were an urban problem; they were caused by the problems of large cities—rapid urban growth; an aging, deteriorating, or decaying city services infrastructure; and large clusters of immigrants and their children. The gangs engaged in violence for its own sake and as a means of securing and protecting their territory, or turf. From the 1930s *Dead-End Kids* movies to the 1950s Broadway musical (and later a movie) *West Side Story*, the public image of youth gangs largely was one of ethnic youths, seeking in the gang a missing sense of neighborhood community and solidarity.

GANGS AND EVOLVING DELINQUENCY THEORY

In postwar America, gangs took on an almost mythical quality in the popular media. Youth gangs—the Sharks (a gang largely of Polish-American youths) and the Jets (a gang of Puerto Rican youths)—were portrayed in somewhat romantic terms in the movie version of *West Side Story*. During this era, other motion pictures featured youths in rebellion (for example, Marlon Brando in *The Wild Ones* and James Dean in *Rebel Without a Cause*), and while many of these youngsters were presumed to be deviant, their activities were seen as a natural part of growing up.

This focus on how children develop led to an explosion of gang-related theories in the 1950s and early 1960s. Whereas the rich tapestry created by Thrasher, Whyte, and Shaw linked gangs to social conditions such as social disorganization, by the 1950s **social disorganization theory** had largely been relegated to the theoretical trash heap. But anomie theory, along with other social-psychological and social-cultural theories, gave new insights into gangs and gang membership. These studies were less about gangs than about understanding problem behavior, much of it associated with youth gangs. For example, in *Delinquent Boys: The Culture of the Gang*, Albert Cohen describes his work as an attempt to be "consistent with the 'known facts' about delinquent subcultures" (1955:170). The goal was to state a theory that could be tested.

Richard Cloward and Lloyd Ohlin's *Delinquency and Opportunity: A Theory of Delinquent Gangs* proposed a theory that was a merger of the anomie and cultural transmission traditions. After a careful presentation of **differential opportunity theory**, Cloward and Ohlin searched existing research for verification of three types of gangs predicted by their theory, examples of what they called **subcultural differentiation**. That is, different neighborhoods should lead to different gang patterns. **Criminal gangs**, groups organized around purely illegal pursuits, they speculated, exist in neighborhoods characterized by close bonding between different age levels of offenders and integration between criminal and conventional elements in those neighborhoods. **Conflict gangs**, formed to engage in fights between competing groups, emerge in neighborhoods that are the opposite of those supporting criminal gangs; that is, neighborhoods with high levels of transience and instability, and weak social controls.

Finally, **retreatist gangs** exemplify Cloward and Ohlin's idea of the **double failure**: Individuals unsuccessful at both the legitimate and illegitimate opportunity structures organize for the pursuit of drugs and other hedonistic pursuits. Retreatist gangs are in neighborhoods not unlike those in which conflict gangs emerge. Retreatists face not only unique social structural forces, but also new associations and values supportive of drug use. It is interesting to note that Cloward and Ohlin (1960:203) predicted that delinquency "will become increasingly aggressive and violent in the future as a result of the disintegration of slum organization."

Gang researchers during the postwar period expanded criminological thinking about delinquency by focusing on gang delinquency. For example, Cloward and Ohlin's work became part of the **Juvenile Delinquency Prevention and Youth Offenses Control Act of 1961**, a federal government effort to reduce delinquency in major cities. While some programs ended in failure, the fact that a theory helped guide a practical response to the gang problem resonates with the ties between social disorganization theory and the **Chicago Area Project** (discussed in chapter 11).

This body of work contributed to another legacy of gang delinquency. Cohen, Cloward, and Ohlin described the locus of gang delinquency in the lower classes, whether it was due to conflict or subcultural values. Perhaps the best articulation of this emphasis is found in a 1958 article by Walter B. Miller entitled, "The Lower Class Culture as a Generating Milieu of Gang Delinquency." Miller maintained that the actions disavowed by middle-class society's social control agents are often endorsed by the lower-class culture. This emphasis on gang delinquency among the lower class, whether or not it constituted a class bias of the researchers, became a fixture of gang studies for more than 20 years. While the golden era of gang research emphasized the immigrant connection, in postwar America gangs were viewed largely as a lower-class concern.

The debate about directionality continued throughout the 1960s. Short and Strodtbeck (1965) "argued that poverty creates socially disabled male youths who feel comfortable only with their fellow gang members" (Inciardi, Horowitz, and Pottieger, 1993:15). Klein (1968), by contrast, shifted the emphasis to middle-class institutional responses to the poor. This transition linked gang studies to a 1970s theoretical perspective that suggested we look at the power of formal social agencies to affect a person's self-concept, or labeling theory (Inciardi et al., 1993:16). By the late 1970s, gang research was largely missing from the social science journals and books. The 1980s would change all that.

RESURGENCE OF GANGS IN THE 1980S

In the 1980s gangs seemed to reappear. As Walter B. Miller noted: "Youth gangs of the 1980s and 1990s are more numerous, more prevalent, and more violent than in the 1950s, probably more so than at any time in the country's history" (1990:263). What caused this resurgence? Were these totally new gangs, or was it simply a resurfacing of gangs that always had existed—but out of the public spotlight?

Two factors in particular seem to explain the renewed interest in gangs. First, gang violence, especially in southern California, graduated from the era of chain-

and-knife fights to an epoch of fully automatic firearms. As gangs such as the Bloods and the Crips battled for physical and economic turf, armed conflict marked the emergence of "new" gangs, and the term *drive-by shooting* began to appear regularly in news accounts (Sanders, 1994:65–84). The second factor that must be acknowledged is the attention paid to gangs by various news media and the entertainment industry. News organizations gave more coverage to gang activity, and with public interest and fascination came a ready market for movies such as *Colors, New Jack City,* and *Boyz in the Hood.* Thus, the public was inundated with fact and fiction about gangs and gang activity around the country.

In this chapter we separate fact from fiction in discussing the state of gang activity in the United States. In the following sections we will consider the definitions of what constitutes a gang, the organization and structural arrangements of many types of youth gangs, the ecological or environmental factors associated with gangs, and the individual motivations of the youngsters who join youth gangs. Subsequent sections will address the ways communities react to gangs, two of the controversial factors associated with gangs (gender and race or ethnicity), the important question of the link between drugs and gangs, and finally, the concern over how we can respond most appropriately to gangs. In the end we hope we can answer some of the most common and persistent questions regarding gangs in contemporary juvenile justice.

DEFINITIONS OF GANGS

Defining what constitutes a gang would seem to be an easy task. Almost 80 years ago Thrasher (1927:45) offered a descriptive definition of a gang, after noting, "no two gangs are alike." He suggested that gangs share a number of common characteristics, including a spontaneous origin, intimate face-to-face interactions, attachment to a home territory, and, to become a "true gang," a threat that is met by force or the threat of force. However, as many social scientists have discovered, providing definitions for gangs is not such a straightforward task (see Curry and Decker, 2003; Esbensen, Winfree, He, and Taylor, 2001). This section deals with the elements that are considered essential for any gang definition.

To begin with, there can be vast differences in explaining what constitutes a gang. Thus, it is essential to remember that the definition for *what* constitutes a gang is dependent on who does the defining. Social scientists and criminal justice practitioners sometimes view the same phenomena and come up with different descriptions or ways to define what they have observed. Gangs and gang behavior provide one of those points of divergence. A few examples drawn from each camp will illustrate the distinctions.

Social scientists provide one source of gang definitions. Miller (1975:121) created one of the most frequently quoted definitions of a gang as a

> self-formed association of peers, bound together by mutual interests, with identifiable leadership, well-developed lines of authority, and other organizational features, who act in concert to achieve a specific purpose or purposes which

generally include the conduct of illegal activity and control over a particular territory, facility, or type of enterprise.

David Curry and Irving Spergel say that a gang "engages in a range of crime but significantly more violence within a framework of norms and values in respect to mutual support, conflict relations with other gangs, and a tradition often of turf, colors, signs, and symbols" (1988:382). In conducting the National Youth Gang Survey, the National Youth Gang Center asked law enforcement agencies to respond by identifying "a group of youths or young adults in your jurisdiction that you or other responsible persons in your agency or community are willing to identify or classify as a 'gang'" (Egley and Major, 2004). Other social scientists (see Horowitz, 1990) warn that to define some groups as "in" is necessarily to define other groups as "out."

The second major group of gang definitions comes from law enforcement or other criminal justice agencies. Jackson and McBride, two law enforcement experts, define a gang as "a group of people that form an allegiance for a common purpose, and engage in unlawful or criminal activity" (1992:20). A National Institute of Justice report entitled *Street Gangs: Current Knowledge and Strategies* notes that a typical law enforcement definition stresses that a gang "is an ongoing, organized association of three or more persons, whether formal or informal, who have a common name or common signs, **colors**, or symbols, and members or associates who individually or collectively engage in or have engaged in criminal activity" (Conly, Kelly, Mahanna, and Warner, 1993:6). This report adopted the definition of street gangs as "groups of youths and young adults who have engaged in a sufficient amount of antisocial activity to warrant attention by the criminal justice system" (Conly et al., 1993:7).

However, as Esbensen et al. (2001) discovered, a great deal of gang research and many law enforcement classification schemes have relied on self-definitions, or what they call "claiming." In other words, "If a person has claimed to be a gang member, that has been adequate grounds for inclusion in a study of gangs or for special prosecution by the justice system" (Esbensen et al., 2001:123). The research by Esbensen and his colleagues was based on a data set derived from the national evaluation of the G.R.E.A.T. Program, and these researchers concluded that self-definition is a powerful predictor of gang involvement. Nevertheless, from the various definitions that have been provided over the years we will try to extract some of the common elements.

AGE

As at least one definition notes, and as many people studying gangs realize, contemporary gangs include members who vary in age from preteens to those in their middle to late twenties. Throughout this chapter we will note the presence and role of adults and young adults in gang activity. Given the focus of this book, however, most of our discussion of gangs will be confined to those individuals who are defined by statutes as juveniles.

NUMBER

Perhaps the issue of number of members is the easiest one to address. To be a gang there must be two or more members. In fact, as we have already seen, some law enforcement agency definitions specify that gangs must have three or more members. Usually this is not a problem since most gangs will have anywhere from six or eight up to hundreds of members. So, in considering the issue of numbers, we can say that all gangs are groups, but not all groups are gangs.

ACTIVITY

One of the things that distinguishes gangs from other groups is the nature of their activity. As we have seen in police definitions, the stress is on illegal activity. That is, gangs are said to exist to engage in, or to facilitate, illegal activity. While this is self-evident to many observers, there is not universal agreement; we shall see later that this element may be a little more elusive than some people would imagine.

ORGANIZATION

With regard to the issue of organization or structure, which we will treat at greater length later, it may be difficult to distinguish gangs from other groups. Gangs may be formal or informal, and often we say of gangs that there may be a loose organizational structure, but that there are individuals within the gang of different perceived status. In this way, gangs are less well differentiated than the Boy Scouts or Girl Scouts, but there is more status differentiation than there might be in a playgroup or clique.

OUTWARD IDENTIFIERS

For most people, outward identifiers are really the factors that distinguish gangs from other groups. As a general rule these outward identifiers are meant to communicate a very specific message: I am a gang member. By outward identifiers we mean, for example, items of clothing such as those with certain sports teams' logos. As an extension of this, many gangs in the 1980s chose particular colors to signify gang membership. Of course, two of the most conspicuous examples were the Bloods (who wore red) and the Crips (who wore blue). Other gangs have used colors or combinations of colors to identify gang subsets, proclaim their allegiance, and provide for quick visual identification of members.

However, focusing on colors as an outward identifier can be misleading. Starbuck, Howell, and Lindquist (2001) note that as "hybrid gangs" have emerged in the past two decades, unique gang status has become more difficult to distinguish. They maintain that the

> "Hybrid gang culture" is characterized by members of different racial/ethnic groups participating in a single gang, individuals participating in multiple gangs, unclear rule or codes of conduct, symbolic associations with more than one well-established gang (e.g., use of colors and graffiti from different gangs), cooperation of rival gangs in criminal activity, and frequent mergers of small gangs. (Starbuck et al., 2001:1)

We will treat the issue of hybrid gangs more fully later in the chapter.

In addition to these symbols, contemporary gangs use visual identifiers such as jewelry, tattoos, and hand signs. Gang jewelry might involve gold necklaces with dollar signs on them, certain numbers (such as 13), or the hood ornaments from a luxury automobile such as a Cadillac or a Mercedes-Benz. The use of jewelry by gang members is meant not only to provide a gang identifier but also to demonstrate something of the gang member's wealth or power.

Tattoos are particularly prominent among Hispanic streets gangs (Jackson and McBride, 1992:78–80) but also are used by black and Asian gangs. The tattoos may display the gang name, the wearer's nickname or *placa*, a female's name, or certain religious symbols (such as a cross, a crown of thorns, or the Virgin of Guadalupe). At times tattoos commemorate a fallen gang member or contain a slogan attesting to the gang's power or prominence. In some gangs tattoos are very common and may be part of the ritual of attaining certain ranks or stature within the gang. Many of the tattoos seen on older gang members have been obtained during incarceration and are less skillful, colorful, or artistic than commercially available tattoos.

Hand signs typically consist of stylized numbers or letters. They may involve a series of characters and may also involve the use of fingers, hands, and arms (Jackson and McBride, 1992:80–83). For instance, the display of a 2-2 (two fingers on each hand) may indicate members of a 22nd Street gang in some city. The letter C often has been associated with the Crips. Multiple signs allow for fuller identifica-

All gangs are groups, but not all groups are gangs. In order to achieve accurate definitions we must often look beyond the outward identifiers—such as clothing, tattoos, and hand signs—and focus on the illegal activities that are associated with gangs and gang behavior.

tion of the gang or set. Sets or cliques (***klickas*** in Hispanic gangs) generally are age-graded subsets of larger gangs.

Hand signs serve several purposes for gangs. First, they are often flashed (or "thrown," in gang jargon) to signify the gang members' presence. Second, hand signs may be displayed for intimidation purposes. This is done in certain contested areas, such as playgrounds, where members of several gangs may be present at one time. Finally, the flashing of hand signs may be considered sufficiently provocative that a physical confrontation may result. In fact, in many areas it is the supreme insult to have one gang throwing their signs in another gang's territory.

We should also add two facts about clothing and other outward gang identifiers. First, some people innocently wear the colors or the clothing, shoes, and hats associated with a particular gang. This act alone, if viewed by members of rival gangs or even the associated gang, could conceivably result in harm or even death to the wearer. Wearing certain types of jewelry and throwing signs can lead to tragic misidentification as a gang member. The innocent display of gang paraphernalia can also lead to unwanted contacts with law enforcement agencies or citizen groups who view such outward identifiers as probable cause of gang membership. Second, *wannabes*[3]—adolescents who want to be in a gang or want others to think that they are in a gang—further confuse the picture. Some youths who want to be associated with the bad-boy gang image may adopt gang clothing and other external identifiers.

TURF OR TERRITORIALITY

Turf may be more or less important for a particular gang. Many New York, Chicago, and Los Angeles gangs have carefully defined turfs, and disputes may arise over control of a particular neighborhood for various reasons. For the gangs that claim control over a certain geographical region, another gang's intrusion or disrespect will not be tolerated. Contests over turf control often result in gang wars.

RECRUITMENT AND INITIATION

Some initiation ritual is typically the last step toward formal gang membership. Gangs vary in the degree to which they recruit members (Conly et al., 1993). In some localities recruiting goes on for new members and is especially prominent in the middle and junior high schools (Curry and Spergel, 1992; Thompson and Jason, 1988; Vigil, 1988). Gangs may seek out youngsters who are known for their fighting ability or who otherwise seem fearless. For some well-established gangs, recruitment may be unnecessary. These groups may have a steady stream of youngsters who want to become members.

On the basis of field interviews with gang members in a New Mexico border community, Mays, Winfree, and Jackson (1993) found that the decision to join a gang is not always a conscious choice. That is, some of these youngsters are following the example of older siblings or other family members, or they find themselves part of groups (that is, gangs) of neighborhood youths with whom they have grown up. The motivations for gang membership will be discussed at length. For the time being, however, we return to the issue of initiation.

Virtually all youth gangs have some rite of passage for those who would be members. The initiation ritual is a test of toughness and loyalty and a way to keep out those who might not be dependable in a tight spot. There are several types of initiation, and in some cases a gang might employ more than one.

First, a very common initiation ritual involves being **jumped in** (Conly et al., 1993; M. Harris, 1994; Winfree et al., 1992). Gang members will administer a beating—with fists, feet, or whatever else they might choose—to the prospective member. The youth seeking membership is expected to fight back vigorously, not fall down, and not cry or show any signs of pain. One member will loudly count to some predetermined number while the beating goes on. If the prospect falls or fails to promptly get up, the counting may start over again. The prospective members are told, "Blood in, blood out": They must endure a beating to join, but they will be subjected to repeated beatings, or worse, if they decide to leave. However, as we will see later in the chapter, getting out of a gang may not be as difficult for some youngsters as it typically has been portrayed.

Second, a few gangs may require prospective members to commit a crime with current members as witnesses. The crime may be one of the recruit's choosing, but often it is specified by gang members. The criminal act might consist of some kind of theft, but in several instances shootings and assaults have been required. For example, a youth gang operating in southern New Mexico in the late 1980s required prospective members to commit a rape (witnessed by others) in order to secure full membership.

A third type of initiation may be less formal than the other two. In such a case the prospective member is a close friend or family member of a long-time and well-respected member. The current member must vouch for the prospect's worthiness, and the gang may observe the prospect's fearlessness or *locura* (that is, craziness), perhaps for an extended time (Vigil, 1988).

GANG ORGANIZATION

Gang organizational style can take several forms. Although there is no single approach that fully describes all gangs, perhaps one of the best ways to understand gang organization is to examine the typology proposed by Carl Taylor (1990). Taylor says that gangs are either *scavenger, territorial,* or *corporate* in nature. In this section we will explore all three types of gangs and what the various types imply about gang activity, organization, and leadership styles.

A **scavenger gang** is the most loosely organized and least hierarchical gang. Taylor (1990) says that these groups generally are composed of younger teens, many of whom have school problems. These gangs almost exclusively are made up of low-intelligence and low-achievement youngsters, and typically no one is recognized as being in control. With scavengers, different members may strive for, or achieve, leadership responsibilities for different activities. Because of their loose organization and lack of consistent leadership, scavenger gangs may dissolve and re-form several times. They may not even stay together long enough to develop a gang name or to adopt some of the outward symbols associated with gang membership.

Scavengers typically lack a unifying purpose. They may be committed to just hanging out, and this makes a lot of their criminal activities unorganized and spontaneous. They tend to be opportunistic, to strike crime targets at hand as opposed to carefully planning a crime over time. They have very little that binds them together over the long term; thus most scavenger gangs never progress further in terms of organization or achievement.

The second type of gang discussed by Taylor (1990) is the **territorial gang**. These gangs are much better organized and are more purposeful in their criminality than the scavenger gangs. Some people might suspect that if members of a scavenger gang stayed together long enough, the group would evolve into a territorial gang. This might be true, but it is not inevitable.

Territorial gangs exist to protect a geographic area (neighborhood, or turf). However, the reasons for this protection may differ depending on the gang's individual circumstances. Some territorial gangs exist essentially as home defense forces. They provide their street or neighborhood and particular gang members with protection from neighboring gangs. More than likely, however, the protection is not simply over space, but over economic issues as well. For instance, some territorial gangs have well-defined turfs over which they exercise economic control for certain criminal activities, such as drug sales. Therefore, their protective efforts are designed to maximize their economic monopoly while keeping out rival monetary enterprises.

Territorial gangs tend to be governed by a small leadership core, as opposed to being controlled by one person. There may be a president or chief, but in most instances there will be a ruling council composed of the oldest, most experienced, and most widely accepted gang members. Many of the leaders actually will be young adults, not teenage members.

To enter into the leadership core, these members will have been initiated—as we mentioned earlier, this is sometimes called being "jumped in" or **ranked in**. Most will have committed serious crimes, and many of them will have served time in either a juvenile facility, county jail, or state prison. As is true in scouting programs nationwide, certain "merit badges" qualify one for a gang leadership position. Some gangs will designate the leaders as **O.G.s**, "original gangsters" or "old gangsters." Hispanic gangs often refer to their leaders as the *veteranos* (veterans).

Outside the leadership core in most territorial gangs are the associate members. This group consists of youngsters in their middle to late teens who have undergone the full gang initiation process and are starting to build a reputation within the gang. They typically have committed crimes, but they may not have served time like the leadership core. Associates constitute the gang's largest group, and in many instances they have been compared to soldiers. They are responsible for carrying out the bulk of gang activities, and the most dangerous associates aspire to leadership positions.

Hispanic gangs often refer to some of the most risk-taking members as *vatos locos*, or crazy guys (Jackson and McBride, 1992; Vigil, 1988). A few of these members add a dimension of danger to the gang's reputation. If the gang has too many locos, the danger level may increase, and so will the level of scrutiny the gang may receive from the police. Moreover, having too many of these members creates instability in the gang's organization and operations.

The outer ring of the territorial gang's organizational structure contains the youngest members. Sometimes these youngsters are as young as 6 or 8 years old and will be called **juniors** or **pee-wees**. They hang around the gang, either by invitation or because a family member is a gang member, but they have not undergone the initiation ritual. Juniors may dress like gang members and use the gang jargon, but they have not yet proved themselves worthy of membership. Occasionally, law enforcement or school officials will dismiss these youngsters as being just a bunch of wannabes. However, it is important to recognize that some wannabes become gang members by proving that they are fearless fighters and risk takers. Therefore, some of the most outrageous gang activities may be undertaken by the youngest members and others who want to establish their status within the gang.

Taylor's (1990) final type of gang is the **corporate gang**. In some ways, these gangs are not a concern of the juvenile justice system at all. Most of Taylor's corporate gangs would fit the definition of organized crime, and they typically consist entirely of adult members (see Shelden, Tracy, and Brown, 2004). Adolescents are not a part of these organizations and are not considered for membership because they are too immature and unpredictable. Corporate gangs are governed by the traditional pyramid hierarchy associated with many noncriminal organizations (the military services, universities, and the Roman Catholic Church, as examples). These groups exist for the purpose of making money. They are exclusively economic enterprises and the emphasis is on maximizing profits through both legal and illegal means. Corporate gang membership generally is earned over a long time period and may be based on some special skill or on family membership; additionally, a current member may vouch for the prospective member's trustworthiness.

ENVIRONMENTAL FACTORS

Gangs might initially appear to be a pervasive problem in the United States. However, a comparison of results from recent National Youth Gang Surveys supports three general observations: (1) the number of communities experiencing youth gang problems actually has decreased since 1996 (Egley, 2002); (2) between 2000 and 2002 the number of gangs decreased from about 24,500 to 21,500 (Egley, 2002; Egley and Major, 2004); and (3) the number of gang members—while still substantial—between 2000 and 2002 decreased from about 750,000 to 731,500.

The 2002 National Youth Gang Survey had 2,182 responding agencies (out of 2,563 originally contacted), and every city with a population of 250,000 or more reported having youth gang problems. Furthermore, 87% of the departments in cities with populations between 100,000 and 249,999, 38% of suburban county agencies, 27% of small city agencies, and 12% of rural county agencies indicated that they were experiencing youth gang problems (Egley and Major, 2004). Consequently, we might ask: What are the environmental factors most frequently associated with gangs and gang activity? Several answers have appeared in the gang literature.

Table 10.1 illustrates two important points related to the location of gangs. First, among those jurisdictions reporting 20 or more gangs, the vast majority had populations in excess of 100,000 people. In fact, jurisdictions with less than 50,000

Table 10.1   Average Number of Youth Gangs and Gang Members per Jurisdiction, by Population Size, 1996, 1997, and 1998

	1996		1997		1998	
Population Size	Gangs	Gang Members	Gangs	Gang Members	Gangs	Gang Members
250,000 or more	80	5,894	85	5,120	83	4,465
100,000–249,999	32	1,016	22	764	21	712
50,000–99,999	10	352	9	289	10	307
25,000–49,999	6	134	6	128	7	151
10,000–24,999	4	84	5	85	5	88
Less than 10,000	3	37	4	55	3	41
Overall average	15	741	14	615	14	559

Source: National Youth Gang Center (2000).

population reported 10 or fewer gangs in 1996, 1997, and 1998. Thus, jurisdictions with large numbers of gangs tended to have large population bases. Second, from all of the jurisdictions responding to the National Youth Gang surveys, the average number of gangs was 14 or 15 for the years displayed. These figures suggest that in most jurisdictions with visible gang activity, the number of gangs causing problems is relatively small; however, a few very large reporting areas have dozens and dozens of gangs. Indeed, three relatively large states—California, Texas, and Illinois—collectively accounted for one reported gang in four and over one-half of all the nation's gang members (National Youth Gang Center, 1997:10,16).

Additionally, much of the gang literature points to the fact that poverty—or at least economic distress of some form—is related to gangs (Shelden et al., 2004; see also Hill, Lui, and Hawkins, 2001). Poverty can affect gang dynamics in several ways. For example, families may be under economic stresses when husbands and fathers are unemployed or only marginally employed. Such a situation may result in the father's abandoning the wife and children. Sometimes both parents and even the older children have to work to provide for the basic necessities. With both parents working and few child-care provisions in some communities, the children are left to fend for themselves.

This lack of surveillance by parents or some other responsible adult figure is another factor associated with gangs. When the parents do not or cannot provide consistent supervision over their children, the streets become socializing agents. Older children provide guidance in these situations, and this guidance may be directed toward neighborhood gangs or groups that may evolve into gangs. Again, many criminologists have observed that parental supervision is crucial to all forms of youthful misconduct, not just gang behavior. Gottfredson and Hirschi (1990), in perhaps the most recent and cogent statement of these ideas, suggest that by the age of 10, poor parental management (a result of poor parenting skills) leads to a predisposition to troublesome conduct, something they call **low self-control**.

Family structure is also an element, and it is related to both urban family economics and lack of surveillance. Very often people say that the lack of a father or father figure is a primary cause of gang involvement. The issue is not so simple. It may not be the lack of a dominant male figure in the home that contributes to gang involvement, but this may be a substantial factor when considered along with economic distress and the lack of supervision. It is also possible that family factors have an impact only in certain types of group-context delinquency or that the influence of the family on gang involvement differs by ethnic group (Winfree and Mays, 1996).

Neighborhood conditions also may contribute in some way to gang creation and persistence. Hagedorn (1991) examined poor African-American neighborhoods in Milwaukee, Wisconsin, that had persistent gang problems. He found that the loss of jobs and a shift from manufacturing to service jobs (what he calls **deindustrialization**) has resulted in members' staying in gangs longer and turning to drug dealing as a means of economic survival. Furthermore, he notes that, at least in the case of Milwaukee, "it is not the absence of working people that defines underclass neighborhoods but more the absence of effective social institutions" (Hagedorn, 1991:538).

Finally, **culture conflict** may also be a factor in the creation of certain kinds of gangs. This idea, first presented in a systematic fashion by Thorsten Sellin (1938), states what many people intuitively understand. An immigrant from a different culture, one that demands the extraction of an immediate and often violent sanction against those who violate certain subcultural norms, can face criminal action by an unsympathetic justice system. Sellin (1938) reports the case of a Sicilian father in New Jersey who kills his daughter's seducer in order to reestablish his family's honor. The father is surprised at the American justice system's stance on his culturally mandated response.

Vigil (1988, 1990) points to transitional communities and families as being especially susceptible to gang formation. In his examination of the Hispanic street gangs of East Los Angeles, he describes the *cholo* culture as being created when youngsters are caught between two cultures: their parents' and grandparents' traditional Mexican culture and the dominant Anglo culture of the United States. The conflict comes in clashes of language (Spanish versus English), values (traditional versus contemporary), socialization agents (the family and the church versus the streets), and the emphasis on material possessions. Vigil says that in response to this cultural conflict, youngsters develop their own set of values and form their own unique and blended culture.

In discussing the features associated with gangs, it is essential to note that in many of the most gang-prone localities in the United States there has been a breakdown in three traditional forces of socialization: the family, the schools, and the police (Goldstein and Huff, 1993). When socialization does not take place by these three institutions, gangs may move into the void to become a community's significant—if not primary—socializing agent.

THE DEMOGRAPHICS OF GANGS

After gangs have formed, we need to pay particular attention to the responses communities manifest in regard to the presence of gangs. In the following section we examine two demographic variables—gender and race or ethnicity—that often shape how the community responds to the real or imagined threats posed by youth gangs.

GENDER

Gang literature traditionally has done little to address the gender issue. Gangs are thought of as primarily male groups, and the 1998 National Youth Gang Survey (National Youth Gang Center, 2000) found nationally 92% of gang members were male. Additionally, recent research involving the Seattle Social Development Project (Hill et al., 2001) found that 90% of the program participants who joined a gang were male. As a result of this level of gender disparity, very few people have addressed the role played by females in gangs. There are some notable exceptions, however. Esbensen and Winfree (1998) conducted a multisite (11 diverse locations) study of 5,935 eighth-grade students and found that nearly 4 in 10 gang members were females; Freng and Winfree (2004) further discovered that almost 45% of the Hispanic females reported gang membership. Therefore, it is clear that youth gangs are not solely the domain of boys.

Moreover, Campbell (1990, 1991) has studied the unique roles played by females in youth gangs (see also Bjerregaard and Smith, 1993; M. Harris, 1994). At one level, females are auxiliaries of male gangs. In these types of arrangements, females are attached to the male gangs but they are not really part of the gangs' leadership or decision-making processes. Campbell (1990, 1991) found that male gang members hold stereotypical views of females, and females hold very traditional roles within the gangs: They are spies, decoys, lures, lookouts, and drug and weapon smugglers.

At the other extreme we find all-female gangs. These groups are typically confined to the largest urban areas, and even then they are somewhat rare. The all-female gang may form for various reasons, and certainly one of the primary reasons is the lack of leadership opportunities in the traditionally all-male gangs.

Esbensen and Huizinga, in their examination of the Denver Youth Survey, noted that "females are more involved in gangs than is generally acknowledged" (1993:571–72). They warn that while there may be greater female gang involvement than has been described by the news media, most females report lower levels of delinquent activity than their male counterparts. Therefore, while there have been reports of increasing involvement and more serious gang activity, there is little indication that we have a new, more virulent form of female gangster. What we do have are youngsters who have come from extremely chaotic and abusive home lives who seek affection and validation in the gang context. The result often is that these young women have children by and even marry male gang members and a family gang lifestyle is created or perpetuated (Conly et al., 1993).

RACE OR ETHNICITY

For all the controversy that surrounds the issue of gender in the discussion of gangs, nothing matches the response caused by raising questions of the degree to which gang activity is associated with certain races or ethnic groups. For instance, the 1998 National Youth Gang Survey found that in the United States 46% of gang members were identified as being Hispanic, 34% were African American, 12% were Caucasian, 6% were Asian, and 2% were from other racial or ethnic groups (National Youth Gang Center, 2000). Furthermore, Esbensen and Winfree's multi-site study of eighth-grade public school students confirms the stereotype of dispro-portionate minority-group participation in youth gangs; however, the fact that 25% of the gang members in the sample were Caucasian calls into question the relative lack of a nonminority focus in gang research (Esbensen and Winfree, 1998; see also Freng and Winfree, 2004). Thus, while there is nothing inherent in these groups that causes them to be more gang-prone, the research into youth gangs clearly points to certain unavoidable conclusions.

First, gangs exist in virtually all racial and ethnic groups, although the gangs in the United States that have received the most attention over the past two decades have been composed of either Hispanic or African-American youngsters (Hill et al., 2001; National Youth Gang Center, 2000; Shelden et al., 2004). This finding does not mean that no other types of gangs exist, but these two groups have been the focus of the bulk of the material published on gangs.

Second, there is some evidence of an increasing presence of what are being called "**hybrid gangs**" (see Starbuck et al., 2001). These are gangs composed of multiple racial or ethnic groups. Nevertheless, much of the evidence on gangs to date indicates that most are composed of only one racial or ethnic group, and one of the primary reasons for this is the largely segregated neighborhood compositions and housing patterns in many communities in the United States (see Shelden et al., 2004:276, 295).

Third, nonminority gangs have appeared with increasing frequency, and these gangs include hate groups, drug and heavy metal music groups, and graffiti-ori-ented groups. Neo-Nazi groups such as the **skinhead gangs** began to appear in some cities in the mid-1980s (Bushart, Craig, and Barnes, 1998; Shelden et al., 2004). These groups have been described as "anti-black, anti-gay, anti-Jewish, anti-Hispanic, anti-Asian, and anti-immigrant," and a few of these groups go so far as to openly advocate violence against minority groups (The Prejudice Institute, 2004; see also Anti-Defamation League, 1999).

Some youth groups committed to a lifestyle of drugs and heavy metal music have evolved into **stoner gangs**. Most sources agree that the name "stoner" came from the regular use of drugs and alcohol by many of these youngsters (Jackson and McBride, 1992:42–45). Wooden says that stoners have developed from merely antisocial youths to groups "increasingly implicated in violent street crimes and numerous homicides" (1995:158). A few of the stoners have become involved in Satanism, and some of their crimes are related to satanic rituals.

The final type of nonminority gang involves tagger **crews** or **posses** (Wooden, 1995:115–28). These are groups whose primary purpose is to place graffiti—partic-ularly their own or their crew's tag—in the most conspicuous places possible. Most of their criminal activity is vandalism, but a group of active taggers can create repeat removal or repair problems. Unlike traditional street gangs that use graffiti to mark territory and to communicate with other gangs, for taggers, placing the graffiti is an end unto itself.

Fourth, it is important to consider that race and ethnicity—rather than being causal factors—are related to other features previously mentioned, such as economics, neighborhood locations and conditions, and family features. All these factors may work together to have a disproportionately strong impact on families in minority communities.

Finally, while gangs are not just a minority problem, Spergel (1995) and others (see for example Shelden et al., 2004) give us insights that indicate that youngsters in racial and ethnic minority communities may be the most socially marginalized. The issue of **marginalization** is significant to our understanding of why some gangs form, why they persist, and why certain youngsters may (or may not) join gangs. In the concluding section of this chapter we will return to marginalization and explore how the environmental forces involved may be reversed in dealing with gang activity. For now, we want to focus on the issue of gangs and drugs, and the various links between the two.

GANGS AND DRUGS

For most people, gang membership and drug use are inseparable: Where you find one, you inevitably find the other. However, recent research has shed new light on the connections between gangs and drug involvement. In this section we will explore the various linkages that might be found. For the sake of simplicity, we classify the connections into three categories based on causal linkages.

First, we might say that joining a gang causes or, more precisely, facilitates drug trafficking and usage. This is a widely accepted relationship by both members of the general public and by law enforcement officials. In fact, in the 1998 National Youth Gang Survey 34% of the law enforcement agencies that responded reported that gangs in their jurisdictions existed for the purpose of drug trafficking. Furthermore, 38% of the agencies serving rural counties reported their youth gangs to be drug gangs (National Youth Gang Center, 2000). A recent report from the Office of Juvenile Justice and Delinquency Prevention (Starbuck et al., 2001) found that youth gang involvement with drugs was most extensive in jurisdictions that saw gang development between 1981 and 1985 and was less extensive in jurisdictions where gangs developed before or after this period.

Second, we might also say that being involved in drugs—either through sales or through purchases and use—might bring an individual into contact with gangs and promote gang membership. Finally, another possible explanation of the gangs-and-drugs relationship is that neither causes the other. In other words, gang activity and drug involvement are both a part of a deviant lifestyle, and they represent a commitment to law-violating or nonconforming behavior. In order to understand the connections more fully, we should explore each of these possible relationships.

The first explanation seems to be the most plausible to many people: Youngsters get involved in gangs, and drug-related activities are a part of who gang members are and what they do. One of the key assumptions is that many gangs are territorial or corporate in nature (Shelden et al., 2004; Taylor, 1990) and that drug involvement is actually an economic enterprise to support gang activities. Indeed, there is evidence from the 1980s that gangs such as the Bloods and Crips used the manufacture and trafficking of crack, or rock cocaine, to finance weapons purchases and to pay for gang activities (Starbuck et al., 2001). We can conclude that in some instances individuals join gangs and are exposed to the economic aspects of drugs. However, as Klein, Maxson, and Cunningham (1991) and Esbensen and Huizinga (1993) found, quite often individual gang members are involved in drug sales and use, but these are not necessarily organized activities involving the gang.

Additionally, the first relationship proposed (that is, that gang involvement facilitates drug involvement) overlooks a very simple but important point: Many youth gangs can be classified into Taylor's (1990) scavenger category. Are these groups involved in drugs? Often the answer is an emphatic yes. Are they trafficking in drugs as an economic enterprise? The clear answer here is no. Why? The very reasons that make scavenger gangs what they are make them relatively unsuccessful as criminal gangs. For these groups, drugs are used almost exclusively for recreational purposes. Members do not sell drugs because they are often too busy using whatever drugs they possess. Therefore, drug use may be one of the elements that brings together some of these low-achievement youngsters and results in the formation of a scavenger gang.

Perhaps the most compelling explanation of the gang-drug connection is that both gang membership and drug involvement are part of an unconventional lifestyle. For many gang-involved youngsters, violence, drugs, and promiscuity define who they are. At some level they are committed to gangs because of what gangs can do for them, and gangs provide many juveniles with protection, recreation, a sense of belonging, and status. As we will see later, to remove the gang identity from some of the most highly committed youths is to leave them with no identity at all. For these youngsters, acceptance of the gang lifestyle means acceptance of all the elements associated with that particular lifestyle, including, in some instances, drugs.

GANG MIGRATION

One of the major concerns associated with gangs and drugs is the degree to which gangs move into new territories to establish economic outposts, a phenomenon referred to as **gang migration** (Starbuck et al., 2001). During the 1980s, law enforcement authorities became greatly concerned that some of the emerging territorial gangs (the Bloods and Crips were frequently mentioned) were establishing **gang franchises** in cities like Portland, Oregon; and Seattle, Washington. These groups were also thought to be moving into America's heartland, into cities such as Dallas, St. Louis, and Kansas City. To what extent has this gang migration taken place? What evidence do we have of gang expansion by exportation?

Although there was some evidence of the most highly organized territorial gangs moving to new cities and establishing new economic territories, the reality is that those groups could be characterized as adult corporate gangs, most having very little juvenile involvement. Much of the available evidence indicates that youth street gangs are composed of locals or youngsters who have moved to a new

Box 10.1   International Perspectives
Another View of "Gang Migration"

Quite often people think of gangs as a phenomenon unique to the United States. However, gangs are found in a number of developed and developing countries around the world. Interestingly, some gangs that formed in other countries have found their way to the United States. This has been the case with certain Asian gangs and a group known as Los Mara Salvatrucha (MS), which formed in the Central American country of El Salvador. Civil war and economic difficulties brought many Salvadorans to the United States, and often these immigrants found themselves in conflict with established Hispanic populations, including well-established gangs. Therefore, the Mara Salvatrucha formed as a street gang initially for protection from other street gangs.

Members of the Mara Salvatrucha have spread from Southern California to at least 14 other states, and they also have been found in Canada, Mexico, and other Central American countries. MS gang members include both juveniles and adults, and they have been implicated in crimes such as aggravated assault, car jacking, murder, drug and weapons sales, and extortion. Law enforcement authorities characterize the MS as "well-organized and extremely violent."

Source: Vaquera and Bailey (2004).

city with their parents. In fact, in assessing gang migration Starbuck and associates (2001:4) note that "gang names are frequently copied, adopted, or passed on. In most instances, there is little or no real connection between local groups with the same name other than the name itself."

If most of these gangs are homegrown, what has created the illusion that gangs are expanding their syndicates into areas traditionally not associated with gang activity? One simple answer is that the names may be the same, but the groups are not. For instance, any gang can call itself the Bloods and wear red clothing; any group of gang members can call themselves the Crips and wear blue clothing. Gang names are not copyrighted, and nothing prevents youngsters in one city from adopting a gang name from another city. Therefore, while we have some evidence of gang expansion or migration, for the most part we find that youth gangs really are local in nature (Weisheit and Wells, 2004).

COMMUNITY REACTIONS

Huff (1989, 1990) says that most communities go through three phases in relation to reports of gang activity. The first response demonstrated by most communities is **denial**. There is a general denial by the police, politicians, and even members of the general public that the community has a gang problem. Commonly, police officials and politicians will note that there are groups of youngsters creating certain types of problems (graffiti and other forms of vandalism, fights, etc.), but that these emphatically are not gangs and that this activity does not demonstrate a gang problem (Huff, 1990).

Denial is the most frequent initial response for several reasons. To admit gang presence is implicit admission that the police are not in control of the situation (Jackson, 1992). So in order to keep up appearances, police officials will deny the presence of gangs or deny that certain activities are related to gangs. Additionally, to admit that gang activity exists in a community is bad for its economy. For example, if the town is a major tourist destination, public acknowledgment of gang presence might undermine the tourist trade. Therefore, not only will denial be the first reaction to reports of gangs, but also in most instances it is a logical reaction.

Denial may continue for some time while gang activity escalates. However, there will come a point when some event shakes the community from its denial stage. At times the catalyst for change will be some dramatic event, such as a shooting. This will be particularly noteworthy if there is an innocent victim, such as a small child or some famous person (Huff, 1990). When such an event occurs the community moves from denial to overreaction.

Overreaction may be thought of as a disproportionate response, given the actual nature of the threat. When the threat is gangs and gang behavior, calls for swift and severe responses to those who belong to gangs are immediate. Politicians, the news media, and citizens' groups will be very vocal in their calls for a law enforcement response to the acknowledgment that gangs exist and that they are now dangerous. The typical response is one of suppression. We will discuss this approach to dealing with gangs and controlling gang activity later in this chapter.

The danger of the overreaction phase is that it will result in what Huff (1990) characterizes as **misidentification**. Misidentification really involves two different dimensions. In the first instance we have misidentification of the causes of gang behavior (e.g., "it's because of all these welfare mothers with children who don't have fathers living at home"). The resulting solutions may be worthwhile but are totally unrelated to the actual causes of gang formation.

This phase also may result in the misidentification of gang members. In other words, some of the youths who appear to be gang members (what we have called wannabes) are classified as members, and the police may apprehend them in gang sweeps. The result may be that the police action backfires. By taking the wannabes into custody, the police have given them confirmation of their gang status. They now will be recognized and identified as real gang members. This type of misidentification may solidify gang identity and commitment to the gang lifestyle among those youngsters who were only marginally committed to the gang.

All three of these phases have implications for the ways we respond to gangs. Indeed, in the next section we will turn to what we can do and have done, at both the local and federal levels, to reduce the threat posed by youth gangs and their unlawful conduct.

RESPONDING TO GANGS

The ultimate question we must ask is: What do we do about gangs? At the most extreme level we could suggest that if we ignore most gang activity, it simply will go away. Most youngsters will mature out of gang involvement, even if we take no action. However, that response is unacceptable to most public policy makers, members of the juvenile justice system, and the general public. This means that we can assume that communities will undertake some type of response when gang activity is finally recognized or admitted. Most of these responses can be classified into one of three categories: prevention, intervention, and suppression (these topics also are discussed more generally in chapter 11).

GANG PREVENTION

In the 1990s, official responses to gang problems relied on the adage that "an ounce of prevention is worth a pound of cure." Major national, state, and local initiatives were aimed at preventing the conditions that lead to gang formation before they occur. This section will examine the "who" and "what" of gang prevention. Most of the delinquency research done over the past decades points to the family as the primary institution of socialization (Home, 1993; Huff, 1993). We would expect, then, that if anything in a society could prevent a child from becoming involved in a gang, it would be the family environment. In this regard, there are both positive and negative aspects of family influence that must be taken into account. As we have mentioned previously, the amount and type of supervision provided by the parents may have a significant effect on the degree to which children become involved in gangs. It is impossible for parents to know where their children are and what they are doing at every minute in the day, but the greater this type of knowledge, the less likely the children are to be involved in deviant or delinquent behaviors (Gottfredson and Hirschi, 1990; Wilson and Herrnstein, 1985). Parents also should provide positive role models for their children, emphasizing what good citizenship actually means. In other words, youngsters should be taught that violating the law is wrong because doing so will cause them trouble with the police and because being a law-abiding citizen is a positive attribute.

On the negative side, we have come to recognize that the system occasionally deals not only with delinquent youngsters but with delinquent families as well. Some gang-involved juveniles come from families with long-standing gang traditions: Their brothers, sisters, and cousins may be in gangs, and the fathers and grandfathers may be gang veterans themselves. If the family is to play a gang prevention role, there must be a consistent message that gangs are bad. Unfortunately, in many instances this is not the message that youngsters receive.

The second major agency associated with gang prevention is the schools. Schools may play a critical role in gang prevention, but two very important statements about schools must be noted. First, in most communities we have not equipped schoolteachers and administrators to deal with gangs. Second, schools have not always been prepared or motivated to deal with those youngsters most at risk for gang involvement. When these two factors are combined, we can see that schools in most communities have done very little to prevent youngsters from joining gangs.

The role played by schools can be illustrated very simply. Many at-risk youngsters come to school with several strikes against them. They may come from impoverished homes, with language deficiencies, and where little or no stress is placed on education. They struggle academically, and their parents give them virtually no academic support or encouragement. In fact, some of these families may encourage the child to leave school and find a job to add to the family's total economic base. Children like this who drop out perpetuate the poverty cycle in which many minority families find themselves.

Some of these at-risk youngsters are not so much dropouts as throw-outs. They exhibit poor academic performance (because of language deficiencies or other learning barriers), they are ridiculed by teachers and other students, their conduct becomes disruptive, and they are expelled or suspended from school for some period of time. In the end, they have achieved what they desired: They have removed themselves from an uncomfortable situation. What becomes of these youngsters once they are out of school? Some gain marginal employment, but most simply hang out together and form scavenger gangs (Taylor, 1990). Given a lack of structure, these youngsters have additional opportunities for deviant and delinquent behavior.

Have schools failed as agents of gang prevention? Yes, but there are other elements within our society that are part of the problem as well. For example, very seldom have we focused on the police as agents for gang prevention. For the most part, we have assumed that the police role in dealing with gangs is fairly well defined: When youngsters violate the law, the police should arrest them and see that a successful prosecution is carried forward. In other words, the police role has been defined almost exclusively in law enforcement terms.

Box 10.2   The Federal Government Develops a Comprehensive Antigang Strategy

The Office of Juvenile Justice and Delinquency Prevention (OJJDP) funded the **National Youth Gang Center** (**NYGC**) in 1994. NYGC serves as a national clearinghouse for all gang-related research, evaluations, legislation, and programs, and it conducts research such as the National Youth Gang Survey.

In 1995, after half a decade of assessing various local, state, and national initiatives on gangs, OJJDP endorsed the **Spergel Model** (after Irving A. Spergel, University of Chicago sociologist) as a linchpin in its response to America's gang problem. The model, formally called the **Comprehensive Community-Wide Approach to Gangs**, consists of 10 component models, each with an identifiable agency partner. Three key partners are a community's policing agency, grassroots organizations within each community, and a jobs program. Other elements, consistent with Spergel's belief that flexible is better, respond to the community's gang problem on an as-needed basis. Currently, this model is undergoing testing at five demonstration sites across the nation, the implementation and review supervised by Spergel, assisted by the NYGC.

Also in 1995, OJJDP adopted an overall plan commonly called the **comprehensive strategy**. The idea is to provide a broad spectrum of services and sanctions while coordinating all protective measures. Aimed at current and potential delinquent youth, from the womb through school and beyond, the plan seeks to diminish or mediate all risk factors for delinquency, including gangs. The effectiveness of this federal government-led effort remains to be seen.

Sources: Curry and Decker (2003); National Youth Gang Center (1997).

However, in recent years this focus has shifted somewhat. The **Gang Resistance Education and Training (G.R.E.A.T.)** Program has been implemented in cities and towns in nearly every state in an effort to bring families, schools, police, and the youngsters themselves into the gang prevention process. This program, already discussed in detail in chapter 3, provides teachers, students, and law enforcement officers with new images of one another. School officials, administrators, teachers, and students have unique opportunities to interact with police officers in a positive learning environment. In fact, the national evaluation of G.R.E.A.T. found that parents and teachers had very positive attitudes toward the program. Similarly, police officers, sometimes for the first time, experience children as something other than units to process as a result of their law enforcement role. The national evaluation of G.R.E.A.T. found that the officers delivering the training materials were supportive of the curriculum and that they felt that this program "improved their relationships with the children, the school, and the community as a whole" (Esbensen, 2004:4). While G.R.E.A.T. neither reduced the number of youngsters who joined gangs nor foreclosed additional delinquency, it did help foster more favorable attitudes toward the police (Esbensen, 2004:4).

Perhaps the best summary of prevention strategies has been provided by an analysis of youth gangs in Seattle, Washington. The authors of this study identified three issues that must be considered when designing programs to prevent youngsters from joining gangs:

1. Prevention efforts should be aimed at youngsters fairly early in life, perhaps as young as 10 to 12 years of age, even before some youngsters consider joining a gang.
2. Prevention efforts should target youngsters who are exposed to multiple risk factors such as neighborhood and family influences, school difficulties, and peer groups.
3. Prevention programs should address a number of dimensions in the lives of youngsters who are most at-risk (Hill et al., 2001:4).

GANG INTERVENTION

When prevention fails, intervention efforts often come into play. Unlike the obvious roles for family, schools, and the police in gang prevention, determining who should take the lead in intervention efforts is a far more difficult proposition. For simplicity's sake, we restrict this discussion to the community context.

Gang intervention programs—however they are organized and implemented—depend on the ability to identify youngsters already committed to gangs or those youngsters who seem to be at greatest risk for gang involvement. The identification problems are significant. For instance, families who have children active in gangs may not know, may not care, or may be reluctant to report such activity to the proper authorities. In such cases, these youngsters may not become gang-identified until some fairly dramatic event, such as a shooting, occurs.

Additionally, we may have the misidentification problem alluded to previously in this chapter. That is, some youngsters may be presumed to be gang members while they actually are wannabes on the periphery of gang activity. However, the

---

Box 10.3   The Family and Community Violence Prevention (FCVP) Program

The Family and Community Violence Prevention Program is one of the nation's most comprehensive initiatives to combat abusive behaviors among minority youths, and this program has direct application to the field of gang prevention and intervention. It is national in scope and a multimillion-dollar (over $60 million) initiative that operates under a cooperative agreement between the Office of Minority Health of the U.S. Department of Health and Human Services and Central State University in Wilberforce, Ohio. The immediate goal of the program is to positively impact the academic and personal development of a select group of youths who are at risk for involvement in violent and other abusive behavior. To achieve this goal, violence prevention activities are provided by Family Life Centers at colleges and universities in 17 states, the District of Columbia, the U.S. Virgin Islands, and Puerto Rico. Each of the centers conducts its activities based on the FCVP Model of six program components: academic development, personal development, family bonding, cultural enrichment, recreational enrichment, and career development. Since the cooperative agreement was finalized in 1994, the program has provided violence prevention services to more than 12,000 community youths and 3,200 college students.

The program has proven to be most effective among socioeconomically disadvantaged minority youths who are at risk for exposure to and/or involvement in violence and other abusive behaviors, such as substance abuse, fighting, possession of firearms and other dangerous weapons. Its holistic approach in combating these antisocial behaviors is based on the precept that when youths are positively immersed in or preoccupied with academic endeavors, cultural activities, positive image formation, recreational activities, and positive family relations, the tendencies toward antisocial behaviors are more likely to be minimized or eliminated.

Source: Rodney (2005).

---

wannabes are at risk for gang attachment, and therefore they are appropriate targets for most intervention programs.

Finally, **school-based programs** have been used in a number of communities, both in terms of intervention efforts and as a part of violence reduction and gang mediation projects (see Hunter, MacNeil, and Elias, 2004; Lawrence, 1998). However, the most difficult problem with intervention programs is that part of the target group may be beyond the reach of the schools, which makes school-based efforts impractical for certain groups:

1. Some gang-involved individuals have turned 18 and are now adults.

2. A few of these youngsters actually have graduated from high school and now are not involved in school activities.

3. Unfortunately, many of these youngsters have dropped out or been thrown out of school, making school-based projects ineffective.

In these cases other community-based organizations must be utilized as intervention agents. Community-based groups might include churches or other religious societies, community action agencies, and youth-oriented groups such as Boys Clubs and Girls Clubs, the scouts, Big Brothers and Big Sisters, and YMCA and YWCA organizations. These groups provide constructive activities for a community's young people through recreation, after-school programs, and in some instances, tutoring and academic support services. They may also have group counseling aimed at juveniles in at-risk situations.

GANG SUPPRESSION

The initial and most frequent response to gang activity is to minimize or eradicate the gangs, a strategy called **gang suppression** (Huff and McBride, 1993). When communities move from denial to reaction or overreaction, the gang situation is generally defined as a law enforcement problem (see Flynn and McDonough, 2004). In such cases, most politicians and members of the public call for aggressive police action. As evidence of the stress on a law enforcement response, the National Youth Gang Center (2000) asked law enforcement agencies if they participated in multi-agency task forces aimed at eradicating youth gangs. Nearly half of the respondents said they participated with other law enforcement agencies, criminal justice agencies, and schools in addressing gang issues.

When responding to gangs in a suppressive manner, police actions may take on a military style, and a specialized police gang unit may be created (Conly et al., 1993; Jackson and McBride, 1992). In some cases these units may be outfitted with distinctive uniforms and may be given a designation that indicates the seriousness of their purpose. For example, in the 1980s the Los Angeles police department created what were designated **CRASH (Community Resources Against Street Hoodlums)** units (Freed, 1986). These units and their tactics were vividly depicted in the movie *Colors*, which showed a very confrontational gang suppression style.

Once a gang unit has been formed, definitions will be developed and programs will be crafted to direct police operations. At this point the concern is with deciding what a gang-related event is and how the police are to respond to such incidents (see Maxson and Klein, 1990). For most police departments, any activity in which a gang member is involved becomes a gang-related occurrence. However, as police departments discover over time, this approach is too inclusive. Some things done by gang members really are not related to their gang status.

Once a police unit is organized, antigang activities commence. **Gang sweeps** are typical suppressive activities. In these operations, police gang units, often supported by uniformed patrol officers, will move in force into a neighborhood and round up all the known or suspected gang members hanging around street corners or other public places. As was mentioned previously in this chapter, gang sweeps and similar activities can have unintended consequences. In some cases these actions misidentify gang members. The most likely to be misidentified are the wannabes who dress and act like gang members.

Police officers may justify sweeps on several bases. First, they believe this approach demonstrates to the community that something is being done about gangs. Second, they hope to drive gangs out of business or at least force them underground by harassing them. Third, they hope that the pressure placed on the gangs may cause some wannabes to become discouraged and drop out before they develop a serious commitment to the gang lifestyle.

Another approach to gang suppression has come through city ordinances aimed at "loitering" and nuisance abatement. For instance, in the mid-1990s Chi-

Box 10.4   Use of Civil Injunctions to Fight Gangs

One of the approaches suggested to suppressing gang activity is to use the legal system against gang members. For instance, civil gang injunctions have been utilized in some communities to prevent gang members "from engaging in specified activities such as loitering at schools, carrying pagers and riding bicycles" (Maxson, Hennigan, Sloane, and Kolnick, 2004:v). This strategy has become popular in several southern California communities, and Maxson and colleagues (2004) used a quasi-experimental research design to evaluate the effectiveness of civil injunctions in the fight against gangs. What were their conclusions? First, community residents responded favorably to the use of civil injunctions and reported fewer acts of intimidation and less fear of gang confrontations. Second, in the control area (the one without civil injunctions) the level of gang fear and intimidation increased. Finally, most of the changes observed in the experimental area occurred in the short term, but these changes did not necessarily translate into intermediate or long-term improvements in communities. Nevertheless, the results from this quasi-experiment indicate that "injunctions can have a positive impact on communities" (Maxson et al., 2004:45). This approach may become another tool in the legal arsenal that cities may use in gang suppression efforts.

Source: Maxson, Hennigan, Sloane, and Kolnick (2004).

cago adopted a "Gang Congregation Ordinance" designed to prohibit the congregation of suspected gang members in public places. Among other things the ordinance provided that "if a police officer observes a person whom he reasonably believes to be a gang member loitering in a public place with one or more persons, he shall order them to disperse." There were a number of challenges to the ordinance that eventually reached the U.S. Supreme Court. In the case of *City of Chicago v. Morales* (119 S. Ct. 1849, 1999), the Court struck down this ordinance as "impermissibly vague" based on the grounds that it gave largely unfettered discretion to police officers as to when and where to apply the law.

RISK-BASED RESPONSES

Not every community can or will adopt OJJDP's comprehensive strategy for dealing with gang delinquency discussed earlier in box 10.2. Regardless of the approach taken, it is important that every community identify the risk factors that may be associated with gang problems. Wyrick and Howell (2004:24–25) identify five different groups of risk factors associated with antisocial behavior:

- *individual risk factors*—conduct disorders, drug use, violence, early dating, precocious sexual activity, school failure, or the death of someone close to the child

- *family risk factors*—broken homes, family poverty, child abuse and neglect, poor parental management including lack of supervision, and family members who are involved in gangs

- *school risk factors*—low school achievement, low academic aspirations, low degree of commitment to school, and negative labels assigned by teachers

- *peer group risk factors*—involvement with delinquent and/or aggressive peers
- *community risk factors*—availability of drugs, lack of safety, high levels of poverty, and community disorganization

As Wyrick and Howell point out, "There are no easy solutions to community gang problems" (2004:27). However, programs aimed at addressing the risk factors associated with gangs and gang membership can help use the resources available in a community to respond to gangs.

STAYING OUT AND GETTING OUT

Earlier in the chapter we mentioned the concept of "blood in, blood out" in terms of gang membership. Additionally, much has been made in the literature relating to gangs about the peer pressure associated with gang membership. However, as we near the end of this chapter, two points should be made about resisting the pressure to join gangs and the consequences of leaving a gang.

First, the Seattle Social Development Project study (Hill et al., 2001:3) found that not all youngsters are susceptible to gang recruitment and that "no single overriding factor explains gang membership." It is the accumulation of risk factors (neighborhood, family, school, and peer group) that increases the likelihood of gang membership. In addition, we should note that even youngsters faced with multiple risk factors may be able to resist gang membership. On this point Starbuck and colleagues note that "it is not as difficult for adolescents to resist gang pressures as is commonly believed. In most instances, adolescents can refuse to join gangs without reprisal" (2001:3).

Second, getting out of gangs may not be as traumatic and deadly as commonly portrayed either. Again, the study of modern gangs by the Office of Juvenile Justice and Delinquency Prevention speaks to this point. The authors of the study assert that gang members, and particularly those who are only marginally involved, "can leave a gang without serious consequences. . . . In fact, most adolescents do not remain in gangs for long periods of time—particularly in areas with emerging gang problems" (Starbuck et al., 2001:3). The Seattle Social Development Project also found that over two-thirds of the gang members in the study were members for less than one year (Hill et al., 2001). Therefore, gang membership and involvement may not imply the lifetime commitment that often is inferred.

Where does this leave us then, in terms of responding to gangs? Should we focus our efforts on prevention, followed by intervention? Is this where we will make the biggest impact in the lives of youngsters who might join gangs, or those already in gangs? Is suppression a more appealing and effective strategy as far as the public and the police are concerned? Not necessarily. Suppression alone will never be effective. However, suppression combined with prevention and intervention may be effective.

SUMMARY

The conclusions that can be drawn about gangs and gang activity are fairly easy to summarize. Gangs have been a part of the juvenile delinquency picture in the United States for much of our nation's history. While gangs were not "invented" in the 1980s, they certainly reemerged and gained a great deal of notoriety. Newspapers, newsmagazines, television, and motion pictures all chose gangs as a subject of extensive coverage. Also during this period social science gang research resurfaced, and a number of established and emerging scholars focused on describing and explaining the contemporary gang phenomenon.

It is impossible to know in advance which youngsters will become gang members, but certain features have been regularly associated with modern youth gangs. An important issue is marginalization. Often, gang-involved or gang-prone youngsters have come from society's most marginalized segments. Many, but far from all, are members of racial or ethnic minorities. They belong to chaotic families under extreme economic and social pressures. One or both parents may be absent as a result of death, abandonment, or imprisonment, and some of the siblings in the family may have followed the family tradition of gang membership and crime.

Vigil (1988) characterizes many of the Hispanic youths he studied from East Los Angeles as being caught between two cultures—the one of their parents and grandparents versus that of the dominant society in which they live. Their response was to create their own culture. In this context, gang involvement becomes merely one way of adapting to an uncertain environment.

Individuals join youth gangs for many reasons, one of the most common being for protection. Another common theme related to gang membership is a sense of belonging. Many youngsters mention that the gang is like a family to them (M. Harris, 1994; Mays, Winfree, and Jackson, 1993). Additionally, gangs provide acceptance. Youths are rewarded by gangs for deviant or delinquent activities condemned by other segments of society.

Gangs also furnish recreational opportunities and activities. They supply their members with alcohol, drugs, parties, and sex. They also provide members with ego support and individual and collective identities. Curry and Spergel characterize gangs as providing "quasi-stable, efficient, meaningful social, and perhaps economic, structures" (1988:401).

Gangs are utilitarian. They provide something to their members. We can assume that if they did not, most youths would not join or continue to belong to them. Clearly, then, gangs are a community problem. The police cannot arrest gangs out of existence, and the schools cannot provide enough programming to prevent gangs. It will take a combined effort of families, the juvenile justice system, schools, churches, and a variety of community agencies and organizations to address the problems created by gangs.

CRITICAL REVIEW QUESTIONS

1. Do you think that Officer Straight was a former gang member or simply a streetwise cop, versed in the adage "you have to know your enemy to win the battle?"

2. What is the common theme (or themes) present in the work of the gang researchers during the golden era of gang studies? What are the implications of this theme (or themes) for the success of the Chicago Area Project?

3. Gang researchers in the postwar era emphasized social class as the key to understanding gang problems in the 1950s and 1960s. Were they correct? If you answered yes to this question, who was "most correct"? If they were wrong, where did they go wrong?

4. Rank the elements of what constitutes a gang from least important to most important. Provide support for each ranking.

5. Gangs, while not exclusively an urban problem, are clearly clustered in large population centers. In your opinion, which environmental factor holds the most promise for explaining this fact? Which one holds the least promise, perhaps because it is not linked to urbanization or population density? Be sure to provide the reasons for each of your selections.

6. Why is it important to consider gender and race or ethnicity when describing the nation's gang problem? What might be missed by criminal justice practitioners and academics who exclude these variables from their policies and analyses?

7. Gangs are clearly "into" drugs. Beyond that statement, however, the picture becomes fuzzy. Which gang–drug connection do you think provides the best insights, and why?

8. Gang migration makes sense—or does it? What do you think? What are the logical ties between gang migration and the various community responses described by Huff?

9. What do we do about gangs? What do you think has the potential to work best: gang prevention, gang intervention, or gang suppression? (*Hint*: Perhaps the type of gang or stage in gang development could be a crucial determinant of which strategy works best.)

RECOMMENDED READINGS

Esbensen, Finn-Aage, Stephen G. Tibbetts, and Larry Gaines (2004). *American Youth Gangs at the Millennium*. Long Grove, IL: Waveland Press. This collection contains 19 works from leading scholars in gang research. They are grouped in four sections that cover terminology and survey information; nontraditional gangs such as female gangs and hybrid gangs; gang activities; and both historical and contemporary responses to gangs.

Shelden, Randall G., Sharon K. Tracy, and William B. Brown (2004). *Youth Gangs in American Society*, 3rd ed. Belmont, CA: Wadsworth. This is frequently used in university classes on gangs. Shelden and his colleagues provide a very valuable service by including a chapter on girls in gangs and by addressing the community-based and national intervention strategies, as well as the legal interventions that may be taken with gangs.

Spergel, Irving A. (1995). *The Youth Gang Problem*. New York: Oxford University Press. The author is one of the major researchers involved with contemporary gang studies. Spergel (along with other colleagues) has conducted gang research nationwide on behalf of the federal Office of Juvenile Justice and Delinquency Prevention. The book provides foundational information on how and why gangs form as well as the types of policies and programs necessary for addressing the gang phenomenon.

KEY TERMS

Chicago Area Project
cholo
colors
Comprehensive Community-Wide
  Approach to Gangs
comprehensive strategy
conflict gang
corporate gang
CRASH (Community Resources
  Against Street Hoodlums)
crews
criminal gang
culture conflict
deindustrialization
denial
differential opportunity theory
double failure
field research
focal concerns
gang franchises
gang migration
Gang Resistance Education
  and Training (G.R.E.A.T.)
gang suppression
gang sweeps
hand signs
hybrid gangs
jumped in

juniors
Juvenile Delinquency Prevention
  and Youth Offenses Control
  Act of 1961
klickas
locura
low self-control
marginalization
misidentification
National Youth Gang Center (NYGC)
O.G.s
overreaction
pee-wees
placa
posses
ranked in
reaction formation theory
retreatist gang
scavenger gang
school-based programs
skinhead gang
social disorganization theory
Spergel Model
stoner gang
subcultural differentiation
territorial gang
vatos locos
veteranos

NOTES

[1] These rankings come from the 1995 National Youth Gang Survey (National Youth Gang Center, 1997). Personal correspondence with Arlen Egley, Jr. from the National Youth Gang Center has confirmed that comparable rankings for subsequent National Youth Gang Surveys are not available. However, on most dimensions there has been relatively little variation in survey results from 1995 to 2002.

[2] There is no mention in the book of 1,313 gangs. The back story is that Thrasher bet a colleague that he could publish a title with the number 13 in it. He went one better: two 13s.

[3] The term wannabe is a contraction of want-to-be and is spelled in a variety of ways. We have chosen this form based on the book by Monti (1994).

chapter

11

DELINQUENCY PREVENTION

* * *

Gently thumping his heavy ceramic coffee mug on the table, John Ellerby called the monthly meeting of the Region V Juvenile Justice Coordinating Board (JJCB) to order. As the JJCB's chair, Ellerby earlier in the week had provided members with an agenda, minutes of the previous meeting, and a staff report, the latter being the key agenda item. He now had the difficult task of guiding the board through the many recommendations contained in the report. Sometimes, like tonight, just getting this group to come to order was an accomplishment.

Two years ago, after a series of home invasions and several gun-related homicides committed by youths the media described as "otherwise normal kids," a group of citizens, educators, judges, and other juvenile justice professionals met in the state capitol at the governor's request. The attendees selected a steering committee from those present. Their task was to establish a statewide response to the "growing menace of violent youth crime and related behaviors." In a unique case of intergovernmental cooperation, the committee included an assistant police chief from the state's largest city, the most senior sheriff in the state, a state Supreme Court justice, a juvenile court judge, a juvenile probation officer, a law professor from the state university, and a criminal justice professor. Two lay members—a prominent member of the clergy and a victims' rights activist— filled out the committee. An aide to the governor chaired the committee, while the senior member of the state legislature's judicial affairs committee served as vice chair. The state director of the Commission on Crime and Delinquency, a not-for-profit organization, was an ex officio member of the committee.

After four months, the steering committee recommended dividing the state into eight geographical areas, each with its own regional Juvenile Justice Coordinating Board. The committee members decided that, given the state's diverse geographical, political, social, and economic nature, the best way to address juvenile justice problems was at the regional level. The chairs of the eight boards, along with ex officio members from the governor's staff and the state legislature's committee on youth and families, formed a statewide Juvenile Justice Coordinating Commission. The commission advised both the governor and legislature on juvenile justice policy and law. For their part, the local boards determined the fate of state and federal funds allocated to their respective regions.

It took another 18 months to move the enabling legislation through the state legislature and get it signed into law. Just setting up the regional boards took almost three months, even after the money began to flow. This was the Region V JJCB's third monthly meeting, each one held in a different city or town in the region. The board's skeleton support staff worked out of a storefront office in an old downtown shopping mall in Region V's largest city. The 16 board members were all volunteers drawn from Region V's eight counties. Now it was Ellerby's task to call them to order, as he again rapped on the table, this time calling out, "Please, come to order, we've got a full plate tonight. I now move that we dispense with the reading of the minutes from the last meeting and accept them as submitted. I see a second to my motion from Dr. Stanton."

"Mr. Chair, actually I have a question about the staff report," spoke Dr. Marsha Stanton, board vice chair and the only member besides the chair to attend the charter meeting two years earlier. Dr. Stanton was a pediatrician; her grandmother had been the victim of one of the home invasions that gave impetus to the original meeting at the state capitol.

"Go ahead, Dr. Stanton, we can return to the minutes later. What was your question?"

"I read the report for the first time last night, so I haven't had a chance to absorb it all. From what I have read, however, it seems that we have at least a dozen different suggestions in this report. If I presented a patient of mine with so many different prescriptions, I would be damned as either a poor practitioner of pediatric medicine or an overly cautious one."

"Dr. Stanton's right," spoke out Sergeant Harry Anderson, a school resource officer employed by the state's second-largest police department. "We need a couple of solid programs that have real teeth. We have to bring these kids into line and do it now, before we have shootings in the schools and kids going on rampages."

"I agree with both Dr. Stanton and Sergeant Anderson," Rick Brown, owner of a chain of movie theaters operating throughout the state, joined in the fray: "We've spent the last two meetings going over the condition of our region's juvenile justice system. What did we learn? I'll tell you. The local police are overworked. Even with overtime pay, they just can't cope with the current workload, let alone any new activities. The juvenile sessions of the trial courts are jammed with so many cases, if you'll excuse me Judge Martinez, that kids who are charged with anything except a really serious crime— and I mean murder, rape, or maybe armed robbery—they just walk. And the correctional system! Now there's an oxymoron if I ever heard one. Right up there with military intelligence and criminal . . ." Brown stopped talking in mid-sentence.

"I assume you were going to say 'criminal justice,' right Mr. Brown? Speaking as the only member of the judiciary and the legal establishment present tonight, I am not insulted personally or professionally by your observations," said Judge Martinez. "They are, taken in sum, quite correct. But aren't you missing the point? Isn't this effort—the primary focus of the JJCB—intended to prevent juvenile delinquency and, when that isn't possible, to intervene in the lives of those who have already taken a few steps toward delinquent misbehavior?"

"Well, yes, you're right, Judge," said Dr. Stanton. "As a physician I understand prevention and intervention. Sergeant Anderson works in an intervention program in his community's public schools, trying to get kids to drop out of gangs. Right, Sergeant Anderson?"

"That's right, Dr. Stanton. And as a police officer, much of my time on the job is spent in crime prevention, stopping it before it starts, like when we do a security survey of people's homes or check out their residences while they're on vacation."

Inwardly, Ellerby smiled. Opening a copy of the staff report, he spoke again for the first time in several minutes: "OK, then we're all on the same sheet of music. So let's turn to the report's first page. Remember, what we want are juvenile prevention and interven-

tion programs that work. At least they worked some place, with some kids and at some point in time. It's up to us to decide if they might work now in our communities. Like I said, page one . . ."

* * *

We have attended meetings such as this one in our academic jobs and in consulting roles. What we hope to make clear by this vignette is that many people begin such enterprises without a clear set of expectations, as appeared to be the case for several Region V JJCB members. Conversely, some members, like Mr. Brown, bring personal agendas with them that may be at odds with the stated goals. Other members may know more than they think they know about the matter under discussion, as was the case with Dr. Stanton and Sergeant Anderson. Translating program-related concepts, even abstract ones such as prevention and intervention, into a new context often is more difficult than even our fictional account suggests.

The vignette should also sensitize you to the problems any agency, formal organization, or even concerned citizen might encounter when proposing changes to the *status quo*. This is the territory of prevention and intervention. When considering delinquency prevention and intervention programs, there are a number of issues to address. In fact, a good place to begin is with the definitions of key terms.

THE CENTRAL IDEAS

Since the 1960s, the juvenile justice system has performed two related functions: (1) prevention and (2) control of delinquency (Lawrence, 1998:224–26; Lundman, 1993:15–17; see also Wheeler and Cottrell, 1966). **Delinquency control** efforts respond to immediate problems. The question is one of reacting responsibly to inappropriate conduct: How should society formally respond to the actions of juvenile delinquents? Therefore, most—but not all—actions by the police, the juvenile court system, and juvenile corrections involve the treatment, regulation, restraint, segregation, or isolation of delinquents. Once it has been determined that suspected or detained youths may be or are involved in delinquency, each successive component of the system addresses a single question: What do we do with them? Prevention is another matter entirely, one which is nonetheless familiar. **Delinquency prevention** refers to the act of keeping something from happening. As such, it is by definition proactive, whereas control is reactive.

Using these criteria, we find that most juvenile justice system activities seek to control delinquency rather than prevent it. In rare instances, as with some police responses to gangs, **eradication**—or the total elimination of the offending behavior—is the goal. However, juvenile justice experts tend to view eradication as an extreme response to delinquency, and the methods necessary to achieve that end completely are so radical that it is rarely used—it remains a kind of "scorched earth" approach to the problem. The combined goals of prevention and control, generally speaking, are to reduce delinquency to a generally more acceptable level.

THE LANGUAGE OF PREVENTION

Prevention is often confused with intervention. Consider the distinction in **disease epidemiology** between intervention and prevention.[1] When medical professionals try to control the spread of a disease that has already surfaced in a population, they use medical interventions. **Intervention** literally means "to come between." Intervention's goal is to modify or change something (Miller, 1997:845).[2] With diseases, medical specialists design treatments for those already infected, but not fatally so, or those about to become infected. Hence, some interventions seek to cure those already infected. Another related goal is to minimize the number of victims among those exposed to the disease *vector,* or the cause of the outbreak or epidemic. Other interventions place physical or chemical barriers between those who are infected and those who are disease-free to limit the spread of the disease. An intervention is a response to a disease outbreak; it is an effort to control its spread, just as social control agencies attempt to control delinquency. In this sense, interventions—like control strategies—are largely reactive.

Prevention means that the disease never has a chance to spread. Prevention specialists quite literally stop the epidemic before it can get started (Miller, 1997:1311). Their efforts target an at-risk population, or a group that has a high likelihood of contracting the disease. Those in charge of prevention programs make a determination of the costs associated with success and failure. In the event that available resources—medicines, treatment procedures, physicians, and the like—are limited, then **secondary prevention**, or targeting seriously at-risk groups, makes sense. Thus, secondary prevention closely resembles control, especially given its reactive nature. The disease—or problem—may be particularly virulent or fast moving. In such a case, secondary prevention that seeks to protect an at-risk group—people identified as having certain risk factors or early stages of the disease—may fail to protect anyone. Relying on secondary prevention may allow the disease to jump from one relatively isolated group to all those susceptible to the disease. The broader-ranging method, then, is **primary prevention**, which seeks to inoculate the entire population against the disease, in rare cases eliminating it.[3]

Are these analogies relevant for social behavior? Consider the following:

- The disease model of crime gained a foothold in correctional philosophy and practice in the 1950s. Criminologists have debated the medical model of crime—in which crime is a disease, the criminal is the patient, and **penology** holds the treatment or cure—for more than 50 years (Mays and Winfree, 2005:47, 121; Winfree and Abadinsky, 2003:42, 62, 121). The sick/well continuum is essential to this model. As MacNamara observed: "In its simplest (perhaps oversimplified) terms, the medical model as applied to corrections assumed the offender to be 'sick' (physically, mentally, and/or socially); his offense to be a manifestation or symptom of his illness, a cry for help" (1977:439–40).

- Prevention and intervention strategies generally use the language of disease epidemiology, including the terms *treatment modalities* for the services rendered and *target population* for the groups served. When it comes to assessment, the language and methods of medical evaluation research abound

(Lundman, 1993). For example, in drug prevention, primary prevention programs target nonusers and experimenters; secondary prevention efforts address the more experienced users; and chronic users and abusers receive treatment (Venturelli, 1994:143–47).

- A major research activity funded by the Justice Department's Office of Juvenile Justice and Delinquency Prevention since the 1980s is the Causes and Correlates program, a longitudinal study of self-reported delinquency in three cities (Rochester, New York; Denver, Colorado; and, Pittsburgh, Pennsylvania). This program's analytic focus has been serious violent behavior. "*Epidemiology* of Serious Violence" (Kelley, Huizinga, Thornberry, and Loeber, 1997; emphasis added) is one report from this research effort.

Clearly, prevention and intervention models speak to criminal justice questions and related issues. How well do they work within the juvenile justice system? We address that question next.

DELINQUENCY: ITS PREVENTION AND CONTROL

Juvenile justice prevention and control have parallel goals. Lundman (1993:15) acknowledges these goals; however, he views them as nearly fused in juvenile justice system responses. Lundman groups the main prevention and control strategies into three categories: predelinquent intervention, preadjudication intervention, and postadjudication prevention.

The intent of **predelinquent intervention** is simple: "*Let's put a stop to delinquency before it begins.*" Hence, it is preventive in nature; the primary challenge for predelinquent interventionists is to identify "juveniles believed headed for trouble with the law" (Lundman, 1993:17). Lundman describes two primary places where these types of interventions occur. The first locus is the individual, whereby the interventionist identifies at-risk youths and subsequently designs a specific treatment to "repair or bolster flawed personalities" (1993:17). Given the previous discussion of prevention, we can best view individual treatment as secondary prevention. Second, interventionists may offer a community-oriented solution. Practitioners of this approach emphasize the social nature of most delinquency and the possible futility of treating the delinquency symptoms and overlooking their cultural or group origins. Since such programs typically do not identify individual at-risk or predelinquent youths as "in need of assistance," most community projects are primary prevention programs.

Preadjudication intervention programming comes between a youth on the path to delinquency and formal designation as a delinquent.[4] Some juvenile justice experts may view this practice as secondary prevention. Intervention specialists—often screening officers in a juvenile court—assess the designated youths as "sick," severely at-risk, or otherwise in need of intervention. The basic philosophy behind such diagnoses and practices is that the disease—delinquency—has not taken hold of the individual sufficiently to warrant treatment. "*You are in real trouble,*" goes the message of this perspective, "*so you had better stop it now before you are adjudicated a* *delinquent!*" The primary form of preadjudication prevention is diversion, a topic covered in chapter 4. The key decisions occur at the juvenile court level; hence, judges and probation officers are essential actors in preadjudication prevention. A clear secondary goal of preadjudication intervention is to limit the youth's penetration into the juvenile justice system.

Lundman's final form is **postadjudication intervention**. All remaining juvenile justice system responses exist at this level, ranging from probation to institutionalization to parole to community treatment. In the language of postadjudication intervention, the message becomes the following: "*Let's see if you've learned your lesson and can avoid a reoccurrence.*" As we described in earlier chapters, some such measures are more punitive and less treatment-oriented than are others. While juvenile justice experts may view preventing future delinquency as a postadjudication intervention goal, the reactive nature is beyond dispute. The choices for juvenile-justice decision makers—Lundman's postadjudication interventionists—are between probation and community treatment and institutionalization, followed by aftercare.

The scope of the juvenile justice system's delinquency prevention activities, then, would seem to be quite limited. The largely reactive and control-oriented system simply is poorly equipped to deal with predelinquents or most preadjudicatory adolescents. Lawrence (1998:224) has claimed that, for the most part, status offenders define the limits of the juvenile justice system's delinquency prevention efforts. In chapters 3 and 9 we learned that the "[p]olice do have the authority to take status offenders into custody and refer them to the juvenile court. Status offenders may not, however, be adjudicated delinquent, and under most state juvenile statutes they may not be committed to a juvenile institution" (Lawrence, 1998:224).

"Pure" primary prevention or predelinquent intervention programs frequently lie outside the juvenile justice system's direct control. For example, rarely do control agents participate in predelinquent prevention, reserving most of their resources for reactive measures.[5] Most predelinquency efforts are the responsibility of "civilians," prevention specialists with no direct ties to the juvenile justice system. This chapter's purpose is to present different prevention programs. Before we begin, however, it is a good idea to review the history of delinquency prevention.

A Brief History of Delinquency Prevention

Systematic delinquency prevention did not occur for more than 30 years after the juvenile court's creation. Over the first three decades of its existence, the emergent juvenile justice system directed its efforts at the creation of control mechanisms, such as police responses, court structure, probation services, correctional institutions, and aftercare. Beginning in the 1930s, several projects attempted to address delinquency prevention, starting in Chicago.

The Chicago Area Project

The University of Chicago's sociology department played a central role in juvenile delinquency's explanation and study early in the twentieth century.[6] Clifford R. Shaw and Henry D. McKay, two Chicago-trained researchers, spent much of their careers at the University's Institute for Juvenile Research. Along with their colleagues, they produced an influential book on what we now call **social ecology**—*Delinquent Areas: A Study of the Geographic Distribution of School Truants, Juvenile Delinquents, and Adult Offenders in Chicago* (1929). More than a decade later, they wrote *Juvenile Delinquency and Urban Areas* (1942), another sociogeographic treatise on delinquency in 23 cities, including Chicago. These works, and a series of **life histories** about delinquents, formed the basis of their theory about delinquency's spread in socially disorganized neighborhoods.

According to **social disorganization theory**, areas—neighborhoods—became disorganized as businesses invaded the physical space and successive waves of poor immigrants moved in and out. These disorganized neighborhoods lacked many of the social support and educational mechanisms found in other areas of their respective cities. Residents subsequently turned to crime since illegal activities "may be regarded as one of the means employed by people to acquire, or attempt to acquire, the economic and social values generally idealized by our culture, which persons in other circumstances acquire by conventional means" (Shaw and McKay, 1942:439).[7] Social ecologists maintained that the propensity for crime passed culturally from one generation of residents to the next. When residents moved, their old neighborhoods were populated with new residents, but because these areas remained disorganized, they continued along the criminogenic path.

Shaw subsequently grounded a major Chicago-based delinquency prevention program in social disorganization theory. Begun in 1932, the **Chicago Area Project (CAP)** was organized around existing community groups, including churches, social clubs, and labor unions. Local community leaders lent the project their names and prestige. The CAP staff selected three ethnically homogeneous white neighborhoods; two near the Chicago Loop, or central business district; and a third on Chicago's southeast side. The Loop sites were high-crime neighborhoods, while the southeast neighborhood had a much lower delinquency rate. Each neighborhood in the study area had a staff consisting of a full-time director, recruited from the neighborhood, and one full-time **detached social worker**, also recruited locally. The social worker had no formal office, working instead on the streets of Chicago.

The CAP was created to enhance and assist neighborhood efforts. Shaw created local committees that shouldered most of the implementation burdens. For example, these self-help organizations sponsored recreation programs for area children. The recreation programs utilized existing resources that neighborhood youths had either ignored or previously underutilized, along with summer camping programs outside the city. Second, the committees addressed local problems associated with health care, sanitation, education, and even police services. The staff and volunteers became advocates for local residents experiencing difficulties obtaining these services. Finally, the CAP detached social workers and other neighborhood volunteers targeted local gangs for special attention. Committee members acted as advocates for local youths who had troubles with law enforcement and the juvenile court system. Their goal was to limit the youths' penetration into the juvenile justice system. When the state released a child from custody, CAP staff and volunteers assisted him or her back into the community.

Did it work? Qualitative, first-person accounts and subjective assessments by CAP contemporaries suggest that the program accomplished its goals, including delinquency prevention. It is interesting to note that Shaw and McKay made no overt efforts to evaluate the CAP. They did continue to collect police arrest data but took no other steps to assess the three neighborhoods. Moreover, the reporting units for these arrest statistics were incompatible with the CAP communities. Meaningful comparisons are impossible. Additionally, by most objective measures a replication of the CAP in Boston's inner-city area—called the **Mid-City Project**—failed to prevent delinquency (Miller, 1962). A third community-level program in Manhattan's Lower East Side, this time based on Cloward and Ohlin's differential opportunity theory of delinquency, also failed to demonstrate positive results. The city cut off funds for that program, called **Mobilization for Youth**, before it yielded conclusive results (Brager and Purcell, 1967; Moynihan, 1969; Weissman, 1969). Assessments of other programs that have utilized the detached social worker concept, a keystone of the CAP and its replications, further suggested that the approach is unlikely to succeed. As Lundman (1993:81) noted, "It seems most accurate to conclude that the Chicago Area Project also failed to prevent juvenile delinquency."

THE CAMBRIDGE-SOMERVILLE YOUTH STUDY

Consider the following statement: If behavioral scientists could learn early in a child's life the likelihood of future troubling behavior, society could concentrate its resources to alter that individual's fate, thereby preventing delinquency. Jackson Toby (1965:1675) observed that most people see early identification and intensive treatment as "breathtakingly plausible." Getting to that point, however, has proved breathtakingly difficult. For example, the schizophrenia scale (Sc) of the **Minnesota Multiphasic Personality Inventory** (**MMPI**) seems closely tied to delinquency. However, tests conducted in the 1940s found prediction errors in three-fourths of the cases.[8] Creating "more powerful" predictor devices from other elements of the MMPI, such as the psychopathic deviation (Pd) and hypomania (Ha) scales, failed to reduce the prediction errors appreciably. Two-thirds of those predictions also were incorrect.

In 1950, Eleanor and Sheldon Glueck published *Unraveling Juvenile Delinquency*, in which they described a social prediction table. They selected five family-related factors: discipline of boys by fathers, supervision of boys by mothers, affection of fathers for boys, affection of mothers for boys, and family cohesiveness. Using a sample of delinquents and nondelinquents, the Gluecks assigned weighted scores to their conditions on the five factors. They classified juveniles who achieved a summary score of less than 250 as "probably nondelinquent," while they called those with 250 or more "probably delinquent." In the 1950s, the New York City Youth Board put the Glueck prediction table to the test. Among those predicted to be nondelinquent, errors occurred in only 2.6 percent of the predictions; however, among those predicted to be delinquent, *more than three-fourths proved to be wrong* (Craig and Glick, 1963; Whelen, 1954).

Even before these "scientific" prediction devices, an experiment tested the idea that delinquency experts can single out predelinquents for special treatment. In

1937, researchers at the **Cambridge-Somerville Youth Study** asked teachers and police officers in the two Boston-area cities to identify two groups of boys: "difficult boys," destined to be delinquents, and "average boys." Researchers then assigned boys randomly to either the experimental group or the control group, irrespective of their defined status.[9]

Experimental subjects received individual counseling, family guidance training, and special tutoring. Counselors with small caseloads made regular contacts with the boys and their families. They saw to it that the boys had the best available medical and psychiatric help. In short, the Cambridge-Somerville staff catered to the experimental subjects' social, physical, intellectual, and spiritual growth (Powers and Witmer, 1951). The controls received no special treatment. Within two years, the experimental group had 325 members, as did the control group. The experiment's goal was to maintain the experimental group's special status for 10 years. In 1939, as the study started in earnest, the subjects averaged 11 years of age. However, World War II threatened the study's integrity and validity as staff and study members entered the armed forces. Although the experiment officially ended on December 31, 1945, large groups of participants had begun to drop out as early as the summer of 1942.

Despite the study's demise, evaluators followed the subjects through 1948. Their conclusion was troubling: "The special work of the counselor was no more effective than the usual forces in the community in preventing boys from committing delinquent acts" (Powers and Witmer, 1951:337). A 1955 follow-up of the Cambridge-Somerville youths revealed essentially the same conclusion. That is, the experimental group's special treatment as children "failed to achieve its fundamental goal of preventing crime" (McCord and McCord, 1959:61). Equally troubling for program proponents was the 1976 finding that the mental hospital visitations, alcoholism treatment, and lifetime court records of experimental subjects differed in no significant ways from those of control group members (McCord, 1978).

THE FEDERAL ROLE IN DELINQUENCY PREVENTION

The first significant federal action directed specifically at delinquency prevention occurred in 1961, more than 60 years after the juvenile court's creation (Wheeler and Cottrell, 1966:5).[10] Called the **Juvenile Delinquency and Youth Offenses Control Act**, it followed many of the recommendations of the President's Committee on Juvenile Delinquency and Youth Crime. This group identified three chief areas for new programs: employment opportunities, educational services, and community organization. The goal of employment opportunities was to integrate school dropouts into the community's occupational structure. The need to provide job-training programs funded by local industry and to instill job skills and social competence skills in a largely unskilled population made such integration even more difficult. Educational services addressed the special needs of youth wavering between staying in school and dropping out. Participants gained access to adult education, special tutoring, reading clinics, and individual and group counseling. Finally, this act provided a national mandate for mobilizing neighborhood and community organizations similar to those of the CAP. However, conservatives in Congress viewed this component as smacking of socialism and too controversial. Pilot projects in community mobilization were unsuccessful or terminated prematurely. Moreover, "The demonstrations had barely got under way before they were virtually inundated by the massive Federal Poverty Program, which so changed the available services and the pressures on the agencies that evaluation programs could not be carried out" (Wheeler and Cottrell, 1966:8).

Throughout the 1960s and 1970s, delinquency prevention remained an elusive goal—as we have seen, one frequently merged with other goals, including diversion and control. Nonetheless, the best statement in support of primary prevention may be one of the earliest:

> Once a juvenile is apprehended by the police and referred to the Juvenile Court, the community has already failed; subsequent rehabilitation services, no matter how skilled, have far less potential for success than if they had been applied before the youth's overt defiance of the law. (President's Commission on Crime in the District of Columbia, 1966:733)

OJJDP AND DELINQUENCY PREVENTION

In the last two decades of the twentieth century, the federal government emerged as a leader in delinquency prevention, largely through the Office of Juvenile Justice and Delinquency Prevention. Beginning with the *Comprehensive Strategy for Serious, Violent and Chronic Juvenile Offenders* (1993), continuing with *Guide for Implementing the Comprehensive Strategy for Serious, Violent and Chronic Juvenile Offenders* (1995), and culminating in its oversight of a series of prevention projects in the late 1990s, OJJDP has exercised a leadership role in the nation's delinquency prevention efforts. Figure 11.1 contains an overview of OJJDP's comprehensive strategy. At the top are the various forms of behavior that bring children to the attention of parents, teachers, and other adults, including the juvenile justice system's key players. Problem behavior, in this model, constitutes an early warning signal. Prevention specialists, parents, and school personnel should not ignore such behavior, as it defines at-risk youths; however, the response to such behavior also should not resemble what we have called reactive control efforts.

What is interesting about this figure is that both problem behavior and noncriminal misbehavior—the latter being status offending—are identified as suitable prevention targets. The strategy clearly defines first-order prevention as "programs for all youths," followed by programs for youths at greatest risk. In our terms, these are examples of primary and secondary prevention. OJJDP identifies these at-risk youths as "in need of development." Programs for them should emphasize a laundry list of goals, including such familiar ones as healthy and nurturing families, school attachment, prosocial peer relations, and healthy lifestyle choices.

The goals of prevention and graduated sanctions represent another interesting feature of the OJJDP agenda. The left side of figure 11.1 represents a developmental model. The emphasis is on those qualities of the youth's social and physical environment that will lead to a "healthy" child. The right side delineates reactions to youthful misconduct. The language associated with the goals is particularly

Figure 11.1
The OJJDP's Comprehensive Strategy

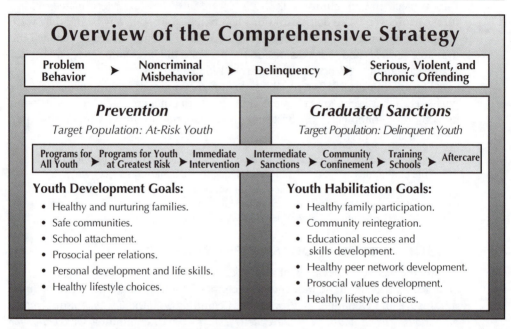

Source: Adapted from Coolbaugh and Hansel (2000).

interesting since it emphasizes correcting the "mistakes" or shortcomings of the past (i.e., not rehabilitation but rather habilitation, to make the child fit to survive in the world). Each of the goals under this section has a parallel developmental goal, the assumption being that those goals not achieved during the child's formative years must now be addressed through graduated sanctions.

Indeed, the figure changes when the behavior transitions to delinquency. OJJDP's comprehensive strategy first calls for intermediate intervention, an approach that Lundman called preadjudication intervention and others call diversion. As behavior moves clearly from noncriminal misbehavior and delinquency to serious, violent, and chronic offending, the strategy enters the domain of previous chapters. These responses are less relevant for delinquency prevention but are important nonetheless to the comprehensive strategy. Their significance for this chapter is that OJJDP's comprehensive strategy incorporates a range of responses, from programs for all youths when the issue is problem behavior, to community confinement and training schools for more serious offenders.

THE LANDSCAPE OF JUVENILE PREVENTION PROGRAMS

The OJJDP Comprehensive Strategy and our review of delinquency prevention's history suggest that to understand delinquency prevention, we need to look mainly in three locations: the community, the schools, and the family.[11] Rather than review general programs suitable for a broad range of nondelinquent and delinquent clients in these three areas, we limit our review primarily to those that serve all youths and at-risk youths. Before we turn to an examination of the three primary loci of prevention, we would like to issue a few cautions.

As a general observation, programs for all youngsters, regardless of legal status, have been relatively rare until the 1990s. Secondary prevention programs for youths at greatest risk are more common but also more problematic, given how various agencies and service providers have defined the term *at-risk*. For review purposes, we have included the following groups of youths in this category, along with the programs intended to prevent their delinquency: predelinquents, at-risk youths, emotionally disturbed and mentally ill offenders, school failures, first-time offenders, and chronic runaways.

Precise definitions for many of these terms are rare. Some youths are clearly suitable secondary prevention targets, for example, school failures and chronic runaways. Deciding exactly when a child is at risk or predelinquent, other than evidence of status offending, is a far more subjective process. This list includes individuals who could potentially be accused of or found involved in serious delin-

As part of a local delinquency intervention or prevention program, and in some cases as a condition of probation or parole, juvenile offenders and those designated as at-risk may be required to work with senior citizens. These interactions may take the form of playing board games, cards, and the like with seniors in their homes or at retirement centers. In other cases, the youths may be required to perform household tasks for seniors. These programs are intended to connect youths to their communities, give them a sense of social responsibility, and to repay the community for its investment in them.

quent acts, for example, first-time offenders and emotionally disturbed and mentally ill offenders. If we erred, it was by including exemplars intended for these latter youths in the review that follows.

In the early 1990s, Montgomery and associates (1994) conducted a thorough review of delinquency prevention programs across the nation. They asked 3,000 experienced judges, court administrators, and chief probation officers to nominate and rate effective treatment programs they recently had used. Tables 11.1 through 11.3 summarize their findings. Each table contains a summary of six primary pieces of information for each program reviewed. That is, regardless of whether the program is community-based, family-oriented, or education-based, we provide the following information:

1. the program's name
2. its geographic location
3. the target population, including age range
4. the program classification (that is, prevention, prevention plus treatment or rehabilitation, and diversion from either the juvenile court or correctional system)
5. participants' average length of involvement
6. the primary intervention offered to program clients (that is, community service or working in the community, adult mentoring or role modeling, academic education or vocational training, and awareness education)

In addition to listing the programs reviewed by Montgomery and associates, we will highlight those that have shown particular promise. Several programs—but not a large number—have earned the designation of either "model" or "working" programs, depending on who is doing the assessing (see box 11.1).

COMMUNITY-BASED DELINQUENCY PREVENTION

Since the 1920s, rightly or wrongly, many policy makers have come to view the community as the locus for successful delinquency prevention. If delinquency has its roots in the community, then that is where we attack it, say the supporters of this perspective. At the end of the twentieth century, many of the nation's cities were **hypersegregated**, meaning that the degree of racial isolation was extreme, with African Americans comprising the main racial group (Massey and Denton, 1993). Poverty and family disruption were greatest in the same relatively small number of urban communities where gang violence, general delinquency, and crime were highest. These communities were also, not coincidentally, high in gun density. As Wilson (1996) observed, these urban communities—where crime levels are highest—are also the ones shunned by the rest of the nation.

Today's community-based programs, including those described in table 11.1, are the programmatic offspring of the CAP, the Mid City Project, and the Mobilization for Youth project. However, about the only common element with those earlier programs is that the youths remain in the community during contact with the program. Contemporary prevention programs provide services to disparate target populations of first-time offenders, predelinquents/at-risk youths, school failures,

Box 11.1   Assessing Prevention: Two Perspectives

In 1996, Congress decided that the "art of crime prevention (*like the art of medicine*) can be evaluated and guided by the science of measuring program effects" (Sherman et al., 1998:2; emphasis added). The National Institute of Justice funded an assessment of the state of crime prevention efforts, conducted under the general leadership of Lawrence Sherman, a University of Maryland criminologist.[12] Prevention was defined as

> any practice shown to result in less crime than would occur without the practice [and] . . . any program that claims to prevent crime or drug abuse, especially youth violence, and, in accordance with the congressional mandate, examined the effects of programs on risk and protective factors for youth violence and drug abuse. (Sherman et al., p. 2)

The research teams created a list of crime prevention program evaluations, mostly from scientific journals. They also identified a series of unpublished evaluations. The Sherman-led team developed the **Maryland Scale of Scientific Methods** for assessing the strength of the evaluations. Research designs were assigned to one of five levels, with level 5 reserved for the strongest design.[13] A program was defined as (1) "working" if it scored at least level 3 for both criteria with "statistical significance tests and the preponderance of evidence showing effectiveness"; (2) "not working" if it scored below level 3 on both dimensions with "statistical significance tests showing ineffectiveness and the preponderance of evidence supporting the same conclusion"; and (3) "promising" if it was found to be "effective in at least one level 3 evaluation and the preponderance of the remaining evidence."

Also in 1996, a team of researchers called the Advisory Board, led by Delbert Elliott at the University of Colorado's Center for the Study and Prevention of Violence, employed a second assessment method. The result of their effort, which is ongoing, is called the **Blueprints for Violence Prevention**, and by 2005 included nearly 400 different programs. Advisory Board members assessed the programs in terms of three criteria. First, they determined whether the program's deterrent effect had been assessed with a "strong design," generally defined as experimental designs with random assignment to treatment and control groups or quasi-experimental designs with matched control groups. Second, the Blueprints researchers included the requirement that the program effects be sustained for at least one year beyond the end of the treatment. Moreover, there could be no subsequent evidence that the effects were lost over time. Third, they included in their assessment model a determination of whether there were replications of the program evaluations. The researchers considered successful replications as a chief means of establishing the strength of a program. Of particular interest was the use of diverse settings (for example, urban, suburban, and rural areas) and diverse populations (for example, different socioeconomic, racial, and cultural groups).

Advisory Board members considered two additional criteria in their evaluations. First, they investigated whether certain risk or protective factors influenced the outcome. If the program assessment considered such mediating factors, the program essentially earned "extra credit." Second, the team considered costs versus benefits. That is, the program costs did not exceed the expected benefits. Again, programs that were cost-effective moved up in the assessment process.

Of the hundreds of programs evaluated, only 11 programs earned Blueprint "model" status, attesting to the rigor of the Blueprint program criteria. In terms of the University of Maryland project, evaluators generally summarized program success, failure, and promise in broader, conceptual terms rather than in a programmatic context.[14] However, seven specific programs were on both lists.[15]

Sources: Sherman et al. (1998); Center for the Study of Prevention and Violence (2005); Mihalic (2005); Mihalic et al. (2004).

runaways, and substance abusers. Even the time duration varies widely, from a few hours to a year or more.

As a rule, most of the community-based antidelinquency programs in table 11.1 are preventive, with a few having mixed goals. Mentoring is the most common service, followed by individual or family counseling and skill development. Many offered their clients little more than mentoring or skill development. Considering the criteria discussed earlier in this chapter, few such programs could achieve primary prevention. At best their goal was secondary prevention, as most dealt with at-risk or predelinquent children.

Sherman (1997a) reported that none of the community-based programs work; however, two approaches—one addressing gang cohesion and one featuring volunteer mentors—show promise. The Blueprints Advisory Board found two programs to be model programs. Big Brothers Big Sisters of America (BBBS) matches youths and volunteer mentors and provides supervision during volunteer-client contact. BBBS is cost-effective as the total expenses are estimated at $1,000 per year per match. In terms of outcomes, illicit substance and alcohol use rates were lower for program participants than those in control groups. The other program—the Midwestern Prevention Program—specifically targeted adolescent drug abuse and achieved similar positive results at relatively low cost.

SCHOOL-BASED AND EDUCATION-RELATED DELINQUENCY PREVENTION

A 2000 study of the nation's schools found that nearly all had incorporated some type of delinquency prevention program.[16] Problem behavior was found to be pervasive in middle schools and in urban schools. However, merely offering a program and having a program that worked turned out to be two different things, as nearly half of the prevention programs failed to meet the study's criteria for quality. That is, using a set of quality indicators ranging from the use of best practices, the number of lessons or sessions, the duration of programming, and the frequency of participation by students and staff, the researchers gave overall failing grades to the nation's school-based programming. Key factors in successful programs were staff training, program monitoring, and other organizational support from school leaders. Interestingly, this study found that it was not for lack of adequate programming that prevention efforts fail to achieve their goals, but rather for lack of effort and attention to detail in their implementation.

Education can play a major role in all forms of prevention. For example, drug prevention programs that target youngsters as early as the elementary-school level rely heavily on several educational models. Consider, by way of example, the three models described in box 11.2. General delinquency prevention that uses education as its chief preventive weapon employs one or more of these tactics. The more children know about delinquency and the costs to society in general and potentially to themselves as individuals, the less likely they are to engage in delinquent behavior (information-based delinquency prevention programs). Less likely to work are those based on instilling fear as a preventive force: "Don't break the law, or you'll end up here in jail with me," says the hardened con, conducting the "scared straight" tour of the local prison or jail.

Table 11.1   Community-Based Delinquency Prevention

Program	Location	Target Population	Age	Program Type	Duration	Primary Intervention
Community Service Early Intervention	Marion, OH	Chronic runaways, school failures, & predelinquents/ at-risk youths	9–16	Prevention	2–12 months	Community service & mentoring
Bismarck Police Youth Bureau	Bismarck, ND	Predelinquents/ at-risk youths & first-time offenders	14–16	Prevention-plus & diversion	NA	Community service
Gateway Outreach	Celina, OH	Substance abusers	8–19	Prevention-plus	2 months	Individual or family counseling
Sentenced to Read	Orlando, FL	School failures & teen parents	4–21	Prevention	2–4 months	Mentoring & skill development
Ottawa Youth Commission	Ottawa, IL	First-time offenders & substance abusers	12–20	Prevention	3–6 months	Mentoring & skill development
Targeted Case Management	Columbia, TN	Emotionally disturbed/mentally ill offenders	2–18	Prevention	1 year	Skill development
Treatment Alternatives to Street Crime (TASC)	Eaton, OH	First-time offenders	12–20	Prevention & diversion	6–9 months	Individual or family counseling & skill development
Street Law	Lewisburg, TN	First-time offenders	12–17	Prevention	1 year	Mentoring
Youth Works	Louisville, KY	First-time offenders	Up to 17½	Prevention & diversion	6 months	Mentoring & skill development
Kids in Need of Development	Monroe, LA	Predelinquents/ at-risk youths	12–17	Prevention-plus	6–7 months	Family counseling & skill development
Project Uplift	Auburn, AL	Predelinquents/ at-risk youths	5–16	Prevention	3 to 4 years	Recreation & fitness, skill development, & mentoring
Teen Fitness Program	Emporium, PA	Predelinquents/ at-risk youths	12–18	Prevention	NA	Recreation & fitness, skill development, & mentoring
Metamorphosis	Natchitoches, LA	Predelinquents/ at-risk youths & substance abusers	5 and older	Prevention	Varies	Nonsecure residential; skill development
Youth Leadership Conference	Vienna, GA	Predelinquents/ at-risk youths	13–15	Prevention	1 year	Skill development

Source: Montgomery et al. (1994).

Box 11.2   Education and Drug Prevention

Prevention seems synonymous with education. Indeed, many prevention programs rely heavily on an educational component. Over the past 40 or more years of drug education, three models have come to dominate school-based programs; each has ties to other delinquency prevention programs.

- *Information model.* The emphasis is on transferring information about drugs. The model assumes that the information received by the students will deter them from using drugs; that is, knowledge yields negative attitudes toward drugs, which in turn leads to nonuse of drugs.

- *Affective model.* This model asks the question, Why do students use drugs? The answer, claim affective model proponents, is the low self-esteem, low self-worth, and inadequate personal communication and decision-making skills children possess. This model, as the name suggests, addresses the improvement of these defective skills by focusing on personal feelings, values, and self-awareness. It may explore, as part of the core content, drug use as a personal choice, along with the personal values associated with that choice.

- *Social influence model.* Why do children use drugs? One answer seemed so self-evident that it generated an entire perspective on drug education. Children use drugs to be like their drug-using peers, to be members of the "in crowd." In this sense, then, drug use is the result of external pressures pushing children toward drugs. The social influence model maintains that educators must arm students with the resistance skills necessary to deflect peer influences. The personification of social influence in its simplest form was Nancy Reagan's "Just Say No" campaign, begun in the late 1980s. Forms that are more sophisticated than this message provide students with conflict-resolution skills.

Each of these formats has its own shortcomings. Drug prevention programs based on the information model may actually stimulate the behavior they intend to prevent, although there is great disagreement on this issue among educators and evaluators. Some social influence models, such as "Just Say No," are far too simplistic in their views of the social forces propelling some youths toward drugs. Part of the problem may be that many educational efforts, including those based on the information model, are actually scare-based education efforts, emphasizing the inherent dangers of drug use. Such programs run into trouble when they employ drug misinformation—insights and messages into drug use that, if not completely wrong, are often based on questionable research. Throughout much of the 1990s, policy makers and prevention specialists largely abandoned the scare-based, informational approach to drug prevention in favor of a cross between the affective model and the social influence model. These blended programs emphasize children's self-esteem, personal development, and personal growth, along with the mechanisms necessary to deflect and blunt peer pressures. According to Victor Kappeler and Gary Potter (2005), a new strategy finding its way into the public lexicon of ideas is to link the "War on Drugs" to the "War on Terrorism," as messages from the Drug Czar's office suggest that those who buy illegal drugs fund those who seek to destroy the American way of life. (For more on this idea, see the discussion in chapter 1 of the media's role in shaping our ideas and information about crime and delinquency.)

Many evaluators of education-based drug prevention programs observe that they work well among those who are at low risk and have little effect among those at higher risk. As Dishion and associates have observed, "Even at age 10, [the] most-at-risk children are already difficult to change, whether by family, teachers or therapists" (1998:90). The same may be true of the most at-risk children for general delinquency as well.

Sources: Abadinsky (1996); Dishion, Patterson, and Reid (1988:90); Ellickson (1995:100–102); Kappeler and Potter (2005:364); Venturelli (1994:143–47).

At least two forms of delinquency prevention rely heavily on educational concepts: school-based programs and education-based programs. The difference is the locus of implementation more than the method of conveying the necessary preventive elements. These types of programs typically follow one of the following models:

- special stand-alone alternative schools or classes within mainstream schools that provide special education classes for dropouts and near-dropouts

- combination education and employment programs, in which job training and education commingle, programs that make us think of the 1961 Juvenile Delinquency and Youth Offenses Control Act

- awareness education sessions of relatively brief duration (one to four hours in length) to lengthy (and intensive) legal education curricula (see our earlier discussion and critique of the G.R.E.A.T. and DARE programs)

- outdoor activities and personal challenge courses to build self-confidence

Table 11.2 contains the education-based primary prevention programs described by Montgomery and associates (1994). They were of relatively brief duration, a couple of hours or less, and relied on awareness education. As a rule, the few primary prevention programs available for the general youth population, including G.R.E.A.T. and DARE, are relatively short in duration, lasting weeks rather than years. Put plainly, stand-alone primary prevention programs in schools, while more common than community-based ones, remain rare.

The University of Maryland team reported that successful programs are generally those that (1) build a school's capacity to initiate and sustain innovation; (2) clarify and communicate norms, including anti-bullying programs; and (3) address a broad range of programs intended to enhance social competency, including self-control, stress-management, responsible decision-making, social problem-solving, and communication skills (Gottfredson, 1997). The Blueprints report includes five model programs that are essentially school-based. Two of the Blueprint programs—Life Skills Training and Project Towards No Drug Abuse—are anti-drug programs (see box 11.2). The remaining three—including Bullying Prevention Program (BPP), Promoting Alternative THinking Strategies (PATHS), and Incredible Years Series (IYS)—address delinquency and related disruptive behavior. Sherman and associates reviewed four of the five and found them effective.[17] IYS targets young children, ranging from 2 to 8 years of age, and provides training for parents, teachers, and children intended to promote emotional and social competence. The children must exhibit conduct problems; however, given the absence of contacts with the juvenile justice system, IYS may be considered a secondary prevention program. PATHS is intended for elementary school children and also promotes emotional and social competencies. It simultaneously addresses the reduction of aggression and behavior problems and the enhancement of educational goals. BPP targets a broad range of school-age children, from elementary to junior high school. This program is a universal intervention intended to reduce and prevent bullying and related victim problems. Participants (students and teachers) learn about bullying and how to deal with the problem in their school.

Getting the prevention message out to school administrators, teachers, parents, and students is a difficult job. Since 1984, the National School Safety Center

Table 11.2   Education-Based Delinquency Prevention Exemplars

Program	Location	Target Population	Age	Program Type	Duration	Primary Intervention
Metropolitan Youth Academy	St. Louis, MO	Chronic runaways, school failures, first-time offenders, & predelinquents/at-risk youths	16–19	Prevention-plus	9 months	Nonsecure residential; academic education
Project Attend	Miami, FL	Chronic runaways, school failures, & predelinquents/at-risk youths	13–21	Prevention	1–4 semesters	Academic education
Youth Education & Employment Program	Chesapeake, VA	Predelinquents/at-risk youths & first-time offenders	16–21	Prevention-plus	3–6 months	Academic education & mentoring
CHOICES (Don't choose crime; don't choose to use)	Huntsville, TX & Georgetown, TX	Predelinquents/at-risk youths & general youths	6–18	Prevention	1 hour	Education
Marshall Middle School	Plymouth, IN	School failures	12–16	Prevention-plus & diversion	18 weeks	Skill development & academic education
Volunteer School Liaison Program	Jeffersonville, IN	School failures	9–17	Prevention-plus & diversion	NA	Mentoring
Spectrum Wilderness Program	Carbondale, IL	Predelinquents/at-risk youths	10–18	Prevention-plus	30 days	Outdoor activity & skill development
Shoplifters Are Very Expensive (SAVE)	Grand Rapids, MI	Predelinquents/at-risk youths & general youth	11–13	Prevention	NA	Awareness education
Bright Young Minds	McComb, MS	School failures & predelinquents/at-risk youths; emotionally disturbed/mentally ill offenders	3–18	Prevention-plus & diversion	9 months	Individual or family counseling
Chemical Awareness Program	Baton Rouge, LA	Substance abusers	12–18	Prevention	3½ hours	Awareness education & skill development

Source: Montgomery et al. (1994).

Theoretical Reflections
School-Based Delinquency Prevention Programs

Richard Lawrence observes that much delinquency is associated with academic failure and school-based problems. He links the school difficulties of troubled youth to two theoretical origins. First, following Cohen's ideas about reaction formation, he notes that much disruptive and delinquent behavior results directly from strains created among those youths unable to meet academic performance standards. While the causal sequencing remains debated, delinquency researchers have firmly established the ties between dropping out of school and delinquency. "Many youths turn to delinquency out of frustration, feelings of failure and low self-esteem" (1998:226). What is unknown is whether they were delinquent before dropping out or because of dropping out.

A second school-based set of forces presents similar causal sequencing problems for delinquency prevention specialists. Earlier in this text, we presented Hirschi's bonding theory: Delinquency is highest among children who exhibit weak bonds or affective attachments to school and similarly low commitments to education. It is unclear whether those who engage in delinquency do so because of weak bonds to school and the values it represents or whether delinquents simply have less interest in and patience for school-related measures of success.

Despite the lack of conclusive evidence about the causal ordering, many school-based prevention programs seem to represent the theoretical ideas found in the works of Cohen and Hirschi, among others. It seems reasonable to conclude that some disjuncture between the schools and the delinquents at least precipitated the youths' movement deeper into the delinquency cycle.

Sources: Cohen (1955); Elliott and Voss (1974); Hirschi (1969); Lawrence (1998).

(NSSC), an entity created by President Ronald Reagan, has provided technical assistance to those schools that have created prevention programs (Lawrence, 1998:249). It serves as a clearinghouse and general resource for schools (today these services are available largely through a Web site). NSSC also conducts training for school safety personnel and helps develop model school-safety codes.

FAMILY-BASED DELINQUENCY PREVENTION

The family has played some role in nearly every chapter in this text. Therefore, it should come as no great surprise that policy makers view the family as essential in prevention efforts. Prevention specialists may define the family as part of both the problem and the solution. For example, in chapter 2 we explored how the changing definitions of the family and children's roles essentially "created" adolescence and, eventually, the condition of delinquency. Kumpfer (1993:1) describes nine specific family correlates of delinquency:

- poor socialization practices, including parents' modeling of antisocial values and behaviors; failure to promote positive moral development; and neglect in teaching the child life, social, and academic skills

- poor supervision of the child, including failure to monitor the child, neglect, latchkey conditions, sibling supervision, and too few adults to care for the number of children

- poor discipline skills, including lax, inconsistent, or excessive discipline; expectations unrealistic for the child's developmental level (which creates a failure syndrome); and excessive, unrealistic demands or harsh physical punishment

- poor parent-child relationships, including rejection of the child by the parents or of the parents by the child, lack of involvement and time together, and maladaptive parent-child interactions

- excessive family conflict and marital discord with verbal, physical, or sexual abuse

- family chaos and stress, often a result of poor family management skills or life skills or poverty

- poor parental mental health, including depression and irritability that cause negative views of the child's behavior

- family isolation and the lack of community support resources

- differential family acculturation and role reversal or loss of parental control over adolescents by parents who are less acculturated than their children

Table 11.3 contains a sampling of family-based prevention programs described by Montgomery and associates (1994). They cluster into two forms. The first form provides heavy counseling for the individual and family, plus skill development and mentoring. A second group relies heavily on skill development alone. More than with community-based and school-based programs, prevention and treatment—plus diversion from the juvenile justice system—drive the family-based programs. When the family is involved, there seems to be a clear recognition that more than just a troubled child is involved, a fact that has caché in the world community as well (see box 11.3).

Sherman (1997b) observed that family-based prevention efforts exhibit a unique ecology of programming, including programs in the home, preschool, school, clinics, hospitals, courts, and battered women's shelters. The ones that work, in Sherman's opinion, were those that used (1) long-term and frequent visits by medical social workers, especially with preschool children, (2) weekly home visitations at any age, and (3) Family Therapy, a specific program also addressed by the Blueprints team. For its part, the Blueprints Advisory Board identified three model programs: Functional Family Therapy (FFT), Nurse-Family Partnerships (NFP), and Multidimensional Treatment Foster Care (MTFC), each with a slightly different emphasis, but all of which fit within the framework identified by Sherman. For example, FFT targets youths aged 11–18 who are at risk or who have engaged in delinquency and disruptive behavior. The program duration is 8–26 hours of direct service. A broad range of medical, mental-health, and juvenile justice professionals provide the direct services, which can include treatment modalities intended to motivate positive behavior and change negative behavior. The locus of treatment varies from client to client and includes in-home, clinic, juvenile court, and post-release residence for youths reentering the community after institutional

Table 11.3   Family-Based Delinquency Prevention Exemplars

Program	Location	Target Population	Age	Program Type	Duration	Primary Intervention
Crisis Intervention	Grand Rapids, MI	Chronic runaways, school failures, & predelinquents/at-risk youths	12–17	Prevention-plus & diversion	NA	Individual or family counseling, skill development & mentoring
Families First	Marquette, MI	Predelinquents/at-risk youths	All ages	Prevention-plus & diversion	4 weeks	Individual or family counseling & mentoring
Family Preservation Services	Fredericksburg, VA	Predelinquents/at-risk youths	Up to 21	Prevention-plus & diversion	3–9 months	Individual or family counseling & mentoring
First Referral Program	Huntsville, TX	First-time offenders	10–16	Prevention	NA	Individual or family counseling, skills development & mentoring
Second Chance Program	Crandon, WI	First-time offenders	8–18	Prevention & diversion	3 months	Skill development & mentoring
Community Treatment Center	Farmington, MO	Predelinquents/at-risk youths & families	12–18	Prevention	3 days	Skill development
Intensive Family Advocate Program	Delaware, OH	Predelinquents/at-risk youths	12–19	Prevention-plus & diversion	6 months	Individual or family counseling, skill development, & mentoring
Teen Crisis Service	Stamford, CT	Predelinquents/at-risk youths, emotionally disturbed & mentally ill offenders	12–17	Prevention-plus & diversion	2 months	Skill development & mentoring
Family Preservation: In-Home Services	New Wilmington, PA	Predelinquents/at-risk youths	12–17	Prevention-plus & diversion	1 year	Skill development & mentoring
Positive Steps	Reno, NV	Predelinquents/at-risk youths & first-time offenders	9–17	Prevention & diversion	5 weeks	Skill development
Preliminary Conferences	Carmi, IL	First-time offenders	5–16	Prevention & diversion	NA	Skill development
Key to Empowering Youth	Morristown, NH	First-time offenders	12–16	Prevention & diversion	2 days	Skill development
Turning Point	Wichita Falls, TX	First-time offenders	9–17	Prevention & diversion	6 weeks	Skill development

Source: Montgomery et al. (1994).

placement. NFP targets low-income, at-risk pregnant women having their first child. Nurse home visitors work with the families during the pregnancy through the first two years of the child's life. Specific goals include prenatal and postnatal health care, and the mother's psychological, social, and work-related needs. Finally, MTFC stands as an alternative to group or residential treatment, incarceration, and hospitalization for teenagers presenting chronic behavioral disorders. The program recruits and trains community foster-care families who care for the problem youth in the near-term, while the family of origin (biological or adoptive) attends training intended to facilitate the return of the child. Coordination and community liaison between MTFC case managers and all other participants is key to the program's success. Many of the programs contained in table 11.3 employ some or all of the programmatic components identified by the Blueprints Advisory Board, but only these three have been subjected to the type of assessment required to be models.

Box 11.3 International Perspectives
Delinquency Prevention in New Zealand

New Zealand experienced a dramatic rise in youthful antisocial behavior in the last decade of the twentieth century. For example, the New Zealand Ministry of Justice reported that apprehensions of youths between 14 and 16 years of age increased by 80% during the 1990s. In particular, apprehensions for violent offenses and property damage offenses increased by even greater amounts. Like many nations, including the United States, New Zealand employed a host of prevention, intervention, and treatment programs at the individual, family, school, and community levels. Multisystemic Therapy (MST), as a family- and community-based treatment, has been shown to have positive outcomes with antisocial youths and has a following among health care professionals in New Zealand.

This support derives from four characteristics of MST that fit with a "best-practices treatment mode" suitable for New Zealand, including:

1. a family preservation model of service delivery, whereby every effort is taken to keep the family unit intact

2. an emphasis on validating the model through well-designed assessments using samples populated by children with serious antisocial behavior

3. a rigorous quality assurance process to insure that the program as designed is the program that is being delivered

4. an ongoing implementation and evaluation of the program within New Zealand, seeking to ground the service delivery within the unique multiculturalism found within that nation

Researchers and practitioners in New Zealand view MST as bridging the gap between isolated programs that fail to take a "total system" view of service delivery to children and families in need of intervention and treatment. While proponents recognize the importance of this intervention strategy, they also recognize that it must "take into account the social, cultural, and ethnic factors that are unique to New Zealand." In the arena of prevention, as in most antidelinquency programs explored from an international perspective, one size does not fit all needs.

Source: Curtis, Ronan, Heiblum, Reid, and Harris (2002).

SUMMARY

Delinquency prevention is an attractive idea—in the abstract. Preventing delinquency means stopping undesired juvenile conduct in its tracks before it can become delinquent, and before adolescents come to the juvenile justice system's attention. If delinquency prevention efforts were perfect, there would be no need for a separate juvenile justice system, and in all likelihood far less adult crime. Of course, the reality is that primary prevention programs designed and implemented to keep otherwise normal children from delinquency are rare. Secondary prevention programs that target at-risk youth, predelinquent children, or first-time offenders and demonstrate to them the error of their ways, along with the promise and potential of law-abiding behavior, are far more common.

Good reasons exist for the lack of primary preventive efforts and the paucity of effective secondary preventive programs. First, delinquency prevention programs are complex and require a great deal of coordination and up-front investments of time, talent, and money. Consider, for example, OJJDP's five-step program for the design, implementation, and evaluation of a successful crime prevention program (see box 11.4). While the focus on local, grassroots efforts described in this bulletin is laudable, a close reading of the steps reveals that getting from an idea to a working program is a difficult and complicated journey.

Second, even when they are well conceived, grounded in the best theoretical understandings of crime and delinquency, widely supported in the community, and adequately implemented, the assessments of prevention programs have tended to be incomplete, or the programs were prematurely curtailed. Perhaps the rush to try something, assess its effectiveness, decide whether it is working, and, if not, move on, is related to our nation's perceived obsession with quick fixes. This tendency also may be related to the politicization of prevention, in which programs that should be based on the best available social scientific knowledge instead are often subject to the whims of political fortune. If liberals are in power, ideas like prevention, treatment, and rehabilitation find support; if conservatives reign, then there is a shift toward reactive responses and graduated sanctions (see for example Walker, 2001).

Third, clear, concise, and widely held definitions are crucial. Unfortunately, the prevention definitions are open to many interpretations, starting with what prevention means. Prevention's benchmark is its response to problem behavior before it becomes more than just problematic. Definitions of problem behavior could vary by part of the country, religious affiliation, race or ethnicity, and other cultural determinants. For example, some adults may view hair and clothing styles as warnings of societal collapse, while others see them as mere expressions of individualism. In the wake of the Columbine school massacre in 1999, many school officials banned so-called "Goth" dress, just as other administrators in the late 1980s banned gang clothes and certain sports apparel. Are these examples of prevention, or they are just knee-jerk reactions and feel-good policies?

Fourth, prevention generally depends on society's ability to predict the next trend in problem behaviors, forerunners of impending noncriminal behavior and true delinquency. The links between gang territory, local drug sales, and high-powered firearms

Box 11.4   Five Steps to a Successful Crime Prevention Program

Who should be involved in prevention? Should it be limited to wise old men and women? How about making teenagers and other young people part of the solution? The latter approach defines the National Youth Network, an OJJDP initiative. OJJDP created *Youth in Action* to encourage the nation's youth to be proactive in preventing crime. Its inaugural volume, aptly entitled "Planning a Successful Crime Prevention Project," outlined a five-step blueprint for action:

Step 1: Assessing your community's needs. Before we can assess needs, the community must be defined. For example, the community could be a geographic unit, such as a block, neighborhood, or school; or it could be group-based, such as a group of peers. Moreover, the bulletin encouraged participants to expand their knowledge about the community by consulting existing information sources, such as police reports, newspapers, school building records, and the like, or by conducting their own survey. These efforts should provide a list of community assets and problems. By contrasting the assets and problems, the youths should be able to identify a specific problem they can address, an activity requiring well-informed, reasonably analytical individuals.

Step 2: Planning a successful project. This step creates an operational plan for attacking the problem. It consists of six interrelated activities: (1) identifying the target, such as a specific group to be helped; (2) spelling out precise goals and objectives; (3) choosing strategies (methods and approaches) to reach the goals and objectives; (4) determining target dates and priorities; (5) dividing specific jobs and responsibilities among group members; and (6) making sure the project can be evaluated properly. All these activities require high analytic skills, particularly if the youths must conduct their own survey.

Step 3: Lining up resources. Key resources include: (1) peer volunteers with needed talents and skills; (2) adult supporters, including teachers, principals, civic leaders, parents, law enforcement officers, and other interested adults; and (3) monetary resources. This step requires well-connected and highly verbal individuals.

Step 4: Acting on your plan. The bulletin maintains that "this is the most exciting part of the success cycle" (1998:2). Adequate training is essential. For example, the bulletin provides estimated times for training people in community cleanup (1 to 4 hours), school crime watch (4 to 6 hours), and teen court (10 to 120 hours).

Step 5: Nurturing, monitoring, and evaluating. This step is heavily dependent upon the skills of the participants. Program employees need to acknowledge, reward, and nurture volunteers. The project must be objectively monitored and evaluated. The bulletin contains guidelines and worksheets for all three activities.

During the 1940s, actor Mickey Rooney sang and danced his way through a series of movies where the basic plot was the same: Some talented kids decide to put on a Broadway-type show. They are successful in spite of tremendous obstacles. In real life, few young people accomplish what Rooney's character did, no matter how talented. The challenge is the same for planning and implementing a successful crime prevention project, even with a blueprint and talented young people. Is it worth trying? Of course it is. Will it meet with success? That depends on how we define success. Simply doing it may have positive consequences for the community and the youths involved, whether or not it prevents criminal behavior by other community youths.

Source: Office of Juvenile Justice and Delinquency Prevention (1998b).

seem obvious in hindsight but were difficult to predict in the early 1980s. The Internet's societal impact, ranging from hard-core pornography to bomb-making technology available in the home, would have been difficult to predict in the early 1990s. Providing a general inoculation for children against what *might* be on the horizon may lie beyond the ability of any society. Indeed, delinquency prediction instruments intended for individuals also have shown little efficacy over the long term. Whether we are predicting the coming trends in misbehavior or predicting who is likely to become a delinquent in the future, we currently lack the skills to bring these ideas to fruition.

Should we give up on prevention? Hardly. Sherman and associates' survey of existing programs demonstrates that much is right with our prevention agenda. Moreover, the future may hold even greater hope for primary and secondary prevention goals. Abandoning prevention because we cannot clearly demonstrate what works may be shortsighted, and given the political nature of such efforts, highly unlikely. As the pundits ask: What would the nation's delinquency problem look like if we made no attempt at prevention?

CRITICAL REVIEW QUESTIONS

1. With whom did you most identify, if anyone, in the opening vignette? Have you altered your position?

2. "The juvenile justice system may be the wrong place to practice delinquency prevention." Support or attack this statement, providing a rational, fact-based argument for your position.

3. Your teacher has asked you to address a group of local concerned citizens on the topic of reducing delinquency in America. How would you explain to them the difference between delinquency control and delinquency prevention?

4. Give two reasons supporting the use of the disease epidemiology analogy and two reasons why its use is a bad idea. Which reasoning is more persuasive, and why?

5. Compare and contrast Lundman's three forms of intervention with the goals of delinquency prevention and control.

6. Given what we described about the Chicago Area Project, provide some reasons why it failed even though the basic premise was sound.

7. Provide reasons for the failure of the Cambridge-Somerville Youth Study.

8. Why do you think it took 60 years for the federal government to take a leadership role in delinquency prevention? Is government involvement a good thing?

9. How do you assess OJJDP's comprehensive strategy? What are its strengths and weaknesses?

10. Delinquency prevention is practiced in the local community, within the family context, and in educational environments, including schools. Do you think that one of these locations has more promise than the rest to reduce delinquency significantly? Would your answer change if we defined the specific target as at-risk children?

11. Looking back over the various prevention programs discussed in this chapter, what is your reaction to the programs described in Sherman's 1998 report, *What Works, What Doesn't, and What's Promising*? Are you optimistic or pessimistic about the future of delinquency prevention?

12. How would you answer the question asked in the last sentence of this chapter's summary?

RECOMMENDED READINGS

Heilbrun, Kirk, Naomi E. Sevin Goldstein, and Richard E. Redding, eds. (2005). *Juvenile Delinquency: Prevention, Assessment, and Intervention*. New York: Oxford University Press. This 15-chapter edited volume covers a broad range of topics related to the prevention, assessment, and intervention of juvenile delinquency. Merging psychological and public health perspectives on juvenile delinquency, each chapter addresses some aspect of law and public policy that impacts the welfare of children that engage in juvenile delinquency and youth antisocial behavior. This work reflects state-of-the-art epidemiological information and delinquency risk factors at the beginning of the twenty-first century.

Lundman, Richard J. (1993). *Prevention and Control of Juvenile Delinquency.* 2nd ed. New York: Oxford University Press. This book is fast becoming a classic—and one of the few works on broad-ranging practices related to delinquency prevention and control. The author contributes valuable insights into the key distinctions among the various formal societal responses to delinquency. He also assesses a large number of specific programs for their ability to accomplish the goals of prevention and control.

KEY TERMS

Blueprints for Violence Prevention
Cambridge-Somerville Youth Study
Chicago Area Project (CAP)
delinquency control
delinquency prevention
detached social worker
disease epidemiology
eradication
hypersegregated
intervention
Juvenile Delinquency and Youth Offenses Control Act of 1961
life histories

Maryland Scale of Scientific Methods
Mid-City Project
Minnesota Multiphasic Personality Inventory (MMPI)
Mobilization for Youth
penology
postadjudication intervention
preadjudication intervention
predelinquent intervention
primary prevention
secondary prevention
social ecology
social disorganization theory

NOTES

[1] Disease epidemiology is a branch of medical science that focuses on disease causes and control. As we shall make clear in this chapter, many social and behavioral sciences employ the language and methods of disease epidemiology.

[2] We use the term *intervention* to describe generally any attempt to reduce or eradicate delinquency, whether the object is society or an individual delinquent.

[3] Disease epidemiologists are always looking for the alpha case, the first one, so that they can determine the vectors by which the disease was spread and, in response, develop both intervention and prevention methods. In addition, they anxiously await the omega case, the last one. However, omega

cases may prove elusive. For example, the United Nations claims the eradication of smallpox. There has not been a new *naturally acquired* smallpox case since 1978 (Centers for Disease Control, 1999). The governments of the world no long vaccinate children against smallpox; nations no longer manufacture the serum. In fact, only two places in the world maintain the live smallpox virus: the U.S. Centers for Disease Control in Atlanta and a Russian medical-weapons laboratory in Koltsovo, Novosibirsk (Henderson, 1998). While it appears that the omega case for smallpox has occurred, we can never be certain. Moreover, the potential to "weaponize" smallpox, discussed so often in the post-9/11 era, threatens to change entirely how we view smallpox and its eradication.

[4] We intend for the language to sound like labeling theory. Since the days of Wheeler and Cottrell (1966), labeling theory has been used as the key support for preadjudication prevention, or diversion.

[5] See the sections in chapter 3 on police-juvenile interaction programs and the presentation and assessment of DARE and G.R.E.A.T. programs.

[6] The discussion of the Chicago Area Project owes much to Lundman's (1993:58–85) insightful treatment.

[7] This statement sounds remarkably like Merton's (1938) discussion of the anomic trap: People seek illegal means to legitimate goals since they are blocked from the legitimate means.

[8] The MMPI-delinquency links are taken from Hathaway and Monachesi (1957, 1963).

[9] Researchers created the two groups in the following manner (Powers and Witmer, 1951): Teachers and police officers recommended 2,000 juveniles. Staff members obtained over 100 pieces of information from 900 potential subjects. Using a primitive but effective two-step selection process, researchers created 325 matched pairs of youths. For each pair, a coin toss determined which child entered the experimental or control group.

[10] The discussion of the Juvenile Delinquency and Youth Offenses Control Act of 1961 is taken from Wheeler and Cottrell (1966:5–10).

[11] The individual might constitute a fourth arena of interest for some people interested in preventing delinquency. Treatment and prevention programs designed for individual offenders are available (see Burns et al., 2003), particularly those that address mental health disorders (see for example Goldstein, Olubadewo, Redding, and Lexcen, 2005); however, these programs largely are beyond the scope of the Comprehensive Strategy and this textbook.

[12] For a summary version of this report see Sherman et al. (1998).

[13] The Maryland team evaluated whether the research design included such things as before- and after-treatment measures, control groups, and randomization of assignment to the treatment or control group. The second dimension, threats to internal validity, refers to the idea that something about how the research was conducted could influence whether we should trust the findings. The researchers assessed each study (and prevention program) in terms of four elements: (1) causal direction, the question of whether crime caused the program or the program caused the observed level of crime; (2) history, whether the passage of time alone may have caused a change in crime rather than the prevention treatment; (3) chance factors, the idea that events within the program (for example, the imprisonment of a few very active offenders) could have caused a change in the crime level; and (4) selection bias, or the idea that the selection of those eligible to receive treatment could independently alter the outcome. Level 1 (weakest) programs had only multiple units, often groups, that were being compared on some behavioral or attitudinal measures, or all four threats to internal validity; level 5 (strongest) programs had all essential research design elements or no threats to internal validity. Level 2 through 4 programs had varying research design flaws or threats to internal validity.

[14] Sherman and associates reported on a broad range of crime-prevention programs, including ones located in courts, corrections and policing. We limit our discussion in this chapter to those located in communities, families, and schools.

[15] In order to simply matters and increase comparability between the two methods, Mihalic (2005) described as "effective" those studies rated by Sherman and associates as promising and working. By this standard, Sherman and associates identified 36 programs that were effective.

[16] The following is taken in part from Gottfredson, Gottfredson, Czeh, Cantor, Crosse, and Hantman (2004).

[17] Gottfredson did not include Project Toward No Drug Abuse in her assessment of school-based prevention programs in the University of Maryland report.

chapter 12

THE FUTURE OF THE JUVENILE JUSTICE SYSTEM

* * *

Judge Albright sat unnaturally upright in her chair and looked down at the 14-year-old standing defiantly before her. After a long pause, the judge began to speak in a quiet, methodical manner. "Jeremiah," she said, her voice betraying a sense of sadness mixed with regret, "you have, by your past and present behavior, shown an unwillingness to abide by your parents' rules and society's laws. You have had many chances to straighten out your life, and you have allowed each one to fall like water on the parched earth: gone without a trace. Now it's your turn."

The judge leaned forward and looked Jeremiah squarely in the eyes, ignoring the child's sobbing parents and two sets of grandparents sitting in the first row of the gallery. She continued: "You are, young man, a threat to the security of the community. Consequently, I am herewith sentencing you to spend the rest of your natural life in the custody of the state. Beginning next week your new home will be the wilderness camp in our state's most inhospitable region. Upon achieving the age of 21, you will be transferred to the state's maximum-security prison.

"What, you may ask, will the state do for you? I have an answer: You will be provided with basic education; humane medical, dental, and psychological treatment; and, of course, adequate food and shelter. You will never see your parents or other family members again. You will never leave the camp or, later, the state penitentiary for any reason, short of your death. And, I should point out that graveyards exist at each facility, where many inmates are buried.

"And what about your 'so-called life,' you might ask? You will be expected to work and to contribute in a meaningful way to the life of the new community in which you will be confined. Your guardians—the state—will become your father and mother. And who will be the rest of your family? The people with whom you are confined will be of roughly your age, and they will have committed offenses similar to those you have committed. It won't be a picnic, but it is a path you have chosen, a path from which there will be no return.

"You can make things easy or hard on yourself. That part, too, is your choice. Do you understand what I am telling you?"

As Jeremiah looked up, he could only mutter: "It's not fair." Despite the soft voice in which it was spoken, Judge Albright heard the youth's comment and responded: "Under the best of circumstances, life is not fair. You have placed yourself in a position where fairness is no longer your concern. What you've received today—and, truthfully, I'm not concerned with whether it is fair or not—is justice. I have given you what I believe you deserve; moreover, it's what you've earned. Bailiff, take this defendant away."

* * *

When did the scene just described take place? In 1906? In 2006? Could it have happened in either year? In both years? How far have we progressed in the last century in terms of juvenile justice? Where will the next 100 years take us? In this chapter we will try to sketch out some likely future courses for juvenile offenders and the juvenile justice system.

This chapter's topics are very real and represent serious dilemmas for the juvenile justice system. Projecting the ongoing nature of these problems into the next few decades is a relatively straightforward task. There is little reason to believe that the next ten or twenty years will witness either catastrophic crime waves or miraculous reductions in crime. Predicting how to respond to these dilemmas is a more difficult task. The bases for our predictions are not mere speculations. We will start with what we do know, then chart a course in the most probable directions for the future of juvenile justice.

THE SEARCH FOR A GUIDING PHILOSOPHY

The original juvenile court, with its benevolent, regenerative philosophy, stressed actions in the child's best interests (Fox, 1996; Gardner, 2003; Mack, 1909). Throughout its first 70 years, the court focused on identifying and dealing with children's problems more than on establishing blame. In the wake of such cases as *In re Gault* and *In re Winship*, the U.S. Supreme Court mandated an increasingly formal **due process orientation** to juvenile court processes (Manfredi, 1998). The result was not the death of a **child-centered orientation** to juvenile justice. However, treatment assumed a secondary priority, with punishment and procedural regularity becoming primary concerns.

In the 1980s there were calls from many quarters for a more adult-like, punitive juvenile court *and* juvenile correctional system (Benekos and Merlo, 1998; Feld, 1999a). McNeece and Jackson note that "between 1992 and 1997, 45 states modified state laws and juvenile justice procedures in order to make their juvenile justice systems more punitive" (2004:42). The general result was a tougher approach to handling juvenile offenders—to the point that in some jurisdictions it is almost impossible to distinguish juvenile hearings from adult trials. The question then becomes: Why have two separate courts? Or even more drastically: Why do we need a separate juvenile justice system?

PAST PRACTICES, FUTURE POLICIES: THE CHALLENGES AHEAD

In this section we examine two issues that illustrate the past practices and future policies of the juvenile court and the entire juvenile justice system. The first of these issues addresses the ongoing search for a guiding philosophy, and the second issue concerns the lingering problem of **disproportionate minority confinement (DMC)**.

The search for an overarching philosophy to guide the juvenile justice system's approach to youthful misconduct will continue the clash between traditional choices; that is, retribution versus rehabilitation, or perhaps some hybrid of the two. Coates (1998) has defined the philosophical choices for juvenile corrections in terms of issue areas. For example, since the early 1980s there has been a general trend toward retribution in the adult system, and juvenile justice policies and programs have mirrored this movement as well (see especially Cullen, 2005). For some juveniles—typically identified as highly violent or repeat personal offenders—the justice system seems increasingly more punitive and oriented toward public safety (see Roberts and Waters, 1998). In 2000, adult courts received just under 6,000 children from juvenile and family courts, and while that number was 58% less than in 1994, states still are moving in the direction of applying adult sanctions to increasing numbers of young offenders (Butts and Mears, 2001; Puzzanchera et al., 2004; Stahl, 2003). A handful of states now threaten the possibility of adult sanctions for youthful offenders as young as 12 or 13 years of age (Sickmund, 2003).

Coates offers three illustrations of the contemporary juvenile justice get-tough movement: (1) the use of secure institutions versus community-based programs, (2) the choice between determinate and indeterminate disposition and release systems, and (3) the debate over rehabilitation versus punishment (1998:434). Regarding corrections, Coates says that secure placements should be reserved for the most violent personal offenders (p. 435). The movement to determinate juvenile sentencing, in which dispositions are often prescribed by sentencing guidelines, means more adult-like sentences for juvenile offenders (see Feld, 2003; Mears, 2002).

The struggle continues between the competing ideologies of punishment and rehabilitation. Rehabilitation has been criticized as a correctional goal by both liberals and conservatives, as well as by correctional personnel and clients. In fact, Coates (1998:439) characterizes rehabilitation as a "much maligned goal." He further asserts that appropriate punishment has a place within rehabilitation, and that many still believe that rehabilitation is a juvenile justice system goal worth preserving.

The reality is that the rehabilitative philosophy that exemplified the early years of juvenile justice continues to be a part of offender processing. Many programs divert youngsters from formal processing. Such diversionary programs signal a continuing concern for less punitive alternatives to the filing of petitions and adjudication before a juvenile court judge.

Where does this leave us then in terms of a guiding philosophy for juvenile justice? Several observers have weighed in on the dilemma. Krisberg and associates (1986:34) noted on the tenth anniversary of the Juvenile Justice and Delinquency Prevention Act that "the nation's juvenile justice system has become more formal, more restrictive, and more oriented toward punishing serious offenders." What did they see for the future? Their conclusion was that the juvenile justice system must be restructured or the result will be "even higher levels of incarceration than is currently the case" (1986:36).

Dawson (1990) asked whether it is time to abolish the juvenile justice system. Ultimately, he concluded that abandoning rehabilitation and abolishing the juvenile justice system would result in substantial losses. For his part, Ferdinand (1991) also believes that rehabilitation is a viable philosophy for the juvenile court. He concludes, "If treatment and rehabilitation are abandoned . . . several untoward consequences would probably result" (1991:219). These consequences would include an increase in the amount and seriousness of delinquency and adult crime, and an increase in the retribution already present in the juvenile justice system.

The second challenge, the issue of disproportionate minority processing—particularly disproportionate minority confinement—is both a past problem and a future policy concern. Since 1988 the Office of Juvenile Justice and Delinquency Prevention has mandated that states assess and address the issue of disproportionate minority confinement in their secure juvenile correctional facilities. Disproportionate confinement exists when the percentage of minorities confined exceeds their percentage in the general population (see Devine, Coolbaugh, and Jenkins, 1998). While there have been some mixed findings, research from around the nation generally has found that there is "significant racial and ethnic disparity in the confinement of juvenile offenders" (Bilchik, 1999:1).

In some cases the disparity between minority and nonminority youngsters is significant, and it increases at each stage of processing from arrest to confinement. In other cases the disparities are significant but the level of disparity stays consistent throughout all stages of processing. Box 12.1 summarizes the experiences of five states in identifying the degree of DMC in their juvenile justice systems.

Pope, Lovell, and Hsia (2002) reviewed the DMC literature from 1989 to 2001 and reached the following conclusions. First, race clearly is a factor in the processing of juvenile cases in the United States. Second, most of the research done to date demonstrates clear racial effects, but there are some mixed research results as well. Third, more research is needed to fully understand this problem. Fourth, decisions made early in the process (like arrests) can be further amplified as cases move through the system (see Pope and Snyder, 2003).

Box 12.1   Understanding Disproportionate Minority Confinement

A report prepared for the Office of Juvenile Justice and Delinquency Prevention (Devine, Coolbaugh, and Jenkins, 1998) examined five states (Arizona, Florida, Iowa, North Carolina, and Oregon) and the status of DMC in each of these states. The report outlined the following conclusions:

- DMC is a pervasive phenomenon, but there is local variation.

- To understand DMC researchers must look at "the juvenile justice system, the educational system, the family, and socioeconomic conditions" since these are all interrelated.

- DMC is not just a phenomenon at the end of juvenile processing; it is related to a series of decisions made earlier in the system.

- Studying DMC heightens awareness of the problem and creates ongoing mechanisms to monitor it.

- Small changes in one part of the juvenile justice system can have "ripple effects" throughout the system.

Source: Devine, Coolbaugh, and Jenkins (1998).

NEW VIEWS OF OLD IDEAS: OLD WINE IN NEW CASKS?

McNeece and Jackson's (2004:46–48) **new-age juvenile justice** is consistent with the juvenile court's traditional goals. Programs in this area include victim-offender mediation and restitution projects, acupuncture and treatment for youngsters involved in drugs, an expanding presence of private-sector service providers, and the use of correctional boot camps. It is interesting to note that boot camps, or shock incarceration programs, combine elements of both retribution and rehabilitation (McNeece and Jackson, 2004).

Another illustration of combined juvenile justice philosophies is balanced and restorative justice (BARJ). The principles behind BARJ have been around for centuries, with the most recent manifestation appearing in the mid-1980s. The idea is that "when a crime has been committed the offender incurs an obligation to restore the victim—and by extension the community—to the state of well-being that existed before the offense" (Freivalds, 1996:1). The BARJ model contains the following key elements (Bazemore and Umbreit, 1998; Umbreit, 1995):

- BARJ is a new paradigm for dealing with adjudicated offenders.
- Balanced and restorative justice programs have been implemented in a variety of jurisdictions with both adult and juvenile offenders.
- This approach represents something of a hybrid (of rehabilitation and punishment) for dealing with offenders.
- BARJ does not discard previously existing programs such as victim-offender mediation and restitution; instead, it builds upon these efforts.
- The three crucial elements that must exist for a balanced and restorative justice approach are (1) offender accountability, (2) development of personal competencies, and (3) emphasis on public safety and community protection.

Table 12.1 illustrates the differences in the accountability assumptions in the retributive model and the restorative justice model.

Under the legal provisions of a retributive juvenile justice approach, the state serves as the **symbolic victim** and the actual victim often serves as just another witness. BARJ and other programs that employ victim-offender mediation personalize and humanize the crime for the victim and the offender (Coates, 1998:443). The result should be greater accountability for the offender and a greater sense of satisfaction for the victim that justice has been done.

THE JUVENILE JUSTICE SYSTEM: A LOOK TO THE FUTURE

So what does the future hold in terms of a guiding juvenile justice philosophy? A likely answer is that *all the current philosophies*—retribution, incapacitation, deterrence, rehabilitation, restoration, and reintegration—*will play some part in juvenile justice policies and practices*. This statement implies that the juvenile justice system will continue to attempt to be all things to all people. It also implies that the failure to accomplish this will cause many individuals—both within the juvenile justice system and on the outside—to continue expressing dissatisfaction with juvenile justice agencies and actors and their apparent failures. The two opposing forces can be

Table 12.1   Accountability: Retributive versus Restorative Justice

Retributive justice	Restorative accountability
• Wrongs create guilt	• Wrongs create liabilities and obligations
• Guilt is absolute	• Degree of responsibility
• Guilt is indelible	• Guilt removable through repentance and reparation
• Debt is abstract	• Debt is concrete
• Debt paid by taking punishment	• Debt paid by making right
• Debt owed to society in the abstract	• Debt owed to victim first
• Accountability as taking one's "medicine"	• Accountability as taking responsibility
• Assumes behavior is chosen freely	• Recognizes differences between potential and actual realization of human freedom
• Free will or social determinism	• Recognizes role of social context of choices without denying personal responsibility

Source: Umbreit (1995:34).

summarized as follows: Hope springs eternal (at least for many working in juvenile justice), but disaster lurks just around the corner.

A number of observers have suggested that the juvenile justice system in the United States is in need of a major overhaul (see for example Hsia and Beyer, 2000; National Criminal Justice Association, 2004). At a conference in March 2000, the chief justice of the Florida Supreme Court said, "I am ashamed of what we have allowed to happen in the State of Florida to our juvenile courts. . . . My answer to the problem is to reform our juvenile courts" ("Supreme Court Justice," 2000). In a similar vein, Butts and Mears add, "For the juvenile justice system to survive another century, policy makers, practitioners, and researchers will need to work together to focus on what works and to avoid the polarizing debates that result in symbolic and ineffective policies" (2001:193). However, Krisberg (2005:193) warns that at the national level juvenile justice issues are "no longer on the radar." Therefore, in regard to the prospect of seeing a reformed and reenergized juvenile justice system, Krisberg asks the question: "Can a redemptive standard of justice reemerge in a political climate dominated by fear of outsiders and the genuine sense of personal vulnerability that followed the attacks on the World Trade Center and the Pentagon?" (2005:194).

The role of juvenile justice personnel in making the system work—whatever its inherent flaws—cannot be overstated. Good people can wring results from a bad system. Conversely, the best policies and most efficient organizational structure cannot make up for poorly trained, unmotivated personnel. The personnel issue is so significant that we next turn our attention to projections and lingering concerns dealing with present and future juvenile justice employees.

JUVENILE JUSTICE PERSONNEL IN THE FUTURE

Several groups of personnel will continue to influence the direction of the juvenile justice system. This section addresses the situations likely to confront judges, attorneys, probation officers, and correctional officers working with accused and adjudicated juvenile offenders.

JUDGES

The past is fairly easy to recount in regard to juvenile judges. In its first 100 years, there was a movement from nonlawyer judges presiding over courts of limited or inferior jurisdiction to judges licensed to practice law presiding over courts that are very similar to their adult counterparts. Of necessity, juvenile court judges have become sensitive to due process protections for the accused offenders coming before them. Consequently, the future may be predictable for juvenile court judges, so much so that two trends seem reasonably certain.

First, it would seem desirable to require that judges have not only a law degree but also additional law-school course work intended for individuals interested in juvenile law practice. Currently, law schools often offer only one elective class in juvenile law. Since legal practice follows the money, most law students concentrate on business-related subjects that are likely to be lucrative. As a consequence, most lawyers—and judges—are exposed to very little, if any, juvenile law in their formative legal education and, as we will discuss in the following section, this leaves lingering doubts about the preparation of attorneys who appear in juvenile courts (see Feld, 1999e). Fortunately, the American Bar Association—through its Juvenile Justice Committee and the National Juvenile Defender Center—provides continuing legal training for attorneys who handle juvenile defense cases (see American Bar Association, 2004b).

Second, organizations such as the National Council of Juvenile and Family Court Judges (mentioned in chapter 1) should expand their role in providing continuing judicial education courses for judges serving in juvenile and family courts. In fact, as states increasingly move toward trying more youngsters as adults, this training should be expanded to adult criminal court.

ATTORNEYS

Since most U.S. juvenile courts draw upon the ranks of practicing attorneys for judges, it is safe to assume that what is true of judges is true of attorneys as well. In some ways the juvenile court due process revolution of the late 1960s and early 1970s was sprung on lawyers as much as on any other actors in the juvenile justice system (Manfredi, 1998). Prior to the decision in the *Gault* case, and some would say for years after it, attorneys were not present and often were not even welcome at juvenile court proceedings. Judges often discouraged attorneys' active involvement in juvenile cases, occasionally relegating them to fairly minor roles in the proceedings (see Fox, 1996; Rubin, 1996).

As previously mentioned, law schools frequently do very little in the way of preparing lawyers to practice juvenile law. Therefore, law schools should give careful consideration to developing, and offering on a regular basis, a course on either juvenile law or family law. Such a course should incorporate a segment on delinquent and non-delinquent youngsters who come before the juvenile court. If juveniles are going to be held to adult protections and punishments, the attorneys defending them and prose-cuting them need to be prepared (American Bar Association, 2004b; J. Jones, 2004).

CORRECTIONAL CUSTODY PERSONNEL

The individuals working in correctional custody positions have not enjoyed the best reputations for talent and ability. This issue is a source of concern among recruiters for agencies in both the adult criminal justice and juvenile justice sys-tems, where people often hear: "If you can't find a job anywhere else, at least you can become a correctional officer." Such musings by the unemployable may be part of the traditional way of thinking about correctional service careers. Juvenile cor-rectional officers today are confronted with three factors—changes in population mix, crowding, and litigation—that will necessitate reexamination of the custodial personnel training and qualifications. For example, since the mid-1970s, the nation's public juvenile correctional facilities have become increasingly populated by serious and violent offenders.[1] When Congress passed the Juvenile Justice and Delinquency Prevention Act of 1974, status offenders were removed from secure custodial care and placed in private or community-based programs. This mandate left behind in secure juvenile institutions only the most serious juvenile offenders. The **distilling effect** caused by deinstitutionalization of status offenders meant that public juvenile correctional facilities incarcerated those youngsters whose offenses were not serious enough to be tried as adults, but were far too serious to be housed in nonsecure placements or put on community supervision status.

As part of the change in the population mix, juvenile correctional authorities have had to deal with more **"state-raised" inmates**, youthful offenders who have spent a substantial part of their adolescence in correctional or other state-operated facilities (Hunt, Riegel, Morales, and Waldorf, 1993). This troubled and troubling population includes youths who have been active in street gangs during their peri-ods of freedom and who bring gang values and orientations into the correctional environment (Winfree, Mays, and Vigil-Backstrom, 1994). Some observers have called the youngsters who have grown up in the California Youth Authority facili-ties part of the "Pepsi generation" of prison gangs (Hunt et al., 1993).

Crowding is also part of the contemporary corrections scene. Both adult and juvenile facilities must deal with the stresses associated with too many inmates in not enough space (Mays and Winfree, 2005). Therefore, correctional officers' per-sonal qualities and training will play a crucial role in being able to manage the problems associated with institutional crowding. Crowding calls for increased expertise in human relations and interpersonal communications skills among those working in this unique work environment.

Litigation has become a third fact of life in contemporary juvenile corrections. While the Supreme Court has yet to address any questions relative to confinement conditions for juveniles, various other appellate courts have created an important body of legal opinions. Consider the types of cases contained in box 12.2.

The pace of juvenile inmate litigation may continue to increase as a result of growth in the population of those incarcerated, the relatively poor conditions in which many youngsters are held, and the successes experienced by adult inmates who have filed similar lawsuits.[2] Moreover, inmate advocacy groups have taken up the cause of juveniles held in state training schools, and confinement conditions such as crowding, medical care, education, substance abuse treatment, and counseling have been addressed by the courts in recent years. While the courts—particularly the federal courts—have become less sympathetic to inmate lawsuits, it is still likely that litigation involving youngsters in secure custody will attract the attention of judges, lawmakers, and the general public for some time to come. Those people attracted to careers in custodial corrections will have to be far more sensitive to the rights of the confined, just as police in the 1960s and 1970s found themselves increasingly under legal scrutiny.

COMMUNITY SUPERVISION PERSONNEL

Some of the greatest changes awaiting juvenile justice employees in the future may well involve community supervision personnel (probation and parole or aftercare officers). In fact, the face of juvenile probation and parole already is starting to change, and the next decade will likely see even greater changes. The challenges confronting community supervision personnel likely will fall into three categories.

Box 12.2   Litigation in Juvenile Corrections: Past and Future

Litigation involving juvenile inmates has addressed two key issues. The first issue centers on confinement conditions. For example, *Inmates of Boys' Training School v. Affleck* (346 F. Supp. 1354, D.R.I., 1972) addressed two constitutional questions: (1) Did placement in dank, dark isolation cells with only a mattress and a toilet constitute cruel and unusual punishment? and (2) Was using a former women's correctional facility for the confinement of youths a violation of the Constitution's equal protection and due process clauses? The appellate court responded affirmatively to both questions. The case is more than a judgment against a Rhode Island youth facility. It signaled a judicial **hands-on orientation** toward juvenile confinement conditions.[3]

The second legal issue is the question of protecting children from harm *while in the state's care and custody*. In the adult system, litigation involving individual rape, assaults, and even prison homicides is rare.[4] Nonetheless, systematic and widespread practices of this nature have caused prison systems, such as those formerly operated in Arkansas and Texas, to be ruled in violation of the Eighth Amendment. In a Kansas case, *C. J. W. by and through L. W. v. State* (853 P.2nd 4, Kansas, 1993), the court was asked two questions: (1) Does the state have an obligation to take reasonable steps to protect a minor placed in its care from other inmates with known records of aggression and sexual assault? and (2) Is the state liable for the minor's injuries sustained as a result of its inattention and inaction? The court answered in the affirmative to both questions. In this case, the state of Kansas was liable for the injuries a 12-year-old inmate suffered at the hands of a 17-year-old youth with a record of aggressive and sexually deviant conduct.

Source: Hemmens, Steiner, and Mueller (2004).

First, caseload sizes will increase for most probation and parole officers. Officers handling "normal" cases will be expected to take on relatively large caseloads, perhaps 200 or more. One exception to this trend is likely to be those officers assigned to intensive supervision with violent offenders, drug offenders, the mentally ill, and sex offenders; they will function as specialists dealing with relatively small numbers of high-risk offenders (Clear, 1997; see also MacKenzie, 2005). Scott says that caseload specialization depends on "an increasingly sophisticated ability to assess risk." The result will be programs that "make community corrections safer, increasingly innovative, and cost-effective alternatives to expensive prisons" (Scott, 1996:172–73).

Second, any vestige of the helping philosophy that has dominated community supervision for decades may grow dimmer or disappear entirely. Expanding caseloads and increasing demands to provide closer surveillance for youngsters on both probation and parole or aftercare will necessitate this change in philosophical orientation. Community supervision officers will either adapt to this change or, because of philosophical and professional disillusionment, may quit and seek other employment where their personal orientations and skills are better appreciated and more likely to have an impact on their clients' lives.

Third, community supervision may rely increasingly on technology (Peak, 1998:395–400). The use of technology will dominate investigation and reporting activities, as well as the active monitoring and tracking of offenders (Voice Interact, 2004). Scott notes that expanded use of laptop computers should help reduce the need for clerical staff and office space, and computers "might allow field officers to safely increase their caseloads and work more efficiently" (1996:174). Further applications of technology "will allow for more flexibility and efficient use of resources, in both space and personnel" (p. 172), particularly in the supervision of high-risk offenders.

The net result is an increased capacity to monitor—and, some would say, to punish—youthful offenders. The problem of funding innovative and technologically intensive programs will remain a constant. Moreover, professionals in the field—along with their supervisors in field offices and central administration—must recognize that, while technology may expand our capacity to punish, it will not eliminate many of the problems now facing the juvenile justice system in general, and community supervision agencies in particular.

BEYOND THE BEST INTERESTS OF THE CHILD: FORCES SHAPING JUVENILE JUSTICE POLICY

Many factors beyond the guiding philosophy of doing what is in the "best interests of the child" will continue to shape juvenile justice policy in the coming years. We have identified three factors that in all likelihood will have as much impact on the shape of the juvenile justice system in the future as the child savers had in its creation. First, because technology currently exerts an expanding influence on society generally, as well as on criminal justice policy in the United States, we explore this force as it relates to juvenile justice practices. Second, we examine the impact of public opinion on the development, implementation, and modification of juvenile justice policy. We live in an information age, driven by changing technologies; hence, we must consider the mass media's potential role in what lies ahead. Third, special types of offenders and offenses likely will continue to hold the attention of the American people, the criminal justice system, and the juvenile justice system, including drug- and firearm-related crimes. A better appreciation of these factors and forces should allow us to understand society's response to juvenile offenders.

TECHNOLOGY AND JUVENILE JUSTICE POLICY

We have illustrated technology's application in monitoring juvenile offenders under probation or parole supervision, but technology may extend well beyond these selected applications. The future may see monitoring devices that can enforce home confinement even more stringently than currently is done. Active monitoring devices may allow youngsters to leave their homes at certain times. Surveillance officers using technology associated with **global positioning satellites** already can determine a released person's location within a few yards (Courtright, 2002). Future technological devices may be able to monitor both where the person is at a

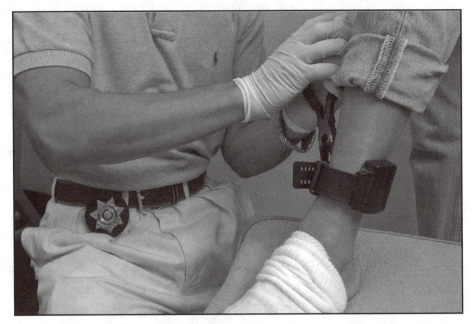

A parole officer inspects a Global Positioning System (GPS) monitoring device on a parolee's leg. Technology is viewed as an important "add-on" feature for many community-based supervision programs. Alaska and California recently contracted for juvenile justice monitoring systems with BI Incorporated, the nation's largest provider of remote sensing technology for community-based corrections. Using third-generation electronic monitoring equipment based on GPS, BI Incorporated can provide its clients with 24-hour monitoring that locates supervisees to within 30 feet. The company automatically alerts juvenile justice officials to violations of supervisee schedules and curfews via the Internet.

given time and the individual's behavior. The degree of effectiveness and unit cost will determine how readily accepted such devices are and the extent to which they are used as alternatives to incarceration.

No discussion of technology and juvenile justice would be complete without a warning about offenders' abilities to beat the system. Most hardware and software manufacturers promote their systems' low failure rates. Nevertheless, some efforts at equipment tampering will be successful, and power outages and satellite communications failures could cause complete system failure—the offenders would be lost to the tracking systems. Juvenile justice policy makers will have to reassess on an ongoing basis whether they are technology's masters or its servants. There is no easy answer to this question; however, it is an issue that society as a whole, not just the juvenile justice system, will have to consider in the coming years.

Public Opinion and Juvenile Justice Policy

In the information age, and with increased reliance on technology to communicate and make decisions, public opinion may emerge as an ever more potent policy-shaping force. However, any time we talk about criminal justice policy and public opinion, we have to ask: Which public? Whose opinion? At least three ingredients influence public opinion in regard to crime, particularly juvenile crime (for extended discussions of these and other factors see Barak, 1995; Coalition for Juvenile Justice, 1997; Fields and Jerin, 1996). First, personal experiences with crime have the potential to influence many members of the public. Crime victims typically hold very strong opinions about what causes crime and what should be done about it. The reality is that while hundreds of thousands of people annually are direct victims of juvenile crime, the vast majority of the public has not personally experienced crime victimization by juveniles.

Second, many in the public "know" about juvenile crime only through statements made by politicians (see Butts and Mears, 2001; Krisberg, 2005). Politicians may shape public opinion as much as they reflect it. Suppose a politician makes the following public statement: "My constituents want tougher penalties for serious juvenile offenders. And if that's what they want, I will work to give it to them." What if the public really does not want tougher penalties? What if the politician has incorrectly gauged the desires of his or her constituents? How can any of us be sure who is "more correct"?

Politicians may base their pronouncements on information from public opinion polls or, worse, on the phone calls and letters they receive from a self-selected and unrepresentative segment of their constituency. At other times, legislative committees and subcommittees hold hearings at which experts and others with relevant evidence give testimony. When held in open session, hearings provide those giving testimony and the politicians with a forum to get out the message. If the topic is interesting enough or the evidence sufficiently sympathetic, sound bites of both the testimony and the questioning may appear on the evening news. By these means, politicians have the power to shape public opinion as much as (if not more than) they are influenced by it. In many cases, public opinion becomes whatever politicians say it is.

Policy makers may be forced to design programs according to what they think the public's aggregate or collective position is on the issue (see chapter 11 and the politicization of prevention). In most cases, beyond vague notions such as public safety, policy makers have great difficulty determining the public's will. For its part, the public may not be well informed about most current juvenile justice system practices. Public attitudes toward juvenile justice often appear to be complex, diffuse, and even contradictory. Many members of the public—the group late President Richard Nixon called the **silent majority**—do not bother to contact their mayors, city councilors, state representatives, governor, or members of Congress about any issues. Achieving consensus in any public on most juvenile justice system issues is a nearly impossible goal (McNeece and Jackson, 2004). Therefore, it is difficult to imagine this unheard segment of the public having any effect on juvenile justice policy in the United States.

Third, the news media play a major role in shaping public opinion toward crime and justice issues (Barak, 1995; Fields and Jerin, 1996; Kappeler and Potter, 2005). The influence of celebrated cases (Walker, 2006), including those involving youngsters shooting groups of schoolmates, selling drugs to their peers on school property, or murdering their newborn children, may shape the public's perceptions of the nature of juvenile crime in general (Coalition for Juvenile Justice, 1997; see also Kotlowitz, 1999; Kappeler and Potter, 2005). Celebrated cases are by definition exceptions rather than the rule (Walker, 2006). Public policy based on such statistical outliers—the aberrant cases—is poor public policy at best, and may prove in the long run to have unintended, negative consequences. In the wake of highly publicized events—such as the shootings in the late 1990s in Littleton, Colorado; Pearl, Mississippi; Paducah, Kentucky; and Jonesboro, Arkansas—many people in this nation believe that youngsters are much more violent than before, and that violence is much more pervasive than at any previous time (see box 12.3). Thousands of parents, if newspaper and other mass media accounts are to be believed, withdrew their children from public schools as a result of these horrific events. Despite the appearance of a recent school-based crime wave, the reality is that schools have become safer places for students and teachers in the past few years (Benekos and Merlo, 1998).

The reality may be that there is no more violence than in past years and perhaps even less, but that many of the violent acts involve a higher degree of lethality (Bjerregaard and Lizotte, 1995; Huff, 1998). The publicity resulting from such acts has an impact on public opinion, which in turn influences public policy. In the aftermath of such incidents, we must consider the impact that guns and drugs have on juvenile crime and violence. Both elements factor into the development and implementation of juvenile justice policy at present and well into the future.

GUNS AND YOUTH CRIME

Researchers (see for example Howell, 1999; Ruddell and Mays, 2003) have addressed the supposed linkage between the possession of firearms and youth crime, particularly in the arena of youth gangs. Huff found that in four research sites—Aurora, Colorado; Broward County, Florida; Cleveland, Ohio; and Denver,

Colorado—almost three-fourths of the respondents surveyed admitted that most of their fellow gang members possessed guns (1998:5). Perhaps more significantly, the weapons of choice were powerful, high-capacity firearms instead of the small-caliber, easily concealable handguns typically characterized as "Saturday night specials." By contrast, research on 1,055 firearms seized from juveniles in St. Louis, Missouri from 1992 to 1999 found that the vast majority were inexpensive, small-caliber weapons in .22, .25, and .32 calibers (Ruddell and Mays, 2003).

Blumstein (1995) suggests that gun possession and use by some youngsters is tied to the next section's topic, drugs. He says that adult drug traffickers look to youngsters for a source of labor. Many juveniles carry weapons for self-protection and for settling disputes. Furthermore, "juveniles also tend to be daring and willing to take risks that more mature adults would eschew" (Blumstein, 1995:30).

Three factors seem to be at work in regard to youth crime and guns. First, some but not all research suggests that use of firearms may be more prevalent among youngsters now committing crimes than in the past. Second, the general level of **lethality**—the power and capacity of the firearms—is much higher than in the past (however, see Ruddell and Mays, 2003). In this regard, it is possible that additional deaths, instead of injuries, result from a higher volume of shots being fired from large-caliber weapons than traditionally has been the case. Third, while many youngsters are exposed to firearms, and there have been several well-publicized shootings involving nongang youngsters, "gang members are significantly more likely to own guns and more likely to own powerful, lethal weapons" than are nongang youths (Huff, 1998:5).

Before leaving the topic of juveniles and guns, we feel compelled to ask: What can be done? Several emerging strategies are worth noting. Blumstein (1995:32) says, "One immediate approach would suggest actions to confiscate guns from juveniles carrying them on the street." In regard to such a policy, Blumstein mentions an experiment conducted in Kansas City, Missouri. This experiment clearly demonstrated that the increased confiscation of guns results in a subsequent reduction in gun crimes. Decker and his colleagues also evaluated this policy approach in St. Louis, Missouri (see Burruss and Decker, 2003; Decker, Rosenfeld, and Burruss, 2005).

Blumstein (1995:33) maintains that another promising strategy is to deal with the source of gun sales to juveniles. These sales, illegal by definition, may be part of an underground trade in both guns and drugs. The Office of Juvenile Justice and Delinquency Prevention echoed many of Blumstein's policy recommendations (Sheppard, 1999). From a review of over 400 local firearms violence-reduction programs, OJJDP issued a report focusing on three points of intervention. The first intervention strategy involves attempts to interrupt illegal gun sources. The OJJDP report summarizes this area as follows:

> Strategies focusing on sources of guns include Federal and local initiatives that disrupt the flow of illegal firearms through gun tracing and monitoring of both licensed and illegal gun dealers. Strategies limiting gun sources also include educational initiatives to prevent at-risk youth from accessing firearms. (Sheppard, 1999:1)

The second intervention point incorporates attempts to deter the illegal possession and carrying of guns. Sheppard says that such strategies include "interventions intended to take guns from adults, juveniles and others at risk for violence, such as probationers, gang members and drug traffickers" (1999:1).

Box 12.3   Safe Schools versus Killing Zones: The "Real" Story

Do you remember where you were when you heard about the 1997 school shootings in Littleton, Colorado; Pearl, Mississippi; West Paducah, Kentucky; Jonesboro, Arkansas; Edinboro, Pennsylvania; Fayetteville, Tennessee; or Springfield, Oregon? If you were at school, you probably do remember. Do you recall talking to your friends about how safe (or unsafe) your school was? Did you start looking at other students as potential mass murderers? Did your parents talk to you about what to do if shooting erupted in your school? We would be surprised if you were unable to answer yes to at least one of these questions, especially given the amount of publicity surrounding these events.[5]

The truth is that the nation's schools are generally safe. School-based injuries to twelfth-grade students have not changed appreciably over the past few decades. Between 1992 and 1994, the latest years for which such numbers are available, 76 students were murdered or committed suicide *at school*, a term that encompasses school property, the journey to and from school, and official school-sponsored events. Nearly 12,000 children aged 5 through 19 were murdered or committed suicide at all locations during this same two-year period.

So student deaths are a bit extreme, you say. What about nonfatal student victimizations? Again, students aged 12 to 18 reported far more nonfatal serious violent crimes (for example, rape, sexual assault, aggravated assault, and robbery) away from school than at school; the difference was nearly 3 to 1. The rates per 1,000 students for thefts, all violent crimes, and serious violent crimes either remained constant or declined between 1992 and 1996. However, theft crime rates were higher at school than away from school.

The truth, or at least the truth as we learn it from the best research available, may not be sufficient to change the minds of people who firmly hold a particular view on crime and justice. Years ago a sociologist observed that if we believe something to be true, it becomes true in its consequences. We often proceed as if what we believe is really true, no matter what the objective truth may be. For example, between 1989 and 1995, the percentage of students who reported that they avoided some areas of their school out of fear increased from 5% to 9%. During this same time, general violent crimes and even thefts declined.

Reducing the deaths of children to impersonal statistics is risky business. The needless death or injury of even one child is tragic. The deaths of dozens or the injury of hundreds is an incalculable loss, even though it may not represent a statistically significant event. Most of us would generally agree that we *expect* our schools to be safe. How else can we expect that students will be able to learn unless they are free of the concern for life and limb? The net result of these social facts is that parents and children will likely continue to view schools as dangerous places, regardless of the fact that students may be safer in school than at home.

Most schools report no serious personal victimizations. Yet some schools are less safe than others, and, still others—the very few—are downright dangerous. Even government reports on the extent and nature of school-based crime agree on this point. The danger is in painting all schools with the same brush.

Sources: Aleem, Moles, and Portner (1997); Kaufman et al. (1998).

The third strategy consists of responses to illegal gun use:

> Strategies focusing on illegal gun use include criminal and juvenile justice inter-
> ventions designed to aggressively prosecute and sentence those who commit
> gun violence and those who illegally sell weapons to juveniles and adults. These
> strategies include court-related programs encompassing sentencing and educa-
> tional options for gun-involved youth. (Sheppard, 1999:1)

The OJJDP report concludes that the communities that have had the most success addressing youngsters and gun violence have developed comprehensive plans.
These plans involve a variety of community agencies and organizations. Moreover,
they incorporate all three of the intervention points highlighted in OJJDP's final
report (Sheppard, 1999:1–2).

DRUGS AND JUVENILE CRIME

Both drug sales and use are assumed to be linked to juvenile crime, especially
gang crime, and violence (Howell and Decker, 2000). The conventional wisdom
held by the public and most politicians is that many juveniles commit property
crimes to make money for drugs. The related assumption is that youth gangs
engage in a conspicuous amount of drug selling to support gang activities.

Huff (1998:4) found that gang members in four different locations were "extensively involved in drug sales, especially cocaine and marijuana." He also determined that gang members are much more likely than a comparable population of
at-risk youths to sell drugs, to "sell more expensive and profitable drugs," and to be
"connected to nonlocal sources" than are drug sellers who are not members of
gangs (Huff, 1998:5). However, he warns that we should not assume that gangs are
the major force in the drug trafficking trade. Huff concluded, "The evidence shows
that drug sales are not controlled by gangs nor do drug sales represent an organized, collective gang activity" (p. 5). Nevertheless, drugs (especially when combined with firearms) tend to be associated with some of the most visible forms of
youth crime, especially in media representations and in the minds of politicians
and members of the general public.

The National Institute of Justice (2003), in its most recent Arrestee Drug
Abuse Monitoring (ADAM) program, reports the following:

- Patterns in drug use by juvenile males were similar in all nine sites where
  data were gathered, and the findings have been consistent in recent years.[6]

- Marijuana was the most commonly used drug for juvenile arrestees (both
  male and female) compared to cocaine, opiates, methamphetamine, and PCP.

- Cocaine was a distant second in use among male arrestees in all sites (and
  second for juvenile females in four sites), except in San Diego and Portland
  where methamphetamine was second; methamphetamine was second for
  female arrestees in Los Angeles, Portland, and San Diego. Cocaine use was
  found in less than 10% of the juvenile male arrestees in all of the sites except
  Denver, Tucson, and Phoenix, where it was greater.

- The use of opiates and PCP was found to be low in all test sites for both male
  and female juvenile arrestees.

Based on the most recent data, the trends appear promising. Drug use in some locations and for some drug categories seems to be leveling off and even declining. Nevertheless, some other drugs appear with regularity across all test sites, and some cities (or regions of the nation) appear to have conspicuous problems with certain drugs.

EVIDENCE-BASED AND THEORY-BASED JUVENILE JUSTICE

Sherman (1998) suggests adopting an evidence-based policing paradigm.[7] He says that police researchers must do more than finish their work and hand in the final reports. They should adopt a more proactive stance to "push accumulated research evidence into practice through national and community guidelines" (Sherman, 1998:1). This practice would lead to evidence-based policing, defined by Sherman as "the use of the best available research on the outcomes of police work to implement guidelines and evaluate agencies, units and others" (p. 3).

Sherman borrows this paradigm from evidence-based medicine, whose proponents have concluded that (1) conflict exists between medical researchers and medical practitioners, (2) this conflict is counterproductive for medicine's advancement, and (3) a medical specialist who can apply research results to the real world and monitor their impact—what Sherman calls an "evidence cop"—can help resolve the conflict. Sherman sees many parallels between practicing doctors who resist the conclusions and recommendations of new medical research and police officers who dismiss research on their profession.

We suggest that juvenile justice practitioners share many characteristics with doctors and police officers. Moreover, the adoption of an evidence-based juvenile justice paradigm could only further our understanding of and insights into the perplexing youth crime problem and the public's formal and informal responses to it. Following Sherman's lead, we would define **evidence-based juvenile justice** as the use of the best available research on the outcomes of juvenile justice system programs and practices to implement guidelines and evaluate agencies, units, and others. Throughout this book, beginning in chapter 1 with an introduction to research methods, our intent has been to provide the best available evidence on the juvenile justice system's operation and demonstrate how practitioners in the field use evidence. The role of theory is a second focus we have maintained throughout this text. We introduced the idea of theory-driven juvenile justice practices and policies in chapter 2. This theme is presented in each chapter's "Theoretical Reflections," brief insights into how theory and research inform us about juvenile justice practices and policies. We believe that it is essential to combine an understanding of the theoretical ideas and processes that undergird our juvenile justice system with the best available and most critically evaluated evidence.

CAREER CRIMINALS AND JUVENILE JUSTICE POLICY

What can we conclude from an evidence-based and theory-based understanding of the juvenile crime problem? For one thing, the juvenile crime problem is really a cluster of problems. For another, *public perceptions play a prominent role in shaping juvenile justice policy.* That statement has been true, is true now, and is likely to remain true for decades to come.

One of the major perceptions held by the public and policy makers is that the United States is in the midst of a major violent crime wave, and that juvenile crime accounts for a disproportionate segment of that wave (Krisberg, 2005; Kappeler and Potter, 2005; Walker, 2006). Although crime has continued to decline in virtually all categories since the early 1990s (Butts, 2000), a small core of adult and juvenile offenders seems disproportionately responsible for crime. These individuals have been labeled **career criminals**. Career criminals who begin their law-violating behavior as juvenile offenders may play a disproportionate role in crime-control policy. Even the term *career criminal* has played a major role in formulating juvenile justice policy over the past three decades and will continue to do so well into the foreseeable future.

One of the reasons career criminals will remain central to crime-control policy formulation is the Attorney General's Task Force on Violent Crime (1981:17) recommendation that the Justice Department "conduct research and development on federal and state career criminal programs, including programs for *juvenile offenders with histories of criminal violence*" (emphasis added). The danger with programs that address career criminals is that they may be applied indiscriminately to all delinquents. Such programs are by nature more punitive and generally are not appropriate for most juvenile offenders (see Krisberg, 2005; Kappeler and Potter, 2005; Walker, 2006).

The juvenile justice system's tendency is to develop and implement policy responses based on the worst crimes, celebrated cases that are in fact behavioral anomalies. For most of the past three decades the system has tended to become more punitive for all youngsters as we have upped the ante for the most serious offenders. In particular, career criminal programs, influenced as they are by public opinion and political fortunes, have two major problems.

First, as we have seen with many other juvenile justice areas, definitions may create their own barriers to program success. Here we must precisely define what a career criminal is, and then decide who fits into the career criminal category. Should the definition be based on:

- the number of arrests?
- the number of delinquency adjudications?
- the amount of time spent incarcerated?
- the seriousness of the offenses committed?
- some combination of these factors?

It is important to arrive at workable definitions because, as Walker (2006:80) notes, "From a practical standpoint, to get some real payoff in terms of crime reduction, it is necessary to identify this small group from among all the other 'serious' offenders."

As we learn in box 12.4, what we think is good policy based on solid research may not be the case. Basing the idea of the serious offender—the one who poses the greatest public safety threat—on the number of prior arrests or even convictions may be, in a word, wrong.

Box 12.4   Career Criminals, Cohort Studies, and Bad Public Policy

More than 30 years ago, the Marvin Wolfgang-directed study of delinquency in a birth cohort appeared in print (Wolfgang, Figlio, and Sellin, 1972). The authors' thesis was that 627 chronic offenders among the Philadelphia cohort's 9,945 subjects—all born in 1945—had, by the age of 18, accumulated five or more police contacts. This 6% subset, which was also only 18% of the delinquent youths in the cohort, accounted for 52% of all arrests for delinquent acts and an astounding 63% of all arrests for index offenses in the entire cohort.

The policy implications of the cohort study were rather straightforward, especially after Robert Martinson's often-misquoted 1974 statement that "nothing works" in corrections. That is, if nothing works and a few offenders, identifiable as repeat offenders, are the source of most of our crime problems, lock them up and throw away the key. Should they ever seek readmission into society, the continuing threat they pose—their "dangerousness"—is a reasonable basis to deny them parole. The sooner one acts to curtail the careers of these offenders, the greater the net reduction in crime. Hence, the lengthy incarceration of young habitual offenders would seem to be a logical extension of these policies and this research. Or is it?

The study's impact on criminal justice policy—which can be seen from habitual offender laws (such as "three-strikes" laws implemented by California and a number of other states) to truth-in-sentencing laws (what a person is sentenced to is what he or she must serve, with fewer options for early release)—is amazing given how few insights we have into the career offender's life of crime. As Joan Petersilia noted earlier in the evolution of these policies, we know little about "how and when the criminal career begins, or how long it is likely to last, why criminal careers persist, and why some persons abandon criminal careers early, others continue into adult crime, and still others begin crime careers late in life" (1980:321). In short, we know precious little about the driving force behind the research and the policies: the habitual offenders themselves.

Elmar G. M. Weitekamp, Hans-Jürgen Kerner, Volkhard Schindler, and Axel Schubert suggest that the policies derived from the career criminal concept are bad policies built on an incomplete understanding of Wolfgang's study. In a sophisticated and extensive reanalysis of the 1945 Philadelphia cohort study, they report that multiple serious offending is not necessarily a precursor to serious crime or index offending. In fact, the offenses of the so-called dangerous 6% generally were what Weitekamp and his associates call cafeteria-style delinquency, in which misbehaving youths show little commitment to a given type of delinquency. These offenders are not as dangerous as others have argued. Finally, Weitekamp and associates found no support for the career offender literature's principal assumption that with increasing career length comes "an escalation in offense severity" (1995:159).

The upshot of the reanalysis of the cohort study is that the criminal justice policies responsible for the current imprisonment binge in the United States are based on a faulty interpretation of perfectly good data.[8] These policies could well have served as the basis for Jeremiah's fictional sentencing in this chapter's opening vignette. In the all-too-real world of criminal sanctioning, claim Weitekamp and his associates, the cohort study findings were "misused by politicians and criminal justice officials with disastrous consequences" (1995:174). As we have stated, we need evidence-based juvenile justice, but we also need to understand clearly what that evidence says before we implement what may be bad policies and practices.

Sources: Austin and Irwin (2001); Martinson (1974); Petersilia (1980); Weitekamp, Kerner, Schindler, and Schubert (1995).

Another problem associated with widespread acceptance of the career criminal concept is its impact on punishment. Most of the research done on this population shows that serious offenders already are treated severely by the justice system (Kappeler and Potter, 2005; Walker, 2006). The consequence of imposing more severe sanctions on chronic offenders is to drive the punishment response upward across the entire system.

If public perceptions on issues such as serious or violent youth crime influence public policy, we must ask: How do we reconcile what the public believes to be true with the realities of delinquent behavior in the United States? Obviously, we need a massive public education effort. However, who should inform the public? The news media? Politicians and policy makers? Your professors? The students taking this course? Again, no easy answers are forthcoming.

DEALING WITH THE HYPER-DELINQUENT

A major juvenile justice system issue for the next several decades may be the repeat violent offender who shows little propensity or willingness to change, like Jeremiah in the opening vignette. Armstrong and Altschuler (1998:449) discuss the notion of a new breed of delinquents who display many psychological and behavioral problems (see also Roberts and Waters, 1998). These youngsters—called **superpredators** or **hyper-delinquents**—are normally found at the juvenile justice system's deep end. In other words, they are housed in secure correctional settings. The warning concerning this group is clear: "There are indications that substantial numbers of this troubling population are today entering the juvenile justice system" (Armstrong and Altschuler, 1998:449).

Most of the developing literature on hyper-delinquents is related to two topics we previously have discussed: the presence of drugs and the increased use of firearms by youngsters. In this section we try to predict a juvenile justice system future dominated by concern over hyper-delinquent offenders. From a theoretical point of view, many of these youthful offenders seem to fit what Gottfredson and Hirschi (1990) label low-self-control individuals. That is, they do not appreciate the long-term potential consequences of their current acts, preferring instead to seek out and engage in risky, thrill-seeking, exciting, and dangerous behaviors. Drugs and guns, separately or in concert, certainly fit within the low-self-control theory's concept of analogous behaviors. Also troubling from a practical viewpoint is what Gottfredson and Hirschi say about the likelihood of change for such low-control youngsters: as a rule they are beyond the point where society can reasonably expect to modify their behavior in all but the most superficial ways.

However, before leaving this topic, it is important to note that not everyone concerned with juvenile justice agrees on the presence or extent of superpredators or hyper-delinquents in the juvenile justice system (see for example Krisberg, 2005). Laurence Steinberg, a clinical psychology professor, comments on the label of "psychopath" often applied to this population of juvenile offenders. He says that "there are many reasons to sound a note of caution within the juvenile and criminal justice systems about the potential overuse of psychopathy as a diagnostic label when applied to juveniles" (Steinberg, 2002:36). Reflecting on the notion of superpredators, Kappeler and Potter (2005:233) conclude that:

there is no empirical evidence to support the view that U.S. society is under siege by a tidal wave of "youthful superpredators." Although this fear has led to a radical transformation of the juvenile justice system, the data indicate that juvenile crime is decreasing.

Therefore, the emotional public alarm over a new breed of hyper-delinquents seems largely misplaced.

The mass media tend to bombard us with messages of juvenile offenders who are more numerous and who commit more serious crimes than at any other time in our nation's history. The hyper-delinquent, although perhaps not known by that label, has become a part of our collective social experience. In fact, we see this notion expanding beyond the United States, as people in other nations begin to complain about delinquency levels that are much higher than societies would expect or accept.

Focusing on the hyper-delinquent produces two results. First, juvenile justice policies are being driven by, and the juvenile justice system is being changed because of, concern over this small group of repeat offenders (Krisberg, 2005). In effect, the celebrated cases are defining hyper-delinquency.[9] Second, we are creating a self-fulfilling prophecy. We expect youngsters to behave badly and to steadily escalate this unlawful behavior. Many of them, if the past is any indication, are not disappointing us. The inevitable result will be policies and system operations geared to deal with the small number of most serious (particularly violent) offenders, while "normal" delinquents will have their needs ignored or will suffer the same fate as the hyper-delinquents.

JUVENILE JUSTICE: ARE RUMORS OF ITS DEMISE PREMATURE?

In 1897, Samuel Clemens, more famously known as Mark Twain, responded to published reports that he had died by cabling the following terse message to the Associated Press: "The reports of my death are greatly exaggerated." Since the early 1970s, the nation's juvenile justice system has faced reports of its imminent demise. It is interesting to note that the early dissent grew from those same qualities and philosophies that made the juvenile justice system unique. Robert O. Dawson (1990:137) suggests that the time frame of the greatest distinction between the adult and juvenile systems, when the juvenile courts and treatment programs exercised the greatest discretion over children, was in the late 1950s and early 1960s. Court decisions such as *Kent v. United States* and *In re Gault* and the general failure of treatment programs to correct adults and children marked the decline of the juvenile justice system's unique mission and its movement closer to the criminal justice system (Butts and Mears, 2001; Fox, 1996; Feld, 2003; but see also Manfredi, 1998).

In the ensuing years, many juvenile justice system critics called for its abolishment, while others, just as adamant in their beliefs, railed against any changes in children's status. Two basic positions have evolved: (1) keep, but improve, the current system; or (2) abandon the bifurcated system of adult and juvenile justice. Let's examine these two positions.

KEEP THE JUVENILE JUSTICE SYSTEM

Ferdinand (1991), who has written extensively about juvenile justice's history and evolution, views the problem as largely stemming from building new programs for status offenders on the backs of existing ones, without any concern for modification or elimination. As a consequence, the old programs and facilities received increasingly hardened offenders. The end product was a bifurcated system: One element was custodial, punitive, and exclusionary; the other, rehabilitative, community based, and inclusionary. Eventually, the entire system devolved to the level of the services provided to the worst delinquents, and it grew ever more punitive (Ferdinand, 1991).

One solution, maintains Ferdinand, is to create a state-level department responsible for the treatment of children, but have service delivery occur at the local level through community-based programs. These programs must address problems beyond those of the "more tractable, responsive clientele. They could focus also on the other end—the more serious predatory offenders" (Ferdinand, 1991:218). Ferdinand believes that the courts are ideally situated to diagnose, classify, and refer children. Much of the current community-oriented programming (for example, probation, community service, and restitution) is operated through the court. The juvenile court "was never given a mandate to sponsor community-based treatment programs" (Ferdinand, 1991:220). As he further observes, the court also "needs an effective right arm to create and evaluate treatment programs throughout the state geared to local needs" (p. 220).

Krisberg has sounded a wake-up call for the juvenile justice system generally, and particularly for juvenile corrections (1995; 2005). He noted that in 1994 various state legislatures introduced over 700 bills to "move troubled youngsters from specialized juvenile facilities to adult prisons" (1995:122). Krisberg is heartened by a few positive steps forward—in states such as Arizona, Indiana, Missouri, Nebraska, New Jersey, and Ohio—to deinstitutionalize juvenile offenders. He also views as steps in the right direction OJJDP's efforts in the late 1990s to blend treatment and public safety concerns in its initiative entitled *A Comprehensive Strategy on Serious, Violent and Chronic Juvenile Offenders*. However, Krisberg and Austin (1993) believe that in order to truly make a difference, the entire juvenile justice system needs to be reinvented, starting with the redefinition of delinquency as a public health issue and ending with treating the whole child, not just the youngster's delinquency.

ONE JUSTICE SYSTEM, ONE SYSTEM OF JUSTICE

A second group of critics calls for the abandonment of the delinquency concept or for the dismantling of the juvenile justice system. McCarthy (1977) identifies *Gault* as the culprit in the demise of delinquency, if not the restructuring of the juvenile justice system. After *Gault*, states redrafted their legal codes so that delinquency was the direct and exclusive equivalent of a criminal law violation. McCarthy further believes that the term "juvenile delinquency" soft-pedaled the idea that what was really being described was criminal conduct. In other words, juvenile delinquency lessened the youthful offenders' accountability for their acts (see also Bradshaw, 1995; Manfredi, 1998).

Rather than calling for the elimination of delinquency by legislative acts (that is, eliminating the legal distinction between delinquent acts and crimes), Bernard (1992) calls for the end of delinquency by rather different means. He believes that society's approach to juveniles produces delinquency. In the past, he notes, juveniles were "firmly embedded in the larger social context" (Bernard, 1992:187). Born and reared in one place, they knew what was expected of them and what they could expect from society. Such contextual imbedding of youths is still possible in modern industrial societies, as evidenced by the lower delinquency rates in other nations.

Box 12.5   International Perspectives
Fragile Families Amidst War, Famine, and Natural Disasters

One of the points we have tried to make throughout this book is that juvenile justice means more than justice for youngsters accused of crimes. It also means justice for those children who have been victimized by crime. Perhaps there is no more dramatic example of this than looking at protections for children who have been the victims of civil wars and famines. For example, the United Nations has warned that in Somalia parents are paying smugglers as much as $10,000 "to take their children abroad, as part of a lucrative and exploitative international child-smuggling business." These children have been "used for benefit fraud in welfare states; others—in the more extreme cases—are used as domestic labor, for prostitution, or fall into the hands of international criminal gangs" (United Nations, 2003). Estimates are that as many as 250 children per month are smuggled out of Mogadishu, Somalia.

Natural disasters in countries such as those in southern Asia (Thailand, Malaysia, Sri Lanka, and Indonesia) struck by the cataclysmic tsunami on December 26, 2004, also create opportunities for the exploitation of children. In the wake of such disasters children are left homeless and oftentimes orphaned. Of great concern to the international community is not only that these surviving children are fed and receive medical attention, but also that they are not exploited by being sold into slavery (including sexual slavery) or that they do not fall into the hands of groups that might sell them into illegal international adoption rings. BBC News (2005) reports that the government of Indonesia has banned children from leaving the province of Aceh for fear that "child traffickers could be trying to exploit the situation." In India, workers from the Save the Children Fund expressed concerns that strangers were removing orphaned or abandoned children from relief centers. Similar concerns have been raised in Sri Lanka as reports have surfaced of family members and others trying to sell children whose parents were killed by the tsunami.

As a result of economic privations, families in many developing nations of the world are very fragile. The governmental and legal structures in these nations are often even more fragile. When disasters like the civil war and famine in Somalia or the December 2004 tsunami strike, the existing infrastructure is not equipped to deal with protecting the youngest and most vulnerable of the victims. In the end, we are left asking: Where is the justice for these children?

Sources: BBC News (2005); Tran (2005); United Nations (2003).

According to Bernard (1992:188),

> Juveniles who engage in delinquency, however, often lack just such a sense of
> having a role and place in the larger society. This is particularly true of juveniles
> in the lowest social classes, who are "left out" of meaningful roles.

Eliminating delinquency—the behavior, not the legal status—claims Bernard, will
come only when society invests the capital necessary to empower and embrace
those presently left out. Bernard is not very optimistic that this will happen; rather,
he proposes that delinquency's demise will come about as a historical fact, much
like "witchcraft in the Middle Ages or the violence of the American 'Wild West'"
(p. 188). As we read about the bygone age of chivalry, someday historians will
write about the equally distant era of delinquency.

Perhaps the most unusual call for abolition and consolidation comes from Hirschi and Gottfredson (1993), the co-creators of self-control theory. In a nutshell, self-
control theory posits that a continuum of self-control is established early in childhood and lasts for a person's entire life. Low-self-control individuals tend to ignore
the long-term consequences of their acts, usually resulting in crime or what Gottfredson and Hirschi (1990) call analogous acts, including illicit drug use, cigarette
smoking, school misconduct, and generally risky behavior. The self-control continuum is related to many factors, but chief among them is the level of parental management and guardianship present in the child's social and physical environment.

Using this theory as a foundation for their arguments, Hirschi and Gottfredson
(1993:269) make the following seven observations about juvenile and adult misbehavior:

1. Adult crimes are not more serious than those of juveniles.

2. The adult offender is not different from the juvenile offender in terms of
   self-control—that is, neither appears to consider the long-term consequences of his or her acts. However, if there is a difference in likelihood of
   subsequent offending, it would appear to favor adults, whose overall rate of
   offending is declining.

3. The idea that young people are more malleable than adults with respect to
   criminal conduct has not been substantiated, and, again, evidence suggests
   that adults have a declining crime rate regardless of treatment.

4. There is no class of acts that reasonably can be considered deviant for children but not for adults. Indicators of criminality among children are also
   indicators of adult criminality. Therefore, for purely crime-control purposes,
   there is no reason to treat acts differentially according to the age of those
   committing the acts.

5. If benefits accrue to children from limiting the stigma attached to criminal
   justice proceedings (through expunging of records and the like), it is hard to
   see why a similar rationale would not apply to adults.

6. The juvenile court's welfare interests would not be affected by its extension
   to adults who, for whatever reason (mental incapacitation, temporary
   homelessness, spousal abuse), are unable to care for themselves.

7. The corruption argument that underlies the use of separate facilities for juveniles and adults can be turned on its head because there are reasons to think that juvenile offenders are as corrupt as adults. The physical danger argument is also usually misguided, because security (or assault) risk classification is already widely practiced.

If, as they contend, these seven often-cited reasons for a separate juvenile justice system are bogus, then what is their recommendation? They *do* believe that one system is better than two, but the one they want to extend to all offenders, regardless of age, is the juvenile justice model. Of the two, the juvenile justice model—with its greater treatment emphasis, less procedural formality, and less concern for the nature of specific offenses—has the greatest hope of helping those offenders who can be helped.

Summary

The juvenile justice system, by its very nature, holds out hope for change and improvement. However, the opinions of those who work in the system and those who do juvenile justice research are less optimistic on this point. In summarizing this chapter, we will finish with some questions that remain to be answered.

First, we must consider whether we will continue on the course of a more punitive juvenile justice system. Is the get-tough movement of the 1980s subsiding? By the same token, is there evidence of increased leniency in juvenile justice? Are we seeing the diversion movement that began in the 1970s now coming to fruition? Where are we going?

Second, related to the question of where we are going, it is important to examine the philosophies or other influences that seem to drive juvenile justice policy. One clear manifestation of the system's philosophical bent is the amount of legislative activity in the 1990s (Torbet et al., 1996). In most states there have been numerous juvenile code changes over the past 15 years. Among those changes are lowering the ages and changing the offenses for which juveniles can be tried as adults. Related to this trend is the complete exclusion of certain offenses—for example, those involving gratuitous acts of personal violence—from juvenile court jurisdiction (Butts and Mears, 2001; Feld, 2003; Gardner, 2003). The result has been a significant number of youngsters tried as adults and sentenced to death or to serve time in adult prisons. Therefore, any prediction of future directions must carefully consider those changes currently taking place in the state and, to a lesser degree, federal legislative arenas.

Third, we already have seen an increasing emphasis on the professionalization of justice system personnel from the time of the President's Commission Report in 1967. Public and private agencies, including those that serve juvenile offenders, now demand more in terms of personal and professional qualifications, including hiring decisions based on psychometric testing and postsecondary educational achievements. Today these organizations provide more training and periodic retraining or exposure to new tactics, techniques, and procedures. The result is increased expectations that juvenile justice system personnel, who in the end are human, will be able to perform superhuman feats and change young law violators' lives.

Fourth, salaries often have not kept pace with work-product expectations and job qualifications. Therefore, we will continue to witness turnover in most juvenile justice system positions. Increased on-the-job stresses and lack of financial rewards produces burnout, or occupational stress, among many juvenile justice professionals. You can see it in their faces and hear it in their voices.

Finally, whatever form the future juvenile justice system takes, there is no doubt that the private sector will play an increasingly larger role. At this point private-sector service providers can be found throughout community-based and institutional corrections. However, as the adult criminal justice system sees more privatization in the areas of the police, courts, and corrections, the juvenile justice system may see the same trends. If privatization expands in juvenile justice, we may see a parallel to health care in the United States: There will be one set of agencies and procedures for those with the ability to pay, and another set of agencies and procedures for those who cannot pay. Such a scenario would widen the gap between the haves and have-nots.

CRITICAL REVIEW QUESTIONS

1. How do you react to the idea of sending juveniles—like Jeremiah—into the state's custody for the rest of their natural lives? Do you think that this practice represents a case of society's just giving up? Would you argue for a bit more optimism, given some of the programs we have discussed in earlier chapters? Or do you think that there is a point beyond which civilized nations cannot be expected to go when it comes to criminal youths?

2. Where do you see the nation's juvenile justice system heading in its search for a guiding philosophy in the next 20 years? Provide supporting documentation for your answer. (Note: Staying right where it is would not be considered an appropriate answer.)

3. What kinds of programming will be necessary to support the philosophy you articulated in your response to question 2?

4. Assume that your community has limited enhancement funds to augment the salaries of current juvenile justice personnel. Assume, further, that you have been told that spreading the money evenly throughout the juvenile justice system is not an option. The policy makers have decided that they want to see significant changes in some segment of the juvenile justice system. Where would you put the money to get the biggest bang for your buck? Pick a group, and then identify what the return must be for augmenting existing salaries.

5. Why do you think that your selection for question 4 is the best choice?

6. This chapter reviewed several cases of actual litigation and identified other areas of possible court action. Which ones do you think have the greatest potential to bring about positive changes in the nation's juvenile justice

system? Include in your answer the reasons behind your selection, as well as what you think those changes may be.

7. Technology likely will affect juvenile justice policies (and practices) in the future. What do you see as the greatest impediments to technology's power to bring about change in the juvenile justice system?

8. In chapter 1, journalism was contrasted with scientific inquiry (and even experiential learning) as a means of understanding the juvenile justice system. There does not seem to be much disagreement that public opinion about juvenile justice is shaped by the way the mass media report on delinquents and delinquency. What do you think about the argument that public opinion is what the politicians say it is?

9. Beginning in the 1980s, firearms emerged as the chief means to secure a drug trafficker's territory. By the early 1990s, gang members gained prestige by possessing (and using) large-caliber, semiautomatic handguns. These developments failed to direct the nation's wrath toward firearms until the deaths of rural and suburban schoolchildren in the late 1990s. By the decade's end, firearms manufacturers, especially those who produce handguns and other weapons with no real purpose other than killing large numbers of human beings, found themselves under siege in the courts. Speculate why this is the case.

10. Respond either affirmatively or negatively to the following assertion: The juvenile justice system's attempts to address the threat posed by career *juvenile* offenders has caused more harm than good. In developing your answer, explain your reasoning.

11. Assuming that there really are hyper-delinquents in society, what can (or should) we do for (or to) them? In answering this complex question, reflect on the likely fate of "throwaway" children like Jeremiah.

12. Consider each of the following positions and indicate which one deserves our serious attention and why:

    (a) Continue the current juvenile justice system and, where possible, improve it.

    (b) Abolish the legal concept of delinquency, but keep the other distinctions for status offenders, children in need of supervision, and the like.

    (c) Abandon the entire juvenile justice system in favor of the criminal justice system.

    (d) Abandon the adult system in favor of the juvenile justice system.

RECOMMENDED READINGS

Bernard, Thomas J. (1992). *The Cycle of Juvenile Justice*. New York: Oxford University Press. We have referred to this slim volume throughout our text, and for good reason. Bernard does a wonderful job of explaining the significance of his title. Especially relevant for the topics covered in this chapter are "What Stays the Same in History" (chapter 3) and "The Lessons of History" (chapter 9). And we would all be enriched by following the advice he offers in "The End of Delinquency" (chapter 10), where he writes (p. 188): "Conscious of our own failings, let us be more gentle with the failings of these juveniles."

Krisberg, Barry (2005). *Juvenile Justice: Redeeming Our Children*. Thousand Oaks, CA: Sage Publications. Krisberg has been the president of the National Council on Crime and Delinquency since 1983. He is a long-time advocate for the rights and protections of juveniles who come into contact with the juvenile justice system. He is a very prolific writer, and his most recent work examines many of the "myths and realities" of the juvenile justice system in the United States. While this book addresses a variety of juvenile justice issues and policies, Krisberg particularly examines the political and policy dimensions of juvenile justice from the founding of the first juvenile court to the present.

McShane, Marilyn D., and Frank P. Williams, III, eds. (2003). *Encyclopedia of Juvenile Justice*. Thousand Oaks, CA: Sage Publications. This one-volume encyclopedia includes over 200 entries from 140 contributors who write and do research in the field of juvenile justice. Throughout this book we have referenced a number of articles taken from this work. Students should check with their college or university libraries to make sure they have this encyclopedia since it provides extremely useful synopses on virtually every topic discussed in the contemporary world of juvenile justice.

KEY TERMS

balanced and restorative justice
career criminals
child-centered orientation
disproportionate minority
   confinement
distilling effect
due process orientation
evidence-based juvenile justice
global positioning satellites

hands-on orientation
hyper-delinquents
lethality
new-age juvenile justice
silent majority
state-raised inmates
superpredators
symbolic victim

NOTES

[1] You might want to review the changes that are occurring in the nation's private correctional facilities. As a hint, they do not look like those in the public sector. For more information see chapter 7.

[2] The distinct possibility exists that if the juvenile justice system loses control over many of its current charges, either through changes in the legal age of juveniles or by the process of waiving jurisdiction to adult court, an increasing number of juveniles will "enjoy" the legal protections provided by judgments against adult correctional systems.

[3] Similarly, *Morales v. Turman* (383 F. Supp. 53, E.D. Tex., 1974) questioned whether the confinement conditions in the Texas Youth Council (TYC) facilities constituted a violation of the cruel and unusual punishment clause of the U.S. Constitution's Eighth Amendment. The key accusations against TYC were directed at physical and psychological abuses commonly practiced at numerous state-run facilities. The court ruled that the practices of TYC denied the confined children the right to treatment. In an interesting legal and historical aside, the judge in this case, Judge William W. Justice, was to gain widespread fame (or notoriety, depending on your viewpoint) in 1980 for ruling the entire adult correctional system in Texas to be in violation of the U.S. Constitution for, among other things, the use of inmate guards (known as building tenders) to help run the internal life of the prisons. As a result of *Ruiz v. Estelle* (503 F. Supp. 1265, 1980), Judge Justice placed the Texas Department of Corrections (now the Texas Department of Criminal Justice) on the long and costly road to change,

under the watchful eye of a court-appointed special master. For a detailed look at Judge Justice and his influence over the Texas correctional system, see Crouch and Marquart (1989).

[4] An exception to this generalization would be if the act was committed by a member of the correctional staff (for example, see *Hudson v. McMillan*, 503 U.S. 1 [1992]) or was witnessed by a member of the staff and that person did nothing to intervene or prevent the act (see *Smith v. Wade*, 461 U.S. 30 [1983]).

[5] Tom Winfree was in Germany on a criminal justice study tour when the school shooting in Oregon took place. German television and newspapers gave the event a high profile. The German law students with whom he was working at the time could not believe that America "would allow such things to happen." The American students in the group, many of whom were from the Midwest, also were shocked by the specific event but unwilling to support drastic actions taken by our federal or state legal systems to block future events of this nature. Specifically, they were nearly unanimous in agreement that more gun-control laws were not needed. This position mystified the Germans. As for the American students, many agreed with Walker's celebrated cases thesis: "Why create public policy based on individual events, no matter how horrible they might be?" they asked.

[6] The nine ADAM test sites were Birmingham, AL; Denver, CO; Cleveland, OH; Los Angeles, CA; Phoenix, AZ; Portland, OR; San Antonio, TX; San Diego, CA; and Tucson, AZ.

[7] Two points of clarification may be needed at this point. First, in this context *evidence* refers to research findings, not evidence in a criminal case. Second, a *paradigm* is an orienting framework that helps us understand the world around us. For example, Sherman (1998:5) notes that policing currently operates under three paradigms. Incident-based policing is the idea that the police respond to high-priority concerns, such as 911 calls. Community-based policing brings the residents of a geographical area in contact with the police in efforts to rid the neighborhood of crime and other unwanted behaviors and to instill a true sense of community back into the neighborhood. Finally, problem-oriented policing moves the focus of the individual police officer from narrow incidents to broad patterns and systems of crime. Of the three, problem-oriented policing is most closely related to evidence-based policing.

[8] Weitekamp, Kerner, Schubert, and Schindler (1996) also reexamined Wolfgang's study of delinquency in the 1958 Philadelphia birth cohort (Tracy, Wolfgang, and Figlio, 1990), and they compared the two cohorts. They were unable to find a severity escalation effect, although there was the beginning of a criminal career-escalation effect in the 1958 birth cohort. However, they concluded that this mild effect did not justify the criminal justice policies that resulted from it and the previous cohort study.

[9] If you have not taken the hint yet, perhaps now would be a good time to read Samuel Walker's (2006) insightful treatment of celebrated cases.

GLOSSARY

abuse (5)   Intentional or unintentional psychological or physical harm to another, possibly including sexual assault.

accuracy (1)   The relative absence of mistakes; often associated with research and data collection efforts.

adjudicatory hearing (5)   Hearing that calls the child into account for alleged delinquent behavior; known as a *trial* in adult court.

adolescence (2)   The stage in life that lasts from puberty through maturity, ending at the legal age of majority; the term was created in the late nineteenth century by psychologists studying childhood development.

Adoption Assistance and Child Welfare Act of 1980 (9)   Act that requires every abused or neglected child to be placed in a safe, permanent, and stable home.

affectional discipline (7)   The use of persuasion, kindness, and empathy as well as shame, guilt, and love instead of physical punishments to discipline a child.

ambivalent enforcers (3)   A policing style where officers make arrests in only the most serious cases; for minor violations they are likely to threaten and release young offenders.

American Bar Association (ABA) (9)   The organization that accredits law schools and represents the professional interests of attorneys in the United States.

Americans with Disabilities Act (ADA) (7)   Act that makes it illegal to discriminate against a person on the basis of a physical or mental disability; includes, but is not limited to, prisons and other correctional facilities, which may not discriminate in either hiring practices or in the participation by inmates in programs.

anarchist criminologists (2)   Criminologists who view hierarchical systems as inherently evil; followers of an extreme form of Marxist criminology.

anomie (2)   1. Concept originated by Durkheim, meaning a generalized sense of normlessness felt throughout a community. 2. Merton's theory about how people respond to imbalances between what they seek in life and the means available to achieve those goals; identifies people who strive to obtain culturally approved goals by socially illegitimate means as innovators, or, in legalistic terms, criminals.

anonymity (1)   In research, a situation in which a subject's identity is unknown to the researcher; often associated with the protection of the research subjects' privacy.

apprenticeship (2)   The binding out of children to learn a trade from a master craftsman.

apprenticeship system (2)   A formal structure for providing children with the opportunity to learn a trade or craft; see *apprenticeship*.

atavists (2)   According to Lombroso, biological throwbacks from earlier times, many of whom are destined to be criminals.

balanced and restorative justice (BARJ) (12)   Sometimes simply known as restorative justice; this philosophy has been applied to both juvenile and adult offenders. It emphasizes three key concepts: accountability, competency development, and public safety.

balanced approach probation model (6)   An approach to probation that emphasizes protecting the community and imposing accountability for offenses while enabling juveniles to live competently, productively, and responsibly.

banishment (8)   The sending away of offenders permanently from their places of residence as a form of penal sanction; under English Law, banished convicts were forbidden to return even after they had served their sentences in penal colonies; see *transportation*.

behaviorism (2)   The theory stating that all behavior is learned and reinforced by consequences.

binding out (2)   The placing of children into work situations for a period of time.

Blueprints for Violence Prevention (11)   Ongoing assessment of crime prevention efforts, led by Delbert Elliott and a team of researchers called the Advisory Board.

bonding theory (2)   Hirschi's theory that delinquency is likely to follow when individuals exhibit weak ties (bonds) to conventional values, low involvement in legitimate activities, and the like; based on the premise that without social controls, we would all naturally engage in norm-violating behavior.

boot camp programs (7)   Military-style alternatives to prison incarceration; participants usually are first-time, nonviolent offenders; sometimes followed by intensive supervision upon release.

Cambridge-Somerville Youth Study (11)   A Boston-area delinquency prevention experiment begun in the late 1930s and canceled in the mid-1940s, owing to researchers' and participants' involvement in World War II. An experimental group (randomly selected from among two groups, one designated predelinquent and the other, normal) received intensive treatment, medical care, and other special treatment; controls (selected randomly from the same two groups), received nothing. Follow-up studies could find no difference between the two groups in terms of delinquency, adult crimes, and mental disorders.

capitalists (2)   People who have capital investments in businesses and, generally, great wealth; viewed as the ultimate enemy by Marxist criminologists.

career criminals (12)   People who have large numbers of arrests or unusually extensive criminal records.

CASA programs (9) (12)   Court Appointed Special Advocate programs found in juvenile and family courts to provide independent support for juvenile litigants.

case classification (6) (7)   Categorizing probation (and parole) cases according to the seriousness of the offense or the amount of supervision required by the offender.

case histories (6)   Reports that contain the essential personal information on youngsters accused of delinquency, typically compiled by court intake workers (or probation officers); include offense history, school status, family situation, and victim statements.

case investigation (6)   The preparation of a case history; see *case history*.

case screening (6)   A review by juvenile court intake workers (sometimes along with an assistant prosecutor) to determine whether a child should be detained, whether a case should be handled informally or formally through filing a petition, and what the appropriate charges may be for petitioned youngsters.

case study (1)   The study of an individual or small group for the purpose of better understanding.

casework service model (6)   A model in which practitioners supervise youths, provide services to youths and families, and make placement recommendations in the criminal justice system; practitioners include probation officers, detention home workers, and detention facility workers.

Center on Children and the Law (9) An organization operated by the American Bar Association that is concerned with the rights of children and the quality of their lives.

chancery law (5) Legal concept of courts that apply the law of equity; see *equity.*

chattel (2) Property that can be transferred to another person; in ancient times, children were considered chattel in that they could be bought, sold, or killed.

Chicago Area Project (CAP) (10) (11) An often-copied program based on the assumption that crime is high in particular neighborhoods, with the goal of developing self-help concepts to improve neighborhoods and foster neighborhood pride.

Child Abuse Prevention and Treatment Act of 1974 (9) Act that made everyone legally responsible to report any abuse or suspected abuse of children.

child-centered orientation (12) 1. Historically, a late nineteenth-century change in outlook from parent-centered families, especially patriarchal families, to ones in which children and families were viewed as important. 2. The perspective of the child savers and the juvenile court, beginning in 1899.

child endangerment (9) The practice, by parents or guardians, of jeopardizing a child, either physically, emotionally, or sexually. See also *physical abuse, emotional abuse, sexual abuse.*

child maltreatment (9) The situation that exists when a parent or guardian causes or permits the abuse or neglect of a child.

child protective services (9) Government agency that investigates reports of neglect and abuse of children.

child savers (2) (7) A Victorian-era group that wanted to help children avoid criminality.

Children's Defense Fund (CDF) (9) A nonprofit organization created in 1973 as an advocate for the welfare of children in the United States.

chivalry hypothesis (3) The notion that the police (and other parts of the criminal justice system) treat suspected female offenders less harshly than their male counterparts.

cholo **(10)** A culture that emerges when youngsters are trapped between the traditional Mexican culture of their families and the dominant Anglo culture in the United States.

Civil Rights of Institutionalized Persons Act (CRIPA) (7) Act that allows the U.S. Department of Justice to sue state and local governments on behalf of institutionalized persons.

colors (10) The color(s) of clothing or other adornments that gang members wear to show their affiliation with a certain gang; for example, Bloods wear red and Crips wear blue.

community disorder (3) Any type of physical deterioration or personal misconduct in a neighborhood that indicates a decline in the sense of community; typically associated with the "broken windows" concept.

community-oriented policing (COP) (3) See *community policing.*

community policing (3) The approach to policing that emphasizes responsiveness to community standards and desires; sometimes identified as problem-oriented policing; stresses the police role in order maintenance above that of law enforcement or "crime fighting."

community protection (6) A county-based program in New York State that diverts prison-bound offenders to intensive supervision and treatment programs.

community risk assessment (8) An assessment tool, similar to the salient factor score, that is applied to juveniles in the state of Washington's Juvenile Rehabilitation Administration.

competency development (6) The development of the skills that will enable a youth to function as an adult, including educational, social, work, and civic skills.

comprehensive community-wide approach to gangs (10) The cooperation of several agencies within a community with the main goal being the elimination of gangs and gang-related problems; see *Spergel Model.*

comprehensive strategy (10)   An orientation for the prevention and control of violent delinquent behavior, officially adopted by the Office of Juvenile Justice and Delinquency Prevention.

confidentiality (1)   In research, a situation in which a researcher knows the respondent's identity but does not reveal it.

conflict gangs (10)   As characterized by Cloward and Ohlin, gangs that have a propensity to engage in fighting with other gangs.

consent decree (6)   The agreement to place a child under the court's supervision without an official finding of delinquency.

containment theory (2)   Reckless's theory that delinquency sometimes results from a push-pull process; children are pushed and pulled by external social forces and internal psychological factors toward and away from delinquency.

control (11)   Treatment efforts designed to deal with delinquent behavior that already is at hand.

corporate gangs (10)   Gangs that are hierarchical in nature and take on the characteristics of organized crime.

CRASH (10)   Acronym for Community Resources Against Street Hoodlums, a confrontational style of law enforcement gang suppression.

crews (10)   Groups of people joined in a common activity; in reference to gangs, crew members are members of the gang or a subset of the gang.

crime waves (1)   As portrayed by the media, widespread and pervasive patterns of crime.

criminal anthropology (2)   An approach to the study of crime that emphasizes the biological and evolutionary nature of crime; often traced to Lombroso.

criminal gangs (10)   According to Cloward and Ohlin, gangs formed solely for the purpose of committing illegal acts.

criminal stigmata (2)   Literally, physical "brands or marks" that Lombroso and other criminal anthropologists associated with criminals.

cult of domesticity (7)   A complex set of beliefs whose main goals were obedience and morality through affectional discipline.

cultural transmission thesis (2)   1. An idea, first proposed by members of the Chicago School, that crime and delinquency are passed from one generation to the next by means of the culture found in a geographic area; people were not viewed as criminal or delinquent, rather the values and norms of a neighborhood essentially created "deviant places." 2. A precursor to Sutherland's *differential association theory.*

culture conflict (10)   The situation that exists when the values of one group conflict with those of another group; can pose problems when a group believes that its norms or rules are exempt from formal social control of the dominant culture.

custodial dispositions (7)   Punishment given out by the juvenile judge after the juvenile has been adjudicated delinquent; includes nonsecure custody, as in a foster home or farm, and secure custody, as in a training school or detention center.

custodial interrogations (3)   The interrogations of juveniles while in the custody of the police; the legality of a custodial interrogation rests on the environment of the interrogation and the characteristics of the juvenile being interrogated.

custody (7)   Restraint or legal, supervisory, or physical responsibility for a person.

dark figure of crime (1)   The portion of law violations unknown to society, which would require self-reporting to become known.

deadly force (3)   The legal authority given police officers to take the life of another person; may be restricted by statute or case law to defense of life situations, or in cases involving a fleeing felon who presents an ongoing threat of harm to others.

decarceration (4) (7)   The practice of diverting juveniles from incarceration by making incarceration the last option for adjudicated juveniles.

deindustrialization (10)   A downward shift in a nation's industrial capacity.

deinstitutionalization of status offenders (4) (7)   The practice of removing juvenile status offenders from secure institutions and providing alternative placement in community-based programs.

delinquency (1) (5)   Actions committed by juveniles that violate criminal laws, juvenile status offenses, or other juvenile behavior as interpreted by the court.

delinquency control (11)   The main efforts of the juvenile justice system intended to reduce or eradicate the delinquency at hand; involves police, courts, and corrections.

delinquency prevention (11)   Efforts by parents, the juvenile justice system, other public institutions, and the general public aimed at stopping delinquency before it starts, largely by employing primary preventions for the general youth population and secondary preventions for children identified as at risk or as predelinquents.

demand waiver (5)   A waiver to adult court requested by a juvenile in order to receive a jury trial or for access to possible treatment resources.

denial (10)   Refusal to accept a fact; communities sometimes exhibit denial with regard to gangs, being unwilling to accept the fact that there is a gang problem.

dependency (5) (9)   The status of a child found in some state of want or need but through no fault of the parents or guardians.

detached social worker (11)   A social worker who provides treatment for at-risk youths (including drug- or gang-involved youngsters) within the context of the community, moving service delivery out of agency offices into the neighborhood (community) setting.

detention (4)   Temporary custody of juveniles in a secure facility prior to case adjudication or disposition.

detention center (7)   Any facility designated for the short-term incarceration of accused juvenile offenders prior to adjudication.

detention hearings (4) (5)   Proceedings to determine the lawfulness of the detainment of a juvenile and to determine whether to forward the petition for processing, to dismiss, or not to file.

determinate sentences (5) (7) (8)   Sentences that set the length of incarceration for a specific amount of time rather than a range of months or years; compare *indeterminate sentences*.

deterrence (7)   The general notion that legal sanctions will prevent potential offenders from violating the law.

deviance amplification (3)   The idea that official police actions, such as arrests, are likely to cause youthful law violators to have an intensified view of themselves as delinquents; a practical example of labeling or a self-fulfilling prophecy.

differential association theory (2)   Sutherland's theory that criminal behavior is not the result of poverty or a mental condition; rather, it is learned in close, intimate contact with others who are disposed to engage in unlawful conduct; what is learned includes not only the "how" of crime, but also the "why."

differential opportunity theory (2) (10)   Cloward and Ohlin's extension of Merton's strain theory, which explains criminal behavior in terms of the variable access to legal or illegal ways of reaching a desired, often legitimate, end.

discretion (3)   The authority of criminal justice officials to make decisions regarding an incident without referring to specific instructions.

discrimination (3)   In the criminal justice system, the practice of using the law to the disadvantage of one person or group but not other persons or groups.

disease epidemiology (11)   The branch of medicine whose goal is to discover origins of diseases, especially those that start epidemics, and provide the means to protect the community.

disposition (5)   The sentence a juvenile will serve, whether that sentence is probation or some period of incarceration.

dispositional options (5)   Options for juvenile sentences, which are much more limited than options for adults; probation, fines, restitution, counseling, and community service are the main sanctions available to juveniles; also, a waiver disposition is available, which moves juveniles into criminal court.

disproportional minority confinement (DMC) (7) (12)   A measure of the degree to which minority youngsters are incarcerated at rates higher than their percentage in the general population.

distilling effect (12)   The process observed especially in juvenile correctional facilities in which the least serious offenders (e.g., status offenders and those committing what would be misdemeanors if the youths were adults) are removed and a concentrated, more serious group of offenders is left behind.

DNA profiling (3)   So-called "fingerprinting" based on DNA pattern evidence; information contained in databanks providing DNA pattern identification for a number of individuals.

double failure (10)   Cloward and Ohlin's term for an individual who is unsuccessful at both legitimate and illegitimate opportunities.

dramatization of evil (2)   Tannenbaum's theory that youths' actions are often labeled "evil" by society, which leads to youths' receiving specialized treatment by society.

Drug Abuse Resistance Education (DARE) (3)   A school-based, police-delivered program created in 1983 by the Los Angeles Police Department and the Los Angeles Unified School District; uniformed police officers deliver 17 weekly lessons designed to decrease the likelihood of youngsters getting involved in drugs.

due process orientation (12)   The approach focusing priority on the legal procedures of the juvenile justice process rather than on the provision of treatment in a helping orientation.

ectomorphic (2)   A body type described by Sheldon as thin, sensitive, and delicate, and the type least likely to be criminal.

educational neglect (9)   Lack of attention for educational needs; may occur in single-parent households where the oldest child has to care for the younger siblings.

emotional abuse (9)   Verbal or emotional assault that occurs at a conscious level, which may result in conduct, cognitive, or other mental disorders.

emotional neglect (9)   Lack of parental nurture and affection for a child; most often found in cases involving parents' mental illness and/or alcoholism and other drug abuse.

equity (7)   A legal doctrine that focuses on fairness in cases in which the law does not apply or is ineffective.

eradication (11)   A process whereby something is completely eliminated or destroyed.

evidence-based juvenile justice (12)   The use of available research in the implementation of the juvenile justice system's programs.

executive privilege (8)   An accepted practice that prevents Congress from interrogating executive officials.

family courts (5)   Courts with jurisdiction over juveniles, divorces, paternity suits, custody cases, and adoption.

family preservation movement (9)   A movement to keep families together and to deal with the distresses and dysfunctions rather than remove the child.

family reform school (7)   A cottage-type setting in which incarcerated youths are placed; inmate groups as small as 10 to 12 or as large as 35 to 50 are placed with surrogate parents in a small reform school setting.

field research (10)   A research method in which the researcher uses personal interviews and direct observations to collect data as opposed to investigating without the subjects' knowledge.

focal concerns (3) (10)   According to Miller, the value orientations of lower-class persons, including the need for excitement, trouble, smartness, and personal autonomy; helps explain the propensity for crime and other misconduct.

formal probation (6)   See *probation*: compare *informal probation*.

foster home (4)   An out-of-home placement with a family willing to accept children who have been found to be delinquent, dependent, neglected, or abused by a court; placements may be determined by, and supervised under the direction of, a child welfare or other social services agency.

free will (2)   The ability to choose the path that will be followed through life; according to Beccaria, people will choose the path that shifts from pain toward pleasure; compare *social determinism*.

gang franchises (10)   The idea that gangs are "businesses," with their products usually being drugs.

gang migration (10)   The movement of gang members into a new area; usually because parents move and take their children (who are in a gang) to a new area.

Gang Resistance Education and Awareness Training (G.R.E.A.T.) (3) (10)   A school-based antigang program that targets sixth- and seventh-graders in an effort to stress methods for resisting peer pressure and avoiding gang involvement; taught by uniformed officers.

gang suppression (10)   An antigang policy that attempts to eliminate gangs in a given jurisdiction, usually by military-style police actions.

gang sweeps (10)   Antigang actions whereby police move into neighborhoods, round up all suspected or known gang members, and arrest or detain them.

gatekeepers (3)   Key individuals who, at critical junctures in any decision-making process, decide what does and does not go forward; in criminal justice, those who determine who will enter and/or exit the criminal justice system; also determine the numbers admitted and the rate at which they are admitted.

general deterrence (2) (7)   Actions taken to prevent crime which target the general public.

general strain theory (2) (9)   Agnew's social-psychological variation of Merton's strain theory; proposes that when youths run away from trouble and troubled lives, they often run afoul of the law.

generalizability (1)   The application of a theory or research findings that were credible with one group or in one setting to other groups or settings.

global positioning satellites (12)   Technology that allows electronic monitoring of parolees or those offenders who are on parole; often called GPS.

group homes (4)   Nonsecure residential placements for small groups of youngsters (typically no more than 8 to 10) under court order or supervision.

guardian (9)   A person who is in legal control of another, either temporarily or permanently.

guardians *ad litem* (9)   Trained volunteers who provide thorough investigations and recommendations to courts.

guardianship (9)   The practice of providing a measure of control over another; see *guardian*.

habeas corpus writs (7)   Writ that challenges the very fact of an inmate's incarceration; has become an often-used legal mechanism for inmates to bring their cases to court.

hand signs (10)   A series of characters, usually including the use of fingers, hands, and arms, which are used for communication or identification in gangs.

hands-on orientation (12)   The active involvement by judges in the operations of executive branch agencies, for example, correctional facilities and programs; particular emphasis on civil rights and inmates' conditions of confinement.

hot spots (3)   The idea developed by the police and police researchers that certain locations are likely to witness higher than expected incidents of crime, delinquency, and disorderly behavior; see also *community disorder*.

house of refuge (7)   Institution that emphasized discipline and hard work.

hybrid gangs (10)   Unlike most traditional gangs, hybrid gangs are composed of more than one racial or ethnic group.

hyper-delinquents (12)   The most delinquent of all juvenile delinquents.

hypersegregated (11)   The extreme degree of racial segregation in many American cities.

incapacitation (7)   The taking away of the ability or opportunity to commit crimes.

indeterminate sentences (5) (7) (8)   Sentences that set the length of incarceration as a range of months or years rather than a specific amount of time; compare *determinate sentences*.

index crimes (1)   The label used by the *Uniform Crime Reports* for the eight Part I offenses with specific criminal intent. These include murder, forcible rape, robbery, and aggravated assault as crimes of violence (manslaughter is an index crime that lacks criminal intent). Crimes against property are burglary, larceny-theft, motor vehicle theft, and arson.

indicated charges (9)   Charges of maltreatment that cannot be substantiated, but for which there were suspicions of maltreatment.

individual case plan (8)   A program based on an assessment of a given youth's individual needs; uniquely designed to address such problems as substance abuse, emotional instability, family problems, school problems, and the like.

individualization (6)   In terms of juvenile probation, the providing of legal classification, treatment, prescription, and risk assessment; a key element in the balanced approach to juvenile justice.

Industrial Revolution (2)   The period of time (between 1760 and 1840) when industry took over as the main production area and led to a decrease in apprenticeships for young children because of the increase in the number of people vying for such positions.

industrial schools (7)   Institutions which provided educational and vocational training to delinquent youths; see *training schools*.

infant (1)   In law, a person in the period between birth and approximately age 10. An infant is incapable of determining right from wrong or of developing the *mens rea* required to be tried for most crimes.

informal adjustments (4)   Any type of nonadjudicatory, nonformal case disposition; many do not provide formal documentation of actions including on-scene actions by police officers or diversion referrals by probation officers.

informal probation (6)   A type of probation, employing selection criteria different from those of formal probation, used as a diversion and imposed before adjudication; may be used for first-time offenders or those accused of minor acts of delinquency; see also *consent decrees*.

in-home placement (9)   The practice of leaving a child in the home and improving the home situation through counseling or treatment.

inmate classification (7)   Efforts conducted by prison administrators to use various tests to determine the best placement for an inmate in terms of treatment level and custody level.

inmate programming (7)   Treatment programs that are designed to aid the offender after release into the community.

institutional environments (7)   The physical and social surroundings of juvenile correctional facilities.

Integrated Automated Fingerprint Identification System (IAFIS) (3)   The FBI's fingerprint storage and retrieval system designed to replace the paper system of fingerprint cards; this system will allow digital recording and electronic transmission of fingerprints.

intensive supervision (6) (8)   Probation or parole program that involves much more supervision of offenders through lower officer-offender ratios and frequent visitation of the offender by the officer.

intermediate sanction (8)   Punishment that lies between incarceration and probation; includes home confinement, electronic monitoring, or intensive supervision.

interstate compact (8)   An agreement between two or more states that allows for the transfer of offenders to a new location while the state with jurisdiction retains its legal authority over the offender.

intervention (11)   A process whereby something is placed in between two other entities; a strategy intended to reduce or eliminate a problem.

Jacksonian era (7)   The period of time when Andrew Jackson was the president of the United States (1829–1837) and shortly thereafter.

jail removal initiative (4)   The nationwide push to remove juveniles from adult jails.

judicial reprieve (6)   Temporary postponement of the imposition of sentence.

judicial transfer (5)   Transfer of juveniles—as a result of hearings conducted under the authority of juvenile court judges—to adult court if there is a public safety issue or the crime is serious enough to justify transfer.

jumped in (10)   To suffer a physical beating as a form of initiation as a gang member; a member may be jumped out—suffer further physical beating—when leaving a gang.

juniors (10)   The youngest gang members; see *pee-wees*.

jurisdiction (5)   The legal authority, with regard to geography, age, and subject matter, to hear cases.

just deserts (7)   The philosophy that legal sanctions should focus on the offense rather than the offender; making the punishment fit the crime.

justice gendering (5)   The imposition of different sanctions based on the accused offender's gender.

juvenile accountability (6)   One of the key concepts in the Balanced and Restorative Justice (BARJ) model; the requirement that youngsters must accept responsibility for their actions and the consequences of those actions.

juvenile aftercare (8)   A supervisory or treatment program into which a juvenile who has been conditionally released from a confinement facility is placed; sometimes called juvenile parole.

Juvenile Delinquency Prevention and Youth Offenses Control Act of 1961 (10) (11)   One of the first acts of federal legislation specifically intended to control and prevent delinquency; based, in part, on the theoretical work of Cloward and Ohlin.

juvenile delinquent (1)   Legally, a minor over whom a court has jurisdiction and who has been found by that court to have committed an act that violates that jurisdiction's penal code.

juvenile detention centers (4)   Short-term, secure facilities designed to hold juveniles prior to case dispositions.

juvenile emancipation hearing (1)   A hearing to determine whether a juvenile can live independently from his or her parents; usually involves minors who want to marry.

Juvenile Justice and Delinquency Prevention Act of 1974 (7)   Federal legislation that prompted the decarceration movement of the 1970s.

juveniles (1)   People who have not reached their majority—ages 18 to 21, depending on state law.

klickas **(10)**   In Hispanic gangs, subsets or cliques of a larger gang.

labeling theory (2) (4)   The idea that people who are called something will live up to (or down to) the name; for example, if a juvenile is officially or unofficially designated as a delinquent, he or she will act delinquent.

LAW Enforcement Assistance Administration (3)   A federal agency created by Congress through the Omnibus Crime Control and Safe Streets Act of 1968. LEAA was designed to improve law enforcement effectiveness in the United States by providing grant funding for training, equipment, and technical assistance for state and local law enforcement agencies. LEAA ceased to exist as a separate federal agency in 1982, although many of its functions were assumed by other organizations in the U.S. Justice Department.

Law Enforcement Explorers (3)   A program affiliated with the Boy Scouts that allows youngsters (both males and females) to explore career options in the field of law enforcement.

least restrictive placement (9)   The notion that youngsters should be placed in the least confining environment possible; occasionally provided for by state juvenile codes; cornerstone of the family preservation movement.

left realists (2)   Criminologists who believe that traditional Marxist criminologists were misguided; as leftists, they argue for left-of-center solutions to crime problems, such as reducing the tendency of the police to misuse their ability to stigmatize youth; as realists, they know they must work within the existing power structure.

legal factors (6)   Factual information about the alleged offense, including any evidence, the type of crime, juvenile record, and the like.

legislative waiver (5)   An automatic waiver mechanism that excludes certain offenses from the juvenile court's jurisdiction, including personal crimes of violence.

lethality (12)   The power and capacity of weapons, especially semiautomatic and automatic firearms.

life histories (11)   A qualitative research technique whereby detailed insights into a community, individual, or group are obtained by learning the details about the subject typically from the subject; may include diaries, letters, biographies, autobiographies, in-depth interviews, and observations.

locura **(10)**   A Spanish word meaning "craziness or insanity."

long-term facilities (7)   Correctional facilities that care for juveniles who have been adjudicated as threats to the community; usually reserved for those serving juvenile life, an incarceration term terminating at the offender's eighteenth or twenty-first birthday, depending on state law.

low self-control (2) (3) (10)   According to Gottfredson and Hirschi's self-control theory, the inability to refrain from an action, a characteristic of those who are more likely to be delinquents.

majority (1)   The age at which a person becomes a legal adult in all respects (usually 21).

marginalization (10)   The condition felt by youngsters and their families existing on the periphery of society; ethnicity, race, socioeconomic status, and location in a geopolitical area can add to the marginalization process; refers also to the condition of any person or group existing outside society's mainstream.

marginalized youths (2)   Youths who are marginalized or share membership in marginalized groups; see *marginalization*.

Marxists (2)   People who believe that deviance is a result of class structure and that capitalist society has built-in conflicts; an ideology derived from Karl Marx.

Maryland Scale of Scientific Methods (11)   The technique developed by Sherman and associates that can be used to determine the quality of evaluations or assessments; rankers assigned values, ranging from 1 (weakest) to 5 (strongest), to (1) the research design, and (2) threats to the project's internal validity. Projects were described as "working" (received high marks on both key elements and were described as having the desired impact), "promising" (received high marks on one of the key elements and the preponderance of evidence suggests the project is having the desired impact), and "not working" (received poor marks on both key elements and was found to be ineffective).

mens rea **(1) (5)**   The criminal intent to commit a crime; "evil mind."

mesomorphic (2)   A body type described by Sheldon as strong, muscular, and aggressive. These people are the most likely to be criminals, according to Sheldon.

Mid-City Project (11)   A Boston-based crime prevention program, modeled on the Chicago Area Project, run for several years in the early 1960s; failed to prevent delinquency.

Minnesota Multiphasic Personality Inventory MMPI (11)   A complex, highly verified, and reliable psychometric testing method, consisting of hundreds of forced choice questions; often used to classify prison inmates and deselect police recruits; used as a predictor of delinquency, in spite of definitional problems with certain subscales, most notably, the schizophrenia scale (Sc), psychopathic deviation scale (Pd), and hyomania scale (Ha).

minors (1)   Persons who have not yet met the age of recognized adulthood (usually between 18 and 21).

misidentification (10)   1. Misclassification of youths as true gang members. 2. Mistaken assumptions as to the causes of gangs.

Mobilization for Youth (11)   A community-based delinquency prevention program run during the early 1960s in Manhattan's Lower East Side; based on Cloward and Ohlin's differential opportunity theory of delinquency; did not prevent delinquency.

Monoamine oxidase (MAO) (2)   A contemporary biogenic theory of crime and delinquency, whereby lower levels of monoamine oxidase, an enzyme found in the bloodstream, are correlated with crime and other "inappropriate" conduct; however, studies to date have been based solely on MAO drawn from the body's bloodstream, not the different form of MAO found in the brain's blood supply.

moral panic (1)   Term popularized by Stanley Cohen to describe a process where a media story takes on a life of its own apart from any basis in reality.

National Crime Victimization Survey (NCVS) (1)   An annual report prepared by the Bureau of Justice Statistics to better reflect the picture of crime in America, including victimizations often hidden from other reports; employs a survey method of self-reporting of crimes among a representative sample of U.S. households.

national defense exception (3)   The statutory provision granting access to the juvenile records of individuals seeking appointment to military service.

National Youth Gang Center (NYGC) (10)   A university-based, government-funded entity that compiles information on gangs, conducts original research, and disseminates gang research, policies, and practices to the nation's policy makers, academics, and related practitioners.

neglect (5)   A deliberate act or the failure to act for their children on the part of the parents.

neighborhood resource officers (3)   Police officers assigned to community policing projects with specific geographical or problem-oriented responsibilities.

net widening (4)   Expanding the reach of social control mechanisms to include more youngsters than otherwise would have been handled by the juvenile justice system.

new-age juvenile justice (12)   Modern programs in juvenile justice, which include victim-offender mediation, restitution, and treatment programs, as well as programs that focus on punishment.

new diversion (4)   The philosophy expressed by Youth Services Bureaus whereby youngsters were removed from the juvenile justice system and placed in noncoercive, client-centered service programs.

nondelinquent children (1) (9)   Youths who have committed status or noncriminal offenses.

observational study (1)   Research method in which the researcher does not directly participate in the study but watches subjects' actions; subjects may or may not know they are being observed.

O.G.s (10)   "Original gangsters" or "old gangsters." Some gangs designate their leaders as O.G.s.

open environments (7)   Facilities that allow easier access, both by the juveniles and by the community; include halfway houses, shelters, and forestry camps.

operant conditioning (2)   The theory, according to behaviorists Watson and Skinner, that reinforcers cause behavior to continue, while punishers stop behavior.

opportunity theory (2)   See *routine activities theory.*

outcomes-based evaluations (7)   Assessments of a program's impact in terms of what it proposed to do, wherein the results are judged on their significance and importance to the problem addressed by the program.

out-of-home placement (9)   The placement of a child in a foster home or group shelter facility when health and safety are jeopardized by leaving the child in the home.

overreaction (10)   The second-stage response to gangs (following denial), in which law enforcement suppression responses are called for; normally precipitated by some dramatic event, such as the killing of an innocent person in a drive-by shooting.

***parens patriae* (5)**   Literally, "father of the country"; English common-law doctrine applied so that the judge is responsible for the fate of youth.

parental management (2) (3)   The ability of parents to monitor their children and provide consistent punishment and reward structures.

parole (8)   The conditional release of a prisoner from custody at the discretion of a parole board, whereby the offender is required to observe conditions of release and remain under supervision of a parole agency for a certain period of time.

parole contracts (8)   Forms used by many parole agencies that spell out the general requirements and special conditions that apply to particular parolees.

Part I offenses (1)   Those offenses that are most likely to be reported and occur with sufficient frequency so as to provide for a basis of comparison, including homicide, rape, aggravated assault, robbery, burglary, larceny-theft, auto theft, and arson; see also *index crimes.*

Part II offenses (1)   Crimes that result in an arrest but are not as serious or as frequent as the Part I offenses; include victimless crimes; three offenses (suspicion, curfew and loitering laws, and running away) are not true criminal offenses.

***paterfamilias* (2)**   A Roman doctrine that recognized the father as the head of the family.

***paterna pietas* (2)**   "Fatherly love"; part of Roman law.

***patria potestas* (2)**   Literally, "power of the father." Under Roman law, the child was under the father's absolute control unless the father wished to emancipate the child.

patriarchal society hypothesis (2)   Chesney-Lind's theory that legal authorities define as delinquent many survival techniques of young girls, such as running away, becoming involved in prostitution, and using drugs.

patriarchal society thesis (9)   See *patriarchal society hypothesis.*

paupers (7)   The condition of receiving aid or support through public funds designated for poor people; the "undeserving" poor.

Pd scale (2) (11)   The psychopathic deviate scale, a subscale of the MMPI, used to try to determine a "delinquent personality."

pee-wees (10)   Young children on the outer fringe of territorial gangs who hang around with the gang, but have not been initiated; see *juniors.*

peer review (1)   Process whereby the editorial staff of a scholarly journal sends a submitted research work to independent experts for careful reading and review.

penology (11)   Branch of criminology dealing with prison management and the treatment of offenders.

personality theory (2)   The theory that the key to understanding human actions lies in the ability to interpret an individual's behavioral patterns, which are expressed physically, mentally, or attitudinally.

physical abuse (9)   Physical actions that result in injury to another person.

physical neglect (9)   Failure to provide adequate food, clothing, shelter, or supervision; includes complete abandonment of a child.

placa **(10)**   Another word for the nickname of a gang member.

Police Athletic Leagues (PALS) (3)   Various team (and individual) sports organizations sponsored by law enforcement agencies.

posses (10)   Large groups of people with a common interest. Gangs oftentimes refer to themselves as posses.

postadjudication intervention (11)   Intervention that occurs after a formal determination of delinquency involvement on the part of the juvenile court; includes all traditional methods from probation to institutionalization and aftercare; see *preadjudication diversion*.

power (2)   The ability of one group to attain its goals despite opposition.

power-control theory (2)   Hagan's theory that males and females are raised differently by parents: Females raised in patriarchal families are more controlled than are males, while females raised in egalitarian families are controlled the same amount as males; consequently, females raised in patriarchal families are less delinquent than the males, while females raised in egalitarian families are equally delinquent as the males.

preadjudication diversion (4)   An attempt to divert juveniles away from court and the delinquent label that is received by being within the criminal justice system.

preadjudication intervention (11)   A method of limiting a youth's penetration into the juvenile justice system; see *preadjudication diversion, secondary prevention*.

predelinquent intervention (11)   Any prevention program designed to stop delinquent behavior before it begins.

predisposition reports (6)   Documents that aid judges in making dispositional decisions by providing background information, facts about the delinquent act, and possible sentence recommendations.

prenatal substance abuse (9)   Drug use, including alcohol, by the mother during pregnancy, which may affect the fetus; may result in the removal of the newborn from the mother.

presentence investigation reports (PSIs) (6)   Reports that are usually used in adult criminal matters; see *predisposition reports*.

presumptive sentences (5)   A form of determinate sentencing by which a normal or presumptive sentence is prescribed to the judge based on the severity of the offense and the offender's criminal history.

prevention (11)   The act of keeping something from happening; a proactive means of influencing the possible occurrence of an event; in delinquency prevention, there are two forms, primary and secondary prevention.

preventive detention (4)   To hold individuals in short-term, secure incarceration facilities while they are awaiting adjudication by a court.

primary deviance (4)   Lemert's term for the original act or acts of delinquency committed by a youth prior to being labeled as delinquent and internalizing that label; the perpetrator has no commitment to the deviance status; compare *secondary deviance*.

primary prevention (11)   The creation of programs intended specifically to keep all youths from becoming involved in delinquency and other troublesome forms of behavior; goal is to "inoculate" all youths against delinquency.

principle of autonomy (1)   In research, the principle that an individual or group being studied does not have the power to shape the outcome of the scientific research being conducted.

prison code (7)   Basic unwritten guidelines for inmates that define acceptable and unacceptable behavior; provides for a sanctioning process for their violation, which can be quite harsh.

prisonization (7)   The adopting, to a greater or lesser extent, of the folkways, customs, and culture of the correctional institution, as promulgated by inmates.

proactive policing (3)   The concept that the police should take the initiative and act before crime, delinquency, or disorderly conduct occurs; contrast with *reactive policing*.

probation (6)   Conditional freedom granted to an offender upon the agreement to abide by certain set guidelines.

probation revocation (6)   Removal of the conditional freedom of probation in response to violations of the set guidelines.

probation violation (6)   A prohibited act or a failure to act according to the guidelines set by the probation agreement that could lead to parole revocation for the probationer.

problem-solving cops (3)   A policing orientation that stresses counseling and personal interaction rather than arrest and law enforcement responses.

Progressive movement (2) (7)   The effort of social activists in the late 1800s through the early 1900s to address youthful misbehavior and other social ills; emphasized the value of industrial training, agricultural education, and social education.

prosecutorial waiver (5)   A waiver determined by the prosecuting attorney, who decides in which court to file a juvenile's case.

Protestant work ethic (7)   An ethic that stresses hard work, thrift, and self-discipline.

psychometrics (7)   The measurement of psychological characteristics using standardized intelligence and personality tests.

psychopaths (2)   People who have apparently no conscience and freely engage in norm-violating behavior without concern for right or wrong.

punishers (2)   Stimuli that eliminate behavior; associated with behavior modification, or the systematic alteration of human behavior by psychological principles of punishments and rewards.

Puritanism (2)   The lifestyle based on the beliefs and practices of the Puritans, which emphasized strictness and austerity.

race-IQ-crime thesis (2)   The thesis stating that various races have different IQ levels, and some races are prone to criminal activity as a result of these differences.

ranked in (10)   Initiated into a gang, usually through the commission of a serious crime; see also *jumped in*.

reactive policing (3)   Actions in response to a law violation that has already occurred; the opposite of a proactive approach, whereby actions prevent crime.

reaction formation theory (10)   Cohen's idea that gangs allow youths to turn the adult (middle-class) world upside-down; gangs provide status and self-respect denied lower-class adolescents by middle-class society in general, but especially, the school system.

reception and diagnostic center (7)   An assessment unit designed to determine the appropriate institutional placement for a youth.

referee (5)   A lawyer who serves as surrogate judge and handles routine matters for the juvenile court.

reform schools (7)   See *reformatories*.

reformatories (7)   Correctional institutions for youthful offenders designed with the idea that delinquency can be corrected.

rehabilitation (7)   The practice of focusing on the individual rather than the offense in an effort to "cure" the offender before release.

reinforcers (2)   Rewards for an act, either positive or negative, that encourage continued action; according to social learning theory, positively reinforced actions are likely to be repeated.

reintegration (8)   A method of returning offenders into the community in a positive manner by involving them in treatment, job placement, educational experiences, and life skills training.

reintegration living placements (8)   The placing of youngsters into facilities that allow greater freedom than in a secure correctional facility but more intensive supervision than traditional parole.

reliability (1)   In research, the situation that exists when repeated measures of some occurrence, event, attitude, or orientation yield the same results.

residential training center (7)   Type of juvenile correctional facility, typically a long-term residential facility that has a lower security level than a training school; includes ranches, camps, farms, and boot camps.

restitution (5) (7)   The court-required payment by the offender of money or services to the offender's victim; often part of restorative justice or alternative sentences.

retreatist gangs (10)   According to Cloward and Ohlin, gangs that are composed of individuals who fail using both legitimate and illegitimate means, and as a result, pursue the use of drugs and engage in other hedonistic pursuits.

retribution (7)   A concept that focuses on punishing the offender for the sake of punishment.

routine activities theory (2)   Cohen and Felson's theory that in order for crime to occur, there must be a suitable target, a lack of guardianship, and a motivated offender, thereby increasing or decreasing criminal activity, depending on the potential victim's ability to become a less suitable target.

routine preventive patrol (3)   Normal patrol patterns followed by uniformed police officers, which typically involve driving in random paths throughout a patrol beat or zone.

rubber-band effect (7)   The idea that any social agency or other formal organization, or even an individual, can stretch the available resources only so far.

rule-applier cops (3)   Police officers who "go by the book" in applying the law; they seldom distinguish between juveniles and adults in their actions.

salient factor score (8)   Numerical classification that aids parole boards in predicting the likelihood of a parolee's success if released early from custody.

scavenger gangs (10)   Gangs that are formed mainly as a means of protection or socializing; they usually form and re-form many times and exhibit very little hierarchal order and no one particular leader.

school-based programs (10)   Delinquency prevention programs (including gang prevention) that are implemented in schools in an effort to deter gang involvement as early as possible.

school resource officers (SROs) (3)   Local police officers assigned to be present in one or more schools as part of their routine duties; officers' salaries often are paid from school system budgets.

second system (4)   The idea that as diversion agencies and programs develop, they become a separate juvenile justice system comprised of private and quasi-private entities.

secondary deviance (4)   Lemert's term for the subsequent deviant acts that may result from being labeled delinquent after an initial act of delinquency, especially as the individual accepts the deviant identity as his or her own; see *primary deviance.*

secondary prevention (11)   Programs intended to reduce or eliminate delinquency among youths identified in some manner as at risk for delinquency or, by behavior, as predelinquent; some programs also target minor delinquents, although some experts argue that the efforts then become a form of diversion and not prevention.

Section 1983 lawsuits (7)   Title 42, Section 1983, of the United States Codes provides an outlet for legal grounds involving civil rights violations of citizens as a result of police action; civil rights suits against government entities.

selective incapacitation (7)   The incapacitation of an individual for a period of time in an effort to prevent any future crimes during that time; based on past behavior.

self-control theory (2)   Hirschi and Gottfredson's theory that people with low self-control engage in risky and law-violating behavior; low self-control is a result of ineffective parenting; see *parental management.*

self-report studies (1)   A method for collecting reliable and valid information about a person's crime or delinquency history, using either confidential or anonymous questionnaires.

sentinel event (7)   An event of great magnitude (e.g. suicide or prison riot) that serves as a "wake-up" call to institutional authorities, often prompting radical reforms at the facility.

service brokers (6)   Probation (and parole) officers used as referral agents to meet clients' treatment and work-related needs.

service delivery (6)   The availability of diversion programs for deinstitutionalized status offenders; includes the availability of alternative places to handle status offenders, such as the social services agencies.

sexual abuse (9)   Illegal sexual acts performed against a minor for gratification of the perpetrator, such as inappropriate touching of the human body, prostitution, and pornography.

shock incarceration programs (7)   Boot camp programs used for first-time, nonviolent offenders as a method of deterring future delinquency.

short-term facilities (7)   Facilities that care for juveniles prior to commitment or adjudication or for those juveniles who are awaiting classification.

silent majority (12)   The majority of the population, who do not contact their mayors, city councilors, or other officials to express their opinions on current issues.

skinhead gangs (10)   Violent gangs that usually support white supremacy; members' hair is usually very closely shorn, or their heads are shaved.

social determinism (2)   The belief that everything results from a sequence of causes that are beyond the control of the individual; often contrasted with free will.

social disorganization theory (2) (10) (11)   The theory that criminal activity is a result of the breakdown of a neighborhood's solidarity, and is most often observed in transition zones between business and residential areas.

social ecology (11)   A branch of science that examines the relationships between human beings and their physical and social environments; also concerned with the spatial distribution of social and cultural traits; the guiding orientation of the Chicago School of Sociology early in the 20th century, especially the criminologists who examined the spatial distribution of crime and delinquency in Chicago.

social factors (6)   Personal demographic information (for example, age, gender, school performance, family situation) compiled as part of a case history; incomplete method of determining intake and case screening needs of a child.

social history (6)   Part of the intake process for juveniles into the probation program that is used to aid in the decision-making process that will determine which probation plan will suit that particular juvenile.

social learning theory (2)   Akers's theory that some behavior is learned from peers, especially that which is highly rewarded by physical, social or sociophysical stimuli.

social prediction table (11)   A technique created by Sheldon and Eleanor Glueck to determine, from a series of five social factors, who is likely to be a delinquent in the future; good at predicting nondelinquents (low false negatives), but poor at predicting delinquents (high false positives).

special conditions (8)   Specific conditions of parole and probation that apply only to certain clients and include certain rehabilitation programs.

specific deterrence (2) (7)   Punishment or other corrective action designed to prevent the individual offender from engaging in future law-violating behavior; also known as special deterrence.

Spergel Model (10)   The perspective on gangs adopted by the OJJDP as a means of combating youth gangs; also called the Comprehensive Community-Wide Approach to Gangs.

standard conditions (8)   General conditions of parole and probation that apply to all clients.

state-raised inmates (7)   Youths who have spent a majority of their adolescence in state-operated facilities, including both correctional facilities and "orphanages."

statistics (1)   1. Numerical facts or data that (in crime statistics) refer to the type and number of complaints, arrest reports, probation and aftercare cases, rates of violations, failures and successes. 2. Mathematical procedures used to reveal characteristics of information or discover patterns between two or more pieces of information. 3. A course of academic study.

status offender (1) (8)   Juvenile who has been adjudicated as having committed a status offense.

status offenses (1) (5)   Acts that are considered offenses only when committed by a juvenile; such acts would not be illegal for adults.

statutory exclusion (5)   Also known as legislative waiver; means through which juveniles are automatically transferred to adult court because statutes exclude certain offenses from juvenile court jurisdiction.

stoner gangs (10)   Gangs whose name originates from members' regular use of drugs and alcohol; such gangs develop from antisocial groups.

strain theory (2)   Merton's theory that society has legitimate goals but does not provide enough legitimate ways to accomplish them; consequently, some people use illegitimate means to attain legitimate ends and are called innovators by some and criminals or delinquents by others. See *anomie*.

subcultural differentiation (10)   Cloward and Ohlin's belief that different neighborhoods exhibit different types of gang members; gangs are associated with the social forces in that sociogeographic area.

subcultural tradition (2)   The perspective found in sociological studies of delinquency that ties certain forms of undesired youthful conduct to the presence of antisocial groups, often characterized as youth gangs; not all subcultural manifestations of youth culture, however, are delinquent or even dangerous to society, but nearly all include a rejection of what are viewed by group members as unattainable middle-class values.

substantiated charges (9)   Charges for which the allegation of maltreatment could be legally established or supported.

superpredators (12)   A term used to describe the most serious juvenile offenders; these youngsters often are viewed as unwilling or unable to change their serious, and particularly violent, behavior.

symbolic victim (12)   The state, which serves as the symbolic victim in the traditional justice system because the state brings charges against the offender, while the real victim has little or no say in the charges that are brought against or the punishment that is given to the offender.

territorial gangs (10)   A gang that exists to protect a certain geographic area where its members exert economic control, either for drugs or other types of criminal activity.

theory of differential oppression (9)   Regoli and Hewitt's theory that the power relationship between parents and their children may result in oppression; parents may use oppressive acts in order to control the child more than is necessary.

third-party custody (4)   Instead of releasing juveniles on bail, typically they are released into the care and custody of their parents or legal guardians.

three stages of penal servitude (8)   Three levels of decreasingly restrictive incarceration. As the prisoner's behavior and willingness to comply improves, he or she is moved to the next lower stage.

ticket of leave (8)   A nineteenth-century penal practice employed in England and Ireland similar to the "good time" credits used in the penal colonies; marks of commendation allowed the inmate to earn his or her way to freedom.

total institution (7)   A term coined by Goffman to refer to formal organizations where rules govern all aspects of behavior and contact with the rest of society is limited.

totality of circumstances test (3)   The method used by courts to examine the legality of a juvenile's testimony. The court examines all the factors surrounding the confession, including the characteristics of the juvenile being interrogated.

traditional diversion (4)   Removal of youngsters from the formal juvenile justice system through the discretionary acts of police officers, probation officers, and other officials within the system; does not necessarily involve placement in, or referral to, treatment programs.

training schools (7)   Secure correctional institutions that provide education and vocational training to delinquent youths.

transfer (5)   Waiver of jurisdiction, certification, or remand; practice includes waiving juveniles to adult courts.

transfer hearing (1) (5)   A preadjudicatory hearing to determine whether the juvenile remains under the authority of the juvenile court or is waived into the adult court.

transportation (8)   Eighteenth and nineteenth century practice in England, France, Russia, and other imperialistic nations whereby convicts were sent to colonies as free labor, and, eventually, became colonists who could never return home. See *banishment*.

treatment (7)   A method of therapy for those incarcerated rather than a punishment method.

validity (1)   In research, the ability to test a theory against future cases and predict the outcome using that theory.

vatos locos **(10)**   Spanish term meaning "crazy guys."

venue (5)   The geographical jurisdiction where a trial is held.

veteranos **(10)**   Term used by Hispanic gangs to refer to their leaders; see *O.G.s.*

voluntary probation (6)   See *informal probation*.

youth at risk population (5)   The number of youths between the ages of 10 and the upper age limit of the juvenile court.

Youth Services Bureaus (YSBs) (4)   Agencies created in the early 1970s, as a result of federal funding, to mobilize community resources to address a wide range of youth problems including delinquency.

REFERENCES

Abadinsky, Howard (2002a). *Law and Justice: An Introduction to the American Legal System*. 5th ed. Upper Saddle River, NJ: Prentice-Hall.

Abadinsky, Howard (2002b). *Probation and Parole: Theory and Practice*. 8th ed. Upper Saddle River, NJ: Prentice-Hall.

Abadinsky, Howard (1996). *Drug Abuse*. 3rd ed. Chicago: Nelson-Hall.

Administration for Children & Families (2005). *Factsheets/Publications: Child Maltreatment 2003*. Washington, DC: U.S. Department of Health & Human Services. http://www.acf.hhs.gov/programs/cb/publications.

Agnew, Robert (1992). "Foundation for a general strain theory of crime and delinquency." *Criminology* 30:47–87.

Agnew, Robert (1985). "A revised strain theory of delinquency." *Social Forces* 64:151–67.

Ainsworth, Janet E. (1999). "Re-imagining childhood and reconstructing the legal order: The case for abolishing the juvenile court." Pp. 8–13 in *Readings in Juvenile Justice Administration*, edited by Barry C. Feld. New York: Oxford University Press.

Akers, Ronald L. (1985). *Deviant Behavior: A Social Learning Approach*. 3rd ed. Belmont, CA: Wadsworth.

Aleem, Diane, Oliver Moles, and Jessica Portner (1997). "Juvenile violence is not a serious problem in the schools." Pp. 36–40 in *Juvenile Crime: Opposing Viewpoints*, edited by D. Bender and B. Leone. San Diego: Greenhaven Press.

Allen, Harry E., Chris W. Eskridge, Edward J. Latessa, and Gennaro F. Vito (1985). *Probation and Parole in America*. New York: Free Press.

Altschuler, Bruce E., and Celia A. Sgroi (1996). *Understanding Law in a Changing Society*. 2nd ed. Upper Saddle River, NJ: Prentice-Hall.

Altschuler, David M., and Troy L. Armstrong (1998). "A summary of intensive aftercare for high-risk juveniles." http://www.tyc.state.tx.us/prevention/intensive.html.

Altschuler, David M., and Troy L. Armstrong (1994). *Intensive Aftercare for High-Risk Juveniles: Policies and Procedures*. Washington, DC: Office of Juvenile Justice and Delinquency Prevention, U.S. Dept. of Justice.

American Bar Association (2004a). http://www.abanet.org/child/about.html.

American Bar Association (2004b). National Juvenile Defender Center. http://www.abanet.org/crimjust/juvjust.jdc.html.

American Correctional Association (2004). *Performance-Based Standards for Adult Local Detention Facilities*. 4th ed. Lanham, MD: American Correctional Association.

American Correctional Association (2003). *2003 Directory: Adult and Juvenile Correctional Departments, Institutions, Agencies, and Probation and Parole Authorities.* Lanham, MD: American Correctional Association.

American Probation and Parole Association (1999). http://www.appa-net.org/issue1.html.

Anderson, Dennis B., and Donald F. Schoen (1985). "Diversion programs: Effect of stigmatization on juvenile/status offenders." *Juvenile and Family Court Journal* 36(2):13–25.

Aniskievicz, R., and E. Wysong (1990). "Evaluating DARE: Drug education and the multiple meanings of success." *Policy Studies Review* 9:727–47.

Anno, B. (1984). "The availability of health services for juvenile offenders: Preliminary results of a national survey." *Journal of Prison and Jail Health* 4:77–90.

Anti-Defamation League (1999). "Nazi Low Riders: A prison gang emerges in California." http://www.adl.org/issue_combating_hate/nazi_low_riders2.asp.

Antler, Stephen (1981). "The rediscovery of child abuse." Pp. 39–54 in *The Social Context of Child Abuse and Neglect*, edited by Leroy H. Pelton. New York: Human Sciences Press.

Apgar, Evelyn (1998). "Satellite tracking: Latest in defendant monitoring." *New Jersey Lawyer*, August 3:5.

Ariès, Philippe (1962). *Centuries of Childhood: A Social History of Family Life.* New York: Knopf.

Armstrong, Troy L., and David M. Altschuler (1998). "Recent developments in juvenile aftercare: Assessment, findings, and promising programs." Pp. 448–72 in *Juvenile Justice: Policies, Programs and Services*, 2nd ed., edited by Albert R. Roberts. Chicago: Nelson-Hall.

Ashbury, Herbert (1928). *The Gangs of New York.* New York: Knopf.

Ashford, Jose B. (1996). "Protecting the interests of juveniles on aftercare/parole." *Children and Youth Services Review* 18(7):637–54.

Ashford, Jose B., and Craig Winston Le Croy (1993). "Juvenile parole policy in the United States: Determinate versus indeterminate models." *Justice Quarterly* 10(2):179–95.

Ashford, Jose B., and Craig Winston Le Croy (1988). "Decision-making for juvenile offenders in aftercare." *Juvenile and Family Court Journal* 39:47–53.

Attorney General's Task Force on Violent Crime (1981). *Final Report.* Washington, DC: U.S. Dept. of Justice.

Austin, James, and John Irwin (2001). *It's About Time: America's Imprisonment Binge.* 3rd ed. Belmont, CA: Wadsworth.

Austin, James, Kelly Dedel Johnson, and Maria Gregoriou (2000). *Juveniles in Adult Prisons and Jails.* Washington, DC: Bureau of Justice Assistance, U.S. Dept. of Justice.

Austin, James, Barry Krisberg, Robert DeComo, Sonya Rudenstine, and Dominic Del Rosario (1995). *Juveniles Taken into Custody: Fiscal Year 1993.* Washington, DC: Office of Juvenile Justice and Delinquency Prevention, U.S. Dept. of Justice.

Babbie, Earl (2004). *The Practice of Social Research.* 10th ed. Belmont, CA: Wadsworth.

Bailey, William C. (1981). "Preadjudicatory detention in a large metropolitan juvenile court." *Law and Human Behavior* 5:19–43.

Bakan, D. (1971). "Adolescence in America: From idea to social fact." *Daedalus* (Fall):979–95.

Barak, Gregg, ed. (1995). *Media, Process, and the Social Construction of Crime.* New York: Garland.

Barbaree, Howard E., and William L. Marshall (2005). *The Juvenile Sex Offender.* 2nd ed. New York: The Guilford Press.

Barry, John Vincent (1958). *Alexander Maconochie of Norfolk Island.* Melbourne: Oxford University Press.

Bartol, Curt R. (1991). *Criminal Behavior: A Psychological Approach.* 3rd ed. Englewood Cliffs, NJ: Prentice-Hall.

Bazemore, Gordon, and Todd J. Dicker (1996). "Implementing detention intake reform: The judicial response." *The Prison Journal* 76:5–12.

Bazemore, Gordon, and Mark Umbreit (1998). "Balancing the response to youth crime: Prospects for a restorative juvenile justice in the twenty-first century." Pp. 371–408 in *Juvenile Justice: Policies, Programs, and Services*, 2nd ed., edited by A. R. Roberts. Chicago: Nelson-Hall.

BBC News (2005). "Aid plea for 'tsunami generation.'" http://www.bbc.co.uk/2/hi/asia-pacific/4147669.stm.

Beccaria, Cesare (1963)[1764]. *On Crimes and Punishments*. Translated by Henry Paolucci. Indianapolis, IN: Bobbs-Merrill.

Becker, Howard S. (1963). *Outsiders: Studies in the Sociology of Deviance*. Rev. ed. New York: Free Press.

Belenko, Steven (1993). *Crack and the Evolution of Anti-Drug Policy*. Westport, CT: Greenwood.

Belknap, Joanne, Merry Morash, and Robert Trojanowicz (1987). "Implementing a community policing model for work with juveniles: An exploratory study." *Criminal Justice and Behavior* 14(2):211–45.

Benekos, Peter J., and Alida Merlo (1998). "Juvenile justice at the crossroads: Waiver policy and the centennial of the juvenile court." Paper presented at the annual meeting of the American Society of Criminology, Washington, DC.

Bernard, Thomas J. (1992). *The Cycle of Juvenile Justice*. New York: Oxford University Press.

Bernstein, Ilene N., Edward Kick, Jan T. Leung, and Barbara Schulz (1977). "Charge reduction: An intermediary stage in the process of labeling criminal defendants." *Social Forces* 56:362–84.

Besharov, Douglas J. (1988). "The need to narrow the grounds for state intervention." Pp. 47–90 in *Protecting Children from Abuse and Neglect*, edited by Douglas J. Besharov. Springfield, IL: Thomas.

Bilchik, Shay (1999). "Minorities in the juvenile justice system." *National Report Series*.

Binder, Arnold (1998). "Juvenile diversion." Pp. 231–49 in *Juvenile Justice*, 2nd ed., edited by Albert R. Roberts. Chicago: Nelson-Hall.

Binder, Arnold, and Gilbert Geis (1984). "Ad populum argumentation in criminology: Juvenile diversion and rhetoric." *Crime and Delinquency* 30(4):624–47.

Binder, Arnold, Gilbert Geis, and Dickson Bruce (2001). *Juvenile Delinquency: Historical, Cultural, Legal Perspectives*. 3rd ed. Cincinnati, OH: Anderson.

Binder, Arnold, Gilbert Geis, and Dickson Bruce (1988). *Juvenile Delinquency: Historical, Cultural and Legal Perspectives*. New York: Macmillan.

Binder, Arnold, Michael Schumacher, Gwen Kurz, and Linda Moulson (1985). "A diversionary approach for the 1980s." *Federal Probation* 49(1):4–12.

Bishop, Donna, Charles Frazier, Lonn Lanza-Kaduce, and Henry George White (1999). "A Study of Juvenile Transfers to Criminal Court in Florida." *OJJDP Fact Sheet*. Washington, DC: Office of Juvenile Justice and Delinquency Prevention, U.S. Dept. of Justice.

Bittner, Egon (1990). "Policing juveniles: The social context of common practices." Pp. 322–47 in *Aspects of Police Work*, edited by Egon Bittner. Boston: Northeastern University Press.

Bjerregaard, Beth, and Alan J. Lizotte (1995). "Gun ownership and gang membership." *Journal of Criminal Law and Criminology* 86(1):37–58.

Bjerregaard, Beth, and Carolyn Smith (1993). "Gender differences in gang participation, delinquency, and substance use." *Journal of Quantitative Criminology* 9(4):329–55.

Black, Donald (1968). "Police encounters and social organization: An observation study." Unpublished doctoral dissertation, University of Michigan, Ann Arbor.

Black, Donald, and Albert Reiss (1970). "Police control of juveniles." *American Sociological Review* 35:63–77.

Black, T. E., and C. P. Smith (1981). *A Preliminary National Assessment of the Number and Characteristics of Juveniles Processed in the Juvenile Justice System*. Washington, DC: U.S. Dept. of Justice.

Black, T. E., and C. P. Smith (1980). *Report of the National Juvenile Justice Assessment Centers: A Preliminary National Assessment of Juveniles Processed in the Juvenile Justice System*. Washington, DC: U.S. Dept. of Justice.

Black's Law Dictionary (2004). Abridged 8th ed. St. Paul, MN: West.

Blumstein, Alfred (1995). "Youth violence, guns, and the illicit-drug industry." *Journal of Criminal Law and Criminology* 86(1):10–36.

Bonnie, Richard J., and Charles H. Whitebread II (1970). "The forbidden fruit and the tree of knowledge: An inquiry into the legal history of American marijuana prohibition." *Virginia Law Review* 56:971–1203.

Bortner, M. A. (1986). "Traditional rhetoric, organizational realities: Remand of juveniles to adult court." *Crime and Delinquency* 32(1):53–73.

Bourque, Blair B., Mei Han, and Sarah M. Hill (1996). *A National Survey of Aftercare Provisions for Boot Camp Graduates*. Washington, DC: National Institute of Justice.

Bradshaw, Judy A. (1995). "The juvenile justice system: Is it working?" *FBI Law Enforcement Bulletin* 64(1):14–16.

Brager, George A., and Francis P. Purcell, eds. (1967). *Community Action Against Poverty: Readings from the Mobilization Experience*. New Haven, CT: College and University Press.

Brantingham, Paul, and Patricia Brantingham (1993). "Environment and routine situation: Toward a pattern theory of crime." Pp. 259–94 in *Advances in Criminal Theory*, edited by R. V. Clarke and M. Felson. New Brunswick, NJ: Transaction.

Breed, Allen F. (1984). "Don't throw the parole baby out with the justice bath water." *Federal Probation* 48(June):11–15.

Brunner, H. G., M. Nelson, Xandra O. Breakefield, H. H. Ropers, and B. A. van Oost (1994). "Abnormal behavior associated with a point mutation in the structural gene for monoamine oxidase A." *Science* 262:578–80.

Bureau of Justice Statistics (1997). *Privacy and Juvenile Justice Records: A Mid-Decade Report*. Washington, DC: U.S. Dept. of Justice.

Bureau of Justice Statistics (1991). *Forensic DNA Analysis: Issues*. Washington, DC: U.S. Dept. of Justice.

Bureau of Justice Statistics (1988). *Report to the Nation on Crime and Justice*. 2nd ed. Washington, DC: U.S. Dept. of Justice.

Bureau of Justice Statistics (1981). *Dictionary of Criminal Justice Data Terminology*. 2nd ed. Washington, DC: U.S. Dept. of Justice.

Burns, Barbara J., James C. Howell, Janet K. Wiig, Leena K. Augimeri, Brendan C. Welsh, Rolf Loeber, and David Petechuk (2003). "Treatment, services, and intervention programs for child delinquents." *Child Delinquency Bulletin Series*. Washington, DC: U.S. Dept. of Justice.

Burruss, George, and Scott Decker (2003). "Gun violence and police problem solving: A research note examining the gun seizure process." *Journal of Criminal Justice* 30(6):567–74.

Bushart, Howard L., John R. Craig, and Myra Barnes (1998). *Soldiers of God: White Supremacists and Their Holy War for America*. New York: Kensington Books.

Butts, Jeffrey A. (2000). *Youth Crime Drop*. Washington, DC: Urban Institute. http://www.urban.org/url.cfm?ID=410246.

Butts, Jeffrey A., and Daniel P. Mears (2001). "Reviving juvenile justice in a get-tough era." *Youth & Society* 33(2):169–198.

Butts, Jeffrey A., Howard N. Snyder, Terrence A. Finnegan, Anne L. Aughenbaugh, and Rowen S. Poole (1996). *Juvenile Court Statistics 1994*. Washington, DC: Office of Juvenile Justice and Delinquency Prevention, U.S. Dept. of Justice.

Cahill, Lisa, and Peter Marshall (2002). *Statistics on Juvenile Detention in Australia: 1981–2001*. Canberra: Australian Institute of Criminology.

Campbell, Anne (1991). *The Girls in the Gang*. 2nd ed. Cambridge, MA: Blackwell.

Campbell, Anne (1990). "Female participation in gangs." Pp. 163–82 in *Gangs in America*, edited by C. Ronald Huff. Newbury Park, CA: Sage.

Carpenter, Mary (1872). *Reformatory Prison as Developed by the Rt. Hon. Sir Walter Crofton in the Irish Convict Prisons*. London: Longmans, Greeb, Reader and Dyer.

Castellano, Thomas C. (1995). "Aftercare." *Corrections Today* 57(5):S1–S8.

Catalano, Shannan M. (2005). *Criminal Victimization, 2004*. Washington, DC: U.S. Dept. of Justice.

Center for the Study and Prevention of Violence (2005). "Blueprints for Violence prevention overview." http://www.colorado.edu/cspv/blueprints/index.html.

Centers for Disease Control (1999). "Smallpox surveillance—Worldwide." *MMWR Supplements* 48(LMRK):41–44. http://www.cdc/gov/epo/mmwr/preview/mmwrhtml/lmrk041.htm.

Chambliss, William J., and Robert Seidman (1982). *Law, Order and Power*. Reading, MA: Addison-Wesley.

Champion, Dean J. (2005). *The American Dictionary of Criminal Justice*. 3rd ed. Los Angeles: Roxbury.

Champion, Dean J. (1998). *Criminal Justice in the United States*. 2nd ed. Chicago: Nelson- Hall.

Champion, Dean J., and G. Larry Mays (1991). *Transferring Juveniles to Criminal Courts*. New York: Praeger.

Charle, S. (1981). "Suicides in the cellblock." *Corrections Magazine* 7:7–16.

Chesney-Lind, Meda (1989a). "Girls' crime and woman's place: Toward a feminist model of female delinquency." *Crime and Delinquency* 35(1):5–29.

Chesney-Lind, Meda (1989b). "Judicial enforcement of the female sex role." *Issues in Criminology* 8:51–69.

Chesney-Lind, Meda (1988). "Girls in jail." *Crime and Delinquency* 34(2):150–68.

Chesney-Lind, Meda, and Randall G. Shelden (2003). *Girls, Delinquency, and Juvenile Justice*. 3rd ed. Belmont, CA: Wadsworth.

Childhelp USA (2004). "Child abuse definitions: Physical abuse, sexual abuse and emotional abuse and neglect." http://www.childhelpusa.net/abuseinfo_definitions.htm.

Children's Defense Fund (2004). http\\www.childrensdefensefund.org/moreinfo.html.

Cicourel, Aaron (1976). *The Social Organization of Juvenile Justice*. New York: Wiley.

Clark, John P., and Larry Tifft (1966). "Polygraph and interview validation of self-reported deviant behavior." *American Sociological Review* 31:516–23.

Clear, Todd R. (1997). "Ophelia the CCW: May 11, 2010." Pp. 399–411 in *Crime and Justice in America*, edited by Paul F. Cromwell and Roger G. Dunham. Upper Saddle River, NJ: Prentice-Hall.

Clear, Todd R. (1988). "A critical assessment of electronic monitoring in corrections." *Policy Studies Review* 7(3):671–81.

Clear, Todd R., and George F. Cole (2002). *American Corrections*. 6th ed. Belmont, CA: Wadsworth.

Clear, Todd R., and George F. Cole (1990). *American Corrections*. Belmont, CA: Wadsworth.

Clear, Todd R., and Edward Latessa (1989). "Intensive supervision: Surveillance vs. treatment." Paper presented at the annual meeting of the Academy of Criminal Justice Sciences, Washington, DC.

Clemmer, Donald (1958). *The Prison Community*. Boston: Christopher.

Cloward, Richard, and Lloyd Ohlin (1960). *Delinquency and Opportunity: A Theory of Delinquent Gangs*. New York: Free Press.

Coalition for Juvenile Justice (1997). *False Images? The News Media and Juvenile Crime*. Washington, DC: Coalition for Juvenile Justice.

Coates, Robert B. (1998). "The future of corrections in juvenile justice." Pp. 434–47 in *Juvenile Justice: Policies, Programs, and Services*, 2nd ed., edited by A. R. Roberts. Chicago: Nelson-Hall.

Coates, Robert B. (1981). "Deinstitutionalization and the serious juvenile offender: Some policy considerations." *Crime and Delinquency* 27(4):477–86.

Cohen, Albert K. (1955). *Delinquent Boys: The Culture of the Gang*. Glencoe, IL: Free Press.

Cohen, Lawrence E. (1975a). *Delinquency Dispositions: An Empirical Analysis of Processing in Three Juvenile Courts*. Washington, DC: U.S. Government Printing Office.

Cohen, Lawrence E. (1975b). *Pre-adjudicatory Detention in Three Juvenile Courts: An Empirical Analysis of the Factors Related to Detention Decision Outcomes*. Washington, DC: U.S. Government Printing Office.

Cohen, Lawrence E., and Marcus Felson (1979). "Social change and crime rate trends: A routine activity approach." *American Sociological Review* 44:588–608.

Cohen, Lawrence E., and J. R. Kluegel (1979). "The detention decision: A study of the impact of social characteristics and legal factors in two metropolitan juvenile courts." *Social Forces* 58:146–61.

Cohen, Stanley (1980). *Folk Devils and Moral Panics: The Creation of Mods and Rockers*. 2nd ed. New York: St. Martin's Press.

Colangelo, Lisa L. (1998, April 17). "Parole: Under a watchful eye." *Asbury Park* (New Jersey) *Press*. http://www.injersey.com/news/younglives/story/1,1783,71199,00.html.

Cole, George (2004). "The decision to prosecute." Pp. 178–88 in *The Criminal Justice System: Politics and Policies*, 9th ed., edited by George F. Cole, Marc C. Gertz, and Amy Bunger. Belmont, CA: Wadsworth.

Community Policing Consortium (2004). "About community policing." http://www.comunitypolicing.org/about2.html.

Community Policing Exchange (1999). *Youth-focused Community Policing: Establishing Partnerships for Addressing Juvenile Crime and Victimization*. January/February, Phase VI, no. 24, pp. 1, 8.

Conly, Catherine H., Patricia Kelly, Paul Mahanna, and Lynn Warner (1993). *Street Gangs: Current Knowledge and Strategies*. Washington, DC: National Institute of Justice.

Connolly, Ceci (2005). "Drug control office faulted for issuing fake news tapes." *Washington Post*, January 7, p. A17.

Coolbaugh, Kathleen, and Cynthia J. Hansel (2000). "The comprehensive strategy: Lessons learned from the pilot sites." *OJJDP Bulletin*. Washington, DC: U.S. Dept. of Justice.

Coordinating Council on Juvenile Justice and Delinquency Prevention (1997). *The National Juvenile Justice Action Plan*. Washington, DC: Office of Juvenile Justice and Delinquency Prevention, U.S. Dept. of Justice.

Courtright, Kevin (2002). "Electronic monitoring." Pp. 610–13 in *Encyclopedia of Crime and Punishment*, edited by David Levinson. Thousand Oaks, CA: Sage.

Craig, Maude M., and Selma Glick (1963). "Ten years' experience with the Glueck prediction table." *Crime and Delinquency* 9:249–61.

Cressey, Donald R. (1955). "Changing criminals: The application of the theory of differential association." *American Journal of Sociology* 61:116–20.

Crouch, Ben M., and James W. Marquart (1989). *An Appeal to Justice: Litigated Reform of Texas Prisons*. Austin: University of Texas Press.

Cullen, Francis T. (2005). "The twelve people who saved rehabilitation: How the science of criminology made a difference." *Criminology* 43(1):1–42.

Cullen, Francis (1997). "Crime and the bell curve: Lessons from intelligent criminology." *Crime and Delinquency* 43(4):387–411.

Cullen, Francis T., Kathryn M. Golden, and John B. Cullen (1983). "Is child saving dead? Attitudes toward rehabilitation in Illinois." *Journal of Criminal Justice* 11(1):1–13.

Cummings, Sue, and Richard W. Clark (1993). "Juvenile diversion programs." *Journal of Extension* 31(1). http://www.joe.org.

Curran, Daniel J. (1988). "Destructuring, privatization, and the promise of juvenile diversion: Compromising community-based corrections." *Crime and Delinquency* 34(4):363–78.

Curry, G. David, and Scott H. Decker (2003). *Confronting Gangs: Crime and Community.* 2nd ed. Los Angeles: Roxbury.

Curry, G. David, and Irving A. Spergel (1992). "Gang involvement and delinquency among Hispanic and African-American adolescent males." *Journal of Research in Crime and Delinquency* 29(3):273–91.

Curry, G. David, and Irving A. Spergel (1988). "Gang homicide, delinquency, and community." *Criminology* 26:381–402.

Curtis, N. M., K. R. Ronan, N. Heiblum, M. Reid, and J. Harris (2002). "Antisocial behaviours in New Zealand youth: Prevalence, interventions and promising new directions." *New Zealand Journal of Psychology* 31:53–58.

Daly, Kathleen (1989). "Gender and varieties of white-collar crime." *Criminology* 27:759–93.

Daly, Kathleen (1987). "Discrimination in the criminal courts: Family, gender, and the problem of equal treatment." *Social Forces* 66:152–75.

Davis, Mark, and Joshua E. Muscat (1993). "An epidemiological study of alcohol and suicide risk in Ohio jails and lockups, 1975–1984." *Journal of Criminal Justice* 21(3):277–83.

Davis, Samuel M. (1980). *Rights of Juveniles.* New York: Clark Boardman.

Dawson, Robert O. (1990). "The future of juvenile justice: Is it time to abolish the system?" *Journal of Criminal Law and Criminology* 81(1):136–55.

de Mause, Lloyd (1975). "The evolution of childhood." Pp. 1–73 in *The History of Childhood*, edited by L. de Mause. New York: Harper Torchbooks.

DeAngelo, Andrew J. (1988). "Diversion programs in the juvenile justice system: An alternative method of treatment for juvenile offenders." *Juvenile and Family Court Journal* 39(1):21–28.

Decker, Scott H., and Janet L. Lauritsen (1996). "Breaking the bonds of membership: Leaving the gang." Pp. 103–122 in *Gangs in America*, 2nd ed., edited by C. Ronald Huff. Thousand Oaks, CA: Sage.

Decker, Scott H., Richard Rosenfeld, and George Burruss (2005). "Evaluating elusive programs: The case of the St. Louis consent to search program." Pp. 42–52 in *Policing and Program Evaluation*, edited by K. Kerley. Upper Saddle River, NJ: Prentice-Hall.

Degler, Carl N. (1991). *In Search of Human Nature: The Decline and Revival of Darwinism in American Thought.* New York: Oxford University Press.

del Carmen, Rolando V., Mary Parker, and Frances P. Reddington (1998). *Briefs of Leading Cases in Juvenile Justice.* Cincinnati, OH: Anderson.

del Carmen, Rolando V., Susan E. Ritter, and Betsy A. Witt (1993). *Briefs of Leading Cases in Corrections.* Cincinnati, OH: Anderson.

DeLucia, Robert C., and Thomas J. Doyle (1998). *Career Planning in Criminal Justice.* 3rd ed. Cincinnati, OH: Anderson.

Department of Justice (1997). *Correctional Populations in the United States, 1995.* Washington DC: U.S. Government Printing Office.

Devine, Patricia, Kathleen Coolbaugh, and Susan Jenkins (1998). *Disproportionate Minority Confinement: Lessons Learned from Five States.* Washington, DC: Office of Juvenile Justice and Delinquency Prevention, U.S. Dept. of Justice.

Dietrich, Shelle G. (1979). "The probation officer as therapist: Examination of three major problem areas." *Federal Probation* 43(2):14–19.

DiIulio, John J., Jr. (1997). "Reinventing parole and probation." *The Brookings Review* 15(2):40–42.

Dishion, Thomas J., Gerald R. Patterson, and John R. Reid (1988). Pp. 69–93 in *Adolescent Drug Abuse: Analysis of Treatment Research*, edited by E. R. Rahdert and J. Grabowski. Rockville, MD: National Institute on Drug Abuse.

Dooley, Elizabeth E. (1978). "Sir Walter Crofton and the Irish or intermediate system of prison discipline." *Journal of Crime and Justice* 1:67–94.

Dressler, Joshua (2001). *Understanding Criminal Law.* 3rd ed. New York: Matthew Bender.

Dundes, Lauren (1994). "Punishing parents to deter delinquents: A realistic remedy." *American Journal of Police* 13:113–33.

Dunford, Franklyn W., D. Wayne Osgood, and Hart F. Weichselbaum (1982). *National Evaluation of Diversion Projects: Executive Summary.* Washington, DC: U.S. Dept. of Justice.

Durkheim, Emile (1951)[1897]. *Suicide.* Translated by J. A. Spaulding and G. Simpson. New York: Free Press.

Egley, Arlen, Jr. (2002). *National Youth Gang Survey Trends From 1996 to 2000.* Washington, DC: Office of Juvenile Justice and Delinquency Prevention, U.S. Dept. of Justice.

Egley, Arlen, Jr., and Mehala Arjunan (2002). *Highlights of the 2000 National Youth Gang Survey.* Washington, DC: Office of Juvenile Justice and Delinquency Prevention, U.S. Dept. of Justice.

Egley, Arlen, Jr. and Aline K. Major (2004). *Highlights of the 2002 National Youth Gang Survey.* Washington, DC: Office of Juvenile Justice and Delinquency Prevention, U.S. Dept. of Justice.

Einstadter, Werner, and Stuart Henry (1995). *Criminological Theory: An Analysis of Its Underlying Assumptions.* Fort Worth, TX: Harcourt Brace.

Eisenstein, James, and Herbert Jacob (1977). *Felony Justice.* Boston: Little, Brown.

Ellickson, Phyllis L. (1995). "Schools." Pp. 83–120 in *Handbook on Drug Prevention*, edited by R. H. Coombs and D. Ziedonis. Boston: Allyn and Bacon.

Elliott, Delbert C., and Suzanne Ageton (1980). "Reconciling race and class differences in self-reported and official estimates of delinquency." *American Sociological Review* 53:890–904.

Elliott, Delbert S., David Huizinga, and Suzanne S. Ageton (1985). *Explaining Delinquency and Drug Use.* Beverly Hills, CA: Sage.

Elliott, Delbert S., and Harwin Voss (1974). *Delinquent and Dropout.* Lexington, MA: Heath.

Ellis, Lee (1991). "Monoamine oxidase and criminality: Identifying an apparent biological marker for antisocial behavior." *Journal of Research in Crime and Delinquency* 28:227–51.

Emerson, Robert M. (1969). *Judging Children.* Chicago: Aldine.

Ennett, Susan, Nancy S. Tobler, Christopher L. Ringwalt, and Robert L. Flewelling (1994). "How effective is drug abuse resistance education? A meta-analysis of project DARE outcome evaluations." *American Journal of Public Health* 84(9):1394–1401.

Esbensen, Finn-Aage (2004). "Evaluating G.R.E.A.T.: A school-based gang prevention program." *NIJ Research for Policy* (June). Washington, DC: U.S. Dept. of Justice.

Esbensen, Finn-Aage (1995). "The national evaluation of the gang resistance education and training (G.R.E.A.T.) program: An overview." Paper presented at the annual meeting of the Academy of Criminal Justice Sciences, Boston.

Esbensen, Finn-Aage, and David Huizinga (1993). "Gangs, drugs, and delinquency in a survey of urban youth." *Criminology* 31(4):565–89.

Esbensen, Finn-Aage, and D. Wayne Osgood (1999). "Gang resistance education and training (G.R.E.A.T.):Results from the national evaluation." *Journal of Research in Crime and Delinquency* 36(2):194–225.

Esbensen, Finn-Aage, Stephen G. Tibbetts, and Larry Gaines (2004). *American Youth Gangs at the Millennium.* Long Grove, IL: Waveland Press.

Esbensen, Finn-Aage, and L. Thomas Winfree, Jr. (1998). "Race and gender differences between gang and non-gang youth: Results from a multi-site survey." *Justice Quarterly* 15:505–26.

Esbensen, Finn-Aage, L. Thomas Winfree, Jr., Ni He, and Terrance J. Taylor (2001). "Youth gangs and definitional issues: When is a gang a gang, and what does it matter?" *Crime and Delinquency* 47(1):105–130.

Eysenck, Hans (1977). *Crime and Personality.* 2nd ed. London: Routledge and Kegan Paul.

Eysenck, Hans (1973). *The Inequality of Man.* San Diego, CA: Edits.

Faulkner, P. L., and W. R. Faulkner (1997). "Effects of organizational change on inmate status and the inmate code of conduct." *Journal of Crime and Justice* 20:55–72.

Federal Bureau of Investigation (2004). "Today's FBI, facts and figures, 2003." <http://www.fbi.gov/priorities/priorities. htm.

Federal Bureau of Investigation (1998). "Uniform Crime Reporting (UCR) summary system: Frequently asked questions." http://www.fbi.gov/ucr/ucrquest.htm.

Feld, Barry C. (2003). *Juvenile Justice Administration.* St. Paul, MN: West.

Feld, Barry C. (1999a). "Criminalizing the American juvenile court." Pp. 356–367 in *Readings in Juvenile Justice Administration*, edited by Barry C. Feld. New York: Oxford University Press.

Feld, Barry C. (1999b). "*In re Gault* revisited: A cross-state comparison of the right to counsel in juvenile court." Pp. 117–26 in *Readings in Juvenile Justice Administration*, edited by Barry C. Feld. New York: Oxford University Press.

Feld, Barry C. (1999c). "Justice by geography: Urban, suburban, and rural variations in juvenile justice administration." Pp. 52–67 in *Readings in Juvenile Justice Administration*, edited by Barry C. Feld. New York: Oxford University Press.

Feld, Barry C. (1999d). "The juvenile court meets the principle of offense: Legislative changes in juvenile waiver statutes." Pp. 228–45 in *Readings in Juvenile Justice Administration*, edited by Barry C. Feld. New York: Oxford University Press.

Feld, Barry C. (1999e). "The right to counsel in juvenile courts: An empirical study of when lawyers appear and the difference they make." Pp. 127–139 in *Readings in Juvenile Justice Administration*, edited by Barry C. Feld. New York: Oxford University Press.

Feld, Barry (1981). "A comparative analysis of organizational structure and inmate subcultures in institutions for juvenile offenders." *Crime and Delinquency* 27:336–63.

Feld, Barry (1977). *Neutralizing Inmate Violence.* Cambridge, MA: Ballinger.

Fenwick, Charles R. (1982). "Juvenile court intake decision making: The importance of family affiliation." *Journal of Criminal Justice* 10:443–52.

Ferdinand, Theodore N. (1991). "History overtakes the juvenile justice system." *Crime and Delinquency* 37(2):204–24.

Ferdinand, Theodore N., and Elmer E. Luchterhand (1970). "Inner city youth, the police, the juvenile court and justice." *Social Problems* 17:510–27.

Ferrell, Jeff (1993). *Crime of Style: Urban Graffiti and the Politics of Criminality.* New York: Garland.

Ferseter, Elyce Z., Edith N. Snethen, and Thomas C. Courtless (1969). "Juvenile detention: Protection, prevention, or punishment?" *Fordham Law Review* 38:161–97.

Fields, Charles B., and Robert A. Jerin (1996). "'Murder and mayhem' in the media: Public perceptions (and misperceptions) of crime and criminality." Pp. 37–45 in *Visions for Change: Crime and Justice in the Twenty-first Century*, edited by R. Muraskin and A. R. Roberts. Upper Saddle River, NJ: Prentice-Hall.

Finckenauer, James O. (1984). *Juvenile Delinquency and Corrections.* Orlando: Academic.

Finkelhor, David, and Lisa M. Jones (2004). *Explanations for the Decline in Child Sexual Abuse Cases.* Washington, DC: Office of Juvenile Justice and Delinquency Prevention, U.S. Dept. of Justice.

Finkelhor, David, and Richard Ormrod (2001). *Homicides of Children and Youth.* Washington, DC: Office of Juvenile Justice and Delinquency Prevention, U.S. Dept. of Justice.

Fishman, Mark (1976). "Crime waves as ideology." *Social Problems* 25:531–43.

Flandrin, Jean-Louis (1979*). Families in Former Times: Kinship, Household, and Sexuality.* Translated by Richard Southern. New York: Cambridge University Press.

Flores, Anthony W., Lawrence F. Travis III, and Edward J. Latessa. (2004). *Case Classification for Juvenile Corrections: An Assessment of the Youth Level of Service/Case Management Inventory (YLS/CMI).* Washington, DC: Dept. of Justice.

Flores, J. Robert (2004). "Truancy reduction: Keeping youth in school and out of trouble." *OJJDP News at a Glance* 3(1)(January/February). Washington, DC: Office of Juvenile Justice and Delinquency Prevention, U.S. Dept. of Justice.

Florida Department of Juvenile Justice (1998). "Aftercare." Chapter 4 in *Program Manual.* http://www.djj.state.fl.us/Program . . . vInterv/Interv%20Services/ch-4.html.

Flynn, William J., and Brian McDonough (2004). "Police work with juveniles." Pp. 200–215 in *Juvenile Justice Sourcebook,* edited by Albert R. Roberts. New York: Oxford University Press.

Folks, Homer (1902). *The Care of Destitute, Neglected, and Delinquent Children.* New York: Macmillan.

Fong, Robert S., and Ronald E. Vogel (1995). "A comparative analysis of prison gang members, security threat groups inmates, and general population prisoners in the Texas Department of Corrections." *The Journal of Gang Research* 2(2):1–12.

Forshee, Vangie, and Karl E. Bauman (1992). "Parental and peer characteristics as modifiers of the bond-behavior relationship: An elaboration of control theory." *Journal of American Health and Social Behavior* 33:66–76.

Forst, Martin L., ed. (1995). *The New Juvenile Justice.* Chicago: Nelson-Hall.

Fox, James G. (1989). "Critical perspectives on selective incapacitation and the prediction of dangerousness." Pp. 136–49 in *U.S. Sentencing Guidelines: Prospects for Criminal Justice,* edited by Dean J. Champion. New York: Praeger.

Fox, Sanford J. (1996). "The early history of the court." *The Future of Children* 6(3):29–39.

Fraser, Steven (1995). *The Bell Curve Wars: Race, Intelligence and the Future of America.* New York: Basic Books.

Frazier, Charles E. (1989). "Preadjudicatory detention." Pp. 143–68 in *Juvenile Justice: Policies, Programs, and Services,* edited by Albert R. Roberts. Chicago: Dorsey.

Frazier, Charles E., and John Cochran (1986). "Detention of juveniles: Its effects on subsequent juvenile court processing decisions." *Youth and Society* 17:286–305.

Frazier, Charles E., Pamela Richards, and Roberto Hugh Potter (1983). "Juvenile diversion and net widening: Toward a clarification of assessment strategies." *Human Organization* 42:115–22.

Freed, David (1986). "Policing gangs: Case of contrasting styles." *Los Angeles Times,* January 19, p.1.

Freivalds, Peter (1996). *Balanced and Restorative Justice Project (BARJ).* Washington, DC: Office of Juvenile Justice and Delinquency Prevention, U.S. Dept. of Justice.

Freng, Adrienne, and L. Thomas Winfree, Jr. (2004). "Exploring race and ethnic differences in a sample of middle school gang members." Pp. 142–62 in *American Youth Gangs at the Millennium,* edited by Finn-Aage Esbensen, Stephen G. Tibbetts, and Larry Gaines. Long Grove, IL: Waveland Press.

Gaines, Larry K., and Victor E. Kappeler (2003). *Policing in America.* 4th ed. Cincinnati, OH: Anderson.

Gaines, Larry K., and Peter B. Kraska (2003). *Drugs, Crime, & Justice.* 2nd ed. Long Grove, IL: Waveland Press.

Galliher, John, and A. Walker (1977). "The puzzle of the social origins of the Marijuana Stamp Act of 1937." *Social Problems* 24:371–73.

Gardner, Martin R. (2003). *Understanding Juvenile Law.* 2nd ed. New York: Matthew Bender.

Garfinkel, Harold (1956). "Conditions of successful degradation ceremonies." *American Journal of Sociology* 61:420–24.

Garry, Eileen M. (1996). *Truancy: First Step to a Lifetime of Problems.* Washington, DC: Office of Juvenile Justice and Delinquency Prevention, U.S. Dept. of Justice.

Geis, Gilbert, and Arnold Binder (1991). "Sins of their children: Parental responsibility for juvenile delinquency." *Notre Dame Journal of Law, Ethics, and Public Policy* 5:303–22.

Giacomazzi, Andrew, and Quint C. Thurman (1994). "Cops and kids revisited: A second-year assessment of a community policing and delinquency prevention innovation." *Police Studies* 17(4):1–20.

Gibbs, J. J., Dennis M. Giever, and J. S. Martin (1998). "Parental management and self-control: An empirical test of Gottfredson and Hirschi's general theory." *Journal of Research in Crime and Delinquency* 35(1):40–70.

Giever, Dennis M. (1995). "An assessment of the core elements of Gottfredson and Hirschi's general theory of crime." Unpublished doctoral dissertation, Indiana University of Pennsylvania.

Gilbert, James (1986). *A Cycle of Outrage: Reaction to the Juvenile Delinquents in the 1950s.* New York: Oxford.

Gillis, John R. (1974). *Youth and History: Tradition and Change in European Age Relations, 1700–Present.* New York: Academic Press.

Glassner, Barry (1999). *The Culture of Fear: Why Americans Are Afraid of the Wrong Things.* New York: Basic Books.

Glaze, Lauren E. (2003). *Probation and Parole in the United States, 2002.* Washington, DC: U.S. Dept. of Justice.

Glueck, Sheldon, and Eleanor Glueck (1950). *Unraveling Juvenile Delinquency.* Cambridge, MA: Harvard University Press.

Glueck, Sheldon, and Eleanor Glueck (1949). *Physique and Criminality.* Cambridge, MA: Harvard University Press.

Goffman, Erving (1963). *Stigma.* Englewood Cliffs, NJ: Prentice-Hall.

Goffman, Erving (1961). *The Asylum: Essays on the Social Situation of Mental Patients and Other Inmates.* Garden City, NY: Doubleday.

Golden, Renny (1997). *Disposable Children: America's Welfare System.* Belmont, CA: Wadsworth.

Goldstein, Arnold P., and C. Ronald Huff, eds. (1993). *The Gang Intervention Handbook.* Champaign, IL: Research Press.

Goldstein, Herman (1993). "The new policing: Confronting complexity." *Research in Brief.* Washington, DC: National Institute of Justice.

Goldstein, N. E. S., O. Olubadewo, R. E. Redding, and F. J. Lexcen. (2005). "Mental health disorders: The neglected risk factor in juvenile delinquency." Pp. 85–110 in *Juvenile Delinquency: Prevention, Assessment, and Intervention*, edited by K. Heilbrun, N. E. S. Goldstein, and R. F. Redding. New York: Oxford University Press.

Goldstrom, I., F. Jaiquan, M. Henderson, A. Male, and R. Manderscheid (2001). "The availability of mental health services to young people in juvenile justice facilities: A national survey." Pp. 248–68 in *Mental Health, United States, 2000.* Washington, DC: Substance Abuse and Mental Health Services Administration, U.S. Dept. of Health and Social Services.

Goodstein, Lynne, and Henry Sontheimer (1997). "The implementation of an intensive aftercare program for serious juvenile offenders: A case study." *Criminal Justice and Behavior* 24(3):332–59.

Gordon, Robert (1987). "SES versus IQ in the race-IQ-delinquency model." *International Journal of Sociology and Social Policy* 7:30–70.

Gottfredson, Denise C. (1997). "School-based crime prevention." Chapter 5 in *Preventing Crime: What Works, What Doesn't, and What's Promising*, edited by Lawrence Sherman,

Denise C. Gottfredson, Doris MacKenzie, John Eck, Peter Reuter, and Shawn Bushway. Washington, DC: National Institute of Justice.

Gottfredson, Gary D., Denise C. Gottfredson, Ellen R. Czeh, David Cantor, Scott B. Crosse, and Irene Hantman (2004). *Toward Safe and Orderly Schools—The National Study of Delinquency Prevention in Schools.* Washington, DC: U.S. Dept. of Justice.

Gottfredson, Michael R., and Travis Hirschi (1990). *A General Theory of Crime.* Palo Alto, CA: Stanford University Press.

Green, Gary S. (1985). "The representativeness of the Uniform Crime Reports: Ages of persons arrested." *Journal of Police Science and Administration* 13(1):46–52.

Greene, Richard, ed. (1991). *Mainstreaming Retardation Delinquency.* Lancaster, PA: Technomic.

Greenwood, Peter W., and Franklin E. Zimring (1985). *One More Chance: The Pursuit of Promising Intervention Strategies for Chronic Juvenile Offenders.* Santa Monica, CA: Rand Corporation.

Greer, William C. (1991). "Aftercare: Community integration following institutional treatment." Pp. 377–390 in *Juvenile Sexual Offending,* edited by G. D. Ryan and S. L. Lane. Lexington, MA: Lexington.

Griffin, P. (2000). *State Juvenile Justice Profiles.* Pittsburgh, PA: National Center for Juvenile Justice.

Griswald, D. B. (1978). "Police discrimination: An elusive question." *Journal of Police Science and Administration* 6(1):61–66.

Hagan, John (1990). "The structuration of gender and deviance: A power control theory of vulnerability to crime and the search for deviant role exits." *Canadian Review of Sociology and Anthropology* 27:137–56.

Hagan, John (1989). *Structural Criminology.* New Brunswick, NJ: Rutgers University Press.

Hagan, John, John H. Simpson, and A. R. Gillis (1979). "The sexual stratification of social control: A gender-based perspective on crime and delinquency." *British Journal of Sociology* 30:28–38.

Hagedorn, John M. (1991). "Gangs, neighborhoods, and public policy." *Social Problems* 38(4):529–38.

Hall, G. Stanley (1904). *Adolescence: Its Psychology and Its Relations to Physiology, Anthropology, Sociology, Sex, Crime, Religion, and Education.* 2 vols. New York: Appleton.

Hanawalt, B. A. (1993). *Growing Up in Medieval London: The Experience of Childhood in History.* New York: Oxford University Press.

Hanson, Roger A., and Brian J. Ostrom (2004). "Indigent defenders get the job done and done well." Pp. 227–50 in *The Criminal Justice System: Politics and Policies,* 9th ed., edited by George Cole, Marc Gertz, and Amy Bunger. Belmont, CA: West/Wadsworth.

Hardt, Robert H., and Sandra Petersen-Hardt (1977). "On determining the quality of the delinquency self-report method." *Journal of Research on Crime and Delinquency* 14:247–61.

Harris, Mary G. (1994). "Cholas, Mexican-American girls, and gangs." *Sex Roles* 30:289–301.

Harris, Paul (2004). "New 'fake stories' row hits US media." *The Observer,* March 21. http//www.guardian.co.uk/print/0,3858,4884801-110878,00/html.

Harrison, Paige M., and Jennifer C. Karberg (2004). *Prison and Jail Inmates at Midyear 2003.* Washington, DC: Bureau of Justice Statistics, U.S. Dept. of Justice.

Hathaway, Starke R., and Elio D. Monachesi (1963). *Adolescent Personality and Behavior: MMPI Patterns of Normal, Delinquent, Dropout, and Other Outcomes.* Minneapolis: University of Minnesota Press.

Hathaway, Starke R., and Elio D. Monachesi (1957). "The personalities of predelinquent boys." *Journal of Criminal Law, Criminology and Police Science* 48:149–63.

Hathaway, S. R., and E. D. Monachesi (1953). *Analyzing and Predicting Juvenile Delinquency with the MMPI.* Minneapolis: University of Minnesota Press.

Hawes, Joseph M. (1971). *Children in Urban Society: Juvenile Delinquency in Nineteenth Century America*. New York: Oxford University Press.

Hayes, Lindsay M. (2004). *Juvenile Justice in Confinement: A National Survey.* Washington, DC: Office of Juvenile Justice and Delinquency Prevention.

Hayes, Lindsay M. (1994). "Juvenile suicide in confinement: An overview and summary of one system's approach." *Juvenile and Family Court Journal* 45(2):65–75.

Heinz, Joseph, Gail D. Ryan, and Steven Bengis (1991). "The system's response to juvenile sex offenders." Pp. 377–90 in *Juvenile Sexual Offending*, edited by G. D. Ryan and S. L. Lane. Lexington, MA: Lexington.

Hemmens, Craig, Benjamin Steiner, and David Mueller (2004). *Significant Cases in Juvenile Justice*. Los Angeles: Roxbury.

Henderson, D. A. (1998). "Bioterrorism as a public health threat." *Emerging Infectious Diseases* 4:1–6.

Herrnstein, Richard, and Charles Murray (1994*). The Bell Curve: Intelligence and Class Structure in American Life*. New York: Free Press.

Hill, Karl, Christina Lui, and J. David Hawkins (2001). *Early Precursors of Gang Membership: A Study of Seattle Youth*. Washington, DC: Office of Juvenile Justice and Delinquency Prevention, U.S. Dept. of Justice.

Hinckeldey, Christopher (1993). *Criminal Justice Through the Ages*. Rothenburg, Germany: Mitterlaterliches Criminalmuseum.

Hindelang, Michael (1973). "Causes of delinquency: A partial replication and extension." *Social Problems* 20:471–87.

Hippchen, Leonard (1978). *Ecologic-Biochemical Approaches to the Treatment of Delinquents and Criminals*. New York: Van Nostrand Reinhold.

Hirschi, Travis (1969). *Causes of Delinquency*. Berkeley: University of California Press.

Hirschi, Travis, and Michael Gottfredson (1993). "Rethinking the juvenile justice system." *Crime and Delinquency* 39(2):262–71.

Hoffman, Peter B., and Sheldon Adelberg (1980). "The salient factor score: A non-technical overview." *Federal Probation* 44 (1):44–52.

Hohenstein, William F. (1969). "Factors including the police disposition of juvenile offenders." Pp. 138–49 in *Delinquency: Selected Studies*, edited by Thorsten Sellin and Marvin E. Wolfgang. New York: Wiley.

Holden, Gwen, and Robert A. Kapler (1995). "Deinstitutionalizing status offenders: A record of progress." *Juvenile Justice* II(2):3–10.

Holten, N. Gary, and Lawson L. Lamar (1991). *The Criminal Courts*. New York: McGraw-Hill.

Home, Arthur M. (1993). "Family-based interventions." Pp. 189–218 in *The Gang Intervention Handbook*, edited by Arnold P. Goldstein and C. Ronald Huff. Champaign, IL: Research Press.

Hooton, E. A. (1939). *The American Criminal: An Anthropological Study*. Cambridge, MA: Harvard University Press.

Horowitz, Ruth (1990). "Sociological perspectives on gangs: Conflicting definitions and concepts." Pp. 37–54 in *Gangs in America*, edited by C. Ronald Huff. Newbury Park, CA: Sage.

Howell, James C. (1999). "Youth gang homicides: A literature review." *Crime & Delinquency* 45(2):208–41.

Howell, James C. (1998). "NCCD's survey of juvenile detention and correctional facilities." *Crime and Delinquency* 44:102–9.

Howell, James C. (1994). "Recent gang research: Program and policy implications." *Crime and Delinquency* 40:495–515.

Howell, James C., and Scott H. Decker (2000). "The youth gangs, drugs, and violence connection." *Juvenile Justice Bulletin*. Washington, DC: Office of Juvenile Justice and Delinquency Prevention, U.S. Dept. of Justice.

Hsia, Heidi M., and Marty Beyer (2000). "System change through state challenge activities: Approaches and products." *Juvenile Justice Bulletin* (March). Washington, DC: Office of Juvenile Justice and Delinquency Prevention, U.S. Dept. of Justice.

Huff, C. Ronald (1998). "Comparing the criminal behavior of youth gangs and at-risk youths." *Research in Brief*. Washington, DC: National Institute of Justice.

Huff, C. Ronald (1993). "Gangs in the United States." Pp. 3–20 in *The Gang Intervention Handbook*, edited by Arnold P. Goldstein and C. Ronald Huff. Champaign, IL: Research Press.

Huff, C. Ronald (1990). "Denial, overreaction, and misidentification: A postscript on public policy." Pp. 300–317 in *Gangs in America*, edited by C. Ronald Huff. Newbury Park, CA: Sage.

Huff, C. Ronald (1989). "Youth gangs and public policy." *Crime and Delinquency* 35:524–37.

Huff, C. Ronald, and Wesley D. McBride (1993). "Gangs and the police." Pp. 401–416 in *The Gang Intervention Handbook*, edited by Arnold P. Goldstein and C. Ronald Huff. Champaign, IL: Research Press.

Hunt, Arnold (1997). "'Moral panic' and moral language in the media." *The British Journal of Sociology* 48(4):629–48.

Hunt, David (1970). *Parents and Children in History: The Psychology of Family Life in Early Modern France*. New York: Basic Books.

Hunt, Geoffrey, Stephanie Riegel, Tomas Morales, and Dan Waldorf (1993). "Changes in prison culture: Prison gangs and the case of the 'Pepsi Generation.'" *Social Problems* 40(3):398–409.

Hunter, Lisa, Gordon MacNeil, and Maurice Elias (2004). "School violence: Prevalence, policies, and prevention," pp. 102–25 in *Juvenile Justice Sourcebook*, edited by Albert R. Roberts. New York: Oxford University Press.

Hurl, Loma F., and David J. Tucker (1997). "The Michigan county agents and the development of juvenile probation, 1873–1900." *Journal of Social History* 30(4):905–35.

Hurst, Hunter, IV, and Patricia McFall Torbet (1993). *Organization and Administration of Juvenile Services: Probation, Aftercare, and State Institutions for Delinquent Youth*. Revised edition. Pittsburgh, PA: National Center for Juvenile Justice.

Inciardi, James (1992). *The War on Drugs II. The Continuing Epic of Heroin, Cocaine, Crack, Crime, AIDS, and Public Policy*. Mountain View, CA: Mayfield.

Inciardi, James A., Ruth Horowitz, and Anne E. Pottieger (1993). *Street Kids, Street Drugs, Street Crime: An Examination of Drug Use and Serious Delinquency in Miami*. Belmont, CA: Wadsworth.

Institute for Judicial Administration/American Bar Association (1996). "Standards Relating to Interim Status: The Release, Control and Detention of Accused Juvenile Offenders between Arrest and Disposition," edited by Robert J. Shepherd, Jr. Chicago: American Bar Association.

Institute for Judicial Administration/American Bar Association (1980). *Juvenile Justice Standards*. Cambridge, MA: Ballinger.

International Associations of Chiefs of Police (1929). *Uniform Crime Reporting: A Complete Manual for Police*. New York: J. J. Little and Ives.

Jackson, Pamela I. (1992). "The police and social threat: Urban transition, youth gangs, and social control." *Policing and Society* 2:193–204.

Jackson, Robert K., and Wesley D. McBride (1992). *Understanding Street Gangs*. Placerville, CA: Copperhouse.

Jeffery, C. Ray (1971). *Crime Prevention through Environmental Design*. Beverly Hills, CA: Sage.

Jensen, Gary F., and Dean G. Rojek (1998). *Delinquency and Youth Crime*. 3rd ed. Long Grove, IL: Waveland Press.

Jerin, Robert A., and Laura J. Moriarty (1998). *Victims of Crime*. Chicago: Nelson-Hall.

Johnson, Herbert A., and Nancy Travis Wolfe (1996). *History of Criminal Justice*. 2nd ed. Cincinnati, OH: Anderson.

Johnson, Kelly Dedel (2004). *Underage Drinking*. Washington, DC: Office of Community Oriented Policing, U.S. Dept. of Justice.

Jolowicz, H. F. (1957). *Roman Foundations of Modern Law*. London: Oxford University Press.

Jones, Judith B. (2004). "Access to counsel." *OJJDP Juvenile Justice Bulletin* (June). Washington, DC: Office of Juvenile Justice and Delinquency Prevention, U.S. Dept. of Justice.

Jones, Mark (2004). *Community Corrections*. Long Grove, IL: Waveland Press.

Justizvollzuganstalt-Adelsheim [Adelsheim Young Offenders' Institution] (1998). *Kurze Information* [*Short Information*]. Adelsheim, Baden-Württemberg, Germany.

Kaplan, Abraham (1964). *Conduct of Inquiry*. Scranton, PA: Chandler.

Kappeler, Victor E., and Gary W. Potter (2005). *The Mythology of Crime and Criminal Justice*. 4th ed. Long Grove, IL: Waveland Press.

Katzman, Gary S. (1991). *Inside the Criminal Process*. New York: W. W. Norton.

Kaufman, Phillip, Xianglei Chen, Susan P. Choy, Kathryn A. Chandler, Christopher D. Chapman, Michael R. Rand, and Cheryl Ringel (1998). *Indicators of School Crime and Safety, 1998*. Washington, DC: U.S. Dept. of Education and U.S. Dept. of Justice.

Kelley, Barbara Tatem, David Huizinga, Terence P. Thornberry, and Rolf Loeber (1997). "Epidemiology of serious violence." *OJJDP Juvenile Justice Bulletin*. Washington, DC: Office of Juvenile Justice and Delinquency Prevention, U.S. Dept. of Justice.

Kelley, Barbara Tatem, Terence P. Thornberry, and Carolyn A. Smith (1997). "In the wake of childhood maltreatment." *OJJDP Juvenile Justice Bulletin*. Washington, DC: U.S. Dept. of Justice.

Kelling, George, and James Q. Wilson (1982). "Broken windows: The police and neighborhood safety." *Atlantic Monthly* 249:29–38.

King County, Washington Superior Court (2004). "Juvenile detention intake criteria." http://www.metrokc.gov/kcsc/juv/detention_criteria.htm.

Klein, Malcolm W. (1968). "Impressions of juvenile gang members." *Adolescence* 3(9):53–78.

Klein, Malcolm W., Cheryl L. Maxson, and Lea C. Cunningham (1991). "'Crack,' street gangs, and violence." *Criminology* 29:623–50.

Kotlowitz, Alex (1999). "The unprotected." *The New Yorker*, February 9, pp. 42–53.

Krause, Wesley, and Marilyn D. McShane (1994). "A deinstitutionalization retrospective: Relabeling the status offender." *Journal of Crime and Justice* 17(1):45–67.

Krisberg, Barry (2005). *Juvenile Justice: Redeeming Our Children*. Thousand Oaks, CA: Sage.

Krisberg, Barry (1995). "The legacy of juvenile corrections." *Corrections Today* 57(5):122, 124, 152, 154.

Krisberg, Barry (1975). *Crime and Privilege: Toward a New Criminology*. Englewood Cliffs, NJ: Prentice-Hall.

Krisberg, Barry, and James F. Austin (1993). *Reinventing Juvenile Justice*. Newbury Park, CA: Sage.

Krisberg, Barry, Robert DeComo, and Norma C. Herrera (1992). *National Juvenile Custody Trends 1978–1989*. Washington, DC: Office of Juvenile Justice and Delinquency Prevention, U.S. Dept. of Justice.

Krisberg, Barry, Deborah Neuenfeldt, Richard Wiebush, and Orlando Rodriguez (1994). *Juvenile Intensive Supervision: Planning Guide*. Washington, DC: Office of Juvenile Justice and Delinquency Prevention, U.S. Dept. of Justice.

Krisberg, Barry, Ira M. Schwartz, Paul Litsky, and James Austin (1986). "The watershed of juvenile justice reform." *Crime & Delinquency* 32 (1):5–38.

Kumpfer, K. L. (1993). *Strengthening America's Families: Promising Parenting Strategies for Delinquency Prevention—User's Guide*. Washington, DC: Office of Juvenile Justice and Delinquency Prevention, U.S. Dept. of Justice.

Latessa, Edward J., and Harry E. Allen (2003). *Corrections in the Community*. Cincinnati, OH: Anderson.

Law Enforcement Assistance Administration (1976). *Traditional Preventive Patrol*. Washington, DC: U.S. Dept. of Justice.

Lawrence, Richard (1998). *School Crime and Juvenile Justice*. New York: Oxford University Press.

Lazar, Cathy (2004). "Model for joint child abuse investigations by law enforcement and child protective services." New Jersey Department of Human Services. http://www.state.nj.us/humanservices/NJTaskForce/gtleccps.html.

Lemert, Edwin (1971). *Instead of Court: Diversion in Juvenile Justice*. Washington, DC: U.S. Government Printing Office.

Lemert, Edwin (1951). *Social Pathology*. New York: McGraw-Hill.

Lieber, Michael J., and Katherine M. Jamieson (1995). "Race and decision making within juvenile justice: The importance of context." *Journal of Quantitative Criminology* 11:363–88.

Lieber, Michael J., Mahesh K. Nalla, and Margaret Farnworth (1998). "Explaining juveniles' attitudes toward the police." *Justice Quarterly* 15(1):151–74.

Lilly, J. Robert, and Richard A. Ball (1987). "A brief history of house arrest and electronic monitoring." *Northern Kentucky Law Review* 13(3):343–74.

Lilly, J. Robert, Richard A. Ball, and Jennifer Wright (1987). "Home incarceration with electronic monitoring in Kenton County, Kentucky: An evaluation." Pp. 189–203 in *Intermediate Punishments*, edited by Belinda R. McCarthy. Mousey, NJ: Willow Tree Press.

Lilly, J. Robert, Francis T. Cullen, and Richard A. Ball (1995). *Criminological Theory: Context and Consequences*. Newbury Park, CA: Sage.

Lipton, Douglas, Robert Martinson, and Judith Wilkes (1975). *The Effectiveness of Correctional Treatment: A Survey of Treatment Evaluation Studies*. New York: Praeger.

Lombroso, Cesare (1876). *L'uomo Delinquente* [*The Criminal Man*]. Milan: Hoepli.

Lundman, Richard J. (1993). *Prevention and Control of Juvenile Delinquency*. 2nd ed. New York: Oxford University Press.

Lundman, Richard J. (1976). "Will diversion reduce recidivism?" *Crime and Delinquency* 22:428–37.

Lundman, Richard J., Richard E. Sykes, and John P. Clark (1978). "Police control of juveniles: A replication." *Journal of Research in Crime and Delinquency* 15:74–91.

Lynch, James P. (2002). "Trends in Juvenile Violent Offending: An Analysis of Victim Survey Data." *OJJDP Juvenile Justice Bulletin*. Washington, DC: Office of Juvenile Justice and Delinquency Prevention, U.S. Dept. of Justice.

Lystad, Mary (1980). *From Dr. Mather to Dr. Seuss: 200 Years of American Books for Children*. Boston: G. H. Hall.

MacDonald, John M. (1999). "Violence and drug use in juvenile institutions." *Journal of Criminal Justice* 27:33–44.

Mack, Julian W. (1909). "The juvenile court." *Harvard Law Review* 23:109–22; pp. 13–20 in *Readings in Juvenile Justice Administration*, edited by Barry C. Feld (1999). New York: Oxford University Press.

MacKenzie, Doris Layton (2005). "Criminal justice and crime prevention." In *Preventing Crime: What Works, What Doesn't, What's Promising*, edited by Lawrence W. Sherman, Denise Gottfredson, Doris MacKenzie, John Eck, Peter Reuter, and Shawn Bushway. Rockville, MD: National Criminal Justice Reference Service. http://www.ncjrs.org/works/.

MacNamara, Donald (1977). "The medical model in corrections." *Criminology* 14:439–47.

Maguire, Kathleen, Ann L. Pastore, and Timothy Flanagan (1993). *Sourcebook of Criminal Justice Statistics—1992*. Washington, DC: U.S. Dept. of Justice.

Maitland, Angela S., and Richard D. Sluder. (1998). "Victimization and youthful prison inmates: An empirical analysis." *The Prison Journal* 78:55–73.

Manfredi, Christopher P. (1998). *The Supreme Court and Juvenile Justice*. Lawrence: University Press of Kansas.

Martinson, Robert (1974). "What works? Questions and answers about prison reform." *Public Interest* 35:22–54.

Massey, Douglas S., and Nancy A. Denton (1993). *American Apartheid: Segregation and the Making of the Underclass*. Cambridge, MA: Harvard University Press.

Mather, Cotton (1690). *Addresses to Old Men, and Young Men, and Little Children*. Boston: R. Pierce.

Matthews, Roger (1987). "Taking realist criminology seriously." *Contemporary Crisis* 11:271–401.

Maxson, Cheryl, Karen Hennigan, David Sloane, and Kathy A. Kolnick (2004). *Can Civil Gang Injunctions Change Communities? A Community Assessment of the Impact of Civil Gang Injunctions*. Washington, DC: National Institute of Justice, U.S. Dept. of Justice.

Maxson, Cheryl, and Malcolm Klein (1990). "Street gang violence: Twice as great, or half as great?" Pp. 71–100 in *Gangs in America*, edited by C. Ronald Huff. Newbury Park, CA: Sage.

Mays, G. Larry (1989). "The impact of federal sentencing guidelines on jail and prison overcrowding and early releases." Pp. 181–200 in *U.S. Sentencing Guidelines: Prospects for Criminal Justice*, edited by Dean J. Champion. New York: Praeger.

Mays, G. Larry (1984). "The Supreme Court and development of federal habeas corpus doctrine." Pp. 55–69 in *Legal Issues in Criminal Justice: The Courts*, edited by Sloan Letman, Dan Edwards, and Daniel Bell. Cincinnati, OH: Anderson.

Mays, G. Larry, and Tara Gray (1996). *Privatization and the Provision of Correctional Services*. Cincinnati, OH: Academy of Criminal Justice Sciences/Anderson.

Mays, G. Larry, and Peter R. Gregware (1996). "The children's code reform movement in New Mexico: The politics of expediency." *Law and Policy* 18 (1, 2):179–93.

Mays, G. Larry, and Michelle Olszta (1989). "Prison litigation: From the 1960s to the 1990s." *Criminal Justice Policy Review* 3(3):279–98.

Mays, G. Larry, and L. Thomas Winfree, Jr. (2005). *Essentials of Corrections*. 3rd ed. Belmont, CA: Wadsworth.

Mays, G. Larry, and L. Thomas Winfree, Jr. (2000). *Juvenile Justice*. Boston: McGraw-Hill.

Mays, G. Larry, L. Thomas Winfree, Jr., and Stacey Jackson (1993). "Youth gangs in southern New Mexico: A qualitative analysis." *Journal of Contemporary Criminal Justice* 9:134–45.

McCarthy, Belinda (1985). "An analysis of detention." *Juvenile and Family Court Journal* 36(2):49–50.

McCarthy, Francis Barry (1977). "Should juvenile delinquency be abolished?" *Crime and Delinquency* 23(2):196–203.

McCarthy, Francis Barry, William Wesley Patton, and James G. Carr (2003). *Juvenile Law and Its Processes: Cases and Materials*. 3rd ed. New York: Matthew Bender.

McCord, Joan (1978). "A thirty-year follow-up of treatment effects." *American Psychologist* 33:384–89.

McCord, William, and Joan McCord, with Irving Kenneth Zola (1959). *Origins of Crime: A New Evaluation of the Cambridge-Somerville Youth Study*. New York: Columbia University Press.

McCorkle, R. C. (1993). "Fear of victimization and symptoms of psychopathology among prison inmates." *Journal of Offender Rehabilitation* 9:27–41.

McCorkle, Richard, and Terence Miethe (2002). *Panic: The Social Construction of the Street Gang Problem*. Upper Saddle Creek, NJ: Prentice-Hall.

McCorkle, R. C., T. D. Miethe, and K. A. Drass (1995). "Roots of prison violence: A test of the deprivation, management, and 'not-so-total' institution model." *Crime and Delinquency* 41:317–31.

McLaughlin, Mary Martin (1975). "Survivors and surrogates: Children and parents the ninth to the thirteenth centuries." Pp. 101–81 in *The History of Childhood*, edited by L. de Mause. New York: Harper Torchbooks.

McNeece, C. Aaron, and Sherry Jackson (2004). "Juvenile justice policy: Current trends and 21st-century issues." Pp. 42–62 in *Juvenile Justice Sourcebook*, edited by Albert R. Roberts. New York: Oxford University Press.

McShane, Marilyn D., and Wesley Krause (1993). *Community Corrections*. New York: Macmillan.

Mears, Daniel P. (2002). "Sentencing guidelines and the transformation of juvenile justice in the 21st century." *Journal of Contemporary Criminal Justice* 18(1):6–19.

Melchiorre, A. (2004). *At what age?* 2nd ed. Retrieved 29 March 2005, from http://www.right-to-education.org/content/age/age.pdf.

Mennel, Robert M. (1973). *Thorns and Thistles: Juvenile Delinquents in the United States, 1873–1940*. Hanover, NH: University Press of New England.

Meriwether, Margaret H. (1988). "Child abuse reporting laws: Time for a change." Pp. 9–45 in *Protecting Children from Abuse and Neglect*, edited by Douglas J. Besharov. Springfield, IL: Thomas.

Merriam-Webster's Collegiate Dictionary (2003). Springfield, MA: Merriam-Webster.

Merton, Robert K. (1938). "Social structure and anomie." *American Sociological Review* 3:672–82.

Meyer, Jon'a F. (2002). "Bail and bond." Pp. 93–97 in *Encyclopedia of Crime and Punishment*, edited by David Levinson. Thousand Oaks, CA: Sage Publications.

Mihalic, Sharon (2005). "Agency and practitioner rating categories and criteria for evidence based programs." www.colorado.edu/cspv/blueprints/matrix/criteria.pdf.

Mihalic, Sharon, Katherine Irwin, Abigail Fagan, Diane Ballard, and Delbert Elliott (2004). "Successful program implementation: Lessons from the Blueprints." *OJJDP Juvenile Justice Bulletin*. Washington, DC: U.S. Dept. of Justice.

Miller, Jerome G. (1991). *Last One over the Wall: The Massachusetts Experiment in Closing Reform Schools*. Columbus: Ohio State University Press.

Miller, Keane (1997). *Encyclopedia and Dictionary of Medicine, Nursing and Allied Health*. 6th ed. Philadelphia: Saunders.

Miller, Walter B. (1990). "Why the United States has failed to solve its youth gang problem." Pp. 263–87 in *Gangs in America*, edited by C. R. Huff. Newbury Park, CA: Sage.

Miller, Walter B. (1975). *Violence by Youth Gangs and Youth Groups as a Crime Problem in Major American Cities*. Washington, DC: U.S. Dept. of Justice.

Miller, Walter B. (1962). "The impact of a 'total community' delinquency control project." *Social Problems* 10:168–91.

Miller, Walter B. (1958). "The lower-class culture as a generating milieu of gang delinquency." *Journal of Social Issues* 14(3):5–19.

Montes, Marisela (1996). "Technological advances in parole supervision." *Corrections Today* 58(4):88.

Montgomery, Imogene M., Patricia McFall Torbet, Diane A. Malloy, Lori P. Adamcik, M. James Toner, and Joey Andrews (1994). *What Works: Promising Interventions in Juvenile Justice*. Washington, DC: Office of Juvenile Justice and Delinquency Prevention, U.S. Dept. of Justice.

Monti, Daniel J. (1994). *Wannabe Gangs in Suburbs and Schools*. Cambridge, MA: Blackwell.

Moorhead-Nord, Tamera (1994). *An evaluation of the Gang Resistance Education and Training (GREAT) program: A model for success?* Unpublished master's thesis, New Mexico State University, Las Cruces.

Mounteer, Carl (1984). "Beginners on the forum: Roman adolescence and youth, 200 B.C. to A.D. 100." *Journal of Psychohistory* 12:251–58.

Moynihan, Daniel P. (1969). *Maximum Feasible Misunderstanding: Community Action in the War on Poverty.* New York: Free Press.

MyLawTerms.com (2004). http://www.mylawterms.com.

Nagel, Ilene (1983). "The legal/extra-legal controversy: Judicial decisions in pretrial release." *Law and Society Review* 17:481–515.

National Advisory Committee on Criminal Justice Standards and Goals (1976). *Juvenile Justice and Delinquency Prevention.* Washington, DC: U.S. Government Printing Office.

National Advisory Committee on Criminal Justice Standards and Goals (1973). *Police.* Washington, DC: U.S. Government Printing Office.

National Advisory Committee on Juvenile Justice and Delinquency Prevention (1980). *Standards for the Administration of Juvenile Justice.* Washington, DC: U.S. Government Printing Office.

National Association of School Resource Officers (2004). http://www.nasro.org.

National Center for Juvenile Justice (2005). *State Juvenile Justice Profiles.* http://www.ncjj.org/stateprofiles/

National Center for Women & Policing (2004). <http://www.womenandpolicing.org>.

National Council on Crime and Delinquency (1998). *NCCD—About the Company.* http://www.nccd.com/company.html.

National Criminal Justice Association (2004). "CASA calls for 'top to bottom' overhaul of the juvenile justice system." *Justice Bulletin* (October). http://www.ncja.org/justice_bulletin.htm.

National Institute of Justice (2003). *Annual Report 2000: Arrestee Drug Abuse Monitoring.* Washington, DC: U.S. Dept. of Justice.

National Institute of Justice (1994). *The D.A.R.E. Program: A Review of Prevalence, User Satisfaction, and Effectiveness.* October, Washington, DC: National Institute of Justice.

National School Safety and Security Services (2004). http://www.schoolsecurity.org/resources'school-resource-officers.html.

National Youth Gang Center (2000). *1998 National Youth Gang Survey.* Washington, DC: Office of Juvenile Justice and Delinquency Prevention, U.S. Dept. of Justice.

National Youth Gang Center (1997). *1995 National Youth Gang Survey.* Washington, DC: Office of Juvenile Justice and Delinquency Prevention, U.S. Dept. of Justice.

Nettler, Gwynn (1978). *Explaining Crime.* New York: McGraw-Hill.

Neubauer, David (1999). *America's Courts and the Criminal Justice System.* 6th ed. Pacific Grove, CA: Brooks/Cole.

New Mexico Criminal and Traffic Law Manual (2004). Charlottesville, VA: Michie.

Newman, Graeme (1978). *The Punishment Response.* Philadelphia: Lippincott.

Norman, Sherwood (1972). *The Youth Services Bureau: A Key to Delinquency Prevention.* Paramus, NJ: National Council on Crime and Delinquency.

Nye, F. Ivan (1958). *Family Relationships and Delinquent Behavior.* New York: John Wiley.

Office of Juvenile Justice and Delinquency Prevention (2004). "OJJDP Model Programs Guide."   http://www.dsgonline.com/mpg_non_flash/intervention_immediate_sanctions.htm.

Office of Juvenile Justice and Delinquency Prevention (2000). "Children as victims." *Juvenile Justice Bulletin.* Washington, DC: U.S. Dept. of Justice.

Office of Juvenile Justice and Delinquency Prevention (1998a). *OJJDP: The Office of Juvenile Justice and Delinquency Prevention.* http://ncjrs.org/offdp/html/mission.html.

Office of Juvenile Justice and Delinquency Prevention (1998b, April). "Planning a successful crime prevention project." *Youth in Action Bulletin,* No. 1.

Office of Juvenile Justice and Delinquency Prevention (1995). *Guide for Implementing the Comprehensive Strategy for Serious, Violent and Chronic Juvenile Offenders*. Washington, DC: U.S. Dept. of Justice.

Office of Juvenile Justice and Delinquency Prevention (1993). *Comprehensive Strategy for Serious, Violent and Chronic Juvenile Offenders*. Washington, DC: U.S. Dept. of Justice.

Ozment, Steven (1983). *When Fathers Ruled: Family Life in Reformation Europe*. Cambridge, MA: Harvard University Press.

Palumbo, Michael G., and Jennifer Ferguson (1995). "Evaluating Gang Resistance Education and Training: Is the impact the same as Drug Abuse Resistance Education (DARE)?" *Evaluation Review* 19(6):597–619.

Parent, Dale G. (2003). *Correctional Boot Camps: Lessons from a Decade of Research*. Washington, DC: U.S. Dept. of Justice.

Parent, Dale G., V. Leiter, S. Kennedy, L. Livens, D. Wentworth, and S. Wilcox (1994). *Conditions of Confinement: Juvenile Detention and Corrections Facilities*. Washington, DC: Office of Juvenile Justice and Delinquency Prevention, U.S. Dept. of Justice.

Parents Anonymous (2004). http://www.parentsanon.org/paindex10.html.

Partington, Angela, ed. (1992). *The Oxford Dictionary of Quotations*. Oxford: Oxford University Press.

Patenaud, Allan (2003). "Diversion programs." Pp. 132–40 in *Encyclopedia of Juvenile Justice*, edited by Marilyn D. McShane and Frank P. Williams, III. Thousand Oaks, CA: Sage.

Paternoster, Raymond, and Paul Mazerolle (1994). "General strain theory and delinquency: A replication and extension." *Journal of Research in Crime and Delinquency* 31(3):235–63.

Patterson, Gerald (1982). *Coercive Family Process: A Social Learning Approach*. Vol. 3. Eugene, OR: Castalia.

Pawlak, Edward J. (1977). "Differential selection of juveniles for detention." *Journal of Research in Crime and Delinquency* 14:152–65.

Peak, Kenneth J. (1998). *Justice Administration: Police, Courts, and Corrections Management*. 2nd ed. Upper Saddle River, NJ: Prentice-Hall.

Peak, Kenneth J., and Ronald W. Glensor (2004). *Community Policing and Problem Solving*. 4th ed. Upper Saddle River, NJ: Prentice-Hall.

Pelz, M. A. (1996). "Gangs." Pp. 213–18 in *Encyclopedia of American Prisons*, edited by M. D. McShane and F. P. Williams, III. New York: Garland.

Pepinsky, Harold (1978). "Community anarchism as an alternative to the rule of criminal law." *Contemporary Crisis* 2:315–27.

Peters, Michael, David Thomas, and Christopher Zamberlan (1997). *Boot Camps for Juvenile Offenders*. Washington, DC: Office of Juvenile Justice and Delinquency Prevention, U.S. Dept. of Justice.

Petersilia, Joan (1997a). "Justice for all? Offenders with mental retardation and the California corrections system." *The Prison Journal* 77(4):358–80.

Petersilia, Joan (1997b). "Unequal justice? Offenders with mental retardation in prison." *Corrections Management Quarterly* 1(4):36–43.

Petersilia, Joan (1980). "Criminal career research: A review of recent evidence." Pp. 321–79 in *Crime and Justice*, Vol. 2, edited by N. Morris and M. Tonry. Chicago: University of Chicago Press.

Petersilia, Joan, and Susan Turner (1990). *Intensive supervision for high-risk probationers: Findings from three California experiments*. Santa Monica: RAND Corp.

Phoenix Police Department (2004). "Gang Resistance Education and Training." http://www.phoenix.gov/police/great1.html.

Pickett, Robert (1969). *House of Refuge*. Syracuse, NY: Syracuse University Press.

Piliavin, Irving, and Scott Briar (1964). "Police Encounters with Juveniles." *American Journal of Sociology* 70:206–214.

Platt, Anthony M. (1977). *The Child Savers: The Invention of Delinquency.* 2nd ed. Chicago: University of Chicago Press.

Poe-Yamagata, Eileen, and Jeffrey A. Butts (1996). *Female Offenders in the Juvenile Justice System.* Washington, DC: Office of Juvenile Justice and Delinquency Prevention, U.S. Dept. of Justice.

Polk, Kenneth (1984). "Juvenile diversion: A look at the record." *Crime and Delinquency* 30(4):648–59.

Pollock, Linda (1983). *Forgotten Children: Parent-Child Relations from 1500 to 1900.* Cambridge: Cambridge University Press.

Poole, Eric D., and Robert M. Regoli (1983). "Violence in juvenile institutions." *Criminology* 21:213–32.

Pope, Carl, and Howard N. Snyder (2003). *Race as a Factor in Juvenile Arrests.* Washington, DC: Office of Juvenile Justice and Delinquency Prevention, U.S. Dept. of Justice.

Pope, Carl, Rick Lovell, and Heidi M. Hsia (2002). *Disproportionate Minority Confinement: A Review of the Research Literature from 1989 through 2001.* Washington, DC: Office of Juvenile Justice and Delinquency Prevention, U.S. Dept. of Justice.

Portwood, Sharon Gross, and N. Dickon Reppucci (1994). "Intervention versus interference." Pp. 3–35 in *When There's No Place Like Home,* edited by Jan Blacher. Baltimore: Brookes.

Powers, Edwin, and Helen Witmer (1951). *An Experiment in the Prevention of Juvenile Delinquency: The Cambridge-Somerville Youth Study.* New York: Columbia University Press.

The Prejudice Institute (2004). "What is a Skinhead?" http://www.prejudiceinstitute.org/skinheadsFS.html.

President's Commission on Crime in the District of Columbia (1966). *Report of the President's Commission on Crime in the District of Columbia.* Washington, DC: U.S. Government Printing Office.

President's Commission on Law Enforcement and Administration of Justice (1967a). *The Challenge of Crime in a Free Society.* Washington, DC: U.S. Government Printing Office.

President's Commission on Law Enforcement and Administration of Justice (1967b). *Task Force Report: Juvenile Delinquency and Youth Crime.* Washington, DC: U.S. Government Printing Office.

"Professor Barry Glassner, The Man Who Knows About Fear in American Culture." http://www.buzzflash.com/interviews/03/04/10_glassner.html. April 10, 2003.

Purcell, Noreen, L. Thomas Winfree, Jr., and G. Larry Mays (1994). "DNA (deoxyribonucleic acid) evidence and criminal trials: An exploratory survey of factors associated with the use of 'genetic fingerprinting' in felony prosecutions." *Journal of Criminal Justice* 22(2):145–57.

Puritz, Patricia, and Mary Ann Scali (1998). *Beyond the Walls: Improving Conditions of Confinement for Youth in Custody.* Washington, DC: Office of Juvenile Justice and Delinquency Prevention, U.S. Dept. of Justice.

Puzzanchera, Charles M. (2003a). "Juvenile delinquency probation caseload, 1990–1999." *OJJDP Fact Sheet.* Washington, DC: U.S. Dept. of Justice.

Puzzanchera, Charles M. (2003b). "Person offenses in juvenile court, 1990–1999." *OJJDP Fact Sheet.* Washington, DC: U.S. Dept. of Justice.

Puzzanchera, Charles, Anne L. Stahl, Terrence A. Finnegan, Nancy Tierney, and Howard N. Snyder (2004). *Juvenile Court Statistics 2000.* Pittsburgh, PA: National Center for Juvenile Justice.

Puzzanchera, Charles, Anne L. Stahl, Terrence A. Finnegan, Nancy Tierney, and Howard N. Snyder (2003). *Juvenile Court Statistics 1999.* Pittsburgh, PA: National Center for Juvenile Justice.

Quinney, Richard (1973). *Critique of the Legal Order: Crime Control in a Capitalist Society.* Boston: Little, Brown.

Rafter, Nicole Hahn (1992). "Criminal anthropology in the United States." *Criminology* 30(4):525–45.

Rankin, Joseph H., and L. Edward Wells (1990). "The effects of parental attachments and direct control on delinquency." *Journal of Research in Crime and Delinquency* 27:140–65.

Reaves, Brian A., and Matthew J. Hickman (2004). *Law Enforcement Management and Administrative Statistics, 2000: Data for Individual and Local Agencies with 100 or More Officers.* Washington, DC: U.S. Government Printing Office.

Reckless, Walter (1967). *The Crime Problem.* New York: Appleton-Century-Crofts.

Reckless, Walter (1961). "A new theory of delinquency and crime." *Federal Probation* 25:42–46.

Regoli, Robert M., and John Hewitt (1997). *Delinquency in Society.* 3rd ed. New York: McGraw-Hill.

Regoli, Robert, and John Hewitt (1994). *Delinquency in Society: A Child-Centered Approach.* 2nd ed. New York: McGraw-Hill.

Ringel, Cheryl L., Ernest L. Cowles, and Thomas C. Castellano (1994). "Changing patterns and trends in parole supervision." Pp. 296–320 in *Critical Issues in Crime and Justice*, edited by Albert R. Roberts. Thousand Oaks, CA: Sage.

Roberts, Albert R. (2004). "The emergence and proliferation of juvenile diversion programs." Pp. 183–95 in *Juvenile Justice Sourcebook*, edited by Albert R. Roberts. New York: Oxford University Press.

Roberts, Albert R., and Judith A. Waters (1998). "The coming storm: Juvenile violence and justice system responses." Pp. 40–70 in *Juvenile Justice: Policies, Programs, and Services*, 2nd ed., edited by A. R. Roberts. Chicago: Nelson-Hall.

Robertson, James B. (1994). "Being a parole agent." Pp. 123–130 in *Inside Jobs: A Realistic Guide to Criminal Justice Careers for College Graduates*, edited by Stuart Henry. Salem, WI: Sheffield.

Rodney, Laxley W. (2005). "Principal investigator, Family and Community Violence Prevention Program" (http://www.fcvp.org). Personal correspondence.

Rogers, Joseph W., and G. Larry Mays (1987). *Juvenile Delinquency and Juvenile Justice.* Englewood Cliffs, NJ: Prentice-Hall.

Roncek, Dennis, and Pamela Maier (1991). "Bars, blocks, and crimes revisited: Linking the theory of routine activities to the empiricism of 'hot spots.'" *Criminology* 29:725–50.

Rothman, David J. (1980). *Conscience and Convenience: The Asylum and Its Alternatives in Progressive America.* Boston: Little, Brown.

Rottman, David B., Carol R. Flango, Melissa T. Cantrell, Randall Hansen, and Neil LaFountain (2000). *State Court Organization, 1998.* Washington, DC: Bureau of Justice Statistics, U.S. Dept. of Justice.

Roush, David W. (2004). "Juvenile detention: Issues for the 21st century." Pp. 218–46 in *Juvenile Justice Sourcebook*, edited by Albert R. Roberts. New York: Oxford University Press.

Rubin, H. Ted (1996). "The role of defense attorneys in juvenile justice proceedings." *Juvenile Justice Update* 2(2):1, 2, 10–11.

Rubin, H. Ted (1985). *Behind the Black Robes: Juvenile Court Judges and the Court.* Beverly Hills, CA: Sage.

Rubin, H. Ted (1980). "The emerging prosecutor dominance of the juvenile court intake process." *Crime and Delinquency* 26(3):299–318.

Rubin, Paula N. (1993). *The Americans with Disabilities Act and Criminal Justice: An Overview.* Washington, DC: National Institute of Justice.

Rubin, Paula N., and Susan W. McCampbell (1995). *The Americans with Disabilities Act and Criminal Justice.* Washington, DC: National Institute of Justice.

Ruddell, Rick, and G. Larry Mays (2003). "Examining the arsenal of juvenile gunslingers: Trends and policy implications." *Crime and Delinquency* 49(2):231–52.

Rush, George (2003). *The Dictionary of Criminal Justice*. 6th ed. Guildford, CT: Dushkin.

Sanborn, Hope Viner (1996). "Kids' crimes can send parents to jail." *ABA Journal* 82:28, 30.

Sanborn, Joseph B., Jr., and Anthony W. Salerno (2005). *The Juvenile Justice System*. Los Angeles: Roxbury.

Sanders, William B. (1994). *Gangbangs and Drive-bys*. Hawthorne, NY: de Gruyter.

Sarri, Rosemary C. (1983). "The use of detention and alternatives in the United States since the Gault decision." Pp. 79–98 in *Current Issues in Juvenile Justice*, edited by R. R. Corrado, M. Le Blanc, and J. Trepanier. Toronto: Butterworth.

Sarri, Rosemary C. (1974). *Under Lock and Key: Juveniles in Jails and Detention*. Ann Arbor: University of Michigan Press.

Schaffner, Laurie (1997). "Families on probation: Court-ordered parenting skills classes for parents of juvenile offenders." *Crime and Delinquency* 43(4):412–37.

Schlossman, Steven L. (1977). *Love and the American Delinquent: The Theory and Practice of "Progressive" Juvenile Justice, 1825–1920*. Chicago: University of Chicago Press.

Schmidt, Rik, Lisa Boesky, Karen Brunson, and Eric Trupin (1998). "Measuring success: The Washington State juvenile rehabilitation model." *Corrections Today* 60(5):104.

Schwartz, Ira M. (1991). "Removing juveniles from adult jails: The unfinished agenda." Pp. 216–26 in *American Jails: Public Policy Issues*, edited by Joel A. Thompson and G. Larry Mays. Chicago: Nelson-Hall.

Schwartz, Ira M. (1989). *(In)Justice for Juveniles: Rethinking the Best Interest of the Child*. Lexington, MA: Lexington Books.

Schwartz, Ira M., Linda Harris, and Laurie Levi (1988). "The jailing of juveniles in Minnesota: A case study." *Crime and Delinquency* 34(2):133–49.

Schwartz, Ira M., and Kimberly J. Merriam (1984). *The Jailing of Juveniles in Minnesota*. Minneapolis: Hubert H. Humphrey Institute of Public Affairs.

Scott, Lori (1996). "Probation: Heading in new directions." Pp. 172–83 in *Visions for Changes: Crime and Justice in the Twenty First Century*, edited by R. Muraskin and A. R. Roberts. Upper Saddle River, NJ: Prentice-Hall.

Scull, Andrew T. (1977). *Decarceration: Community Treatment and the Deviant—A Radical View*. Englewood Cliffs, NJ: Prentice-Hall.

Sellin, Thorsten (1938). *Culture Conflict and Crime*. New York: Social Science Research Council.

Selph, Andrew F., L. Thomas Winfree, Jr., and G. Larry Mays (1996). "Serving juvenile time in New Mexico: A comparison of institutionalized and reintegrated male offenders." *Juvenile and Family Court Journal* 47(2):1–14.

Shaw, Clifford R. (1938). *Brothers in Crime*. Philadelphia: Saifer.

Shaw, Clifford R. (1931). *The Jack-Roller: A Delinquent Boy's Own Story*. Philadelphia: Saifer.

Shaw, Clifford R., and Henry D. McKay (1972). *Juvenile Delinquency and Urban Areas: A Study of Rates of Delinquency in Relation to Different Characteristics of Local Communities in American Cities*. Chicago: University of Chicago Press.

Shaw, Clifford R., and Henry D. McKay (1942). *Juvenile Delinquency and Urban Areas*. Chicago: University of Chicago Press.

Shaw, Clifford R., Frederick M. Zorbaugh, Henry D. McKay, and Leonard S. Cottrell (1929). *Delinquent Areas: A Study of the Geographic Distribution of School Truants, Juvenile Delinquents, and Adult Offenders in Chicago*. Chicago: University of Chicago Press.

Shelden, Randall G., Sharon K. Tracy, and William B. Brown (2004). *Youth Gangs in American Society*. 3rd ed. Belmont, CA: Wadsworth.

Sheldon, William (1949). *Varieties of Delinquent Youth*. New York: Harper and Row.

Sheppard, David (1999). *Strategies to Reduce Gun Violence*. Washington, DC: U.S. Dept. of Justice.

Sherman, Lawrence W. (1998). "Evidence-based policing." *Ideas in American Policing*. Washington, DC: Police Foundation.

Sherman, Lawrence W. (1997a). "Communities and crime prevention." Chapter 3 in *Preventing Crime: What Works, What Doesn't, and What's Promising,* edited by Lawrence W. Sherman, Denise Gottfredson, Doris MacKenzie, John Eck, Peter Reuter, and Shawn Bushway. Washington, DC: National Institute of Justice.

Sherman, Lawrence W. (1997b). "Family-based crime prevention." Chapter 4 in *Preventing Crime: What Works, What Doesn't, and What's Promising,* edited by Lawrence W. Sherman, Denise Gottfredson, Doris MacKenzie, John Eck, Peter Reuter, and Shawn Bushway. Washington, DC: National Institute of Justice.

Sherman, Lawrence W., Patrick R. Gartin, and Michael E. Bueger (1989). "Hot spots of predatory crime." *Criminology* 27:27–55.

Sherman, Lawrence W., Denise Gottfredson, Doris MacKenzie, John Eck, Peter Reuter, and Shawn Bushway, eds. (1998). *Preventing Crime: What Works, What Doesn't, and What's Promising*. National Institute of Justice Research Brief. Washington, DC: National Institute of Justice.

Shichor, David (1995). *Punishment for Profit*. Thousand Oaks, CA: Sage.

Short, James F., Jr., and Fred L. Strodtbeck (1965). *Group Process and Gang Delinquency*. Chicago: University of Chicago Press.

Sickmund, Melissa (2004). *Juveniles in Corrections*. Juvenile Offenders and Victims, National Report Series. Washington, DC: Office of Juvenile Justice and Delinquency Prevention, U.S. Dept. of Justice.

Sickmund, Melissa (2003). *Juveniles in Court*. Juvenile Offenders and Victims, National Report Series. Washington, DC: Office of Juvenile Justice and Delinquency Prevention, U.S. Dept. of Justice.

Sickmund, Melissa (2000). "Census of juveniles in residential placement." *OJJDP Fact Sheet*. Washington, DC: U.S. Dept. of Justice.

Sickmund, Melissa, T. J. Sladky, and Wei Kang (2004). "Census of juveniles in residential placement databook." http://www.ojjdp.org/ojstabb/cjrp/.

Sickmund, Melissa, Howard N. Snyder, and Eileen Poe-Yamagata (1997). *Juvenile Offenders and Victims: 1997 Update on Violence*. Washington, DC: Office of Juvenile Justice and Delinquency Prevention, U.S. Dept. of Justice.

Sickmund, Melissa, Anne L. Stahl, Terrence A. Finnegan, Howard L. Snyder, Rowen S. Poole, and Jeffrey A. Butts (1998). *Juvenile Court Statistics 1995*. Washington, DC: Office of Juvenile Justice and Delinquency Prevention, U.S. Dept. of Justice.

Simonsen, Clifford E., and Marshall S. Gordon (1982). *Juvenile Justice in America*. 2nd ed. New York: Macmillan.

Simpson, Sally (1989). "Feminist theory, crime and justice." *Criminology* 27:605–27.

Smith, Beverly A. (1989). "Female admissions and paroles of the Western House of Refuge in the 1880s: An historical example of community corrections." *Journal of Research in Crime and Delinquency* 26:36–66.

Smith, David, Christy A. Visher, and L. A. Davidson (1984). "Equity and discretionary justice: The influence of race on police arrest decisions." *Journal of Criminal Law and Criminology* 75:234–59.

Smithburn, J. Eric (2002). *Cases and Materials in Juvenile Law*. Cincinnati: Anderson.

Snyder, Howard N. (2005). *Juvenile Arrests 2003*. OJJDP Juvenile Justice Bulletin. Washington, DC: Department of Justice.

Snyder, Howard N. (2001). *Law Enforcement and Juvenile Crime*. Washington, DC: Office of Juvenile Justice and Delinquency Prevention, U.S. Dept. of Justice.

Snyder, Howard N. (1997). *Juvenile Arrests 1996*. OJJDP Juvenile Justice Bulletin. Washington, DC: U.S. Dept. of Justice.

Snyder, Howard N., and Melissa Sickmund (1999). *Juvenile Offenders and Victims: 1999 National Report*. Washington, DC: Office of Juvenile Justice and Delinquency Prevention, U.S. Dept. of Justice.

Snyder, Howard N., Melissa Sickmund, and Eileen Poe-Yamagata (2000). *Juvenile Transfers to Criminal Court in the 1990s: Lessons Learned From Four Studies*. Washington, DC: Office of Juvenile Justice and Delinquency Prevention, U.S. Dept. of Justice.

Snyder, Howard N., and Monica H. Swahn (2004). *Juvenile Suicides, 1981–1998*. OJJDP Youth Violence Research Bulletin. Washington, DC: U.S. Dept. of Justice.

"Some states target parents of kids who commit crimes" (1999). *Sun-News* (Las Cruces, NM), May 1, p. A-9.

Sontheimer, Henry, and Lynne Goodstein (1993). "An evaluation of juvenile intensive aftercare probation: Aftercare versus system response effects." *Justice Quarterly* 10(2):197–227.

Spencer, Herbert (1961)[1864]. *The Study of Sociology*. Ann Arbor: University of Michigan Press.

Spergel, Irving A. (1995). *The Youthful Gang Problem*. New York: Oxford University Press.

Stahl, Anne L. (2003). *Delinquency Cases in Juvenile Courts, 1999*. OJJDP Fact Sheet. Washington, DC: Office of Juvenile Justice and Delinquency Prevention, U.S. Dept. of Justice.

Starbuck, David, James C. Howell, and Donna J. Lindquist (2001). *Hybrid and Other Modern Gangs*. Washington, DC: Office of Juvenile Justice and Delinquency Prevention, U.S. Dept. of Justice.

Steinberg, Laurence (2002). "The juvenile psychopath: Fads, fictions, and facts." Pp. 35–64 in *Perspectives on Crime and Justice: 2000–2001 Lecture Series*. Washington, DC: National Institute of Justice, U.S. Dept. of Justice.

Stephan, James J. (2001). *Census of Jails 1999*. Washington, DC: Bureau of Justice Statistics, U.S. Dept. of Justice.

Stol, Wouter, and Eric Bervoets (2002). "Policing Dutch-Moroccan youths." *Police and Society* 12(3):191–200.

Stops, Maria, and G. Larry Mays (1991). "Treating adolescent sex offenders in a multicultural setting." *Journal of Offender Rehabilitation* 17(1, 2):87–103.

"The Story" (1981). *Washington Post*, April 19, pp. A12–A15.

Streib, Victor (1995). "The death penalty today." Unpublished manuscript. Cleveland-Marshall College of Law, Cleveland, Ohio.

"Subordinate Courts of Singapore—Juvenile Justice" (2004). http://www.juvenilecourtofsingapore.gov.sg/.

Sullivan, Jacqueline (2002). "Widening the net in juvenile justice and the dangers of prevention and early intervention." San Francisco: Center on Juvenile and Criminal Justice. http://www.cjcj.org/pubs/net/netwid.html.

"Summary of the Uniform Crime Reporting (UCR) Program." http://www.fbi.gov/ucr/cius_02/html/web/summary/summary.html. Retrieved November 3, 2005.

"Supreme Court justice calls for overhaul of juvenile court system" (2000). http://www.pdmiami.com/justice_anstead.htm.

Sutherland, Edwin (1947). *Principles of Criminology*. Philadelphia: Lippincott.

Sykes, Gresham (1958). *The Society of Captives: A Study of a Maximum Security Prison*. Princeton, NJ: Princeton University Press.

Tannenbaum, Frank (1938). *Crime and the Community*. New York: Ginn.

Taylor, Carl (1990). "Gang imperialism." Pp. 103–115 in *Gangs in America*, edited by C. Ronald Huff. Newbury Park, CA: Sage.

Taylor, Ian, Paul Walton, and Jock Young (1973). *The New Criminology*. New York: Harper and Row.

Taylor, William B. (1978a). "Alexander Maconochie and the revolt against the penitentiary." *Southern Journal of Criminal Justice* 3(Spring):42–54.

Taylor, William B. (1978b). "The separate system under fire: Alexander Maconochie and prospective prison discipline." *Journal of Crime and Justice* 1:133–51.

ten Bensel, Robert W. (1984). "Definitions of child neglect and abuse." *Juvenile and Family Court Journal* 35(4):23–31.

Tennenbaum, David J. (1977). "Personality and criminality: A summary and implications of the literature." *Journal of Criminal Justice* 5:225–35.

Terrill, Richard J. (2003). *World Criminal Justice Systems: A Survey.* Cincinnati: Anderson.

Terry, Robert M. (1967). "Discrimination in the handling of juvenile offenders by social control agencies." *Journal of Research in Crime and Delinquency* 4:218–30.

Theodorson, George A., and Achilles G. Theodorson (1969). *Modern Dictionary of Sociology.* New York: Crowell.

Thomas, Charles W. (1971). "Are status offenders really so different? A comparative and longitudinal assessment." *Crime and Delinquency* 22:438–55.

Thomas, Charles W., Jeffery M. Hyman, and L. Thomas Winfree, Jr. (1981). "The impact of confinement on juveniles." *Youth and Society* 14:251–62.

Thompson, David W., and Leonard A. Jason (1988). "Street gangs and preventive interventions." *Criminal Justice and Behavior* 15(3):323–33.

Thornberry, Terence (1979). "Race, socioeconomic status and sentencing in the juvenile justice system." *Journal of Criminal Law and Criminology* 70:164–71.

Thrasher, Frederick (1927). *The Gang: A Study of 1,313 Gangs in Chicago.* Chicago: University of Chicago Press.

Toby, Jackson (1965). "An evaluation of early identification and intensive treatment programs for predelinquents." *Social Problems* 12:1650–75.

Toby, Jackson (1957). "The differential impact of family disorganization." *American Sociological Review* 47:435–38.

Torbet, Patricia McFall (1996). *Juvenile Probation: Workhorse of the Juvenile Justice System.* Washington, DC: Office of Juvenile Justice and Delinquency Prevention, U.S. Dept. of Justice.

Torbet, Patricia, Richard Gable, Hunter Hurst IV, Imogene Montgomery, Linda Szymanski, and Douglas Thomas (1996). *State Responses to Serious and Violent Juvenile Crime.* Pittsburgh, PA: National Center for Juvenile Justice.

Tracy, Paul E., Marvin E. Wolfgang, and Robert M. Figlio (1990). *Delinquency in Two Birth Cohorts.* New York: Plenum.

Tran, Tini (2005). "Police in Sri Lanka accuse man of trying to sell his daughter." Associated Press news release, January 12, p. 1. http://www.news.yahoo.com/news?tmpl= story&cid=535&u=/ap/20050112/ap_on_re_as/tsunami.

Travis, Lawrence F., III, and Edward J. Latessa (1984). "'A summary of parole rules—Thirteen years later': Revisited thirteen years later." *Journal of Criminal Justice* 12(6):591–600.

Trester, Harold B. (1981). *Supervision of the Offender.* Englewood Cliffs, NJ: Prentice-Hall.

Trojanowicz, Robert (1983). *An Evaluation of the Neighborhood Foot Patrol Program in Flint, Michigan.* East Lansing: Michigan State University.

Trojanowicz, Robert, and B. Bucqueroux (1990). *Community Policing: A Contemporary Perspective.* Cincinnati: Anderson.

Trumbach, Randolph (1978). *The Rise of the Egalitarian Family: Aristocratic Kinship and Domestic Relations in Eighteenth Century England.* New York: Academic Press.

Tucker, M. J. (1975). "The child as beginning and end: Fifteenth and sixteenth century English childhood." Pp. 229–57 in *The History of Childhood*, edited by L. de Manse. New York: Harper Torchbooks.

Tzeng, Oliver C. S., Jay W. Jackson, and Henry C. Karlson (1991). *Theories of Child Abuse and Neglect*. New York: Praeger.

U.S. Department of Justice (1981). *Dictionary of Criminal Justice Data Terminology*. 2nd ed. Washington, DC: U.S. Government Printing Office.

Umbreit, Mark S. (1995). "Holding juvenile offenders accountable: A restorative justice perspective." *Juvenile and Family Court Journal* 46(2):31–42.

UNICEF's Convention on the Rights of Children (1997). "Progress of nations 1997 special protections: Progress and disparity." Retrieved March 29, 2005 from http://www.unicef.org/pon97/p56a.htm.

United Nations (2003). "Somalia: The experience of separated Somalia Children." http://www.unsomalia.net/media/2003/stories/20030117_1.asp.

United Nations (1986). *Standard Minimum Rules for the Administration of Juvenile Justice*. New York: U.N. Department of Public Information.

"U.S. population covered by NIBRS." http://www.as.wvu.edu/~jnolan/nibrsparticipation.htm. Retrieved November 3, 2005.

Vaquera, Tony, and David W. Bailey (2004). "Latin gang in the Americas: Los Mara Salvatrucha." *Crime & Justice International* 20(83):4–10.

Venturelli, Peter J. (1994). *Drug Use in America: Social, Cultural, and Political Perspectives*. Boston: Jones and Bartlett.

Vigil, James Diego (1990). "Cholos and Gangs: Culture Change and Street Youth in Los Angeles." Pp. 116–128 in *Gangs in America*, edited by C. R. Huff. Newbury Park, CA: Sage.

Vigil, James Diego (1988). *Barrio Gangs*. Austin: University of Texas Press.

Visher, Christy A. (1983). "Gender, police arrest decisions, and notions of chivalry." *Criminology* 21:5–28.

Vito, Gennaro F., Richard Tewksbury, and Deborah G. Wilson (1998). *The Juvenile Justice System*. Long Grove, IL: Waveland Press.

Voice Interact (2004). http://www.voiceinteract.com/Community_Supervision.htm.

Waldo, Gordon, and Simon Dinitz (1967). "Personality attributes of the criminal: An analysis of research studies." *Journal of Research in Crime and Delinquency* 4:185–202.

Walker, Nigel (1983). "Childhood and madness: History and theory." Pp. 19–35 in *Providing Criminal Justice for Children*, edited by Allison Morris and Henri Giller. London: Edward Arnold.

Walker, Samuel (2006). *Sense and Nonsense about Crime and Drugs*. 6th ed. Belmont, CA: West/Wadsworth.

Walker, Samuel (2001). *Sense and Nonsense about Crime and Drugs: A Policy Guide*. 5th ed. Belmont, CA: Wadsworth.

Walker, Samuel (1998a). *Popular Justice: A History of American Criminal Justice*. 2nd ed. New York: Oxford University Press.

Walker, Samuel (1998b). *Sense and Nonsense about Crime and Drugs*. 4th ed. Belmont, CA: West/Wadsworth.

Walker, Samuel, and Charles M. Katz (2005). *The Police in America*. 5th ed. New York: McGraw-Hill.

Watson, Alan (1970). *The Laws of Ancient Romans*. Dallas: Southern Methodist University Press.

Weisheit, Ralph A., and L. Edward Wells (2004). "Youth gangs in rural America." *National Institute of Justice Journal* 251 (July):2–6.

Weissman, Harold H., ed. (1969). *Community Development in the Mobilization for Youth Experience*. New York: Association Press.

Weisz, Virginia G. (1994). "Consequences of placement for children who are abused." Pp. 63–100 in *When There's No Place Like Home*, edited by Jan Blacher. Baltimore: Brookes.

Weitekamp, Elmar G. M., Hans-Jurgen Kerner, Volkhard Schindler, and Axel Schubert (1995). "On the dangerousness of chronic/habitual offenders: A reanalysis of the 1945 Philadelphia birth cohort data." *Studies of Crime and Crime Prevention* 4(2):159–75.

Weitekamp, Elmar G. M., Hans-Jurgen Kerner, Axel Schubert, and Volkhard Schindler (1996). "Multiple and habitual offending among young males: Criminological and criminal policy lessons from a re-analysis of the Philadelphia birth cohort studies." *International Annals of Criminology* 34(1/2):9–53.

Welch, Michael, Eric A. Price, and Nana Yankey (2002). "Moral panic over youth violence: Wilding and the manufacture of menace in the media." *Youth & Society* 34(1):3–30.

Wheeler, Stanton, and Leonard S. Cottrell, Jr. (1966). *Juvenile Delinquency: Its Prevention and Control*. New York: Sage.

Whelen, Ralph (1954). "An experiment in predicting delinquency." *Journal of Criminal Law, Criminology and Police Science* 45:432–41.

Whyte, William Foote (1943). *Street Corner Society: The Social Structure of an Italian Slum*. Chicago: University of Chicago Press.

Widom, Cathy Spatz (1995). "Victims of childhood sexual abuse—Later criminal consequences." *NIJ Research in Brief*. Washington, DC: U.S. Government Printing Office.

Wiebush, Richard G. (1993). "Juvenile intensive supervision: The impact of felony offenders diverted from institutional placement." *Crime and Delinquency* 39(1):68–89.

Wiebush, Richard G., Dennis Wagner, Betsie McNulty, Yanqing Wang, and Thao N. Le (2005). *Implementation and Outcome Evaluation of the Intensive Aftercare Program: Final Report*. Washington, DC: Office of Juvenile Justice and Delinquency Prevention.

Wilbanks, William (1987). *The Myth of a Racist Criminal Justice System*. Monterey, CA: Brooks/Cole.

Willing, Richard. (2005). "U.S. prisons to end boot-camp program." *USA Today,* February 3. http://www.usatoday.com/news.nation/2005-02-03-boot-camps_x.htm.

Wilson, James Q. (1983). *Thinking about Crime*. Rev. ed. New York: Basic Books.

Wilson, James Q. (1973). *Varieties of Police Behavior*. New York: Atheneum.

Wilson, James Q., and Richard Herrnstein (1985). *Crime and Human Nature*. New York: Simon and Schuster.

Wilson, William Julius (1996). *When Work Disappears: The World of the New Urban Poor*. New York: Knopf.

Winfree, L. Thomas, Jr., and Howard Abadinsky (2003). *Understanding Crime: Theory and Practice*. Belmont, CA: Wadsworth.

Winfree, L. Thomas, Jr., Finn-Aage Esbensen, and D. Wayne Osgood (1996). "Evaluating a school-based gang-prevention program: A theoretical perspective." *Evaluation Review* 20(2):181–203.

Winfree, L. Thomas, Jr., Kathy Fuller, Teresa Vigil, and G. Larry Mays (1992). "The definition and measurement of 'gang status': Policy implications." *Juvenile and Family Court Journal* 43(1):29–37.

Winfree, L. Thomas, Jr., and Dana Lynskey (1999). "A brief history of the gang resistance education and training program: From idea to implementation of G.R.E.A.T." Unpublished report, Department of Criminal Justice, New Mexico State University, Las Cruces.

Winfree, L. Thomas, Jr., and G. Larry Mays (1996). "Family and peer influences on gang involvement: A comparison of institutionalized and free-world youth in a southwestern state." Pp. 35–53 in *Gangs: A Criminal Justice Approach*, edited by J. Mitchell Miller and Jeffrey P. Rush. Cincinnati, OH: Anderson/Academy of Criminal Justice Sciences.

Winfree, L. Thomas, G. Larry Mays, and Teresa Vigil-Backstrom (1994). "Youth gangs and incarcerated delinquents: Exploring the ties between gang membership, delinquency, and social learning theory." *Justice Quarterly* 11(2):229–56.

Wolfgang, Marvin E., Robert M. Figlio, and Thorsten Sellin (1972). *Delinquency in a Birth Cohort.* Chicago: University of Chicago Press.

Wooden, Wayne S. (1995). *Renegade Kids, Suburban Outlaws.* Belmont, CA: Wadsworth.

"Writer says drug story faked, paper surrenders Pulitzer Prize" (1981). *The Globe and Mail,* April 16, p. 1.

Wyrick, Phelan A., and James C. Howell (2004). "Strategic risk-based response to youth gangs." *Juvenile Justice* 9(1):20–29.

Young, Jock (1971). "The role of the police as amplifiers of deviancy, negotiators of reality, and translators of fantasy: Some consequences of our present system of drug control as seen in Notting Hill." Pp. 24–46 in *Images of Deviance,* edited by S. Cohen. Middlesex, England: Penguin.

Young, Jock, and Roger Matthews, eds. (1991). *Rethinking Criminology: The Realist Debate.* Newbury Park, CA: Sage.

AUTHOR INDEX

SUBJECT INDEX